Handbook of Critical Race Theory in Education

This handbook illustrates how education scholars employ critical race theory (CRT) as a framework to bring attention to issues of race and racism in education. It is the first authoritative reference work to provide a truly comprehensive description and analysis of the topic, from the defining conceptual principles of CRT in the law that gave shape to its radical underpinnings to the political and social implications of the field today. It is divided into three parts, covering innovations in educational research, policy and practice both in schools and in higher education, and the increasing interdisciplinary nature of critical race research. With 28 newly commissioned pieces written by the most renowned scholars in the field, this handbook provides the definitive statement on the state of critical race theory in education and on its possibilities for the future.

Marvin Lynn is Dean of the School of Education at Indiana University, South Bend, USA.

Adrienne D. Dixson is an Associate Professor of Critical Race Theory in Education in the Department of Educational Policy, Organization and Leadership in the College of Education at the University of Illinois at Urbana-Champaign, USA.

Handbook of Critical Race Theory in Education

Edited by
Marvin Lynn and Adrienne D. Dixson

Routledge
Taylor & Francis Group

NEW YORK AND LONDON

First published 2013
by Routledge
711 Third Avenue, New York, NY 10017

Simultaneously published in the UK
by Routledge
2 Park Square, Milton Park, Abingdon, Oxon OX14 4RN

Routledge is an imprint of the Taylor & Francis Group, an informa business

© 2013 Taylor & Francis

The right of the editors to be identified as the author of the editorial material, and of the authors for their individual chapters, has been asserted in accordance with sections 77 and 78 of the Copyright, Designs and Patents Act 1988.

All rights reserved. No part of this book may be reprinted or reproduced or utilised in any form or by any electronic, mechanical, or other means, now known or hereafter invented, including photocopying and recording, or in any information storage or retrieval system, without permission in writing from the publishers.

Trademark notice: Product or corporate names may be trademarks or registered trademarks, and are used only for identification and explanation without intent to infringe.

Library of Congress Cataloging in Publication Data
Handbook of critical race theory in education /
edited by Marvin Lynn and Adrienne D. Dixson.
pages cm
Includes bibliographical references and index.
1. Critical pedagogy—Handbooks, manuals, etc.
2. Racism in education—Handbooks, manuals, etc.
3. Discrimination in education—Handbooks, manuals, etc.
I. Lynn, Marvin, 1971– editor of compilation.
II. Dixson, Adrienne D., editor of compilation.
LC196.H364 2013
370.11'5—dc23
2012037238

ISBN: 978–0–415–89995–6 (hbk)
ISBN: 978–0–415–89996–3 (pbk)
ISBN: 978–0–203–15572–1 (ebk)

Typeset in Minion
by Swales & Willis Ltd, Exeter, Devon

Certified Sourcing
www.sfiprogram.org
SFI-00453

Printed and bound in the United States of America
by Edwards Brothers Malloy

"A disciple is not above his teacher, but everyone when he is fully trained will be like his teacher."

(Luke, 6:40)

We dedicate this book to the memory of Derrick A. Bell, the Father of Critical Race Theory. His unwavering commitment to truth, justice and serving the "least of these" is an unparalleled model of scholar-activism that we aspire to become. We hope that this contribution honors his legacy.

Marvin dedicates this book to the memory of Selma Stewart White: a teacher among teachers. He also dedicates the book to his sons: Kwabena, Naasei and Nana Yaw. You continue to inspire me to do this work.

Adrienne dedicates this book to her sons, Jordan Cameron and Jameel Amman Paulin. You are my constant sources of inspiration.

CONTENTS

List of Figures and Tables   xi

Acknowledgments   xii

About the Editors   xiii

Contributors   xiv

Introduction   1
ADRIENNE D. DIXSON AND MARVIN LYNN

Part I   **THE GENEALOGY OF CRITICAL RACE THEORY AND
               CRITICAL RACE THEORY IN EDUCATION**   7

Chapter 1   The History and Conceptual Elements of Critical Race Theory   9
               KEVIN BROWN AND DARRELL D. JACKSON

Chapter 2   Discerning Critical Moments   23
               RICHARD DELGADO AND JEAN STEFANCIC

Chapter 3   Critical Race Theory—What It Is Not!   34
               GLORIA LADSON-BILLINGS

Chapter 4   Critical Race Theory's Intellectual Roots: My Email Epistolary
               with Derrick Bell   48
               DANIEL G. SOLÓRZANO

Chapter 5   W.E.B. Du Bois's Contributions to Critical Race Studies in
             Education: Sociology of Education, Classical Critical Race Theory,
             and Proto-Critical Pedagogy   69
             REILAND RABAKA

Chapter 6   Tribal Critical Race Theory: An Origin Story and Future Directions   88
             BRYAN MCKINLEY JONES BRAYBOY

Chapter 7   Origins of and Connections to Social Justice in Critical Race
             Theory in Education   101
             THANDEKA K. CHAPMAN

Chapter 8   Doing Class in Critical Race Analysis in Education   113
             MICHAEL J. DUMAS

Part II   INTERSECTIONAL AND INTERDISCIPLINARY METHODS
             TO CHALLENGING MAJORITARIAN POLICIES AND STOCK
             STORIES IN EDUCATION   127

Chapter 9   The Policy of Inequity: Using CRT to Unmask White Supremacy
             in Education Policy   129
             DAVID GILLBORN

Chapter 10   Educational Policy Contradictions: A LatCrit Perspective on
             Undocumented Latino Students   140
             NEREIDA OLIVA, JUDITH C. PÉREZ, AND LAURENCE PARKER

Chapter 11   Badges of Inferiority: The Racialization of Achievement in
             U.S. Education   153
             SONYA DOUGLASS HORSFORD AND TANETHA J. GROSLAND

Chapter 12   The Racialization of South Asian Americans in a Post-9/11 Era   167
             BINAYA SUBEDI

Chapter 13   Blurring the Boundaries: The Mechanics of Creating Composite
             Characters   181
             DANIELLA ANN COOK

Chapter 14   Education as the Property of Whites: African Americans' Continued
             Quest for Good Schools   195
             JAMEL K. DONNOR

Chapter 15   The Inclusion and Representation of Asian Americans and
             Pacific Islanders in America's Equity Agenda in Higher Education   204
             ROBERT T. TERANISHI AND LONI BORDOLOI PAZICH

Chapter 16   Let's Be For Real: Critical Race Theory, Racial Realism,
              and Education Policy Analysis (Toward a New Paradigm)   216
              KRISTEN L. BURAS

Chapter 17   Examining Black Male Identity through a Raced, Classed,
              and Gendered Lens: Critical Race Theory and the Intersectionality
              of the Black Male Experience   232
              TYRONE C. HOWARD AND REMA REYNOLDS

Chapter 18   Expanding the Counterstory: The Potential for Critical Race Mixed
              Methods Studies in Education   248
              JESSICA T. DECUIR-GUNBY AND DINA C. WALKER-DEVOSE

Chapter 19   A Critical Race Policy Analysis of the School-to-Prison Pipeline for
              Chicanos   260
              BRENDA GUADALUPE VALLES AND OCTAVIO VILLALPANDO

Chapter 20   Critical Race Quantitative Intersectionality: An Anti-Racist Research
              Paradigm that Refuses to "Let the Numbers Speak for Themselves" 270
              ALEJANDRO COVARRUBIAS AND VERÓNICA VÉLEZ

Part III   **CRITICAL RACE PRAXIS IN COMMUNITIES, SCHOOLS,
              AND THE UNIVERSITY**   287

Chapter 21   "Fightin' the Devil 24/7": Context, Community, and Critical
              Race Praxis in Education   289
              DAVID O. STOVALL

Chapter 22   Arizona on the Doorstep of Apartheid: The Purging of the
              Tri-Dimensionalization of Reality   302
              AUGUSTINE F. ROMERO

Chapter 23   Other Kids' Teachers: What Children of Color Learn from White
              Women and What This Says about Race, Whiteness, and Gender   313
              ZEUS LEONARDO AND ERICA BOAS

Chapter 24   Critical Race Methodological Tensions: *Nepantla* in Our
              Community-Based Praxis   325
              ENRIQUE ALEMÁN, JR., DOLORES DELGADO BERNAL, AND SYLVIA MENDOZA

Chapter 25   Critical Race Theory, Interest Convergence, and Teacher Education   339
              H. RICHARD MILNER IV, F. ALVIN PEARMAN III, AND EBONY O. MCGEE

Chapter 26   CRT's Challenge to Educators' Articulation of Abstract Liberal
              Perspectives of Purpose   355
              KENNETH FASCHING-VARNER AND ROLAND MITCHELL

Chapter 27   Post-Racial Critical Race Praxis   368
            SABINA VAUGHT AND GABRIELLE HERNANDEZ, WITH IKENNA ACHOLONU,
            AMBER FROMMHERZ, AND BEN PHELPS

Chapter 28   What Is "Urban"? A CRT Examination of the Preparation of
            K-12 Teachers for Urban Schools   386
            CELIA ROUSSEAU ANDERSON AND BEVERLY E. CROSS

Index   397

FIGURES AND TABLES

FIGURES

4.1 A genealogy of critical race theory in education   51

4.2 *The Puppeteer* (artist unknown) (1972), corner of Whittier Blvd. and Eastern Avenue in East Los Angeles   54

4.3 *Unidos Carnal* (Brothers United) (artist unknown) (1972), Brooklyn Avenue in East Los Angeles   55

4.4 A genealogy of critical race theory in education, critical race tools, and transformational resistance   58

4.5 Delgado Bernal's dimensions of grassroots leadership   59

4.6 Notes on Freire and Giroux's oppositional behavior (1983)   60

4.7 Defining the concept of resistance   61

4.8 Letty's figure in progress   63

13.1 Composite counterstory (CCS) storyline   189

24.1 *Adelante* goals and programmatic components   327

24.2 Alvaro's picture story   331

25.1 An emerging picture of the teacher preparation pipeline: race and ethnicity of full-time faculty in professional education programs, Fall 2007   347

25.2 An emerging picture of the teacher preparation pipeline: race and ethnicity of adjunct faculty in professional education programs, Fall 2007   348

TABLES

11.1 Multi-step progression from racial literacy to racial reconciliation   162

19.1 District percentages of all discipline infractions: distribution by race/ethnicity, 2007 and 2008   266

19.2 Type of disciplinary infraction by race/ethnicity and violation type, 2007–08   266

25.1 Summary of keyword search: "anywhere"   341

25.2 Summary of keyword search: "title"   341

ACKNOWLEDGMENTS

We would like to thank everyone who helped to make this project possible. First, to the contributors—thank you for sharing your groundbreaking scholarship. Without you, this handbook would not be possible. Many thanks to the members of the editorial board whose advice helped to keep the project on track. We especially want to thank Gloria Ladson-Billings, William F. Tate IV, Daniel G. Solorzano, and Laurence Parker. In one way or another, each of you is responsible for the vast majority of those who regard themselves as critical race scholars in education, including many of the contributors to this handbook. Beyond helping us find our way within the legal literature at the start of our scholarly journeys, to this point in our academic careers, you have offered guidance, ideas, support, and encouragement. We also want to thank our editor, Catherine Bernard, and her staff at Taylor & Francis. We are very appreciative for your constructive and critical feedback on the direction of the handbook in its very early stages to its completion. Finally and most importantly, we want to thank God for giving us the inspiration, courage, strength, and fortitude to see this project through to its glorious end. We are forever grateful for the grand opportunity we have been given.

Marvin Lynn and Adrienne D. Dixson

ABOUT THE EDITORS

Marvin Lynn is an Associate Professor of Education Studies and Associate Dean for Teacher Education at the University of Wisconsin-Eau Claire. Recently named Professor and Dean of the School of Education at Indiana University, South Bend, he coined the term "critical race pedagogy" while conducting research on the work and lives of African American male teachers. He is co-founder and past president of the Critical Race Studies in Education Association and the South Shore Opera Company of Chicago.

Adrienne D. Dixson is an Associate Professor of Critical Race Theory in Education in the Department of Educational Policy, Organization and Leadership in the College of Education at the University of Illinois at Urbana-Champaign. Her research focuses primarily on educational equity and race in urban schooling contexts, especially those in the urban south. She has published extensively in the areas of culturally relevant pedagogy, qualitative research methodologies, and educational equity.

CONTRIBUTORS

Enrique Alemán, Jr. is an Associate Professor of Educational Leadership and Policy in the College of Education and a Faculty Affiliate in the Ethnic Studies Program at the University of Utah. His research agenda includes studying the effects of educational policy on Latina/o and Chicana/o students and communities and the utilization of critical race theory (CRT) and Latina/critical theory (LatCrit) frameworks in educational research.

Celia Rousseau Anderson is an Associate Professor in the Department of Instruction and Curriculum Leadership at the University of Memphis. Her scholarly interests include equity in mathematics education, urban education, and critical race theory.

Erica Boas is a Ph.D. candidate in the Social and Cultural Studies Program at the University of California, Berkeley's Graduate School of Education. Her dissertation explores the organization of sexuality in elementary schools.

Loni Bordoloi Pazich is a Ph.D. candidate in Higher and Postsecondary Education at the New York University Steinhardt School of Culture, Education, and Human Development. Her research interests focus on the role of the state in facilitating equitable outcomes for students of color and immigrant students in higher education.

Bryan McKinley Jones Brayboy (Lumbee) is Borderlands Associate Professor of Indigenous Education, co-director of the Center for Indian Education and co-editor of the *Journal of American Indian Education* at Arizona State University. His research focuses on the experiences of Indigenous students and faculty in institutions of higher education, Indigenous knowledge systems, and the intersections between race, law, and education.

Kevin Brown is the Richard S. Melvin Professor of Law at Indiana University Maurer School of Law and the Emeritus Director of the Hudson and Holland Scholars

Program at Indiana University-Bloomington. He was an original participant in both the first Critical Race Theory Workshop held in Madison, Wisconsin in 1989 (as well as the next three annual workshops) and the first People of Color Conference held in Chicago in 1991. His research interest for more than a quarter of a century has been primarily in the area of race, law, and education.

Kristen L. Buras is an Assistant Professor in the Department of Educational Policy Studies at Georgia State University. Her research centers on the race and class dynamics of neoliberal policy in cities throughout the South. She is co-founder and Director of the Urban South Grassroots Research Collective for Public Education and was granted the Distinguished Scholar-Activist Award by Critical Educators for Social Justice of the American Educational Research Association.

Thandeka K. Chapman is an Associate Professor of Education Studies in the Division of Social Sciences at the University of California, San Diego. She has conducted research on policy implementation in desegregated schools, urban small school reforms, teaching and learning in racially diverse classrooms, and evaluating social justice curricula.

Daniella Ann Cook, Ph.D., is an Assistant Professor in the School of Education at the University of Tulsa and an Affiliate Professor in African American Studies. She is an accomplished organizer, educator, former public school teacher, and facilitator, whose work has been published in the *Journal of Culture and Mathematics*, *Southern Anthropologist* and *Voices in Urban Education*.

Alejandro Covarrubias is the founder and former Executive Director of Los Angeles Communities Advocating for Unity, Social Justice and Action (LA CAUSA), an East Los Angeles non-profit organization that is one of the leading producers of local and nationally recognized young leaders of color. His research examines the philosophical foundations, pedagogical commitments, and networks of organizations that lead in intentionally engaging those most impacted by unjust relations of power.

Beverly E. Cross is the Lillian and Morrie Moss Chair of Excellence in Urban Education at the University of Memphis. She provides leadership in the College of Education's mission to enhance educational success for urban learners. She has conducted research in the areas of teacher diversity, urban education, multicultural and anti-racist education, and curriculum theory, and she has written frequently on urban education, particularly issues of race, class, and culture in urban schools and achievement.

Jessica T. DeCuir-Gunby is an Associate Professor and Program Coordinator of Educational Psychology in the Department of Curriculum, Instruction, and Counselor Education at North Carolina State University in Raleigh, North Carolina. Her research and theoretical interests include race and racial identity development, critical race theory, mixed methods research, and emotions in education.

Richard Delgado is University Professor of Law at Seattle University, where he writes and teaches in the areas of civil rights, critical race theory, and civil procedure. He is a founding member of the critical race theory movement.

Dolores Delgado Bernal is Professor of Education and Ethnic Studies at the University of Utah. Her research contributes to the fields of education and Chicana/o studies by examining the socio-cultural context of the educational pipeline and by investigating alternative definitions of knowledge, teaching, and learning.

Jamel K. Donnor is an Assistant Professor in Curriculum and Instruction in the School of Education at the College of William and Mary. His research covers three areas: theory, education policy, and African American student achievement.

Michael J. Dumas is Assistant Professor of Educational Leadership in the Steinhardt School of Culture, Education, and Human Development at New York University. His scholarly interests focus on three interrelated areas of inquiry: the cultural politics of Black education, the cultural political economy of urban education, and public discourses and policy-making related to Black boyhood and the education of young Black boys.

Kenneth Fasching-Varner is the Shirley B. Barton Assistant Professor of Elementary Education and Foundations in the College of Human Sciences and Education at Louisiana State University. His research draws on critical race theory and culturally relevant pedagogy to examine the nature of White pre-service teachers' racial identity.

David Gillborn is Professor of Critical Race Studies at the University of Birmingham. He is founding editor of the international journal *Race Ethnicity and Education*.

Tanetha J. Grosland is an Assistant Professor of Education at Morgan State University. Her research interests involve bringing postmodern/poststructuralist, cultural, and critical perspectives to bear on curriculum issues, particularly social justice pedagogy.

Gabrielle Hernandez is a graduate student in the Educational Studies program at Tufts University. Her research focuses on the intersection of race, gender, and government, exploring structures of inequity across U.S. institutional policy contexts. She is currently working as a research assistant on a political prisoner project.

Sonya Douglass Horsford is The Senior Resident Scholar of Education at the Lincy Institute at the University of Nevada, Las Vegas. She conducts research on school desegregation and the politics of race in education.

Tyrone C. Howard is a Professor at the University of California, Los Angeles in the Graduate School of Education and Information Studies' Urban Schooling Division. He also serves as the Faculty Director of Center X and the Director of the Black Male Institute at UCLA. His research interests focus on issues of access and equity in urban schools, the role of race and culture in teaching and learning, and the educational experiences of African American students.

Darrell D. Jackson is Visiting Professor of Law and Director of the Prosecution Assistance Program at the University of Wyoming College of Law. His research interests surround supporting historically marginalized communities (HMCs) as they struggle to obtain an equitable share of power within truly democratic societies. His theoretical framework is formed at the intersections of three primary disciplines—law; education; and race, cultural, or ethnic studies—and primarily utilizes critical race theory. Using counter-narratives from HMCs and legal analysis that suggests protecting those whose interests are often overlooked and overwhelmed, he critically analyzes the institutional status quo through research, writing, teaching, commentary, and community service.

Gloria Ladson-Billings is the Kellner Family Chair in Urban Education in the Department of Curriculum and Instruction at the University of Wisconsin-Madison and Faculty Affiliate in the Departments of Educational Policy Studies and Afro-American Studies and the African Studies Program.

Zeus Leonardo is Associate Professor of Education and Affiliated Faculty of the Critical Theory Designated Emphasis at the University of California, Berkeley. He is the author of *Ideology, Discourse, and School Reform* (Praeger) and editor of *Critical Pedagogy and Race* (Blackwell).

Ebony O. McGee is Assistant Professor of Diversity and Urban Schooling at Vanderbilt University's Peabody College. She is a former electrical engineer, whose research focuses on the role of racialized biases in educational and career attainment, resiliency, mathematics identity, and identity development in high-achieving marginalized students of color in STEM fields.

Sylvia Mendoza is a doctoral student at the University of Utah in the Department of Education, Culture and Society. Her research interests include decolonizing pedagogies and Chicana feminisms.

H. Richard Milner IV is Associate Professor of Education in the Department of Teaching and Learning and a founding director of the graduate program Learning, Diversity and Urban Studies at Peabody College of Vanderbilt University. He is also a Policy Fellow of the National Education Policy Center. His research, teaching, and policy interests concern urban education, teacher education, African American literature, and the sociology of education. He is editor-in-chief of *Urban Education*.

Roland Mitchell is the Assistant Director of the School of Education in the College of Human Sciences and Education at Louisiana State University. He is an Associate Professor and currently serves as the Higher Education Administration Program Leader and Co-Director of the Curriculum Theory Project. His current research interests include theorizing the impact of historical and communal knowledge on pedagogy.

Nereida Oliva is a doctoral student in the Department of Educational Leadership and Policy in the College of Education at the University of Utah. Her area of interest is critical educational leadership and Latina parent involvement in schools.

Laurence Parker is on the faculty in the Department of Educational Leadership and Policy at the University of Utah, and his research and teaching interests are in the area of critical race theory, education, and social justice leadership.

F. Alvin Pearman III is a doctoral student at Peabody College of Vanderbilt University. His research focus is the social context of education and the social aspects of opportunities to learn.

Judith C. Pérez is a doctoral student in the Department of Educational Leadership and Policy at the University of Utah. Her area of interest is in Latino student involvement in school university partnerships as the pipeline to college access and success.

Reiland Rabaka is an Associate Professor of African, African American, and Caribbean Studies in the Department of Ethnic Studies at the University of Colorado at Boulder, where he is also an Affiliate Professor in the Women and Gender Studies Program and the Humanities Program. He is a Research Fellow at the Center for Studies of Ethnicity and Race in America (CSERA) at the University of Colorado at Boulder. His ongoing teaching and research interests in the arts, specifically the social and political implications of African, African American, and Caribbean music and popular culture, include: Harlem Renaissance Studies; Jazz Studies; Negritude Studies; the Black Arts Movement; the Feminist Art Movement; Reggae Music and the Rastafari Movement; Hip Hop Studies; and the Hip Hop Feminist Movement.

Rema Reynolds is a former teacher, counselor, and administrator, and currently organizes Black parents for the improvement of student achievement in various schools. She is a Postdoctoral Fellow at the University of California, Los Angeles and an Associate Professor of Education at Azusa Pacific University, whose research interests center on issues of equity and access for underrepresented students and families in U.S. public schools.

Augustine F. Romero is Tucson Unified School District's Director of Student Equity, co-founder of the Social Justice Education Project, and the architect and founder of TUSD's Mexican American Studies Program in Tucson, Arizona. He created the Critical Compassionate Intellectualism Model of Transformative Education, which has led to high academic achievement, graduation rates, and college matriculation rates for its students and has been recognized internationally as a model of effective transformative education.

Daniel G. Solórzano is a Professor of Social Science and Comparative Education in the Graduate School of Education and Information Studies at the University of California, Los Angeles. He also has a joint appointment as Professor in the Chicana and Chicano Studies Department and Affiliated Professor in the Women's Studies Department. He is the Director of the University of California All Campus Consortium on Research for Diversity (UC/ACCORD), an interdisciplinary, multi-campus research center devoted to a more equitable distribution of educational resources and opportunities in California's public schools and universities. His teaching and research interests include: critical race and gender theory in education; critical race pedagogy; racial microaggressions in education; and the educational access, persistence, and graduation of students of color in the United States.

Jean Stefancic is Research Professor of Law at Seattle University, where she writes and teaches in the area of race and civil rights. She is the author of numerous books and articles on critical thought, Latino legal issues, and conservative think tanks and foundations, including *No Mercy: How Conservative Think Tanks and Foundations Changed America's Social Agenda* (Temple University Press, 1996).

David O. Stovall is an Associate Professor of Educational Policy Studies and African-American Studies at the University of Illinois at Chicago. His scholarship investigates four areas: critical race theory; concepts of social justice in education; the relationship between housing and education; and the relationship between schools and community stakeholders. In the attempt to bring theory to action, he has spent the last ten years working with community organizations and schools to develop curricula that address issues of social justice.

Binaya Subedi teaches classes on issues of diversity and equity, particularly in relation to issues of race, gender, ethnicity, and sexuality at the Ohio State University. He also teaches courses on global education, postcolonial theory, qualitative research, and immigrant narratives. His research has examined the racial identities and experiences of immigrants in mid-western cities.

Robert T. Teranishi is Associate Professor of Higher Education at New York University, Co-Director for the Institute for Globalization and Education in Metropolitan Settings, and Principal Investigator for the National Commission on Asian American and Pacific Islander Research in Education. In 2011, he was appointed by Secretary of Education Arne Duncan to the U.S. Department of Education's Equity and Excellence Commission.

Brenda Guadalupe Valles works for the Office for Equity and Diversity at the University of Utah conducting research, assessment, and teaching. She is a mixed-methods researcher who draws from critical race theory and LatCrit to better understand the educational pipeline, pedagogies of the home and community, and PK-20 policies and practices.

Sabina Vaught is an Associate Professor of Education at Tufts University, where she teaches courses on critical race theory, pedagogical theory, and qualitative research methodologies. Her scholarship examines the institutional contexts and dynamics of race, gender, schooling, and power. Specifically, she has conducted institutional ethnographic studies in a large urban school district and in a state division of juvenile affairs and its prison schools.

Verónica Vélez is a Postdoctoral Research Fellow for the Center for Latino Policy Research at the University of California, Berkeley. Her research focuses on critical race theory, the political agency of Latina/o families in educational reform, participatory action research, popular education, and the use of GIS technologies to further a critical race research agenda on the study of space.

Octavio Villalpando is the Associate Vice President for Equity and Diversity, and Professor of Educational Leadership and Policy at the University of Utah. His scholarship draws from critical race theory to examine racial inequality in U.S. higher education.

Dina C. Walker-DeVose is a doctoral candidate in the Department of Curriculum, Instruction, and Counselor Education at North Carolina State University in Raleigh, North Carolina. She works as an Adjunct Instructor at North Carolina State University, serves as a University Supervisor for student teachers in the Birth–Kindergarten Teacher Education Program at North Carolina Central University, and is completing the requirements for her Ph.D. expected in May 2013. Her research area focuses on parental school involvement, parent–teacher trust, and home–school collaboration.

INTRODUCTION

Adrienne D. Dixson and Marvin Lynn

"The problem of the color line," as described so vividly by W.E.B. Du Bois in his 1903 text *The Souls of Black Folk*, has been the focus of scholarly attention for academics in a variety of disciplines and fields for well over one hundred years. In education, race has primarily functioned as one of many variables used by scholars to examine educational outcomes. In the mid-1990s, critical race theory (CRT) emerged as a way to engage race as both the *cause* of and the *context* for disparate and inequitable social and educational outcomes. CRT scholars in both the law and education argued that scholars must place race at the center of their analyses. The *Handbook of Critical Race Theory in Education* provides examples of key scholarship that draws on CRT and other related frameworks, concepts, and methods as tools to analyze, investigate, document, and describe the impact of race and racism in education.

> And we know that all things work together for good to them who love God, who have been called according to his purpose.
>
> (Romans, 8:28)

THE ROAD TO CRT

In this brief chronicle, Adrienne Dixson will document her "road to CRT." I spent the summer of 1993 as the Dean of Students in a program that brought together students from the city's elite private schools and public schools. My job, as the Dean of Students, was ostensibly to help the instructors, all of whom were undergraduates from elite private universities and mostly White, develop lesson plans, manage their classrooms, and make "learning fun" for the students in the program. The common refrain recited by both kids and staff was: "Education Crossover[1] is not like regular school." I was new to the program, and connected to it because of my participation in a national teacher corps. That phrase bothered me, as a classroom teacher in one of the city's public schools, especially since the program was designed to meet the academic needs of the city's mostly African American population. The inclusion of the students from the city's elite private schools, most of whom were White, was a recent change in the program's policy and that also bothered me. The program was housed in one of the premier private schools in the city, which boasts two Superbowl champions among its alumni. The stark contrast between the haves and the have-nots was striking. The kids who attended public school were bussed in, and the kids who lived near the program either walked every morning or their parents dropped them off. The refrain of "This is not like regular school," I thought, was a constant reminder to the African American students of how unobtainable and temporary wealth and Whiteness were for them, no matter how close they were to it. In addition, that refrain, at least from my perspective, was a reminder of the inferiority of their Black schools with mostly Black teachers. In other words, and as we say in the vernacular, it was a diss. The contrast between the White students and the mostly White faculty and the African American students was shockingly uneven. It was during this summer that I was introduced, almost by accident, to Derrick Bell's (1992) groundbreaking book *Faces at the bottom of the well*. Interestingly, and what I understood after reading *Faces* and other work by Bell, the mostly White and self-described liberal ("Progressive" was a term that was in vogue in the early 1990s) faculty raved about how insightful *Faces* was for them in terms of "understanding racism in America." What I found so profoundly ironic was that they could not see how the entire program and indeed their actions during the program were also racist. In the Treme[2] and miles away from the uptown location of Summer Stroll, I purchased the book from the local Black-owned bookstore, the Community Book Center. I read it one day. I couldn't put it down. Bell's masterful storytelling interwoven with case law and historical information was so captivating and vivid that I felt as though I was reliving each event that he described. I also felt that I had more clarity on what I had been experiencing as a person of color in the U.S. It became even more clear to me that I had no real framework or vocabulary to describe what I believed was racism but that I had been socialized not to name racism explicitly. It would be several years before I would have an opportunity to engage Bell's work in a "scholarly" manner as a graduate student and have new vocabulary with which to talk about and examine race and racism: critical race theory. For the time being, *Faces* helped me make sense of what I was witnessing as structural racism at its most pervasive both within the Summer Stroll program and in my work as a teacher in a severely under-resourced school district.

CRITICAL RACE THEORY IN EDUCATION

The genealogy of CRT and CRT in education has been well documented and often recited in nearly every article and book chapter on the topic (Dixson & Rousseau, 2005). Indeed, in this handbook, several scholars offer perspectives on the genealogy of CRT and CRT in education (Brown & Jackson, Chapter 1; Delgado & Stefancic, Chapter 2; Ladson-Billings, Chapter 3). It is important to note however that, since the introduction of CRT to education in 1995 first by Gloria Ladson-Billings and William F. Tate IV and shortly thereafter with important contributions by Daniel G. Solórzano and Laurence Parker, scores of scholars across the academic spectrum have used CRT to examine a range of educational issues and the way they are informed and impacted by race and racism. We, the editors of this volume, along with other colleagues, have examined this emerging body of literature in our reviews of the literature on CRT in education (DeCuir & Dixson, 2004; Dixson & Rousseau, 2005; Lynn & Parker, 2006).

The expansion of CRT into education is significant because it has helped to illuminate the ubiquitous nature and "permanence of race" in the U.S. (Bell, 1992). Indeed, despite the 1954 *Brown v. Board of Education* decision that officially ended *de jure* racial segregation in education and other public facilities, public schools in most U.S. cities remain mostly separate and mostly unequal (Bell, 2004; Ladson-Billings, 2007; Orfield, 2009). Beyond just the critique of racial segregation in public schools, scholars have sought to uncover the ways that race manifests itself to create oppressive educational experiences for students of color (and their families) in seemingly "race neutral" contexts relative to pedagogy, policy, and curriculum. In this way, CRT scholars in education seek to show the inextricable relationship between educational inequity and race. In addition, CRT scholars in education have also challenged commonsense beliefs about people and communities of color that essentially cite cultural practices and poverty as reasons for educational disparities. Rather, CRT scholars in education call into question schooling practices that perpetuate Whiteness through expectations for student behavior and narrowly constructed curricular content, among other factors. CRT scholars in education have also sought to challenge and expand our understanding of research methods and methodologies such that we can capture, analyze, and represent racialized educational inequity. Thus, CRT scholars in education have made significant contributions to the field of education writ large.

PURPOSE

The purpose of the *Handbook of Critical Race Theory in Education* is to be both a "state of the art" discussion of CRT in education and exemplar scholarship. We invited education and legal scholars to examine a range of issues in education to illustrate both the "how" of CRT research and "why" CRT is an important way to understand persistent educational inequity. Despite the push by CRT scholars in education to center race and push the field to consider race as more than just a variable, far too many scholars who have an interest in examining race and racism in education misunderstand and misuse CRT.

While it is beyond the scope of this introduction to fully explain the misuses and misperceptions of CRT in education, it is important to note that some scholars claim a CRT project simply because their sample may be primarily composed of people of color. Far too often, scholars have invoked CRT in the introductory sections of their paper never to revisit the theory or even utilize any of its tenets in their analysis. As CRT scholars, we have both had our fair share of reviewing manuscripts submitted to a journal or for a conference that purport to use CRT but do so in a manner that is superficial, if utilized at all. By the same token, we have both had the pleasure of reading the work of both junior and senior scholars who not only demonstrate a rigorous and robust use of CRT but do so in a manner that moves the field forward in an exciting and significant way. It is for this reason that we believed it was time to compile, in one volume, scholarship by our CRT colleagues. We believe the work presented in this handbook represents both the standard-bearing rigorous scholarship and the "cutting-edge" scholarship of CRT in education. Readers who are interested in how particular CRT tenets apply to particular aspects of educational practice and theory will find the handbook helpful. Others who are interested in scholarship that departs from what has become tradition in the CRT in education literature will find a number of chapters that move the field forward, particularly as it pertains to issues of intersectionality and research methodologies. Our goal was to create a handbook that would speak to a number of constituencies within and across the educational community. We believe we have reached that goal.

ORGANIZATION OF THE HANDBOOK

The handbook is organized into three parts that address broad and overlapping topics. This is in large part due to the nature of CRT as an explanatory and analytical theory: race never operates in isolation of other factors. Thus, while a scholar may have an interest in language minorities, it is difficult to examine linguistic differences outside of the context of how language functions as a racializing agent. That is, language often serves as a racial marker. Thus, we could not create parts that were narrowly focused on single ideas. Instead, we created categories that were broad enough to capture the diversity of thought and use of CRT on particular educational issues. This is a testimony to the intellectual acuity of the scholars who contributed their work to this project.

The first part of the handbook, "The Genealogy of Critical Race Theory and Critical Race Theory in Education," describes the key conceptual principles of CRT in the law that gave shape to its departure from mainstream and critical legal scholarship. This part includes chapters that describe, in great detail, the key conceptual and methodological domains within CRT such as the interest convergence principle, Whiteness as property, the racial realism thesis, intersectionality, and chronicles and storytelling/counter-narrative. After each of these areas is described in rich detail, the authors examine the particular ways in which these frameworks have been utilized in the law and in the field of education and discuss how other scholars and policy-makers can use these frameworks in the development of transformative policy and practice in education.

This part also includes chapters that move beyond the discussion of the conceptual elements of CRT, to focus on the interdisciplinary origins of critical race theory and education (referred to by some as critical race studies in education) as a field. The chapters illustrate how fields in Ethnic Studies such as Black Studies, Chicano Studies, Asian American Studies, and Native or American Indian Studies have influenced the field. Radical race scholarship in education has also borrowed heavily from critical social theory. Critical race scholars in education have followed a path that is similar to that of their counterparts in the law: they have spent a great deal of time critiquing the racial blind spots apparent in education theory and practice. In this part, contributors provide some definition of these fields and describe and illuminate their relationship to critical race studies in education research. In explaining these disciplines and their relationship to CRT, the handbook situates CRT as an interdisciplinary, intersectional discourse that draws on multiple lines of inquiry as a means to construct a critique of race and racism that incorporates issues of ethnicity, language, social class, gender, sexuality, and nation.

The next part of the handbook, "Intersectional and Interdisciplinary Methods to Challenging Majoritarian Policies and Stock Stories in Education," highlights critical race intersectional and interdisciplinary research that illuminates broader social, political, and economic concerns that emerge from analyses of the impact of race in education. This research examines not only the experiences of both faculty and students of color in higher education but the ways in which public policy has shaped what happens in schools and universities. The research in this area draws on a variety of qualitative and quantitative methods, including person-centered narratives, composite chronicles, and legal policy analyses. Many of the chapters in this part draw on the concept of intersectionality, a concept advanced by Kimberlé Crenshaw that argues for an examination of discrimination that takes into account how multiple forms of oppression like race, ethnicity, class, gender, language, immigrant status, and sexuality work in concert to form a unique set of experiences for people of color globally. This part examines the methods and tools CRT scholars have engaged in, but also how they have innovated, enhanced, or transformed methods to examine and theorize on and about research into race in education. The chapters explore how CRT has informed both the form and the function of educational research that moves beyond the goal of "generating understanding" toward the goal to "create interdisciplinary knowledge" about race and racism that has the impact of changing the social and political landscape.

Finally, Part III, "Critical Race Praxis in Communities, Schools, and the University," examines the ways in which CRT is used as a framework to explore the multiple and varied ways that pedagogy and praxis both develop and are contested within schools, universities, and communities. Critical race praxis challenges current constructions of "high-quality teaching" while constructing a transformative vision for America's schools and universities. The chapters in this part explore the various political, social, and economic issues taken up by these organic discourses and practices and explore the role of culture, identity, civic agency, and social action as important variables that shape and impact the outcomes of various forms of praxis in these contexts and in their surrounding communities. These chapters begin the important process of articulating how CRT might aid scholars, teachers, activists, and others committed to examining race in education to construct a vision for a more democratic, egalitarian, and just society.

NOTES

1 A pseudonym.
2 The Faubourg Treme is the oldest African American neighborhood in the U.S. This historic site was an important site of Black commerce and cultural activity for much of the history of New Orleans. It experienced some challenges with the building of the I-10 freeway system that literally divided the Treme in half and dispersed homeowners. It also experienced some challenges owing to the levee failures after Hurricane Katrina. News coverage at that time that showed the city underwater featured aerial shots of the Treme. Like much of the city that experienced the brunt of the flooding, the Treme is still rebuilding even seven years after Hurricane Katrina.

   The Community Book Center has been serving the Treme area for 25 years as the only independent bookstore in the New Orleans metropolitan area. It specializes in books about African and African American culture and serves as a meeting site for many of the city's community groups. The store's motto, "More than just a bookstore," aptly describes its central role in community affairs and politics.

REFERENCES

Bell, D.A. (1992). *Faces at the bottom of the well: The permanence of racism.* New York: Basic Books.

Bell, D.A. (2004). *Silent covenants: Brown v. Board of Education and the unfulfilled hopes for racial reform.* New York: Oxford University Press.

DeCuir, J., & Dixson, A.D. (2004). "So when it comes out, they aren't that surprised that it is there": Using critical race theory as a tool of analysis of race and racism in education. *Educational Research, 33*(5), 26–31.

Dixson, A.D., & Rousseau, C.K. (2005). And we are still not saved: Critical race theory in education ten years later. *Race, ethnicity and education, 8*(1), 7–27.

Du Bois, W.E.B. (1903/1995). *Souls of Black folks.* New York: Signet Classic.

Ladson-Billings, G.J. (2007). Can we at least have *Plessy*? The struggle for quality education. *North Carolina Law Review, 85*, 1279–1292.

Ladson-Billings, G.J., & Tate, W.F. (1995). Toward a critical race theory of education. *Teachers College Press, 97*, 47–68.

Lynn, M., & Parker, L. (2006). Critical race studies in education: Examining a decade of research on US schools. *Urban Review, 38*(4), 257–290.

Orfield, G. (2009). *Reviving the goal of an integrated society: A 21st century challenge.* Los Angeles, CA: Civil Rights Project/Proyecto Derechos Civiles at UCLA.

Part I

The Genealogy of Critical Race Theory and
Critical Race Theory in Education

1

THE HISTORY AND CONCEPTUAL ELEMENTS OF CRITICAL RACE THEORY

Kevin Brown and Darrell D. Jackson

While the roots of the scholarship of critical race theory (CRT) can be traced to earlier writings, the first meeting occurred in the summer of 1989 in Madison, Wisconsin. Twenty-three legal scholars of color met for a weeklong workshop (Crenshaw, 2011).[1] As with any intellectual movement, CRT was born out of the confluence of historical developments of the time and the need to respond to those developments. Thus, in order to understand the scholarship produced by CRT, it is necessary to start with those historical events.

THE HISTORY BEHIND CRITICAL RACE THEORY

The Supreme Court's unanimous 1954 opinion in *Brown v. Board of Education* overturned the doctrine of "separate but equal" embraced by the Court in its infamous 1896 *Plessy v. Ferguson* decision. In *Brown*, the Court struck down statutes that authorized racial segregation of public school students, which existed in 21 states, because the statutes violated the equal protection clause of the Fourteenth Amendment. This Amendment was added to the Constitution in 1868. In its 1873 decision in the *Slaughterhouse Cases*, the first opinion addressing the reach of the Fourteenth Amendment, the Court originally stated that its "one pervading purpose ... [was] the freedom of the slave race, the security and firm establishment of that freedom, and the protection of the newly-made free-man and citizen from the oppressions of those who had formerly exercised unlimited dominion over him" (Slaughterhouse Cases, 1873).[2]

The *Brown* decision ushered in a dramatic 15-year period of unprecedented legal, political, economic, and educational measures directed towards dismantling the structures of racism and oppression instituted as a result of segregation. The Court quickly followed its opinion in *Brown* with a string of decisions which struck down segregation practices by governmental entities that involved public parks, beaches, golf courses, transportation, and other public facilities. Ten years after *Brown*, Congress passed the

Civil Rights Act of 1964, the most sweeping civil rights legislation in the nation's history, followed the next year by passage of the Voting Rights Act and the Elementary and Secondary Education Act. In 1968, Congress passed the Fair Housing Act, outlawing discrimination in the real estate industry. In that same year, the Supreme Court issued another major school desegregation decision, *Green v. New Kent County* (1968). Frustrated by the lack of progress in the dismantling of dual school systems, one for whites and the other for people of color, in *Green* the Court ordered school districts to eliminate segregation root and branch in all aspects of their public schools and to do so immediately. Also, many selective higher education institutions established affirmative action admission policies in the mid- to late 1960s, which brought large numbers of black and other minority students to their campuses. Furthermore, governmental units, as well as private entities, established set-aside programs for minority contractors and race conscious hiring and promotion plans in order to increase the diversity of their contractors, workforces, supervisors, and managers.

The inauguration of Richard Nixon in 1969 quickly led to changes in the justices who sat on the Supreme Court bench. By the end of his first term, Nixon had appointed four justices to the Court, and these justices were decidedly less sympathetic to the concerns and interests of underrepresented minorities.[3] Thus, as Nixon started his second term, a far more conservative Supreme Court was in place. As a result, the Court began to halt, and then reverse, many of the hard-won legal victories obtained for underrepresented minorities.

The first major indication of this change in direction of the Supreme Court was its 1973 decision in the case of *Keyes v. School District No. 1* (Skiba et al., 2009). In *Keyes*, the Court concluded that an unconstitutionally segregated school system was not one where the students attended racially identifiable schools, *de facto* segregation. Rather it was one where the racially identifiable schools resulted from intentional conduct by school authorities directed toward segregating the schools. Thus, many *de facto* segregated schools were not unconstitutionally segregated. In addition, establishing the existence of a dual school system became a complicated and arduous affair for black plaintiffs. Petitioners for black schoolchildren had to comb through mounds of government documents and interview countless witnesses to prove that the segregated schools resulted from discriminatory motives.

The *Keyes* decision was followed the next year by the Court's decision in *Milliken v. Bradley* (1974), which dealt the deathblow to the hopes of ever successfully desegregating America's public schools. In a five to four decision,[4] with all four Nixon justices in the majority, the Supreme Court rejected a lower court's inter-district school desegregation remedy for the Detroit public school system. According to the lower court, in a school system where 63 percent of the student body was black, there were not enough white students to successfully desegregate the schools (Milliken v. Bradley, 1974, p. 765). So the lower court reassigned many of Detroit's students to suburban school systems, even though there was no evidence of actions by the suburban schools that fostered segregation in Detroit. The lower court felt justified in doing this because it had found that the State of Michigan was also responsible for the segregation in Detroit public schools. Since school district boundary lines were products of decisions by the State, the lower court reasoned that these boundaries should not limit a desegregation remedy. However, the Supreme Court concluded, in general, that a school desegregation remedy was limited to the offending school system and overturned the lower court inter-district desegregation order. As a result of the *Milliken* decision, most of the nation's major urban school districts such as Atlanta, Chicago, New York, Newark, and Philadelphia could not be effectively integrated, because there were not enough white students left in the districts (Bell, 1980; Coleman, 1975).

In the Court's 1976 *Washington v. Davis* decision, a case that behind *Brown v. Board of Education* may be the most significant race discrimination decision in the past 116 years, the Court was presented with the need to determine what constitutes unconstitutional race discrimination. In this case, the Court addressed a challenge by black police officers to the use of a written civil service exam designed to test verbal ability, vocabulary, reading, and comprehension, because blacks were far more likely to fail the exam than whites. Five years earlier, in another case of first impression, the Court addressed the definition of what constituted employment discrimination under Title VII of the 1964 Civil Rights Act. In *Griggs v. Duke Power Co.* (1971), the Court concluded that a complainant could establish a *prima facie* case of employment discrimination by establishing that a given employment policy or practice, such as requiring a high school diploma or successfully passing a standardized general intelligence test, produced a discriminatory effect on minorities. An employer could rebut the *prima facie* case of discrimination by showing that the employment policy or practice was related to successful job performance. However, in *Washington v. Davis* (1976),[5] the Court rejected discriminatory effects as the basis of determining unconstitutional discrimination. Instead, the Court concluded that only governmental actions motivated by discriminatory intent violated the Constitution. In justifying its decision to reject discriminatory effects, the Court stated:

> A rule that a statute designed to serve neutral ends is nevertheless invalid, absent compelling justification, if in practice it benefits or burdens one race more than another would be far reaching and would raise serious questions about, and perhaps invalidate, a whole range of tax, welfare, public service, regulatory, and licensing statutes that may be more burdensome to the poor and to the average black than to the more affluent white …
>
> (p. 248)

To emphasize just how far reaching a decision that based unconstitutional discrimination on proof of discriminatory effects could be, the Court included a footnote that quoted portions of a law review article. The article suggested that the discriminatory effect analysis could invalidate "tests and qualifications for voting, draft deferment, public employment, jury service, and other government-conferred benefits and opportunities … sales taxes, bail schedules, utility rates, bridge tolls, license fees, and other state-imposed charges" (p. 248, n. 14). The Court pointed out that "it has also been argued that minimum wage and usury laws as well as professional licensing requirements would require major modifications in light of the unequal-impact rule" (p. 248, n. 14).

The Supreme Court followed up *Washington v. Davis* with its decision two years later in *Bakke v. Regents of the University of California* (1978). In *Bakke*, the Court struck down an admission plan adopted by the University of California at Davis Medical School because it reserved 16 of its 100 admissions seats for blacks, Native Americans, Hispanics, and Asians. The justices split on the decision, with four justices willing to uphold the admissions plan against challenges under the equal protection clause and Title VI of the 1964 Civil Rights Act, which prohibits discrimination in federally funded programs. Four other justices concluded that Title VI barred any consideration of race in the admissions process. They also felt that it was unnecessary to address the equal protection challenge. Justice Powell provided the deciding opinion.

Before turning to his analysis of the admissions plan, Powell addressed the governing purpose behind the equal protection clause. He rejected the Court's original statement of the purpose of the Fourteenth Amendment in its 1873 *Slaughterhouse Cases* decision. Powell also rejected the argument first articulated by the Supreme Court in footnote 4 of a famous 1942 opinion, *U.S. v. Carolene Products Co.*, that the purpose of the clause was to protect discrete insular minorities who required extraordinary protection from the majoritarian political process. Such an understanding would require the Supreme Court to be more differential to measures intended to benefit minority groups, like blacks and Latinos, than it would be to measures that would harm those groups. Rather, Powell concluded that the purpose of the equal protection clause was to protect the rights of individuals, regardless of race. As a result, for Powell, the use of racial classifications that disadvantaged whites would receive the same strict scrutiny that the use of racial classifications that disadvantaged underrepresented minority groups would receive.

For Powell in order for colleges and universities to consider race in the admissions process they needed to have a constitutionally permissible and substantial reason. Powell concluded that reducing the historical deficit of traditionally disfavored minorities in medical school and the medical professions, countering the effects of societal discrimination on minorities, and increasing the number of physicians who would practice in currently underserved minority communities were not sufficiently compelling reasons to justify the consideration of race. The only rationale Powell found worthy was obtaining the educational benefits that flow from an ethnically diverse student body. Thus, Powell concluded that an admission plan that took account of race or ethnicity as one factor among many in an effort to obtain a diverse student body would survive challenges under both the equal protection clause and Title VI. However, one that reserved a certain quota of admissions seats for members of these groups would not.

THE EMERGENCE OF CRITICAL RACE THEORY

All of the law professors who met at the original CRT workshop taught in predominantly white law schools and most of them were among the first persons of color hired to teach at their respective institutions. Consistent with Powell's opinion in *Bakke*, the faculties that hired them were allowed to give positive considerations to their candidacy because of their race in making the hiring decision. Many of these professors had also participated in various Critical Legal Studies (CLS) conferences.

In the late 1970s, a movement composed of predominately white neo-Marxist, New Left, and counter-culturalist intellectuals emerged within the legal academy. CLS sought to expose and challenge the view that legal reasoning was neutral, value-free, and unaffected by social and economic relations, political forces, or cultural phenomena. Rather CLS pointed out that the law tends to enforce, reflect, constitute, and legitimize the dominant social and power relations through social actors who generally believe that they are neutral and arrive at their decisions through an objective process of legal reasoning. Thus, for CLS proponents, American law and legal institutions tend to serve and to legitimize an oppressive social order. CLS scholars also effectively demonstrated that legal decisions were indeterminate, incoherent, and deeply embedded in both politics and the personal biases of the deciding judges.

The first meeting of CRT emerged out of a sense that, while CLS had developed some very significant insights about how the legal process worked, the movement did not adequately address the struggles of people of color, particularly blacks. As Harlan Dalton pointed out in a special issue of the *Harvard Civil Rights–Civil Liberties Law Review* devoted to minority critiques of CLS, there was an absence of a positive program for how to address the concerns of people of color on the part of many CLS scholars. This was one of the central difficulties that scholars of color had with the movement (Dalton, 1987; Matsuda, 1987). In addition, CLS scholars were too dismissive of legal rights. For people of color, it was legal rights and their enforcement by the Supreme Court that led to the end of segregation, anti-discrimination legislation, and voting rights for people of color.

Beyond the sense of frustration with CLS, major legal and political events shaped the first meeting of CRT. George Bush handily defeated Michael Dukakis in the November 1988 elections. Bush's inauguration in January of 1989 assured the continued appointment of conservative judges like the ones Ronald Reagan had selected, including Supreme Court justices, to the federal bench for the foreseeable future. Also, during its 1988–89 term, the Supreme Court issued seven major opinions that further restricted or eliminated hard-won legal gains for underrepresented minorities. These decisions made it more difficult for minority plaintiffs to win employment discrimination lawsuits under Title VII, created uncertainty regarding the validity of many consent decrees to resolve claims of discrimination, narrowed the interpretation of certain civil rights statutes, and limited the situations where discrimination plaintiffs could collect attorney's fees (Spann, 1990). However, the most significant of these decisions was the Court's opinion in *City of Richmond v. Croson* (1989). In that decision, the Court struck down the set-aside program for minority contractors established by the city of Richmond, Virginia, the former capital of the Old Confederacy. Blacks made up over 50 percent of the population of Richmond. Over the five years before the adoption of the set-aside program, however, the City had only awarded 0.67 percent of the dollar volume of its prime construction contracts to minority businesses (pp. 479–480). Despite Richmond's long history of discrimination against blacks and figures regarding the awarding of prime construction contracts, the Supreme Court concluded that the set-aside program discriminated against the rights of non-minority contractors under the equal protection clause. For the first time in the 121-year history of the equal protection clause, a majority of the justices followed Justice Powell's proclamation: that the purpose of the equal protection clause was to protect the rights of individuals. As a result, the Court concluded that strict judicial scrutiny would apply to the use of racial classifications by state and local governmental entities, regardless of the race of the beneficiaries. In doing so, the Supreme Court concluded that there was little constitutionally significant difference between segregation statutes that confined minorities to inferior schools and various governmental policies and programs adopted to dismantle the continuing societal effects on these minority groups of America's history of racial discrimination. By depriving governmental entities of the ability to institute policies and programs that took account of race as a means to dismantle the continuing effects of racial oppression and the ability to order private parties to do the same, the Court was freezing into place the status quo of prior discrimination.

While the Supreme Court's decision in *City of Richmond* specifically addressed set-asides for minority contractors created by state and local governmental units, the Court's rationale suggested that race conscious hiring and promotion plans enacted by governmental entities, as well as affirmative action admissions programs instituted by selective colleges and universities, were also constitutionally suspect. As a result, the rationale of the *City of Richmond* decision called into question the very legal grounds for the consideration of race in the hiring process that brought many of these scholars of color to their legal institutions. Furthermore, it cast doubt upon the affirmative action admissions programs that continued to bring most of their students of color to their law schools. Thus, the first meeting of CRT was held at a time of crisis for these scholars. It was also clear that the Supreme Court and the federal courts had turned from friend of people of color to foe.

While the legal scholars who met at the first CRT meeting were looking for a community of like-minded individuals, they were also motivated by a desire to understand how a regime of white supremacy and its subordination of people of color had been created and maintained in America. More importantly, they wanted to develop the understandings that would change it. These legal scholars sought to comprehend how the signature statement of civil rights rhetoric, to judge individuals "by the content of their character, not the color of their skin," was turned on its head. They wanted to understand how this rhetoric, which had been so effective for underrepresented minorities in the 1950s, 1960s, and early 1970s, could now be used to strike down the very programs instituted to help America undo the effects of its history of racial oppression. Basically, what distinguished these CRT scholars from conventional liberal scholarship about race and inequality was a deep dissatisfaction with the traditional civil rights discourse. Thus, their mission necessarily required understanding the very foundational ideas of traditional legal discourse and formulating criticisms of those ideas.

CHALLENGING THE NEUTRALITY AND ABILITY OF TRADITIONAL CIVIL RIGHTS DISCOURSE IN THE LAW

One important aspect of CRT seeks to reveal that the conceptions of racism and racial subordination as understood by traditional legal discourse are neither neutral nor sufficient to overcome the effects of centuries of racial oppression on people of color. Indeed, the appearance of neutrality primarily operates to obscure the fact that the perspective of the white majority is embedded within this view. In addition, the concept of discrimination is so limited that remedies for it cannot adequately recognize all forms of discrimination nor overcome the continuing effects that it has had on our society.

In a 1978 article, which legal scholars of color found to be one of the best-written CLS pieces, Alan Freeman pointed out that the view of racism and racial oppression embedded in traditional legal thinking is that of the perpetrators of racial oppression, as opposed to its victims. In a 1987 article, Charles Lawrence noted that the Supreme Court's definition of race discrimination as the product of consciously racially motivated decision making is inadequate because it overlooks the impact of unconscious forms of racism. Derrick Bell's interest convergence principle and racial realism went a step beyond Lawrence. In his interest convergence principle, Bell asserted that blacks only make substantial progress against racial oppression when their interests align with those of white elites. From this interest convergence principle comes Bell's racial realism—that racism is an integral, permanent, and indestructible part of American society.

The Victim's Perspective and the Perpetrator's Perspective

The victim's perspective and the perpetrator's perspective were introduced in an article written by Alan Freeman (1978). When the Supreme Court addresses an issue for the first time, there is no prior judicial opinion to guide the decision of the justices. Thus, in cases of first impression, the Supreme Court is left to choose which legal principle will govern. In the 1976 case of *Washington v. Davis*[6] noted above, the Court was presented with the need to choose between using discriminatory effects or discriminatory intent as the means by which to determine what constitutes unconstitutional race discrimination for purposes of the equal protection clause. The Court concluded that discrimination is the result of actions that are motivated by a discriminatory intent.

Given the definition of discrimination articulated by the Court in *Washington v. Davis*, actions motivated by racially neutral justifications which, nevertheless, generate a disproportionately negative impact upon racial minorities are not considered to be discriminatory. Thus, for example, application of various educational policies and procedures such as the use of high-stakes tests as part of the requirements to obtain a high school diploma, minimum competency tests for teachers, various disciplinary policies and procedures, using seniority to determine teacher layoffs, and ability skills grouping, which disadvantage the educational and employment opportunities of underrepresented minorities more than majority individuals, normally survive a discrimination legal challenge. The reason they do is because what constitutes discrimination is based on whether the actions by the perpetrators are motivated by discriminatory intent, not whether such actions or decisions have a discriminatory effect upon underrepresented minority populations. Since educational officials can usually justify their educational policies and practices with reference to legitimate educational concerns, these practices are seldom struck down by federal courts. As a result, regardless of the extent of the negative disparate impact of school policies and practices upon underrepresented minorities, federal courts will tend to view such outcomes as the unfortunate result of racially neutral decision making.

Freeman's article noted how the distinction between defining discrimination in terms of the effects of actions as opposed to the intent that motivated the actions represented a distinction between the victim's perspective of discrimination as opposed to the perpetrator's perspective. For victims, "racial discrimination describes the actual social existence as a member of a perpetual underclass. This perspective includes both the objective conditions of life (lack of jobs, lack of money, lack of housing) and the consciousness associated with those objective conditions" (Freeman, 1978, pp. 1052–1053).

Thus, for the victims, if racial discrimination is eliminated, then there would be some significant changes in the conditions of life that were associated with racial discrimination. These changes would include substantial improvements in their employment and educational opportunities, income, wealth, and ability to obtain adequate affordable housing. In contrast, the perpetrator's perspective views racial discrimination as the result of conscious discriminatory actions by individuals, not as a social phenomenon. From the perpetrator's perspective, society needs to eliminate its villains, those whose actions are motivated by racial animus. Thus, racial discrimination is the fault of a limited group of individuals; however, those who are not perpetrators are innocent and share no responsibility to ameliorate the problems caused by racism. Once the actions of the misguided perpetrators have been remedied, then what remains in terms of the socioeconomic order is presumed to be the just condition of society. The point of Freeman's piece was to establish that the legal system's view of racism and race discrimination was neither neutral nor objective.[7] Rather it represented the courts choosing the perspective of the perpetrators regarding what is considered discrimination over that of the victim.

Unconscious Discrimination Does Not Exist in Traditional Legal Discourse

Charles Lawrence, in his pathbreaking article "The Id, the Ego, and Equal Protection Clause: Reckoning with Unconscious Racism" (1987), extended the critique of the concept of discrimination that Freeman had made. Lawrence pointed out the inherent failings of a legal system that views race discrimination as a product of conscious racial decision making. As Lawrence notes, the Supreme Court's race discrimination jurisprudence views apparently neutral actions that are not motivated by conscious racial animus as legal. This motive-centered approach makes it difficult, if not impossible, for victims to prove discrimination. Perpetrators can easily hide improper discriminatory purposes. In addition, the behavior of individuals normally results from a combination of a number of different motives. As a result, there are likely to be racially neutral motives to explain a person's actions, as well as racially discriminatory ones. However, the injury of racial inequality suffered by the victims exists regardless of the motives of the actors. For example, the harms inflicted upon underrepresented minority schoolchildren who are constrained in low-achieving, under-resourced schools, provided with less skilled teachers or systematically left out of gifted and talented classes, exist regardless of the reasons provided by the educational officials for allowing these circumstances to occur.

Lawrence rejects the dichotomy of the Court's race discrimination jurisprudence, which views actions motivated by discriminatory intent as illegal, but actions motivated by racially neutral considerations that generate a negative discriminatory effect as legal. Drawing on insights from psychology, Lawrence argues that:

> Americans share a common historical and cultural heritage in which racism has played and still plays a dominant role. Because of this shared experience, we also inevitably share many ideas, attitudes and beliefs that attach significance to an individual's race and induce negative feelings and opinions about nonwhites. To the extent that this cultural belief system has influenced all of us, we are all racists. At the same time, most of us are unaware of our racism. We do not recognize the ways in which our cultural experience has influenced our beliefs about race or the occasions on which those beliefs affect our actions. In other words, *a large part of the behavior that produces racial discrimination is influenced by unconscious racial motivations.*
>
> (Lawrence, 1987, p. 322, emphasis added)

There is a fundamental difference between the way traditional legal discourse views individuals and the way that Lawrence sees them. For traditional legal discourse, individuals are products of self-determination. Individuals become who they are through interacting with the world and learning about the world on their own. Thus, individuals come to develop their own ideas and act based solely on their self-determined motivations. In contrast, Lawrence views individuals as products of culture. Rather than individuals coming to know what they know as the result of an individualized learning process, individuals are acculturated into a dominant cultural system of beliefs about race and ethnicity. Thus, defining racial discrimination as the product of intentionally motivated decision making is inadequate. Such a narrow view of discrimination fails to address a large part of the potent aspects of racism, which are the products of unconscious motivations derived from an acculturation process into the dominant cultural set of beliefs that view people of color more negatively than whites.[8]

Interest Convergence Principle

Professor Derrick Bell, the first tenured black professor at Harvard Law School, pointed out the limitation of the Supreme Court's decisions to dismantle the effects of America's history of racial discrimination with his pathbreaking idea of the interest convergence principle. Bell first put forth his principle as a dilemma in 1980, when he did a retrospective review of the Supreme Court's school desegregation jurisprudence (Bell, 1980). Bell stated:

> The interest of blacks in achieving racial equality will be accommodated only when it converges with the interests of whites. However, the fourteenth amendment, standing alone, will not authorize a judicial remedy providing effective racial equality for blacks where the remedy sought threatens the superior societal status of middle and upper class whites.
>
> It follows that the availability of fourteenth amendment protection in racial cases may not actually be determined by the character of harm suffered by blacks or the quantum of liability proved against whites. Racial remedies may instead be the outward manifestations of unspoken and perhaps subconscious judicial conclusions that the remedies, if granted, will secure, advance, or at least not harm societal interests deemed important by middle and upper class whites.
>
> (p. 523)

Bell went on to show that the Court's decision in *Brown v. Board of Education* could easily be justified in terms of advancing the interest of elite whites as opposed to protecting the constitutional rights of black schoolchildren. In *Brown*, attorneys for both the NAACP and the federal government made the argument that segregation of people of color provided the Soviet Union with a huge rhetorical advantage in trying to garner support from the independent nations that were emerging or would emerge in Africa and Asia (Dudziak, 1988). Thus, Bell noted that the *Brown* decision immediately improved America's credibility in its struggle against communism for the hearts and minds of people in emerging third world countries. Bell also pointed out that many elite whites understood that the South could not make the transition from a plantation economy to an industrialized economy without discarding segregation. Thus, substantial economic progress in the southern states depended upon rejecting segregation. Third, Bell noted that the segregation decision could help to assuage the disillusionment experienced by blacks with so many having recently participated in World War II's efforts to assure freedom and equality in Europe, yet finding it denied to them at home.

Bell also applied his theory of interest convergence to President Abraham Lincoln's decision to issue the Emancipation Proclamation. He pointed to Lincoln's September 1862 letter to the editor of the *New York Times*, Horace Greely, written shortly before Lincoln announced his intention to issue the Proclamation. In the letter Lincoln explained: "What I do about slavery and the colored race, I do because I do believe it helps to save the Union. I shall do less whenever I shall believe that what I am doing hurts the cause, and I shall do more whenever I believe that doing more will help the cause" (Bell, 2008,

p. 22). Bell goes on to note that three reasons justified Lincoln issuing the Proclamation, which had nothing to do with the interest of the black slaves. First, as the war dragged on, Lincoln's military advisers urged emancipation as a way to disrupt the Southern economy, which relied on slave labor. Second, there were indications that foreign governments might be willing to recognize the Confederacy and supply it with financial aid and arms. However, foreign abolitionists in these countries might oppose such an effort if the North made abolition one of its war objectives. Third, with the enlistment of whites in the Union army lagging, emancipation could open up the opportunity to enlist thousands of black soldiers. As Bell concludes, abolition of slavery had to wait until it coincided with the best interest of elite whites.

Racial Realism

The interest convergence principle is inherently conservative, because it strongly implies another point about the centrality of racism in American society and law: that it is permanent. Bell had spoken of the principle of racial realism earlier, and the tenor of his 1987 book *And We Are Not Saved: The Elusive Quest for Racial Justice* suggested this point. However, racial realism took center stage in Bell's 1992 book *Faces at the Bottom of the Well: The Permanence of Racism*. In it Bell rejected the hopes of civil rights organizations, the black community, and social justice advocates by asserting that "racism is an integral, permanent, and indestructible component of this society" (Bell, 1992, p. ix). As Bell goes on to state:

> Black people will never gain full equality in this country. Even those herculean efforts we hail as successful will produce no more than temporary "peaks of progress," short-lived victories that slide into irrelevance as racial patterns adapt in ways that maintain white dominance. This is a hard-to-accept fact that all history verifies.

(p. 12)

Bell suggests one obtains a certain freedom from knowing the truth. He further argues that blacks should struggle against racial oppression even though, ultimately, the struggle is futile, because the struggle will empower blacks.

CRITICAL RACE THEORY STRATEGIES TO DEMONSTRATE THE LIMITED ABILITY OF TRADITIONAL LEGAL DISCOURSE TO ADEQUATELY REVEAL THE NATURE OF RACIAL OPPRESSION

CRT scholars sought to expose the limited ability of traditional legal scholarship to adequately reveal how integral racism and racial subordination are in the everyday lives of people of color. CRT authors employed techniques of chronicles, storytelling, and counter-narratives to point this out. Cheryl Harris's (1993) article discussing the concept of whiteness as property is an excellent example of this critique.

Chronicles, storytelling, and counter-narratives

Many dominant group members presuppose that racial or ethnic inequality is the result of cultural problems of minority groups or the lack of adequate enforcement of existing discrimination laws. However, because social and moral realities are socially constructed, they are indeterminate and subject to multiple interpretations. One way to demonstrate that racial and ethnic phenomena are interpreted differently based on the positionality of your particular group in the social hierarchy is to tell stories, parables, chronicles, or narratives. Thus, CRT scholars use chronicles, storytelling, and counter-narratives to undermine the claims of racial neutrality of traditional legal discourse and to reveal that racism and racial discrimination are neither aberrant nor occasional parts of the lives of people of color. Rather racism and racial discrimination are deep and enduring parts of the everyday existences of people of color. Thus, chronicles, storytelling, and counter-narratives are used to make visible the racial biases that are deeply embedded in the unstated norms of American law and culture.

Several CRT authors tell stories to convey the ubiquitous nature of racism and racial discrimination. Nor is the solution to continuing racial oppression and subordination merely the better enforcement of existing anti-discrimination laws. Because discrimination comes in many forms, such as institutional, unconscious, and cultural, which are not addressed by current antidiscrimination laws, those laws are inadequate. Some of the early examples and uses of chronicles, storytelling, and counter-narratives include Derrick Bell's book *And We Are Not Saved: The Elusive Quest for Racial Justice* (1987), Patricia Williams's book *Alchemy of Race and Rights: Diary of a Law Professor* (1987), and Richard Delgado's *Rodrigo Chronicles: Conversations about Race in America* (1995).

Cheryl Harris's 1993 article "Whiteness as Property"

While our concept of race is socially constructed and, thus, represents a state of mind, in this article Cheryl Harris conceptualizes whiteness as an intangible property interest and speaks of how the legal system protected a vested interest in white skin. Harris discusses the story of her light-skinned grandmother, who passed as white in the 1930s in order to gain employment at a department store that catered to upper middle class whites. Harris uses this story to go on to note that being white means gaining access to a set of public and private privileges that allow for greater control over the critical aspects of one's life. As a result, whiteness automatically carries with it greater economic, political, and social security. Harris goes on to argue that American law has long protected the settled expectations based on white privilege and thereby converted whiteness into a valuable property interest that, "although unacknowledged, now forms the background against which legal disputes are framed, argued and adjudicated."

INTERSECTIONALITY

Another concept associated with CRT is intersectionality. This concept was first articulated by Kimberlé Williams Crenshaw, one of the principal organizers and founders of CRT, in a 1991 *Stanford Law Review* article. Crenshaw noted that identity-based politics has been a source of strength, community, and intellectual development. However, one of the problems with such politics is that it often conflates or ignores intragroup differences. Crenshaw goes on to note:

> Feminist efforts to politicize experiences of women and antiracist efforts to politicize experiences of people of color have frequently proceeded as though the issues and experiences they each detail occur on mutually exclusive terrains. Although racism and sexism readily intersect in the lives of real people, they seldom do in feminist and antiracist practices. Thus, when the practices expound identity as women or person

of color as an either/or proposition, they relegate the identity of women of color to a location that resists telling.

(p. 1242)

Crenshaw points out that, frequently, the experiences of women of color are the result of the intersection of patterns of racism and sexism. As a result of this intersectionality, discourse shaped by women of color tends to get marginalized in discussions about the issues that impact women and people of color. In her discussions about intersectionality, Crenshaw notes that other characteristics such as class or sexuality also are important in shaping the experiences of women of color. Thus, her focus on intersections of gender and race is only meant to highlight the need to take account of the multiple identities when considering how to restructure the social world.

CONCLUSION AND FUTURE DIRECTION

CRT major success in changing the debate about the role of race in American jurisprudence can be seen in the comparison of the Supreme Court's justifications for school desegregation with its rationale for approving affirmative action. School desegregation and affirmative action are similar in that both involve integrating students. In *Brown*, the Court explained its rationale for striking down segregation statutes by approvingly quoting the district court opinion in the Kansas case:

Segregation of white and colored children in public schools has a detrimental effect upon the colored children ... [f]or the policy of separating the races is usually interpreted as denoting the inferiority of the negro group. A sense of inferiority affects the motivation of a child to learn. *Segregation with the sanction of law, therefore, has a tendency to [retard] the educational and mental development of negro children.*

(Brown, 1954, p. 494, emphasis added)

Thus, in *Brown*, the Court viewed black people as psychologically damaged because of segregation. As a result, white students who attended desegregated schools with blacks could expect to receive little, if any, educational benefit from a diverse classroom. Nor was there any reason to incorporate the perspectives and understandings of blacks into the education process, because those were the consequences of the detrimental effect suffered by blacks as a result of their separation from whites. However, consistent with the rationale of critical race theorists, a majority of the justices in *Grutter* concluded that obtaining a critical mass of underrepresented minorities with a history of discrimination improves the educational environment for all students. Thus, having everyone exposed to the different perspectives and points of view of minority groups with a history of discrimination is beneficial to all students.

Unfortunately, beyond affirmative action for selective higher education programs, the Supreme Court did not either fundamentally change the legal definition of race discrimination, which is still limited to actions motivated by discriminatory intent, or expand the ability to use racial classifications to ameliorate the conditions of underrepresented minorities in other contexts. Thus, as an intellectual movement, CRT succeeded beyond all realistic expectations at the time of its founding. However, its ultimate impact on American race jurisprudence has been limited.

In education, CRT remains extraordinarily useful. Ladson-Billings and Tate (1995) provided the initial introduction in their seminal piece. They used CRT tenets and research "as an analytic tool for understanding school inequality" (p. 48). Since that time, CRT analysis has been honed by numerous other authors. Each author enhanced the relevance of a CRT perspective on past, present, and future educational issues. More specifically, in the field of education, CRT can be used to question the variables chosen (or ignored) in quantitative research as well as establish counter-narratives in qualitative research.

Moving onward, educational issues like school re-segregation, the school-to-prison pipeline, and special education studies will be able to utilize CRT in their assessment of educational policy. As an example, the normalcy of racism tenet helps one understand why schools continue to become more and more segregated (with or without intent). *Brown* (1954), while politically expedient, provided few if any tools for significant social change. Without affirmative measures forcing change in student populations, the status quo would inevitably revert to a pre-desegregation era. The school-to-prison pipeline and special education labels merely facilitate the reversion. These, and myriad other educational issues, are part of the responsibility borne by the newest wave of CRT scholars who are challenged to carry the baton forward.

NOTES

1 Those attending that meeting were: Anita Allen, Taunya Banks, Derrick Bell, Kevin Brown, Paulette Caldwell (New York University), John Calmore, Kimberlé Crenshaw, Harlon Dalton, Richard Delgado, Neil Gotanda, Linda Greene, Trina Grillo, Isabelle Gunning, Angela Harris, Mari Matsuda, Teresa Miller, Philip T. Nash, Elizabeth Patterson, Stephanie Phillips, Benita Ramsey, Robert Suggs, Kendall Thomas, and Patricia Williams.

2 The Court was actually speaking about the purposes of the three Amendments added to the Constitution after the Civil War, the 13th, 14th and 15th Amendments.

3 Nixon appointed Warren E. Burger as Chief Justice (1969–86), Harry Blackmun (1970–94), Lewis F. Powell, Jr. (1972–87), and William H. Rehnquist (1972–2005). (Reagan elevated Rehnquist to Chief Justice in 1986.)

4 The four Nixon-appointed justices and Justice Potter Stewart constituted the five-person majority.

5 The equal protection clause of the Fourteenth Amendment only applies to actions by states and local governments, not the federal government. Washington v. Davis involved a claim of discrimination by the federal government. Thus, the equal protection clause did not apply. Instead, the Court addressed the issue of race discrimination as part of the due process clause of the Fifth Amendment. The following year in Village of Arlington Heights v. Metropolitan Housing Development Corp., the Court adopted the same intent test to determine unconstitutional discrimination under the equal protection clause that it articulated in Washington v. Davis.

6 The equal protection clause of the Fourteenth Amendment only applies to actions by states and local governments, not the federal government. Washington v. Davis involved a claim of discrimination by the federal government. Thus, the equal protection clause did not apply. Instead, the Court addressed the issue of race discrimination as part of the due process clause of the Fifth Amendment. The following year in Village of Arlington Heights v. Metropolitan Housing Development Corp. (1977), the Court adopted the same intent test to determine unconstitutional discrimination under the equal protection clause that it articulated in Washington v. Davis.

7 In an early article, Brown (1993) contrasted the difference between the view of public education held by the courts and that of an Afrocentric educator's.

8 For further analysis, see Harvard University, the University of Virginia, and the University of Washington's work on implicit bias at https://implicit.harvard.edu/implicit/ (last retrieved on June 20, 2012).

REFERENCES

Bakke v. Regents of the University of California, 438 U.S. 265 (1978).

Bell, D. (1980). Brown v. Board of Education and the interest convergence dilemma. *Harvard Law Review*, *93*(3), 518–533.

Bell, D. (1987). *And we are not saved: The elusive quest for racial justice.* New York: Basic Books.

Bell, D. (1992). *Faces at the bottom of the well: The permanence of racism.* New York: Basic Books.

Bell, D. (2008). *Race, racism, and American law* (6th ed.). New York: Aspen Publishers.

Brown v. Board of Education, 347 U.S. 483 (1954).

Brown, K. (1993). Do African-Americans need immersion schools? The paradoxes created by the conceptualization by law of race and public education. *Iowa Law Review, 78*(4), 813–882.

City of Richmond v. Croson, 488 U.S. 469 (1989).

Coleman, J.S. (1975). Recent trends in school integration. *Educational Researcher, 4*(7), 3–12.

Crenshaw, K. (1991). Mapping the margins: Intersectionality, identity politics, and violence against women of color. *Stanford Law Review, 43*(6), 1241–1299.

Crenshaw, K.W. (2011). Twenty years of critical race theory: Looking back to move forward. *Connecticut Law Review, 43*(5), 1253–1352.

Dalton, H.L. (1987). The clouded prism: Minority critique of the critical legal studies movement. *Harvard Civil Rights–Civil Liberties Law Review, 22*(2), 435–447.

Delgado, R. (1995). *Rodrigo chronicles: Conversations about race in America.* New York: New York University Press.

Dudziak, M.L. (1988). Desegregation as a cold war imperative. *Stanford Law Review, 41*(1), 61–120.

Freeman, A.D. (1978). Legitimizing racial discrimination through antidiscrimination law: A critical review of Supreme Court doctrine. *Minnesota Law Review, 62*(6), 1049–1119.

Green v. New Kent County, 391 U.S. 430 (1968).

Griggs v. Duke Power Co., 401 U.S. 424 (1971).

Harris, C. (1993). Whiteness as property. *Harvard Law Review, 106*(8), 1709–1791.

Ladson-Billings, G., & Tate, W.F. (1995). Toward a critical race theory of education. *Teachers College Record, 97*, 47–68.

Lawrence, C.R., III (1987). The id, the ego, and equal protection clause: Reckoning with unconscious racism. *Stanford Law Review, 39*(2), 317–388.

Matsuda, M.J. (1987). Looking to the bottom: Critical legal studies and reparations. *Harvard Civil Rights–Civil Liberties Law Review, 22*, 323.

Milliken v. Bradley, 418 U.S. 717 (1974).

Plessy v. Ferguson, 163 U.S. 537 (1896).

Skiba, R.J., Eckes, S.E., & Brown, K. (2009). African American disproportionality in school discipline: The divide between best evidence and legal remedy. *New York Law School Law Review, 54*, 1072–1104.

Slaughterhouse Cases, 86 U.36, 71 (1873).

Spann, G.A. (1990). Pure politics. *Michigan Law Review, 88*(7), 1971–2033.

U.S. v. Carolene Products Co., 304 U.S. 144 (1942).

Village of Arlington Heights v. Metropolitan Housing Development Corp., 429 U.S. 252 (1977).

Washington v. Davis, 426 U.S. 229 (1976).

Williams, P. (1987), *Alchemy of race and rights: Diary of a law professor.* Cambridge, MA: Harvard University Press.

2

DISCERNING CRITICAL MOMENTS
Richard Delgado and Jean Stefancic

How can we recognize critical moments, in personal life or the broader world? And what can we do when we recognize one?

The 1960s, for example, were a time of social ferment, when minorities, women, prisoners, and other disempowered groups challenged long-standing social structures and relations (Gitlin, 1993). Yet, at the time, not everyone recognized the significance of those challenges. Some, even on the left, dismissed them as fads that would not last. Others saw them for what they were, but opposed them, just as conservatives today urge that with the election of the nation's first African American president the United States is a postracial society with no need for additional soul-searching (Brown et al., 2005).

We are living, perhaps, through a critical moment for the right wing, like others in the recent past. Recall, for example, how William Simon, secretary of the treasury under Presidents Nixon and Ford, urged the right to rise above the platitudes of both classical liberalism and Goldwater-era conservatism and create institutions capable of leading America into a new age (Simon, 1978).

A few years earlier, in 1971, corporate lawyer and future Supreme Court justice Lewis Powell had warned, in a confidential memorandum to the U.S. Chamber of Commerce, that the free enterprise system was endangered and that American businesses needed to dedicate themselves anew to its preservation (cited in Blodgett, 1984). Those calls led to the formation of a host of well-funded conservative think tanks, foundations, and training centers and, eventually, to the Reagan revolution (Stefancic & Delgado, 1996, pp. 137–146). The late 1970s and early 1980s were a critical moment for the right, yet few recognized it as such at the time.

A few years ago, financiers developed mortgage backed securities and collateralized debt obligations to capitalize on the housing boom and prices that looked as though they would never stop rising. That was a critical moment, although few realized it then. Recently, Latinos overtook African Americans as the nation's largest minority group. The press took note, but relatively few readers, even those on the left, seem to have appreciated its meaning.

THE CHALLENGES OF DISCERNING CRITICAL MOMENTS CONTEMPORANEOUSLY

Critical moments are generally easy to discern in retrospect, but less so at the time one is living through them. Sometimes appreciating them requires knowledge of events that are not widely known, such as a speech and memo by two conservative icons and the gusher of corporate money that followed.

Other times, the challenge is interpretive or conceptual, requiring a predictive judgment. For example, is the Tea Party Movement a major shift in U.S. politics or a momentary fad that will end after an election cycle or two (Krugman, 2009)?

Existential philosopher Soren Kierkegaard wrote that we are doomed to lead life forward, but only to understand it in reverse (Kierkegaard, 1967, p. 450). Similarly, Aristotle noted that happiness is the quality of a life well lived, so that one often cannot say that a person was happy until close to the end (Aristotle, 1998, bk. 1, at 17). Understanding one's times—or even one's own life—is no simple task.

DISCERNMENT AND COURAGE

Sometimes one may understand events full well, but lack the courage or energy to confront them. For example, Derrick Bell, the prominent African American legal scholar, writes, in *The Derrick Bell Reader,* of a stunning episode that befell him in mid-career (Bell, 1986, p. 5; Bell, 2005, pp. 10–13). The first African American tenured professor at Harvard Law School and one of the founding figures of the critical race theory movement, Bell had been serving as dean of the University of Oregon law school in the early 1980s when he resigned over his faculty's refusal to hire a promising Asian American female law professor. The timing of Bell's resignation left him with a gap to fill. His former school, Harvard, was prepared to take him back, but his wife held a satisfying position at Oregon which she was not prepared to leave right then. So Bell was overjoyed when he received an offer to teach for a semester as a visiting professor at Stanford Law School while his wife completed her duties in Eugene, after which they would return to Cambridge.

At Stanford, Bell was enjoying teaching constitutional law to a group of first-year students when, a few weeks into the semester, he received an invitation from the dean to deliver a public lecture in a new series on constitutional law. Seeing the invitation as an expression of confidence by his new colleagues, he gratefully accepted.

His pleasure changed to chagrin, however, when, a short time later, a delegation of black students informed him that the lecture series was aimed at his own deficiencies as an instructor. Evidently, a number of his students had complained about having to take a required first-year course from this unassuming black man from "Oregon State." Bell, who had taught that subject all his life, did so in slightly unorthodox fashion, beginning with the Slavery Compromises—six provisions, still in the document, which guaranteed the continuation of the institution of slavery. Bell showed how those clauses shaped the American legal system during its formative years, leaving traces even today.

The students were discontent. They had expected to take that important course from one of two prominent professors, on leave that year, who taught the course in a more conventional fashion. The administration had responded by scheduling the lecture series so as to guarantee the students their money's worth. And they had invited Bell to participate to dispel any suspicion that the series was aimed at him.

Most readers might have felt like hiding under a rock. Bell instead took the occasion to write a long column for the Stanford student newspaper. Entitled "The Price and Pain of Racial Perspective," the essay addressed the racist subtext of the lecture series and called on the law school to reckon with its own race and class biases (Bell, 2005, p. 12). This led to a series of town-hall meetings that continued long after Bell had left and resulted in significant changes at the law school.

Life confronts us with countless challenges and irritations, so that the challenge often lies in determining which ones are worth confronting and speaking out quickly enough to do some good. With Bell, we suspect that his years as a litigator with the NAACP Legal Defense Fund told him that the Stanford incident was a time for action. But personal courage entered into it, as well as, we suspect, his familiarity with critical theory.

We begin by recounting the origins of that school of scholarship, for it illustrates the very recognition of new possibilities that is the subject of this chapter. Then we show how tools such as interest convergence, intersectionality, differential racialization, and revisionist history can assist in understanding events and controlling their direction. No one wants to be thought of as an alarmist, much less a conspiracy theorist who sees trouble and plots everywhere. Yet we do not want to miss out on "teachable moments" and opportunities to show courage and be on the right side.

ORIGINS OF CRITICAL RACE THEORY

The late 1960s and early 1970s were a time of retrenchment (Gitlin, 1993). The gains of the heady civil rights era had stalled and were beginning to be rolled back. Across the country, groups of civil rights lawyers and scholars realized that new tools were needed to deal with the insidious forms of institutional or veiled racism that were developing and an American public that seemed tired of hearing about race (Delgado & Stefancic, 2011, pp. 3–5).

NEW TOOLS AND CONCEPTS

Interest Convergence

Scholars like Derrick Bell and Alan Freeman had already posited that racism is normal—the usual way American society does business—and that racial oppression serves important majoritarian interests (Bell, 2005, pp. 25–91, 369–378; Freeman, 1978). Bell applied this insight in a groundbreaking article entitled "Brown v. Board of Education and the Interest Convergence Dilemma" in the *Harvard Law Review* (Bell, 1980). Taking as his main example this crown jewel of American Supreme Court jurisprudence, he posited that *Brown* arrived not from a belated spasm of judicial conscience on the part of the Supreme Court, but from majoritarian self-interest. He noted that the NAACP Legal Defense and Education Fund had been attacking school segregation in the South and getting nowhere for years or registering, at most, narrow victories.

Yet, in 1954, the sky opened when the Supreme Court granted them everything they wanted. Why just then? Bell posited that, when the Supreme Court decided *Brown* in 1954, the United States was in the early stages of a Cold War against the atheistic, materialist forces of monolithic Soviet communism, competing for the hearts and minds of the Third World, most of which was brown, black, or Asian. When the world press splashed photos of Klan violence and lynching on the front pages of major newspapers around the world, the United States' adversaries made capital at its expense. It behooved the U.S. establishment to arrange a spectacular breakthrough for blacks, thereby burnishing America's image abroad.

Years later, legal historian Mary Dudziak corroborated what Bell had posited. Through archival research and Freedom of Information Act requests, she showed that the State Department had sent a series of memos to the Justice Department, imploring them to intervene on the side of the blacks (Dudziak, 1988, pp. 65–67, 73, 88). Research by the two of us revealed that, when the justices were deciding a companion case, *Hernandez v. Texas*, a major breakthrough for Latino rights, they were gripped by concern over left-wing forces in Latin America and domestically, including among the pecan shelling workers under the leadership of communist organizer Emma Tenayuca (Delgado, 2006, pp. 23, 43).

Unconscious Discrimination

Building on Bell's work, scholars such as Charles Lawrence put forward legal theories for combating unconscious racism (Lawrence, 1987, pp. 329–344). One of us coined a new term—hate speech—and proposed legal remedies for it (Delgado, 1982). Alan Freeman showed how traditional civil rights law, proceeding through a series of small incremental steps, legitimized racial discrimination (Freeman, 1978, pp. 1052–1098).

Intersectionality

Critical race theorists Kimberlé Crenshaw and Angela Harris developed the notion of intersectionality to explain how antidiscrimination law fails women of color (Crenshaw, 1989; Harris, 1990). Existing statutes, such as the 1964 Civil Rights Act, prohibit discrimination on the basis of race and also of sex. What about the variety that targets black women? One might think they would be doubly protected, but research showed that they often fell between the cracks. Intersectionality called attention to how current law is poorly equipped to redress discrimination targeting individuals like black women, gay Latinos, or others who sit at the intersection of two or more categories.

Narrative Analysis and Storytelling

Other critical race theorists examined the role of legal narratives such as the story of white innocence that opponents deploy to oppose black reparations and affirmative action (Delgado, 1989, pp. 2413–2435; Ross, 1990). These scholars delved into racial stereotypes and tropes such as the welfare queen, the lazy Mexican, or the wise, all-knowing white settler or administrator. Some have applied the teachings of postcolonial writings on subaltern co-optation, resistance, the mind of the oppressor, and the notion of an internal colony to the experience of minorities of color in the United States and Latin America (Acuña, 1988).

Revisionist History

Revisionist historians examined the zigs and zags of racial progress, showing how society racialized different groups at different times, sometimes pitting them against each other (Delgado & Stefancic, 2011, pp. 6–9, 20–21). Recently, critical race theory has expanded to other fields, including education, sociology, psychology, and communications studies.

Critical race theory illustrates how a small group of scholars—only 24 attended its founding workshop in Madison, Wisconsin in 1989—can sometimes seize the moment in a way that turns out to be useful and analytically helpful.

USING CRITICAL ANALYSIS TO DISCERN CONNECTIONS AMONG DISPARATE EVENTS

Critical moments may arrive when an observer notes connections among seemingly disparate events. For example, consider the Columbine school shootings of a few years ago. When these broke out in Littleton, Colorado, columnists and cultural critics scrambled to find the meaning or cause, some placing it in peer pressure and bullying, others in a culture of guns, still others in overindulgent parents or violent video games (Delgado, 2003, p. 1214).

The two of us saw a different connection, harkening back to the period when, in the years following *Brown v. Board of Education*, school desegregation finally expanded beyond the South. The first major challenge to northern school segregation took place in Denver, a few miles from Littleton, when a coalition of Latino and black parents sued the city school district for intentional discrimination in pupil school assignments (Keyes, 1973). The case was long and heated, featuring angry white mobs, fire bombs that damaged 49 school buses, and an explosion outside the home of the federal judge presiding over the case.

Years later, after a series of hearings and appeals, the writing was on the wall: Busing would come to the first major U.S. city outside the South. White families began moving out of Denver in large numbers and settling in surrounding cities such as Aurora, Littleton, and Boulder. This wave of white flight changed the nature of these surrounding cities. Formerly commuter towns with a small mixed population including blacks, Latinos, and working class people, they now became much whiter and wealthier.

The schools in these towns changed as well, becoming much more competitive, with the newcomers vying for the highest grades and places on the cheerleading squad and student government, and to see who could earn the highest SAT scores and gain admission to the most elite college or university. Social pressures increased, as students competed to see who could wear the latest clothes, drive the best cars, or belong to the most popular cliques.

Unsurprisingly, a few years later, two Goth kids, after months of being bullied, marginalized, bumped in the halls, and labeled weird, exploded in a paroxysm of deadly rage, killing a teacher and 12 of their classmates and finally themselves.

Paradoxically, the parents who had fled Denver in search of safety found the opposite for their children in the suburbs. Nor is Littleton unique. Practically every serial shooting has taken place in suburban schools that were all-white and highly competitive.

It turns out that, for a child going through the turbulent years of adolescence, the safest and healthiest school is one with a diverse student body. Kids at that age fear social ostracism more than practically anything else. In a mixed school, most students will be able to find kindred souls. A teen crazy about theater, for example, is apt to find groupies who share that interest. One interested in heavy metal or Chicano rap is likely to find a like-minded group. Goths will find Goths, and so on.

Schools like Berkeley High School or Santa Monica High School in California, or Garfield in Seattle, with large numbers of minorities and kids from all classes, professor and banker families all the way to janitor and homeless families, are both academically excellent and multiracial. Few shootings or serious mayhem take place in schools like these, because almost every kid is apt to have a peer group in which he or she feels secure. The schools may see fist fights and shouting matches, but they are apt to be safer than all-white suburban schools where a social isolate can brood and nurse a grievance for months, suffering ridicule every day. Paradoxically, the Denver parents who fled desegregation for fear of their children's safety found, instead, a school with hidden menace (Delgado, 2003, pp. 1214–1215).

AVOIDING TRIUMPHALISM AND PREMATURE CELEBRATION

Critical theory counsels that we avoid triumphalism and premature celebration. Derrick Bell and others have pointed out how this country's legal system often supplies breakthroughs ("contradiction-closing cases") just when white self-interest requires one (Bell, 2005, p. 184). Black people predictably celebrate and take to the streets in a joy born of years of waiting. Then, when no one is watching, the judiciary cut the breakthrough decision back by narrow judicial construction, foot-dragging, and delay, so that blacks end up worse off than before. The decision legitimizes a judicial system that affords precious little lasting protection. It comforts liberals, who then relax their efforts and move on to another front, such as saving the whales. Meanwhile conservatives, believing that the courts have once again catered to undeserving minorities, redouble their resistance. As everyone knows, more black children attend dominantly minority schools than did before *Brown v. Board of Education* came down.

POSTRACIALISM

When Americans celebrated the election of the first black president, a few took it as a sign that the United States had entered a postracial era. In fact, Obama was the far superior candidate, who deserved to win by an even wider margin than he did. Only about 43 percent of whites voted for him, despite his clear-cut superiority to his Republican opponent. His margin of victory was due almost entirely to the black and Latino vote.

If the United States is a postracial nation, it is difficult to tell this from the statistics on black and Latino employment, school achievement, family wealth, and access to health care. A recent United Nations study, for example, reported that, on a combined measure of social wellbeing that included years of schooling, income, access to health care, infant mortality, longevity, and a few other factors, African Americans, if considered as a separate country, would rank 46th in the world and Latinos 68th. (U.N., 2001, pp. 15, 141–142).

ADVENT OF A LARGE LATINO POPULATION

At other times, a development may be obvious, but not its meaning. A recent example is the news that Latinos have overtaken African Americans as the nation's largest group of color. Some have reacted to this announcement with a form of intellectual inertia reminiscent of those social workers in Vine Deloria's *Custer Died for Your Sins* who, upon first encountering Indian clients, treated them in light of their own book learning about African Americans (Deloria, 1988, pp. 168–174). Of course those two groups have little in common other than poverty and a history of mistreatment at the hands of Anglo society.

Much the same is true of Latinos. Omi and Winant's differential-racialization hypothesis holds that each group of color is racialized in different ways from the others (Omi & Winant, 1994). Thus, when a new group comes to light, it may be tempting to assume that they will resemble the ones you know. But, with Latinos, thinkers need to consider new issues such as language rights, nativism, immigration status, NAFTA, and the role of U.S. meddling in Latin America's economy as a source of displacement and misery.

Most Latinos may vote much the same way other minority groups do and favor some of the same programs, including well-funded schools, job programs, and universal health insurance, but their situation and needs differ in many respects. Mexican immigration, for example, consists largely of single, healthy young men who consume few social services, pay taxes, and contribute to a region economically through their labor. The average immigrant consumes about $80,000 less than he contributes in the form of taxes during his life.

Much the same is true for crime. Areas experiencing an increase of immigrants generally report a *reduction* in the crime rate, according to Harvard researcher Robert Sampson, which is pretty much what you would suspect from a population that is largely Catholic, pious, from small villages, and eager to avoid coming to the attention of the authorities (Sampson, 2006).

A great deal of misinformation circulates about their effects on the labor market, as well. Complementarity, a tool of analysis in labor economics, holds that if I am a surgeon living in a town and performing ten operations a week and mowing my yard on Saturday, and a new surgeon moves to town, I am apt to be worse off and the town not much better (Delgado et al., 2008, pp. 457–458). But if the newcomer is a skilled gardener, I can hire him to mow my grass on Saturday and perform an extra operation that week, and both he and I are better off, and probably the town is, too. Most of the new immigrants add to complementarity, because the services they perform—gardening, landscaping, busing dishes in a restaurant, laying carpet, installing dry wall—are in undersupply in the regions where they settle.

The typical Latino immigrant has six or seven years of formal education and does not speak English. The average African American worker, by contrast, has a high school degree and speaks native English. Because of their high degree of complementarity, the two groups are unlikely to be in competition for most jobs. Indeed, African Americans may well find their job prospects improved as a result of immigrations. Not only will they benefit from improvement in the local economy, but they may find new jobs opening up as supervisors of gardening crews, as waiters or maitre d's in the newly prosperous restaurants, or as owners of small construction or moving companies (Delgado et al., 2011).

Black unemployment has stayed largely the same or improved during the years of heavy Latino immigration, beginning around 1990. It has worsened markedly since the economic downturn began a few years ago, but this is the period when Latino immigration began to decline. So the relation between Mexican labor and black jobs is complex.

MISSING OPPORTUNITIES

One can easily miss all this interesting action, as well as the many possibilities for coalition with the new group over such issues as police profiling, school funding, and reform of health care, if one persists in seeing America's racial scene in terms of two principal actors only. Paradigms resist change even when the evidence is piling up against them. It does seem to us quite possible that whites will try to recruit light-skinned Latinos and Asians as middle men and brokers, much as the British colonial service did when it used highly educated Indians to help administer and rule their own fellow citizens and prolong the British reign in return for secure jobs and status (Delgado, 2010, pp. 1302, 1333). The mass of Latinos are not apt to participate in this tactic, however, because they see little future in it and also see how poorly it has served African Americans.

COUNTERSTORYTELLING

A related critical tool that can enable one to recognize a critical moment and do something about it is storytelling, including oral history and slave narratives. Oppressed people have always resisted their oppression by recounting tales of disgraceful sheriffs and developers, or of heroic resistance figures like Paul Robeson, Gregorio Cortez, or John Brown who stood up to unlawful authority and defended the rights of their countrymen (Delgado et al., 2008, pp. 36–41, 303–304). Teachers and scholars can use these tales to convey what life looks like from below. Sometimes, we can deconstruct a comforting master narrative, such as the legal maxim "without intent, no discrimination" or the idea that, with Obama's election, we are entering a postracial period. The tools can include facts and statistics, showing, for example, that black and Latino wellbeing has dropped, not risen, in the years since conservatives began proclaiming a colorblind order. The tools can also include mockery, satire, and debunking, such as by showing the self-interest behind a comforting platitude and how differently the world looks to someone at the bottom (Delgado, 1989, pp. 2412–2434).

Sometimes, challenging a prevailing myth requires careful historical research. For example, the High Court of Australia announced a major decision in the area of indigenous land rights when, in 1992, it handed down a decision entitled *Mabo v. Queensland* (1992). The case began when Eddie Mabo, a Torres Strait indigenous gardener, asserted legal ownership to land that his tribe had inhabited and occupied beginning long before Admiral Cook arrived and claimed all of Australia for the British Crown.

Before then, the aborigines inhabited Australia in a series of small villages with a basic government and set of rights, many of them communal. The British settlers unceremoniously displaced them from the most valuable lands and, over time, built cities, farms, and ranches, pushing the aborigines to the less desirable areas where their numbers and living conditions languished.

In *Mabo*, the Australian Supreme Court revisited the question of aboriginal land title, which until then had rested on the notion of *terra nullius*—null or empty land. Somewhat related to the American notion of Manifest Destiny and the Discovery Doctrine, *terra nullius* provided that all of Australia was, essentially, up for grabs during the settlement period because no one was really occupying it. Accordingly it was lying there fallow, fair game for any industrious white settler willing to fence and develop it (Perea et al., 2007, pp. 271–282).

It was that notion that came before the court in *Mabo*. Aided by the research of historian Henry Reynolds, whose book *Law of the Land* subjected the doctrine of *terra nullius* to searching analysis, the Supreme Court declared that the principle by which Australians had asserted title to indigenous lands for nearly 200 years was invalid. The Crown had not, in fact, asserted *terra nullius* over Australia at the time of the settlers' arrival. Instead it expected the settlers to negotiate with the aborigines and reach an accommodation with them that was appropriate in light of what they found. Because of their failure to do this, a commission has been adjudicating several hundred indigenous claims to large stretches of Australian land, much to the consternation of the mining industry.

Similar developments are taking place in the United States and Canada. In Canada, in response to the *Calder* Supreme Court decision, the country recently returned large reaches of Canadian land to native people (Calder, 1973). And, in the U.S., the Colorado Supreme Court recently upheld property rights of Mexican American farmers in the large Taylor Ranch, which required determining the validity of an ancient land grant predating the region's becoming a part of the United States (Lobato, 2002). Acting at the request of Congress, the Government Accountability Office recently issued a 500-page report on long-standing land claims throughout the Southwest, concluding with five options, including returning the land to the Mexicans who owned it originally. Academic historians played key parts in all these decisions (G.A.O., 2004).

MONEY AND INFLUENCE

As mentioned, critical moments can take a conservative form. Colleges and universities are seeing a determined attack on faculty autonomy by conservative organizations like the American Council of Trustees and Alumni, who press for monitoring outputs, testing for graduating students, and more student contact hours and less research for the faculty. Tenure is under attack, as is the idea of full-time core faculty (Ennis, 2011). Ethnic studies is under siege, and one state, Texas, passed a law requiring professors to post their lesson plans, c.v.s, and travel itineraries online (Mangan, 2010).

In 2010, the newly conservative Supreme Court, in *Citizens United v. Federal Elections Commission*, held that money is speech and that corporate donors are individuals, too, who are free to contribute unlimited amounts to political campaigns. This has led to a sudden inflow to the campaigns of business-friendly candidates.

Finally, consider a series of developments taking place in California, the most ethnically diverse U.S. state. The state's population recently reached a tipping point, with Asian Americans, blacks, and Mexicans together outnumbering whites. Early in its history, the same situation prevailed, as a small number of white settlers wrested control over a larger population of Indians and Mexicans, and then ruled over it during territorial days and into statehood. The discovery of gold and, a little later, the completion of the transcontinental railroad brought increasing numbers of Anglos, so that whites then could rule by sheer force of numbers, wielding power through ordinary means, passing legislation such as alien land laws, ordinances against Chinese laundries, and school segregation laws (Delgado, 2010, pp. 1303–1305).

In recent years, however, California has been approaching a point when minorities will again outnumber whites. The school population in the state became dominantly nonwhite some years ago and now is nearly two-thirds minority. Faced with the threat of nonwhite control, California Anglos have been putting in place mechanisms to enable them to continue to rule far into the future. Some of those mechanisms resemble ones from its own colonial past and that of classically colonial regimes, such as the British in India and the French in Algeria, including co-optation of light-skinned, educated minorities for middle-management and assistant dean positions, ruling over their fellows and keeping the lid on for the benefit of their colonial overlords, as well as maintaining control over official ideology in schools, Hollywood, and the news. To understand California and what it portends for America's future, we may need to re-read scholars such as Frantz Fanon, Albert Memmi, Rodolfo Acuña, and Robert Allen on the colonized mind, resistance, and preserving sanity in the face of hostile occupation. Developments in California allow one to see what may lie ahead for other states, such as Arizona, and, eventually, the rest of the country (Delgado, 2010, pp. 1313–1330).

This chapter has provided examples and tools to help discern critical moments. It has discussed barriers to discernment, including lack of knowledge, the challenge of spotting relationships between disparate events, failure of courage, and the problem of interpreting events while living through them. Critical theory can sometimes help, as can close observation of what your adversaries are doing. In general, oppressed people turn out to be better at spotting critical moments than those who are satisfied with the current order. As Georg Hegel pointed out, the slave tends to know the master better than the other way around (Hegel, 1967, pp. 229–240). Professors, teachers, and scholars desiring to sharpen their pedagogy can do well to heed outsider voices, scholarship, and concerns. Our teaching will be the better for it, and, through our students, society too.

REFERENCES

Acuña, Rodolfo. (1988). *Occupied America: A history of Chicanos* (3rd ed.). London: Longman-Pearson.

Aristotle (1998). *Nichomachean ethics* (J.L. Ackrill & J.O. Urmson, Eds., David Ross, Trans.). New York: Oxford University Press.

Bell, Derrick, Jr. (1980). Brown v. Board of Education and the interest convergence dilemma. *Harvard Law Review, 93*, 518–533.

Bell, Derrick. (1986). The price and pain of racial perspective. *Stanford Law School Journal*, April, 5.

Bell, Derrick. (2005). *The Derrick Bell reader* (Richard Delgado & Jean Stefancic, Eds.). New York: New York University Press.

Blodgett, Nancy. (1984). The Ralph Naders of the right. *American Bar Association Journal, 70*, 71.

Brown, Michael, et al. (2005). *Whitewashing race*. Berkeley: University of California Press.

Calder v. British Columbia (Attorney General) [1973] S.C.R. 313, [1973] 4W.W.R.1.

Citizens United v. Federal Elections Commission, 558 U.S. 8 (2010).

Crenshaw, Kimberlé. (1989). Demarginalizing the intersection of race and sex: A black feminist critique of anti-discrimination doctrine, feminist theory, and antiracist politics. *University of Chicago Legal Forum, 1989*, 139–169.

Delgado, Richard. (1982). Words that wound: A tort action for racial insults, epithets, and name-calling. *Harvard Civil Rights–Civil Liberties Law Review, 17*, 133–181.

Delgado, Richard. (1989). Storytelling for oppositionists and others: A plea for narrative. *Michigan Law Review, 87*, 2411–2441.

Delgado, Richard. (2003). White interests and civil rights realism: Rodrigo's bittersweet epiphany. *Michigan Law Review, 101*, 1204–1215.

Delgado, Richard. (2006). Rodrigo's roundelay: Hernandez v. Texas and the interest-convergence dilemma. *Harvard Civil Rights–Civil Liberties Law Review, 41*, 23–65.

Delgado, Richard. (2010). Rodrigo's portent: California and the coming neocolonial order. *Washington University Law Review, 87*, 1293–1344.

Delgado, Richard, & Stefancic, Jean. (2011). *Critical race theory: An introduction* (2nd ed.). New York: New York University Press.

Delgado, Richard, Perea, J.F., & Stefancic, J. (2008). *Latinos and the law: Cases and materials*. St. Paul, MN: Thomson-West.

Delgado, Richard, Gonzalez, Carmen, & Stefancic, Jean. (2011). Setting the record straight: Latinos are not a "problem group." *Seattle Times*, May 22.

Deloria, Vine. (1988). *Custer died for your sins: An Indian manifesto*. Norman: University of Oklahoma Press.

Dudziak, Mary. (1988). Desegregation as a Cold War imperative. *Stanford Law Review, 41*, 61–118.

Ennis, Daniel J. (2011). The last of the tenure track. *Chronicle of Higher Education*, July 3.

Freeman, Alan. (1978). Legitimizing racial discrimination through anti-discrimination law: A critical review of Supreme Court doctrine. *Minnesota Law Review, 62,* 1049–1120.

G.A.O. (Government Accountability Office). (2004). *Report to governmental requesters, Treaty of Guadalupe Hidalgo: Findings and possible options regarding longstanding community land grant claims in New Mexico.* Washington, DC: Government Printing Office.

Gitlin, Todd. (1993). *The sixties: Years of hope, days of rage.* New York: Bantam.

Harris, Angela. (1990). Race and essentialism in feminist legal theory. *Stanford Law Review, 42,* 581–616.

Hegel, Georg. (1967). *The phenomenology of mind* (J.B. Baillie, Trans.). New York: Harper Torchbooks.

Keyes v. Denver School Dist. No. 1, 413 U.S. 189 (1973).

Kierkegaard, Soren. (1967). *Kierkegaard's journals and papers* (Howard V. Hong & Edna H. Hong, Eds.). Bloomington: Indiana University Press.

Krugman, Paul. (2009). Tea parties forever? *New York Times,* April 2.

Lawrence, Charles, III. (1987). The id, the ego, and equal protection: Reckoning with unconscious racism. *Stanford Law Review, 39,* 317–388.

Lobato v. Taylor, 71 P.3d 938 (Colo. 2002).

Mabo v. Queensland (No. 2), 1992 WL 1290806 (HCA 1992).

Mangan, Catherine. (2010). Professors in Texas protest law that requires them to post teaching details online. *Chronicle of Higher Education,* May 6.

Omi, Michael, & Winant, Howard. (1994). *Racial formation in the United States* (2nd ed.). London: Routledge.

Perea, Juan, Delgado, R., Harris, A.P., & Wildman, S.M. (2007). *Race and races: Cases and materials for a diverse America* (2nd ed.). St. Paul, MN: Thomson-West.

Ross, Thomas. (1990). The rhetorical tapestry of race: White innocence and black abstraction. *William and Mary Law Review, 32,* 1–40.

Sampson, Robert J. (2006). Open doors don't invite criminals: Is increased immigration behind the drop in crime? *New York Times,* March 11.

Simon, William. (1978). *A time for truth.* New York: Reader's Digest Press.

Stefancic, Jean, & Delgado, Richard. (1996). *No mercy: How Conservative think tanks and foundations changed America's social agenda.* Philadelphia, PA: Temple University Press.

U.N. (2001). *U.N. Human Development Report.* New York: United Nations.

3

CRITICAL RACE THEORY—WHAT IT IS NOT!

Gloria Ladson-Billings

THE BEGINNING OF CRT IN EDUCATION

In the summer of 1993, William F. Tate and I submitted a proposal for the 1994 annual meeting of the American Educational Research Association (AERA). AERA was soliciting new forms of presentation so we selected a different format—the advanced paper session. This format called for prospective attendees to write authors in advance for their papers so that these sessions would be in-depth discussions of papers all the session attendees had previously read. Unfortunately, no one wrote for a copy of our paper, and Tate and I believed no one would show up to our session. It turned out that we were wrong. The session, bearing the title of the paper, "Toward a Critical Race Theory of Education" (TCRTE), was standing room only, and we had to discuss its substance with a group who were unfamiliar with the paper.

During the question and answer section of the presentation it was clear that some of the attendees were hostile to this new theoretical perspective. Surprisingly, the hostility came from some scholars who were typically allies—scholars whose work focused on multiculturalism and diversity. Apparently, our focus on race as a primary tenet of inequality violated the sacred rule of maintaining the race, class, and gender triumvirate. The "friendly fire" we received as a result of making race the axis of understanding inequity and injustice in the US spurred us to write what became the first article on CRT in education (Ladson-Billings & Tate, 1995).

While I have described the "public" introduction of CRT in education, it is important to include the less public foundational moves that made that first publication possible. Sometime in early 1992 William Tate shared a *Harvard Law Review* article by Professor Kimberlé Crenshaw (1988), "Race, Reform and Retrenchment: Transformation and Legitimation in Antidiscrimination Law." That article transformed how I thought about civil rights and race. Rather than accept the slow and incremental progress of traditional civil rights legislative and judicial processes or the notion that race was "just another variable," Crenshaw's article challenged my thinking and pushed me intellectually in new and important ways. To be sure, I had previously read Derrick Bell's *And We Are*

Not Saved: The Elusive Quest for Racial Justice (1989), but I did not connect Bell's use of literary imagination with what was becoming an important movement in legal studies.

Reading the Crenshaw article forced Tate and me into the law library, where we found an entire group of scholars working in this tradition. Of course it was a wonderful irony that we were working at the University of Wisconsin-Madison, the place where the movement started. Both Professors Patricia Williams and Linda Greene were on our law school faculty, which gave us a bit of an advantage despite our outsider status as non-legal scholars. Williams's book *The Alchemy of Race and Rights: Diary of a Law Professor* (1991) was another entry way into this new legal genre. Professor Greene pointed us to a variety of other scholars—Richard Delgado, Mari Matsuda, Charles Lawrence III, Neil Gotanda, Gary Peller, and Cheryl Harris, to name a few. The first thing we learned as we began this quest was just how much we did not know. Our challenge was not merely the density of legal writing but our ignorance about the precedents upon which many of the arguments rested. Thus, our work was not merely reading these scholars; it was reading them in relation to the legal cases they were citing.

After extensive reading Tate and I wrote a draft of a paper that tried to both explain CRT and describe its relevance and application to education. Tate and I had worked together on an earlier paper, "The Brown Decision Revisited: Mathematizing Social Problems" (Tate et al., 1993), where we tried to examine the way the *Brown* decision proposed a mathematical solution to a problem that was much more complex than mere numbers. In the midst of writing this paper Tate and I realized our perspectives about race were converging and moving away from that of other "diversity" scholars.[1] Because we knew we were undertaking what would be a radical departure from traditional work on inequity we thought it best to "test out" our work in our own department. Fortunately, we worked at a place where colleagues were eager to hear each other's ideas, and we distributed the paper widely throughout the department to colleagues and graduate students alike. We then convened a colloquium on a Friday afternoon.[2] We presented our main argument and then opened it up for questions. Those questions came fast and furious. What was surprising was that they were not hostile. People were genuinely trying to understand what our analysis meant for the future of educational disparities. Were we saying that the inequities were intractable? Yes, we were. Were we saying that the civil rights movement was a failed project? To some extent it was. Were we saying that racism would endure? Indeed we were.

Given the pessimism of our argument our colleagues pushed us to provide more evidence and to at least present people with a way to reconcile the belief in progress towards greater equality and the racial realism that we were promoting. No one said we had a flawed argument. Instead, people were worried that our argument might be so jolting that others would reject it out of hand. Over the next few weeks colleagues gave us scribbled notes on their copies of the manuscript to consider so that we might offer a tighter thesis—whether they agreed with us or not. I found that support some of the most helpful I have ever received in the academy. Even though people did not wholeheartedly agree, they were at least willing to provide good questions that forced us to bolster our position.

So, by the time we arrived at the AERA session, we felt as though we had already been through a rigorous vetting. The questions raised at that session were no tougher than what we had already endured. What was different about the AERA session was the hostility that we felt from supposed friends and allies. I suggested to Tate at the end of the session that we get the paper out for publication as soon as possible—before the detractors began to publish pieces against ours. We wanted a journal outlet that had a wide readership and good standing in the field. We decided on *Teachers College Record* and were pleased that the editor saw it as a promising article. With some minor edits the editor accepted the article for publication. To date that article has had over 1,000 citations and has been reprinted in several other volumes. Within a few years of publication of TCRTE a number of other CRT in education articles and book chapters began to appear. Tate (1997) published a comprehensive overview of the field and its major proponents that became an important baseline document for understanding the terrain of CRT in education. The following year I (Ladson-Billings, 1998) published an article that attempted to dissuade education researchers from delving into CRT without adequate grounding in the field. During this time Derrick Bell, Kimberlé Crenshaw, and Richard Delgado made visits to the University of Wisconsin-Madison and we had opportunities to sit and talk with them about our project. Bell also urged caution. Crenshaw encouraged us to keep reading in the field and keep spreading the word. Delgado was especially excited to hear about the work and was interested in possible collaborations. He was fearful that CRT might not go any farther in law and saw education as a logical extension of the work. In fact, Delgado developed an interest in publishing a CRT volume that would be accessible to high school students.

At about this same time Solorzano (1997) began publishing on CRT and building the project at UCLA. Since Kimberlé Crenshaw had two positions—one at Columbia Law School in the fall and another at UCLA Law School in the spring—the CRT project naturally spread from the early summer workshops at the University of Wisconsin-Madison to both coasts. Also, Solorzano had access to Neil Gotanda and Gary Peller at UCLA. Later Parker et al. (1999) began engaging the methodologies that CRT recruited to illuminate and illustrate its case. Afterwards, Lynn (1999), Taylor (1999), Solorzano and Yosso (2001), and Delgado Bernal (2002) were among the scholars who contributed to this literature.

The previously cited works laid the foundation for critical race theory in education. The field was in its infancy and like any new movement it was attracting many young scholars who were looking for new ways to think about their work and new methodologies for race scholarship. However, we must be clear that just because a scholar looks at race in her work it does not make her a critical race theorist. In "Through a Glass Darkly: The Persistence of Race in Education Research and Scholarship" (Ladson-Billings, 2012), I argued that all of the social sciences were infused with conceptions of race and racist notions, and since education draws heavily from the social sciences those views of race find their way into education scholarship and research. For example, most scholars of gifted and talented education do not focus on the fact that much of the field is build on the eugenicist perspectives of Lewis Terman (1925–59). Clearly, these scholars do not consider themselves race scholars, let alone critical race scholars.

Many scholars study disproportionality in special education designations, expulsion, and suspension but they would not call themselves critical race scholars. Scholars such as Skiba and Rausch (2006) carefully document issues of unequal disciplinary procedures and school exclusion. Although they document differential treatment based on race, these scholars would not call themselves critical race theorists. They use quantitative data to demonstrate the adverse impact of school rules and policies on African American and Latina/o students. The point is that writing about race and racial issues does not necessarily make one a critical race theorist. Those who are CRT scholars subscribe to a number of tenets that Delgado and Stefancic (2001) identify as hallmarks of CRT:

- belief that racism is normal or ordinary, not aberrant, in US society;
- interest convergence or material determinism;
- race as a social construction;
- intersectionality and anti-essentialism;
- voice or counter-narrative.

RACISM AS NORMAL

What do critical race theorists believe? … First, that racism is ordinary, not aberrational—"normal science," the usual way society does business, the common, everyday experience of most people of color in this country.

(Delgado & Stefancic, 2001, pp. 6–7)

The first tenet of CRT is the notion that racism is not some random, isolated act of individuals behaving badly. Rather, to a CRT scholar racism is the normal order of things in US society. This is the thing that distinguishes CRT scholars from others who investigate race. Some focus on specific instances of racism or might admit to institutional racism. However, few outside of CRT would declare that racism is normal. Most argue that racism resides in individual (and sometimes corporate) beliefs and behaviors regarding the inferiority of people of another race. According to Delgado and Stefancic (2001), CRT scholars believe that racism "is the usual way society does business, the common, everyday experience of most people of color in this country" (p. 7).

In 1944 Swedish Nobel prize-winning social scientist Gunnar Myrdal concluded that racism was simply the failure of liberal democratic practices to align with liberal democratic theory. This concept was what Hochschild (1984) termed an "anomaly thesis," i.e., "race discrimination is a terrible and inexplicable anomaly stuck in the middle of our liberal democratic ethos" (p. 3). For more than two generations civil rights advocates and social scientists subscribed to this notion. Hochschild further opines that racism's ongoing presence long beyond slavery, Reconstruction, two world wars, and the landmark *Brown v. Board of Education* case (1954) "is not simply an excrescence on a fundamentally healthy liberal democratic body but is a part of what shapes and energizes the body" (p. 5). Further, Hochschild argues, "liberal democracy and racism in the United States are historically, even inherently, reinforcing; American society as we know it exists only because of its foundation in racially based slavery, and it thrives only because racial discrimination continues" (p. 5). Instead of Myrdal's "anomaly thesis" Hochschild says that this is a "symbiosis thesis." In a nutshell, this difference between anomaly and symbiosis forms the basis of the difference between most race theory and critical race theory.

INTEREST CONVERGENCE

Most racial remedies, however, when measured by their actual potential, will prove of more symbolic than substantive value to blacks.

(Bell, 1992, p. 646)

The late Professor Derrick A. Bell is considered the "Father of Critical Race Theory," perhaps because of his prolific writing on the topic, his instrumental role in educating many cohorts of law scholars who fostered the movement, and the principles by which he lived his life and his career.[3] One of Bell's theoretical propositions that accompany CRT is interest convergence. According to Bell (1980), White people will seek racial justice only to the extent that there is something in it for them. In other words, interest convergence is about alignment, not altruism. We cannot expect those who control the society to make altruistic or benevolent moves toward racial justice. Instead, civil rights activists must look for ways to align the interests of the dominant group with those of racially oppressed and marginalized groups.

A policy example of interest convergence came about when President John F. Kennedy issued Executive Order 10925 in March 1961 that included a provision that government contractors "take affirmative action to ensure that applicants are employed, and employees are treated during employment, without regard to their race, creed, color, or national origin." The intent of the order was to affirm the government's commitment to equal opportunity. Four years later, President Lyndon Johnson issued Executive Order 11246 prohibiting discrimination based on race, color, religion, and national origin by those organizations receiving federal contracts and subcontracts. However, in 1967 Johnson amended the order to include sex. That one move changed affirmative action from a racial justice policy to an interest convergence whose major beneficiaries are White women (and by extension other Whites—men, women, and children).

A second example of interest convergence occurred when former Arizona Governor Evan Meacham cancelled the state's Martin Luther King, Jr. Holiday. According to Meacham, the state could not afford another paid holiday and Dr. King was undeserving of a holiday. This move caused the cancellation of 45 conventions, with an estimated loss of $25 million. The most high-profile cancellation was the National Basketball Association's All Star Game. The reversal of the MLK Holiday decision was not a result of a change of heart on the part of Governor Meacham but rather a need to align the state's economic interests with the hope and symbolism the holiday represented for African Americans (Gross, 1993).

RACE AS A SOCIAL CONSTRUCTION

Race has been a constitutive element, an organizational principle, a "praxis" and structure that has constructed and reconstructed world society since the emergence of modernity, the enormous historical shift represented by the rise of Europe, the founding of modern nation-states and empires, the "conquista," the onset of African slavery, and the subjugation of much of Asia.

(Winant, 2001, p. 19)

Biologists, geneticists, anthropologists, and sociologists all agree that race is not a scientific reality. Despite what we perceive as phenotypic differences, the scrutiny of a microscope or the sequencing of genes reveals no perceptible differences between what we call races. As members of the same species, human beings are biologically quite similar. Just as a tabby cat and a calico cat are the same species with the ability to reproduce within their species so it is with humans. However, humans have constructed social categories and organization that rely heavily on arbitrary genetic differences like skin color, hair texture, eye shape, and lip size. They have used these differences as a mechanism for creating hierarchy and an ideology of White supremacy.

Smedley (1993) points out that there is a deep paradox between the scientific notion of "no-race" and the "social parameters of race by which we conduct our lives and structure our institutions" (p. 19). Thus, while critical race theorists accept the scientific understanding of no-race or no genetic difference, we also accept the power of a social reality that allows for significant disparities in the life chances of people based on the categorical understanding of race.

One of the most interesting instances of race as a social construction is that of President Barak Obama. During the 2008 presidential campaign, candidate Obama was regularly confronted by the notion that he was not "Black enough." Born of a "White" mother and a "Black" Kenyan father, many considered the circumstances of Barak Obama's upbringing so far outside of the experiences of most African Americans that he could not possibly be "really" Black. Some questioned his legitimacy to be president, presumably based on Article II Section I of the United States Constitution that states the office can only be held by a natural born citizen of at least 35 years of age who has lived in the country at least 14 years prior to election. There was no question about Barak Obama's age or length of residence but he was constantly dogged by the allegation that he was not born in the US. Interestingly, his opponent, Senator John McCain, was born in the Panama Canal Zone, yet no one ever questioned his legitimacy to be president. While we insist that race no longer matters in our society, President Obama's entire presidency has been suffused in race—even when he has worked hard to steer clear of race and race related issues in policy making and governing.

INTERSECTIONALITY AND ANTI-ESSENTIALISM

As CRT developed, scholars began to see "race" itself as the product of other social forces—for example as the product of heteropatriarchy in a post-industrial, post-colonial, capitalist society—or as in the United States, in a Euro-American heteropatriarchy.

(Valdes et al., 2002, p. 2)

According to Delgado & Stefancic, "Intersectionality means the examination of race, sex, class, national origin, and sexual orientation and how their combinations play out in various settings" (2001, p. 51). Because our society is organized along binaries, intersectionality is a difficult concept to research. We see things as black or white, east or west, rich or poor, right or left. When we move into the complexities of real life we recognize that we each represent multiple identities—race, class, gender, sexuality, ability, religion, and many more. We perform our identities in myriad ways and can never be certain to which of those identities others react. However, since race has been such a flashpoint in this society we almost always believe that our challenges stem solely from racial injustice. Imagine the following scenario:

A Black woman walks into a luxury car dealer. She has just come from a strenuous workout and is sweating in an old pair of sweat pants and a ratty T-shirt. She is not wearing makeup and her hair is pulled back in a ponytail. She does not look like a "typical" luxury car buyer.

During her time in the showroom she notices that the salespeople introduce themselves to everyone but her. She has stood by a high-end model for at least 10 minutes but no salesperson has asked the customary "Can I answer any questions about this car for you?" Instead she is starting to feel invisible. Car salespeople are talking to everyone else in the showroom, including those who have arrived after she did. What seems to be the problem?

Because of the way race structures our everyday life experiences it is reasonable for most people to believe that the reason the woman is not receiving any attention is her race. However, one might also argue that her less than professional appearance might make class the reason the salespeople are ignoring her. Perhaps the obvious class markers—dress, hair, and overall appearance—make her an unlikely candidate for a sale. Thus, class not race may be operating here. Or, since our society continues to maintain sexual asymmetry, perhaps the woman's gender has closed her off from receiving serious consideration as a luxury car buyer. However, CRT scholars are urged to look at the way all three identity/status categories may be operating simultaneously.

That same showroom might have been more welcoming had the woman arrived in high-end clothing and a nicely coiffed hairdo. It might have been more welcoming if the person in those same workout clothes were a man. We do not know which individual or combination of identity categories is at work here. Rather than attempting to simplify and strip down to a single explanation, CRT scholarship is willing to engage in the "messiness" of real life.

Because of increasing globalization we should expect to see even more complexities. We see people we categorize as Black who speak what we perceive as European languages (e.g. French, Spanish, Portuguese, etc.). Or we try to neatly categorize who is Muslim or Jewish or Christian only to learn that people cross many traditional boundaries and align themselves in different groups and categories. CRT scholars recognize that the neatness was always artificial and arbitrary. If someone is gay or lesbian, is his or her racial identity thrown into question? Is race or sex privileged? Are these identities ever in conflict? These questions are a part of the work of CRT scholarship.

Do all oppressed people have the same thing in common?

(Delgado & Stefancic, 2001, p. 56)

The other side of intersectionality is essentialism. Critical race theory scholarship decries essentialism. Essentialism is a belief that all people perceived to be in a single group think, act, and believe the same things in the same ways. Such thinking leads to considerable misunderstanding and stereotyping. On the one hand there is the need for people to participate in group solidarity for social, cultural, and political purposes (Guinier & Torres, 2003). Thus, to identify as African American or a woman or an immigrant can be useful as a way to organize and garner political clout and social benefits. However, on the other hand, people do not relinquish their individual rights, perspectives, and lifestyles because they share group identities.

Recently, a well-known historically Black college/university declared that male students entering its business school would not be permitted to wear their hair in dreadlocks (Davis, 2012). This declaration sparked a lively debate among African Americans on social networking sites like Facebook and Twitter. Some agreed with the business school dean. Others vehemently opposed the decision. Still others offered mixed opinions that suggested the school was trying to protect its students from the harsh realities of a mainstream, corporate workplace and what it takes to "get ahead." There was not a "Black" position on this issue.

During the days after the O.J. Simpson trial verdict, when the former football star, sports commentator, and actor was acquitted of murdering his ex-wife and her male friend, tensions were high in many communities. The talk show hosts on both television and radio were discussing O.J. non-stop. The day the verdict was announced I was teaching a class of pre-service teachers. Our room did not have a television monitor so I took a portable radio to class, plugged in my earphone, and when the verdict was announced repeated it verbatim to the class. No sooner had I shared the verdict than a young White student sitting in the front row of the class began to cry. What about this murder—given the thousands of murders that occur in the US every year—made it personal to my student?

At the same moment one of our graduates (who happens to be White) was collecting data for her dissertation at a historically Black college/university. When the verdict was announced the students gathered around the student union big screen television jumped up in a triumphant shout when the announcement came. What was it about this verdict—given the thousands of court trials in the US—that had the Black students assembled in solidarity to receive it?

After a few days when it seemed that all people could talk about was the O.J. Simpson verdict, a White colleague stopped me in the corridor and asked, "So, Gloria, what *do* Black people think about the O.J. Simpson verdict?" For once I had what I think was the correct response. I smiled slowly and replied, "I don't know. What do *White* people think about it?" At that moment my colleague realized just how ridiculous the question was. There was no uniform "White" response to the verdict, and there certainly was no uniform "Black" response. The amount of within-group differences for any racial or ethnic group are greater that the between-group differences. CRT scholars guard against essentializing the perspectives and experiences of racial groups.

VOICE OR COUNTER-NARRATIVE

In the mid-sixties, Archie Shepp took his "fundamentally critical" tenor saxophone and stepped outside of the commercially laden mainstream's musical community of assumption and voiced his dissent beyond the ways it would be tolerated within the constraints of conventional jazz. Twenty-five years or so later, some legal scholars of color … are voicing … dissent from many of the law's underlying assumptions.

(Calmore, 1995)

Storytelling is one of the oldest human art forms. Ancient cultures maintained their histories and cultural sense of self through the stories they told and retold. Stories or narratives have been shared in every culture as a means of entertainment, education, and cultural preservation and to instill moral values. The very discipline we call history is about the cultural narrative that cultures, nations, and societies tell, particularly about themselves. The African proverb says, "Until lions have their historians, tales of the hunt shall always glorify the hunter." It captures the ethnocentric and hegemonic way stories can and do operate. Stories reflect a perspective or point of view and underscore what the teller, audience, society, and/or those in power believe to be important, significant, and many times valorizing and ethnocentric.

For example, many German school students went through school learning nothing about the Third Reich and Adolph Hitler's "final solution" to rid Germany (and indeed Europe) of Jews and others he deemed undesirable. The story Germans hoped to tell about themselves focused more on their post-war achievements in arts, culture, innovation, and economic prosperity. Similarly, some West African nations tell an official story in their school textbooks that omits any acknowledgement of the transatlantic slave trade and its devastating impact on the development of the continent. The issue of embellishing or valorizing one's history and/or culture is common. However, the acceptance of that presentation as "truth" and "universal" can be deeply problematic (Ladson-Billings, 2000). When one group describes its worldview or story as "real history," "truth," or "objective science" and others' worldviews as myth, legend, and lore we validate one narrative while simultaneously invalidating the other.

In American jurisprudence opposing lawyers allegedly have the same evidence from which to construct a narrative—a story to tell a judge and/or jury. Both sides claim to be telling the "truth." Despite what story is presented to the public, the "counter-story" is a contrasting story that describes the story from a different vantage point. The ability to tell that story is important not just as a defense strategy but also as a way to unmoor people from received truths so that they might consider alternatives.

At the end of apartheid in South Africa it became important to construct "Truth and Reconciliation" panels for those who had been harmed by a brutal system of separation and oppression (Theissen, 1999). The painful experience had to be articulated by victims and acknowledged by perpetrators. The storytelling of the victims represented a series of counter-stories to the narrative the country had told itself and others for years. Telling the stories was both therapeutic and cathartic. It became one of the ways the new nation could reconstitute itself and move ahead. Unfortunately, the US tends to devalue the role of storytelling in social science. A story represents an instance and does not include enough "empirical" data points or a large enough sample to conform to Western science notions of "truth."

Critical race theorists use storytelling as a way to illustrate and underscore broad legal principles regarding race and racial/social justice. The point of storytelling is not to vent or rant or be an exhibitionist regarding one's own racial struggle. Unfortunately, far too many would-be critical race theorists in education use the narrative or counter-story in just that way. There is little or no principled argument to be made. The writer is mad because of an affront and the pen becomes a retaliatory weapon. The story does not advance larger concerns or help us understand how law or policy is operating.

Derrick Bell's "The Chronicle of the DeVine Gift" (1999) is an example of how a counter-story can be written that has personal reference but broader social justice meaning. In this chronicle Bell's alter ego, Geneva Crenshaw, is frustrated about the amount of work she has as the only African American law professor in a prestigious law school. This is exactly the situation in which Bell found himself at Harvard. But rather than rant about being overburdened he constructs a story or chronicle about what life might be like if a mysterious donor continued to steer high-quality candidates of color to the law school. Bell's chronicle suggests that a high-profile predominately White law school would reach a "tipping point" if "too many" candidates of color were hired.

Bell's story starts with his experience but quickly branches off into a speculative tale that points out the disingenuous way predominately White institutions that claim to be seeking to "diversify" their faculty and staff actually have no real intention of achieving true diversity, even when candidates of color are meritorious.

In another chronicle Bell (1989) describes what he calls "The Black crime cure," where a group of young Black men discover a magic pill that changes them from petty street criminals to outstanding citizens. They no longer do drugs, rob and steal, cut school, or participate in gang activity. They become model citizens as long as they keep taking the pills. Unfortunately law enforcement has less work to do—the gang task force is no longer needed, the drug enforcement task force has no purpose, and the nightly patrols in Black communities yield no suspects. At first, the larger community is delighted, but soon people begin to realize how lucrative crime is for the rest of the society. Now they must lay off police officers and prison guards. The security firms sell fewer security devices and need to cut back their work forces. The alternative schools and juvenile detention centers are without youth. The town's entire economy was based on the by-products of crime. To return things to their previous state, the police follow the Black youth to a cave outside of town and discover the source of the magic pills. After the youth leave, the police raid the cave, confiscate all the remaining pills, and blow up the site.

Again, Bell is not telling a story about himself. Instead he is exposing the ways that Black crime serves the interests of Whites. First, Black crime is rarely perpetuated on Whites, i.e., the victims of most Black crime are Black. Second, Black crime creates work opportunities for Whites—police officers, probation officers, prison construction firms, prison guards, lawyers, judges, and court workers all benefit from high rates of crime. The point of the chronicle is to get readers to consider Black crime from a very different perspective beyond the notion of pathological Black people to the economic benefits the "so-called pathology" provides for the White middle class.

In an attempt to develop chronicles and counter-stories that were more expansive and linked to broader educational policy issues I tried to write a chronicle that explained the way current education reform efforts were designed to subvert real reform in urban communities (Ladson-Billings, 2007). In this chronicle, which I titled "The Case of the Sacrificed Black Children—Part 2," I used Bell's (1989) earlier story about school deseg-regation ("The Case of the Sacrificed Black Children") to discuss how modern attempts at urban renewal made schools their centerpiece. Here draconian testing regimes and severe promotion and retention policies that everyone knew were designed to fail were a proxy for displacing urban families in order to provide corporate interests greater access to prime land and tax deductions in the form of TIFs (tax incremental financing). I tell this story not as a personal story but rather as a broader motif for explaining what citizens in urban areas across the nation were experiencing in the neighborhoods and schools, especially Black and Brown citizens.

Similarly, in a chapter in the book William Tate and I edited (Ladson-Billings, 2006) I wrote a story that predicted how the rebuilding in post-Katrina New Orleans would occur. When I shared the story in one audience one person said I was a "prophet." I was quick to correct him. There was nothing prophetic about what I was saying. I was merely articulating what was predictable, since it had happened so many times before. The chronicle did come to pass. Redevelopment in New Orleans emphasized middle and upper income residents, and poor people have been left to fend for themselves. The primary point here is that the chronicle or counter-story is about racial justice principles, not personal affront.

CODA

This chapter attempts to address central tenets of CRT that education scholars who want to work in this area must adhere to if they want to be true to the concepts developed by CRT innovators. I set out to write this chapter not merely to chastise scholars who have grabbed hold of CRT as a "sexy," "trendy," "new" thing that absolves them of the responsibility to do quality work. The point is not to have a rant or to claim that racial "navel gazing" is any more substantive than Eurocentric, positivist, functionalist navel gazing is. CRT scholars cannot rail against the failure of positivist research to be objective or neutral when our own scholarship is so specific to our personal concerns that it fails to help us grasp important principles of racial justice. To illustrate my concern, I end this chapter with what might be called a CRT "anti-chronicle."

A Game of Spades ... or, "Are You Really Going to Play that Card?"

Khalia Winston sat in her office and placed her feet comfortably on her desk. She could hardly believe it. She had landed a tenure track position at a research-intensive university. She would teach one course each of the first two semesters, and receive two months of summer support, a graduate assistant, and a $25,000 research grant as a part of her start-up package. Her salary was about $5,500 higher than the other two new hires in her department. Her research focused on race and its impact on teacher education.

In her first few months Khalia learned her way around the university. She taught her graduate course and received good feedback from the graduate students who were looking for faculty members whose primary focus was on race. Her faculty mentor told her that, although she'd done excellent work on her dissertation, at this university she would have to develop a new data set with which to pursue her line of inquiry. When the internal research funds competition came around Khalia did not get her proposal completed in time and could not receive campus research funds. Undaunted, Khalia continued working on her proposal and submitted it for an external grant. Unfortunately, it was not selected for funding.

As the years passed Khalia continued to have success with her graduate courses. She was popular among graduate students, particularly graduate students of color. Her undergraduate courses were a different story. The undergrads thought she was too strident and left them guilt-ridden about their privilege and lack of exposure to other cultures. Every semester her teaching evaluations were bifurcated: high graduate course evals and low undergrad evals. Swinging back and forth between these two poles, Khalia became stressed out and struggled to focus on her writing.

Because she was one of two Black faculty members in her school, Khalia was regularly called on to serve as a speaker or facilitator for professional development throughout the community. Although she enjoyed this attention she felt the need to get away from campus and started going to conferences in big cities that dealt specifically with race, diversity, and Black issues. A few times she had a paper to present, but rarely did she turn the papers into manuscripts for publication. When the time for her third-year review rolled around Khalia had published only one book review and a short opinion piece for an obscure newspaper. Her review chair informed her that things were not looking good and he could not guarantee a vote for renewal.

At this point Khalia grew quite angry and started working on a "manuscript" about her experience as a "Black" scholar in a "White" institution. Throughout the manuscript Khalia castigated her undergraduate students, colleagues who didn't "help" her, the "unreasonable" demands on her time, and the failure of her chair to provide her with accurate information about what she needed to do to earn tenure. She submitted her manuscript without sharing it with any senior scholars for feedback. When she received a "reject" letter from the editors that included detailed reviews of the limitations of her work she declared that all of academe was "racist" and it was "impossible" for Black scholars to get their work published.

In a tearful conversation with the only senior Black colleague in her department Khalia grew angrier as he asked her some pointed questions—"How many original manuscripts did you write and get out the door?" "What did you do about the poor teaching evaluations?" "What did you do to protect your time for writing and research?" "How many of your conference papers are in good enough shape to be turned into manuscripts?"

Khalia's eye's burned with anger and the corners of her mouth turned into a snarl. "Oh, you too, huh?" she snapped.

"Me too, what?" her senior colleague asked.

"You're just as whitewashed as the rest of them. You ain't nothin' but a sell-out!" she barked as she rose to leave.

"Now you just wait a minute, young lady," her colleague's baritone voice reverberated throughout the office. Khalia stopped in her tracks. "One of the reasons you got this job is that I put my credibility on the line. It's not that you didn't have solid credentials, but they had a White candidate with an equally stellar resume. When she gave her job talk she knocked it out of the park. Your talk was mediocre at best, but I reminded my colleagues that few people give good 'job talks.' I convinced them to look carefully at your whole body of work and the 'promise' it offered. I lobbied to get you a higher salary because indeed you had 'rare bird status'—an African American woman graduate of a prestigious graduate program. But from the moment you arrived you dismissed any advice I gave you. You insisted that you knew what you were doing. When I cautioned you about going to too many conferences you insisted that you needed to get away from all of this "Whiteness." When I said you should at least turn your conference papers into publishable manuscripts you said you'd do it but you did not. When I advised you to try to work with your undergraduates and meet them where they were you dismissed me. Now I understand you're writing what amounts to a rant—and, yes, I know a lot of editors who share things with me—and you want to suggest that I'm the sell-out? No, honey, you don't get to use that card with me!"

This brief "chronicle" is a composite of instances I have heard throughout the country. The work of the critical race scholar must be as rigorous as that of any other scholarship (or perhaps more so). We have an obligation to point out the endemic racism that is extant in our schools, colleges, and other public spaces. We must deconstruct laws, ordinances, and policies that work to re-inscribe racism and deny people their full rights. And we must be careful to guard this movement that is entering its "academic adolescence." We must be willing to say what critical race theory is not.

NOTES

1 I am using the term "diversity scholars" to describe a number of scholars whose research takes a more inclusive approach (i.e. class, gender, race, ability, linguistic, etc. differences). This is not a critique of such scholarship, but I do distinguish it from the more race-focused approach Tate and I began undertaking in this work.
2 I must confess we called it on a Friday afternoon presuming few people would come. To our surprise the room was packed.
3 See Bell (2003).

REFERENCES

Bell, D. (1980). Brown v. Board of Education and the interest-convergence dilemma. *Harvard Law Review, 93*, 513.

Bell, D. (1989). *And we are not saved: The elusive quest for racial justice.* New York: Basic Books.

Bell, D. (1992). *Race and racism in American law.* New York: Aspen Law and Business.

Bell, D. (1999). The civil rights chronicles: The chronicle of the DeVine Gift. In R. Delgado & J. Stefancic (Eds.), *Critical race theory: The cutting edge* (2nd ed., pp. 468–478). Philadelphia, PA: Temple University Press.

Bell, D. (2003). *Ethical Ambition: Living a Life of Meaning and Worth.* New York: Bloomsbury Press.

Brown v. Board of Education, 347 U.S. 483, 492 (1954).

Calmore, J. (1995). Critical race theory, Archie Shepp, and fire music: Securing an authentic intellectual life in a multicultural world. In K. Crenshaw, N. Gotanda, G. Peller, & K. Thomas (Eds.), *Critical race theory: The key writings that formed the movement* (pp. 315–329). New York: New Press.

Crenshaw, K. (1988). Race, reform, and retrenchment: Transformation and legitimation in antidiscrimination law. *Harvard Law Review, 101*(7), 1331–1387.

Davis, K. (2012). Hampton Univ. students question continued ban on dreadlocks, cornrows in MBA program. *Afro American,* August 25 (retrieved August 26, 2012 from http://www.afro.com/sections/news/afro_briefs/story.htm?storyid=75974).

Delgado, R., & Stefancic, J. (2001). *Critical race theory: An introduction.* New York: NYU Press.

Delgado Bernal, D. (2002). Critical race theory, LatCrit theory and critical race gendered epistemologies: Recognizing students of color as holders and creators of knowledge. *Qualitative Inquiry, 8*(1), 105–126.

Gross, J. (1993). Arizona hopes holiday for King will mend its image. *New York Times,* January 17, p. 16.

Guinier, L., & Torres, G. (2003). *The miner's canary: Enlisting race, resisting power, transforming democracy.* Cambridge, MA: Harvard University Press.

Hochschild, I.J. (1984). *The New American dilemma: Liberal democracy and school desegregation.* New Haven, CT: Yale University Press.

Ladson-Billings, G. (1998). Just what is critical race theory and what's it doing in a *nice* field like education? *International Journal of Qualitative Studies in Education, 11*(1), 7–24.

Ladson-Billings, G. (2000). Racialized discourses and ethnic epistemologies. In N. Denzin & Y. Lincoln (Eds.), *Handbook of qualitative research* (2nd ed., pp. 257–277). Thousand Oaks, CA: Sage.

Ladson-Billings, G. (2006). Introduction. In G. Ladson-Billings & W.F. Tate (Eds.), *Education research in the public interest: Social justice, action, and policy* (pp. 1–13). New York: Teachers College Press.

Ladson-Billings, G. (2007). Can we at least have Plessy? The struggle for quality education. *North Carolina Law Review, 85*, 1279–1292.

Ladson-Billings, G. (2012) Through a glass darkly: The persistence of race in education research and scholarship. *Educational Researcher, 41*(4), 115–120.

Ladson-Billings, G., & Tate, W.F. (1995). Toward a critical race theory of education. *Teachers College Record, 97*(1), 47–68.

Lynn, M. (1999). Toward a critical race pedagogy: A research note. *Urban Education, 33*(5), 606–627.

Myrdal, G. (1944). *The American dilemma: The Negro problem and American democracy.* New York: Harper & Bros.

Parker, L., Deyhle, D., & Villenas, S. (1999) *Race is … race isn't: Critical race theory and qualitative studies in education.* Boulder, CO: Westview.

Skiba, R., & Rausch, M.K. (2006). Zero tolerance, suspension, and expulsion: Questions of equity and effectiveness. In C. Evertson & C. Weinstein (Eds.), *Handbook of classroom management: Research, practice and contemporary issues* (pp. 1063–1089). Mahwah, NJ: Lawrence Erlbaum.

Smedley, A. (1993). *Race in North America: Origin and evolution of a worldview.* Boulder, CO: Westview Press.

Solorzano, D. (1997). Images and words that wound: Critical race theory, racial stereotyping and teacher education. *Teacher Education Quarterly,* Summer, 5–19.

Solorzano, D., & Yosso, T. (2001). From racial stereotyping and deficit discourse toward a critical race theory of teacher education. *Multicultural Education, 9*, 2–8.

Tate, W.F. (1997). Critical race theory in education: History, theory, and implications. *Review of Research in Education, 22*, 195–247.

Tate, W.F., Ladson-Billings, G., & Grant, C.A. (1993). The Brown decision revisited: Mathematizing social problems. *Educational Policy, 7*, 255–275.

Taylor, E. (1999). Critical race theory: A primer. *Journal of Blacks in Higher Education, 19*, 122–124.

Terman, L.M. (1925–59). *Genetic studies of genius* (Vols. I–V). Stanford, CA: Stanford University Press.

Theissen, G. (1999). Common past, divided truth: The Truth and Reconciliation Commission in South African public opinion. Paper presented at International Institute for the Sociology of Law, Oñati, Spain, September.

Valdes, F., Culp, J.M., & Harris, A. (2002). Battles waged, won, and lost: Critical race theory at the turn of the millennium. In F. Valdes, J.M. Culp, & A. Harris (Eds.), *Crossroads, directions, and a new critical race theory* (pp. 1–6). Philadelphia, PA: Temple University Press.

Williams, P. (1991). *The alchemy of race and rights: Diary of a law professor.* Cambridge, MA: Harvard University Press.

Winant, H. (2001). *The world is a ghetto: Race and democracy since World War II.* New York: Basic Books.

4

CRITICAL RACE THEORY'S INTELLECTUAL ROOTS
My Email Epistolary with Derrick Bell
Daniel G. Solórzano

INTRODUCTION

I am an educational archaeologist. I never identified myself as such, but in retrospect I've been an educational archaeologist for most of my life. But what is an educational archaeologist? If an archaeologist is a person who discovers, collects, and analyzes the material remains of past cultures, among other things, an educational archaeologist is a person who discovers, collects, and analyzes the written and visual materials of our educational past (and present). I have spent most of my academic life searching for, collecting, and analyzing books, journal articles, newspapers and magazines, and other written and visual materials on the experiences of communities of color. I have spent many hours, days, months, and years in libraries and archives of all sizes practicing my archaeological craft. I have searched in bookstores, video stores, second-hand stores, antique stores, estate sales, yard sales, and photo archives looking for materials that help me better understand communities of color.

This chapter is a story on how I used my educational archaeological skills to understand critical race theory (CRT) and how CRT led me to identify and analyze various concepts within the fields of education, sociology, ethnic studies, women's studies, and the law. To help tell the story, I will use a real and fictional email correspondence I had with Derrick Bell in April of 2009 on his use of "racism hypos."[1] In fact, this chapter was inspired by and loosely modeled on an article Derrick Bell wrote in 1989 titled "An Epistolary Exploration for a Thurgood Marshall Biography." At first I didn't know what "epistolary" meant. After searching I found it defined as a form of writing that utilizes a letter or a series of letters to tell a story. In his "epistolary" Bell (1989) recreates a series of letters between himself and a fictitious Asa Bookman, the President of *Real World Books.* In a sequence of letters they discuss the possibility of writing a Thurgood Marshall biography. Here I begin my email "epistolary" with Professor Bell on my journey to critical race theory in education generally and CRT and transformational resistance in particular.[2]

MY EMAIL EPISTOLARY WITH PROFESSOR BELL

April 30

Dear Professor Bell:[3]

I am a Professor of Social Science and Comparative Education at UCLA's Graduate School of Education and Information Studies. I have read your *Race, Racism, and American Law* (4th ed.) (Bell, 2000) and was really inspired by your use of "racism hypos" as a pedagogical tool. I do some work with Paulo Freire's "problem-posing pedagogy" and see real connections. I went to your website (https://its.law.nyu.edu/courses/description. cfm?id=6176; last retrieved May 18, 2012) and noticed that you use hypotheticals as part of your "Constitutional Law" course description. I would love to work them into my seminar on "Critical Race Theory in Education." Have you written anything on how to create hypotheticals—especially racism hypotheticals—and how you use them as pedagogical tools. Any resources or other "racism hypos" would be truly appreciated.

On a side note, I met you in April of 2004 at the Eso Won Bookstore in Los Angeles, where you read from your book *Silent Covenants* (2004). I'm the one who asked about the future of Geneva Crenshaw in your writing. You mentioned at the time that we probably wouldn't be seeing her in future work. Your work has truly influenced my students and me.

Thank you for all you do.

Take care,
Daniel Solorzano

May 1

Hi Daniel:

Good to hear from you and thanks for your kind words about my racism hypos. *Race, Racism and American Law* is now in its 6th edition, and if you are using it in your teaching I am sure that the publisher, now Wolters Kluwer, Law and Business under the Aspen Publishers name, will be happy to send you an examination copy (see Bell, 2008a). Be sure to ask for the *Teacher's Manual* (see Bell, 2008b). I based my constitutional law course on a series of hypothetical cases, some of which are written by students. The idea is to stretch the existing law into a new set of facts that test the existing rules. I am attaching the hypo cases I used this past semester. The ones dealing with race directly or indirectly include hypos 3, 4, 9, 10, 16, 17, 19, 20, and 25.[4]

You mention in your previous email that you're teaching a seminar on critical race theory in education. How have you come to use CRT? I am really interested in how it has made its way to the field of education. I'm familiar with the works of Gloria Ladson-Billings and William Tate (1995) and would like to know how you have been influenced by CRT.

Sincerely,

Derrick

May 2

Dear Professor Bell:

Thank you for your kind response to my request for information on the "racism hypos." They have been influential in my teaching and research in critical race theory in education. Over the years I have been working on developing the field of critical race pedagogy. Two of my former graduate students—Marvin Lynn[5] and Tara Yosso[6]—have been instrumental in its evolution (see Lynn, 1999; and Solorzano and Yosso, 2001). I see the "racism hypos" as an important tool in the continuing development of critical race pedagogy. But I'm getting ahead of myself. You asked how I came to CRT.

I was first introduced to critical race theory in June of 1993 by an article in the *Chronicle of Higher Education.*[7] by Peter Monaghan (1993) titled "'Critical Race Theory' Questions Role of Legal Doctrine in Racial Inequality." Although I didn't know it at the time, this was my first "critical race moment."[8] The article introduced me to an emerging field that was challenging the orthodoxy of race, racism, and the law and mentioned you along with other legal scholars such as Richard Delgado, Linda Greene, Lani Guinier, Patricia Williams, and Mari Matsuda. Critical race theory seemed to be a framework that began to answer some of the questions that had been troubling me—especially questions on how we center race and racism in our academic research and teaching. Yet two reactions also went through my mind as I read the article: Reaction 1: This is really a new and powerful way of looking at race and racism in the law and probably in education, and Reaction 2: I've seen this before. In the days that followed I realized the language of CRT in the law resonated with my previous training in race, ethnic, and women's studies, and Freirean pedagogy. At that point I returned to some of these early foundational writings and tried to connect them to CRT. In order to secure time for this academic excavation, I asked for and received a sabbatical to get to the law libraries to immerse myself in the CRT legal artifacts and incorporate them to my background and training in race, ethnic, and women's studies, and Freirean pedagogy. This is how my journey began in CRT.

Take care,

Daniel

May 3

Hi Daniel:

Thanks for that initial background on your journey to CRT. As you know, in the law CRT had its roots in critical legal studies and other critical legal traditions. How were you able to connect the fields of race, ethnic, and women's studies, and Freirean pedagogy with CRT and the field of education?

Sincerely,

Derrick

May 4

Dear Professor Bell:

As an undergraduate student in the late 1960s and early 1970s I majored in Chicana/o studies and sociology and considered these disciplines as areas of critical social inquiry. Chicana/o studies examines the lives, histories, and cultures of Mexican-origin people living in the United States.[9] Like other ethnic studies programs of study, Chicana/o studies was developed in the context of the civil rights movements of the late 1960s. In those years we also read foundational works in African American, Native American, Asian American, and women's studies. When I graduated from college in 1972, I began my career as a high school social science teacher and was introduced to the work of Paulo Freire (1970a, 1970b). It was these two educational experiences that were foundational to my intellectual and pedagogical development. I'll elaborate.

THE INTELLECTUAL ROOTS OF CRITICAL RACE THEORY IN EDUCATION

From my standpoint, as scholarly and activist traditions, race and ethnic studies, women's studies, and Freirean pedagogy each inform the CRT framework in education (see Figure 4.1).[10] As an analytical framework, CRT draws on the strengths of these traditions by connecting them to the study of race and racism in education. CRT also learns from blind spots of some of these disciplinary fields. For instance, there are the tendencies to decenter or de-emphasize race in women's studies, to ignore gender in race and ethnic studies and Freirean pedagogy, and to overlook race and gender in class based analyses (see McGrew, 2011; Sleeter & Delgado Bernal, 2004).

RACE, ETHNIC, AND WOMEN'S STUDIES

As I began to learn about CRT in the law, I drew upon race, ethnic, and women's studies, which examine the complex issues of race, gender, ethnicity, racism, and sexism from an interdisciplinary perspective. My interdisciplinary training in these fields led me to reflect back and re-analyze the cultural nationalist frameworks (see Asante, 1987, 1991), the internal colonial models (see Barrera et al., 1972; Blauner, 1969, 1972, 2001; Bonilla & Girling, 1973), Marxism and neo-Marxism (see Barrera, 1979; Bowles & Gintis,

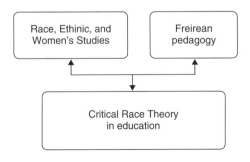

Figure 4.1 A genealogy of critical race theory in education

1976), women of color feminisms (see Anzaldúa, 1987; Hill Collins, 1990; hooks, 1990; Hurtado, 1996), Freirean pedagogy (see Freire, 1970a, 1970b, 1973), and intersectional models (see Crenshaw, 1991). These works helped me see them as part of my intellectual roots of CRT in education.

As I now reflect on this period I am drawn to Terry Curry's (2008) article on your work on racial realism titled "Saved by the Bell: Derrick Bell's Racial Realism as Pedagogy." He pushes me to re-visit questions on who to recognize as we tell the story of the intellectual roots of the CRT tree in education. Throughout my academic career these questions constantly came up.[11] Indeed, Curry (2008) addressed this very issue when talking about your work:

> It is also relevant to discuss the tendency of whites to read into Bell's scholarship non-existent continuities with traditional white figures. In this regard whites attempting to understand the works of Bell align him with what they take to be radical figures in the Western tradition, like Michel Foucault, Karl Marx, and Jacques Derrida, *instead of confront[ing] the racism inherent in assuming that it is only through white thinkers that Black thoughts can be understood or philosophical.* To my claim that his [Bell's] work should be understood as a continuation of Black thought, exclusive of white influence, Bell replied:
>
>> You have it exactly right. I consider myself the academic counterpart of Errol Garner, the late jazz pianist from my hometown, Pittsburgh, who never learned to read music fearing, as I understand it, that it would ruin his style. I think there must be value in Marxist and other writings, but I did not really read them in college and have had little time since. I am writing this in Pittsburgh where I have been celebrating my 50th law school reunion from Pitt Law School. *I do care more about the thought and writings and actions of Du Bois, Robeson, Douglass, et al.* I think, during my talk at UCLA, I read from the 1935 essay by Ralph Bunche about the futility of using law to overcome racism. It made more sense than so much of the theoretical writings on law, past and present, that I can barely understand and have great difficulty connecting with my experience. And you are right. At almost 77, I do not care to write in ways that whites can vindicate (personal interview, October 2, 2007).
>>
>> (Curry, 2008, p. 44, emphasis added)

My genealogy of CRT in education takes a similar route. The foundational works in race and ethnic studies, women of color feminisms, and Freirean pedagogy heavily influenced my journey to CRT in education and I must name and honor that contribution. To continue, here is what I learned from Freire's work.

FREIREAN PROBLEM-POSING PEDAGOGY

Paulo Freire's *Pedagogy of the Oppressed* (1970b) guided my analysis of CRT in the law and its application for a CRT in education. For instance, one of the foundational tools of Freirean pedagogy is problem-posing pedagogy. This is where I also saw one of the initial connections to your use of "racism hypos" (see Bell, 2008a, 2008b). Freire's (1970a, 1970b) problem-posing method starts from the premise that all education is political and thus schools are never neutral institutions. He asserts that schools either function to maintain and reproduce the existing social order or empower people to transform themselves and/or society.[12] Freire argues that, when schools domesticate, they socialize students into accepting as legitimate the ideology and values of society's dominant class. According to Freire (1970b), schools use the banking method to domesticate students and treat them as passive receptacles waiting for knowledge to be deposited by the teacher. They are taught in a pedagogical format where the teacher communicates with the students in one-way monologues. This approach leads students to feel their thoughts and ideas are not important enough to warrant a two-way dialogue with the teacher. Students are also dependent on the teacher for their acquisition of knowledge. Finally, teachers are seen as conduits through which the ideology and values of the dominant social class are transmitted to the students.

Conversely, when schools liberate, students are viewed as subjects willing and able to act on their world. To create a liberating education, Freire developed the problem-posing method, in which two-way dialogues of cooperation and action between the student and the teacher are the focus, content, and pedagogy of the classroom. Freire's method includes three general phases: 1) identifying and naming the problem, 2) analyzing the causes of the problem, and 3) finding solutions to the problem (Freire 1970a, 1970b; Smith and Alschuler 1976).

In the naming phase, the educator enters the community or social setting. While in the community, the teacher learns about the major issues and problems of the area by listening and speaking to the people and observing community life. After gathering the needed information, the educators develop generative codes. Most often, these codes can be visual or physical renditions—as in pictures, drawings, stories, articles, films, or other artifacts—of the significant themes or problems identified by members of the community. The codes are at the heart of the problem-posing process because they are used to begin critical dialogue among the participants. When I first started teaching high school social studies in a correctional facility in Los Angeles I used my camera to take pictures of places in the community that my students described and found significant. I would go out after school or on weekends and take photos of the themes students described as important in their lives. Many of these photos became my initial documentation of the Chicano Public Art Mural Movement in Los Angeles in the 1970s.[13]

In the second or analytic phase, I brought these pictures back to the classroom and they became our generative codes. We used these codes to describe and analyze the causes of the problem through dialogue with the participants. Figure 4.2 (*The Puppeteer*) is an example of a photo generative code and was taken in 1972. I used the *Puppeteer* photo to involve the young men in a dialogue on who benefits from conflicts within and between the African American and Chicana/o communities. Using the photo with the puppeteer's hands and strings helped us continue a dialogue on social and political power in the larger Los Angeles community. Figure 4.3 (*Unidos Carnal* [United Brothers]) was another generative code used to challenge the message of the *Puppeteer* photo and resume the dialogue on issues that bring neighborhoods and youth together and unite them for the common good. These photos were used to engage the youth in critically reading both their words and their worlds (see Freire, 1970a, 1970b, 1973).[14]

In the final or solution phase, participants—in collaboration with the educators—find and carry out solutions to the problem. This process of critically reflecting and acting on one's reality by describing and defining a problem clearly, analyzing its causes, and acting to resolve it is a key element of Freire's problem-posing method. Participants

Figure 4.2 *The Puppeteer* (artist unknown) (1972), corner of Whittier Blvd. and Eastern Avenue in East Los Angeles
Source: Daniel Solórzano personal photo archive.

are encouraged to view issues as problems that can be resolved, not as a reality to be accepted. Hence participants feel that their ideas are recognized as legitimate and that the problem posed can be resolved in a constructive manner. In addition, participants and educators become dependent on each other for knowledge.

Freire felt that one of the processes of learning in a problem-posing format is when a person moves from one level of consciousness to the next—from magical, to naïve, to critical (see Freire, 1970b; Solorzano and Yosso, 2001). For instance, in the magical stage participants may blame educational inequality on luck, fate, or God. Whatever causes the inequality seems to be out of the student's control, so she/he may be resigned to do nothing about it. For example, a person at a magical stage of consciousness may explain her/his condition this way: "In the U.S., if Chicanas do not get a good education it is because God is in control of my destiny. If he wills it then it will be." In the naïve stage, participants

Figure 4.3 *Unidos Carnal* (Brothers United) (artist unknown) (1972), Brooklyn Avenue in East Los Angeles

Source: Daniel Solórzano personal photo archive.

place the blame on themselves, their culture, or their community for educational inequality. Because they're informed by a naïve consciousness, participants try to change themselves, assimilate to the White, middle class, mainstream culture, or distance themselves from their community in response to experiencing inequality. For instance, a person at a naïve stage of consciousness may say: "In the U.S., if African Americans do not do well in life, it is because the Black community and Black culture don't value education."[15] At the critical stage, participants look beyond fatalistic or cultural reasons for educational inequality and focus on structural or systemic explanations. A person with a critical level of consciousness looks toward the overall social system and its educational structures as a response to educational inequality. For example, a person at a critical stage of consciousness may explain, "In the U.S., if Native Americans don't go to college, it is because from kindergarten through high school they are being socialized for working class or low status occupations that don't require a college degree" (see Bowles & Gintis, 1976).

Freire also argues that in the process of learning literacy skills, the participant also develops:

- the capacity to name and analyze the causes and consequences of the social conditions that they face;
- the ability to look at other possibilities or alternatives to their problems; and
- a disposition to act in order to change a problematic situation.

Freirean pedagogy situates curriculum in issues, examples, and language from the everyday life of participants. Freirean pedagogy fosters the development of a critical race, gender, and class consciousness. In fact, as we develop our generative codes for our classrooms, we must try to identify those examples that depict the intersection of race, gender, and class subordination and engage our students in a dialogue at those intersections. When I went on to teach at the community college I continued to use my camera to take pictures of the community to bring them back into the classroom to engage in a problem-posing pedagogy (see Solorzano, 1989).

Take care,

Daniel

May 5

Hi Daniel:

I can see how these frameworks are coming together. What did you do next?

Sincerely,

Derrick

May 6

Hi Professor Bell:

With the power of historical hindsight and the strength of the multiple intellectual and community traditions, I worked with others to use CRT as a framework to help shape our methodologies as researchers and practices as educators. I found that CRT informs our praxis (where theory and practice meet) in multiple ways.

In 1993 and 1994 I continued to comb the law archives reading and analyzing the CRT literature for insight and connections to work in the social sciences and education. I went on to define critical race theory as the work of scholars who are attempting to develop an explanatory framework that accounts for the role of race and racism in education and that works toward identifying and challenging racism as part of a larger goal of identifying and challenging all forms of subordination. With this definition in hand and my reading in CRT in the law, I further developed and applied these five tenets of CRT in education:

1 CRT foregrounds race and racism and challenges separate discourses on race, gender, and class by demonstrating how racism intersects with other forms of subordination (i.e. sexism, classism, euro-centrism, monolingualism, and heterosexism) which impact students of color.
2 CRT challenges traditional research paradigms and theories, thereby exposing

deficit notions about students of color and educational practices that assume "neutrality" and "objectivity."

3 CRT focuses research, curriculum, and practice on experiences of students of color and views these experiences as sources of strength.

4 .CRT offers a transformative solution to racial, gender, and class discrimination by linking theory with practice, scholarship with teaching, and the academy with the community.

5 CRT challenges ahistoricism and acontextualism, and insists on expanding the boundaries of the analysis of race and racism in education by using contextual, historical, and interdisciplinary perspectives to inform praxis.

These five themes are not new in and of themselves, but collectively they represent a challenge to the traditional modes of scholarship. In the Freirean tradition, CRT names racist injuries, identifies their origins, and seeks remedies for the injury.

My first introduction to CRT in education was an article by William Tate in 1994 titled "From Inner City to Ivory Tower: Does My Voice Matter in the Academy?" Soon after, Tate co-authored an article with Gloria Ladson-Billings in 1995 titled "Toward a Critical Race Theory of Education."[16] My first article was written in 1997 and titled "Images and Words That Wound: Critical Race Theory, Racial Stereotyping, and Teacher Education."[17]

In CRT in education we are often told that we must return to the legal foundations and tenets of CRT. Although I feel that CRT in the law has been critical and foundational in CRT in education, I've tried to show how it also has foundational roots in race, ethnic, and women's studies and Freirean critical pedagogy. I believe it is our responsibility to reinvent CRT for the various fields and contexts in which it finds itself. Again, Freire helped us in our thinking here. I have heard him respond to this very issue in various settings.[18] For instance, in a question from Donaldo Macedo (Freire & Macedo, 1987), Freire addresses this question of reinvention:

Macedo: Explain in concrete terms how one reinvents one's practice and experience.
Freire: … I cannot, then, simply use Lenin's text and apply it literally to the Brazilian context without rewriting it, without reinventing it.

(p. 92)

Professor Bell, I would take Freire's advice and apply it to CRT in education and state: "I cannot simply use CRT's text in the law and apply it to the education context without rewriting it, without reinventing it." Years later Macedo (1994) recounts another conversation on this topic when Freire states: "Donaldo, I don't want [my methodology] to be imported or exported. It is impossible to export pedagogical practices without re-inventing them. Please, tell your fellow American educators not to import me. Ask them to recreate and rewrite my ideas" (p. xiv). I believe that is what CRT scholars in education are doing. They are engaging with CRT in the context of the structures, processes, and discourses of educational research and praxis. In a Freirean sense, CRT has to continue to "reinvent" itself so as to work for the communities they serve.

Over the years, my colleagues and I have worked to "reinvent" CRT in education by developing critical race tools to help understand the ways people and communities of color experience racism, the ways they respond to racism, and the wealth and assets they possess to survive racism and other forms of oppression. One such tool is CRT and transformational resistance theory.

Take care,

Daniel

May 7

Hi Daniel:

I see how your genealogy of CRT is different to that of most of us in the law. However, when you read the *Race, Racism, and American Law Teacher's Manual* (Bell, 2008b) you see how I too have been influenced by the works of Paulo Freire.[19] Tell me more about transformational resistance theory. As you know, I've spent my adult life engaged in various forms of oppositional behavior.[20] Tell me what you've learned by linking CRT and transformational resistance.

Sincerely,

Derrick

May 8

Dear Professor Bell:

I'll share how Dolores Delgado Bernal and I came to develop one of our critical race tools: transformational resistance theory (see Figure 4.4).[21] In the last 17 years some of our col-

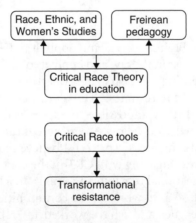

Figure 4.4 A genealogy of critical race theory in education, critical race tools, and transformational resistance

leagues have been developing various transformational resistance tools (see Camangian, 2009; Collatos, 2005; Covarrubias, 2005; Covarrubias and Revilla, 2003; Delgado Bernal, 1997; Morrell, 2001; Revilla, 2004; Romero, 2008; Talavera-Bustillos, 1998).[22]

CRITICAL RACE THEORY AND TRANSFORMATIONAL RESISTANCE

In the mid-1990s I was having a conversation in my office with Dolores Delgado Bernal[23]—a doctoral student at the University of California, Los Angeles, and I was her advisor. As part of her dissertation research, she was examining the 1968 East Los Angeles walkouts (blowouts) (see Delgado Bernal, 1997). These were student-organized demonstrations against unequal educational conditions and opportunities in the public schools of East Los Angeles. As we talked about the social historical texts that Dolores had been analyzing, she was concerned that the role of women was not present in the student activist literature generally and the blowouts in particular. She asked me if I knew of women who participated and were leaders in this historic movement for educational rights. Since I was a high school senior in 1968 and had lived in the Lincoln Heights community of East Los Angeles,[24] I mentioned two women I knew were involved in the blowouts. Over the next weeks and months we discussed how women's leadership roles were ignored or downplayed in the academic and historical research. Indeed, in Figure 4.5 we see Delgado Bernal's model of grassroots leadership (Delgado Bernal, 1997, 1998). Through her research Dolores Delgado Bernal was able to identify, define, and give examples of five dimensions of women's leadership emanating from the 1968 blowouts. The first two were traditional roles—holding office and acting as spokesperson; and the final three were more non-traditional—developing consciousness, organizing, and networking. Her research opened up important discussions and insights on women's roles in leadership and the ways we identify and define them (Delgado Bernal, 1997, 1998).

This discussion of grassroots leadership also led to discussions of student oppositional behavior during this period and particularly the East Los Angeles blowouts.[25] We had been looking at Henry Giroux's (1983) and Paul Willis's (1977) work on resistance theory. However, we had both been influenced by the historical research in race and ethnic

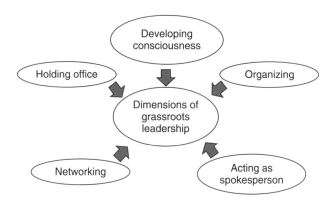

Figure 4.5 Delgado Bernal's dimensions of grassroots leadership

Source: Delgado Bernal (1997, 1998)

studies on individual and collective forms of resistance in such books as Rodolfo Acuna's (1972) *Occupied America*, Vine Deloria's (1969) *Custer Died for Your Sins*, W.E.B. Du Bois's (1903) *The Souls of Black Folk*, Ronald Takaki's (1989) *Strangers from a Different Shore*, and Paulo Freire's (1970b) *Pedagogy of the Oppressed*.[26]

As a doctoral student at the Claremont Graduate School I wrote a doctoral qualifying paper on Paulo Freire and critical pedagogy in 1983. In the paper, I was trying to create a visual model of how the oppositional behaviors of youth could be explained using either reactionary or progressive logics (frameworks) (see Figure 4.6). This early thinking on my part was clearly leading toward a bimodal model of oppositional behaviors that either reinforced (reactionary) or challenged (transformative) structures of social domination. My reasoning on this topic shows the influence of critical Freirean pedagogy on our model of transformational resistance (see Solorzano and Delgado Bernal, 2001).

In subsequent meetings Dolores Delgado Bernal and I visually sketched out our initial thinking on a two-dimensional (and later three-dimensional) model of oppositional behavior that took into consideration one's critique of oppression (y axis) and one's motivation for social justice (x axis). Influenced by Freire (1970a, 1970b, 1973), we

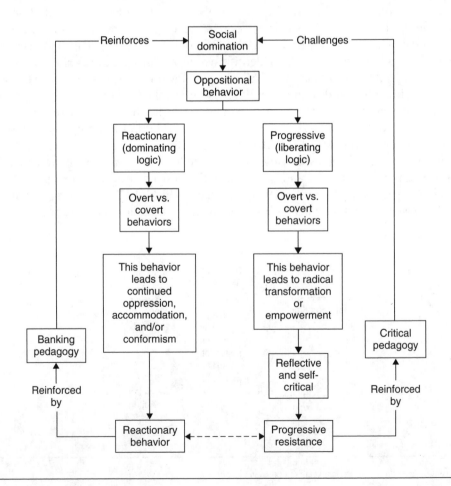

Figure 4.6 Notes on Freire and Giroux's oppositional behavior (1983)

initially defined resistance as the oppositional behavior of students that meets one of two intersecting criteria. They are: (1) students have a critique of social oppression (liberating ideology), and (2) students are interested in working toward social justice (liberating practice). In this early model we were also struggling with how to account for overt and covert forms of resistance.[27]

These initial discussions led to the final model that appears in Dolores Delgado Bernal's 1997 dissertation titled "Chicana School Resistance and Grassroots Leadership: Providing an Alternative History of the 1968 East Los Angeles Blowouts" and our 2001 *Urban Education* article titled "Examining Transformational Resistance through a Critical Race and LatCrit Theory Framework: Chicana and Chicano Students in an Urban Context" (Solorzano and Delgado Bernal, 2001) (see Figure 4.7). The fundamental question of a resistance framework is: How do individuals and groups respond to and negotiate structures of subordination? The basic assumptions of resistance models are that (1) individuals and groups can and do resist subordination, (2) students often resist subordination through forms of oppositional behavior that are empowering, transformative, reflective, and self-critical, and (3) not all oppositional behavior is resistance. Indeed, Dolores Delgado Bernal and I see transformational resistance as:

> student behavior that illustrates both a critique of oppression and a desire for social justice. In other words, the student holds some level of awareness and critique of her/ his oppressive conditions and structures of domination and must be at least somewhat motivated by a sense of social justice. With a deeper level of understanding and a social justice orientation, transformational resistance offers the greatest possibility for social change.
>
> (Solorzano & Delgado Bernal, 2001, p. 15)

Take care,

Daniel

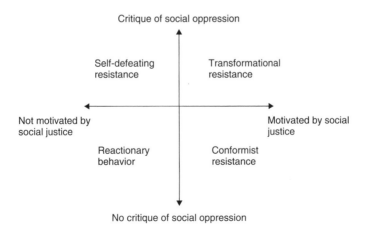

May 9

Hi Daniel:

Did you write anything else on Freirean influences on the development of transformational resistance theory? From my reading of Freire, I think I can see where this is heading.

Sincerely,

Derrick

May 10

Dear Professor Bell:

In another collaboration with Tara Yosso[28] we began to explicitly link Freirean pedagogy with resistance theory. The article was titled "Maintaining Social Justice Hopes within Academic Realities: A Freirean Approach to Critical Race/LatCrit Pedagogy" (Solorzano & Yosso, 2001). We published this paper as part of our participation in the LatCrit V Conference in Colorado in 2000. In this article we tried to answer the question: How do we as critical educators maintain a sense of integrity as we attempt to work for social change within the confines of the academy? In Section VI of the article, titled "An Algebraic Approach to Resistance?," Tara Yosso and I created a counterstory where we treat the original resistance model as an algebraic lesson along the x and y coordinates. Specifically, along the y coordinate we substitute "critique of social oppression" with Freire's "levels of consciousness"—magical, naïve, and critical (see Figure 4.8) (this was discussed in my May 4th email to you). In the article we discuss the challenges that educators face while working for social justice at all levels of the educational pipeline.

Take care,

Daniel

May 11

Hi Daniel:

Are you finding that other groups are using transformational resistance theory in and out of the classroom?

Sincerely,

Derrick

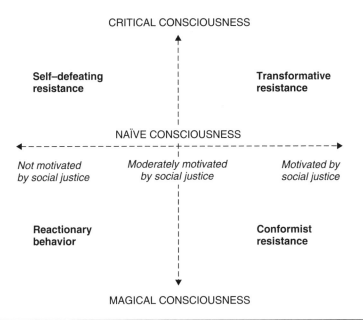

CRITICAL CONSCIOUSNESS

Self–defeating resistance

Transformative resistance

NAÏVE CONSCIOUSNESS

Not motivated by social justice

Moderately motivated by social justice

Motivated by social justice

Reactionary behavior

Conformist resistance

MAGICAL CONSCIOUSNESS

Figure 4.8 Letty's figure in progress

Source: Solorzano & Yosso (2001, p. 607)

May 12

Dear Professor Bell:

In the 17 years since Dolores Delgado Bernal and I started working in this area I have found that young students—middle and high school—and their teachers have used the model in ways that initially we hadn't anticipated. The transformational resistance model seems to allow students to place themselves on this "oppositional behavior" or "resistance matrix," but also provides a set of tools to reflect on that placement and how one moves from one quadrant to another. It appears that over time they gravitate or aspire toward the "transformative resistance" quadrant: that space where they feel they are moving toward a "critique of social oppression" and their oppositional behaviors are becoming "motivated by social justice." Educators who work with these students provide the curricular and pedagogical supports to both understand the resistance framework and work toward a transformative agenda in and out of the classroom.

Recently, I received an email from a ninth grade algebra teacher who read the two articles (Solorzano and Bernal, 2001; Solorzano and Yosso, 2001) and shared them with her students. Here is an excerpt of what she said:

Hi Danny. I taught my math students about the coordinate plane using the forms of resistance theory. I used resistance theory to introduce and provide relevance to the Cartesian coordinate system … I wanted students to understand that the coordinate system can show the presence (or positive value) of one variable and the absence (or negative value) of a second variable—all in one diagram. This made using the coordinate system with numbers more of a valuable tool and more meaningful for them. They got the idea of negative and positive *x* with the absence or presence of *motivation for social justice*, and the idea of negative and positive *y* with the absence or presence of *critique of oppression* … I also had them do some writing about a *time they resisted* and to *place themselves on the coordinate system* … We are going to re-visit this in March once students are done with their research (Food for Justice Campaign in East Los Angeles) and are planning for action—so they can decide how they can resist in a *transformative way* regarding the quantitative data they collect on health.[29]

(Emphasis added)

Initially, Dolores Delgado Bernal, Tara Yosso, and I were not thinking of how creative and committed educators might use this transformational resistance framework to engage students to (in Freirean terms) "read the word and their world." We now know of and speak to many other teachers and students who are using the transformational resistance framework in and out of their classrooms.[30]

CONCLUSION

Professor Bell, as you can see, I came to CRT from the transdisciplinary fields of race, ethnic, and women's studies and Freirean pedagogy. CRT in education draws on these and other schools of progressive scholarship and merges them with the works in CRT and the law. CRT utilizes the strengths of these various critical frameworks and has the benefit of hindsight in addressing some of their weaknesses, blind spots, and/or underdeveloped areas. That's not to say that CRT doesn't have its own blind spots. Indeed, Latino critical theory (LatCrit) emerged in the law because of CRT's inability to incorporate issues of language, immigration status, and citizenship into the race discourse. LatCrit draws on the strengths outlined in CRT, and emphasizes the intersectionality of experience with oppression, and the need to extend conversations about race and racism beyond the Black/White binary. So CRT and LatCrit theory are not new in and of themselves, but instead are a synthesis of many critical and transformative frameworks.

In this short autobiography, I've tried to show how my background in race, ethnic, and women's studies, Freirean pedagogy, and CRT in the law, with the collaboration of my colleagues, helped us build a model of transformational resistance within an educational context. This transformational resistance model extends the works of Paulo Freire (1970a, 1970b, 1973), Henry Giroux (1983), and Paul Willis (1977) by incorporating historical and contemporary examples of resistance in the fields of African American, Chicana/o, Native American, Asian American, and women's studies (see Acuna, 1972; Deloria, 1969; Du Bois, 1903; Hill Collins, 1986, 1990; and Takaki, 1989).[31] CRT in the law was and continues to be pivotal in my work. I am forever grateful for your contributions, along with the many legal colleagues I have, and continue to read, analyze, and incorporate into my work in CRT in education. I want to thank you for encouraging me to document my own intellectual genealogy and hope my colleagues and I have done justice to your work and its many contributions to liberatory education across many domains.

Take care,

Daniel

EPILOGUE

Professor Bell passed on from this world on October 5, 2011. To view the many tributes for Professor Bell you can go to the official Derrick Bell website.[32] I end this chapter with my tribute to Professor Bell taken from the Book of Daniel (12:3): "They that instruct many to justice shall shine as stars for all eternity."

NOTES

1 Bell (2008b) defines racism hypos as "hypothetical cases providing a detailed set of facts that can provide the basis for simulated appellate case arguments with students representing each side. This is an excellent way to facilitate discussion of both the depths and the parameters of racial issues in each of the subject areas" (p. xxii).

2 It should be noted that this is my personal journey to CRT in education: an amazing journey that continues.

3 Although this initial email correspondence took place in April of 2009, I have edited and expanded it to include a conversation I wanted to share with Professor Bell.

4 These nine "racism hypotheticals" were among the 27 hypotheticals Professor Bell sent me titled "Spring 2009 Docket—Court of Bell."

5 Marvin Lynn is an Associate Dean for Teacher Education and Associate Professor at the University of Wisconsin-Eau Claire.

6 Tara Yosso is an Associate Professor of Chicana and Chicano Studies at the University of California, Santa Barbara.

7 The *Chronicle of Higher Education* is a weekly newspaper that addresses the latest news and information in the field of higher education.

8 I credit this term to my colleague Professor Lawrence Parker at the University of Utah.

9 In the 1960s and 1970s the field was called the Mexican American studies. It is now called Chicana/o studies.

10 For an excellent historicizing of CRT in education see Lynn and Parker (2006).

11 See Rosaldo (1994) on the challenge to traditional genealogy of cultural studies, and also Delgado (1984, 1992) on the challenge to White male "imperial scholars" in the field of civil rights law.

12 Here Freire pre-dates both social reproduction (Bowles & Gintis, 1976) and resistance (Giroux, 1983) frameworks in education.

13 For a brief history of the Chicano Mural Movement see: http://www.sparcmurals.org:16080/sparcone/index.php?option=com_content&task=view&id=14&Itemid=44&limit=1&limitstart=0 (last retrieved June 12, 2012).

14 We used Roach Van Allen's (1965, 1967) language experience approach to teach the word or basic literacy skills to the students. We also helped teach the word and the world by examining the 1961 Cuban Literacy Campaign (see Fagan, 1969, ch. 3).

15 In the magical and naïve stages of consciousness, people have internalized these racist and cultural deficit explanations for their unequal condition (see Kohli and Solorzano, 2011 and Perez Huber et al., 2006 for a critical race examination of internalized racism).

16 An earlier version of this article was presented in April 1994 at the annual American Education Research Association Conference in New Orleans, Louisiana.

17 I presented my first CRT paper (with Octavio Villalpando) on November 2, 1995 at the annual meeting of the Association for Studies in Higher Education in Orlando, Florida titled "Critical Race Theory, Marginality, and the Experience of Minority Students in Higher Education" (see Solorzano and Villalpando, 1998).

18 In the winter of 1991 Paulo Freire visited the Graduate School of Education at the University of California, Los Angeles. During his visit he also engaged in dialogues with other groups outside of UCLA. In these situations the question of application and reinvention of Freirean pedagogy came up on numerous occasions.

19 See Bell (2008b, p. 9) on Freire's influence of his views on educator–student collaborative learning. See also Bell and Edmonds (1993); and Lawrence (1991).

20 For instance, see Bell (2002).

21 Although I chose the tool of transformational resistance for this chapter, there are many more tools that have become an important part of our arsenal to understand and combat racism and other forms of oppression (e.g. racial microaggressions, community cultural wealth, and racist nativism).

22 For instance, in addition to Dolores Delgado Bernal's (1997) seminal dissertation on transformational resistance, Valerie Talavera-Bustillos (1998) developed the concept of "triggers of resistance," and Alejandro Covarrubias (2005) and Anita Revilla (2004) developed the concept of "agencies of transformational resistance" (see Covarrubias and Revilla, 2003). I served as chair for all four dissertations.

23 Dolores is now a Professor of Education and Ethnic Studies at the University of Utah.
24 I attended local Catholic elementary and high schools in the Lincoln Heights and Chinatown communities of Los Angeles.
25 We found another African American student led high school "walkout" 17 years earlier in 1951 in the Davis v. The School Board of Prince Edward County legal case (103 F. Supp. 337 (1952)). This case was one of five that were part of the 1954 Brown v. Board desegregation case (347 U.S. 483 (1954)).
26 These five works represent a larger body of race and ethnic studies research in its early days.
27 These overt and covert forms of resistance evolved into active and passive forms of resistance. We finally settled on external and internal forms of resistance (see Solorzano and Delgado Bernal, 2001).
28 I was Tara Yosso's dissertation chair, and she is now an Associate Professor of Chicana and Chicano Studies at the University of California, Santa Barbara.
29 As I walked into the teacher's classroom, I was met with two large x and y blue axes that took up the whole classroom and created four large quadrants. I was impressed with how the teacher physically set up the room to engage her students with both mathematics and transformational resistance.
30 For instance, see how raza studies students in the Tucson Arizona Unified School District used the framework in Romero et al. (2009). See also Camangian (2009); Collatos (2005); Morrell (2001); and Romero (2008) for research with high school students using the transformational resistance framework.
31 These works are used to represent a body of race and ethnic studies scholarship that tells the historical and contemporary story of resistance.
32 http://professorderrickbell.com/tributes/ (last retrieved May 21, 2012).

REFERENCES

Acuna, R. (1972). *Occupied America: The Chicano's struggle toward liberation.* San Francisco, CA: Canfield.
Anzaldúa, G. (1987). *Borderlands—La frontera: The new mestiza.* San Francisco, CA: Spinsters/Aunt Lute.
Asante, M. (1987). *The Afrocentric idea.* Philadelphia, PA: Temple University Press.
Asante, M. (1991). The Afrocentric idea in education. *Journal of Negro Education, 60,* 170–180.
Barrera, M. (1979). *Race and class in the Southwest: A theory of racial inequality.* Notre Dame, IN: University of Notre Dame Press.
Barrera, M., Muñoz, C., & Ornelas, C. (1972). The barrio as internal colony. *Urban Affairs Annual Reviews, 6,* 465–498.
Bell, D. (1989). "An epistolary exploration for a Thurgood Marshall biography." *Harvard BlackLetter Journal, 6,* 51–67.
Bell, D. (2000). *Race, racism, and American law* (4th ed.). New York: Aspen Law and Business.
Bell, D. (2002). *Ethical ambition: Living a life of meaning and worth.* New York: Bloomsbury.
Bell, D. (2004). *Silent covenants: Brown v. Board of Education and the unfulfilled hopes for racial reform.* New York: Oxford University Press.
Bell, D. (2008a). *Race, racism, and American law* (6th ed.). New York: Wolters Kluwer.
Bell, D. (2008b). *Race, racism, and American law: Teacher's manual* (6th ed.). New York: Wolters Kluwer.
Bell, D., & Edmonds, E. (1993). Students and teachers, teachers as learners. *Michigan Law Review, 91,* 2025–2052.
Blauner, R. (1969). Internal colonialism and ghetto revolt. *Social Problems, 16,* 393–408.
Blauner, R. (1972). *Racial oppression in America.* New York: Harper & Row.
Blauner, R. (2001). *Still big news: Racial oppression in America.* Philadelphia, PA: Temple University Press.
Bonilla, F., & Girling, R. (Eds.). (1973). *Structures of dependency.* Stanford, CA: Stanford Institute of Politics.
Bowles, S., & Gintis, H. (1976). *Schooling in capitalist America: Educational reform and the contradictions of economic life.* New York: Basic Books.
Camangian, P. (2009). Teaching like our lives matter: Critical pedagogy and classroom research. Unpublished doctoral dissertation, University of California, Los Angeles.
Collatos, A. (2005). Critical college access: Reframing how we empower urban youth toward higher education and social change. Unpublished doctoral dissertation, University of California, Los Angeles.
Covarrubias, A. (2005). Agencies of transformational resistance: Transforming the intersections of race, class, gender, and sexuality oppression through Latino critical race theory (LatCrit) and praxis. Unpublished doctoral dissertation, University of California, Los Angeles.
Covarrubias, A., & Revilla, A. (2003). Agencies of transformational resistance: Dismantling injustice at the intersection of race, class, gender, and sexuality through LatCrit praxis. *Florida Law Review, 55,* 459–477.
Crenshaw, K. (1991). Mapping the margins: Intersectionality, identity politics, and the violence against women of color. *Stanford Law Review, 43,* 1241–1299.

Curry, T. (2008). Saved by the Bell: Derrick Bell's racial realism as pedagogy. *Philosophical Studies in Education, 39*, 35–46.

Delgado, R. (1984). The imperial scholar: Reflections on a review of civil rights literature. *University of Pennsylvania Law Review, 132*, 561–578.

Delgado, R. (1992). The imperial scholar revisited: How to marginalize outsider writing, ten years later. *University of Pennsylvania Law Review, 140*, 1349–1372.

Delgado Bernal, D. (1997). Chicana school resistance and grassroots leadership: Providing an alternative history of the 1968 East Los Angeles blowouts. Unpublished doctoral dissertation, University of California, Los Angeles.

Delgado Bernal, D. (1998). Grassroots leadership reconceptualized: Chicana oral histories and the 1968 East Los Angeles school blowouts. *Frontiers: A Journal of Women Studies, 19*, 113–142.

Deloria, V. (1969). *Custer died for your sins: An Indian manifesto.* New York: Avon.

Du Bois, W.E.B. (1903). *The souls of black folk: Essays and sketches.* Chicago, IL: A.C. McClurg.

Fagan, R. (1969). *The transformation of political culture in Cuba.* Stanford, CA: Stanford University Press.

Freire, P. (1970a). *Cultural action for freedom.* Cambridge, MA: Harvard Educational Review Monographs.

Freire, P. (1970b). *Pedagogy of the oppressed.* New York: Continuum.

Freire, P. (1973). *Education for critical consciousness.* New York: Seabury.

Freire, P., & Macedo, D. (1987). *Literacy: Reading the word and the world.* London: Routledge.

Giroux, H. (1983). Theories of reproduction and resistance in the new sociology of education: A critical analysis. *Harvard Educational Review, 53*, 257–293.

Hill Collins, P. (1986). Learning from the outsider within: The sociological significance of black feminist thought. *Social Problems, 33*, S14–S32.

Hill Collins, P. (1990). *Black feminist thought: Knowledge, consciousness, and the politics of empowerment.* New York: Routledge.

hooks, b. (1990). *Yearning: Race, gender, and cultural politics.* Cambridge, MA: South End Press.

Hurtado, A. (1996). *The color of privilege: Three blasphemes on race and feminism.* Ann Arbor: University of Michigan Press.

Kohli, R., & Solorzano, D. (2011). Black and brown high school student activism. In L. Urrieta & A. Revilla (Eds.), *Marching students: Chicana/o identity and the politics of education 1968 and the present* (pp. 131–147). Reno: University of Nevada Press.

Ladson-Billings, G., & Tate, W. (1995). Toward a critical race theory of education. *Teachers College Record, 97*, 47–68.

Lawrence, C. (1991). Doing "the James Brown" at Harvard: Professor Derrick Bell as liberationist teacher. *Harvard BlackLetter Journal, 8*, 263–273.

Lynn, M. (1999). Toward a critical race pedagogy: A research note. *Urban Education, 33*, 606–626.

Lynn, M., & Parker, L. (2006). Critical race studies in education: Examining a decade of research on U.S. schools. *Urban Review, 38*, 257–290.

Macedo, D. (1994). Preface. In P. McLaren & C. Lankshear (Eds.), *Politics of liberation: Paths from Freire* (pp. xiii–xviii). London and New York: Routledge.

McGrew, K. (2011). A review of class-based theories of student resistance in education: Mapping the origins and influence of *Learning to Labor* by Paul Willis. *Review of Educational Research, 81*, 234–266.

Monaghan, P. (1993). "Critical race theory" questions role of legal doctrine in racial inequality: Lani Guinier, ill-fated Justice Dept. nominee, is one of its traditional adherents. *Chronicle of Higher Education*, July 23, pp. A7, A9.

Morrell, E. (2001). Transforming classroom discourse: Academic and critical literacy development through engaging popular culture. Unpublished doctoral dissertation, University of California, Berkeley.

Perez Huber, L., Johnson, R., & Kohli, R. (2006). Naming racism: A conceptual look at internalized racism in U.S. schools. *UCLA Chicana/o–Latina/o Law Review, 26*, 183–206.

Revilla, A. (2004). Raza womyn re-constructing revolution: Exploring the intersections of race, class, gender, and sexuality in the lives of Chicana/Latina student activists. Unpublished doctoral dissertation, University of California, Los Angeles.

Romero, A. (2008). Towards a critically compassionate intellectualism model of transformative education: Love, hope, identity, and organic intellectualism through the convergence of critical race theory, critical pedagogy, and authentic caring. Unpublished doctoral dissertation, University of Arizona.

Romero, A., Arce, S., & Cammarota, J. (2009). A barrio pedagogy: Identity, intellectualism, activism, and academic achievement through the evolution of critically compassionate intellectualism. *Race Ethnicity and Education, 12*, 217–233.

Rosaldo, R. (1994). Whose cultural studies? *American Anthropologist, 96*, 524–529.

Sleeter, C., & Delgado Bernal, D. (2004). Critical pedagogy, critical race theory, and antiracist education: Implications for multicultural education. In J. Banks & C. Banks (Eds.), *The Handbook of Research on Multicultural Education* (pp. 240–258). New York: Macmillan.

Smith, W., & Alschuler, A. (1976). How to measure Freire's stages of conscientizacao: The C Code manual. Unpublished manuscript, University of Massachusetts, Amherst.

Solorzano, D. (1989). Teaching and social change: Reflections on a Freirean approach in a college classroom. *Teaching Sociology, 17,* 218–225.

Solorzano, D. (1997). Images and words that wound: Critical race theory, racial stereotyping, and teacher education. *Teacher Education Quarterly, 24,* 5–19.

Solorzano, D., & Delgado Bernal, D. (2001). Examining transformational resistance through a critical race and LatCrit theory framework: Chicana and Chicano students in an urban context. *Urban Education, 36,* 308–342.

Solorzano, D., & Villalpando, O. (1998). Critical race theory, marginality, and the experience of minority students in higher education. In C. Torres & T. Mitchell (Eds.), *Emerging issues in the sociology of education: Comparative perspectives* (pp. 211–224). New York: SUNY Press.

Solorzano, D., & Yosso, T. (2001). Maintaining social justice hopes within academic realities: A Freirean approach to critical race/LatCrit pedagogy. *Denver Law Review, 78,* 595–621.

Takaki, R. (1989). *Strangers from a different shore: A history of Asian Americans.* New York: Little, Brown.

Talavera-Bustillos, V. (1998). Chicana college choice and resistance: An exploratory study of first generation college students. Unpublished doctoral dissertation, University of California, Los Angeles.

Tate, W. (1994). From inner city to ivory tower: Does my voice matter in the academy? *Urban Education, 29,* 245–269.

Van Allen, R. (1965). *Attitudes and the art of teaching reading.* Washington, DC: National Education Association (retrieved from ERIC database, ED 038240).

Van Allen, R. (1967). *How the language experience works* (retrieved from ERIC database, ED 012226).

Willis, P. (1977). *Learning to labor: How working class kids get working class jobs.* New York: Columbia University Press.

5

W.E.B. DU BOIS'S CONTRIBUTIONS TO CRITICAL RACE STUDIES IN EDUCATION

Sociology of Education, Classical Critical Race Theory, and Proto-Critical Pedagogy

Reiland Rabaka

INTRODUCTION: DU BOIS'S RACE-CENTERED SOCIOLOGY OF EDUCATION

W.E.B. Du Bois's writings on race remain relevant and contribute to both contemporary racial and educational discourse—especially the emerging field of critical race studies in education—for four fundamental reasons. First, his sociology of race has been often interpreted as an "ideology of race," that is, as an inert, inflexible, fixed and fast, singular notion of what race is, and which groups constitute constituent races. This is not only a gross misinterpretation of Du Bois's constantly evolving sociology of race, but an example of the type of intellectual disingenuousness and, let it be said, epistemic apartheid that has long plagued African American intellectuals of every political persuasion.

Critically engaging Du Bois's sociology of race offers objective interpreters and critics of race and racism an opportunity to analyze a theoretically rich and thoroughgoing series of ruminations on race and racism by an undisputed pioneer critical race theorist who almost infinitely harbored a hardnosed skepticism toward the supposed "scientific" and/or "biological" bases of race. This skepticism, coupled with his own homegrown pragmatism, often led Du Bois to contradictory conclusions regarding race. However, he repeatedly reminded his readers that he was not searching for a sound, "scientific" concept of race as much as he was on a quest to either locate or create a vehicle for African American socio-political survival and, ultimately, African American liberation.

The meaning of race has always meandered, as the very idea of race has consistently traveled far and wide since its inception. As witnessed in his discussions of race in "The Negroes of Farmville" (1898a) and *The Philadelphia Negro* (1899), Du Bois has the distinction of being one of the first persons of African descent to empirically research and write on race and anti-black racism. His Africanity or blackness is important insofar as Africans or blacks have historically been and continue currently to be considered one of the most thoroughly and oppressively racially colonized groups—although under-theorized from their own cultural perspectives and radical political positions—in the history of race and racism. From an increasingly insurgent empirical and critical theoretical perspective, he studied the history of race with an intense interest in its origins and originators, and the purpose(s) of its origination. This alone should distinguish Du Bois's writings on race as more than mere intellectual artifacts, but, truth be told, there is much more, so much more.

Du Bois's concepts of race harbor an inherent and radical humanism that is often complex and seemingly contradictory, but which nonetheless is part and parcel of his overarching transdisciplinary trajectory. In specific, he developed what I have crudely called a "gift theory," which, in short, elaborated that each race has specific and special "gifts" to contribute to national and international culture and civilization. In works such as *The Souls of Black Folk* (1903a), "The People of Peoples and Their Gifts to Men" (1913), and *Darkwater* (1920a), and, most especially, in later works like *The Gift of Black Folk* (1924), "The Black Man Brings His Gifts" (1925), *Black Reconstruction in America, 1860–1880* (1995a), *Black Folk Then and Now* (1939), *Dusk of Dawn* (1968a), and *The World and Africa* (1965), Du Bois put forward concepts of race that were not biologically based, but predicated on social, political, historical, and cultural "common" characteristics and "common" experiences shared by continental and diasporan Africans. In Du Bois's "gift theory," these characteristics represent continental and diasporan African peoples' "gifts" or race- and culture-specific contributions to the wider world and the ongoing development of civilization.

Second, and falling fast on the heels of the first point, it is important for us to revisit Du Bois's concepts of race, because what we now know of his sociology of race is almost utterly predicated on, and relegated to, his early writings. For instance, most contemporary critics of Du Bois's sociology of race begin and often end with his 1897 address to the American Negro Academy, "The Conservation of Races." Some critics go as far as his early career classics, "The Study of the Negro Problems" (1898b), *The Philadelphia Negro* (1899), and, of course, *The Souls of Black Folk* (1903a). Further than these texts, however, contemporary race critics do not dare venture, which to my mind seems absurd considering the fact that Du Bois continued to publish for another 60 years. Scant attention has been given to Du Bois's writings on race and racism after *The Souls of Black Folk*, and when on rare occasions they are engaged more is made of his infamously alleged and highly controversial collapsing of race into class in his 1935 classic *Black Reconstruction in America* (1995a). Maybe those who argue that Du Bois (1982) collapsed race into class and that he uncritically accepted communism have never read his 1936 essay "Social Planning for the Negro, Past and Present," where he roared against the supposed racelessness and political panacea thesis of white socialists and communists: "There is no automatic power in socialism to override and suppress race prejudice ... One of the worst things that Negroes could do today would be to join the American Communist Party or any of its many branches" (p. 38). Du Bois, then, was a much more astute interpreter of Marxian philosophy and class theory than many contemporary race theorists, especially sociologists of race and critical race theorists, may be aware of. Without a thorough understanding of why and the ways in which he critically engaged—as opposed to uncritically embraced—Marxism many critics of his concepts of race are doomed to do Du Bois a disservice by misinterpreting his motivations for emphasizing certain aspects of race and racism at specific socio-historic and politico-economic intervals. It may not be too much of an overstatement to say that Du Bois empirically developed a discourse on race in order to critique racism and provide a philosophical foundation for anti-racist radical politics and social movements. This is the second reason his work has import for contemporary race and racism discourse, especially sociology of race: because it may offer models for us to further our critiques of race and to combat the seemingly omnipresent and omnipotent racism of the twenty-first century.

The third reason Du Bois's writings on race are important for contemporary race and racism discourse is because of the recent emergence of critical white studies and the emphasis on whiteness, white racelessness or white racial neutrality and universality, and white supremacy. In several pioneering publications in historical sociology, sociology of race, sociology of culture, and political economy he deftly and defiantly hit at the heart of whiteness, chronicling its rise alongside the concept of race, noting that to be white is to be raceless, to be powerful, or, at the least, to have privileged access to power or people in positions of power. In the logic of the white world, race is something that soils the social status of sub-humans, that is, non-whites; it politically pollutes their thinking, thus rendering them powerless, irrational, and in need of clear conceptions concerning themselves and the world. Since whites are the only group purportedly not plagued by race, they then have been burdened by God (who, within the racist logic of the white supremacist world, is also, of course, white) with the task of leading the lost, raced "natives," "barbarians," "savages," and sub-humans to the higher level or lily-white "heaven" of humanity. Du Bois resented whites' racial mythmaking, and directed a significant portion of his writings on race and racism to critiquing whiteness and white supremacy. His writings, such as "Race Friction between Black and White" (1908), "The Souls of White Folk" (1910c), "Of the Culture of White Folk" (1917), "White Co-Workers" (1920b), "The Superior Race" (1923), "The White Worker" (1995c), "The White Proletariat in Alabama, Georgia, and Florida" (1995b), "The White World" (1968b), and "The White Folk Have a Right to Be Ashamed" (1949b), represent and register as early innovative efforts aimed at critiquing and combating whiteness and white supremacy. Du Bois's work in this area, then, can be said to prefigure and provide a paradigm and point of departure for the contemporary discourse and debates of critical white studies.

Finally, Du Bois's writings on race are relevant with regard to contemporary race and racism criticism, as they contribute significantly to the discursive arena of critical race theory. No longer considered the exclusive domain of legal studies scholars and radical civil rights lawyers and law professors, critical race theory has blossomed and currently encompasses and includes a wide range of theory and theorists from diverse academic disciplines. In a nutshell, the core concerns of critical race theory include: race and racism's centrality to European imperial expansion and modernity; racism's intersections and interconnections with sexism, capitalism, and colonialism; white supremacy; white normativity and white neutrality; state-sanctioned (or legal) racial domination and discrimination; and revolutionary anti-racist race and cultural consciousness amongst non-whites (Crenshaw et al., 1995; Delgado, 1995; Delgado & Stefancic, 2001; Essed & Goldberg, 2001; Goldberg & Solomos, 2002). Du Bois's sociology of race in many senses foreshadows contemporary critical race theory and, therefore, contributes several paradigms and points of departure to its discursive community as well. However, as with so many other aspects of his thought, Du Bois's writings on race and racism have been relegated to the realm of, at best, ethnic and racial studies, which downplays and diminishes their trenchant transdisciplinarity and significance for sociology of race and sociology of culture in specific, and contemporary radical politics and critical social theory in general. Therefore, his writings on race have been virtually overlooked and/or rendered intellectually invisible by critical race theorists.

As Susan Gillman and Alys Eve Weinbaum argued in their ground-breaking anthology *Next to the Color-Line: Gender, Sexuality, and W.E.B. Du Bois* (2007), and as I have discussed in greater detail in *Against Epistemic Apartheid: W.E.B. Du Bois and the Disciplinary Decadence of Sociology* (2010a), Du Bois was critically conscious of many of the ways in which *race is gendered* and *gender is raced.* Emerging in the fifteenth century, and coinciding with European imperial expansion around the globe, racial domination threw fuel on the wildfire of preexisting gender discrimination. An astute student of gender relations, Du Bois eventually accented the intersections and interconnections of racism and sexism, specifically white supremacy and patriarchy. This means, then, that at the least some of his anti-racist social theorizing may serve as a model for contemporary critical race theory in the sense that it seeks a similar goal: to make visible the long-invisible connections between racial, gender, and class domination and discrimination, not only in law but in medicine, politics, education, and religion, among other aspects and areas of contemporary society. What is intellectually amazing is that Du Bois developed a sexism-sensitive conception of race and racism almost a hundred years prior to the current critical race theory movement, which is to say that much of Du Bois's work in sociology of race and sociology of culture, for all theoretical and practical purposes, could (and, I honestly believe, should) be considered *classical critical race theory.*

Du Bois was also an early exponent of the race/class thesis that contended that, although class struggle had been a part of human history for several centuries, the modern concept of race and the insidious socio-political practice of racism—of course, coupled with capitalism and colonialism—exacerbated class conflicts among both the racial colonizers and the racially colonized. Although often unacknowledged, similar to C.L.R. James (1994, 1996, 1999) and Oliver C. Cox (1948, 1976, 1987), Du Bois was a pioneer in terms of analyzing the political economy of race and racism, which is to say that he often argued against studying race independently of class. Race and class, as we have seen with race and gender in Du Bois's sexism-sensitive and/or gender-centered conception of race, are inextricable and incessantly intersecting and reconfiguring, constantly forming and reforming, creating a racial or racist dimension in modern class theory and class struggle, and a classist or economically exploitive dimension in racial politics and racial struggle.

Race and racism were European modernity's weapons of choice in its efforts to establish global (racial colonial) capitalism. A (sub)person, from the modern white world's frame of reference, was capitalized on or, rather, economically exploited based on biology or ethnicity. That is to say, the degree(s) to which one was dominated and/or discriminated against was predicated on European-invented racial classifications and ethno-cultural categorizations. Du Bois's writings on the political economy of race and racism, therefore, provide an alternative paradigm for contemporary critical race theory to build on and bolster its calls for racial, economic, and gender justice. But at this point critical race theory is not the exclusive domain of law professors and civil rights lawyers. Along with humanities and social science scholars, several education scholars have embraced and directly contributed to the discursive development of critical race theory.

As with most other critical race theorists, those in the field of education often seem to be oblivious to Du Bois's classic critical race theory, which is most visible when and where his sociology of race overlaps with his sociology of education. Hence, educational and intellectual historian Derrick Alridge (2008) opens his watershed work *The Educational Thought of W.E.B. Du Bois* stating: "No other African American or other American scholar has ever offered as comprehensive a set of educational ideas for black people as did Du Bois" (p. 1). However, Alridge quickly quipped, "[d]espite his contributions ... Du Bois has been for the most part neglected as an educational thinker in twentieth century American history, and his educational ideas have been largely ignored by the fields of educational and intellectual history" (p. 1). Something similar could be said concerning the ongoing omission of Du Bois's critical educational theory with regard to the sociology of education. When Du Bois is acknowledged within the sociology of education, it is most frequently in reference to his intellectual history-making debate with Booker T. Washington concerning an optimal educational strategy for African Americans, or completely collapsed into what can be gathered from his most popular publications, both published in 1903, *The Souls of Black Folk* (1903a) and "The Talented Tenth" (1903b) (Frantz, 1997; Freedman, 1975; Greco, 1984; Harris, 1993; Hwang, 1988; Johnson, 1976; Moore, 2003; Wortham, 1997).

In 1903 Du Bois was 35 years old and would go on to live another extremely eventful 60 years. Needless to say, his ideas grew and changed greatly over the course of his long and productive life. To start and stop investigations of Du Bois's educational thought with *The Souls of Black Folk* and "The Talented Tenth" is to put into play a kind of logical reductionism that seems to be almost exclusively reserved for either non-white or non-male intellectuals. In order to seriously grasp and grapple with Du Bois's educational thought (see Du Bois, 2002), one must be willing to go into discursive depth and to rigorously research not only Du Bois's educational ideas, but also the epoch in which he put forward his educational theories and praxes. In other words, to start and stop investigations of Du Bois's educational thought with *The Souls of Black Folk* and "The Talented Tenth" would mean overlooking important contributions to the sociology of education published both prior to and long after *The Souls of Black Folk* and "The Talented Tenth." For instance, prior to his aforementioned 1903 classics, Du Bois published "Careers Open to College-Bred Negroes" (1989), *The Philadelphia Negro* (1899), *The College-Bred Negro* (1900a), *Memorial to the Legislature of Georgia on Negro Common Schools* (1900b), "The Freedmen's Bureau" (1901c), *The Common School* (1901b), "The Burden of Negro Schooling" (1901a), and "The Higher Education of the Negro" (1902), among many others. Special mention must be made of the often-overlooked fact that *The College-Bred Negro* was the first social scientific study of African Americans in higher education (Glascoe, 1996; Mielke, 1977; Neal, 1984; Nwankwo, 1989; Okoro, 1982; Smith, 1975; Sumpter, 1973).

Du Bois's major contributions to educational thought after the publication of *The Souls of Black Folk* and "The Talented Tenth" include: "What Intellectual Training Is Doing for the Negro" (1904), "Atlanta University" (1905), "The Hampton Idea" (1906), *College-Bred Negro Communities* (1910b), *The College-Bred Negro American* (1910a), *The Common School and the Negro American* (1911), "Negro Education" (1918), "Education in Africa" (1926), "Education and Work" (1931), *The Field and Function of a Negro College* (1933), "Does the Negro Need Separate Schools?" (1935), "A Program for Land-Grant Colleges" (1941), and "The Freedom to Learn" (1949a), among many others. It is, of course, important to observe the fact that five of the 14 chapters of *The Souls of Black Folk* were exclusively devoted to education, which made the book arguably the most audacious and eloquent statement concerning African American education at the turn of the twentieth century. However, it is equally important to observe that, of the 16 Atlanta University studies Du Bois edited, four were exclusively focused on education: *The College-Bred Negro, The Common School, The College-Bred Negro American,* and *The Common School and the Negro American* (Du Bois, 1969a, 1969b). Although the Atlanta University studies on African American education are not in any way unblemished, they are indisputably the first comprehensive studies of African American education. Often lacking adequate data and revealing serious interpretive limitations (i.e., elitist, Euro-centric, and masculinist interpretive limitations), the Atlanta University studies on African American education still represent an unprecedented achievement. This fact is even more obvious when Du Bois's lack of research funds, the recentness of social scientific research methodologies at the turn of the twentieth century, and his undeniably over-ambitious intellectual aspirations are taken into critical consideration (Horne, 2009; Lewis, 1993, 2000; Marable, 1986).

It is, perhaps, common knowledge at this point that at the conceptual core of Du Bois's social scientific discourse lies his searing search for solutions to social, political, and cultural "problems" (see Du Bois, 1898b). In fact, it could be easily averred that Du Bois spent the sweep of his publishing life—an almost unfathomable 80 years (from 1883 to 1963)—searching for solutions to problems, and not just "Negro" or black problems, but problems which plagued humanity as a whole. These "problems" varied in nature and nuance, but each emerged from the incontrovertible fact(s) of modern (and/ or postmodern) imperialism—and specifically as experienced and endured in various forms of racism, sexism, capitalism, and colonialism. According to Du Bois, one of the most pressing problems confronting humanity, and non-whites (in capitalist, communist, and colonialist countries) in particular, is, as he himself put it, "the problem of education" (Anderson & Massey, 2001; Anderson & Zuberi, 2000; Gordon, 2000; Rabaka, 2007).

According to Du Bois, education is "by derivation and in fact a drawing out of human powers." It involves, or, at the least, education from Du Bois's point of view *should* involve, essentially three things. First, education requires a critical knowledge of the past, that is, critical study of history, continental and diasporan African history, as well as "world" history. Du Bois (1920a, 1924, 1939, 1945, 1995a) argued that *history,* as conventionally conceived in white supremacist capitalist and colonialist contexts, was often an ideological ruse in the hands of the ruling race/gender/class/religion. Over time he, therefore, developed a critical theory of history or *counter-history,* if you will, that chronicled the insidious agenda of European imperialism and African American and other non-white peoples' radical politics and unceasing social movements *against apartheid,* epistemic or otherwise.

Second, education entails questions of culture, "cultural study"—as Du Bois (1973, pp. 9, 28) put it—and critical cultural inquiry. History and culture go hand in hand, and to rob and reframe a people's history and culture from an oppressive point of view, or in the interest of imperialism, is to distort and deny that which is most human in each of us: our right to live decent and dignified lives, to walk unmolested in the world, and to develop (freely and to our fullest potential) our own unique contributions to the various traditions and heritages that constitute human culture and civilization. Lastly, Du Bois's sociology of education demands a critical understanding of present and future vital needs—the needs of not simply this or that specific cultural group, class, race, or gender, but humanity and our fragile ecology as a whole. This means, then, that Du Bois's sociology of education (as with Du Bois's sociological discourse in general) is inherently and radically humanist, multicultural, and transethnic, and often uses history and culture as a basis to apprehend, interpret, and create critical consciousness concerning life- and world-threatening conflicts and contradictions. Considering Du Bois's above definition of education, this chapter endeavors an exploration of Du Bois's evolving sociology of education and considers its import for contemporary sociology of education, critical race theory, and what I have elsewhere termed *Africana critical pedagogy* (see Rabaka, 2008, pp. 43–80).

In what follows I will, first, discuss Du Bois's historical sociology and its impact on his sociology of education. Next, I examine Du Bois's sociology of culture and the distinct style of cultural criticism he developed for its centrality to his sociology of education and his critical race theory more generally. Finally, I conclude this chapter commenting on the contributions Du Bois's sociology of education continues to make to contemporary critical race studies in education. Let us begin, then, by hitting at the heart of Du Bois's sociology of education, his historical sociology.

DU BOIS, CRITICAL RACE THEORY, HISTORICAL SOCIOLOGY, AND EDUCATIONAL HISTORY

For Du Bois (1973), African American education "should be founded on a knowledge of the history of their people in Africa and in the United States [and other parts of the African diaspora], and their present condition[s]" (p. 93). Du Bois's sociology of education is distinguished in that it was one of (if not "the") first to maintain that "the whole cultural history of Africans in the world" should be taken into consideration when one is seeking to grasp and grapple with the "present condition[s]" of continental and diasporan Africans. To begin, according to Du Bois, one needs to know about "the history of their people in Africa," "the slave trade and slavery," "abolition," and "the struggle for emancipation" (p. 150). Only after a careful and critical study of classical, colonial, and contemporary continental and diasporan African history did Du Bois deem an educator minimally prepared to proceed with the pedagogical process where continental and diasporan Africans are concerned.

Knowledge of "the whole cultural history of Africans in the world" is a necessity in Du Bois's sociology of education on account of the complexities and conundrums of the colonial, neocolonial, and, some would go so far as to add, "postcolonial" African condition (see Eze, 1997; Olaniyan, 2000; Quayson, 2000a, 2000b). Africana education "starts from a different point," because continental and diasporan Africans' historicity—that is, their concrete historical endurances and cultural experiences—have been and continue to be ones which require, and oft-times demand, as Du Bois (1973) put it, "a different starting point" (p. 95). Du Bois's demand for a different point of departure for Africana education rests on the realities of continental and diasporan Africans' situatedness in the modern world. In other words, he understood continental and diasporan Africans to be "facing a serious and difficult situation," one that was at once "baffling and contradictory," and:

> made all the more difficult for us because we are by blood and descent and popular opinion an integral part of that vast majority of mankind which is the Victim and not

the Beneficiary of present conditions; which is today working at starvation wages and on a level of brute toil and without voice in its own government or education in its ignorance, for the benefit, the enormous profit, and the dazzling luxury of the white world.

(pp. 48, 75)

Africana education, according to Du Bois, "cannot begin with history and lead to Negro history. It cannot start with sociology and end with Negro sociology" (1973, p. 95). It "must be grounded in the condition and work of ... black men [and women]" (p. 95). This is to say, Africana education, educators, and students "must start where we are and not where we wish to be" (p. 94). Drawing parallels between African American education and European education, Du Bois argued that, much in the same manner that education and educational institutions function in England, France, Germany, Spain, and Russia, they have a similar task and must play a comparable role in African American life and culture. As he understood it, education and educational centers in the aforementioned countries used the history of the country and the culture of its people as aids in the socialization and acculturation of its citizens. As with education and educational centers elsewhere, Du Bois admonished Africana educators and educational institutions to utilize continental and diasporan African history and culture as their foundation and grounding point of departure.

It is the history of continental and diasporan Africans that is at the heart of Du Bois's (1996) sociology of education, and it is the harsh realities of that history which demand a "different program" and require Africana education to "start ... from a different point" (pp. 416–418). As with contemporary Africana Studies theory and research methods, Du Bois's prophetic pedagogy utilized Africana history and culture and Africana thought, spiritual traditions, and value systems to "interpret and understand" "all history" and "all mankind in all ages" (p. 418; Warren, 1984, 2010, 2011). For Du Bois (1897), Africana perspectives and points of view and Africana interpretations and explanations of the human experience (i.e., history) and the human condition (i.e., actuality) are viable and valid insofar as it is understood that "the Negro people, as a race, have a contribution to make to civilization and humanity, which no other race can make" (p. 15).

Each human group has its philosophy, which is to say that each group of human beings harbors a certain "habit of reflection" that helps them "interpret and understand" the world in which they live. As the Ghanaian philosopher Kwasi Wiredu (1991) put it, "Any group of human beings will have to have some world outlook, that is, some general conceptions about the world in which they live and about themselves both as individuals and as members of society" (p. 87). In Du Bois's critical social theory, it is Africana "world outlook[s]," Africana conceptions of history, society, politics, economics, religion, and art, among other important issues, that have afforded and continue to offer continental and diasporan Africa's "contributions" to human culture and civilization. Indeed, for Du Bois (1897) Africana people have a "great message ... for humanity," and it is only through careful, critical, and concerted study of their history and culture that they (and ethically committed anti-imperialist others) will be able to discover, as well as extend and expand, not only what it means to be black in a white supremacist capitalist-colonialist world, but also, and perhaps more importantly, what it means to be human and deeply devoted to the search for social justice in the neocolonial and/or (post)modern moment (p. 10).

DU BOIS'S SOCIOLOGY OF CULTURE AND ITS IMPACT ON HIS CRITICAL EDUCATIONAL THEORY

Du Bois's sociology of education involves not only reclamation of Africana historical memory in the interest of radically re-educating critical educators and students about Africa's creation of, and contributions to, civilization, but also a struggle over the meaning of culture and cultural meanings. In order to resist the imperialist impulse, continental and diasporan Africans, along with other oppressed people, must do more than merely rediscover their long-hidden history. They are obliged to also—as Amilcar Cabral (1972, 1973, 1979) succinctly put it—critically "return to the source" of their history, which is their culture, the distinct thought- and practice-traditions that they have developed to sustain and enhance their life-worlds and lived experiences (see also Rabaka, 2009). For Du Bois, culture plays a special part in the critical consciousness-raising process (what Paulo Freire [1996, pp. 41–58] calls "conscientização"), and its degradation helps to highlight the white supremacist and Eurocentric cultural hegemonic dimension of what is currently being variously called "globalization," "global capitalism," "transnational capitalism," and/or "corporate capitalism." Capitalism and racism, as with capitalism and sexism, are inextricable and constantly influencing and exacerbating each other. They are interlocking systems of exploitation, oppression, and violence that conceal a kind of cultural racism deeply embedded in the language(s) and logic(s), mores and twisted morals, institutions, and individual imperialist expressions of the ruling race/gender/class/religion and its (neo)colonized "colored" lackeys. Concerning cultural racism and its ongoing effects on every aspect of the lives of the racially colonized, Du Bois (1973) revealingly wrote:

To kidnap a nation; to transplant it in a new land, to a new language, new climate, new economic organization, a new religion and new moral customs; to do this is a tremendous wrenching of social adjustments; and when society is wrenched and torn and revolutionized, then, whether the group be white or black, or of this race or that, the results are bound to be far reaching.

(p. 33)

Two of the many "far reaching" results of the African holocaust, African enslavement, and racial colonization have been historical amnesia and cultural dislocation. In light of the fact that the preceding section was devoted to the role history plays in Du Bois's sociology of education, I will forgo a discussion of historical amnesia here and focus instead on how Du Bois's sociology of culture informs his sociology of education. In the passage above, Du Bois observed that Africans were taken from Africa and coerced into a "new" culture and, in point of fact, their (classical or "pre-colonial") culture was "wrenched and torn and revolutionized." In the "new land"—and often in the "old land," Africa—the diasporan Africans (or "blacks," if you prefer) were "trained" only "grudgingly and suspiciously," and often without "reference to what we can be, but with sole reference to what somebody [else] wants us to be" (p. 9). Two of the "far reaching" results of this type of "training" were and continue to be cultural degradation and cultural dislocation.

Because continental and diasporan Africans' culture has been and continues to be "wrenched and torn and revolutionized," there is a decisive and dire need to break with and go beyond the borders and boundaries of the culture of the established imperialist order (i.e., the white supremacist–patriarchal–capitalist–colonialist world), and discover and recover those aspects of classical and traditional African culture which, in Wiredu's (1991) words, "may hold some lessons of moral significance for a more industrialized society" (p. 98). Looking at this issue from the perspective of Du Bois's sociology of education, we are wont to ask a question that Du Bois (1973, p. 10) asked long ago: How can we use "the accumulated wisdom of the world for the development of full human power" and to "raise the black race to its full humanity"? What bothered Du Bois was the fact that Africana contributions to "the accumulated wisdom of the world" were often either utterly left out of, or claimed by whites (i.e., both Europeans and/or European Americans) in, discussions of issues that he felt they had direct and practical bearing on. He was also perplexed by the fact that so many persons of African origin and descent knew few or "no norms" that were not "thoroughly shot through with [European imperialist] ideals," and relied so heavily on European thought-traditions, religious conceptions, and cultural values. Du Bois's (1970, vol. 2) critical comments are worth quoting at length:

> With few exceptions, we are all today "white folks' niggers." No, do not wince. I mean nothing insulting or derogatory, but this is a concrete designation which indicates that very very many colored folk: Japanese, Chinese, Indians, Negroes; and, of course, the vast majority of white folk; have been so enthused, oppressed, and suppressed by current white civilization that they think and judge everything by its terms. They have no norms that are not set in the nineteenth and twentieth centuries. They can conceive of no future world which is not dominated by present white nations and thoroughly shot through with their ideals, their method of government, their economic organization, their literature and their art; or in other words their throttling of democracy, their exploitation of labor, their industrial imperialism and their color hate. To broach before such persons any suggestion of radical change; any idea of intrusion, physical or spiritual, on the part of alien races is to bring down upon one's devoted head the most tremendous astonishment and contempt.
>
> (p. 137)

When continental and diasporan Africans "think and judge everything by [their own] terms," they share the perspective or point of view of their particular people or cultural group with the wider world; they extend and expand what it means to be both African and human; they add to "the accumulated wisdom of the world"; and they take Du Bois's (1897) weighted words to heart when he said: "[I] believe that the Negro people, as a race, have a contribution to make to civilization and humanity, which no other race can make" (p. 15). In order to contribute to "civilization and humanity," Africana and other oppressed and anti-imperialist people have to know not only *their* history, as was pointed out in the preceding section, but also *their* culture, which includes continental and diasporan traditions of critique, resistance, radical politics, and projects of multicultural, transethnic, and democratic social transformation. Without knowledge of cultural "norms" and "terms"—by which I take Du Bois to mean Africana views and values—prior to, and in defiance of, European imperial conquest and various forms of racial colonization, which continue well into the contemporary "postcolonial" period, blacks and other non-whites are racistly rendered the very "cultural foundlings" and "social wards" that the acclaimed African American philosopher Alain Locke (1968) and many members of the New Negro Movement and Harlem Renaissance perceptively prophesied, unrepentantly resented, and warily warned against (p. 247; see also Rabaka, 2011, 2012).

Africana education in its best sense should expose continental and diasporan Africans not simply to their "distinct and unique" history and culture, but also to their problems and the historical circumstances and situations that imperially produced and neo-imperially perpetuate those problems. Also—and I should like to place special emphasis on this—education should expose continental and diasporan Africans, as well as other struggling people, to ways in which they can solve their problems. As Du Bois (1946) put it: "Plans for the future of our group must be built on a base of our problems, our dreams and frustrations; they cannot stem from empty air or successfully be based on the experiences of others alone" (p. 235). This means, then, that Du Bois's sociology of education is ultimately directed at rescuing and reclaiming the denied humanity of continental and diasporan Africans and other oppressed people by critiquing and combating domination and discrimination and extending and expanding the prospects and promises of critical multicultural and radical democratic social transformation.

Education, liberation, and leadership are not the exclusive domain of the ruling race, gender, and/or class; they are vital human needs just as food, clothing, and shelter are human necessities. But, without critical education and authentic liberation thought that speaks to the specificities of continental and diasporan Africans' and other subjugated souls' life-worlds and life-struggles, ongoing hardships and unspeakable hurts, long-held utopian hopes and deep-seated radical democratic desires, then all oppressed and racially colonized people have are abstract and empty inquiries into Eurocentric notions of "justice," "freedom," "democracy," "liberation," "peace," and, perhaps most importantly, what it means to be "human." Capitalist, racial colonialist, and/or global imperialist "democracy" is a deformation of democracy that enables the ruling race, gender, and/or class to put the premium on *what* the oppressed are fighting for and *how* they should fight for what they are fighting for. Africana education must not simply expose and introduce us and tyrannized others to Africana history and culture and Africana thought-, belief-, and value-systems and traditions, but must also aid us in our efforts to engage, explore, and ethically alter the world in our own and other downtrodden and dispossessed peoples' anti-imperialist interests. What I am calling for here is nothing short of a critical multiculturalist, revolutionary humanist, and radical democratic socialist transgression and transcendence of Eurocentric-ideological-imperial education, socialization, and globalization.

AFRICANA CRITICAL PEDAGOGY: DU BOIS, SOCIOLOGY OF EDUCATION, AND CRITICAL RACE, GENDER, AND CLASS STUDIES IN EDUCATION

Du Bois serves as an ideal point of departure for contemporary sociology of education when and where he asserted that continental and diasporan Africans "have a contribution to make to civilization and humanity, which no other race can make," and insofar as he stressed the necessity and importance of Africana education beginning with and being rooted in Africa—its people and problems, its history and culture, its thought-, belief-, and value-systems and traditions—and ever expanding "toward the possession and the conquest of all knowledge." Du Bois also poses a paradigm for critical pedagogy, particularly in terms of recent efforts geared toward de-domesticating and reconstructing it to reflect constructive criticisms of its inattention to racism, sexism, radical politics, and revolutionary democratic socialist transformation. For example, critical pedagogues frequently reproach racism, but very rarely systematically analyze it and incorporate philosophy of race, sociology of race, and, especially, critical race theory into their educational theory (Chapman & Hobbel, 2010; Dixson & Rousseau, 2006; Parker et al., 1999). Such a synthesis (i.e., one of critical pedagogy *and* critical race theory) has precedent in Du Bois's sociology of education in particular, and the history of African American educational theory and praxis in general (Jennings & Lynn, 2005; Lynn, 1999, 2004; Lynn & Jennings, 2009; Oatts, 2003, 2006). What Du Bois's educational thought and Africana critical pedagogy urge conventional critical pedagogues to do is broaden their critical theoretical base by making it more multicultural and expanding the range of pedagogical (and social and political) problems to which they seek solutions.

Paulo Freire's (1985, 1989, 1993, 1996, 1998) philosophy of education has long served as the fountainhead and foundation for critical pedagogy, but the politics of postmodernism or, rather, postmodern politics have downplayed and diminished its inherent radical humanism and promotion of revolutionary democratic socialist projects. Postmodern pedagogues have pointed out that Freire's formulations often raise important issues but do not adequately provide the necessary philosophical foundation for putting forward more progressive and programmatic alternatives to the (mostly European, bourgeois, modernist, and masculinist) pedagogical perspectives he criticizes (Darder et al., 2008; Steiner et al., 2000). For instance, Freire provides few concrete (as opposed to abstract) accounts of ways in which critical educators progress from critical thought to critical practice and support radical politics and critical multicultural social movements. However, I should obstinately observe, Freire's pedagogical pronouncements are often purposely universal, and this gives them their intellectual and political potency (much like Du Bois's critical educational thought) such that they can be conscripted by progressive educators to criticize and counterpoint imperial-ideological pedagogical practices worldwide.

Indeed, many of the postmodern pedagogues may have misread Freire's philosophy of education, but perhaps part of the confusion is due to the fact that there has been a mounting debate amongst Freirean critical pedagogues concerning how to best interpret and apply his radical pedagogy and radical politics (McLaren & Lankshear, 1994). However, and this must be made clear, even before postmodernism taunted and tantalized pedagogues lost in the theoretical labyrinths of the last couple of decades, Freirean critical pedagogy failed to adequately engage race and racism, and the same should be said of its silence regarding gender and sexism (hooks, 1994, 2003, 2009; Luke, 1996; Luke & Gore, 1992). Peter McLaren (2000) mused:

> The legacy of racism left by the New World European oppressor—that Blacks and Latino/as are simply a species of inferior invertebrates—was harshly condemned but never systematically analyzed by Freire. And while Freire was a vociferous critic of racism and sexism, he did not, as Kathleen Weiler points out, sufficiently problematize his conceptualization of liberation and the oppressed in terms of his own male experience.
>
> (p. 14; see also Weiler, 1994, 2001)

Unfortunately, in all of the recent theoretical wrangling amongst Freireans, few have indexed the important deficiencies that could be developed were they to do as Freire admonished them to before the massive heart attack that claimed his life—"reinvent me," Freire said solemnly. In one of his last works he wrote, "the progressive educator must always be moving out on his or her own, continually reinventing me and reinventing what it means to be democratic in his or her own specific cultural and historical contexts" (quoted in McLaren, 2000, p. 14; see also Darder, 2002). What I am advocating here is a "reinvention" and radical reconstruction of critical pedagogy, a return to its critical theoretical roots, if you will, and also a critical theoretical branching out that will bring it into dialogue with: W.E.B. Du Bois's insurgent intersectional sociology; Gloria Ladson-Billings's culturally relevant pedagogy; Frantz Fanon's discourse on decolonization; Patricia Hill Collins's black feminist sociology; bell hooks's critical black feminist pedagogy; critical race theory; and contemporary racism-sensitive, sexism-sensitive, and heterosexism-sensitive articulations of revolutionary democratic socialism.

Almost unanimously regarded as the preeminent sociologist of race of the twentieth century, Du Bois with his anti-racist sociology of education helps to fill one of the major critical theoretical lacunae of Freire's philosophy of education and, therefore, a yawning intellectual chasm in contemporary critical pedagogy. Where Freire's work is weak when it comes to the critique of racism and sexism, Du Bois's educational discourse is particularly powerful and distinguished by its simultaneous emphasis on racial, gender, and economic justice. For instance, although many read him as an archetypal "race man," according to Joy James in *Transcending the Talented Tenth* (1997) Du Bois actually practiced "a politics remarkably progressive for his time and ours" (p. 36). James further noted: "Du Bois confronted race, class, and gender oppression while maintaining conceptual and political linkages between the struggles to end racism, sexism, and war" (pp. 36–37). Both his social scientific and critical socio-theoretical discourses were dynamic and constantly integrated diverse components of African American liberation and critical race theory, anti-colonial and decolonization theory, women's decolonization and women's liberation theory, peace and disarmament theory, and Marxist critiques of capitalism and revolutionary democratic socialist theory, among others (Rabaka, 2007, 2008, 2010a, 2010c).

Although complicated and brimming with contradictions, Du Bois indeed does make several significant contributions to the sociology of gender and intersectional sociology (see Rabaka, 2010a, pp. 175–222). These contributions could aid both contemporary sociologists of education and critical pedagogues in their efforts to either develop or deepen their respective discursive formations' understanding of the interrelation between education and racism, on the one hand, and education and sexism, on the other hand. What is more, perhaps the most remarkable aspect of Du Bois's sociological discourse is that it offers an early example of intersectional sociology that seriously considers and is self-consciously connected to educational thought (Neal, 1984; Rabaka, 2010a; Sumpter, 1973). Often in the rush to critique race, gender, and class, contemporary intersectional sociologists leave education (among other important issues, such as religion, social ecology, and state-sanctioned violence) out of the equation.

In terms of developing critical educational theory, and Africana critical pedagogy in particular, what I am most interested in here is how Du Bois maintained, as J. James (1997, pp. 36–37) put it, "conceptual and political linkages" between various anti-racist, anti-sexist, anti-colonialist, and anti-capitalist thought-traditions and socio-political movements. Unlike most of the critics in the Frankfurt School tradition of critical theory and Freirean critical pedagogues, Du Bois did not downplay racial domination and gender discrimination. On the contrary, remarkably foreshadowing Fanon's critique of racial colonization in *Black Skin, White Masks* (1967) and *The Wretched of the Earth* (1968), Du Bois's early insurgent intersectional sociology repeatedly placed the critique of sexism, colonialism, and racism right alongside Marxism and its critique of capitalism (Rabaka, 2009, 2010b; see also Fanon, 1965, 1969). In tune with the thinking of many Marxist feminists and socialist feminists, Du Bois was critical of both capitalism *and* patriarchy. He understood women, in general, to have great potential as agents of social transformation because of their simultaneous experience of, and resistance efforts against, capitalist and sexist oppression. However, similarly to contemporary black feminist sociologists—for example, Patricia Hill Collins (1998, 2000, 2005, 2006), Bonnie Thornton Dill (1979, 1983), and Deborah King (1988, 1992)—Du Bois understood women of African descent, in particular, to have even greater potential as agents of radical social change on account of their simultaneous experience of, and revolutionary praxis against, racism, sexism, and economic exploitation, whether under capitalism or colonialism. Du Bois's social scientific and critical socio-theoretical discourses, therefore, have immense import for the discussion at hand insofar as they provide contemporary sociology of education and critical pedagogy with a paradigm and point of departure for developing a critical race-centered educational theory that is simultaneously critical of racism, sexism, capitalism, and colonialism.

Although there is much more in Du Bois's educational thought that warrants our critical attention, I believe that the major issues—issues of historical and cultural grounding, intellectual insularity, pedagogical pitfalls, and the relationship between critical race theory, critical pedagogy, and radical political praxis—have been adequately addressed. Therefore, despite the conundrums of, and contradictions in, his sociology of education, I believe that Du Bois was one of the most important critical pedagogues of the twentieth century, and that his life-work harbors an unrivaled relevance and crucial significance for African American, critical multicultural, feminist, democratic socialist, and radical humanist sociologists of education attempting to grasp and grapple with the problems of the twenty-first century.

In conclusion, then, it could be said that, as Du Bois came to see historical and cultural grounding, anti-imperialist ethics, and radical resistance as the cornerstones of African American education and leadership, he grew increasingly critical of bourgeois (both conservative and liberal) African American educators and leaders and, ironically, his own antecedent thought on African American education and leadership. This was a consequence of his evolving critical consciousness and ultimate break with Eurocentric, elitist, and bourgeois conceptions of Africa and its diaspora. Hence, at the heart of Du Bois's sociology of education is an intense emphasis on continental and diasporan African history, culture, and struggle.

Consequently, as Derrick Alridge (2008) argued, Du Bois "believed that black intellectuals worldwide should take an active role in [both developing and] disseminating knowledge about Africa and African peoples" (p. 130). Du Bois's sociology of education, like critical theory in its most general sense, critiques the ideology of the established imperial order. It provides contemporary sociologists of education with a paradigm to identify both the "problems" and the "solutions" revolving around critical race studies in education.

However, as intimated throughout this chapter, Du Bois's sociology of education is inextricable from the whole of his unique brand of intersectional sociology. It is with this in mind that we end where we began, returning to Alridge's work, which accented that Du Bois "believed firmly that education was the most effective strategy for correcting misinformation about Africa and for helping people of African descent around the world unite politically to overthrow outside oppression" (p. 129). More than anything else, this chapter, faithfully following Du Bois's discourse, was researched and written to help "people of African descent around the world unite politically to overthrow [both inside and] outside oppression." Instead of attempting to reinvent the wheel each time we are confronted with racism or sexism or classism in education, I honestly believe we should turn to the wisdom-filled words and works of our intellectual ancestors. Consequently, even our most eminent educators may have to be re-educated, and the life and legacy of W.E.B. Du Bois—among other honored, albeit often-overlooked, intellectual ancestors—provides us with both a paradigm and a point of departure for educational decolonization and educational re-Africanization. In light of Du Bois's insurgent intersectional sociology of education, it could be solemnly said that what is most needed now is much more than "critical race studies in education" but, more appropriately, *critical race, gender, and class studies in education.*

REFERENCES

Alridge, Derrick P. (2008). *The educational thought of W.E.B. Du Bois: An intellectual history.* New York: Teachers College Press.

Anderson, Elijah, & Massey, Douglas S. (Eds.). (2001). *The problem of the century: Racial stratification in the United States.* New York: Russell Sage Foundation.

Anderson, Elijah, & Zuberi, Tukufu. (Eds.). (2000). *The study of African American problems: W.E.B. Du Bois's agenda, then and now.* Thousand Oaks, CA: Sage.

Cabral, Amilcar. (1972). *Revolution in Guinea: Selected texts.* New York: Monthly Review Press.

Cabral, Amilcar (1973). *Return to the source: Selected speeches of Amilcar Cabral.* New York: Monthly Review Press.

Cabral, Amilcar (1979). *Unity and struggle: Speeches and writings of Amilcar Cabral.* New York: Monthly Review Press.

Chapman, Thandeka K., & Hobbel, Nikola (Eds.). (2010). *Social justice pedagogy across the curriculum: The practice of freedom.* New York: Routledge.

Collins, Patricia Hill. (1998). *Fighting words: Black women and the search for social justice.* Minneapolis: University of Minnesota Press.

Collins, Patricia Hill. (2000). *Black feminist thought: Knowledge, consciousness, and the politics of empowerment* (2nd ed.). New York: Routledge.

Collins, Patricia Hill. (2005). *Black sexual politics: African Americans, gender, and the new racism.* New York: Routledge.

Collins, Patricia Hill. (2006). *From black power to hip hop: Racism, nationalism, and feminism.* Philadelphia, PA: Temple University Press.

Cox, Oliver C. (1948). *Caste, class, and race: A study in social dynamics.* New York: Monthly Review Press.

Cox, Oliver C. (1976). *Race relations: Elements of social dynamics.* Detroit, MI: Wayne State University Press.

Cox, Oliver C. (1987). *Race, class, and the world system* (Herbert M. Hunter and Sameer Y. Abraham, Eds.). New York: Monthly Review Press.

Crenshaw, Kimberlé, Gotanda, Neil, Peller, Gary, & Thomas, Kendall (Eds.). (1995). *Critical race theory: The key writings that formed the movement.* New York: New Press.

Darder, Antonia. (2002). *Reinventing Paulo Freire: A pedagogy of love.* Boulder, CO: Westview.

Darder, Antonia, Baltodano, Marta, & Torres, Rodolfo D. (Eds.). (2008). *The critical pedagogy reader* (2nd ed.). New York: Routledge/Falmer.

Delgado, Richard (Ed.). (1995). *Critical race theory: The cutting edge.* Philadelphia, PA: Temple University Press.

Delgado, Richard, & Stefancic, Jean. (2001). *Critical race theory: An introduction.* New York: New York University Press.

Dill, Bonnie Thornton. (1979). The dialectics of black womanhood: Towards a new model of American femininity. *Signs: A Journal of Women and Culture in Society, 4*(3), 543–555.

Dill, Bonnie Thornton (1983). Race, class, and gender: Prospects for an all-inclusive sisterhood. *Feminist Studies*, 9(1), 131–150.

Dixson, Adrienne D., & Rousseau, Celia K. (Eds.). (2006). *Critical race theory in education: All God's children got a song*. New York: Routledge.

Du Bois, W.E.B. (1897). The conservation of races. *American Negro Academy Occasional Papers, 2*, 1–15.

Du Bois, W.E.B. (1898a). The negroes of Farmville, Virginia: A social study. *Bulletin of the Department of Labor*, 3(14), 1–38.

Du Bois, W.E.B. (1898b). The study of the negro problems. *Annals of the American Academy of Political and Social Science, 11*, 1–23.

Du Bois, W.E.B. (1899). *The Philadelphia negro: A social study*. Philadelphia, PA: University of Pennsylvania Press.

Du Bois, W.E.B. (Ed.). (1900a). *The college-bred negro*. Atlanta, GA: Atlanta University Press.

Du Bois, W.E.B. (1900b). *Memorial to the legislature of Georgia on negro common schools*. Atlanta, GA: Atlanta University Press.

Du Bois, W.E.B. (1901a). The burden of negro schooling. *Independent, 53*, July, 1667–1668.

Du Bois, W.E.B. (Ed.). (1901b). *The common school*. Atlanta, GA: Atlanta University Press.

Du Bois, W.E.B. (1901c). The Freedmen's Bureau. *Atlantic Monthly, 57*, March, 354–365.

Du Bois, W.E.B. (1902). The higher education of the negro. *Talladega College Record, 10*, November, 2–3.

Du Bois, W.E.B. (1903a). *The souls of black folk: Essays and sketches*. Chicago: A.C. McClurg.

Du Bois, W.E.B. (1903b). The talented tenth. In Booker T. Washington (Ed.), *The negro problem: A series of articles by representative American negroes of today* (pp. 33–75). New York: James Pott & Co.

Du Bois, W.E.B. (1904). What intellectual training is doing for the negro. *Missionary Review of the World, 17*, August, 578–582.

Du Bois, W.E.B. (1905). Atlanta University. In R.C. Ogden (Ed.), *From servitude to service* (pp. 155–197). Boston, MA: American Unitarian Association Press.

Du Bois, W.E.B. (1906). The Hampton idea. *Voice of the Negro, 3*, September, 332–336.

Du Bois, W.E.B. (1908). Race friction between black and white. *American Journal of Sociology, 13*, May, 835–836.

Du Bois, W.E.B. (Ed.). (1910a). *The college-bred negro American*. Atlanta, GA: Atlanta University Press.

Du Bois, W.E.B. (1910b). *College-bred negro communities*. Atlanta, GA: Atlanta University Press.

Du Bois, W.E.B. (1910c). The souls of white folk. *Independent*, August 18.

Du Bois, W.E.B. (Ed.). (1911). *The common school and the negro American*. Atlanta, GA: Atlanta University Press.

Du Bois, W.E.B. (1913). The people of peoples and their gifts to men. *Crisis, 6*, November, 339–341.

Du Bois, W.E.B. (1917). Of the culture of white folk. *Journal of Race Development*, April.

Du Bois, W.E.B. (1918). Negro education. *Crisis, 15*, February, 173–178.

Du Bois, W.E.B. (1920a). *Darkwater: Voices from within the veil*. New York: Harcourt, Brace & Howe.

Du Bois, W.E.B. (1920b). White co-workers. *Crisis, 20*, 6–8.

Du Bois, W.E.B. (1923). The superior race. *Smart Set, 70*, April.

Du Bois, W.E.B. (1924). *The gift of black folk: The negroes in the making of America*. Boston, MA: Stratford.

Du Bois, W.E.B. (1925). The black man brings his gifts. *Survey Graphic, 6*(6), 655–657, 710.

Du Bois, W.E.B. (1926). Education in Africa. *Crisis, 33*, June, 86–89.

Du Bois, W.E.B. (1931). Education and work. *Howard University Bulletin, 9*, January, 1–22.

Du Bois, W.E.B. (1933). *The field and function of a negro college*. Nashville, TN: Fisk University Press.

Du Bois, W.E.B. (1935). Does the negro need separate schools? *Journal of Negro Education, 4*, July, 328–335.

Du Bois, W.E.B. (1936). Social planning for the negro, past and present. *Journal of Negro Education, 5*(1), 110–125.

Du Bois, W.E.B. (1939). *Black folk then and now: An essay in the history and sociology of the negro race*. New York: Henry Holt.

Du Bois, W.E.B. (1941). A program for land-grant colleges. In *The Proceedings of the Nineteenth Annual Conference of the Presidents of Negro Land Grant Colleges* (pp. 42–56). Washington, DC: Howard University Press.

Du Bois, W.E.B. (1945). *Color and democracy: Colonies and peace*. New York: Harcourt Brace.

Du Bois, W.E.B. (1946). The future and function of the negro private college. *Crisis, 53*, 234–246, 253–254.

Du Bois, W.E.B. (1949a). The freedom to learn. *Midwest Journal, 2*, 9–11.

Du Bois, W.E.B. (1949b). The white folk have a right to be ashamed. *National Guardian*, February 7.

Du Bois, W.E.B. (1965). *The world and Africa: An inquiry into the part which Africa has played in world history*. New York: International Publishers.

Du Bois, W.E.B. (1968a). Dusk of dawn: An essay toward an autobiography of a race concept. New York: Schocken.

Du Bois, W.E.B. (1968b). The white world. In *Dusk of dawn: An essay toward an autobiography of a race concept* (pp. 134–172). New York: Schocken.

Du Bois, W.E.B. (Ed.). (1969a). *Atlanta University publications, 1896–1916*, Nos. 1–20 (2 vols.). New York: Arno Press.

Du Bois, W.E.B. (Ed.). (1969b). *Atlanta University publications*, Nos. 12–15. New York: Russell & Russell.

Du Bois, W.E.B. (1970). *W.E.B. Du Bois speaks: Speeches and addresses, 1899–1963* (2 vols., Philip S. Foner, Ed.). New York: Pathfinder Press.

Du Bois, W.E.B. (1973). *The education of black people: Ten critiques, 1906–1960* (Herbert Aptheker, Ed.). New York: Monthly Review Press.

Du Bois, W.E.B. (1982). *Writings in periodicals edited by others* (vol. 3, Herbert Aptheker, Ed.). Millwood, NY: Kraus-Thomson.

Du Bois, W.E.B. (1989). Careers open to college-bred negroes. In W.E.B. Du Bois and H.H. Proctor, *Two addresses delivered by alumni of Fisk University, in connection with the anniversary exercise of their alma mater* (pp. 1–14). Nashville, TN: Fisk University Press.

Du Bois, W.E.B. (1995a). *Black reconstruction in America, 1860–1880*. New York: Touchstone.

Du Bois, W.E.B. (1995b). The white proletariat in Alabama, Georgia, and Florida. In *Black reconstruction in America, 1860–1880* (pp. 487–525). New York: Touchstone.

Du Bois, W.E.B. (1995c). The white worker. In *Black reconstruction in America, 1860–1880* (pp. 17–31). New York: Touchstone.

Du Bois, W.E.B. (1996). *The Oxford W.E.B. Du Bois reader* (Eric Sundquist, Ed.). New York: Oxford University Press.

Du Bois, W.E.B. (2002). *Du Bois on education* (Eugene F. Provenzo, Jr., Ed.). Walnut Creek, CA: Altamira.

Essed, Philomena, & Goldberg, David Theo (Eds.). (2001). *Race critical theories: Texts and contexts*. Malden, MA: Blackwell.

Eze, Emmanuel Chukwudi. (Ed.). (1997). *Postcolonial African philosophy: A critical reader*. Malden, MA: Blackwell.

Fanon, Frantz. (1965). *A dying colonialism*. New York: Grove.

Fanon, Frantz. (1967). *Black skin, white masks*. New York: Grove.

Fanon, Frantz. (1968). *The wretched of the earth*. New York: Grove.

Fanon, Frantz. (1969). *Toward the African revolution*. New York: Grove.

Frantz, Nevin R., Jr. (1997). The contributions of Booker T. Washington and W.E.B. Du Bois in the development of vocational education. *Journal of Industrial Teacher Education*, 34(4), 87–91.

Freedman, Martin Neil. (1975). The rhetorical adaptation of social movement leaders: Booker T. Washington and W.E.B. Du Bois. Ph.D. dissertation, Purdue University, Lafayette, IN.

Freire, Paulo. (1985). *The politics of education: Culture, power, and liberation*. South Hadley, MA: Bergin & Garvey.

Freire, Paulo. (1989). *Learning to question: A pedagogy of liberation*. New York: Continuum.

Freire, Paulo. (1993). *Pedagogy of the oppressed*. New York: Continuum.

Freire, Paulo. (1996). *Education for critical consciousness*. New York: Continuum.

Freire, Paulo. (1998). *The Paulo Freire reader* (Ana Maria Araujo Freire & Donaldo Macedo, Eds.). New York: Continuum.

Gillman, Susan, & Weinbaum, Alys E. (Eds.). (2007). *Next to the color-line: Gender, sexuality, and W.E.B. Du Bois*. Minneapolis: University of Minnesota Press.

Glascoe, Myrtle G. (1996). W.E.B. Du Bois: His evolving theory of education. *Research in Race and Ethnic Relations*, 9, 171–188.

Goldberg, David Theo, & Solomos, John (Eds.). (2002). *A companion to racial and ethnic studies*. Malden, MA: Blackwell.

Gordon, Lewis R. (2000). What does it mean to be a problem? W.E.B. Du Bois on the study of black folk. In Lewis R. Gordon, *Existentia Africana: Understanding Africana existential thought* (pp. 62–95). New York: Routledge.

Greco, Rose Dorothy. (1984). The educational views of Booker T. Washington and W.E.B. Du Bois: A critical comparison. Ph.D. dissertation, Loyola University of Chicago.

Harris, Thomas E. (1993). *Analysis of the clash over the issues between Booker T. Washington and W.E.B. Du Bois*. New York: Garland.

hooks, bell. (1994). *Teaching to transgress: Education as the practice of freedom*. New York: Routledge.

hooks, bell. (2003). *Teaching community: A pedagogy of hope*. New York: Routledge.

hooks, bell. (2009). *Teaching critical thinking: Practical wisdom*. New York: Routledge.

Horne, Gerald. (2009). *W.E.B. Du Bois: A biography*. Westport, CT: Greenwood Press.

Hwang, Hae-Sung. (1988). Booker T. Washington and W.E.B. Du Bois: A study in race leadership, 1895–1915. Ph.D. dissertation, University of Hawaii.

James, C.L.R. (1994). *C.L.R. James and revolutionary Marxism: Selected writings of C.L.R. James, 1939–1949* (Scott McLemee and Paul Le Blanc, Eds.). Atlantic Highlands, NJ: Humanities Press.

James, C.L.R. (1996). *C.L.R. James on the "negro question"* (Scott McLemee, Ed.). Jackson: University of Mississippi Press.

James, C.L.R. (1999). *Marxism for our times: C.L.R. James on revolutionary organization* (Martin Glaberman, Ed.). Jackson: University of Mississippi Press.

James, Joy A. (1997). *Transcending the talented tenth: Black leaders and American intellectuals*. New York: Routledge.

Jennings, Michael E., & Lynn, Marvin. (2005). The house that race built: Critical pedagogy, African American education, and the re-conceptualization of a critical race pedagogy. *Journal of Educational Foundations, 19*(3–4), 15–32.

Johnson, Adolph, Jr. (1976). A history and interpretation of the William Edward Burghardt Du Bois–Booker Taliaferro Washington higher education controversy. Ph.D. dissertation, University of Southern California, Los Angeles.

King, Deborah K. (1988). Multiple jeopardy, multiple consciousness: The context of a black feminist ideology. *Signs, 14*(1), 42–72.

King, Deborah K. (1992). Missing the beat, unraveling the threads: Class and gender in Afro-American social issues. *Black Scholar, 22*(3), 36–44.

Lewis, David Levering. (1993). *W.E.B. Du Bois: Biography of a race, 1868–1919*. New York: Henry Holt.

Lewis, David Levering. (2000). *W.E.B. Du Bois: The fight for equality and the American century, 1919–1963*. New York: Henry Holt.

Locke, Alain L. (Ed.). (1968). *The new negro*. New York: Atheneum.

Luke, Carmen. (Ed.). (1996). *Feminisms and pedagogies of everyday life*. Albany: State University of New York Press.

Luke, Carmen, & Gore, Jennifer (Eds.). (1992). *Feminisms and critical pedagogy*. New York: Routledge.

Lynn, Marvin. (1999). Toward a critical race pedagogy: A research note. *Urban Education, 33*(5), 606–627.

Lynn, Marvin. (2004). Inserting the race into critical pedagogy: An analysis of race-based epistemologies. *Journal of Educational Philosophy and Theory, 37*(2), 153–165.

Lynn, Marvin, & Jennings, Michael E. (2009). Power, politics and critical race pedagogy: A critical race analysis of black male teachers' pedagogy. *Race, Ethnicity and Education, 12*(2), 173–196.

Marable, Manning. (1986). *W.E.B. Du Bois: Black radical democrat*. Boston, MA: Twayne.

McLaren, Peter. (2000). Paulo Freire's pedagogy of possibility. In Peter McLaren, Robert Bahruth, Stan Steiner, & Mark Krank (Eds.), *Freirean pedagogy, praxis, and possibilities: Projects for the new millennium* (pp. 1–22). New York: Falmer Press.

McLaren, Peter, & Lankshear, Colin (Eds.). (1994). *Politics of liberation: Paths from Freire*. New York: Routledge.

Mielke, David Nathaniel. (1977). W.E.B. Du Bois: An educational critique. Ph.D. dissertation, University of Tennessee, Knoxville.

Moore, Jacqueline M. (2003). *Booker T. Washington, W.E.B. Du Bois, and the struggle for racial uplift*. Wilmington, DE: Scholarly Resources.

Neal, Terry Ray. (1984). W.E.B. Du Bois's contributions to the sociology of education. Ph.D. dissertation, University of Cincinnati.

Nwankwo, Henry C. (1989). The educational philosophy of W.E.B. Du Bois: A Nigerian interpretation. Ph.D. dissertation, East Texas State University.

Oatts, Terry O'Neal. (2003). W.E.B. Du Bois and critical race theory: Toward a Du Boisian philosophy of education. Ed.D. dissertation, Georgia Southern University.

Oatts, Terry O'Neal. (2006). *W.E.B. Du Bois and critical race theory: Toward a Du Boisian philosophy of education*. Sydney: Exceptional Publications.

Okoro, Martin Umachi. (1982). W.E.B. Du Bois's ideas on education: Implications for Nigerian education. Ph.D. dissertation, Loyola University of Chicago.

Olaniyan, Tejumola. (2000). Africa: Varied colonial legacies. In Henry Schwarz & Sangeeta Ray (Eds.), *A companion to postcolonial studies* (pp. 269–281). Malden, MA: Blackwell.

Quayson, Ato. (2000a). *Postcolonialism: Theory, practice or process?* Malden, MA: Polity.

Quayson, Ato (2000b). Postcolonialism and postmodernism. In Henry Schwarz & Sangeeta Ray (Eds.), *A companion to postcolonial studies* (pp. 87–111). Malden, MA: Blackwell.

Parker, Laurence, Deyhle, Donna, & Villenas, Sofia (Eds.). (1999). *Race is … Race isn't: Critical race theory and qualitative studies in education*. Boulder, CO: Westview.

Rabaka, Reiland. (2007). *W.E.B. Du Bois and the problems of the twenty-first century: An essay on Africana critical theory*. Lanham, MD: Lexington Books.

Rabaka, Reiland. (2008). *Du Bois's dialectics: Black radical politics and the reconstruction of critical social theory.* Lanham, MD: Lexington Books.

Rabaka, Reiland. (2009). *Africana critical theory: Reconstructing the black radical tradition, from W.E.B. Du Bois and C.L.R. James to Frantz Fanon and Amilcar Cabral.* Lanham, MD: Lexington Books.

Rabaka, Reiland. (2010a). *Against epistemic apartheid: W.E.B. Du Bois and the disciplinary decadence of sociology.* Lanham, MD: Lexington Books.

Rabaka, Reiland. (2010b). *Forms of Fanonism: Frantz Fanon's critical theory and the dialectics of decolonization.* Lanham, MD: Lexington Books.

Rabaka, Reiland (Ed.). (2010c). *W.E.B. Du Bois: A critical reader.* Farnham, Surrey, UK: Ashgate.

Rabaka, Reiland. (2011). *Hip hop's inheritance: From the Harlem Renaissance to the hip hop feminist movement.* Lanham, MD: Lexington Books.

Rabaka, Reiland. (2012). *Hip hop's amnesia: From blues and the black women's club movement to rap and the hip hop movement.* Lanham, MD: Lexington Books.

Smith, Eddie Calvin. (1975). Educational themes in the published work of W.E.B. Du Bois, 1883–1960: Implications for African American educators. Ph.D. dissertation, University of Wisconsin-Milwaukee.

Steiner, Stanley F., Krank, H. Mark, McLaren, Peter, & Bahruth, Robert (Eds.). (2000). *Freirean pedagogy, praxis and possibilities: Projects for the new millennium.* New York: Falmer Press.

Sumpter, Richard David. (1973). A critical study of the educational thought of W.E.B. Du Bois. Ph.D. dissertation, Peabody College for Teachers of Vanderbilt University.

Warren, Nagueyalti. (1984). The contributions of W.E.B. Du Bois to Afro-American studies in higher education. Ph.D. dissertation, University of Mississippi.

Warren, Nagueyalti. (2010). *An intellectual biography of W.E.B. Du Bois: Initiator of black studies in the university.* Lewiston, NY: Edwin Mellen Press.

Warren, Nagueyalti. (2011). *W.E.B. Du Bois: Grandfather of black studies.* Trenton, NJ: Africa World Press.

Weiler, Kathleen. (1994). Freire and feminist pedagogy of difference. In Peter McLaren & Colin Lankshear (Eds.), *Politics of liberation: Paths from Freire* (pp. 12–40). New York: Routledge.

Weiler, Kathleen (Ed.). (2001). *Feminist engagements: Reading, resisting, and revisioning male theorists in education and cultural studies.* New York: Routledge.

Wiredu, Kwasi. (1991). On defining African philosophy. In Tsenay Serequeberhan (Ed.), *African philosophy: The essential readings* (pp. 87–110). New York: Paragon House.

Wortham, John M. (1997). The economic ideologies of Booker T. Washington and W.E.B. Du Bois: 1895–1915. Ph.D. dissertation, Boston University.

6

TRIBAL CRITICAL RACE THEORY
An Origin Story and Future Directions
Bryan McKinley Jones Brayboy

THE AWAKENINGS

In the mid-1960s my father enlisted in the U.S. Army, where he served honorably for three years. After completing his term of service he attended and graduated from college, enrolling in an officer training school afterward. It was at this time that he began his career as a military professional, serving in the capacity of commissioned officer. He would serve 33 years as a hospital administrator for the United States Navy.

As a child, I distinctly remember watching in the evenings as he carefully laid out his uniform for the following day. He would whistle (badly, I might add) as he went about the task of laying out his tunic or uniform shirt on the bed, pulling out a ruler, measuring, and meticulously pinning his medal ribbons in the appropriate places. I was ten years old when my father came home one Friday—still wearing his "whites." His uniform was a significant departure from the "tans" he wore regularly, indicating he had attended a significant function that day. He walked into the kitchen, greeted my mother with a kiss, removed his tunic—taking time to place it carefully on a hanger—and opened a can of Black Label beer. He proceeded down to the den, where our family's eight-track player was located, and before we knew it Floyd Westerman's rich baritone voice began to emanate through the speakers. Accompanied by his guitar, Westerman warbled the (hi)story of Indigenous peoples in the U.S. in the style of the country and western music my father loves. Echoing throughout the house we could hear "Custer Died for Your Sins!"

The song, indeed the album, is overtly political, pro-Indian, and unapologetically confrontational regarding the relationship between the U.S. government and tribal nations and peoples:

> All the lies that were spoken
> All the blood we have spilled
> All the treaties that were broken
> All the leaders you have still

Custer died for your sins!
Custer died for your sins!
Oh, a new day must begin
Custer died for your sins

It wasn't until I was in my twenties that I came to understand the complexity of what I had witnessed that day. My father, with shorn hair and U.S. naval uniform pants and polished shoes, joined the much longer-haired Lakota-born political activist, whose clothing proudly reflected his Indigenous heritage, in reminding politicians and Anglo listeners of the importance and consequence of U.S. history on Indigenous peoples. Together they proclaimed:

For the truth that you pollute
For the life that you have tossed
For the good you prostitute
And for all that we have lost

Custer died for your sins!

Their call for "a new day" was an anthem of resistance in which Indigenous peoples spoke back to mistreatment suffered at the hands of the U.S. government—which also happened to be my father's employer. Although some might see my father's actions as contradictory, I see them as a mechanism of relief for a person who gave his life to the U.S. government.[1] His actions reflected how he made sense of the inherent contradictions in his work and his day-to-day existence as an Indigenous man. My father's active engagement with the music of an artist singing about resistance while working for the U.S. government became a personal moment of awakening; it highlighted his liminal space as both a military and a tribal man. In many ways, this memory became one of the origin stories for what would later become tribal critical race theory (TribalCrit). In this chapter I re-visit the narrative and intellectual origins of the theory and offer my present-day thinking, as it has evolved from the theory's initial published iteration. Owing to space limitations, however, I can only skim the surface of these evolutions, but will further elaborate them in a book-length manuscript in the near future.

THE EARLY INTELLECTUAL INFLUENCES

While the framework of TribalCrit has been attributed to the piece I authored in 2005, facets of the theory predate that time. The theory is constructed from ideas rooted in my own experiences as well as the experiences and writings of other Indigenous peoples. Perhaps the earliest published influence comes from the work of Seneca intellectual Arthur C. Parker. In 1916 Parker presented a list of grievances or "charges" against the U.S. as a result of the spiritual, physical, and intellectual dislocation experienced by Indigenous peoples at the hands of forcibly imposed Western colonial notions of jurisprudence and religious civilizing missions. "We wish to lay down seven charges, out of perhaps many more that the Indian makes at the bar of American justice" (p. 254). He continued: "Whether the white man believes them or not, true or not, he cannot discharge his obligation to the red man until he considers them and understands that the Indian makes them because he at least feels that they are just" (p. 254). These seven charges included the right of Indigenous peoples to their own identity as Indigenous peoples, economic freedom, land, and a vibrant intellectual life based on Indigenous worldviews. Parker's work suggests that, if these charges are not resolved in meaningful and culturally appropriate ways, the resulting disruption creates a fissure, or liminal space, wherein Indigenous peoples (will) remain in the struggle of being in between. Foreshadowing some of Westerman's work, Parker explains the physical and cognitive dissonance that arises from forcefully imposed political, legal, and social liminality and exclusionary practices levied against Indigenous societies in their own home(land)s. He writes, "There can be nothing but bewilderment and anarchy when a man knows not what his status in his country is. This is especially true when the individual has property interests and matters at hazard in the courts—handled at the initiative of others" (1916, p. 264). Parker's work appears to respond to a series of Congressional debates that took place around 1866. James Anderson's (2007) cogent analysis of the 14th amendment and its colorblind application frames this debate well. Additionally, the debates include dialogue between Representatives James Brooks and Thaddeus Stevens as they debated whether Indigenous peoples had the "right" to receive benefits and protections under the Constitution, like citizens.

> "Why exclude the Indian? Is he not a man and a brother?" asked Brooks. "The Constitution of the United States has always excluded them," replied Stevens (*CG 39th*, p. 376). Not satisfied with the answer, Brooks countered, "Why not, as we amend the Constitution, embrace the Indian as a man and a brother?" Stevens responded, "Because they are a tribal race, have their separate governments, and, as a general rule, are not citizens."[2]
>
> (Anderson, 2007, p. 252)

At the core of this debate is one of the basic notions that frames TribalCrit, that of the liminality of the American Indian.[3] In this instance, lack of citizenship and "tribal race" became factors that framed American Indians as separate and excluded from conversations of belonging and at the mercy of others' decision-making. The resulting decisions come to dictate every aspect of our lives, including how we can/must live, eat, worship, and teach and educate our children, including the language we use to communicate with one another.

The question of how to frame American Indians' place in society and, more specifically, in schools led me to undertake an examination of how critical race theory might relate to Indigenous peoples. The theory's focus on the ubiquity of racism makes it ideal for examining the experiences of Indigenous peoples in educational institutions, although at the time of my writing CRT had not quite evolved to the point of fully addressing the unique status of Indigenous peoples. TribalCrit was intended to build on and extend CRT in order to more directly account for the history and role of U.S. colonization on the modern-day experiences of Indigenous peoples.

As a Lumbee person, whenever I meet another Lumbee person that I may not know, two questions (or variations) are invariably asked: Who are your people? (or a variation would be: Who are your kin?) and Where do you stay at? These questions are rooted in notions of relationality and allow Lumbee peoples to make sense of how, if at all, we are related to one another (whether through blood, kinship, family homeplace, or some other way). In this same way, it is important for me to note here that, in response to the question Who are your kin?, TribalCrit would immediately recognize its relation to critical race theory.

In 1999, as a new assistant professor, I was exposed to CRT and then introduced to its application to the field of education. Its organic nature—that is, CRT emerged from scholars of color and was often rooted in community knowledges and the experiences of people and communities of color—offered me a new set of possibilities to think about, express, and analyze my own experiences and those of the communities of color with whom I worked. In many ways, my own training as an educational anthropologist prepared me for certain conversations; I was literate in very particular ways within the academy. That is, I could discuss Bourdieu, Foucault, Giddens, Marx, Durkheim, Weber, and other (post-)structural and (post)modern scholars, their theoretical frames, and contributions to "the field," and integrate their ideas into my scholarship. These conversations and theories, while intellectually satisfying, did not really provide me with the kinds of necessary tools to dig into, explore, and explain what I was seeing in the communities and peoples with whom I was working. In short, it was like dressing in a generic hospital gown, when what I needed was something comfortable, useful, compelling, and inspiring.

My experiences as a racialized and tribal person, however, were either ignored or romanticized/fetishized by those around me in graduate school. Being exposed to the work of Bell, Delgado, Matsuda, Crenshaw, Olivas, Lawrence, and others opened up new possibilities for me. Later, when I read the work of Ladson-Billings, Tate, Parker, Solorzano, Yosso, Dixson, Lynn, and others using CRT to analyze racial and methodological disparities in the field of education, it opened up a whole new world of possibilities for me. They demonstrated ways that I could explain what was happening with racialized peoples in educational institutions. Ultimately, CRT, and more specifically CRT scholars in the field of education, provided a framework that felt like my favorite pair of jeans, T-shirt, and shoes—it fit beautifully and felt comfortable and natural, as if it had been made specifically for me.

A THEORY OR SOMETHING ELSE?

Shortly after accepting my first faculty job, as part of a foundation-funded series of conversations connecting social science disciplines and the field of education, I was invited to participate in a small cohort of "up and coming" scholars. Part of the appeal for the gathering was that "junior" scholars were joined in these conversations by a small group of well-established "senior" scholars. One day, after a long day of discussing what some might call "high theorists" (e.g. Bourdieu, Foucault, Giddens), I joined the junior scholars for a meal. A few hours later we found ourselves in a noisy, smoky pub, where we ran into a group of the senior scholars. I sat next to one of these scholars who had clearly been in the pub for quite some time, judging from the glaze covering her eyes and slurred speech. At one point, she leaned over to me as if to impart some bit of worldly knowledge and said, "Bryan, you'll never be a great theorist but you tell really good stories!" Stunned and unwilling to believe she had just engaged in what felt like an unprovoked attack, I asked her to repeat herself. As it turns out, I had, in fact, heard her correctly the first time.

After the weekend, I did what any strong, twentieth-century, Indigenous man would do: I went home to speak with the wisest person I know—my mother. After listening carefully to my story and pausing to reflect on what I had just shared, she looked at me thoughtfully and frowned. "Baby, doesn't she know that our stories are our theories? And she thinks she's smarter than you because she can't tell stories ..." In one swift move, she had put into words what I had suspected all along: for Indigenous people(s), narratives and stories are an important form of theorizing and imparting important ancestral knowledge. What the professor at the bar failed to realize is that, when we share stories, we create and share theory. Her comment helped me understand what the "new day" that Westerman calls for must include. It must begin with re-centering the work and philosophies of Indigenous peoples, with the voices and stories of Indigenous peoples.

TribalCrit begins by recognizing the unique, liminal position of American Indian tribal peoples in education and in their relationship to the U.S. government. The theory offers new ways to examine the concepts of theory, culture, knowledge, and power from the perspective of American Indian people and their communities. Ultimately, it seeks to build upon the strong foundation provided by CRT by specifically addressing the multiple, nuanced, and historically located experiences of tribal peoples today. The basic tenets of the theory can be summarized as follows:

1 Colonization is endemic to U.S. society.
2 U.S. policies toward Indigenous peoples are rooted in imperialism, colonization, white supremacy, and a desire for material gain.
3 Indigenous peoples occupy a liminal space that accounts for both the political and the racialized nature of our identities.
4 Indigenous peoples have a desire to obtain and forge tribal sovereignty, tribal autonomy, self-determination, and self-identification.
5 The concepts of culture, knowledge, and power take on new meaning when examined through an Indigenous lens.
6 Governmental policies and educational policies toward Indigenous peoples closely follow each other toward a problematic goal of assimilation.
7 Tribal philosophies, beliefs, customs, traditions, and visions for the future are central to understanding the lived realities of Indigenous peoples; they also illustrate the differences and adaptability among individuals and groups.
8 Stories are not separate from theory; they make up theory and are, therefore, real and legitimate sources of data and ways of being.
9 Theory and practice are connected in deep and explicit ways such that scholars must work towards social change.

THE TENETS UNPACKED

TribalCrit begins with the recognition that colonization is endemic to society. By *colonization*, I am referring to the idea that European American thought, knowledge, economic structures, and power structures dominate and frame present-day society in the United States. The focus on Eurocentric ideology has been used to establish hierarchies wherein the philosophies, worldviews, and languages of Indigenous people(s) have been stripped of value and relegated to the periphery as archaic or irrelevant. "Eurocentric thinkers dismissed Indigenous knowledge in the same way they dismissed any socio-political cultural life they did not understand: they found it to be unsystematic and incapable of meeting the productivity needs of the modern world" (Battiste, 2002, p. 5). Although one of CRT's primary tenets includes the belief that racism is endemic to society, TribalCrit rests on the notion that colonization is also endemic. For Indigenous peoples, this notion became fully articulated by the legislatures of the 1860s (Anderson, 2007) and the early 1900s (Parker, 1916).[4] As a result of colonizing effects experienced under U.S. occupation, Indigenous peoples have been plagued by not knowing our place in the modern world or by having that place defined at the "initiative of others" (Parker, 1916, p. 264). By naming colonization as a persistent problem, TribalCrit seeks to begin moving toward constructing measures to directly confront and dampen the effects of colonization. The recognition of colonization as endemic to society is at the heart of TribalCrit; all other tenets are offshoots of this vital concept.

Second, TribalCrit recognizes that the policies of the United States toward American Indians are rooted in imperialism, colonization, white supremacy, and a desire for material gain. Lumbee[5] law professor Robert A. Williams (1987, 1989) has methodically examined the early policies set forth by the U.S. and its treatment of American Indians. According to Williams, historical policies such as Manifest Destiny and the Norman Yoke were rooted in a self-interested reading of legal concepts that encouraged white settlers to rationalize and legitimate their decision to steal lands from the Indigenous peoples already inhabiting them. According to Manifest Destiny, it was God's destiny for the new settlers to have the land; this concept armed European-Americans with the belief they had the moral authority to expand the U.S. by taking over lands throughout the North American continent through whatever means necessary. The Norman Yoke, originally established by Adam Smith as an economic term, was also employed to justify taking lands and property from Indigenous people. Loosely defined, the concept argues that individuals not only have a *right* to utilize and exploit natural resources on lands that are considered "vacant," but they have a *moral obligation* to do so. Both concepts are rooted in heteropatriarchal notions of white supremacy. *White supremacy* refers to the idea that the established European or Western way of doing things has both moral and intellectual superiority over non-Western ways (e.g. see Mills, 1999 for a historical analysis of this concept).[6]

I have already begun to address the third tenet of TribalCrit: that Indigenous peoples occupy a liminal space that accounts for both the political and the racialized conceptualization of our identities. Currently, the different circulating discourses around what it means to be Indian, as well as what constitutes American Indian education, establish a context in which American Indians must struggle for the right to be defined as both a legal/political and a racial group. It is this place of liminality that accounts for the political nature of Indigenous peoples' relationship with the U.S. government and with our embodiment as racialized beings. There are three planes at work that both complement and oppose one another. The first is the legal status that Indigenous peoples have rooted in the Constitution.[7] The second is the social/racial terrain that Indigenous peoples occupy. The third plane is the potentially fatal intersection between the first two. It is in this space where tribal nations, not recognized by the federal government,[8] are potentially framed by law- and policy-makers as well as other tribal nations as somehow "not real" in spite of the long history of relations with other tribal nations and the federal government (see Lowery, 2009 for an interesting and insightful analysis of how this third plane is actualized).

An additional complication with the third intersecting plane is that legal/political status depends upon the Constitution, Supreme Court rulings from the early nineteenth century, and legal statutes and treaties from the sixteenth and seventeenth centuries which locate Indigenous peoples in the past (yet our status as racialized peoples make us distinctly modern). That is, our political/legal standing is located in "old pieces of paper," while our status as members of a racialized group of people is rooted in twentieth- and twenty-first-century policies and legislative acts. The conflict between the old and the new is easily viewed when thinking about gaming communities. Combine our modern identity with the advent of casinos and a cognitive dissonance is formed such that many individuals struggle in making sense of how a racialized group can have the "unfair benefits" of no taxation and casino revenue. TribalCrit recognizes the liminality of our position, legally *and* socially, but never as one expression at the exclusion of another. I want to be clear here in stating I understand there are dangers in presenting what might be considered a position of "exceptionality" by separating American Indians from other racialized groups. Nationhood (and the statuses associated with it), sovereignty, and self-determination (that is, the enactment of sovereignty)—and all of the political machinations that attend to the bestowing or denial of a particular kind of status—complicate the experiences and day-to-day realities of Indigenous peoples in ways that are both similar to and unique from other racialized peoples. I stand in solidarity with my brothers and sisters of color and don't deny that Indigenous people are racialized peoples. However, I am simply arguing that we are a political and legal group as well.

Fourth, TribalCrit is rooted in a belief in and desire to obtain and forge tribal autonomy, self-determination, self-identification, and ultimately tribal sovereignty. *Tribal autonomy* is the ability of communities and tribal nations to have control over existing land bases, natural resources, and tribal national boundaries. Autonomy is also linked to the ability to interact with the U.S. and other nations on a nation-to-nation basis. *Self-determination* is the enactment or operationalization of sovereignty; it refers to the inherent right of Indigenous peoples and nations to be independent and to engage as a separate political, spiritual, and legal entity. Self-determination, guided by sovereignty, includes the ability to define what happens with autonomy, how, why, and to what ends, without the need to solicit permission from the United States. Self-determination rejects the guardian–ward relationship which currently dominates the thinking among federal policy- and law-makers in the U.S. government. Finally, self-determination entails the ability and legitimacy for groups to define themselves and to create what it means to be Indian.

Fifth, TribalCrit problematizes the concepts of culture, knowledge, and power and offers alternative ways of understanding them through an Indigenous lens. TribalCrit departs from Western/European notions of culture, knowledge, and power and moves toward notions that have been circulating among Indigenous peoples for thousands of years. I understand that *culture* is a highly contested term; I choose, however, to invoke it nevertheless. Culture is simultaneously fluid or dynamic and fixed or stable. Like an anchor in the ocean, it is tied to a group of people and often a physical place; for many Indigenous people, culture is rooted to lands on which they live as well as to ancestors who lived on those lands before them. However, just as the anchor shifts and sways with changing tides and the ebbs and flows of the ocean, culture shifts and flows with changes in contexts, situations, people, and purposes. Like all humans, Indigenous people are shaped by their cultural inheritance and they engage in cultural production.[9]

There are at least three forms of knowledge that I want to address which must, subsequently, exist in accord with one another. *Cultural* knowledge is an understanding of what it means to be a member of a particular tribal nation; this includes particular traditions, issues, and ways of being and knowing that make an individual a member of a community. *Academic* knowledge is acquired from educational institutions; in many of our communities this is often referred to as "book knowing" or "book smarts." Finally, knowledge of *survival* includes an understanding of how and in what ways change can be accomplished and the ability and willingness to change, adapt, and adjust in order to move forward as an individual and community. These different forms of knowledge do not need to be in conflict. In fact, knowledge learned in school can be used in conjunction with tribal knowledge toward social justice and survival for these communities.

For many Indigenous peoples, power appears throughout the world and it is something that is sacred. Power must be handled with care; if power is abused or misused, it will decrease in its vitality over time. If we don't examine power in all of its manifestations—including the power to define what is good, true, right, and beautiful—then we are lost in this work that we do. Power is rooted in a group's ability to define themselves, their place in the world, and their traditions (Deloria, 1970; Vizenor, 1998; Warrior, 1995). According to the late Lakota scholar Vine Deloria, Jr. (1970), "few members of racial minority groups have realized that inherent in their peculiar experience on this continent is hidden the basic recognition of their power and sovereignty" (p. 115). Power is the ability to survive rooted in the capacity to adapt and adjust to changing landscapes, times, ideas, circumstances, and situations. However, for Indigenous peoples, survival is more than simply staying together as a group; it is the thriving (educationally, politically, spiritually, and many other ways), both as individuals and as a group.

Determining how to best attend to issues of sovereignty is governed by the group's own sense of themselves. Culture is the base for knowledge that ultimately leads to power. There is a dialogical relationship between culture, knowledge, and power. While I believe that culture serves as a basis for the relationship, there are clear reciprocal ties to knowledge and power. Culture reminds individuals, in a group, who they are; its dynamic nature allows for adaptability to change. Knowledge relates to culture in that it offers links to what people know. Ultimately, knowledge is important in the process of recognizing that no single culture has solutions to the myriad problems encountered by groups. Knowledge also allows groups to distinguish change, adapt, and move forward in a vision related to power in the form of sovereignty. The way that groups define themselves, their places in the world (at least in part, recognizing that places are co-constructed by many things), and their cultures is a form of power. Importantly, power lies outside of individuals, making the tribe the subject in the dialogic rather than individual tribal members.

The sixth key component of TribalCrit is a recognition that governmental policies and educational policies toward Indigenous peoples have, historically, closely followed each other toward the problematic goal of assimilation. TribalCrit rejects the past and present rhetoric calling for assimilation of American Indian students in educational institutions. Throughout the history of U.S. governmental policies, the approach taken toward Indigenous peoples has been to "kill the Indian and save the man." Historically, this call for assimilation has also been present for American Indians in higher education. Since 1637 when the College of William and Mary hoped to "educate the infidels of the forest," higher education has been replete with calls for students to "integrate" into their academic communities in order to "succeed" (e.g. see Pascarella & Terenzini, 1991; Tinto, 1986). Two years later, Harvard was founded with one of its explicit goals being to become the "Indian Oxford." Benjamin Franklin hoped to educate some of the tribal peoples of the Haudenosaunee (commonly known as the Iroquois Confederacy) at the University of Pennsylvania. He found these people to be gifted—so gifted that his plan for the governmental set-up for what would become the United States is grounded in the constitution of this Confederacy. TribalCrit recognizes and highlights the past and present rhetoric calling for integration and assimilation of American Indian students in institutions of higher education, rejecting it and calling for a reframing of policies to recognize the wisdom of Indigenous knowledge systems as well as the fact that formal education can be used toward tribal nation building and local capacity building (Brayboy et al., 2012).

The seventh tenet of TribalCrit centers tribal philosophies, beliefs, customs, traditions, and visions for the future; it honors the adaptability of groups and recognizes the differences in and between people and groups. Diné philosopher Brian Yazzie Burkhart (2005) explains the central role of tribal epistemologies and cultures by contrasting them with Descartes's Cartesian principle. The principle "I think; therefore I am" points to the centrality of the individual in the larger U.S. society and legal code. This focus on the importance of the individual also points to ways that the U.S. government has worked to assimilate tribal nations—by moving the focus away from communal living, sharing, and engagement with the world to one rooted in individuals. This is evidenced in the Dawes Act, where reservations were broken up into parcels of 160-, 80-, and 40-acre individual plots, thereby moving to assimilation through individual land ownership. Burkhart (2005) argues that an Indigenous perspective of the Cartesian principle would be "We are; therefore I am,"[10] which re-centers the importance of a community, as Indigenous people(s) are defined by our membership in the community, not simply by being individuals. Placing the individual at the center of societal epistemologies and ontologies illuminates much of the U.S.'s democratic foundation; placing the community at the center of our epistemologies and ontologies points to the foundations of many tribal nations. Indigenous beliefs, thoughts, philosophies, customs, and traditions serve as a foundation from which to analyze the schooling practices and experiences of Indigenous peoples. These concepts must be recognized as being viable and important for the lives of the individuals and members of the group and lead to different ways of examining experiences and theoretical frames through which to view the experiences.

Contrary to recent calls for "scientifically based" research as being the only justifiable form of research, the eighth tenet of TribalCrit honors stories and oral knowledge as real and legitimate forms of data and ways of being. In this view, stories are not separate from theory; rather, they make up theory. Many Indigenous peoples have strong oral traditions, which are used as vehicles for the transmission of culture and knowledge. Oral stories remind us of our origins and serve as lessons for the younger members of our communities; they have a place in our communities and in our lives (e.g. see Basso, 1996; Battiste, 2002; Olivas, 2000). Stories serve as our moral and practical guideposts in life. My mother's observation about my colleague's telling me that I'd never be a good theoretician illustrates the importance of this tenet.[11]

The final component of TribalCrit is a call to action or activism—a way of connecting theory and practice in deep and explicit ways. It is my contention that no research should be conducted with Indigenous peoples that is not in some way directed by the community and aimed toward improving the life chances and situations of specific communities and American Indians writ large. Deloria warns against the dangers of conducting research that has little relevance and/or no benefit for Indigenous communities: "abstract theories create abstract action. Lumping together the variety of tribal problems and seeking the demonic principle at work is intellectually satisfying. But it does not change the real situation" (1969/1988, p. 86). Ultimately, then, we have come full circle, because Tribal-Crit research and practice—or better still, praxis—move us away from colonization and assimilation and towards a more real self-determination and tribal sovereignty.

TribalCrit endeavors to expose the inconsistencies in structural systems and institutions—like colleges and universities—and make the situation better. By legitimizing and hearing stories, while connecting power, knowledge, and culture, TribalCrit users take part in the process of self-determination and in making universities and colleges more understandable to Indigenous students and Indigenous students more understandable to the institutions.

CRITIQUES AND NEW BEGINNINGS

Many of the ideas I have introduced in this chapter have been developed and evolved considerably since I first introduced the concept of tribal critical race theory in 2005. My work has developed in interesting ways, with a deeper consideration of sovereignty and self-determination, and significant interest in returning to or re-centering indigenous knowledge systems. I have encouraged scholars to engage with this work in hopes that they would build, extend, and complicate the theory. One issue that has been raised is that this theory backs itself into a corner on the subject of sovereignty. The argument goes that placing too much emphasis on a legal status, rooted in the Constitution, appears to buy into the system of the federal government possessing too much power to define who belongs where, when, and how. I respond to these criticisms by turning to the work of Mohawk scholar Gerald Taiaiake Alfred (1999, 2005) wherein he declines to address sovereignty in relation to other nation-states; rather, he focuses on the inherent rights of tribal nations, with an emphasis on the spiritual aspects of sovereignty. In many ways, his work is directly related to Comanche intellectual Wallace Coffey and Yaqui scholar Rebecca Tsosie's concept of *cultural sovereignty*. Coffey and Tsosie (2001) write: "The concept of cultural sovereignty encompasses the spiritual, emotional, mental, and physical aspects of our lives. Because of this, only Native peoples can decide what the ultimate contours of Native sovereignty will be" (p. 210). This critique is well taken. My primary response to this is that I honor the spiritual components of sovereignty, understanding and agreeing with Alfred as well as Coffey and Tsosie. I also recognize the legal relationship that Indigenous peoples have with the federal government, educational institutions, and their laws and policies. There is a practical component to TribalCrit, which requires that I seek to address challenges and barriers placed in front of Indigenous peoples on a plane that can directly respond to these challenges.

The second critique has focused on my lack of engagement with gender. My work has always focused on the plight of Indigenous peoples in schools and society. If I have overlooked one area it is, admittedly, around issues of gender. Clearly, there are differences in the ways that boys and girls and men and women engage and are engaged by school and society. My primary interest has been on the engagement around conceptions of indigeneity in these interactions and relationships. What TribalCrit may offer is a way to examine the differentiating ways that gender intersects with sovereignty and self-determination. For example, Guerrero (2003) cogently and powerfully outlines a concept that she calls *patriarchal colonialism*, whereby the engagement of tribal politics is dominated by men in unhealthy and non-traditional ways. In short, her work points to the ways that Indigenous men have moved away from "traditional" ways of engaging Indigenous women on an equal and culturally differentiated status and toward one rooted in European patriarchy. Future iterations of TribalCrit would benefit from a deeper engagement in these kinds of politics. My hope is that those who understand the role of gender engage it through this lens in new, interesting, and important ways. Although my original intent was not to focus on gender specifically, I readily believe this critique is noteworthy and warranted.

CONCLUSIONS

When I advanced the concept of tribal critical race theory, it was an attempt for me to create a theoretical suit that was custom made for my projects, rather than the generic, off-the-rack suit offered by theorists like Bourdieu, Foucault, Giddens, and others. My intent was not necessarily to create something that others would use as a paradigm; rather, the intent was to offer a concentration of issues to consider when engaging in work that seeks to understand and/or benefit Indigenous peoples. In retrospect, I believe that the suit still fits, although it clearly needs to be let out in some places and taken in elsewhere. That is my next academic exercise: to tailor the theory a bit more. That others have found it useful and instructive has been surprising and humbling.

ACKNOWLEDGMENTS

This paper is better because of the extensive comments made by Adrienne Dixson and Marvin Lynn. I am grateful to them both. All mistakes remain my own.

NOTES

1 In fairness, my father also gave his life—and continues to do so—serving Indigenous peoples, opening health clinics for American Indians, sponsoring young, Indigenous medical and dental students, and actively serving the health crisis in Indian Country. In his seventh decade of life, he works as an elementary school counselor, walking through the same elementary school that he attended as a child, like the Lumbee pied piper, with a legion of Native children in tow.

2 It would not be until 1924, under the auspices of the Citizenship Act, that the majority of American Indians in the U.S. were granted citizenship in the U.S.

3 Although I use the term "[American] Indian" throughout this chapter, it is important to note I use this language to mirror the official language used in many of the sources I cite/refer to. However, other Indigenous groups, sometimes considered separate from American Indians (e.g. Alaska Natives, Native Hawaiians, and/or, at times, Chicanos/as), have also faced similar legal, political, and racial tensions in U.S. politics and jurisprudence (see for example the work of Tsosie, 2005).

4 It should be clear that colonization is raced. That is, the ways that legislative, educational, social, and judicial bodies construct the rules that govern them are inherently rooted in the maintenance of racial superiority. This connection becomes evident in TribalCrit's second tenet. I do not want to be misunderstood here; reframing the conversation around colonization does not reject or erase/"erace" race and racism. Instead, it points to a different side of the same coin—that is colonialism—that I believe brings racism and policies toward Indigenous peoples into a clearer, more refined light when the notion of liminality is introduced.

5 Lumbee peoples and our history demonstrate the complicated nature of how policies have been enforced to benefit the U.S. government. Although we were granted federal recognition by the federal government in 1956—in a legislative era when Congress was disestablishing, or "terminating," tribal nations—the recognition

was hollow in that it denied any federal benefits. In short, it was a hollow form of recognition and only serves to further frustrate and leave Lumbee peoples in a form of political and legal limbo. Others have written eloquently on this (see in particular Lowery, 2009).

6 For example, see hooks (1995); Ladson-Billings (1998, 2000); Richardson and Villenas (2000); Thompson (1999); Villenas and Deyhle (1999).

7 American Indians are the only racialized group mentioned in the Constitution. In this context, American Indians have argued, successfully in many arenas, that they have a government-to-government relationship with the U.S. government, recognizing their political/legal status.

8 This could be terminated tribes, state-recognized tribes, or those tribes that are "non-recognized." The issue here is that the status of recognition comes from the federal government, invoking once again the implication that a group's status is dependent on the whims and definitions of Congress. The colonial implications of this are significant, when considering that others (Alfred, 2009; Coffey & Tsosie, 2001; Deloria & Lytle, 1984; Wilkins & Lomawaima, 2001) have argued convincingly that sovereignty is extra-Constitutional (that is, tribal sovereignty existed long before the U.S. Constitution was constructed) and that nations like the U.S. and Canada actually gained their sovereignty through their connections to tribal nations, rather than the other way around (see Alfred, 2005 and Tsosie, 2005 for especially convincing arguments along these lines).

9 For a full outlining and contestation of culture, see Borofsky et al. (2001). The article in *American Anthropologist* highlights the contested nature of culture. I recognize the term is contested; as an educational anthropologist, however, I choose to utilize it in this chapter.

10 Not surprisingly, there are other Indigenous manifestations of these sentiments. For example, the Zulu people have a proverb, "I am because we are," which is quite similar. Importantly, these sentiments cross national and continental borders.

11 As I noted at the beginning of this chapter, TribalCrit is intimately related to critical race theory. Perhaps nowhere is this linkage and connection more apparent than in the concept of storytelling. Derrick Bell's foundational work (1987) highlights this connection. Others (Chang, 1996; Culp, 1996; Delgado, 1989; Montoya, 1994; Olivas, 2000) have also served as inspiration for me.

REFERENCES

Alfred, T. (G.R.). (1999). *Peace, power, righteousness: An indigenous manifesto.* Don Mills, Canada: Oxford University Press.

Alfred, T. (G.R.). (2005). *Wasase: Indigenous pathways of action and freedom.* Peterborough, Canada: Broadview Press.

Alfred, T. (2009). *Peace, power, righteousness* (2nd ed.). Oxford: Oxford University Press.

Anderson, J.D. (2007). Race-conscious educational policies versus a "color-blind Constitution": A historical perspective. *Educational Researcher, 36*(5), 249–257.

Basso, K.H. (1996). Wisdom sits in places. In *Wisdom sits in places: Landscape and language among the Western Apache* (pp. 105–149). Albuquerque: University of New Mexico Press.

Battiste, M. (2002). *Indigenous knowledge and pedagogy in First Nations education: A literature review with recommendations.* Ottawa: Indian and Northern Affairs Canada.

Bell, D. (1987). *And we are not saved: The elusive quest for racial justice.* New York: Basic Books.

Borofsky, R., Barth, F., Shweder, R.A., Rodseth, L., & Stoltzenberg, N.M. (2001). A conversation about culture. *American Anthropologist, 103*(2), 432–446.

Brayboy, B.M.J. (2005). Toward a tribal critical race theory in education. *Urban Review, 37*(5), 425–446.

Brayboy, B.M.J., Fann, A., Castagno, A.E., & Solyom, J.A. (2012). *Postsecondary education for American Indian and Alaska Natives: Higher education for nation building and self-determination.* San Francisco, CA: Jossey-Bass.

Burkhart, B.Y. (2005). What coyote and thales can teach us: An outline of American Indian epistemology. In A. Waters (Ed.), *American Indian thought: Philosophical essays* (pp. 15–26). Oxford: Blackwell.

Chang, R.S. (1996). The nativist's dream of return. *La Raza Law Journal, 9,* 55–59.

Coffey, W., & Tsosie, R. (2001). Rethinking the tribal sovereignty doctrine: Cultural sovereignty and the collective future of Indian nations. *Stanford Law and Policy Review, 12*(2), 191–221.

Culp., J.M., Jr. (1996). Telling a black legal story: Privilege, authenticity, "blunder," and transformation in outsider narratives. *University of Virginia Law Review, 82,* 69–94.

Delgado, R. (1989). Storytelling for oppositionists and others: A plea for narrative. *Michigan Law Review, 87,* 2411–2441.

Deloria, V., Jr. (1969/1988). *Custer died for your sins: An Indian manifesto (Civilization of the American Indian).* New York: Macmillan.

Deloria, V. (1970). *We talk, you listen: New tribes, new turf.* New York: Macmillan.

Deloria, V., & Lytle, C.M. (1984). *The nations within: The past and future of American Indian sovereignty.* Austin: University of Texas Press.

Guerrero, M.A.J. (2003). "Patriarchal colonialism" and indigenism: Implications for Native feminist spirituality and Native womanism. *Hypatia, 18*(2), 58–69.

hooks, b. (1995). *Killing rage: Ending racism.* New York: Holt & Co.

Ladson-Billings, G. (1998). Just what is critical race theory and what's it doing in a nice field like education? *International Journal of Qualitative Studies in Education, 11*(1), 7–24.

Ladson-Billings, G. (2000). Racialized discourses and ethnic epistemologies. In N. Denzin & Y. Lincoln (Eds.), *Handbook of qualitative research* (2nd ed.). Thousand Oaks, CA: Sage.

Lowery, M.M. (2009). Telling our own stories: Writing Lumbee history in the shadow of the BAR. *American Indian Quarterly, 33*(4), 499–522.

Mills, C.W. (1999). *The racial contract.* Ithaca, NY: Cornell University Press.

Montoya, M.E. (1994). Máscaras, trenzas y greñas: Un/masking the self while un/braiding Latina stories and legal discourse. *Chicano-Latino Law Review, 15*(1), 1–37.

Olivas, M.A. (2000). The chronicles, my grandfather's stories, and immigration law: The slave traders' chronicle as racial history. In R. Delgado & J. Stefancic (Eds.), *Critical race theory: The cutting edge* (2nd ed., pp. 9–20). Philadelphia, PA: Temple Press.

Parker, A.C. (1916). The social elements of the Indian problem. *American Journal of Sociology, 22*(2), 252–267.

Pascarella, E.T., & Terenzini, P.T. (1991). *How college affects students: Findings and insights from twenty years of research* (1st ed.). San Francisco, CA: Jossey-Bass.

Richardson, T., & Villenas, S. (2000). "Other" encounters: Dances with whiteness in multicultural education. *Educational Theory, 50*(2), 255–273.

Thompson, A. (1999). Colortalk: Whiteness and off white [book review]. *Educational Studies, 30*(2), 141–160.

Tinto, V. (1986). Theories of student departure revisited. In J. Smart (Ed.), *Higher education: Handbook of theory and research* (vol. II). New York: Agathon Press.

Tsosie, R. (2005). Engaging the spirit of racial healing within critical race theory: An exercise in transformative thought. *Michigan Journal of Race and Law, 11*, 21–49.

Villenas, S., & Deyhle, D. (1999). Critical race theory and ethnographies challenging the stereotypes: Latino families, schooling, resilience and resistance. *Curriculum Inquiry, 29*(4), 413–445.

Vizenor, G. (1998). *Fugitive poses: Native American Indian scenes of absence and presence.* Lincoln: University of Nebraska Press.

Warrior, R.A. (1995). *Tribal secrets: Recovering American Indian intellectual traditions.* Minneapolis: University of Minnesota Press.

Wilkins, D.E., & Lomawaima, K.T. (2001). *Uneven ground: American Indian sovereignty and federal law.* Norman: University of Oklahoma Press.

Williams, R.A., Jr. (1987). Jefferson, the Norman Yoke, and American Indian lands. *Arizona Law Review, 28*, 165–202.

Williams, R.A., Jr. (1989). Documents of barbarism: The contemporary legacy of European racism and colonialism in the narrative traditions of federal Indian law. *Arizona Law Review, 31*, 231–278.

7

ORIGINS OF AND CONNECTIONS TO SOCIAL JUSTICE IN CRITICAL RACE THEORY IN EDUCATION

Thandeka K. Chapman

INTRODUCTION

After sending the editors my abstract, I struggled to begin this chapter. I was overwhelmed by the numbers of ERIC articles using "social justice and education" as key words, and underwhelmed by articles using "social justice and critical race theory." The bulk of these 3,000-plus articles merely referenced the term in their conclusions when making suggestions for future work or to assert the need for social justice. I could not find the foothold I was seeking in the literature. Perhaps my struggle was also because I was misinterpreting the connection between critical race theory (CRT) and social justice. I was looking for enactments of activism, rather than the deeply embedded understanding of how critical race theorists assert social justice through their works in the academy.

I realized my mistake when I finally returned to the original texts and compilations of critical race theory. I tell my students all the time to go back to their primary sources. I had to heed my own advice and start with the father of CRT, Derrick A. Bell: "If we are to seek new goals for our struggles, we must first reassess the worth of the racial assumptions on which, without careful thought, we have presumed too much and relied on too long" (1992, p. 14). The irony of Derrick Bell's words being the ones to clarify my thinking, when these same words inspired my professional pathway, was not lost on me. Since we lost Derrick Bell in 2011, it seems only fitting that I continue to be reminded of the legacy of his work. After returning to Bell's work (1989), I began a journey to better understand how CRT defined the elusive term "social justice."

I read the works of various CRT scholars and discovered that they did not define social justice. I went to the roots of the theory and explored the writings of "race men and women" of the twentieth century to find the words I so desired to quote. They were not in the texts. But I was not disappointed. What I found was the many calls to action for doing the work of scholarship in the quest for justice. I found rationales for disseminating knowledge that challenges stock stories and majoritarian tales, offers re-tellings of history, deconstructs litigation and policy, and analyzes the outcomes of policy and law. In this chapter I show the reader how social justice is not a separate call for action in

101

CRT, but an embedded function of scholarship that combats the pervasive and punishing presence of race and racism in social and institutional contexts.

DEFINING SOCIAL JUSTICE FOR CRITICAL RACE THEORY

The term "social justice" is rarely defined in the field of education. Sadly, the editors of three prominent edited books on social justice, my own included, do not provide definitions of social justice (Adams et al., 2010; Ayers et al., 2009; Chapman & Hobbel, 2010). These texts assume a level of understanding and agreement on the term that does not exist. Moreover, Boyles et al. maintain that, because of the disagreements concerning social justice, "there are groups promoting educational reform in order to perpetuate status quo norms of power and privilege acting in the name of social justice. Yet, and at the same time, there are other groups who wish to dismantle such privilege under the auspices of social justice" (2009, p. 30).

Perhaps because there are multiple components of social justice, scholars shy away from a full articulation of its meaning. Many education scholars use John Rawls's (1972) articulation of social justice to bind the terminology to issues of access and equity. Although it has been heavily critiqued by critical race scholars such as Mari Matsuda (1986) for focusing on abstractions and not realities, I use it because the two principles of social justice articulated by Rawls also align with the goals of CRT to eradicate injustice based on undeserved, systemic inequalities. Rawls contends that "The justice of a social scheme depends essentially on how fundamental rights and duties are assigned and on the economic opportunities and social conditions in various sectors of society" (1972, p. 7). In the case of the United States, his definition of social justice would include the ability to fully access both constitutional rights and opportunities for financial success. The push in CRT for equitable access and equitable treatment under the law resonates with Rawls's theory of justice. Rawls breaks his definition of social justice into two principles:

> First: each person is to have an equal right to the most extensive basic liberty compatible with a similar liberty for others.
> Second: social and economic inequalities are to be arranged so that they are both (a) reasonably expected to be to everyone's advantage, and (b) attached to positions and offices open to all.
>
> (1972, p. 60)

These two principles must be applied together, with the first principle always being in place before the second principle can be enacted. Rawls's principles leave room for some interpretation when we contemplate his use of the word "similar" in the first principle and "reasonably expected" in the second principle. Moreover, Rawls poses his second principle as a balance of "inequities" to recognize that there will always be uneven distributions of social power and economic resources. These words demonstrate that Rawls is not speaking of a social ideal or utopia, and notes that the fallacies of society prevent perfection. Thus Rawls presents his principles as both abstract understandings of social justice and goals for society.

Rawls states that principle one covers a citizen's political liberties. These liberties include "freedom from arbitrary arrest and seizure as defined by the concept of the rule of law" (p. 61) as an example of "pure procedural justice." Pure procedural justice occurs when "there is no independent criterion for the right result: instead there is a correct or fair procedure such that the outcome is likewise correct or fair, whatever it is, provided that the procedure is fairly followed" (p. 86). CRT relates to the notion of pure procedural justice because it challenges the commonsense belief that our current justice system is "blind" and objective. In a just society, the U.S. justice system would be an example of pure procedural justice in which the judicial process worked the same for everyone and produced fair results. Here CRT shares Rawls's definition of social justice and the goal of pure procedural justice. CRT exposes the hypocrisy of the current U.S. justice system by highlighting the racialized injustice within the system and challenging the focus of justice on "procedure" rather than tangible, lasting outcomes.

Similarly, CRT interrogates the ways in which the societal function of White privilege works to maintain White supremacy in various forms. CRT views White privilege as an uneven distribution of social capital, or property, which can be parlayed into greater social and economic advantages for White citizens. Scholars of CRT challenge Whiteness as property because it exists to the detriment of anyone who is not White, thus creating an unequal advantage for White citizens. Rawls's statement that the distribution of wealth must be attuned to the "liberties of equal citizenship and equality of opportunity" (1972, p. 61) resonates with the position of CRT concerning the need to dismantle White privilege in order to create a more just society. Rawls asserts:

> All social values—liberty and opportunity, income and wealth, and the basis of self-respect—are to be distributed equally unless an unequal distribution of any, or all, of these values is to everyone's advantage.
> Injustice, then, is simply inequalities that are not to the benefit of all.
>
> (p. 62)

If Rawls's line of reasoning is used, in connection with CRT, White privilege should be abolished, because it benefits one group of citizens to the detriment of others.

Additionally, CRT resonates with Rawls's theory of justice because both recognize the roots of injustice as political, economic, and social. Rawls remarks:

> In this way the institutions of society favor certain starting places over others. These are especially deep inequalities. Not only are they pervasive, but they affect men's initial chances in life; yet they cannot possibly be justified by an appeal to the notions of merit or desert. It is these inequalities, presumably inevitable in the basic structure of any society, to which the principles of social justice must in the first instance apply.
>
> (1972, p. 7)

In CRT, these "starting places" are rooted in the history of race and racism in the United States. Given the histories of slavery, manifest destiny, and westward expansion, the "basic structure" of U.S. society was built upon the maintenance of White supremacy and the oppression of people of color. Institutional racism causes deep inequities by affecting where people can live and attend school, and the future opportunities available to them. Therefore, for CRT, exploring the permanence of race and racism is the first instance to which social justice must be applied.

Lastly, the call for policies and laws, such as affirmative action, by critical race scholars ties with Rawls's theory of justice. He states that the claims of "redress" (1972, p. 101) must be taken into account when creating a just society. Rawls asserts that, in order for social justice to occur, society must provide more opportunities for success to those groups who have most often been the victims of institutional inequity.

The concept of redress is woven into the scholarship and actions of critical race theorists. It is visible in the push by legal scholars to racially diversify schools of law and calls for coalition building (Williams, 2000), the drive to reform the laws and procedures in legal systems, and Derrick Bell's resignation from Harvard Law School. In CRT in education, redress abounds in calls to help teachers teach students of color through professional development, to reform teacher education programs and PK-16 curricula, and to reform policies and practices at all levels of education—school, district, state, and federal. Redress as a criterion of social justice is indivisible from CRT.

In this discussion of social justice, I must mention that both Rawls's theory of justice and CRT recognize the difficulties in obtaining justice. Social justice hinges upon the ideas of equity and equality, opportunities for economic, social, and moral growth and development, and the ability to choose one's own pathway (Clark, 2006). Tensions arise when the theory of justice is put into practice, because it almost always means a redistribution of power and privilege must take place. How much, how little, and at whose expense are questions that often go under-examined when scholars espouse a social justice position (Clark, 2006). Because of the entrenchment of racism in U.S. society, critical race scholars understand that social justice with regard to the dismantling of race and racism is an unobtainable goal; yet it is worth the lifetime of struggle to fight for equity (Bell, 2004).

CRITICAL RACE THEORY AND JUSTICE

Roots of Justice in Critical Race Theory

Critical race theory is rooted in critical studies, ethnic studies, and women's studies. To expand intersections of race, class, and gender, CRT has borrowed theoretical concepts from postmodernists, poststructuralists, and postcolonial thought. Critical race scholars such as Patricia Hill Collins (1998) and Kimberlé Crenshaw (1995) continue to explore the complexities of racial struggle as a social construction whose signifiers and reproduction are dependent upon other social constructions of gender, class, and sexuality. Crenshaw explains:

> To say that a category such as race or gender is socially constructed is not to say that that category has no significance in our world. On the contrary, a large and continuing project for subordinate people—and indeed, one of the projects for which postmodern theories have been helpful—is thinking about the way in which power has clustered around certain categories and is exercised against others.
>
> (1995, p. 375)

Crenshaw's (1995) conception of intersectionality is most closely associated with CRT because it continues to position race as the central concept. The exploration of intersectionality is an integral aspect to social justice, because the discourses of race and gender as they have traditionally been written "are often inadequate even to the discrete tasks of articulating the full dimensions of racism and sexism" (Crenshaw, 1995, p. 360). Black and Third World feminist writers offer a strong message of social action that has been incorporated into the foundations of CRT. In her book *Women, Culture and Politics*, Angela Davis (1990) uses the motto "Lift as we climb" of the National Association of Colored Women's Clubs to express the push for justice by scholars:

> We must strive to "lift as we climb." In other words, we must climb in such a way as to guarantee that all our sisters, regardless of social class, and indeed all of our brothers, climb with us. This must be the essential dynamic of our quest for power—a principle that must not only determine our struggles as Afro-American women, but also govern all authentic struggles of disposed people. Indeed, the overall battle for equality can be profoundly enhanced by embracing this principle.
>
> (1990, p. 5)

Davis's call to action takes into account the privileged nature of the middle class professional as the socially mobile subject in communities of color. She tells the educated person who is able to move forward and gain power and prestige that she must not forget to help those people who have fewer resources and opportunities. Davis states:

> Black women scholars and professionals cannot afford to ignore the straits of our sisters who are acquainted with the immediacy of oppressions in a way many of us are not. The process of empowerment cannot simplistically be defined in accordance with our own particular class interests. We must learn to lift as we climb.
>
> (1990, p. 9)

Davis does not assume an innate knowledge among Black women professionals for helping others succeed. Instead, she suggests it is a learned trait. Other Black feminists suggest that using scholarship to fight for a more just society is a necessity, not a choice. Hull and Smith assert: "Because we are so oppressed as Black women, every aspect of our fight for freedom, including our teaching and writing about ourselves, must in some way further our liberation" (1982, p. xxi). Similarly, Anzaldua affirms the power of scholarship when she states: "For positive social change to occur we must imagine a reality that differs from what already exists ... Empowerment comes from ideas—our revolution is fought with concepts, not guns, and it is fueled by vision" (2002, p. 5). Critical race feminist Adrienne Wing draws on the works of her foremothers and forefathers in Black feminist thought and CRT to offer an explanation for why women of color are often compelled to work towards justice:

> Since many of us come from disenfranchised communities of color, we feel compelled to "look to the bottom," to involve ourselves in the development of solutions to our people's problems. We cannot afford to adopt the classic, detached, ivory tower model of scholarship when so many are suffering, sometimes in our own extended families. We do not believe in praxis instead of theory, but believe both are essential to our people's literal and figurative future.
>
> (2000, p. 6)

Wing moves the call for women of color to join struggles for equity to a more personal level, and maintains the need for scholarship to create a more just society. Wing asserts the need for theoretically complex explications of women's multiple identities, oppressions, and privileges as a means to disclose racism, sexism, heterosexism, and other barriers to women's empowerment. The calls from Black and Third World feminists to right our wrongs and challenge injustice through scholarship inform the foundations of CRT as social justice. They resonate with CRT beyond a gender binary and can be applied to all CRT scholars.

Role of Critical Race Theory as Social Justice

Critical race theory was created to "expose and dismantle this social and legal status quo from an explicitly race-conscious and critical 'outsider' perspective" (Valdes et al., 2002, p. 1). CRT counters the stock stories and misrepresentations of past and present texts that have sought to position people of color as derelicts and victims. Bell explains the role of CRT:

> We must see this country's history of slavery, not as an insuperable racial barrier to blacks, but as a legacy of enlightenment from our enslaved forebears reminding us that if they survived the ultimate form of racism, we and those whites who stand with us can at least view racial oppression in its many contemporary forms without underestimating its critical importance and likely permanent status in this country.
> (1992, p.12)

Bell insists on disclosing that the complex connections between the past experiences of people of color and their current situations are a significant goal in CRT. Uncovering and rewriting our racialized past are among many goals that center on racial empowerment. Crenshaw et al. (1995) focus on addressing the immediate contexts of race and racism as a key goal of the theory. They explain that "we argued that Critical Race Theory does not simply understand the complex condominia of law, racial ideology, and political power. We believe that our work can provide a useful theoretical vocabulary for the practice of progressive racial politics in contemporary America" (p. xxvii). They believe a task of CRT is to remind people of the deep and complex current nature of racial ideology and power.

Valdes et al. (2002) share three goals for CRT. They state that CRT "continues to reject at least three entrenched, mainstream beliefs about racial injustice" (Valdes et al, 2002, p. 1). CRT rejects colorblindness, racism as individual and not systemic, and essentialism. By exploring the discourses of race, law and policy enactments, and racially stratified outcomes in society, CRT becomes a vehicle to dismantle these three mainstream beliefs and move towards social justice. Rupturing long-standing processes of racism and uncovering the various enactments of race and racism provide new opportunities for people of color to overcome systemic barriers that prevent people of color from leading more successful lives. The goal to move marginalized peoples forward by challenging stock stories and stereotypes and offering new, contextualized stories and perspectives is part of the challenge to achieve justice.

CRT provides scholars with the tools to critique and question the ways in which people of color are represented, the resources that schools receive, and the public mandates structuring their lives. "Questioning regnant visions of racial power, critical race theorists seek to fashion a set of tools for thinking about race that avoids the traps of racial thinking" (Crenshaw et al., 1995, p. xxxiii). The tools used in CRT shift the focus from the individual plight to institutional constrictions impacting majority-marginalized populations.

For example, storytelling as an analytic tool in CRT performs specific functions. "Critical Race Theory's challenge to racial oppression and the status quo often takes the form of storytelling in which writers analyze the myths, presuppositions, and received wisdom that make up the common culture about race and invariably render blacks and other minorities one-down" (Delgado and Stefancic, 2000, p. xvii). Wing supports the use of storytelling as a method to speak to people outside the context of the academy without using the "hypertechnical" language often used in academic texts (Wing, 2000). Connecting with people from outside the academy strengthens the power of the scholarship and allows for diverse coalitions to be created within and among groups.

ROLE(S) OF CRITICAL RACE THEORISTS

The act of writing cannot be overvalued, nor should it be underemphasized. Words have moved individuals and groups to do amazing tasks and challenge unbelievable odds. It is not by accident that scholars throughout time have feared for and lost their lives because those in power deemed them too dangerous to live. Book burnings and banning books continue to occur in today's society to staunch the flow of ideas and limit intellectual freedom. Gloria Anzaldua states: "Books saved my sanity, knowledge opened the locked doors in me and taught me first how to survive and then how to soar" (1999, p. 19). This is the powerful legacy of words.

Historically, intellectuals of color have used their scholarship to counter racism and discrimination. In the early twentieth century, writings about the role(s) of African American scholars, or Negro intellectuals, emphasized the responsibility of scholars to use their access to knowledge to speak against injustice:

> Again, we may decry the color-prejudice of the South, yet it remains a heavy fact. Such curious kinks in the human mind exist and must be reckoned with soberly. They cannot be laughed away, nor always successfully stormed at, nor easily abolished by act of legislature. And yet they must not be encouraged by being let alone. They must be recognized as facts, but unpleasant facts, things that stand in the way of civilization and religion and common decency. They can be met in but one way— by the breadth and broadening of human reason.
>
> (Du Bois, 1904/1999, p. 63)

This quote echoes the very foundations of CRT as a tool to combat racism through scholarship and "human reasoning." Traditionally African American scholars have used their writing to defy stereotypes and speak out against systemic racism as a means to invoke justice. Du Bois is a recognizable example of the implicit connection between the Negro intellectual and social justice.

Additionally, W.E.B. Du Bois demands that education provide former slaves with the option to become philosophers to help eradicate ignorance of culture and history. He states that education must "teach the workers to work and the thinkers to think; make carpenters of carpenters, and philosophers of philosophers, and fops of fools" (1904/1999, p. 61). Du Bois asserts that the African American people need philosophers of color just as much as they need workers who provide the infrastructures for the movement of goods and services. He states that African American people have to hold the United States accountable to the words of the Declaration of Independence by "every civilized and peaceful method" (p. 45). The use of scholarship becomes one of those methods.

Interestingly, in his critique of scholarly men, such as Du Bois, Cruse (1967) shares his opinion of the role of the Negro intellectual:

> He [the Negro intellectual] should explain the economic and institutional causes of his American cultural depravity. He should tell black America how and why Negroes are trapped in this cultural degeneracy, and how it has dehumanized their essential identity, squeezed the lifeblood of their inherited cultural ingredients out of them, and relegated them to the cultural slums.
>
> (1967, p. 455)

This quote must be contextualized in its historical understanding that deficit discourses concerning African American men, women, and families inundated conversations about race in ways that were meant to both facilitate and deter social justice. Cruse's stance, although problematic, illustrates earlier calls to challenge the economic and institutional causes of poverty, the barriers to societal growth and political power, and the struggle to command our own cultural products. His words resonate with the role of critical race scholars as race advocates, because he demands that Negro intellectuals enlighten others by "defining their own roles as intellectuals within *both* worlds" (p. 455, author's italics)—Black and White—as a means to provide a more accurate depiction of African Americans.

Critical race theorists have embraced the legacy of intellectual accountability that comes with their status and privilege. For critical race theorists, our primary power is our words. As scholars who serve in positions of power and privilege, our primary form of enacting justice is writing papers, books, and monographs, and speaking in public. Delgado and Stefancic state:

> Our social world, with its rules, practices, and assignments of prestige and power, is not fixed; rather, we construct it with words, stories, and silence. But we need not acquiesce in arrangements that are unfair and one-sided. By writing and speaking against them, we may hope to contribute to a better, fairer world.
>
> (2000, p. xvii)

For the critical race theorist, words are our weapon of choice. Black historian Roger Wilkins compared fighting racism to "hand-to-hand combat" and scholars of color to "warriors" (in Lawrence, 2002, p. xv) to emphasize the embattled nature of working against racism in White institutions. Black feminist and Third World scholars previously quoted speak of scholarship as a "fight for our freedom" and "revolution" to emphasize the combative nature of doing race work.

The voice of the critical race theorist is unique because of the principles espoused in the theory. As part of his CRT call to action, Derrick Bell states: "We must reassess our cause and our approach to it, but repetition of time-worn slogans will not do. As a popular colloquialism puts it, it's time to "get real" about race and the persistence of racism in America" (1992, p. 5). Asserting the centrality of race and racism is one way critical race theorists push the boundaries of academic scholarship. Critical race theorists must defend the centrality of race through rigorous scholarship that melds past manifestations of race and racism with present contexts of society and public institutions. "We cannot prepare realistically for our future without assessing honestly our past" (1992, p. 11). The assessment of our past serves to highlight points of strength, survival, and success, ahistorical re-tellings of people of color, the omission of people of color, and our historical missteps. Re-presenting our stories is one of the important roles critical race theorists have in the quest for social justice, because the act of re-presentation and the power to re-present people's histories impacts how new generations view their race and their individual and collective future.

CRITICAL RACE THEORISTS AS EMBATTLED SCHOLARS

To the extent that we are in the picture, it is only as cannon fodder. As a result, the interests we champion have been under attack for some time.

(Crenshaw, 2002, p. 23)

Being a critical race theorist can impact a scholar's ability to be successful in institutions of higher education. Academics take their ideological power and currency very seriously, and will fight to maintain privilege by attacking the intellectual work of others who counter or bring a new nuanced approach to their work. "Critical Race Theory was born as part of the resistance to reentrenchment, and it is not surprising that we and our work have been subject to relentless attack throughout the past ten years" (Lawrence, 2002, p. xv). The scholars who claim CRT as part of their intellectual identity, for it is most certainly a choice, understand that they may have to be more strategic to get published, promoted, and primed for leadership opportunities in the academy (Delgado Bernal & Villalpando, 2002). However, should a person choose the route of CRT, "… we must also speak the simple and radical truths of White supremacy and patriarchy and class oppression and heterosexism, even when we know we will pay a price for speaking them" (Lawrence, 2002, p. xv). As with any work that leads towards greater justice for a marginalized population, there is a price to be paid. The willingness of CRT scholars to continue their work, in the face of easier choices and options, speaks to the embedded nature of social justice among critical race theorists.

ENACTMENTS OF PRAXIS

In harmony with the intellectual work of critical race scholars is the theory of praxis, and enacting social justice on a daily basis. Without people willing to do the work of struggle and change, the words are meaningless. In times of progress and regression, people transform ideas and theories into policies and practices. These people do not necessarily call themselves activists; in fact, many can be people who stand firm to the status quo. Regardless of political or other societal affiliations, most people rely on words to shape their rationales for behavior and understanding.

Scholars may debate whether or not CRT scholars are political activists by the very nature of their work, or whether CRT scholars must go beyond their academic careers to be considered activists. Williams (2000) insists that CRT scholars must be actively engaged in their communities by using their academic resources and their intellect to help foster tangible change. He simply states: "You know the drill. Your elders taught it to you. Get off your butt, go out and make a difference in the world. Or, think independently, act for others" (2000, p. 621). Williams's call to make a difference is wide open for interpretation, with the understanding that a person's actions must benefit other people. In regard to critical race theorists, the questions are:

> In what ways can race scholars and political lawyers, working together, contribute to a progressive, social-justice movement? What is our role, not only in the academy and the courts, but also in neighborhoods, schools, workplaces, churches, city councils, and legislatures?
>
> (Su & Yamamoto, 2002, p. 387)

Scholars continue to question the ways in which they should be engaged with battles over power and privilege beyond the purview of their scholarship. As Williams (2000) points out, the pressure to publish and remain active in academic conversations is very real in higher education. But, "to whom much is given, much is expected" (Luke 12:48, New International Version), and many scholars have made their peace with these questions by balancing their roles as activist scholars and advocates for change.

Many times the praxis of critical race theorists goes unseen and unrewarded (Culp, 2000). Although Derrick Bell's political activism was highly publicized when he resigned from academic institutions in defiance of university hiring policies, the institutional battles of CRT scholars are generally far less public or, perhaps, publicized. Critical race theorists advocate for students and scholars of color on a daily basis. They become the people others hate to see sit down in university meetings, because they are known for their "race" politics and "radical" ideas. Critical race theorists are often the burr in the saddle of "business as usual" and "it's always been that way" conversations over resources and access in their departments and colleges.

It seems that only as CRT moved into education did the specific term "social justice" become identified with the theory. William Tate joined the terms of CRT and social justice when he wrote: "Critical race scholars are engaged in a dynamic process seeking to explain the realities of race in an ever-changing society. Thus, their theoretical positions and, more specifically, these elements should be viewed as a part of an iterative project of scholarship and social justice" (1997, p. 235). In this moment, the connection between CRT and social justice became indelibly linked and often misinterpreted. Tate links the scholarship of CRT with the process of seeking equity and exposing injustice through academic discourse. However, as the field has evolved, social justice and CRT have come to mean enactments of praxis, rather than the scholarship itself.

Several critical race theorists in education have questioned the connection between CRT and praxis as a form of activism and intentional intervention (Alemán & Alemán, 2010; Gillborn, 2006; McKay 2010; Parker & Stovall, 2004). To contextualize the lives of teachers and administrators, critical race theorists in education document the work of PK-12 teachers and school leaders in schools and classrooms (Chapman, 2007; Dixson & Dingus, 2007; Evans, 2007; Lynn, 2002; McCray et al., 2007; Morris, 2001). Critical race theorists also counter majoritarian tales of deficit behavior and dysfunction by highlighting the experiences of students of color in various school settings (Berry, 2008; DeCuir-Gunby, 2007; Duncan, 2002).

The goals of CRT in education vary widely, but reflect the same types of variation found in the conceptualizations of CRT articulated earlier in this chapter. Crenshaw states that "the notion of CRT as a fully unified school of thought remains a fantasy of our critics" (2002, p. 20). Just as critical race scholars in the legal arena do not all share the same ideology and understandings of race and racism, critical race scholars in education have different understanding of CRT and how it can be used in the field. These variations of CRT in education demonstrate the breadth of the field and the need to further explore issues of race and education. Although scholars may not share the same concepts of critical race theory nor agree on the ways to attack racism, they agree that striving for justice is the elusive goal.

REFERENCES

Adams, M., Blumenfeld, W., Castaneda, C., Hackman, H., Peters, M., & Zuniga, X. (Eds.). (2010). *Readings for diversity and social justice* (2nd ed.). New York: Routledge.

Alemán, E., Jr., & Alemán, S.M. (2010). Do Latin@ interests always have to "converge" with White interests? (Re)claiming racial realism and interest-convergence in critical race theory praxis. *Race, Ethnicity and Education, 13*(1), 1–21.

Anzaldua, G. (1999). *Borderlands/La frontera.* San Francisco, CA: Aunt Lute Books.

Anzaldua, G. (2002). Preface. In G. Anzaldua & A. Keating (Eds.), *This bridge we call home* (p. 5). New York: Routledge.

Ayers, W., Quinn, T., & Stovall, D. (Eds.). (2009). *Handbook of social justice in education.* New York: Routledge.

Bell, D.A. (1989). *And we are not saved: The elusive quest for racial justice.* New York: Basic Books.

Bell, D.A. (1992). *Faces at the bottom of the well: The permanence of racism.* New York: Basic Books.

Bell, D.A. (2004). *Silent covenants: Brown v. Board of Education and the unfulfilled hopes for racial reform.* New York: Oxford.

Berry, R.Q. (2008). Access to upper-level mathematics: The stories of successful African American middle school boys. *Journal for Research in Mathematics Education, 39*(5), 464–488.

Boyles, D., Carusi, T., & Attick, D. (2009). Historical and critical interpretations of social justice. In W. Ayers, T. Quinn, & D. Stovall (Eds.), *Handbook of social justice in education* (pp. 30–42). New York: Routledge.

Chapman, T.K. (2007). Interrogating classroom relationships and events: Using portraiture and critical race theory in education research. *Educational Researcher, 36*(3), 156–162.

Chapman, T., & Hobbel, N. (Eds.). (2010). *The practice of freedom: Social justice pedagogy in the United States.* New York: Routledge.

Clark, J. (2006). Social justice, education, and schooling: Some social justice issues. *British Journal of Educational Studies, 54*(3), 272–287.

Collins, P.H. (1998). *Fighting words: Black women and the search for justice.* Minneapolis: University of Minnesota Press.

Crenshaw, K. (1995). Mapping the margins: Intersectionality, identity politics, and violence against women of color. In K. Crenshaw, N. Gotanda, G. Peller, & K. Thomas (Eds.), *Critical race theory: The key writings that formed a movement* (pp. 357–383). New York: New Press.

Crenshaw, K. (2002). The first decade: Critical reflections or "a foot in the closing door". In F. Valdes, J.M. Culp, & A.P. Harris (Eds.), *Crossroads, directions, and a new critical race theory* (pp. 9–31). Philadelphia, PA: Temple University Press.

Crenshaw, K., Gotanda, N., Peller, G., & Thomas, K. (1995). Introduction. In K. Crenshaw, N. Gotanda, G. Peller, & K. Thomas (Eds.), *Critical race theory: The key writings that formed a movement* (pp. xiii–xxxii). New York: New Press.

Cruse, H. (1967). *The crisis of the Negro intellectual.* New York: William Morrow & Co.

Culp, J.M., Jr. (2000). Autobiography and legal scholarship and teaching: Finding the me in the legal academy. In R. Delgado & J. Stefancic (Eds.), *Critical race theory: The cutting edge* (2nd ed., pp. 487–496). Philadelphia, PA: Temple University Press.

Davis, A. (1990). *Women, culture and politics.* New York: New Vintage Books.

DeCuir-Gunby, J.T. (2007). Negotiating identity in a bubble: A critical race analysis of African American high school students' experiences in an elite, independent school. *Equity and Excellence in Education, 40*(1), 26–35.

Delgado, R., & Stefancic, J. (Eds.). (2000). *Critical theory: The cutting edge* (2nd ed.). Philadelphia, PA: Temple University Press.

Delgado Bernal, D., & Villalpando, O. (2002). An apartheid of knowledge in academia: The struggle over the "legitimate" knowledge of faculty of color. *Equity and Excellence in Education, 35*(2), 169–180.

Dixson, A.D., & Dingus, J.E. (2007). Tyranny of the majority: Re-enfranchisement of African-American teacher educators teaching for democracy. *International Journal of Qualitative Studies in Education (QSE), 20*(6), 639–654.

Du Bois, W.E.B. (1904/1999). *The souls of Black folks* (H.L. Gates and T.H. Oliver, Eds.). New York: W.W. Norton & Co.

Duncan, G.A. (2002). Beyond love: A critical race ethnography of the schooling of adolescent Black males. *Equity and Excellence in Education, 35*(2), 131.

Evans, A.E. (2007). School leaders and their sensemaking about race and demographic change. *Educational Administration Quarterly, 43*(2), 159–188.

Gillborn, D. (2006). Critical race theory and education: Racism and anti-racism in educational theory and praxis. *Discourse: Studies in the Cultural Politics of Education, 27*(1), 11–32.

Hull, G., & Smith, B. (1982). Introduction. In G. Hull, P.B. Scott, & B. Smith (Eds.), *All the women are White, all the men are Black, but some of us are brave* (pp. xvii–xxxi). New York: Feminist Press.

Lawrence, C. (2002). Foreword: Who are we? And why are we here? Doing critical race theory in hard times. In F. Valdes, J.M. Culp, & A.P. Harris (Eds.), *Crossroads, directions, and a new critical race theory*. Philadelphia, PA: Temple University Press.

Lynn, M. (2002). Critical race theory and the perspectives of Black men teachers in the Los Angeles public schools. *Equity and Excellence in Education, 35*(2), 119.

Matsuda, M. (1986). Liberal jurisprudence and abstracted visions of human nature: A feminist critique of Rawls' theory of justice. *New Mexico Law Review, 16*, 613–624.

McCray, C.R., Wright, J.V., & Beachum, F.D. (2007). Beyond Brown: Examining the perplexing plight of African American principals. *Journal of Instructional Psychology, 34*(4), 247–255.

McKay, C.L. (2010). Community education and critical race praxis: The power of voice. *Educational Foundations, 24*(1/2), 25–38.

Morris, J.E. (2001). Forgotten voices of Black educators: Critical race perspectives on the implementation of a desegregation plan. *Educational Policy, 15*(4), 575.

Parker, L., & Stovall, D.O. (2004). Actions following words: Critical race theory connects to critical pedagogy. *Educational Philosophy and Theory, 36*(2), 167–182.

Rawls, J. (1972). *A theory of justice*. Cambridge, MA: Harvard University Press.

Su, J.A., & Yamamoto, E.K. (2002). Critical coalitions: Theory and practice. In F. Valdes, J.M. Culp, & A.P. Harris (Eds.), *Crossroads, directions, and a new critical race theory* (pp. 379–392). Philadelphia, PA: Temple University Press.

Tate, W.F. (1997). Critical race theory and education: History, theory, and implications. *Review of Research in Education, 22*, 191–243.

Valdes, F., Culp, J.M., & Harris, A.P. (2002). Introduction: Battles waged, won, and lost: Critical race theory at the turn of the millennium. In F. Valdes, J.M. Culp, & A.P. Harris (Eds.), *Crossroads, directions, and a new critical race theory* (pp. 1–6). Philadelphia, PA: Temple University Press.

Williams, R., Jr. (2000). Vampires anonymous and critical race practice. In R. Delgado and J. Stefancic (Eds.), *Critical race theory: The cutting edge* (2nd ed., pp. 614–622). Philadelphia, PA: Temple University Press.

Wing, A.K. (Ed.). (2000). *Global critical race feminism: An international reader*. New York: New York University Press.

8

DOING CLASS IN CRITICAL RACE ANALYSIS IN EDUCATION

Michael J. Dumas

Village Voice columnist Greg Tate, in his commentary on the lack of Black involvement in the Occupy Wall Street (OWS) movement, quotes one of the young Black men he spoke to, who told him, "I ain't about to go get arrested with some muhfuhkuhs who just figured out yesterday that this shit ain't right" (Tate, 2011). For Tate, this young man's reluctance to participate in the nascent movement reflects a broader wariness among African Americans about social analyses and political action which seemingly have little to say—at least explicitly—about race and racism. Implicit in this critique is a sense that White people are just beginning to resist state policies, corporate interests, and hegemonic cultural-ideological logics that have long wreaked havoc in Black communities. The problem, as these skeptical observers see it, is that, in reframing the debate solely in terms of class, in which the so-called 99 percent stand in solidarity against the abuses of the economically elite 1 percent, supporters of the OWS movement collapse the 99 percent in ways that ignore differential access to economic and political resources, delegitimize race-based appeals for social redress, privilege the interests and voices of those (middle-class Whites) most recently hurt by inequitable policies and practices, and problematically posit class dominance as more disastrous, more explanatory, and more material than racial dominance.

Historically, Black people have understood their oppression—including their economic oppression—through the lens of race. Thus race and racism are situated at the center of Black popular analyses of the social policies and everyday institutional and cultural practices that so heavily inform Black life and Black life chances (Cohen, 1999; Dawson, 1994, 2001; Gordon, 2000; Marable & Mullings, 1994). As the young man quoted by Tate points out, "shit ain't [never been] right" for Black people in the United States. Black unemployment has consistently been double that of White US citizens. Housing and employment discrimination on the basis of race has long been codified in a number of federal, state, and local policies (Massey & Denton, 1993; Wilson, 1997, 2009). Access to well-resourced schools has been a struggle since the end of slavery, with stark differences between the educational opportunities available to Black and White children and young adults (Anderson, 1988; Walker, 1996; Watkins, 2001). For most African Americans, the latest economic downturn may have exacerbated, but did not mark the beginning of, their social and financial woes, or serve as their first awareness of how powerful corporate and state interests collude in social policy. For this young man, that so many of the 99 percent appear in the streets only now, and with such newfound surprise and dismay, only highlights their whiteness, and all the privilege and naiveté that that connotes (Leonardo & Porter, 2010). As Greg Tate (2011) notes in his piece, "Black folk got wise to the game back in 1865 when we realized neither 40 acres nor a mule would be forthcoming."

Critical race theory (CRT), consistent with this popular-cultural imagination, situates race at the center of social analysis. Differences such as social class, gender, ethnicity, and language are acknowledged, and understood as dimensions of intersectionality that impact how race shapes policy and everyday life; however, race is the primary object of analysis, and explanations of social phenomena are primarily offered through a racial lens. That is to say, in CRT, inquiry revolves around understanding how race and racism work in the formation and implementation of social policy, and how racist (or White supremacist) ideologies act to establish and continually justify the political and moral "rightness" of these policies.

As we have witnessed an increase in CRT scholarship in education, it has become subject to critique from Marxian[1] scholars, who argue that CRT problematically prioritizes race over class, fails to account for the political-economic foundations of racial inequities and racialized processes, and focuses on White supremacy as the explanation for the persistent oppression of people of color, without due attention to the impact of capitalism and market forces. Some of these critics have argued that, in their advancement of the notion of race, CRT scholars only lend credence to a discredited construct, and reinforce essentialist understandings of racial identity that misstate and perhaps romanticize racial collective identification. Further, they would contend, such investment in viewing the world through the lens of race undermines efforts to imagine a politics that transcends the "false" boundaries of race and moves toward a more material, and therefore "real," politics that brings *all* poor and working people together in solidarity to struggle for more equitable social and economic conditions. Ultimately, for Marxian scholars, CRT may usefully highlight racial dimensions of social inequality, but its race-based analyses and solutions miss the (material) point (Cole, 2009, 2011; Darder & Torres, 2009).

Critical race theorists have responded to these critiques in a number of ways, challenging what they contend are a number of reductionist misrepresentations of CRT, and reasserting the need to interrogate White supremacy as a "totalizing" frame for understanding racism, akin to the scrutiny of capitalism in critical class analyses.

In this chapter, rather than attempting to resolve this contentious debate, or somehow pick a "winner" between race and class, I highlight the primary tensions between Marxian and critical race approaches. Drawing on this discussion, I offer some persistent and emerging challenges for critical race theorists who wish to richly and incisively take up and explain class within decidedly *racial* policy analyses that—and this is important—are situated within and aim to inform a broader leftist project. In short, how do we sustain a critical race theory that speaks in radical ways about class in policy discussions of what "ain't right" in the lives of people of color in general and, more specifically here, in the lives of Black people?

THE MARXIAN CRITIQUE OF CRITICAL RACE THEORY

The Marxian critique of CRT, it must be said at the outset, is not a denial of the political and economic significance of race and racism, or an attempt to dismiss the validity of anti-racist theorizing and activism. In fact, as I will explain below, Marxian scholars account for race as a social construct, and racism as an oppressive practice, within the framework of their critique of capitalism. However, this is not to say that their analysis of race and racism is necessarily satisfactory or adequate. To be sure, as we shall see in the response from critical race scholars, there may be reason to doubt the capacity of Marxian theory to fully explain or even acknowledge certain dimensions of racism; at very least, to say that Marxian theory addresses race is not to say that it addresses it in a manner or to the extent that critical race scholars believe necessary. Indeed, many Black Marxists have contended that Marxism must address racism as an integral part of its project, and have critiqued the racism of White workers as an impediment to socialist revolution (Du Bois, 1935/1998; Kelley, 2002; Robinson, 1983/2000). My point here is that the contention between Marxian and critical race scholars is not a matter of choosing between race and class, but of how to best explain the relationship between race and class, and how to situate and engage race and racism within a critical social critique and political praxis.

The Marxian critique in education has been expressed most prominently in the US by Antonio Darder and Rodolfo Torres (2004, 2009) and in the UK by Mike Cole (2009, 2011) and Dave Hill (2009). Here, I use their writings to enumerate the primary Marxian contentions with CRT, fully cognizant that there may be other critics and critiques that might be mentioned. However, these are Marxian critiques from within the field of education, so it makes sense to highlight them in this chapter. Also, the texts discussed here are the ones referred to most often in responses from critical race scholars.

First, Marxian scholars argue that CRT erroneously assumes that race provides a totalizing explanation for persistent social inequities equal to or in place of class. For Marxian scholars, the foundation of social inequities is rooted in capitalism, in the political economy, and in class exploitation. Class is central, global, and pervasive in ways that make it exceptional, and exceptionally capable of explaining the human condition, oppression, and the very idea of freedom. Darder and Torres see "power as unrelentingly anchored in external material conditions" (2009, p. 152). For them, race (or gender or sexuality) simply does not "have the same meaning or constitutive power" (p. 161). As they explain, "It is the *material* domination and exploitation of populations, in the interest of perpetuating a deeply entrenched capitalist system of world dominion, which serves as the impetus for the construction of social formations of inequality" (p. 160). In the view of Darder and Torres, a theory which helps us understand systems of power, and their material effects in the world, on human populations, must be regarded as transcending, as "more total" than, a theory which revolves around a social construction, a fiction that is not, in the end, real.

For Mike Cole, although CRT offers important social insights, it cannot provide the kind of comprehensive analysis or program of political action needed to combat capital. CRT is not, in his estimation, "up to such a gargantuan task" (2009, p. 119), because it is not situated in a class analysis, but instead seeks to offer a project of anti-racism as if race is its own totalizing system. For Marxists, Cole contends, "the debate between class *or* racism becomes redundant, in that … the struggle is against racialized (and gendered) capitalism" (2009, p. 37). In this sense, class becomes the broader framework within which race means or effects anything.

Second, and proceeding from this point, Marxian scholars critique CRT because it fails to theorize capitalism as a force in the construction of race and operationalization of racism. Two points need to be made here, one about race and racism, and the other related to theorizing capitalism. Marxian scholars suggest that, once we acknowledge that race is a social construction, we need to understand that racism is intended to exploit and dominate those marked as "Other" for the benefit of capitalists. As Darder and Torres (2004) note, "Racism is one of the primary ideologies by which material conditions in society are organized and perpetuated in the service of capitalist accumulation" (p. 101).

Marxian theorists would emphasize that this stands in contrast to class, which unlike race "is more than a constructed category. It refers to real, historical, material relations. The social mechanisms that give rise to the various historical expressions of 'racism' lie deep in class relations" (Banfield, quoted in Hill, 2009, p. 25). If indeed racism is founded in class relations, and in the logics and institutions of capital, then any analysis of the construct of race or institutional and cultural practices of racism must be based in a class critique. Put another way, in Marxian analysis, discussion of race is only critical, and only makes sense, when racism is understood as a powerful instantiation of capitalism.

Given the relationship between racism and capitalism in a Marxian framework, it becomes imperative to theorize how capital works in processes of racialization and racial exploitation and violence. For Marxian scholars, such theorizing is absent in CRT, and this limits the ability of CRT to effectively and fully explain just what is happening racially in the world. While they acknowledge that CRT scholarship makes some mention of social class, these references are "generally vague and undertheorized." Thus, CRT has "done little to further our understanding of the political economy of racism and racialization" (Darder & Torres, 2004, p. 99).

Rather—and this brings us to the third critique—in CRT, class is most often presented as a dimension of intersectionality, in which class (alongside such categories as nationality, gender, and ability) is a social identity and descriptor of personal life experience, rather than a pervasive and structural exercise of the power of capital. Intersectionality has been advanced within CRT as a way to capture the dynamic relationships between race and other "differences," including gender, sexual identity, disability, and, of course, social class (Crenshaw, 1995). However, as should be clear by now, Marxian scholars reject the idea that class is an identity akin to a range of countless others which might be put forth. Not only does this deny the powerful structural dimensions of class, but it also dangerously mischaracterizes the relationship of social class to other differences, which, for Marxian scholars, are all constituted and serve their oppressive functions within (and not aside from or in addition to) capitalism. As Darder and Torres explain, intersectionality "ignores the fact that notions of identity result from a process of identification with a particular configuration of historically lived or transferred social arrangements and practices tied to material conditions of actual or imagined survival" (2004, p. 106). In shifting our focus to race, they argue, CRT furthers an identity-based politics that "glosses over class differences and/or ignores class contradictions, in an effort to build a political base" (p. 106). The problem for Marxian scholars is that this serves to separate the political and economic into two separate and independently operational spheres, which only obscures and deemphasizes class relations in capitalist societies.

Fourth, Marxian scholars are concerned that CRT's focus on White supremacy reifies racial identities in ways that legitimize broad generalizations about Whites that fail to account for the ethnic and economic diversity within this population, and ignore the significance of class differences amongst people of color. Mike Cole argues that the concept of White supremacy, as employed in CRT, conflates the differences among White people. For Cole, "White supremacy" suggests that all White people wield the power of being White, regardless of class or ethnicity, which positions Whites differently in relation to the modes of production. Further, Cole maintains, while Marxists fully acknowledge racism across hundreds of years, White supremacy "does not in itself *explain* this continuity [of racism], since it does not need to connect to modes of production and developments in capitalism" (2009, p. 113). CRT scholars thus fall short in their analysis of the trajectory of racism, because White supremacy alone cannot account for its reproduction. Cole laments that, while Marxian analysis includes interrogation of racialization, there is no corresponding attention to class within CRT. Although some CRT scholars may indeed note the significance of class relations in their discussion of race, "there is no *a priori* need in CRT formulations [e.g., White supremacy] to connect with capitalist modes of production" (p. 113).

Darder and Torres (2004) contend that "White supremacy," in addition to naturalizing the "black–white binary" of race discourse, advances the flawed and (over)psychologized race-relations paradigm, in which racism is seen as an ideological or attitudinal problem that needs to be addressed through appeals to Whites. Their fear is that CRT, in its conceptualization of White supremacy, locates racism primarily in the ideological-discursive realm, as a matter primarily of combating ignorance and building multicultural understanding.[2] Instead, they argue, we need an analysis of racism that acknowledges the fictive nature of race, and the power of racial(ized) discourse, but keeps our attention on "the complex nature of historically constituted social relations of power and their material consequences" (p. 112). Racial inequities, then, are not a result of White supremacy pursued for its own sake—that is, for the advantage of Whites as a social group. Rather, they can be explained as a result of racism employed to foment agitation among working people and maintain the advantage of class elites.

Fifth, Marxian scholars argue, CRT counterproductively advances a racial-political project that undermines the possibilities of a truly multiracial mass solidarity movement among poor and working people. As noted above, Marxian critics of CRT worry that an emphasis on (racial) identity politics, and specifically a critique of White supremacy, serves to alienate working-class Whites who should be part of the alliance pushing back against the forces of capital. Indeed, Darder and Torres (2004) call for a new "cultural citizenship" which, contrary to a politics centered on race, "seeks not only to establish a collectivity in which no one is left outside the system, but [is extended] the rights of first-class citizenship" (p. 23).

Although CRT includes similar aims related to opportunity and justice, Cole contends, most of its proponents are far too vague about what the "struggle" or "transformation" is really about, or how to get there from here. He states, "no indication is given of what they are struggling towards, what liberation means to them, or what is envisioned by social transformation and the end of all forms of oppression" (2009, p. 117). Ultimately, for Cole, CRT, despite its consideration of class oppression, falls short of presenting a pathway toward realization of a radical vision because it has no inherent critique of class relations themselves. "While challenging the *oppression* of people that is based on their social class (classism) is extremely important, and is championed by Marxists," he notes, "the fundamental point is to also challenge the *exploitation* of workers at the point of production, for therein lies the economic relationship that sustains and nurtures the capitalist system" (p. 118).

THE RESPONSE FROM CRITICAL RACE THEORISTS

The essence of the critical race response to Marxian critics is perhaps foretold in CRT's emergence years ago as a critique of critical legal studies (CLS) (Matsuda, 1995). Although CRT shares with CLS a radical commitment to challenging normative explanations of power, rights, and justice, early writings in the field of CRT lament the marginalization and erasure of the voices of people of color in CLS, and detail CLS's failure to account for how racism heavily informs the public imagination of whom policy is for and whom laws are meant to protect. CRT scholars have also raised serious concerns about the tendency within CLS to engage questions of law only in the abstract, and not in solidarity (or even in dialogue) with oppressed communities at the center of the storm.

These same tensions reemerge in the more recent CRT response to Marxian critiques. First, CRT scholars insist that, just as capitalism is regarded as totalizing in analysis of class relations, White supremacy should be regarded as equally totalizing in the sphere of racial analysis and lived experience. As David Stovall (2006) argues, while socialist critique might emphasize, for example, that the majority of members of the US Senate are among the wealthiest individuals in the nation, "a CRT critique would remind us that this ruling class continues to be White" (p. 248). Stovall acknowledges that there are certainly individual people of color among this ruling elite, but "their actions as people of color in serving the interests of the conservative right reifies current racialized power structures in that those who control the resources and social status to which they emulate remain White" (pp. 248–249).

In his introduction to David Gillborn's (2008) book, which offers a critical race analysis of education in the United Kingdom, Richard Delgado notes that White supremacy has all the "structure of a conspiracy" (p. xv). Indeed, Gillborn spends the greater part of the book detailing how White supremacy in education is, ultimately, a set of "concerted actions" for a common purpose "always to the benefit of the racist status quo. It's a web of actions by teachers, policymakers, right-wing commentators, uncritical academics and the media—all working in one direction, day after day and to incredibly powerful effect" (p. 192). In this sense, then, White supremacy is, like capitalism, pervasive, invasive, expansive, and devastating in its ideological and material destruction—or, in a word, totalizing.

It follows from this that, second, racism is not entirely dependent on capitalism. It has its own logics, its own hegemonic frames, and its own material effects. Stovall notes that critics of CRT such as Darder and Torres insist that we need to focus on the material conditions of poor people of color, but do not acknowledge that these material conditions are just as much a result of White supremacy as they are of class domination (Stovall, 2006, p. 251). And, as Ladson-Billings and Tate (1995) explain, the problem with relying solely on a class-based (or gender-based) approach is that race is likely to be left untheorized:

By arguing that race remains untheorized, we are not suggesting that other scholars have not looked carefully at race as a powerful tool for explaining social inequity, but that the intellectual salience of this theorizing has not been systematically employed in the analysis of educational inequality … Class- and gender-based explanations are not powerful enough to explain all the difference (or variance) in school experience and performance.

(pp. 50, 52)

Although Marxian scholars would likely respond by pointing to their own analysis of race and racism, CRT scholars would contend that a Marxian approach is limited from the beginning in its theoretical denial of racism as a system of its own and not simply an ideological dimension of capitalist modes of production.

Third, CRT scholars push back against the assumption by Marxian critics that CRT situates all White people as equally positioned in relation to power. Gillborn, in his own work on the White working class in the UK, insists that critics are flatly wrong on this count:

CRT does not imagine that all White people are uniformly racist and privileged. However, CRT *does* view all White-identified people as implicated in relations of racial domination: White people do not all behave in identical ways and they do not all draw similar benefits—but they *do* all benefit to some degree, whether they like it or not.

(2010, p. 4)

Because they do benefit, even as they may be exploited for their labor, it becomes important to investigate how they become complicit, however unwittingly, in the system of domination. In turn, this racial analysis helps us understand more complexly how ruling-class elites employ race to legitimize and maintain their economic dominance.

Fourth, CRT scholars insist that, despite the claims of Marxian critics, CRT does offer a meaningful class analysis. Stovall (2006) points to Cheryl Harris's (1993) explication of whiteness as property as a prime example of CRT's engagement of social class. In her seminal piece, Harris offers a detailed historical account of whiteness as one of the most significant foundations of the US economy. Whiteness, she explains, accorded (White) citizens an important set of privileges in the market and in civil society, including the right to own (that is, to accumulate) Black people as one's property and, beyond that, to claim superiority over all other racialized groups in legal proceedings and everyday social interactions. Taking the *Brown* decision as one exemplar, Harris points to the Court's refusal to acknowledge whiteness as a form of material property that not only subjected Black citizens to (past) subordination, but also ensured that Whites would maintain and actually strengthen their hold on educational resources long after desegregation was declared unconstitutional. As Stovall (2006) explains:

"Property" in Harris' sense operates on material and social levels, expressed in common assumptions on race. Contrary to Darder and Torres's point on CRT as divorcing itself from the "realities of class struggle," it makes room for the realities of class while discussing them in the context of what race means historically and what it has come to mean in contemporary analysis.

(p. 249)

Within CRT, Stovall contends, Marxian class analysis is credited for its contribution, but is complicated by interrogating how racial myths of White entitlement, including the entitlement to exclude, facilitate the reproduction of class inequities. In this way, then, racism is not merely a function of class domination; we must also acknowledge that class domination serves to maintain and legitimize systems of White racial supremacy. (For a detailed explanation of the concept of whiteness as property, see Harris, 1993.)

Fifth, CRT pushes back against the Marxian tendency to view the politics of identity as merely an obsession with fictive notions of affiliation. In CRT, validating and nurturing racial identities are a meaningful and valid response to the experience of everyday life in racialized bodies and enduring the material effects of racism in racialized communities. Also, importantly, identity is a crucial frame through which people of color give voice to their lived experiences, and make sense of resistance against the forces acting against them individually and collectively. "To critique CRT simply as 'identity politics,'" David Stovall states, "ignores the necessity of narrative in developing coalitions across racial and class boundaries" (2006, p. 251).

In CRT, of course, counterstories are the primary way of articulating and developing a coherent (and ultimately collective) narrative. As Dixson and Rousseau (2006) note, "This, then, is the essence of 'voice'—the assertion and acknowledgement of the importance of the personal and community experiences of people of color as sources of knowledge … Thus, voice scholarship provides a 'counterstory' to counteract or challenge the dominant story" (p. 35). If the only "dominant story" were offered by class elites (and not also racial elites), Marxian analysis might suffice. However, from the perspective of CRT, White supremacy (again, as an equally impactful totalizing frame) necessitates a decidedly racial politics that, while eschewing crude racial essentialisms, embraces "the common experience of racism that structures the stories of people of color" (p. 35) and provides a way to organize their words into communities of resistance.

Finally, following from this, CRT rejects the assertion by Marxian scholars that CRT has no concrete or transformative praxis. Precisely because CRT places such a strong emphasis on voice, critical race theorists maintain, it is able to connect theory with everyday experience and politics at the community level. Stovall explains, "Through counter story we are able to discover the relationships between nuanced experience, individual responses and macro-policy" (2006, p. 253). In fact, Stovall offers a case example in which critical race scholars, informed by both CRT and socialist critique, have been able to work with a specific school community to initiate political resistance to educational inequities. In this case and others, CRT did not serve as an impediment to praxis, as some Marxian scholars have maintained; rather, it was a crucial piece in creating a theoretical synergy (of race and class) that facilitated action in racialized communities.

Gillborn (2008), writing about his own responsibilities as a White anti-racist scholar, notes that he uses CRT to help influence policy in the UK at the governmental level, and in strategizing for action with community-based and advocacy organizations. While CRT offers a cogent intellectual analysis of racism, Gillborn points to the extensive work on critical race praxis (McKay, 2010; Stovall et al., 2009; Yamamoto, 1997) to stress that CRT scholars "do not imagine for a second that an analysis of racism alone is a sufficient contribution to the struggle for racial equality" (2008, p. 202).

In calling for a "ceasefire" between class-based analyses and CRT, Stovall concludes that what it ultimately needed is for each side to acknowledge and incorporate the strengths of the other, not to win some academic argument, but to effectively respond to social and educational inequality. He states:

The social justice project in education will require the recognition of the interplay of race and class … Doing so will require those of the side of CRT to recognize that there may be intra-racial issues that need class analysis, while not separating them from the larger construct of White supremacy. Those who engage class analysis will have to recognize the dynamics of racialization in discussions of the ruling classes, in understanding that racism is not the sole byproduct of capitalism.

(2006, p. 257)

However, Stovall does point to what may be irreconcilable differences when he insists that "the dynamics of race inextricably identify a system of shifting hierarchies that are not married to a stringent interpretation of class analysis" (2006, p. 257). And indeed Mike Cole, in his critique of CRT, suggests that ultimately "Marxist conceptions of racialization … [have] the *best purchase* in explaining manifestations of racism, Islamaphobia and xeno-racism in contemporary Britain" (2009, p. 33, emphasis added). Surely, much has been written and will continue to be written about the (in)compatibility of Marxian and critical race analyses. What I wish to do in the final section of this chapter is bypass that theoretical wrangling, largely because I believe there may indeed be—if not clear contradictions—what we might call *necessary tensions* between the two camps. Mindful of those tensions, which I have detailed throughout this chapter, I want to identify some persistent and emergent priorities facing critical race scholars as we move forward, both in our development of CRT and in pursuit of a transformative critical race praxis.

CLASS-RELATED PRIORITIES FOR CRITICAL RACE THEORY AND PRAXIS

In an article in the *Iowa Law Review*, Richard Delgado (2011) worries that critical race scholars may have "failed to expand analytically or even to keep up with the times" (p. 1288). Here, he cautions that CRT, in an effort to attend ever so carefully to the diverse voices of people of color, has pursued intersectionality at the expense of analysis of the material effects of racism, and the broader exercise of power. He explains: "By itself, intersectionality does not mount a challenge to anything important. Moreover, in focusing on smaller and smaller units of analysis, you can easily overlook large-scale processes that are working to the disadvantage of large classes, say, workers vis-à-vis management or women vis-à-vis men" (pp. 1264–1265). I do not mean to engage his complex critique of intersectionality here. However, for the purpose of this discussion, I am taken with two ideas underlying his argument. First, strategies or analyses that may have made sense 10 or 15 years ago may be inadequate or even counterproductive today, given the shifting terrain of racial identities and affiliations and, importantly, changes in how ruling elites engage the politics of race for their own purposes, and in ways that have real ramifications for the life chances of people in racialized communities. In other words, there can be no CRT that is not also critical of its own historicity—that is not, in Delgado's words, keeping up with the times.

Second, Delgado points us toward the need to recommit to an analysis and politics that is as concerned about economic justice as it is about combating White racism. He insists, "Unless one dismantles both systems, white privilege and outright oppression of minorities, workers, and the poor, *class and racial lines will remain the way they are forever*" (p. 1287, emphasis added). CRT must, at its core, also offer a critical class analysis or it is, in the end, useless. This reinforces a point he made some years before, in the *Texas Law Review* (Delgado, 2003). Noting improving racial attitudes in the US over the past several years, he notes, "Yet the black–white gap in income, family wealth, educational attainment, and health and longevity is as great as ever" (p. 144). Lamenting a sharp turn toward discursive analysis of the social construction of race, Delgado calls on critical race theorists to "examine the relationship between class and race more carefully than they have done," with a focus on issues that "span race, class, and the profit motive" (p. 151).

CRT was envisioned as a leftist, activist intellectual project. This should mean that it is critical not only about race, but about class as well. Although this is certainly open to debate, I would argue that a CRT that has an inadequate critique of capitalism is not worthy of the name: Not only is it *not* critical, but it cannot even offer us a meaningfully transformative analysis of race. Even so, I believe we need a robust conversation about the meaning of "critical" in critical race theory, in which we consider the possibility of whether one can advocate radical action against White supremacy while keeping the foundations of capitalism intact. Or, put another way, how do we theorize—not merely acknowledge or address—class in CRT? What are our responsibilities here, if we understand that the lives of people of color are (also) governed by class relations, which are materially imbricated with race, largely through the (mal)distribution of economic and human resources (Dumas, 2009, 2011)?

CRT may also need to move toward greater sophistication in its analysis of middle-class people of color vis-à-vis poor and working-class people of color. This is not merely a matter of intersectionality, in which we readily acknowledge the diversity of racialized experiences. Instead, we also need to theorize what it means for a small number of people of color—including most critical race theorists!—to have a different relationship to the modes of production than the masses of people of color. Again, this is not simply about being culturally different, but also about being starkly different in power, in access to resources, and importantly in our (class) interests.

I am not denying what political scientist Michael Dawson (1994, 2001) has called "linked fate," in which Black people—and this may be true for other peoples of color as well—see their own well-being as connected to that of the racial group as a whole. I part ways with many, but not all, Marxists in embracing collective politics informed by notions of racial communality, even as I understand this communality to be fluid, indeterminate, and fictive (Dumas, 2010). Following Stuart Hall, I have called for a Black cultural politics of education without guarantees, in which we are constantly reexamining "our representation(s) of 'Black' in education to ensure that Black people have the freedom to imagine all that we now need (and need to *do*) at this historical moment in our struggle" (2010, p. 404). So I do in fact believe there are some ways in which Black people reasonably and necessarily see their fates as linked across social class.

However, I also fully agree with Cathy Cohen's (1999) assessment that certain Black political interests are more likely to be regarded as more valid than others:

> While there is a history of contestation around the definition of a broad and expansive black political agenda, one that includes issues affecting all segments of the community … the political issues that continue most often to be pursued and embraced publicly by community institutions and leaders are those thought to be linked to, or to conform to, middle-class/dominant constructions of moral, normative, patriarchal citizenship.
>
> (p. 19)

Thus, it becomes that much more important for critical race theorists to understand how Black class elites can shape and determine what counts as racial injustice, on the one hand, and, on the other, what issues are deemed to be—in Cohen's term—"cross-cutting issues," those that only affect certain, and usually marginalized, segments of the racial group. Cohen contends that the further we get from the Civil Rights Movement, the more our racial concerns become local and specific, and the more our experiences become less likely to be shared broadly over the entire group. I have a sinking suspicion that access to public education may become, if it isn't already in some places, one of these cross-cutting issues, in which the class interests of affluent and middle-class people of color lead them to very different analyses and engagement of the problem, and that, since they are more likely to hold the economic and political purse strings in communities of color, critical race theorists and activists may increasingly be called upon to highlight and address these divisions, and speak (class) truth to (racial) power even in the face of calls by these elites for loyalty to their self-serving notions of racial solidarity (Carbado & Gulati, 2004; Cohen, 1999; Dawson, 2011; Dyson, 2006; Marable & Mullings, 1994).

Finally, returning to Delgado's concern about connecting racial analysis to economic justice, we may be seeing a resurgence of critical race research that directly takes on persistent racialized economic inequities in specific spaces—a kind of convergence of CRT and (urban) political economy. Legal scholar Elizabeth Iglesias (2000), most notably, proposes the concept of "racial spaces" to explain how neoliberal economics reimagines communities as "networks of markets" to be primed for the flow of capital. Such racial spaces are both created by, and simultaneously the result (at least in part) of, White supremacy, which not only constricts where people of color can live, but also privileges White racial spaces for advantage in the "free" marketplace. Thus, neoliberal formations, while on the surface racially disinterested, attribute value to certain spaces, and lack of value to others, and ultimately contribute to patterns of development, marginalization, and exploitation aligned with the racial composition of different communities.

"Racial spaces," Iglesias explains, "are visible artifacts of both racial segregation and the relations of investment, production and exchange that are reflected in the export of capital; monopolies of political and economic power; and the restricted circulation of goods, services and capital within racially subordinated communities." With this conceptualization of the relationship between race and class—as both cultural and political-economic constructs—critical race theorists can offer a more incisive intervention at the point of analysis and then again at the point of policy intervention.

One exemplar in educational research is a study by Janet Smith and David Stovall (2008) of the intersection of housing and education policies in the Kenwood-Oakland area of Chicago, and how race plays a central role in determining the allocation of resources in ways that are ultimately detrimental to people of color, across lines of social class. Through their analysis, they emphasize how racism acts to powerfully inform policies and sense-making in the interest of Whites as a group, in ways that simultaneously, and by design, benefit ruling elites. "The argument is not that the developers in Kenwood-Oakland are racist," the authors conclude, "but rather that their contribution to a system of displacement contributes to a larger racist system, centered in making the city 'safe again' for its returning white residents" (p. 149). Importantly, in Smith and Stovall's study, the focus is not so much on the individual racial attitudes of Whites, and doesn't stop at deconstruction of racial discourses. Rather, they aim to impact how researchers, policymakers, and youth and community activists might improve the material well-being of people of color. The article ends with a series of concrete questions, informed by a critical race analysis, intended to push back against policies of containment that deprive working-class communities of color of educational resources.

Here, and in the best critical race research, we see an approach to the intersectionality of race and class that is far more than a passing nod to the significance of class. Rather, these critical race scholars incorporate class into their theorizing about race and racism, and explicate what their findings mean for critical race praxis. As Gillborn states, "Serious critical work on intersectionality requires us to do more than merely *cite* the difficulties and complexities of intersecting identities and oppressions, it challenges us to *detail* these complexities and account for *how* categories and inequalities intersect, through what processes, and with what impacts" (2010, p. 5). This is the work we need, to enrich an ongoing dialogue amongst critical scholars from varying traditions and, more importantly, to develop the knowledge needed to help our folks where they live.

NOTES

1 I use the term "Marxian" here to denote a sociopolitical theoretical orientation that emphasizes the inherent destructive material and cultural impacts of capitalism, views the relationships between individuals and modes of production as the most significant social (group identity) differentiation, and foregrounds a politics of struggle in which working people (i.e., those who make their living through their own labor, rather than the labor of others) must collectively unite to demand concessions from the ruling class, who employ physical force and/or ideological formations in order to justify their own class dominance, and exploit the labor of working people for their own economic gain. I fully acknowledge various forms of, and conflicts amongst, Marxisms and that many who agree with these basic Marxian ideas may themselves not choose to identify as Marxists, for a variety of reasons. For the purpose of this chapter, I chose the term "Marxian" because most of the critics of CRT have identified as Marxists, and/or have acknowledged being most heavily influenced by Marxian thought.

2 This claim that CRT does not engage the materiality of race is certainly refuted by critical race theorists. I will elucidate this later, in my discussion of CRT responses to Marxian critics.

REFERENCES

Anderson, J.D. (1988). *The education of Blacks in the South, 1860–1935.* Chapel Hill: University of North Carolina Press.

Carbado, D.W., & Gulati, M. (2004). Race to the top of the corporate ladder: What minorities do when they get there. *Washington and Lee Law Review, 61*(4), 1645–1693.

Cohen, C. (1999). *The boundaries of blackness: AIDS and the breakdown of Black politics.* Chicago: University of Chicago Press.

Cole, M. (2009). *Critical race theory and education: A Marxist response.* New York: Palgrave Macmillan.

Cole, M. (2011). *Racism and education in the U.K. and the U.S.: Towards a socialist alternative.* New York: Palgrave Macmillan.

Crenshaw, K.W. (1995). Mapping the margins: Intersectionality, identity politics, and violence against women of color. In K.W. Crenshaw, N. Gotanda, G. Peller, & K. Thomas (Eds.), *Critical race theory: The key writings that formed the movement* (pp. 357–383). New York: New Press.

Darder, A., & Torres, R.D. (2004). *After race: Racism after multiculturalism.* New York: New York University Press.

Darder, A., & Torres, R.D. (2009). After race: An introduction. In A. Darder, M.P. Baltodano, & R.D. Torres (Eds.), *The critical pedagogy reader* (2nd ed., pp. 150–166). New York: Routledge.

Dawson, M. (1994). *Behind the mule: Race, class, and African American politics.* Princeton, NJ: Princeton University Press.

Dawson, M. (2001). *Black visions: The roots of contemporary African-American political ideologies.* Chicago: University of Chicago Press.

Dawson, M. (2011). *Not in our lifetimes: The future of Black politics.* Chicago: University of Chicago Press.

Delgado, R. (2003). Crossroads and blind alleys: A critical examination of recent writings about race. *Texas Law Review, 82,* 121–152.

Delgado, R. (2011). Rodrigo's reconsideration: Intersectionality and the future of critical race theory. *Iowa Law Review, 96*(4), 1247–1288.

Dixson, A.D., & Rousseau, C.K. (2006). And we are still not saved: Critical race theory in education ten years later. In A.D. Dixson & C.K. Rousseau (Eds.), *Critical race theory in education* (pp. 31–54). New York: Routledge.

Du Bois, W.E.B. (1935/1998). *Black reconstruction in America, 1860–1880.* New York: Free Press.

Dumas, M. (2009). How do we get dictionaries at Cleveland? Theorizing redistribution and recognition in urban education research. In J. Anyon (Ed.), *Theory and educational research: Toward critical social explanation.* New York: Routledge.

Dumas, M. (2010). What is this "Black" in Black education? Imagining a cultural politics without guarantees. In Z. Leonardo (Ed.), *Handbook of cultural politics and education.* Boston, MA: Sense.

Dumas, M. (2011). A cultural political economy of school desegregation in Seattle. *Teachers College Record, 113*(4), 703–734.

Dyson, M.E. (2006). *Is Bill Cosby right? Or has the Black middle class lost its mind?* New York: Basic Books.

Gillborn, D. (2008). *Racism and education: Coincidence or conspiracy?* London: Routledge.

Gillborn, D. (2010). The White working class, racism and respectability: Victims, degenerates and interest-convergence. *British Journal of Educational Studies, 58*(1), 3–25.

Gordon, L.R. (2000). *Existentia Africana: Understanding Africana existential thought.* New York: Routledge.

Harris, C.I. (1993). Whiteness as property. *Harvard Law Review, 106*(8), 1707–1791.

Hill, D. (2009). Race and class in Britain: A critique of the statistical basis for critical race theory in Britain. *Journal for Critical Education Policy Studies, 7*(2), 1–40.

Iglesias, E.M. (2000). Global markets, racial spaces and the role of critical race theory in the struggle for community control of investments: An institutional class analysis. *Villanova Law Review, 45*(5), 1037–1073.

Kelley, R.D.G. (2002). *Freedom dreams: The Black radical imagination.* Boston, MA: Beacon.

Ladson-Billings, G., & Tate, W.F. (1995). Toward a critical race theory of education. *Teachers College Record, 97*(1), 47–68.

Leonardo, Z., & Porter, R.K. (2010). Pedagogy of fear: Toward a Fanonian theory of "safety" in race dialogue. *Race, Ethnicity and Education, 13*(2), 139–157.

Marable, M., & Mullings, L. (1994). The divided mind of Black America: Race, ideology and politics in the post Civil Rights era. *Race and Class, 36*(1), 61–72.

Massey, D.S., & Denton, N.A. (1993). *American apartheid: Segregation and the making of the underclass.* Cambridge, MA: Harvard University Press.

Matsuda, M. (1995). Looking to the bottom: Critical legal studies and reparations. In K.W. Crenshaw, N. Gotanda, G. Peller, & K. Thomas (Eds.), *Critical race theory: The key writings that formed the movement* (pp. 63–79). New York: New Press.

McKay, C.L. (2010). Community education and critical race praxis: The power of voice. *Educational Foundations,* Winter/Spring, 25–38.

Robinson, C.J. (1983/2000). *Black Marxism: The making of the Black radical tradition.* Chapel Hill: University of North Carolina Press.

Smith, J.J., & Stovall, D. (2008). "Coming home" to new homes and new schools: Critical race theory and the new politics of containment. *Journal of Education Policy, 23*(2), 135–252.

Stovall, D. (2006). Forging community in race and class: Critical race theory and the quest for social justice in education. *Race, Ethnicity and Education, 9*(3), 243–259.

Stovall, D., Lynn, M., Danley, L., & Martin, D. (2009). Introduction: Critical race praxis in education. *Race, Ethnicity and Education, 12*(2), 131–132.

Tate, G. (2011). Top 10 reasons why so few Black folk appear down to Occupy Wall Street. *Village Voice,* October 19 (retrieved from http://www.villagevoice.com).

Walker, V.S. (1996). *Their highest potential: An African American school community in the segregated South.* Chapel Hill: University of North Carolina Press.

Watkins, W.H. (2001). *The White architects of Black education: Ideology and power in America, 1865–1954.* New York: Teachers College Press.

Wilson, W.J. (1997). *When work disappears: The world of the new urban poor.* New York: Knopf.

Wilson, W.J. (2009). *More than just race: Being Black and poor in the inner city.* New York: Norton.

Yamamoto, E.K. (1997). Critical race praxis: Race theory and political lawyering practice in post-Civil Rights America. *Michigan Law Review, 95*(4), 821–900.

Part II

Intersectional and Interdisciplinary Methods to Challenging Majoritarian Policies and Stock Stories in Education

9

THE POLICY OF INEQUITY

Using CRT to Unmask White Supremacy in Education Policy
David Gillborn

… much of our policy making is evidence free, prejudice driven and hysteria driven (particularly hysteria generated by the press).

This startling assessment of how policy is made comes from *inside* the public policy-making process in the UK. The words were spoken by Paul Flynn, a Member of Parliament for the then ruling Labour Party and a member of the Public Administration Select Committee, i.e. a group of politicians *specializing* in issues of governance and law-making. The statement came as Flynn summed up the views of several senior politicians who had just given evidence about the policy-making process in their departments of state (House of Commons 2009, Q138). Flynn's summary stands in diametric opposition to the official version of policy contained in briefings, legislation, and official statements, where policy is presented as an almost scientific, neutral weighing of evidence to arrive at the most effective response to whatever "problem" is top of the day's agenda. Unfortunately, the very definition of what counts as "problematic" (like the assumptions that determine what counts as an "appropriate" response) is shaped by dominant ideologies, including widespread assumptions about race and racism in society.

Education policy has become a major focus of academic attention over recent years: at the annual meeting of the American Educational Research Association (AERA), for example, the number of sessions designated as relating to education policy increased by more than 600 per cent in less than 20 years.[1] In this chapter, I review the major concerns that have emerged as critical race scholars turn their attention to understanding education policy. The chapter begins with a brief note about the nature of "policy" and then provides a case study concerning Arizona statutes that directly address the question of racism and what counts as appropriate curriculum content. The case study offers a concrete example that illustrates several key elements in a CRT perspective on policy. This is followed by a consideration of three crucial CRT concepts: interest convergence, contradiction-closing cases; and interest divergence. These concepts provide the essential tools for a CRT analysis of education policy, that is, a perspective that radically challenges the taken-for-granted traditional view of policy as an incremental process moving toward greater justice and inclusion. CRT reveals policy as a central tool in the continuing struggles for racial justice against a regime of White supremacy.

WHAT IS POLICY AND WHO DOES IT?

"Policy" is one of those obvious terms we all use but use differently and often loosely.
(Ball, 2008, p. 6)

When most people think of "policy" they probably have in mind some explicit statement of government intent (such as a landmark political speech) or a formal piece of legislation. In recent decades, however, the analysis of education policy has become a major academic preoccupation; dedicated articles, books, and journals have multiplied and, with the increased attention, a more sophisticated and contested array of understandings has emerged. While some writers continue to focus primarily upon policy texts (such as legislative proposals, speeches, regulations, and the like), others have broadened their conception of policy to include not only formal texts and official pronouncements but also the wider debates and controversies that surround the process by which policies are shaped (see Rizvi & Lingard, 2010). Stephen Ball, one of the leading education policy scholars internationally, has expanded the concept to include multiple sites or contexts (where policy is produced, contested, (re)shaped) and forms of discourse (including texts and ways of speaking about particular issues and possibilities for action). This perspective, therefore, includes the widest possible spectrum of "policy," from pieces of national (and international) legislation to informal institutional practices which—although not written down formally—become what Ball calls "little-p policies" that nevertheless influence beliefs and practices. This is a view of policy that is self-consciously "messy" and uncertain, emphasizing that policy is dynamic, contested, and always in flux:

> we need to remain aware that policies are made and remade in many sites, and there are many little-p policies that are formed and enacted within localities and institutions … policy that is "announced" through legislation is also reproduced and reworked over time through reports, speeches, "moves," "agendas" and so on … Policies are contested, interpreted and enacted in a variety of arenas of practice and the rhetorics, texts and meanings of policy makers do not always translate directly and obviously into institutional practices.
>
> (Ball, 2008, p. 7)

Ball's observations are especially pertinent in the field of race and education, where policies are constantly contested and the passing of legislation is neither the start nor the end of the process by which policy influences the everyday experiences and life chances of racially minoritized students and their families. Many of CRT's insights are surprising, even shocking, to readers schooled in the traditional view of policy as a consensual and rational process of debate and compromise. I want to begin by looking at a real-world example of racism and education policy; this case provides a concrete basis for understanding the broader concepts discussed later in the chapter. The case involves recent attacks on Mexican American/Raza Studies in the state of Arizona.

A POLICY CASE STUDY: RACISM AND "RESENTMENT" IN ARIZONA: NEO-LIBERALISM BY LAW

Prohibited courses and classes; enforcement

A school district or charter school in this state shall not include in its program of instruction any courses or classes that include any of the following:

1　Promote the overthrow of the United States government.
2　Promote resentment toward a race or class of people.
3　Are designed primarily for pupils of a particular ethnic group.
4　Advocate ethnic solidarity instead of the treatment of pupils as individuals.

(Arizona State Legislature, 2012)

In May 2010 House Bill 2281 (HB2281) was signed into legislation in Arizona, effectively banning ethnic studies throughout the state (Martinez, 2012, p. 177). This was the culmination—but not the end—of a policy process that had been underway for many years. Augustine Romero and Martine Sean Arce (2010) explain that the establishment, in 1998, of the Mexican American Studies Department (MASD) within the Tucson Unified School District (TUSD) was the result of a grassroots community movement spanning several decades. The MASD pioneered a form of critical pedagogy that honored the voices and experiences of the Latino community and responded to the expressed needs and desires of the students. The formal outcomes of the approach were stunning:

students have outperformed all other students on the state's high stakes graduation exam and have graduated at a higher rate than their Anglo peers. In addition … students have matriculated to college at rate that is 129% greater than the national average for Chicana/o students.

(Romero & Arce, 2010, p. 181)

Despite—or possibly because of—these outcomes, there was a vociferous campaign against multicultural education in the state. One of the leading advocates for HB2281 was Tom Horne (now Arizona Attorney General). As Cammarota and Aguilera (2012, p. 5) document, Horne's "crusade" began when he was State Superintendent of Public Instruction (2003–11) with a promise to eradicate Arizona's remaining bilingual education programs. Horne's campaign grew into an assault on any program that centered the voices and experiences of minoritized people, viewing such courses as anti-American and anti-White. Predictably, the attack found favor in parts of the national media:

when an ethnically based education, which is bad enough, transmogrifies into an ethnically based education of grievance and oppression that vilifies the United States and anyone with white skin—well, this is simply untenable. And yet this product is exactly that which goes by the name Raza Studies and that Tucson blithely pushes.

(Julian, 2009)

Although Horne was the public face of the campaign, its success cannot be understood in isolation. The moves that led to the outlawing of race-conscious education (and the banning from the curriculum of books such as Paulo Freire's (1996) *Pedagogy of the*

Oppressed, Delgado and Stefancic's (2001) primer *Critical Race Theory: An Introduction*, and William Shakespeare's *The Tempest*) drew strength from the growing anti-immigration lobby in the US and the success locally of the libertarian Tea Party (Arizona Ethnic Studies Network, 2012; Cammarota & Aguilera, 2012). The entire process generated considerable controversy locally, nationally, and even internationally—Arizona's education and immigration statutes were condemned by United Nations experts as amounting to a "disturbing pattern of legislative activity hostile to ethnic minorities and immigrants" (UN News Centre, 2010, quoted in Martinez, 2012, p. 200).

The wording of the Arizona statutes is bold and revealing; the articles enforce a *neoliberal* world view as the only permissible basis for action. Neo-liberalism is a conservative perspective that stresses the importance of individual self-interest and free market operations as the basis for the most efficient and just form of society (Lauder et al., 2006, pp. 25–30). This view has come to prominence in policy across most advanced capitalist societies, but the Arizona moves enshrine it in a very obvious way. The supremacy of an individualistic and "color-blind" perspective is guaranteed by law where advocating "ethnic solidarity" is prohibited. Perhaps most revealingly, the fears and interests of White people are placed at the forefront of policy. In the public discussions by policymakers and in their official pronouncements, reference to "resentment toward a race or class of people" has been widely interpreted as an explicit attempt to protect White people (as a group and individually) from accusations of bias and race discrimination. In his official judgment that the TUSD was in violation of the statutes, Tom Horne (then Superintendent of Public Instruction) cited curriculum materials that included critical understandings of whiteness:

> These materials go on to state: "Anger, guilt, and shame are just a few of the emotions experienced by participants as they move toward greater understanding of Whiteness." If one were to substitute any other race for "Whiteness," it would be obvious how this promotes resentment toward a race or a people.
>
> The materials go on to state: "White Americans often feel a unique sense of entitlement to Americanism, partly because many never travel beyond the borders of the United States." All of these kinds of racist propaganda are fed to young and impressionable students, who swallow them whole.
>
> (Horne, 2010, p. 9)

Horne neatly conflates a critique of white*ness* with an attack on all White-identified *people*, seen clearly in his argument that, "If one were to substitute any other race for 'Whiteness,' it would be obvious how this promotes resentment." The key, of course, is that "whiteness" is *not* a race; "whiteness" (as discussed in the critical literature) is a form of belief, a system of assumptions and practices; it is not a description of a people:

> "Whiteness" is a racial discourse, whereas the category "white people" represents a socially constructed identity, usually based on skin color … many white subjects have fought and still fight on the side of racial justice. To the extent that they perform this act, they disidentify with whiteness. By contrast, historically, the assertion of a white racial identity has had a violent career.
>
> (Leonardo, 2002, pp. 31, 32)

Horne and the Arizona statutes, therefore, outlaw any critical commentary on whiteness and the actions of White-identified people as a group (historically and contemporaneously). Arizona's legislative changes make explicit what has already become routine (but less obvious) elsewhere in policy (including, but not exclusive to, education); the changes put the interests, fears, and feelings of White people at the centre of policy. In Europe, for example, recent years have seen growing controls on the wearing of face veils by Muslim women, which is now illegal in public places in France and Belgium and viewed as outside school dress codes in England (*BBC News*, 2011). The entire history of policy and debate on multiculturalism in England has been characterized by a central concern with the interests, feelings, and fears of White people, from the earliest decisions about the need to limit the number of "immigrant" students in any one school (for fear of upsetting White parents) to new requirements making English language competence mandatory for new citizens (Gillborn, 2008, pp. 86–89).

RACISM AS POLICY: SOME WIDER LESSONS

In addition to evidencing the role of policy as a context for the preservation of White supremacy, events in Arizona point to several important lessons about policy and the policy-making process.

First, although policy is often presented as a contest between high-profile antagonists, a critical race perspective highlights the necessity of taking a historically contextualized perspective. In this case, the continuing legislative battles are the latest skirmishes in a long line of moves and counter-moves as the Latino community campaign for racial justice against a White supremacist system keen to enforce a color-blind individualistic discourse that excuses (and even celebrates) White domination as the result of individual merit not systemic oppression. The establishment of the Raza courses was a huge victory for the Latino community, and the restrictive statutes represent a strike-back by the forces of White supremacy in the state. This highlights the constant tensions that surround racial progress (see below in relation to the "interest convergence" principle).

Second, heightened racism in public debate can operate independently of any legal success/failure. At the time of writing the legislative changes in Arizona are still subject to legal challenge. Regardless of whether the anti-Raza statutes ultimately stand or fall, the racist impact of the debates has been powerful and lasting—demonstrating with brutal clarity the realities of racial domination in the state. As Romero and Arce conclude:

> TUSD's Mexican American Studies Department … have, for the last two and a half years, fallen victim to acts by the state's Republican Superintendent of Public Instruction and the Republican led State Legislature … as a means of eliminating Mexican American Studies … with the intent of securing and perpetuating the American (and in this case specifically Arizona's) racial order. From our perspective, there is no other conclusion.
>
> (2010, p. 182)

Similarly, in the UK it is known that, whenever a mainstream politician (of any political party) delivers a speech about the supposed "dangers" of immigration, there is generally an increase in racial harassment on the streets (Ahmed & Bright, 2001). A further example can be found in recent moves in the US, by the Tea Party and others, to challenge the legitimacy of people of color as valid citizens for the purposes of voting. Although claims of "voter fraud" have yet to gain widespread success in terms of the number of states imposing restrictive voter ID requirements, the wider debates about "fraud" and demonstrations targeting or questioning voters as they attend polling booths in Black and Latino neighborhoods are unquestionably acts of racist harassment that will impact on voter numbers (see *ColorLines*, 2012).

Finally, the Arizona case points to the importance of follow-up in the aftermath of legislative change. The Arizona changes have been enforced through the credible threat to remove funding from schools that violate the new statutes; as a result, the ethnic studies courses have ended. As I explore in the following section, however, when legislative change is won by minoritized groups, in the name of race equity, the impacts have a habit of being much slower and more uncertain.

CRT AND EDUCATION POLICY: KEY CONCEPTS

Traditional mainstream approaches to education tend to imagine the history of policy as a series of incremental steps leading gradually towards improved attainments and ever greater degrees of equity and social inclusion. Critical perspectives, however, view policy very differently. CRT views policy not as a mechanism that delivers progressively greater degrees of equity, but a process that is shaped by the interests of the dominant White population: a situation where genuine progress is won through political protest and where apparent gains are quickly cut back. This section of the chapter looks at some key ideas that inform a CRT analysis of policy, beginning with two concepts coined by the late African American legal scholar Derrick Bell.

Interest Convergence

Edward Taylor (1998) summarizes the concept of interest convergence as follows: "The interests of blacks in achieving racial equality have been accommodated only when they have converged with the interests of powerful whites" (p. 123).

Interest convergence points to the *politics* involved in social change and—most importantly—the concept highlights the uncertain nature of even the most impressive-looking victories. For example, when reviewing the key civil rights decisions of the US Supreme Court, Bell shows how, in retrospect, these famous victories can be seen to have operated in much more complex ways than is popularly imagined. Although they were hailed as epochal victories that would change the social landscape forever, Bell argues that not only was their progressive impact uncertain and short-lived but, in the long run, their consequence may be to further protect the racial status quo. Bell argues (and subsequent examination of the public record supports the view) that the famous *Brown v. Board of Education* legal decision, which was hailed as ending segregated education, served the interests of the White elite by removing the most obvious and crass forms of apartheid-style public segregation, while leaving the fabric of *de facto* economic, residential, and educational segregation largely untouched (Bell, 1980a, 1980b; Dudziak, 2000). In this way, the US could continue to present itself globally as the home of democracy while engaged in a Cold War struggle with the Soviet Union to win economic and political allies in Africa. George Martinez (2012) views a similar process in operation concerning current federal challenges to the Arizona statutes; the challenges stress the needs of US foreign policy and overseas relations rather than any concern for the material inequities in Arizona (pp. 199–200).

The interest convergence principle is probably the most frequently cited concept in CRT, but it is prone to a great deal of misunderstanding. In particular it is necessary to clarify two key aspects, namely, the central place of conflict in the concept and the importance of social class distinctions in understanding interest convergence in practice.

First, it is vital to understand that interest convergence, as set out by Bell, does *not* envisage a rational and balanced negotiation between minoritized groups and White power holders, where change is achieved through the mere force of reason and logic. History suggests that advances in racial justice must be won, through political protest and mobilization that create a situation where—for White interests—taking some action against racism becomes the lesser of two evils because an even greater loss of privilege might be risked by failure to take any action at all. For example, the *Brown* decision may have served certain White interests, but it is inconceivable that there would have been any such change without the civil rights protests that brought the issue to the top of the international news agenda.

Second, Bell did not view Whites as a single homogeneous group, and an understanding of class dynamics was central to his own application of the interest convergence principle. Bell was clear that lower class White interests are likely to be the first to be sacrificed. Richard Delgado has described the interest convergence principle as a theory that "explains the twists and turns of blacks' fortunes in terms of the *class* interests of *elite* whites" (Delgado, 2007a, p. 345, emphasis added). In the original *Harvard Law Review* article that coined the concept, Bell wrote: "Racial remedies may instead be the outward manifestations of unspoken and perhaps subconscious judicial conclusions that the remedies, if granted, will secure, advance, or at least not harm societal interests deemed important by *middle and upper class whites*" (Bell, 1980b, p. 523).

The interest convergence principle, therefore, is crucially about an intersectional analysis of race and class interests. It views non-elite Whites as a kind of buffer (or safety zone) that secures the interests of elite Whites, especially when challenged by high-profile race equality or civil rights campaigns. The concept offers a critical way of understanding the dynamics of racism and social policy at key points, especially where a landmark event *appears* to have advanced the cause of race equality. The less well-known, but no less insightful, idea of "contradiction-closing cases" helps to explain what happens after the news headlines have died down and racism returns to its business-as-usual.

Contradiction-Closing Cases

This concept refers to shifts in policy that appear to address an obvious injustice; hence they remove the apparent contradiction between, on one hand, a clear injustice and, on the other hand, the official rhetoric of equality and fairness. However, the cases' long-term impact is by no means as progressive as is usually assumed. Richard Delgado and Jean Stefancic argue that a clear pattern tends to emerge:

> after the celebration dies down, the great victory is quietly cut back by narrow interpretation, administrative obstruction, or delay. In the end, the minority group is left little better than it was before, if not worse. Its friends, the liberals, believing the problem has been solved, go on to something else ... while its adversaries, the conservatives, furious that the Supreme Court has given way once again to undeserving minorities, step up their resistance.

(2001, p. 24)

According to Delgado, landmark victories may actually come to operate in ways that protect the racist status quo by ensuring "just the right amount of racism":

> Contradiction-closing cases provide the solution when the gap grows too large between, on one hand, the liberal rhetoric of equal opportunities and, on the other hand, the reality of racism.
>
> [Contradiction-closing cases] are a little like the thermostat in your home or office. They assure that there is just the right amount of racism. Too much would be destabilizing—the victims would rebel. Too little would forfeit important pecuniary and psychic advantages for those in power.
>
> (Delgado, 1995, p. 80)

These landmark cases *appear* to have removed the inequality, but in reality little or nothing changes. Indeed, such cases are sometimes used as yet another weapon against further reform, because they "allow business as usual to go on even more smoothly than before, because now we can point to the exceptional case and say, 'See, our system is really fair and just. See what we just did for minorities or the poor'" (Delgado, 1999, p. 445).

More than 50 years after the *Brown* decision it has been argued that US schools are even more segregated than they were at the time of the original case (Delgado & Stefancic, 2001, p. 33). Similarly, the most famous race equality case in recent UK history concerns Stephen Lawrence, a Black teenager stabbed to death by a gang of racist White youths (Gillborn, 2008, pp. 118–145; Lawrence, 2006; Rollock, 2009). After years of campaigning by Stephen's parents, a public inquiry eventually found overwhelming evidence of institutional racism across public services such as the police and education. The then Labour government instigated widespread changes in race equality laws behind the prime minister's claim that the Lawrence Inquiry Report "must lead to new attitudes, to a new era in race relations, and to a new more tolerant and more inclusive Britain" (*Hansard*, 1999, cols. 380–381). Unfortunately, the legal changes were rarely enforced and, in the face of widespread condemnation from race equality activists, a decade later (with Black school students still being failed by the education system and Black prisoners disproportionately dying in police custody) the official verdict was that the term "institutional racism" was no longer "appropriate or useful" (National Policing Improvement Agency et al., 2009, p. 12).

Interest Divergence

It is strange that so much attention has focused on interest convergence (which describes an exceptional set of social and political conditions) rather than its reverse, the much more common position, where racial interests are assumed to diverge. In fact, Bell wrote of the dangers of growing interest divergence in the same *Harvard Law Review* article that launched the concept of interest convergence (Bell, 1980b). It was Lani Guinier, however, who placed interest divergence at the centre of analysis when she addressed the reasons for the failure of the *Brown* decision to lead to long-lasting change. Guinier argues that interest divergence holds the key to understanding "racism's ever-shifting yet ever-present structure" (2004, p. 100). She places the concept at the heart of a critical perspective (which she calls "racial literacy") and views it as a powerful explanatory device in understanding how White supremacy is protected and emboldened through the creation and manipulation of apparent interest divergence between racial groups:

Those most advantaged by the status quo have historically manipulated race to order social, economic, and political relations to their benefit ... The racialized hierarchies that result reinforce divergences of interest among and between groups with varying social status and privilege, which the ideology of white supremacy converts into rationales for the status quo. Racism normalizes these racialized hierarchies; it diverts attention from the unequal distribution of resources and power they perpetuate. Using race as a decoy offers short-term psychological advantages to poor and working-class whites, but it also masks how much poor whites have in common with poor blacks and other people of color.

(Guinier, 2004, p. 114)

Although the concept has received less attention, the global economic crisis that began in 2008 points to the particular dangers of interest divergence, by which I mean a situation where White people imagine that some benefit will accrue from the further marginalization and oppression of racially minoritized groups. Just as Bell (1980b) and Guinier (2004) highlight the important psychological benefits that poor Whites draw from their sense of racial superiority (despite their own continued economic marginalization), so periods of economic downturn make interest divergence an even greater threat to racial justice. When economic conditions become harder, we can hypothesize that White elites will perceive an even greater need to placate poor Whites by demonstrating the continued benefits of their whiteness.

This form of interest divergence is clearly evident in the UK, where recent years have witnessed a campaign by politicians and the media to present the true racial victims in education as "White working class" children, especially boys (see Gillborn, 2010; Sveinsson, 2009). As a direct result, multicultural education programs have been cut and special programs targeted at supporting poor White students have multiplied across the country (Gillborn, 2010). In the US, the popularity of the Arizona statutes among White voters seems also to reflect a strong sense of interest divergence, especially where the Raza studies programs were delivering such positive outcomes for Latino students. The education statutes and related moves to increase the surveillance and routine harassment of people of color (based on the need to demonstrate their legal immigration status) also reflect this position in what Richard Delgado describes as a form of colonialism aimed at securing ever greater control over the Latino population as a means of preventing political control shifting away from Whites as they become a numerical minority in certain states (Delgado, 1996, 2007b).

Legal theorist George Martinez has taken these insights to a further level in his development of his "state of nature theory" of racial oppression (2010, 2012):

This theory posits that the dominant group tends to relate to racial minorities as if it were in a state of nature—i.e., there is a tendency to act as if there were no legal or moral constraints on their actions or to move to a situation where there are fewer constraints in contexts in which it deals with racial minorities.

(2010, p. 202)

According to Martinez's theory, the actions of White powerholders can be understood—and predicted—on the basis that they will tend to act in relation to their perceived "self-interest or self-preservation" and to adopt "an amoral perspective" when deciding on the most advantageous course of action (2012, p. 195). Hence, both interest convergence and divergence are wrapped together in a theory that makes sense of policy as a never ending campaign to secure ever greater control and benefit to White powerholders.

CONCLUSION

Critical race scholars argue for a fundamentally different interpretation of the role of education policy. Far from being a gradual movement towards ever greater equality and social justice, a CRT perspective on race and education views policy as at best acting to preserve the status quo and defend as normal the state of White supremacy. When calls for change become so great as to threaten the stability of the system, then (temporarily at least) the interests of the White majority are seen to converge with those of the protesting minority group and certain concessions may be granted. However, once the apparent contradiction between rhetoric and reality has been addressed, then the real-world impacts of the changes are reined in or removed completely. Far from advancing equity, therefore, a critical perspective views public policy as largely serving to *manage* race inequality at sustainable levels while maintaining, and even enhancing, White dominance of the system.

NOTE

1 In 1995 a total of 16 separate 'policy' sessions were listed; this rose to 99 sessions in 2012 (AERA, 1995, 2012).

REFERENCES

Ahmed, K., & Bright, M. (2001). Labour failing to meet pledges on race. *Observer*, April 22, p. 1.

AERA (American Educational Research Association). (1995). *Annual meeting program (AERA 1995)*, April 18–22, San Francisco. Washington, DC: AERA.

AERA (American Educational Research Association). (2012). *Annual meeting program: Non satis scire, To know is not enough, April 13–17, 2012, Vancouver, British Columbia, Canada*. Washington, DC: AERA.

Arizona Ethnic Studies Network. (2012). *Banned books list* (retrieved July 10, 2012 from http://azethnicstudies. com/banned-books).

Arizona State Legislature. (2012). *Arizona revised statutes, 50th legislature, 1st regular session, Title 15 (Education)*, chapter 1, article 1, 15–122 (retrieved July 10, 2012 from http://www.azleg.gov/FormatDocument. asp?inDoc=/ars/15/00112.htm&Title=15&DocType=ARS).

Ball, S.J. (2008). *The education debate*. Bristol: Policy Press.

BBC News. (2011). The Islamic veil across Europe (retrieved July 10, 2012 from http://www.bbc. co.uk/news/world-europe-13038095).

Bell, D. (1980a). *Race, racism and American law*. Boston, MA: Little, Brown.

Bell, D. (1980b). Brown v. Board of Education and the interest convergence dilemma. *Harvard Law Review, 93*, 518–533.

Cammarota, J., & Aguilera, M. (2012). "By the time I get to Arizona": Race, language, and education in America's racist state. *Race, Ethnicity and Education*, DOI:10.1080/13613324.2012.674025.

ColorLines. (2012). Latinos accused of voter fraud feeling the Willie Horton ill effect (retrieved July 10, 2012 from http://colorlines.com/archives/2012/04/latinos_accused_of_voter_fraud_feeling_the_willie_horton_effect. html).

Delgado, R. (1995). *The Rodrigo chronicles: Conversations about America and race*. New York: New York University Press.

Delgado, R. (1996). *The coming race war? And other apocalyptic tales of America after affirmative action and welfare*. London: New York University Press.

Delgado, R. (1999). Rodrigo's committee assignment: A skeptical look at judicial independence. *Southern California Law Review, 72*, 425–454.

Delgado, R. (2007a). Rodrigo's roadmap: Is the marketplace theory for eradicating discrimination a blind alley?

In A.K. Wing & J. Stefancic (Eds.), *The law unbound! A Richard Delgado reader* (pp. 338–355). London: Paradigm.

Delgado, R. (2007b). Rodrigo's corrido: Race, postcolonial theory, and U.S. civil rights. *Vanderbilt Law Review, 60,* 1689–1745.

Delgado, R., & Stefancic, J. (2001). *Critical race theory: An introduction.* New York: New York University Press.

Dudziak, M.L. (2000). Desegregation as a Cold War imperative. In R. Delgado & J. Stefancic (Eds.), *Critical White studies: Looking behind the mirror* (pp. 106–117). Philadelphia, PA: Temple University Press.

Freire, P. (1996). *Pedagogy of the oppressed.* London: Penguin.

Gillborn, D. (2008). *Racism and education: Coincidence or conspiracy?* London: Routledge.

Gillborn, D. (2010). The White working class, racism and respectability: victims, degenerates and interest-convergence. *British Journal of Educational Studies, 58*(1): 2–25.

Guinier, L. (2004). From racial liberalism to racial literacy: Brown v. Board of Education and the interest-divergence dilemma. *Journal of American History, 91,* 92–118.

Hansard. (1999). Prime Minister's questions, February 24, cols. 379–387 (retrieved May 3, 2007 from http://www.publications.parliament.uk/pa/cm199899/cmhansrd/vo990224/debtext/90224-20.htm#90224-20_spmin0).

Horne, T. (2010). *Finding by the State Superintendent of Public Instruction of violation by Tucson Unified School District pursuant to A.R.S. §15–112(B)* (retrieved July 10, 2012 from http://saveethnicstudies.org/assets/docs/the_opposition/Final_Supplement_to_Open_Letter_to_Tucson.pdf).

House of Commons (2009). *Public Administration Select Committee: Good government,* Eighth report of the session 2008–09, Vol. II: *Oral and Written Evidence.* HC 97-II. London: Stationery Office.

Julian, L. (2009). "Raza studies" defy American values. *CBS News Opinion* (retrieved July 10, 2012 from http://www.cbsnews.com/2100-215_162-4227721.html).

Lauder, H., Brown, P., Dillabough, J.-A., & Halsey, A.H. (2006). *Education, globalization and social change.* Oxford: Oxford University Press.

Lawrence, D. (2006). *And still I rise: Seeking justice for Stephen.* London: Faber and Faber.

Leonardo, Z. (2002). The souls of White folk: Critical pedagogy, whiteness studies, and globalization discourse. *Race, Ethnicity and Education, 5*(1): 29–50.

Martinez, G.A. (2010). Race, American law and the state of nature. *West Virginia Law Review, 112,* 799–838.

Martinez, G.A. (2012). Arizona, immigration, and Latinos: The epistemology of whiteness, the geography of race, interest convergence, and the view from the perspective of critical theory. *Arizona State Law Journal, 44,* 175–211.

National Policing Improvement Agency, Ministry of Justice, & Home Office. (2009). *Stephen Lawrence Inquiry 10 years on: Conference report.* London: NPIA.

Rizvi, F., & Lingard, B. (2010). *Globalizing education policy.* London: Routledge.

Rollock, N. (2009). *The Stephen Lawrence Inquiry 10 years on: A critical review of the literature.* London: Runnymede Trust.

Romero, A., & Arce, M.S. (2010). Culture as a resource: Critically compassionate intellectualism and its struggle against racism, fascism, and intellectual apartheid in Arizona. *Hamline Journal of Public Law and Policy, 31,* 179–217.

Sveinsson, K.P. (Ed.). (2009). *Who cares about the White working class?* London: Runnymede Trust.

Taylor, E. (1998). A primer on critical race theory. *Journal of Blacks in Higher Education, 19,* 122–124.

UN News Centre. (2010). Independent UN rights experts speak out against Arizona immigration (retrieved July 10, 2012 from http://www.un.org/apps/news/story.asp?NewsID=34663&Cr=migration&Cr1).

10

EDUCATIONAL POLICY CONTRADICTIONS
A LatCrit Perspective on Undocumented Latino Students
Nereida Oliva, Judith C. Pérez, and Laurence Parker

INTRODUCTION

Undocumented individuals living in the United States have found themselves excluded from many opportunities including a post-secondary education (Perez Huber & Malagon, 2007). While the exact number of undocumented individuals is unknown, it is estimated that there are 1.7 million undocumented immigrants under the age of 18 living in the United States (Annand, 2008, p. 685). Of those, an estimated 65,000 undocumented students graduate from public high schools each year (Gonzales, 2009) with a diploma and the hope that they too can have the same equitable access to higher education as their K-12 classmates. The undocumented immigrant population is composed of many nationalities and ethnic groups; however, the most contested policy debates have been around the status of undocumented immigrants from Mexico and other Central American countries. Broadly speaking, they are considered undocumented Latinos, and the U.S. public policy debate has voiced two polarizing and contradictory opinions about this group. On the one hand, they are viewed as hard-working, willing to take on labor intensive jobs (e.g., construction, farm work, food and hospitality service work), upholding strong Christian religious values centered on family, and valuing education; on the other hand, they have been portrayed as criminals, lazy, and unwilling to learn English or become American citizens, with high birthrates that threaten to change the U.S. population, who will drain public services and therefore should face deportation (Aleman & Aleman, 2012; Dávila, 2008). We can see evidence of this contradiction in President Obama's executive order to grant partial rights to undocumented students who have been in the U.S. for at least five years and have no criminal record (Love, 2012). Yet some states continue to limit the experiences of undocumented students as they face state legal barriers to citizenship through threats of arrest by local and state police, bans on educational opportunities at the K-12 and post-secondary levels, and denials of access to health and social services (Filindra et al., 2011).

The purpose of this chapter is to review Derrick Bell's (1980) interest convergence theory, critical race theory, and the major themes of LatCrit (Hernandez-Truyol et al., 2006;

Haney Lopez, 1996; Mutua, 1999; Trucios-Haynes, 2000–01), to explain and provide a perspective regarding how these two contradictory political positions are representative of how Latinos[1] are perceived in the U.S. In addition, we posit that these contradictory positions serve as a form of neo-racism or ethno-racism when one takes a critical lens and looks at the underlying ideology of current educational policy (Alcoff, 2005; Dávila, 2008; Goldberg, 2009). A liberal position on race and racism is that it is a horrible thing of the past that is now behind us and that we as a society can move past this history to have a truly color-blind society. This assertion is maintained by a concerted effort of racial denial and ignorance, but still maintaining the structure of White supremacy and racism in the form of the conflicting policy intentions (Soss et al., 2011). We argue that the debate concerning Latinos and undocumented students and educational opportunity is part of a larger and more fundamental struggle around interest convergence/divergence forms of racism in the twenty-first century, as Latinos, who now constitute the largest numerical minority group, are viewed contrastingly as an asset and as a threat to U.S. society (Cobas et al., 2009).

We will first briefly review the salient concepts that undergird CRT and LatCrit and make a connection to policy contradictions in education when one looks at Latinos in general and undocumented Latino students in particular. Legal scholar Derrick Bell's (1980) idea of interest convergence in CRT is particularly useful for theorizing how Latinos are seen in contradictory ways as an asset to the nation but as a cultural and social threat to the U.S. way of life. Interest convergence can shift into "interest divergence" when one applies this concept to educational policy issues and Latinos (Alemán & Alemán, 2010). Using the Latino undocumented student policy debate, we will then attempt to show how education policy agendas are partially set by a convergence of special interest groups and political events that can trigger a policy change either for or against Latinos (Dougherty et al., 2010), and that a LatCrit and interest convergence/divergence analysis of this change is necessary to see and understand the underlying roots of White supremacy in educational policy. We will conclude with a discussion of how the contradictions of educational policy issues for Latinos represent the next generational CRT/LatCrit shift to a different debate around race and racism, and what the federal and state governments should do to truly align policy interests for educational beneficial results for Latino students.

LATCRIT AND THE POLICY CONTRADICTIONS OF UNDOCUMENTED LATINO STUDENTS

As CRT has evolved, it has begun to take up new positions regarding the operations of racial discourse and its impact on law and policy with respect to persons of color and structural analysis of racism and economic disparities. One of the powerful strands that has branched off into its own unique powerful theory has been LatCrit. This movement has been grounded in the use of narrative storytelling as a tool to examine how other aspects of race, ethnicity, language, and national origin converge to "otherize" and politically disenfranchise Latinos/as in the U.S. For example, Haney Lopez (1996) argued for using a critical race lens to assess the experiences of Latino groups in the U.S. even though they include different ethnicities and nationalities. Haney Lopez pointed out that, under the legal construction of race and citizenship law, "White" has historically stood not only for members of the White race but for a set of concepts and privileges associated with it, while "Black" has been defined by the legal denial of those privileges. According to Haney Lopez, many Latinos don't occupy neatly defined racial categories: instead, they often stand at the intersection and cultural and national borders that defy assimilation into the total American mainstream. Mutua (1999) also cited the historical nature of the Black–White paradigm to show how Latinos constitute a broad spectrum of ethnicities and nationalities, but that certain aspects of their experiences in the U.S. have made them a racialized group subject to different types of racial discrimination, from the backlash against Spanish and the "English only movement" to periodic attacks on immigration (p. 1216).

A LatCrit analysis in education examines ways in which race and racism explicitly and implicitly impact educational structures, processes, and policy discourse that affect Latinos. Using the histories, research, and counter-stories of Latinos, LatCrit in education looks at places where racism intersects with other forms of subordination such as sexism or class bias. A LatCrit analysis in education acknowledges that schools and colleges operated in contradictory ways in terms of their potential to be oppressive institutions that marginalize Latino students, but also how these same institutions offer the potential of real hope and opportunity. LatCrit in education is grounded in an ethos of social justice and action for change, and there are major efforts to link scholarship to teaching and higher education to schools and communities (Alemán and Alemán, 2010). Finally, LatCrit in education explicitly relies on interdisciplinary analyses of race and racism to explain the everyday acts of racial micro- and macro-aggression directed toward Latino students (Solórzano & Yosso, 2001).

The duality of particular forms of racism directed at Latinos and the opportunity to pursue the American Dream through educational directives such as the No Child Left Behind Act of 2001 (NCLB) and the promise of educational accountability is contradicted by the oppositional political struggle over immigration and allowing in-state tuition for undocumented students who resided in states and graduated from state high schools (Gonzales, 2011). In addition some states have created smoother paths than others for these undocumented students to obtain higher education past the rhetorical promise of NCLB (Dougherty et al., 2010; Flores, 2010). For instance, in 2001 Texas enacted legislation that would allow undocumented students to pay in-state tuition rates. However, Arizona enacted Proposition 300 in 2007. Proposition 300 "prohibits students who are not legal residents from receiving in-state tuition rates at public colleges and universities" (Robinson, 2007). During the first six months that the Arizona law was in effect, more than 4,600 people in Arizona were denied state-based financial aid and were prevented from paying lower in-state tuition, or were rejected from adult-education classes (Hebel, 2007). Oklahoma followed this current trend of implementing laws that deny undocumented students access to a more affordable post-secondary education by enacting the Oklahoma Taxpayer and Citizen Protection Act in 2007. This statute requires all applicants for state and local public services and benefits over the age of 14 to have their immigration status verified.

Bell's (1980) concept of interest convergence and Harris and Ranson's (2005) tracing of the contradictions of educational policy in the UK present useful frameworks through which to examine the ways that educational policy in public higher education and K-12 public schooling often does contradict in ways that reinforce social class inequities and racial bias. Furthermore, this particular form of interest convergence and educational policy contradiction has a direct, deleterious impact on the status of Latinos in the U.S.

and how they are viewed politically and culturally (Dávila, 2008). The concept of interest convergence in CRT emerged in a 1980 article by Derrick Bell. He posited that we should view the *Brown v. Board of Education* (1954) U.S. Supreme Court ruling against racially segregated public schooling as not only a landmark case of a new era of civil rights progress, but also a strategic legal decision that had major global ramifications for the image of the U.S. Bell argued that the U.S. politically had much to gain in terms of global interest and image of a country that was finally making world progress in treating its citizens with equality after WWII and the continual racism faced by African Americans and other men and women of color who served in the armed forces and yet faced discrimination after the war. According to Bell (1980), the interests of African Americans in obtaining racial equality will only be tolerated when they converge with the interests of Whites; and Whites will still insist on more substantive privileges than African Americans through this interest convergence. Bell's thesis has undergone different interpretations given political changes that have occurred (see Guinier, 2004), but the central theme of interest convergence lends itself to understanding the ways in which educational policy contradictions and Latinos can be viewed in the interest both of Whites and of Latinos, but only when and if Whites will benefit more, and if Latinos are viewed as a threat then they will be targeted, particularly if they are undocumented students.

The second part of our analytical framework draws on the work of Harris and Ranson (2005) and policy contradiction in education. Highlighting examples of how the British government in the late 1990s and early 2000s engaged in a series of policies with the stated intentions of closing the educational achievement gap, Harris and Ranson documented the political rhetoric as to how the government would provide equality of opportunity for all students under a market-based neo-liberal policy ideology. But this was not achieved, in part because no efforts were really made to include the youth served by these policies as full participants in their development and implementation. Therefore, the policy contradiction process gave the appearance that the government was doing something about the problem. This policy contradiction process is one we wish to map on to the problem of the ideological goals of laws such as NCLB and the push for achievement and accountability for all students, particularly racial minorities such as Latinos, versus the higher education barriers of political and legal discrimination, particularly toward undocumented students. The contradictions of the education policy perspective create a duality of racism against Latinos. Dávila (2008) pointed out that Latinos in the U.S. are seen as a racial minority group that is not as problematic as African Americans or Tribal Nation groups in terms of their past racial history with Whites. Latino families have traditional values that appeal to White Americans, such as hard work, the value of family, and strong religious ties to churches. Furthermore, they are a valued part of the workforce economy of most communities in the U.S. and are becoming valued consumers to be targeted for marketing purposes. At the same time, Latinos are seen as a threat, because they are now the largest racial minority group in the U.S., they are seen as taking away employment and higher education opportunities from other Americans and as the source of the undocumented immigration problem, and they are blamed for urban ills such as crime and overburdening health and social services. Dávila (2008) argued that this type of policy contradiction is due in large part to the contradictory ways in which Latinos are viewed: they are valued for their hard work and sense of family and religious roots, but racially vilified in policy discourse and law because they are seen as contributing to a host of social and economic problems (e.g., immigration, use of Spanish, higher birthrates as the fastest growing minority group, crime, strain on social services). It is this current contradiction rooted in historical racial tensions in which we find LatCrit and interest convergence/divergence in education as a useful framework of policy analysis to interrogate its impact on Latino undocumented students.

Undocumented Immigrants in the United States: The New Terrorists

Dávila (2008) argued that the political and cultural debates around Latinos are shaped by a process she termed "Latino spin." This is a concept defined by media sound-bites, interpretation of public opinion polls by the media and politicians, and marketing management for corporate products. The "spin" process can take the dual form of projecting the image of Latinos as hard-working newcomers who embrace the American Dream or as clear threats to U.S. society and life. For example, the Christian values of hard work and family are seen as a plus for courting Latinos into the mainstream culture and assimilation. However, when there is a downturn in the economy and the job market is at risk, it is easier to blame the presence of undocumented individuals, making them the problem for the economic crisis. Such blame is transferred to the students by anti-immigrant associations who perceive undocumented students as morally corrupt, or even dangerous, modifiers, often associating them as criminals based on their status (Annand, 2008, p. 689).

In addition, Latinos are also at higher risk of being profiled as immigrants or undocumented immigrants. A research study demonstrates how between April 2000 and July 2007, Latinas/os accounted for more than half (50.5 percent) of the overall population growth in the United States, a growth of 29 percent and an increase of 10.2 million (Fry, 2008). Although the majority of undocumented individuals in the U.S. are shown to come from Mexico and Latin American, there are also a significant number of immigrants from Asia. The Asian American and Pacific Islander communities have had a 63 percent increase from 1990 to 2000, also making them one of the fastest growing racial/ethnic groups in the U.S. (Gonzales, 2009). However, when concerns are raised about the incoming undocumented populations, the common assumption is that of undocumented "Mexicans" to refer to all Latinas/os as the only people coming to the U.S. illegally.

As a result, undocumented students are often victims of multi-layered federal and state laws that aim to limit their experience in the U.S. The provisions and acts that bar undocumented students from having access to post-secondary education and financial aid are also discriminatory, as these services were available up until the 1960s as the demographics of immigrants changed from a Eurocentric body to a more non-White group (Alfred, 2003). As the number of undocumented people of color increased, laws were used to target this specific group in hopes of pushing them out of the U.S. (Olivas, 2004). The undocumented population (who happened to be of color) not only had to deal with discriminatory immigration laws that disproportionately impacted them but also had to face criminal accusations and assumptions.

LEGAL DECISIONS, POLICY AGENDA SETTING, AND RACIAL IMPLICATIONS OF POLICY DEVELOPMENT

Political context at both the national and the state/local level plays a major role in shaping the ways in which from a LatCrit and education policy contradiction perspective we can view the duality of undocumented Latino students being accepted on the one hand, but feared and facing discrimination on the other hand (Filindra et al., 2011). By looking at key legal decisions and then at the role of special interest groups in state level acceptance or hostility toward undocumented students, we will use these examples to highlight how racism undergirds policy decisions at state and national levels.

Plyler v. Doe

In 1982, the U.S. Supreme Court struck down a 1975 Texas law that sought to deny undocumented immigrant children a free elementary and secondary public education by charging them tuition to attend state schools. *Plyler v. Doe* (1982) was the first case that focused on educational access for undocumented immigrant students. While the Supreme Court focused this case only as a K-12 educational matter separate from issues in higher education, the case still represents a stepping-stone for educational access, as it was one of the first cases to care for undocumented immigrant students.

The Court in the *Plyler* case determined that undocumented children of unauthorized immigrants have the right to free public primary and secondary education. The Court held that states must show compelling interest for limiting access to education for particular groups, and there was no significant financial burden imposed on the state because of undocumented immigrants. The decision effectively rejected the claim that preventing undocumented immigrants from accessing education would be an effective deterrent to further illegal immigration. The Court indicated that education was not a fundamental right but acknowledged that depriving undocumented students of a K-12 education would create an "underclass of individuals." Therefore, a K-12 education was granted for undocumented immigrant children as a way to balance and avoid the creation of a new underclass in society.

Toll v. Moreno

Consequently, in 1982, the issue of access to higher education for undocumented students reached the U.S. Supreme Court. *Toll v. Moreno* (1979) was the first Supreme Court case that addressed post-secondary education for undocumented and foreign students. The Court ruled that the University of Maryland could not deny in-state tuition rates to "legal alien" status students, as:

> in light of Congress' decision in the Immigration and Nationality Act of 1952 to allow G-4 aliens to establish domicile in the United States, the state's decision to deny "in-state" status solely on account of the G-4 aliens' immigration status amounted to an ancillary "burden not contemplated by Congress" in admitting these aliens to the United States, and since, by imposing on un-domiciled G-4 aliens higher tuition and fees than are imposed on other domiciliaries of the state, the university's policy frustrated the federal policies embodied in the special tax exemptions offered G-4 aliens by various treaties, international agreements, and federal statutes.
>
> (Toll v. Moreno, 1979)

Article IV of the Constitution, which stated that the federal government has power over immigration policies, and that they are not left for interpretation by any state, supported the Court's decision. This court case "marks the first time that the federal government interfered with the residency policies of a public higher education institution and allowed a non-U.S. citizen access to in-state tuition" (Janosik & Johnson, 2007, p. 27).

Several years later, in an effort to regulate immigration, the federal government enacted the Illegal Immigration Reform and Immigrant Responsibility Act of 1996 (IIR-IRA). Owing to the ambiguity found in IIRIRA, states were given the right to give or not to give residency benefit to students identified as undocumented in their public institutions. The bill states:

> [A]n alien who is not lawfully present in the United States shall not be ineligible on the basis of residence within a state (or political subdivision) for any postsecondary education benefit (in no less an amount, duration, and scope) without regard to whether the citizen or national is such a resident.
>
> 8 U.S.C. § 1623(S) (2000)

As a result, the federal government could not interfere with any state legislation regarding in-state tuition benefits for undocumented students. In addition, undocumented students were not allowed to receive any federal or public funding.

Undocumented Students in Higher Education

Undocumented students usually enter the United States at a very young age with their families. In academic literature these students are referred to as the "1.5" generation. They are not first generation immigrants because they did not choose to migrate, but neither do they belong to the second generation, because they were born and spent part of their childhood outside of the United States (Gonzales, 2009, p. 7). Members of the 1.5 generation are left to navigate two worlds: one that is a distant memory and one that refuses to accept them. This generation has learned how to speak English and has adopted American customs. In addition, many are honor roll students, athletes, class presidents, valedictorians, and aspiring teachers, engineers, and doctors (Gonzales, 2009, p. 8).

Amaya et al. (2007) compiled a report on a conference and hearing that was held in 2009 in California to address the educational attainment of undocumented students. Several of California's politicians, community members, and students gathered to hear testimonies of those who were denied full access to a post-secondary education. Twelve students were courageous enough to make themselves vulnerable in front of hundreds of people and told their story. Students expressed their commitment and dedication to a college education. More importantly, students' testimonies "offered a human face to hundreds of thousands of undocumented high school and college students throughout the state and nation" (Amaya et al., 2007, p. 3). Research focused on the experiences of undocumented college students would not be as insightful without student voices.

Diaz-Strong and Meiners (2007) have contributed to the research arena of undocumented students in higher education by conducting a study on the experiences of undocumented students in Chicago. Their study found that the undocumented students in their study often faced trouble with immigration policies. For many, it took years for their residency paperwork to be completely processed. Because of the long period of time between when the papers were submitted and when they were processed, some of the students were not able to establish residency. Furthermore, the study showed that students were sometimes "unmotivated" to go to college because of their status. However, students found support in family members and teachers to continue their education after high school. It was also found that students received little support from high school counselors.

Students' major concerns were found to be lack of financial resources and the uncertainty of their futures. Because of their status, undocumented students are ineligible for federal grants or loans and are not permitted to legally work; thus they cannot afford the cost of college tuition (Connolly, 2005, p. 206). Some students in the study considered going back to their home country or to another country where they would be able to put their knowledge into practice, because their college degree in the U.S. could not be used unless they had legal work authorization (Annand, 2008). Despite the immigration policies and other policies that infiltrate the lives of undocumented students, the study showed their continuous resiliency to continue their education, with hopes of one day being legally able to work in the U.S.

Contreras (2009) also conducted a study on the experiences of undocumented students in higher education in Washington state. Similar to Diaz-Strong and Meiners (2007), Contreras found commonalities among the students' experiences. The themes that were found through her study were:

1 the pervasive presence of fear in the lives of undocumented students and their families, especially regarding the prospect of separation;
2 the financial difficulty of paying for college with limited access to financial aid;
3 campus experiences that were often discriminatory, as well as exposure to resources and supportive individuals whom students could trust to help them navigate the college;
4 the will to persist, as seen in the determination to overcome challenges in their personal and academic lives as well as the determination to give back to their communities;
5 concerns about the future.

Students also expressed the need to not do anything that might attract too much attention in fear of being separated from their families. Moreover, students were hesitant to apply for scholarships, because several scholarships required proof of legal residency. The requirement to provide proof of legal residency was seen as a roadblock for students and made them feel that their presence in the U.S. was not wanted. The legal status of individuals has the potential to elevate levels of isolation and discouragement and incidents of discrimination by individuals who possess anti-immigrant sentiments (Contreras, 2009, p. 12).

DISCUSSION AND POLICY RECOMMENDATIONS

What the No Child Left Behind Act Means for Undocumented Students

Like many schools worldwide, U.S. schools are being altered by steady high flows of newcomers as children of immigrants tripled their share of the K-12 student population between 1970 and 2000 (Fix & Capps, 2005). The numbers have only increased in the last decade and will continue to increase. As for their U.S.-born peers, the future of immigrant children, documented or not, relies heavily on federal and local policies and practices. However, for undocumented children, their immigration status sometimes takes them on a different path that may limit their overall access to an equitable education. Dougherty et al. (2010), in their study of how legislation in favor of undocumented students being accepted into public higher education institutions in Texas passed but how this same issue faced a political backlash in Arizona, explained the different policy context as that of policy advocacy coalition building versus policy entrepreneurship. In each state, external shocks played a role in setting a political agenda, either for or against undocumented students. In the Texas situation, it was the politics of how education can be used to increase the human capital potential of an emerging workforce that can help the state economy, and the political power of the Latino legislative members in the state. In Arizona, the numbers of undocumented individuals and families coming into the state created a xenophobia against all forms of immigration and a push-back against immigrants by the state. A policy advocacy coalition approach also takes the view that change happens over long periods of time and that the special interest groups involved have a deep set of core beliefs about how citizens should be treated by state governments. This was more of the approach in Texas, which resulted in favorable legislation for undocumented students. On the other hand, as exemplified in Arizona, the policy entrepreneurship approach was in operation, with a coalition of short-term groups who developed common interests. However, it was not enough to stop the policy change in the state that led to the restrictions on undocumented Latino students attending public higher education.

These policy approaches in the case of undocumented Latino students can also be seen through the racial classification model of policy choice (RCMPC). This model was developed by Soss et al. (2011, pp. 75–82) and their analysis of how welfare policy worked against low-income African Americans in Florida. They developed this policy model to look at how policies that are seemingly racially neutral turn out to have racially deleterious effects in terms of how welfare laws are enacted and enforced, from the legislature and state agencies to the local bureaucratic agencies that administer state support. The application of the RCMPC to this issue reveals that theories of unconscious racism and racial schemas developed through cultural discourse play a role in the initial stages of policies designed to target a specific group. Furthermore, when the particular group (i.e., African Americans or Latinos) is salient in a policy context, race will be used as a basis for social classification to accomplish policy goals. Finally, if the overall political/social context views the racial group as a threat and there is a contrast between the racial minority group and the White majority, race-neutral, color-blind patterned policy choices become more likely, but with the effect being that racial and cultural characteristics are intuitively expressed by legislators through an implicit process of racial cuing.

When taken together, these two frameworks of policy enactment provide us with a lens with which to view "how" some states have restrictive laws against undocumented Latino students. As political battles over immigration loom larger, the context of how Latinos are viewed in the U.S., as an asset or a threat, serves as the "why" lens regarding how LatCrit and contradictory education policy analysis can be used to explain the deep-seated ideological roots of racism directed at Latinos but in contradictory and interest-convergent ways. Undocumented students, like those students with legal immigration status, have aspirations of continuing to a post-secondary education to make something of themselves and eventually to contribute to society and their community. But because of their status, which is "spun" by the mainstream media and shaped by political leaders in racially coded ways, this is not always an achievable goal when policy restrictions are placed on how far they can pursue higher education after the rhetorical promise of NCLB.

Given the political context of undocumented students, LatCrit, and policy contradictions, we propose the policy recommendations:

- *All states should support the version of the DREAM Act enacted by President Obama in 2012:* Make college accessible. This change in U.S. immigration policy allows for people who are no more than 30 years old and who were brought to the U.S. by their parents before the age of 16 to obtain renewable, two-year deferments on any action that could lead to deportation and to apply for work permits. This policy change is a step in a more socially just direction for undocumented students, as it potentially makes college access easier for them because of the previous additional challenges they face owing to their immigration status (Love, 2012).
- *History of immigration in the United States:* Acknowledge the history of immigration in the United States and racism toward Latino immigrants (Cobas et al., 2009).
- *Awareness of the growing undocumented student population:* Be conscious about the ongoing population of undocumented students and their contributions to society. This situation is exacerbated by the fact that many low-income Latina/o students are the children of immigrants and/or come from homes where English is not spoken, neither parent has attended college, and there is little knowledge about the formal educational system in the United States (Chavez et al., 2007; Valenzuela, 1999).
- *Additional resources:* Provide additional resources for newly arrived undocumented students without taking deficit pedagogies by acknowledging that the new incoming students are entering schools with knowledge. Conversely, students who attend segregated minority schools are likely to have fewer qualified teachers, weaker academic climates, poorer, non-English-speaking, and homeless peers, fewer gifted classmates, and fewer options to enroll in college preparatory courses than peers at racially balanced schools (Southworth & Mickelson, 2007, p. 498).
- *Graduation rate accountability:* The need to align K-12 and higher education accountability structures together under one governance structure as a way to promote students' college access by integrating federal and state accountability from the bottom up.
- *Inform undocumented students about their post-secondary opportunities:* Many undocumented students are under the impression that they are not allowed to go to college. As institutional contexts, K-12 schools influence the decision-making process of students as they think about whether college is an option and, if so, where to apply and where to go (Louie, 2005, p. 80). As undocumented students get closer to their high school graduation day, the pressure to make future plans arises. Some are determined to pursue post-secondary education and some do not see the point of continuing their education because of their immigration status. More-over, they are discouraged from considering post-secondary education because they do not have the financial resources to pay for tuition. Undocumented students are allowed to attend public and private universities and/or colleges. Advisors, college counselors, financial aid staff, and outreach support staff are all in the front line interacting with students; a critical element of their position is to assist students navigate college (Alfred, 2003, p. 628).
- *Become a social justice ally:* Teachers and school and university administrators are often at the forefront of efforts to support students on campus from subordinate

social groups as well as confront the negative oppressive behaviors of students from privileged social identities (Edwards, 2006). Teachers and school administrators have a lot of contact with students and can support their efforts in combating social injustices. Reasonably, teachers and administrators must also be aware of their own privileges to better understand some of the inequities certain students combat on a daily basis. When it comes to students, it is vital that teachers and administrators detach themselves from their own prejudices and biases to better serve the students. In addition, practitioners should also break away from campus culture that has historically oppressed certain groups of students. By becoming more aware and making a more visible effort to become allies, practitioners can help create a more socially conscious campus. This can also lead to continuous institutional efforts to advocate for the DREAM Act or for any other federal reform that will allow undocumented students to attend post-secondary institutions, work towards residency, and receive federal financial aid if eligible (Olivas, 2009).

CONCLUSION

As the growing estimated numbers of undocumented students are increasing, this population needs to be considered in the federal, state, and local context, at both the K-12 and the higher education level (Sharron, 2007; Stevenson, 2004). The educational future of this population depends greatly on federal and state policies and practices. There is a contradiction in laws such as No Child Left Behind and the rhetorical promise of no child being left behind that needs to be squared against the legal resistance of granting access to higher education in some states. Removing the deficit approaches that assume that undocumented students enter with no education and are less prepared than their classmates is rooted in a LatCrit analysis of how racism works against Latinos. In changing such policies to best support undocumented students we further conclude for such policy changes to be taken up at the federal and state levels to begin implementing these policies to challenge deficit ideologies on undocumented students. Instead, we support a true interest convergence and equitable change by providing additional resources in the K-12 level and supporting undocumented Latino students in higher education so they no longer face the epistemology of racial ignorance in educational policy.

NOTE

1 In this chapter we are using the term "Latino(s)" for political definitional purposes to incorporate all groups who have been racialized based on their national origin and language immigration bias based on their "Latino" cultural heritage (e.g., Chicano/Chicana, Mexicano/a, Central American, etc.). For more on this see Cobas et al., 2009).

REFERENCES

Alcoff, L. (2005). *Visible identities: Race, gender, and the self*. Oxford: Oxford University Press.

Alemán, E., Jr., & Alemán, S.M. (2010). Do Latin@ interests always have to "converge" with White interests? (Re)claiming racial realism and interest-convergence in critical race theory praxis. *Race, Ethnicity and Education, 13*(1), 1–21.

Alfred, J. (2003). Denial of the American Dream: The plight of undocumented high school students within the U.S. educational system. *New York Law School Journal of Human Rights, 19*, 615–650.

Amaya, L., Escobar, W., Gonzales, M., Henderson, H., Mathay, A., Ramirez, M., & Yamini, N. (2007). *Undocumented students: Unfulfilled dreams*. Los Angeles, CA: UCLA Center for Labor Research and Education.

Annand, K. (2008). Still waiting for the DREAM: The injustices of punishing undocumented immigrant students. *Hastings Law Journal, 59*, 683–710.

Bell, D.A., Jr. (1980). Brown v. Board of Education and the interest-convergence dilemma. *Harvard Law Review, 93*, 518–533.

Brown v. Board of Education, 347 U.S. 483 (1954).

Chavez, M.L., Soriano, M., & Oliverez, P. (2007). Undocumented students' access to college: The American Dream denied. *Latino Studies, 5*, 254–263.

Cobas, J.A., Duany, J., & Feagin, J.R. (2009). *How the United States racializes Latinos: White hegemony and its consequences.* Boulder, CO: Paradigm.

Connolly, K.A. (2005). In search of the American Dream: An examination of undocumented students, in-state tuition, and the DREAM Act. *Catholic University Law Review, 55*, 193–226.

Contreras, F. (2009). Sin papeles y rompiendo barreras: Latino students and the challenges of persisting college. *Harvard Educational Review, 79*(4), 610–631.

Dávila, A. (2008). *Latino spin: Public image and the whitewashing of race.* New York: NYU Press.

Diaz-Strong, D., & Meiners, E. (2007). Residents, alien policies, and resistances: Experiences of undocumented Latina/o students in Chicago's colleges and universities. *UCLA Journal of Education and Information Studies, 3*(2), 1–22.

Dougherty, K.J., Nienhusser, H. Kenny, & Vega, B.E. (2010). Undocumented immigrants and state higher education policy: The politics of in-state tuition eligibility in Texas and Arizona. *Review of Higher Education, 34*(1), 123–174.

Edwards, K.E. (2006). Aspiring social justice ally identity development: A conceptual model. *NASPA Journal, 43*(4), 39–59.

Filindra, A., Blanding, D., & Garcia Coll, C. (2011). The power of context: State-level policies and politics and educational performance of the children of immigrants in the United States. *Harvard Educational Review, 81*(3), 407–438.

Fix, M., & Capps, R. (2005). Immigrant children, urban schools, and the No Child Left Behind Act. Migration Policy Institute (retrieved November 18, 2010 from http://www.migrationinformation.org/Feature/print.cfm?ID=347).

Flores, S.M. (2010). State Dream Acts: The effect of in-state resident tuition policies and undocumented Latino students. *Review of Higher Education, 33*(2), 239–283.

Fry, R. (2008). *Latino settlement in the new century.* Washington, DC: Pew Hispanic Center.

Goldberg, D.T. (2009). *The threat of race: Reflections on racial neoliberalism.* Malden, MA: Blackwell.

Gonzales, R.G. (2009). *Young lives on hold: The college dreams of undocumented students.* New York: College Board Advocacy.

Gonzales, R.G. (2011). Learning to be illegal: Undocumented youth and shifting legal contexts in transition to adulthood. *American Sociological Review, 76*(4), 602–619.

Guinier, L. (2004). From racial liberalism to racial literacy: Brown v. Board of Education and the interest convergence dilemma. *Journal of American History, 92*(1), 92–118.

Haney Lopez, I.F. (1996). *White by law.* New York: NYU Press.

Harris, A., & Ranson, S. (2005). The contradictions of education policy: Disadvantage and achievement. *British Educational Research Journal, 31*(5), 571–587.

Hebel, S. (2007). Arizona's colleges are in the crosshairs of efforts to curb illegal immigration. *Chronicle of Higher Education, 54*(10), A15.

Hernandez-Truyol, B., Harris, A., & Valdés, F. (2006). Beyond the first decade: A forward-looking history of LatCrit theory, community and praxis. *Berkeley LaRasa Law Journal, 17*(1), 169–216.

Janosik, S.M., & Johnson, A.T. (2007). Undocumented students and access to public higher education: Legislative acrimony, confusion, and stagnation. *Virginia Issues and Answers: A Public Policy Forum*, Fall, 24–31.

Louie, V. (2005). Immigrant newcomer populations, ESEA, and the pipeline to college: Current considerations and future lines of inquiry. *Review of Research in Education, 29* (L. Parker, Ed.), 69–105.

Love, J. (2012). Undocumented dreamers in college welcome policy change on immigration. *Chronicle of Higher Education*, July 6, A13–A14.

Mutua, A.D. (1999). Shifting bottoms and rotating centers: Reflections on Lat Crit III and the Black–White paradigm. *University of Miami Law Review, 53*, 1177–1217.

Olivas, M.A. (2004). IIRIRA, the DREAM Act, and undocumented college student residency. *Journal of College and University Law, 30*, 435–464.

Olivas, M.A. (2009). Undocumented students and financial aid: A technical note. *Review of Higher Education, 32*(3), 407–416.

Perez Huber, L., & Malagon, M.C. (2007). Silenced struggles: The experiences of Latina and Latino undocumented college students in California. *Nevada Law Journal, 7*, 841–861.

Plyler v. Doe, 457 U.S. 202 (1982).

Robinson, J. (2007). *In-state tuition for undocumented students in Utah*. Policy brief. Salt Lake City, UT: Center for Public Policy and Administration.

Sharron, J. (2007). Passing the DREAM Act: Opportunities for undocumented students. *Santa Clara Law Review, 47*, 559–643.

Solórzano, D.G., & Yosso, T.J. (2001). Critical race and LatCrit theory and method: Counter-storytelling Chicana and Chicano graduate school experiences. *International Journal of Qualitative Studies in Education, 14*(4), 471–495.

Soss, J., Fording, R.C., & Schram, S.F. (2011). *Disciplining the poor: Neoliberal paternalism and the persistent power of race*. Chicago: University of Chicago Press.

Southworth, S., & Mickelson, R.A. (2007). The interactive effects of race, gender and school composition on college track placement. *Social Forces, 86*(2), 497–523.

Stevenson, A. (2004). Dreaming of an equal future for immigrant children: Federal and state initiatives to improve undocumented students' access to postsecondary education. *Arizona Law Review, 46*, 551–650.

Toll v. Moreno, 441 U. S. 458 (1979).

Trucios-Haynes, E. (2000–01). Why "race matters": LatCrit theory and Latina/o racial identity. *LaRaza Law Journal, 12*, 1–42.

Valenzuela, A. (1999). *Subtractive schooling*. New York: SUNY Press.

11

BADGES OF INFERIORITY

The Racialization of Achievement in U.S. Education

Sonya Douglass Horsford and Tanetha J. Grosland

In his 2010 book *Brainwashed: Challenging the Myth of Black Inferiority*, marketing communications pioneer Tom Burrell argues that, in America, the wholesale marketing and branding campaign of blacks as subhuman not only has reinforced white superiority and black inferiority to justify slavery within a democracy, but also perpetually "weakens the impulse to understand or help those still scorched at the bottom of America's melting pot" (p. 4). From colonial times and reconstruction well into the Civil Rights era and twenty-first century, this marketing campaign has functioned as a "tsunami of words and images that promote an image of black inferiority" and echoes W.E.B. Du Bois's (1903/1989) observation that, "In propaganda against the Negro since emancipation in this land, we face one of the most stupendous efforts the world ever saw to discredit human beings." He noted that this effort included the participation of universities, spanning "history, science, social life, and religion."

Indeed, the field of education proves no exception to the reproduction of this myth of black inferiority. In fact, one could argue that the perpetuation of this myth within the U.S. public education system is most dangerous and damaging given the well-documented link between educational expectations, educator efficacy, student achievement, and future life chances (Darling-Hammond, 2010; Delpit, 1995; Duncan & Murnane, 2011; Reardon, 2011). To suggest that black children and youth are inherently inferior in terms of intelligence, knowledge, and/or academic prowess introduces a host of troubles far beyond the scope of what one steadfast parent, culturally relevant educator, or organized community can tackle. This is not to diminish the significance of engaged and activist parents (Cooper, 2009, 2010; Howard & Reynolds, 2008, 2009; Lightfoot, 1980; Tillman, 2003), self-efficacious teachers (Ball, 2006; Ladson-Billings, 2004; Lynn et al., 2010), and supportive communities (J. Anderson, 1988; Horsford, 2010, 2011b; Morris, 1999, 2009), who together have provided the social-emotional support, high expectations, and access to quality educational opportunities that have consistently produced well-educated and highly successful blacks throughout American history (Horsford, 2010; Morris, 2008, 2009; Walker, 1996). Rather it is to underscore the powerful historical, political, and social forces that have developed and sustained a narrative of black inferiority, which most recently has manifested itself in the form of an "achievement gap," successfully using data to racialize achievement.

In this chapter, we interrogate the majoritarian narrative of the "achievement gap" and black student underachievement in U.S. education. Drawing from related research on achievement by race and the schooling experiences of black K-12 students in the U.S., we argue that mainstream discourses highlighting black underachievement serve as contemporary *badges of inferiority*, which undermine black student educational experiences and outcomes. We begin with a brief discussion of black student underachievement within the context of black inferiority, followed by a review of the origins of the contemporary "achievement gap" narrative and its role in using data to sustain the stock story of black educational inferiority. We conclude the chapter with Horsford's (2011a, 2011b) critical race approach to equal education—a multi-step progression from racial literacy and racial realism (Bell, 1992) to racial reconstruction and racial reconciliation as a way of rebranding the narrative of black student achievement in U.S. schools.

THE BRANDING OF EDUCATIONAL INFERIORITY

In his book *Inheriting Shame: The Story of Eugenics and Racism in America* (1999), Steven Selden reminded us that "Humankind's desire to construct an explanation for its varying levels of performance dates back at least to Plato's *Republic*" (p. xiii). Given the longstanding narrative of black inferiority in the U.S., grounded largely in the need to justify slavery and segregation through scientific racism, the story of black student underachievement has a deep and unrelenting history (J. Anderson, 1988; Perry et al., 2003). In the early twentieth century in the U.S., "many eugenicists, anxious about their social status as well as about immigration-driven demographic changes, saw in eugenics a legitimation of their racial interpretations of differential human worth" (p. xiii)—a hierarchy in which whites reigned supreme and blacks represented a problem to be studied, analyzed, and relegated as inferior to whites in every way.

Long before such anxieties surfaced, Thomas Jefferson expressed his hypothesis of black inferiority in the *Notes on the State of Virginia* (1781), where he concluded:

> I advance it therefore as a suspicion only, that the blacks, whether originally a distinct race, or made distinct by time and circumstances, are inferior to the whites in the endowments both of body and mind. It is not against experience to suppose, that different species of the same genus, or varieties of the same species, may possess different qualifications.

This founding father and third President of the United States' "suspicion" ushered in the development and publication of scientific studies intended to prove a racial hierarchy in which Caucasians enjoyed "decided and unquestioned superiority over all the nations of the earth" (PBS, 2003). Indeed, it was prominent American leaders—presidents, Supreme Court justices, social scientists, and respected university professors—who publicly and confidently propagated this narrative of black inferiority for mainstream consumption. In 1854, Jefferson's suspicion became scientifically based "fact" when pro-slavery scientist Josiah Nott reported: "Nations and races, like individuals, have each an especial destiny: some are born to rule, and others to be ruled … No two distinctly-marked races can dwell together on equal terms" (PBS, 2003).

A similar sentiment was presented in 1896 by U.S. Supreme Court justice Henry Billings Brown in the historically significant *Plessy v. Ferguson* case, which codified the practice of "separate but equal" in American public life. On behalf of the court, Justice Brown's rejected plaintiff Homer Plessy's contention that separate facilities stamped a "badge of inferiority" on the colored race. He disagreed:

> We consider the underlying fallacy of the plaintiff's argument to consist in the assumption that the enforced separation of the two races stamps the colored race with a badge of inferiority. If this be so, it is not by reason of anything found in the act, but solely because the colored race chooses to put that construction upon it. If one race be inferior to the other socially, the constitution of the United States cannot put them upon the same plane.

While *Plessy v. Ferguson* did not address education directly, its formalization of the "separate but equal" facilities and public spaces also sanctioned the development of a dual system of education expensive to maintain, "but not too high for advocates of white supremacy" (Franklin & Moss, 1988, p. 238). Although the *Brown v. Board of Education* decision of 1954 legally dismantled this system by declaring "separate schools inherently unequal," the goal of meaningful school integration is yet unfulfilled (Horsford, 2011a, 2011b), largely because of the reality that the belief and mainstream narrative that black students are inherently unequal remain intact. Much like "the brand that the early ruling class literally and figuratively burned onto black Americans" as "the permanent identifier of 'subhuman inferiority'" (Burrell, 2010, p. 11), so is the brand of black student underachievement as propagated through the late-twentieth- and early-twenty-first-century mainstream narrative of the "achievement gap."

THE ACHIEVEMENT GAP: A CRITICAL RACE PERSPECTIVE

The term "achievement gap" made its debut in 1964 in the Hauser Report, a report commissioned by the Chicago Board of Education intended to "analyze and study the school system in particular regard to schools attended entirely or predominately by Negroes," "define any problems that result therefrom," and "formulate … a plan by which any education, psychological and emotional problems or inequities can be eradicated" (Hauser et al., 1964). It determined that "intensified educational opportunities for Negro boys and girls would result in a major closing of the achievement gap between group performances of Negro students and other groups of students." Just two years later, the U.S. Department of Health, Education, and Welfare released its *Equality of Educational Opportunity* report, more commonly called the Coleman Report, and used the phrase "gap in achievement" to describe the variance between white and minority student academic performance (Coleman, 1966). In 1970, the *American Economic Review* described a "widening achievement gap between white and nonwhite students as the general level of education increases" (Gwartney, 1970).

Nearly 50 years since its first mention, education researchers, reformers, and policymakers have helped to make the "achievement gap" a household phrase. While there are many and varied definitions for the term, it is generally understood to describe "the disparities in standardized test scores between Black and White, Latina/o and White, and recent immigrant and White students" (Ladson-Billings, 2006, p. 3). Despite this more recent framing of the achievement gap as educational disparities according to class, immigrant status, language, or any difference between groups, the majority of research on the achievement gap has concentrated on test score variances between black and white students (S. Anderson et al., 2007, p. 548), while ignoring the history of racial exclusion, segregation, and discrimination in U.S. schools. Cross (2007) characterized the mainstream narrative or "conventional story" of the achievement gap as:

> an internal threat to the imminent, competitive advantage of the United States of America, and it resides in urban school districts. The threat is so large that it places the nation in danger of losing its leadership position more so than other educational gaps. This gap, no this threat, is one between the low educational achievement … of poor children in urban schools, many of whom are children of color and linguistically diverse, and their suburban white, middle class counterparts who are intelligent and high achieving.
>
> (p. 248)

Critical analyses of the achievement gap as majoritarian narrative (Love, 2004), metaphor (Cross, 2007), and "crossover hit" (Ladson-Billings, 2006, p. 3), informed by a "national ideology about Black intellectual inferiority" (Perry et al., 2003, p. 8), have shed much needed light on this multifaceted dilemma. Not only have such researchers conducted and called for more rigorous and historical examinations of the origins of gaps in educational achievement by race; they also have warned us of risks associated with noncritical, ahistorical interpretations of contemporary variances in standardized test scores, grades, and graduation rates (Cross, 2007; Horsford, 2011b; Ladson-Billings, 2006; Love, 2004; Perry et al., 2003). According to Ladson-Billings (2006), "this all-out focus on the 'Achievement Gap' moves us toward short-term solutions that are unlikely to address the long-term underlying problem" (p. 4).

We believe that addressing this deeper, more fundamental issue of educational inequality based in a branding of black educational inferiority necessitates a theoretical framework that centers race in the analysis. The problem of an achievement gap, much less an opportunity gap or resource gap, cannot be properly framed, investigated, or "closed" without a substantive understanding of the role and function of race and racism in American society. This is where critical race theory (CRT) and a critical race perspective on the achievement gap bring great value. CRT acknowledges racism as a permanent aspect of life in the U.S. (Bell, 1992) and the "means by which society allocates privilege and status" (DeCuir & Dixson, 2004, p. 27). This allocation correlates heavily to whiteness and what Harris (1995) found to be an "entangled relationship between race and property" (p. 277) where whiteness affords unique rights and privileges, to include serving as the normal and neutral measure by which all other groups are defined and compared (Delgado & Stefancic, 2001). Whiteness also reaps the rewards of interest convergence, Derrick Bell's theory that "the majority group tolerates advances for racial justice only when it suits its interest to do so" (Delgado & Stefancic, 2001, p. 149).

Given the enduring and cumulative benefits of whiteness, CRT recognizes the significance and value of telling the untold stories that reflect the experiential knowledge of people of color (Delgado & Stefancic, 2001; Solórzano & Yosso, 2002). It also takes issue with liberal conceptions of colorblindness, meritocracy, and neutral applications of laws and policies, which undermine efforts to address race-based problems in effective and meaningful ways. For these reasons, the scholarship of critical race theorists in education has made significant theoretical and empirical contributions to our understanding of educational inequality, opportunity, and achievement in the U.S. (e.g., DeCuir & Dixson, 2004; Dixson & Rousseau, 2005, 2006; Horsford, 2010, 2011a, 2011b; Ladson-Billings & Tate, 1995; G. López & Parker, 2003; N. Lopez, 2003; Lynn, 2002; Lynn & Parker, 2006; Lynn et al., 2002; Milner, 2008; Parker & Villalpando, 2007; Parker et al., 1999; Solórzano & Yosso, 2002; Tate, 1997). In particular, research on racially marginalized students, their teachers, and their educational environments has greatly increased our knowledge of what schooling is like for these students. In the next section, we focus our attention on the research on black student achievement and the racialization of their achievement in K-12 contexts.

EXPECTING LESS THAN SUCCESS: DILEMMAS OF BLACK STUDENT ACHIEVEMENT

In the case of the education of black students and their achievement, researchers have studied: teachers' beliefs and perceptions about black students (Lynn et al., 2010; Tyson, 2003); voices, characteristics, and behaviors of high-achieving or gifted black students (Ford, 1996, 2010; Perry et al., 2003; Stinson, 2008, 2011); the burden of "acting white" (Fordham & Ogbu, 1986; Horvat & Lewis, 2003; Horvat & O'Connor, 2006; Ogbu, 2004; Stinson, 2011; Tyson, 2003; Tyson et al., 2005); and the impact of racism on their educational experiences (Allen, 2010; Bell, 1980, 2004; DeCuir & Dixson, 2004; Lynn et al., 2002). Unfortunately, much of the research literature illustrates how much less is expected of black students in terms of academic success in comparison to their peers. In this section, we focus on the racialization of black student achievement in three select areas: (a) schools as "arenas of risk and failure" (Roderick, 2003); (b) teacher perspectives on student ability and achievement; and (c) student perspectives on black underachievement to bring to bear the multiple challenges and dimensions that contribute to the persistent dilemma facing black students and their academic achievement.

Schools as Arenas of Risk and Failure: Institutional Expectations and Outcomes

During the era of school segregation, the black segregated school served as a "safe house" (Horsford, 2011b, p. 32) where students enjoyed caring yet demanding teachers who held high expectations for academic success, alongside parents, within a supportive community environment (Horsford, 2010, 2011b; Morris, 1999, 2008; Walker, 1996, 2000). In the post-*Brown* era, however, (1) black school closings, (2) lost jobs for black teachers and administrators, (3) the disproportionate burden of desegregation on black students and families, and (4) the dismantling of the black community ushered in, ironically, a new host of problems related to the education of black students (Horsford, 2011b). These post-desegregation challenges, what Horsford (2011a, 2011b) described as *vestiges of desegregation*, included and still include (1) sifting, sorting, and tracking students by perceived ability, (2) disproportionate special education placements, (3) cultural mismatch and incongruence between home and school, and (4) school–family–community disconnects, all of which have significant implications for black student achievement (Horsford, 2011a, 2011b).

In many ways, the achievement gap narrative exacerbates these more recent manifestations of education inequality in schools. Black students (and their white and non-white peers) are bombarded with messages emphasizing differences in academic achievement by race and, oftentimes, how the underachievement of black students hurts overall school performance indicators. While high-achieving white and Asian students are expected to move from school to college and career, black and Latino students are reminded of a school-to-prison pipeline that claims nearly one in three black or one in six Latino boys within their lifetimes (Children's Defense Fund, 2007). Indeed, Roderick's (2003) observation that, for black males, high school is an "arena of risk and failure" (p. 580) rings true given the condemnation of black bodies, which are constantly being contained, controlled, and criminalized—a process that starts as early as the elementary years (Allen, 2010; K. Muhammad, 2010). The resultant overrepresentation of black students, particularly black males, in contained special education classrooms, controlled for being disciplinary problems (Monroe, 2005), and criminalized through alternative educational and behavioral programs, demonstrates that, while schools are sites of imagination and opportunity for some students, they serve as arenas of risk and failure for others.

A Crisis of Faith: Teacher Perspectives on Student Ability and Achievement

Research points to a strong and direct correlation between a teacher's perceptions of her or his students and her or his capacity to teach them successfully (Darling-Hammond, 2004; Delpit, 1995; Ladson-Billings, 1994; Lynn et al., 2010; Noguera, 2007). According to Noguera (2007), for students of color, "of all the factors most consistently cited as influencing the achievement and motivation … teacher efficacy consistently ranks the highest" (p. 45). Conversely, qualified teachers with low rates of efficacy have the potential to dishearten and dissuade students, which is disproportionately the case for black students, who often attend schools with both unqualified teachers (Darling-Hammond, 2004) and teachers who are not confident in their ability to educate black children and youth (Lynn et al., 2010). A positive academic identity, particularly for those children representing racially marginalized groups and cultures, is critical to their academic achievement and can be quickly compromised and undermined when teachers are unable to move beyond their own racialized biases or assumptions (Comer & Pouissant, 1992; Delpit, 1995; Horsford et al., 2011; King, 2005; Ladson-Billings, 2004; Lynn et al., 2010; Tyson 2003).

Tyson's (2003) examination of black elementary teacher perspectives and practices in a black independent school explained how the two main goals of schooling—teaching academic knowledge and cultural socialization—were often in conflict and revealed how some of these teachers unwittingly placed conformity to white, middle-class cultural norms over positive black identity development and academic success. This was especially the case for black teachers who stressed academic achievement through an "exaggerated emphasis on behavior" (p. 333). Tyson found that, in doing so, these teachers unwittingly undermined the affirmation of their students' intelligence, aptitude, and culture (Tyson, 2003). What she characterized as the "hidden" nature of the second goal of schooling—cultural socialization—may explain the cultural disconnects between home and school, since the second goal is not clearly explained to students. The challenging part of this reality is that "Underlying this sentiment is the idea that the consequences of bad behavior and poor school performance are disastrous for black students and the black community more so than they are for students of other racial groups"

(p. 335). She concluded, much like scholars such as Asa Hilliard, Lisa Delpit, and Gloria-Ladson-Billings, that "positioning minority students for mainstream success requires a delicate balance of explanation *and* affirmation" (p. 339) such that students understand "how or why they may be falling short of the school's expectations" (p. 328).

Unfortunately, explaining the goal of cultural socialization and affirming students in their blackness while countering the mainstream narrative of black educational inferiority is a paradox for not only black teachers and black students, but students and teachers of all races. What becomes even more problematic is what Lynn et al. (2010) discovered in their study of teacher beliefs of black male students in a Mid-Atlantic high school. Their critical race ethnography revealed a "crisis of faith" among teachers who failed to believe they could improve the academic achievement of their black students, especially males. The authors suggested this to be a nationwide crisis where most black and Latino students are made to feel that they do not have what it takes to be considered intelligent, academically successful, or high-achieving. While some teachers are consciously working to remove badges of inferiority from their students, others are replacing those badges of inferiority with new ones.

"I'd Rather Not Talk about It": Student Perspectives on Black Underachievement

"If I were white I would be good."
"If I were white I would be nice."
"If I were white I would speak proper English."
"If I were white I would go to class."
"If I were white I would spell words right."

> (Written statements from black elementary students at a black independent school in response to a writing assignment from their teacher asking them to complete the sentence: "If I were white, I would …" Tyson, 2003, p. 336)

These twenty-first-century badges of inferiority share both similarities and differences with their nineteenth- and twentieth-century counterparts. While the similarities are obvious (white is good, nice, and right; black is altogether bad), the differences exist greatly in context, for these new badges of inferiority exist in desegregated, integrated, and diverse yet "colorblind" educational settings (Bonilla-Silva, 2006; Horsford, 2011b). Beyond the widely documented practices of within-school segregation, resegregation, and disproportionate discipline practices aimed at black students, and the racialization of black educational inferiority through the achievement gap metaphor, even black students who enjoy privileged class status are made to feel invisible, uncared for and undervalued, and misunderstood (Allen, 2010). In Allen's (2010) examination of how social and institutional racism mediated the ways in which black middle-class males fared in an integrated Arizona high school, Allen reaffirmed the notion that black male students are better motivated in school when they feel their teachers care about them (Irvine, 1991; Lynn et al., 2010; Polite, 1993, 1994). "Racial microaggressions" evidenced by differential treatment by student race, such as a teacher not knowing the name of the only black student in class (invisibility), unfair discipline practices and lack of academic support and guidance (uncared for and undervalued), and the inability to understand and respond to the beliefs, values, and culture of black youth (misunderstood), undermined black student achievement (Allen, 2010).

Although the parents of these black males expended their middle-class social and cultural capital "to create moments of inclusion for their sons" (p. 136), Allen's (2010) study provided yet another example of how "middle-class standing in and of itself does not shield people of color from racist encounters" (p. 138). To be sure, the black student perspective of black underachievement varies greatly from student to student. It also depends greatly on its intersection with class, gender, immigrant status, ability, and/or context. For example, C. Muhammad and Dixson's (2008) study of black female high school students described teacher perceptions of black girls (e.g., independent, self-reliant) markedly different from teacher perceptions of their male peers (e.g., lazy, dangerous), resulting in different types of interactions between teachers and students (i.e., black males may be "overly monitored" while black girls are "routinely ignored"; p. 166). Additionally DeCuir-Gunby's (2007) qualitative study of six African American adolescents in a predominately white, elite, independent school expands our knowledge on how black youth negotiate their racial identity in what they described as a "bubble" of colorblindness that privileged the culture and experiences of white students while ignoring the culture and needs of its African American students.

The cultural diversity embodied within the black race also informs the schooling experiences of black students, as documented in N. Lopez's (2003) study of second-generation black Caribbean high school students in New York City. Upon entering elementary school, study participants were placed in high tracks, only to be placed in low tracks in high school, exposing them to irrelevant and meaningless curriculum and instructional experiences. She found this to be especially the case for males, sharing the account of one student who became disengaged from school and dropped out in the eleventh grade because of boredom, frustration, and being taught things he already knew. Regardless of their academic achievement, the young men in her study recalled having difficult and tense interactions with teachers, so much so that, when asked to discuss his relationships with his teachers, one high-achieving student refused to answer, bowed his head, and replied, "I'd rather not talk about it" (p. 53).

These student voices and perspectives or, in the case of the young man who preferred to "not talk about it," unspoken words underscore the power and value of counterstorytelling and how these stories can positively inform educational policies and practices in important ways. Lynn et al. (2010) recommended: "we must begin to take seriously students' beliefs about what constitutes a high-quality teacher and use their assessments as part of the criteria for determining how we define high-quality teaching ... particularly in urban contexts" (p. 323). As black students continue to "face the threat of confirming or being judged by a negative stereotype—a suspicion—about their group's intellectual ability and competence" (p. 797), it is no surprise that the racialization of their achievement could pose challenges to their ability to succeed academically.

It could also, however, serve as the motivation and inspiration for positive racial socialization, which Sanders (1997) found correlated to high student achievement. In her study of 40 black middle school students in the southeastern U.S., Sanders discovered that the students who demonstrated high awareness of racism and the racialization of achievement were also high-achieving academically. She concluded:

> By transmitting an awareness of racial discrimination and an achievement orientation that has been a central part of the African American experience, Black students' family members, teachers, ministers, and others responsible for their upbringing and

socialization may diminish the likelihood that these youth will have a negative orientation toward schooling and academic achievement. Such practices of positive racial socialization may be aptly and usefully conceived of as an important and heretofore under-researched form of parental and community involvement in the education of African American and other minority youth.

(p. 10)

Sanders's call to increase positive racial socialization practices as a strategy for improving educational achievement among black students in the U.S. is certainly worthy of response. Failure to acknowledge this unrelenting narrative of black educational inferiority renders ineffective policies and initiatives designed to advance equality and equity in the education of black students. As we continue to spend time conceptualizing, introducing, developing, and evaluating the best practices for "closing the achievement gap" and increasing the educational achievement of black students, we lose valuable time that should be spent countering the stock story of black educational inferiority and rebranding black achievement as a narrative of educational triumph and excellence.

BADGES OF EXCELLENCE: TOWARD RACIAL EQUALITY AND JUSTICE IN SCHOOLS

Schools are not exempt from the negative stereotypes, media messages, and "propaganda" (Burrell, 2010; Du Bois, 1903/1989) reinforcing the ideology of black inferiority in the U.S. According to Burrell (with respect to Du Bois):

though black progress is more visible today than ever before, I maintain that the unwritten, audacious promotion of white superiority and black inferiority was (and still is) the most effective and successful marketing/propaganda campaign in the history of the world. African Americans, no matter how savvy, educated, or financially privileged, could not completely avoid the conditioning that resulted from increasingly sophisticated bombardment of subtle and not-so-subtle messages created to reinforce how different and inherently inferior blacks are when compared to whites.

(Burrell, 2010, p. 5)

In fact, such large-scale marketing and branding campaigns coupled with everyday references to the "achievement gap" make matters worse, serving as the prime vehicle for reproducing "badges of inferiority" in twenty-first-century schools. Ahistorical interpretations of standardized test data and an unyielding focus on racial comparisons have helped to construct the achievement gap metaphor, which, as Cross (2007) explained, "is part of a powerful enduring narrative that functions to stigmatize certain groups as deviant and abnormal, based largely in race, class, and language" (p. 249) and that "To focus on a gap, paradoxically sustains it" (p. 253).

Regretfully, short-term efforts to "close the achievement gap" have themselves fallen short, because they refuse to account for the substantial historical evidence that explains largely why so much inequality exists within and among U.S. public schools. Without taking a serious look at race and the history of educational inequality in America, no gaps will be closed and the racial wounds resulting from the not-so-soft "bigotry of low expectations" (Bush, 2004) will remain opened. For these reasons and more, as previously discussed in this chapter, many researchers have underscored the importance of explicitly explaining the schooling objective of cultural socialization to black students (Delpit, 1993; Tyson, 2003), accounting for student perspectives and voices concerning the qualifications and attributes of a successful teacher (Lynn et al., 2010), and engaging positive racial socialization practices to ensure black students understand the role and function of race and racism in schools and society (Ladson-Billings, 1994; Sanders, 1997). At the end of the day, it is critically important how black students (and all students for that matter) see themselves. Thus, dismantling the narrative of black educational inferiority requires a powerful counterstory.

The positive racial identity and achievement orientation of any student depends largely upon the racial awareness and consciousness of the adults in their lives, especially teachers. As the research states, there is a decisive correlation between how teachers perceive the ability of their students and their teaching efficacy on student motivation, learning, and outcomes (Darling-Hammond, 2004; Delpit, 1995; Ladson-Billings, 1994; Lynn et al., 2010; Noguera, 2007). Although developed with educational leaders and administrators in mind, Horsford's (2011b) multi-step progression of race consciousness from *racial literacy* to *Derrick Bell's concept of racial realism* (1992) and *racial reconstruction* to *racial reconciliation* (see Table 11.1) could also be applied to a broader, community-based approach toward positive racial socialization and, in turn, improved black student achievement.

Race permeates the large majority of discussions around educational opportunity and equality, social mobility, school success, and student achievement, and according to racial realists this will always be the case. Whether researchers are examining the relative difference in achievement between students by race, the reasons for such gaps, or their causes, there exists a variety of social, psychological, cultural, political, and ecological explanations for why whiteness continues to be associated with high student achievement and blackness is not. Even more troubling are the ways in which the reporting of student and school achievement by racial subgroups has solidified the notion of a racial "achievement gap" in U.S. education—normalizing academic success for some and failure for others.

Using this model would require all education stakeholders, from parents and school officials to researchers and policymakers, to be conscious of the black educational inferiority narrative. Through a critical race orientation, they could see better and more clearly how achievement has been racialized in U.S. schools and reveal how contemporary badges of inferiority remain invisible to those who do not yet understand (or choose

Table 11.1 Multi-step progression from racial literacy to racial reconciliation

Racial literacy	Ability to understand what race is, why it is, and how it is used to reproduce inequality and oppression.
Racial realism	Drawn from critical race theory's focus on acknowledging the history, pervasiveness, and salience of race and racism in U.S. society, including its schools, and the pitfalls associated with liberal education ideology, policy, and practices.
Racial reconstruction	The process of ascribing new meaning to race in order to transform the ways we think about, and subsequently act on, our racial assumptions, attitudes, and biases.
Racial reconciliation	Process that seeks to heal the soul wounds and the damage that has been done in schools and society as it relates to race and racism.

Source: Horsford (2011b).

not or refuse to acknowledge) what race is, how it functions, and why and how it remains such a force in American life. In fact, this represents the first dimension of *racial literacy* (see Guinier, 2004; Horsford, 2009) or "the ability to understand what race is, why it is, and how it is used to reproduce inequality and oppression" (Horsford, 2011b, p. 95). The next step is *racial realism*, which is the recognition that racism is not "shocking or aberrant" (Horsford, forthcoming), but to be expected (Bell, 1992; Ladson-Billings, 2011), prompting individuals and institutions to become more mindful and intentional about how they interpret and tackle racial inequality and injustice in schools and school communities.

Racial realism is followed by *racial reconstruction*, which is where the difficult work of assigning new meanings to racial categories holds promise for countering narratives of black inferiority with messages that foster positive racial socialization and mutual respect across racial differences. Questioning how individuals and organizations define phrases like the "achievement gap" and understanding the implications of those meanings for students of all races and achievement levels inform the racial reconstruction process. This compels us to think differently about racial group membership in ways that reflect equal standing and regard (Horsford, 2011b). As Warikoo and Carter (2009) proposed, "new studies should incorporate an understanding of the process of racialization if they seek to attribute social and academic outcomes to race" (p. 384). Racial reconstruction aims not only to understand this process, but to transform and rebrand the message of black student achievement through counterstorytelling that disrupts and supplants stereotypes and deficit thinking with positive constructions of blackness.

The last step is *racial reconciliation*, which is far more aspirational and arguably less attainable than the others (Horsford, forthcoming). The wounds associated with badges of inferiority are painful and real, fostering an expectation of black student underachievement encouraged by the belief that "blacks … are inferior to the whites in endowments both of body and mind" (Jefferson, 1781) and tacitly accepting Justice Billings Brown's contention that if racial segregation "stamps the colored race with a badge of inferiority … it is … solely because the colored race chooses to put that construction upon it" (Plessy v. Ferguson, 1896). As the end of the progression from racial literacy to racial realism, on to the reconstruction of what it means to be black (or any race) in America, racial reconciliation's primary aim is to find common ground and heal racial wounds through meaningful positive racial socialization, cross-racial dialogue and praxis, and self-reflection. By engaging this work seriously and steadfastly, we can tell a new story—one that does not ignore, devalue, or misunderstand the intelligence, culture, ability, and achievement of black students, but expects success, marking them not with a *badge of inferiority* but with a *badge of excellence*.

REFERENCES

Allen, Q. (2010). Racial microaggressions: The schooling experience of black middle-class males in Arizona's secondary schools. *Journal of African American Males in Education, 1*(2), 125–143.

Anderson, J.D. (1988). *The education of blacks in the South, 1860–1935.* Chapel Hill: University of North Carolina Press.

Anderson, S., Medrich, E., & Fowler, D. (2007). Which achievement gap? *Phi Delta Kappan, 88*(7), 547–550.

Ball, A.F. (2006). *Multicultural strategies for education and social change: Carriers of the torch in the United States and South Africa.* New York: Teachers College Press.

Bell, D. (1980). *Shades of Brown: New perspectives on school desegregation.* New York: Teachers College Press.

Bell, D. (1992). *Faces at the bottom of the well: The permanence of racism.* New York: Basic Books.

Bell, D. (2004). *Silent covenants: Brown v. Board of Education and the unfulfilled hopes for racial reform.* New York: Oxford University Press.

Bonilla-Silva, E. (2006). *Racism without racists: Color-blind racism and the persistence of racial inequality in the United States* (2nd ed.). Lanham, MD: Rowman & Littlefield.

Brown v. Board of Education of Topeka, Kansas, 347 U.S. 483 (1954).

Burrell, T. (2010). *Brainwashed: Challenging the myth of black inferiority.* New York: Smiley Books.

Bush, G.W. (2004). *Text: President Bush's acceptance speech to the Republican National Convention* (retrieved from http://www.washingtonpost.com/wp-dyn/articles/A57466-2004Sep2.html).

Children's Defense Fund. (2007). *Annual Report 2007* (retrieved from http://www.childrensdefense.org/child-research-data-publications/data/cdf-2007-annual-report.pdf).

Coleman, J. (1966). *Equality of educational opportunity.* U.S. Department of Health, Education, and Welfare. Washington, DC: U.S. Printing Office.

Comer, J.P., & Pouissant, A.F. (1992). *Raising black children: Two leading psychiatrists confront the educational, social and emotional problems facing black children.* New York: Penguin.

Cooper, C.W. (2009). Parent involvement, African American mothers, and the politics of educational care. *Equity and Excellence in Education, 42*(4), 379–394.

Cooper, C.W. (2010). Educational leaders and cultural workers: Engaging families and school communities through transformative leadership. In S.D. Horsford (Ed.), *New perspectives in educational leadership: Exploring social, political, and community contexts and meaning* (pp. 173–195). New York: Peter Lang.

Cross, B.E. (2007). Urban school achievement gap as a metaphor to conceal U.S. apartheid education. *Theory into Practice, 46*(3), 247–255.

Darling-Hammond, L. (2004). The color line in American education: Race, resources, and student achievement. *W.E.B. Du Bois Review: Social Science Research on Race, 1*(2), 213–246.

Darling-Hammond, L. (2010). *The flat world and education: How America's commitment to equity will determine our future.* New York: Teachers College Press.

DeCuir, J.T., & Dixson, A.D. (2004). "So when it comes out, they aren't that surprised that it is there": Using critical race theory as a tool of analysis of race and racism in education. *Educational Researcher, 33*(5), 26–31.

DeCuir-Gunby, J.T. (2007). Negotiating identity in a bubble: The experiences of African American high school students at Wells Academy. *Equity and Excellence in Education, 40*(1), 26–35.

Delgado, R., & Stefancic, J. (Eds.). (2001). *Critical race theory: An introduction.* New York: New York University Press.

Delpit, L. (1993). The silenced dialogue: Power and pedagogy in educating other people's children. *Harvard Educational Review, 58*(3), 280–298.

Delpit, L. (1995). *Other people's children: Cultural conflict in the classroom.* New York: New Press.

Dixson, A.D., & Rousseau, C.K. (2005). And we are still not saved: Critical race theory in education ten years later. *Race, Ethnicity and Education, 8*(1), 7–27.

Dixson, A.D., & Rousseau, C.K. (2006). *Critical race theory in education: All God's children got a song.* New York: Routledge.

Du Bois, W.E.B. (1903/1989). *The souls of black folk.* New York: Bantam Books.

Duncan, G.J., & Murnane, R.J. (Eds.). (2011). *Whither opportunity? Rising inequality, schools, and children's life chance.* New York: Russell Sage Foundation Press.

Ford, D.Y. (1996). *Reversing underachievement among gifted black students: Promising practices and programs.* New York: Teachers College Press.

Ford, D.Y. (2010). *Reversing underachievement among gifted black students: Theory, research and practice* (2nd ed.). Waco, TX: Prufrock Press.

Fordham, S., & Ogbu, J. (1986). Black students' school success: Coping with the burden of "acting white." *Urban Review, 18*(3), 176–206.

Franklin, J.H., & Moss, A., Jr. (1988). *From slavery to freedom: A history of Negro Americans* (6th ed.). New York: McGraw-Hill.

Guinier, L. (2004). From racial liberalism to racial literacy: Brown v. Board of Education and the interest-divergence dilemma. *Journal of American History, 91*(1), 92–118.

Gwartney, J. (1970). Changes in the nonwhite/white income ratio: 1939–67. *American Economic Review, 60,* 872–883.

Harris, C.I. (1995). Whiteness as property. In K. Crenshaw, N. Gotanda, G. Peller, & K. Thomas (Eds.), *Critical race theory: The key writings that formed the movement.* New York: New Press.

Hauser, P.M., McMurrin, S.M., Nabrit, J.M., Nelson, L.W., & Odell, W.R. (1964). *Integration of the public schools: Chicago.* Chicago: Board of Education, Chicago Public Schools.

Horsford, S.D. (2009). The case for racial literacy in educational leadership: Lessons learned from superintendent reflections on desegregation. *UCEA Review, 50*(2), 5–8.

Horsford, S.D. (2010). Mixed feelings about mixed schools: Superintendents on the complex legacy of school desegregation. *Educational Administration Quarterly, 46*(3), 287–321.

Horsford, S.D (2011a). Vestiges of desegregation: Superintendent perspectives on inequality and (dis)integration in the post-Civil Rights era. *Urban Education, 46*(1), 34–54.

Horsford, S.D. (2011b). *Learning in a burning house: Educational inequality, ideology, and (dis)integration.* New York: Teachers College Press.

Horsford, S.D. (forthcoming). When race enters the room: Improving educational leadership through racial literacy. Manuscript submitted for publication.

Horsford, S.D., Grosland, T.J., & Gunn, K.M. (2011). Pedagogy of the personal and professional: Toward a framework for culturally relevant leadership. *Journal of School Leadership, 21*(4), 582–606.

Horvat, E.M., & Lewis, K. (2003). Reassessing the "burden of acting white": The importance of black peer groups in managing academic success. *Sociology of Education, 76, October*, 265–280.

Horvat, E.M., & O'Connor, C. (Eds.). (2006). *Beyond acting white: Reframing the debate on black student achievement.* Lanham, MD: Rowman & Littlefield.

Howard, T.C., & Reynolds, R. (2008). Examining parent involvement in reversing the underachievement of African American students in middle-class schools. *Educational Foundations*, Winter–Spring, 79–98.

Howard, T.C., & Reynolds, R.E. (2009). Parental involvement and engagement to improve the school achievement of African American students. *Educational Foundations, 22*(1–2), 79–98.

Irvine, J.J. (1991). *Black students and school failure: Policies, practices, and prescriptions.* Westport, CT: Praeger.

Jefferson, T. (1781). *Notes on the State of Virginia.*

King, J.E. (Ed.). (2005). *Black education: A transformative research and action agenda for the new century.* New York: Routledge.

Ladson-Billings, G. (1994). *The dreamkeepers: Successful teachers of African American children.* San Francisco, CA: Jossey-Bass.

Ladson-Billings, G. (2004). Landing on the wrong note: The price we paid for Brown. *Educational Researcher, 33*(7), 3–13.

Ladson-Billings, G. (2006). From the achievement gap to the education debt: Understanding achievement in U.S. schools. *Educational Researcher, 35*(7), 3–12.

Ladson-Billings, G. (2011). Interview with Gloria Ladson-Billings [Video file] (retrieved from http://www.aera.net/AnnualMeetingsOtherEvents/AnnualBrownLectureinEducationResearch/2011BrownLectureEventPhotos/InterviewwithGloriaJLadsonBillings/tabid/12763/Default.aspx).

Ladson-Billings, G., & Tate, W.F. (1995). Toward a critical race theory of education. *Teachers College Record, 97*(1), 47–68.

Lightfoot, S.L. (1980). Families as educators: The forgotten people of Brown. In D. Bell (Ed.), *Shades of Brown: New perspectives on school desegregation* (pp. 3–19). New York: Teachers College Press.

López, G., & Parker, L. (Eds.). (2003). *Interrogating racism in qualitative research methodology.* New York: Peter Lang.

Lopez, N. (2003). *Hopeful girls, troubled boys: Race and gender disparity in urban education.* New York: Routledge.

Love, B.J. (2004). Brown plus 50 counter-storytelling: A critical race theory analysis of the "majoritarian achievement gap" story. *Equity and Excellence in Education, 37*, 227–246.

Lynn, M. (Ed.). (2002). Critical race theory and education: Recent developments in the field. *Equity and Excellence in Education, 35*(2), Special Issue.

Lynn, M., & Parker, L. (2006). Critical race studies in education: Examining a decade of research in U.S. schools. *Urban Review, 38*, 257–290.

Lynn, M., Yosso, T.J., Solórzano, D.G., & Parker, L. (Eds.). (2002). Critical race theory and education: Qualitative research in the new millennium. *Qualitative Inquiry, 8*(1), Special Issue.

Lynn, M., Bacon, J.N., Totten, T.L., Bridges, T.L., III, & Jennings, M.E. (2010). Examining teachers' beliefs about African American male students in a low-performing high school in an African American school district. *Teachers College Record, 112*(1), 289–330.

Milner, H.R., IV. (2008). Critical race theory and interest convergence as analytical tools in teacher education politics and practices. *Journal of Teacher Education, 63*(3).

Monroe, C.R. (2005). Why are "bad boys" always black? Causes of disproportionality in school discipline and recommendations for change. *Clearing House: A Journal of Educational Strategies, Issues, and Ideas, 79*(1), 45–50.

Morris, J.E. (1999). A pillar of strength: An African American school's communal bonds with families and community since Brown. *Urban Education, 33*(5), 584–605.

Morris, J.E. (2008). Research, ideology, and the Brown decision: Counter-narratives to the historical and contemporary representation of black schooling. *Teachers College Record, 110*(4), 713–732.

Morris, J.E. (2009). *Troubling the waters: Fulfilling the promise of quality public schooling for black children.* New York: Teachers College Press.

Muhammad, C.G., & Dixson, A.D. (2008). Black females in high school: A statistical educational profile. *Negro Educational Review, 59*(3–4), 163–180.

Muhammad, K.G. (2010). *The condemnation of blackness: Race, crime, and the making of modern urban America.* Cambridge, MA: Harvard University Press.

Noguera, P. (2007). Extended view: Race, student achievement and the power and limitations of teaching. *Sage Race Relations Abstracts, 32*, 44–47.

Ogbu, J. (2004). Collective identity and the burden of "acting white" in black history, community, and education. *Urban Review, 36*(1), 1–35.

Parker, L., & Villalpando, O. (2007). A race(cialized) perspective on education leadership: Critical race theory in educational administration. *Educational Administration Quarterly, 43*, 519–524.

Parker, L., Deyhle, D., & Villenas, S. (Eds.). (1999). *Race is … Race isn't: Critical race theory and qualitative studies in education.* Boulder, CO: Westview.

PBS (Public Broadcasting Service). (2003). *Race: The power of an illusion. Go deeper: Race timeline, explore race, science and social policy* (retrieved from http://www.pbs.org/race/000_About/002_03_a-godeeper.htm).

Perry, T., Steele, C., & Hilliard, A.G., III (Eds.). (2003). *Young, gifted, and black: Promoting high achievement among African-American students.* Boston, MA: Beacon Press.

Plessy v. Ferguson, 163 U.S. 537 (1896).

Polite, V.C. (1993). If only we knew then what we know now: Foiled opportunities to learn in suburbia. *Journal of Negro Education, 62*, 337–354.

Polite, V.C. (1994). The method in the madness: African American males, avoidance schooling, chaos theory. *Journal of Negro Education, 63*, 588–601.

Reardon, S.F. (2011). The widening academic achievement gap between the rich and the poor: New evidence and possible explanations. In G.J. Duncan & R. Murnane (Eds.), *Whither opportunity? Rising inequality, schools, and children's life chance.* New York: Russell Sage Foundation Press.

Roderick, M. (2003). What's happening to the boys? Early high school experiences and school outcomes among African American male adolescents in Chicago. *Urban Education, 38*, 538–607.

Sanders, M.G. (1997). Overcoming obstacles: Academic achievement as a response to racism and discrimination. *Journal of Negro Education, 66*(1), 83–93.

Selden, S. (1999). *Inheriting shame: The story of eugenics and racism in America.* New York: Teachers College Press.

Solórzano, D.G., & Yosso, T.J. (2002). Critical race methodology: Counter-storytelling as an analytical framework for education research. *Qualitative Inquiry, 8*(1), 23–44.

Stinson, D.W. (2008). Negotiating sociocultural discourses: The counter-storytelling of academically (and mathematically) successful African American male students. *American Educational Research Journal, 45*(4), 975–1010.

Stinson, D.W. (2011). When the "burden of acting white" is not a burden: School success and African American male students. *Urban Review, 43*, 43–65.

Tate, W. (1997). Critical race theory and education: History, theory and implications. *Review of Research in Education, 22*, 195–247.

Tillman, L.C. (2003). African American parental involvement in urban school reform: Implications for leadership. *Challenges of Urban Education and Efficacy of School Reform, 6*, 295–312.

Tyson, K. (2003). Notes from the back of the room: Problems and paradoxes in the schooling of young black students. *Sociology of Education, 76*, October, 326–343.

Tyson, K., Darity, W.A., Jr., & Castellino, D. (2005). "It's not a black thing": Understanding the burden of acting white and other dilemmas of high achievement. *American Sociological Review, 70*, 582–605.

Walker, V.S. (1996). *Their highest potential: An African American school community in the segregated South.* Chapel Hill: University of North Carolina Press.

Walker, V.S. (2000). Valued segregated schools for African American children in the South, 1935–1969: A review of common themes and characteristics. *Review of Educational Research, 70*(3), 253–285.

Warikoo, N., & Carter, P.L. (2009). Cultural explanations for racial and ethnic stratification in academic achievement: A call for a new and improved theory. *Review of Educational Research, 79*(1), 366–394.

12

THE RACIALIZATION OF SOUTH ASIAN AMERICANS IN A POST-9/11 ERA

Binaya Subedi

Educational scholars argue that there is a larger need to scrutinize the foundational thinking that positions Asian Americans as the Other: as subjects who do not have claims to national citizenship because of their Other status (Coloma, 2006; Rhee, 2006; Subedi, 2008). Historical and contemporary constructions of Asian Americans as being the Other (exotic, foreign, deviant, etc.) have functioned to racialize Asian American bodies. Omi and Winant (1994) argue that conceptions of race have shifted over time, since "racial categories are created, inhabited, transformed and destroyed" (p. 55). As Palumbo-Liu (1999) demonstrates, scientific racism, racist immigrant laws, and various kinds of political/economic thinking have historically shaped "particular understanding and imagining of the racial Asian/American body and psyche, and the ways Asian Americans might occupy, or should occupy, a particular place in America" (p. 7).

Considering that race has always been a part of the Asian American experience in the United States, the scholarship on critical race theory (CRT) is a productive space to explore how racism has shaped the making of the master narratives on who an Asian American is and what an Asian American should be. The legal framework advocated by critical race theorists enables the critique of the racialized norms that perpetuate violence against Asian Americans (Chang, 1993). It is the commitment to documenting everyday experiences, analyzing the impact of racial structures, and the commitment to social justice that make CRT transformative as a theoretical construct. In the field of education, the infusion of CRT legal scholarship has engendered productive dialogue on how race continues to play a significant role in shaping school inequities. Scholars who utilize CRT as a lens to analyze educational research argue that class and gender analysis cannot fully explain why students of color continue to face academic challenges and continue to be racialized as the Other (Ladson-Billings & Tate, 1995; Tate, 1997). By situating race as a compelling analytical category, CRT "can be used to theorize, examine and challenge the ways race and racism implicitly and explicitly impact on social structures, practices and discourses" (Yosso, 2005, p. 70). "The CRT legal literature offers a necessary critical vocabulary for analyzing and understanding the persistent and pernicious inequity in education that is always already a function of race and racism" (Dixson & Rousseau, 2005, p. 18). Educators who utilize a CRT framework advocate how questions of curriculum, pedagogy, and school culture cannot ignore how race shapes questions of privilege, racial violence, and exclusion. As an extension of U.S. society, the schooling process and in general the discipline of education are deeply implicated in racialized discourses. Linking Asian American educational issues and CRT concepts, Teranishi et al. (2009) argue that CRT scholarship enables educators: (1) to analyze Asian American voices that have been historically silenced in education settings; (2) to critique how interest convergence supports dominant ideas about Asian Americans; and (3) to enable praxis that supports social justice projects within Asian American communities.

Theorizing within the context of tribal critical race theory, Brayboy (2006) examines how indigenous people's conception of reality is based on "multiple, nuanced, and historically- and geographically-located epistemologies and ontologies found in Indigenous communities" (p. 427). Brayboy proposes that the examination of indigenous experiences sheds light on the racial reality within the United States and that the reality cannot be situated outside of larger questions on colonialism and imperialism that have shaped indigenous history and experience. What Brayboy argues is relevant in analyzing the situated and multilayered experiences of marginalized people that have come into existence because of particular historical formations. In this discussion, I argue that we consider the discourse on war as an analytical category that influences the discussion on race about Asian Americans. In particular, I explore the impact of the War on Terror in relation to two tenets of critical race theory: interest convergence and whiteness as property. I argue that war as an analytical lens enables us to further explore concepts such as interest convergence and whiteness as property vis-à-vis how Asian Americans are positioned in school and in society. Firstly, I explore the master narratives on Asian Americans and how the narratives elide critical perspectives on war, since it through the dominant narratives on war that Asian Americans have often been racialized as the Other (Lowe, 1996). Secondly, I explore interest convergence and whiteness as property discourse in relation to (a) a critical media curriculum and (b) the specific ways South Asian Americans are racialized in school and in society. Overall, I argue that there is a larger need to use CRT frameworks in theorizing the racialized experiences of the South Asian and Asian American population. Considering that CRT scholars advocate the need to examine broader historical issues that have shaped the contemporary racial order (Solórzano & Yosso, 2002b), I propose that educators analyze the particularities of racialization in post-9/11 contexts not as isolated events or episodes but as effects of the larger civilizational racism that profoundly influenced the rise of racist epistemologies and which has subordinated the epistemologies of people of color (Scheurich & Young, 1997). Said (1979) termed the larger western project of domination as Orientalism: a systematic process to redefine, to catalogue, "to control, manipulate, even to incorporate, what is manifestly a different (or alternative and novel) world" (p. 12). New and old forms of Orientalism have shaped post-9/11 anti-Muslim or anti-Asian racialization, thus enabling us to recognize that "racist representations and practices are continually changing, being challenged, interrupted, and reconstructed, and that all forms of racism are historically specific" (Rizvi, 2005, p. 170).

Although Asian American and South Asian American designations are useful in speaking about the common or the collective struggles of cultural communities, there are differences within various ethnic and cultural groups within Asian American communities. My use of the term "South Asian American" includes people who trace their background to Bhutanese, Nepali, Indian, Pakistani, Sri Lankan, and Bangladeshi identity. There is much value in conceptualizing identities within ethnic, racial, or cultural groups as being heterogeneous, considering that individuals negotiate their identities differently based on gender, race, ethnicity, social class, sexual orientation, etc. (Asher, 2003). For instance, Pakistani American women who wear headscarves may have different racial experiences than Pakistani American men or Pakistani American women who do not wear headscarves. Similarly, Sikh American men who wear turbans face different dimensions of racism than Sikh American men who do not wear turbans.

MASTER NARRATIVES ON ASIAN AMERICANS AND WAR

The "model minority" framework is a master narrative on race about Asian Americans. It is a model created by whites to benefit a/the white power structure. Its popularity can be attributed more to what it says about whiteness and white systems than to what it says about Asian Americans. The model minority discourse corresponds with white claims to supporting diversity and tolerance. It is popular because it explicitly avoids questions of racialization. In other words, the model minority thesis may be embraced by dominant entities if it parallels the institutions' self-interest in promoting a specific political or cultural ideology. Although the thesis claims to support diversity, the model minority structure is an attempt to secure white interests and policies. In the educational context, the model minority proposition represents Asian Americans as being academically successful subjects who have "progressed" by embodying the ethic of self-help and meritocracy. The thesis selectively ignores the differences within Asian American groups and represents Asians Americans as being "better" than other racial groups (Lee, 2005; Ng et al., 2007; Pang et al., 2011).

As Osajima (1988) writes, the popularity of the model minority thesis coincided with the rise of the East Asian economies in the 1970s and early 1980s and the subsequent migration of Asians in the United States. Formulated after the civil rights movement of the 1960s, the model minority thesis was designed to marginalize the progress made by people of color in the U.S. and was formulated to show how racial minorities can succeed if they follow the meritocracy framework, suggesting that anyone could succeed if they persevered through individual bootstrap effort. Consequently, the model minority construct served as a disciplinary measure on how other racial minorities ought to emulate the Asian American experience. Thus, Asian Americans were given "honorary" white status, suggesting that being a successful minority meant that one ought to assimilate to white cultural norms.

The model minority thesis benefits whites, since it serves as a "divide and conquer" strategy: a ploy to create divisions within people of color who had united during the 1960s struggle for civil rights. Similarly, the model minority construct justifies the need to dismiss "the unique discrimination faced by Asian Americans" (Chang, 1993, p. 1259). In the context of schooling, the model minority framework renders Asian American youth invisible, and the construct has become a license to ignore the discriminations faced by Asian Americans. Consequently, Asian American groups are not seen as a marginalized or racialized community, and educators have difficulty recognizing that "to accept the myth of the model minority is to participate in the oppression of Asian Americans" (Chang, 1993, p. 1264).

Secondly, the master narrative on perpetual outsiders or "forever foreigners" (Tuan, 1998) shapes the experience of Asian Americans in schools and in society. Despite their having a long history in the United States, the narrative represents Asian Americans as individuals who lack national claims or national citizenship (Okihiro, 1994). Since whiteness is often conflated with authentic citizenship, the foreigner designation represents Asian Americans as not being "real" U.S. subjects: always global, always outsiders, and always foreign. If the model minority thesis pejoratively gave Asian Americans a sense of local identity, the foreigner thesis erases any sense of national claims Asian American subjects may claim. And, unfortunately, it is the use of the dehumanizing framework of exotic/deviant foreignness that denies Asian American students their sense of identity in schools. This is not to suggest that Asian American students do not negotiate diasporic or global identities or resist school practices. But it is the framing of Asian Americans as only being global subjects that denies them their sense of national or local identities that are negotiated in various geographies of the United States. It is worth noting that the racialized vocabulary associated with the model minority and that associated with foreignness are often mobilized in relation to each other. Clearly, political, economic, and cultural imperatives influence how and when they are mobilized, but both function as master narratives positioning Asian Americans as monolithic and homogeneous and as being lesser racial, cultural, or ethnic beings. Lowe (1996) argues that Asian American experience is marked by heterogeneity, considering that there are multiple differences within the category of Asian American, which have historically functioned "within relationships of unequal power and domination" (p. 67). Lowe suggests that, when Asian Americans claim their identities as being heterogeneous, it serves to "destabilize the dominant discursive construction and determination of Asian Americans as a homogenous group" (p. 68).

It is not surprising that dominant narratives on the model minority and the perpetual foreigner avoid discourses on war. I recognize that the very idea of (re)examining the nature of Asian American identities within the context of war can further perpetuate their experiences and histories as being non-domestic or foreign. Yet, as Lowe (1996) argues, Asian American experiences cannot be understood without interrogating U.S. involvement in wars in Asia (Korea, the Philippines, Vietnam, etc.), particularly in relation to how it has shaped anti-Asian racism in the United States. U.S. involvement in wars (whether domestic or international) cannot be separated from U.S. interest or complicity in empire. Empires operate via political, cultural, economic, or military means, and war functions to support imperial agendas (Hardt & Negri, 2000). Maira (2010) argues that empire is invisible yet ever-present in our society and that one becomes complicit within the imperial discourse without even recognizing it as an "imperial feeling" (p. 33). This is because, according to Maira, questions of empire and war are often packaged as being about national allegiance, democracy, and freedom. As Maira explains, the post-9/11 apparatus of the War on Terror can be understood as a means to secure imperial interests. It is presented as a benevolent, well-meaning exercise for freedom, for cultural preservation, and for democracy: in order to make "us" safe from "them." It is through the category of war that we can understand how Asian Americans are situated within the discourse on War on Terror that operates in national as well as international contexts. In what follows, I examine how key concepts in CRT (interest convergence and whiteness as property) and the War on Terror can be interconnected to explore South Asian American experiences in school and society.

INTEREST CONVERGENCE, TOLERANCE, AND WAR

Theorized by Bell (1980), interest convergence theory argues that whites may be willing to support diversity efforts if they have the potential to enhance white economic, political, and cultural interests; and the alignment with white interests is a cost for people of color. There is never full parity or equity. Whites, ultimately, will continue to be advantaged when people of color align their interests with whites. In other words, self-interest plays a key role in shaping how whites may decide or not decide to support issues advocated by people of color. Bell argued that the U.S. Supreme Court was willing to support *Brown v. Board of Education*, considering that it wanted the United States represented as a democratic nation-state in the world. Since it critically examines white interests, interest convergence is a useful space to examine the motives that may shape white commitment to racial justice. This is not to assume that white identity or whiteness is a homogeneous category, considering white supremacy operates in complex ways (Leonardo, 2002).

Along with promoting racial profiling and the surveillance of Arab, Asian, and Muslim populations, an important corollary of the War on Terror was promoting tolerance. What constitutes tolerance and the extent to which it can be a tool to promote social change are debatable. The framework of tolerance often operates with the belief that whites need to tolerate or be open-minded about differences rather than focusing on white intolerance. In the post-9/11 context, dominant entities were willing (to a certain degree) to promote tolerance as long as it fit within the dominant interpretation of national citizenship and its notions of patriotism. In other words, the call for white "tolerance" paralleled Asian American efforts to promote anti-racism and social justice in light of post-9/11 racialization and state-sponsored racial profiling. The dominant call to promote religious and cultural tolerance cannot be separated from the U.S. interest in claiming itself as the epicenter of democracy and freedom. The occupation of Iraq and Afghanistan was rationalized based on the need to promote democracy and freedom around the world (Mohanty, 2003). The tolerance construct functioned to show to the world that the United States protected freedom of speech and democratic rights, and in many ways the tolerance narrative was promoted as a social justice discourse.

The case of Mohammad Salman Hamdani illustrates how dominant representations appropriate the identities of people of color and how white self-interest on tolerance attempts to silence the racialized reality that South Asian Americans face. Salman's case explores broader issues of Islamophobia and how it created a culture of surveillance and white resentment of Muslim subjects who were viewed as potential terrorists and as a threat to national security. Considering that Islam is often represented as a deviant religion in western mainstream discussions, Islamophobia is a "term designed to highlight the specificities of contemporary forms of racism directed against Muslims" (Rizvi, 2005, p. 171). Salman's case is documented in Mira Nair's (2003) short film included within the short-film collection titled *11'9"01*. The film explores the complex interplay of religious and racial identities and how the dominant narratives represented Muslims in times of national crisis. I examine the film/media narrative as a way to explore the relationship between pedagogy and CRT tenets (Lynn & Jennings, 2009). The film is a counter-story, a marginalized knowledge that has remained invisible in mainstream discussions on racial profiling, citizenship rights, and Islamophobia. The film addresses, as CRT scholars have argued, the need to narrate the experiences of people of color within the context of power and racialization (Solórzano & Yosso, 2002a). The film, despite dominant claims of tolerance and inter-faith dialogue, traces the operations of racial profiling of suspected terrorists after the events of 9/11 in New York City.

The racial narrative in the film is explored when Salman does not return home following the destruction of the Twin Towers and when his mother posts pamphlets seeking the whereabouts of her son in the local community. Realizing Salman's absence, the FBI opens up an investigation into his potential ties to terrorism. His mother explains in the film about her son being investigated simply because of his Muslim and Pakistani identity. The dissenting voice is the speech of the mother: a Muslim, Pakistani woman searching for the whereabouts of her son, who is being pursued by the U.S. government for potential ties to terrorism. The film documents the hysteria around racial and religious profiling and the active promotion of a surveillance culture of people affiliated with Muslim, Asian, and Arab communities. It explores how Salman was being constructed as a figure of a potential terrorist or as a monster. In the post-9/11 context, in an attempt to incite fear about the global Other, an embodiment of a monster was a Muslim terrorist figure who sought (western) civilization's destruction and one who worked against democratic ideals (Puar & Rai, 2002).

Prashad (2007) argues that the post-9/11 aspect of racialization needs to be understood in relation to broader issues of racial profiling, war, and Islamophobia. Considering the range of issues the War on Terror aimed to promote and silence, Muslims, for instance, found themselves having to respond to questions such as: "How religious of a Muslim are you? How many times a day do you pray? At what Mosque do you pray? How do you feel about the war in Afghanistan? The war in Iraq? What do you think about U.S. foreign policy? How do you feel about Israel?" (Hashad, 2004, p. 742). These questions enable us to recognize the broad nature of racial discourse in which various racial and religious communities come under surveillance and become targets of racial and religious profiling. It helps us recognize how space becomes an important category of analysis, considering how suspected individuals were asked to respond to where they attended a mosque and what they felt about events in geographies such as Iraq, Afghanistan, and Israel. The kinds of scrutiny suspected people were subjected to help us recognize the coupling of domestic and global politics on war and how local/international formations influence racialization in the United States (Zia, 2001).

As a way to foreground racial and religious profiling, the film exposes how the body of Salman was found yet how the knowledge of the discovery of the body was withheld from his family for months. It is worth asking what the intentional silence or the withholding of information around the death may signify in relation to questions of racialization and dominant narratives on monstrosity, terrorism, and war. Salman's body was found in the rubble under the Twin Towers and it was discovered that he had, in fact, rushed to the scene of the destruction to assist with the rescue effort, since he was trained as a police cadet and as an emergency medical assistant. The film critiques the racial and religious profiling efforts of the U.S. state and the post-discovery narrative of tolerance that produced Salman as the "good" Muslim/Pakistani subject who had come to the aid of a national tragedy. He was not only posthumously (and briefly) declared as an assimilated "hero" but was represented as an embodiment of the diverse, multiracial make-up of the nation-state. The herofication suggested that the nation-state needed to be tolerant of the diversity of the nation-state, including those who were not Christians. As often reflected in historical and contemporary contexts, people of color have to claim their good subjectivity or citizenship, as otherwise they will be read as objects who are outside of the normative interpretation of "good" citizens. Mamdani (2004) suggests that Muslim subjects often have to prove that they are good Muslims; otherwise they become, by default, "bad" subjects.

The post-9/11 framework of white tolerance supports the arguments made by critical race theorists that dominant entities may support diversity if it parallels their interest (Bell, 1980). The film addresses how a racialized subject, once represented as a terrorist, can be renamed (even if for a brief moment) as a national hero and the difficulties racialized subjects face in claiming their citizenship. Although the herofication narrative certainly gives the impression that a South Asian American, a person of Pakistani descent, a Muslim, can be a national hero, the film examines how the state-sponsored Muslim-Pakistani-as-hero designation can appropriate minority identities for the purpose of valorizing a specific interpretation of national identity. The film describes how Salman was posthumously read as a domestic subject who had come to the aid as a model minority.

One can speculate why the herofication was needed during this period of intense xenophobia and immigrant surveillance. The film, as a counter-story, helps us recognize how Muslim or South Asian American subjects' claims to national affiliation are often fragile, tenuous, and temporary. It raises questions around what it means to be appropriated by the U.S. nation-state that valorizes itself as a multicultural democracy yet simultaneously racializes citizens by promoting "tolerance" and "freedom." Abu-Lughod (2002) argues that it was during the post-9/11 period that the U.S. reasserted itself as the bastion of democracy by representing the nation-state as a multiracial democracy that valued gender and ethnic diversity. For instance, emphasis was placed on how the cabinet level of the U.S. executive branch under George Bush was reflective of the national demographics. As Eisenstein (2008) argues, such representations, claiming diversity, served undemocratic purposes in which "females and people of color become decoys" (p. 27). The story on how a Muslim, Pakistani subject assimilated and served the United States fits the framework of a multicultural nation-state invested in promoting specific notions of tolerance and freedom at home and abroad.

SCHOOLS AS WHITE PROPERTIES

Scholars who utilize CRT as a theoretical lens argue that questions of property rights have always been connected to racial politics and that whiteness is often affirmed through property discourses. One way the property rights issue enters the educational arena is through property values, taxation, and its relationship to reproducing school inequities. In a similar way to Ladson-Billings and Tate (1995), I want to propose the subtle ways the property rights narrative may help us recognize how people of color are impacted by "the construction of whiteness as the ultimate property" (p. 59). Thus, property in the broader sense includes how one may frame questions on what counts as legitimate identities, knowledge, and practices that can be spoken or practiced and "the idea that whiteness—that which whites alone possess—is valuable and is property" (p. 59). For this reason, schools are constructed as white properties, since they emphasize white norms (Lewis, 2001). Similarly, white property can be emphasized via the framework of the nation-state: who counts as an authentic citizen within the nation-state is connected to white constructions of property. The white property narrative calls for the need for preservation: preserving democracy, preserving freedom, and preserving "our way of life." With the context of the War on Terror, I want to explore the recurring use of preservation rhetoric and how it frames the nation-state and schools as white properties to be protected and how this impacts the experience of South Asian American youth and the communities they affiliate with.

Historically, the question of who counts as an authentic citizen in schools has privileged the norms and values (or properties) of whites. In the post-9/11 context, an important corollary of the property discourse was how the nation-state needed to be safe from potential terrorists. It emphasized ideas of security and surveillance of communities being suspected of having "foreign" affiliations, particularly Muslim affiliations. In other words, the rhetoric on the need to make the country and the school safe meant that those deemed "dangerous" could be or should be scrutinized and profiled. Individuals were asked to give up individual rights for the sake of national security and freedom.

Lewis (2001) argues that schools often reinforce white norms by claiming to have a color-blind school culture. Considering schools are often represented as white property or as (white) national, (white) intellectual space to be preserved, students of South Asian ancestry found themselves more frequently answering questions such as: "Where are you from?" or "When are you going back?" Such queries are not innocent, since they catalogue those who are considered insiders and outsiders, and such questions can leave students befuddled, considering that "home" might be a local space and not outside of U.S. geographical borders. Within the peer interactions in schools in the post-9/11 racial scene, students of South Asian descent faced more blatant questions on their legal status or if their family had potential terrorist connections (Maira, 2010). The events of 9/11 certainly shed light on their racial status in schools, considering that their racial and religious identity had become a source of anxiety and uncertainty. Clearly, the peer use of terms such as "terrorist" or "bomber" or their being somewhat connected to the 9/11 destruction carries a visceral meaning. The frequent use of names such as Osama and Muhammad to refer to South Asian American students frames the students within the categories of potential terrorist and fundamentalist. The uses of those names are not innocent, since they represent the students as being the enemies of the U.S. nation-state.

Verma (2011) documents Sikh American students being harassed and questioned on the legitimacy of their Sikh identity, including being taunted for being potential hijackers and terrorists in school. Verma documents how racial violence ranged from students being taunted concerning "We don't want you, get out you Sikh!!" (p. 187) to students being physically violated in schools for embodying unpatriotic bodies (wearing a turban, etc.). It is worth asking what strategies students may deploy to counter the constructs that position them as the Other within the white property framework. Verma's study points out how, in an attempt to avoid racism, students resorted to changing school, avoiding school, and making attempts to not attend events that promoted hyper-patriotic discourse at the expense of their identities. The study documents how students resorted to hiding their identities in the wake of 9/11 events and the subsequent War on Terror. This meant resorting to giving up wearing a turban and cutting their hair to avoid being read as having a certain religious or cultural identity. For Sikh communities, the act of "dethroning one's turban is the paramount insult to the wearer, the most humiliating form of disrespect, the sheer force of which is usually unknown to hate-crime perpetrators" (Puar, 2008, p. 56). Most importantly, Verma's study illustrates how students mobilized to counter media and public perception of Sikh identities. This meant contacting media, holding dialogue sessions, and correcting mainstream knowledge about Sikh communities. Clearly, as Verma argues, learning the vocabulary to counter racialization can be difficult, considering that there was often little or no support in schools to counter the racist discourse fueled by the War on Terror. The study indicates how there are risks associated with such actions, yet how students mobilized themselves amidst the kinds of racial violence they were enduring in everyday contexts. We can read such forms of actions as forms of counter-stories that critique school cultures and as attempts to reclaim one's cultural dignity and cultural citizenship.

Thus, it is not surprising that the reproduction of schools as white properties forced South Asian American students to enter a world of disclaimers. Students had to disclaim or to clarify that their families did not affiliate with fundamentalists or that they did not support terrorism. Similarly, students had to disclaim that they were from certain nation-states that promoted anti-U.S. policies, or they had to hide the fact that they negotiated religions such as Islam, Buddhism, or Sikhism or that they had ethnic roots in Africa, Asia, or the Middle East. This meant entering a world, to use Yoshino's (2006) term, "covering" or learning to make constant disclaimers to fit within the school system. The racialized condition forced students to disavow suspected affiliations or identities before they would be accepted within school peer culture, or to enter or affiliate with the white property framework so that they would be able (somewhat) to negotiate everyday experiences in school.

NATIONAL SUFFERING AND DISPLACED WHITE ANGER

School cultures that promote citizenship ideals are not innocent, and the hidden curriculum of schools functions to promote and to "preserve" specific values that are aligned with white, middle class norms or property narratives (Yosso, 2005). Joshi (2006) argues that, although schools may claim to promote race-neutral and religious-neutral values, schools overtly or subliminally promote whiteness and mainstream Christianity as the norm. Thus, when students are discriminated against based on their racial background, schools may adopt the color-blind approach: thus claiming the absence of race or racial bias in schools. In other words, when schools are accused of being racist, schools often claim the color-blind response. Not surprisingly, schools may articulate the religious neutrality response as a way to discount the presence of Islamophobia in schools. South Asian American students, especially Muslim and Sikh students, find little comfort in schools considering that they are rendered invisible by the neutrality logic that privileges the knowledge and the norms of white, middle class students.

The discourse on preserving democracy, preserving freedom, and preserving "our way of life" has overt property-related connotations. This is because the narrative on preservation advocates the need to imagine the geography of the nation-state as white spaces. Considering the emphasis on white norms or white notions of citizenship in schools, it is not surprising the extent to which racial discrimination and in general Islamophobia, xenophobia, or anti-immigrant acts are overlooked in schools. The de-emphasis of the racial violence against Muslims and Sikhs is a reflection of how schools socialize students in thinking about the nation-state: as white properties to be preserved. Clearly, schools, homes, and the communities play a crucial role in socializing youth into the rituals on how they ought to affiliate with the nation-state. Too often, as Giroux (2002) maintains, students learn to conform to the nation-state rather than to be critical of the actions of people in power who attempt to define how citizenship should be idealized and practiced. In other words, the unquestioned love for the nation-state is learned very early in life, yet how one is socialized into aspects of this love varies depending on the context (ethnicity, culture, etc.).

The lack of response to the violence endured by people of South Asian background, within and outside of school, is a function of their foreigner status: subjects who are positioned outside of the white interpretation of citizenship. Since the students are viewed as outsiders, school cultures, whether consciously or unconsciously, neglect to respond to the difficulties faced by such students. What if schools operate with the unintentional or intentional thinking that some violence for the love of the nation-state ought to be subliminally tolerated? Ahmad (2002) argues that the countless instances of violence, including murders against immigrants of color, that have taken place in the last decade (whether at gas stations, small towns, suburbs, etc.) are often interpreted in the mainstream context as being a "result of displaced anger" (p. 108) of whites: actions that are reprehensible, considering the psychic damage the nation-state has endured since 9/11. Consequently, dominant society represents such violence as "crimes of passion" (p. 108) that are born out of the love for the country. Such violence is overlooked, since it is constructed as a result of the understandable white anger that justifies the larger purposes of "preserving" democracy and freedom. In other words, there is (ir)rationality and (lack of) logic to this violence against Asian Americans. Thus, whites may disapprove of the violence yet they may interpret the violence as:

> social transgressions … mitigated by our sympathy and shared love for the country; we don't like that this has happened, but we understand why it did, because we, too, have been loyal, we too, have been humiliated. We might even be able to imagine acting out such violence ourselves.
>
> (Ahmad, 2002, p. 108)

In other words, such a perspective, according to Ahmad, tacitly approves, as "the violence being done, while not fully sanctioned, escapes the fullness of moral condemnation one would otherwise expect, and offers the perpetrators a kind of solace, even a form of encouragement" (p. 108). For this reason, what would be codified as unacceptable in social contexts becomes acceptable if certain racial groups endure the violence within and outside of school properties.

Ahmad's argument is relevant in analyzing school culture that implicitly or explicitly may condone verbal or physical violence against students of color. This sort of "sanctioned violence" (Spivak, 1988), although occasionally deplored but not openly and actively condoned, becomes subliminally acceptable, since it involves protecting the nation-state from the Other. In the schooling context, the absence of a clear response to Islamophobia or xenophobia fosters the belief that such actions are acceptable. This does not mean that teachers or school officials sanction such events, but it is the consistent silence around questions of Islamophobia and the racialization of religion that creates the atmosphere of fear and suspicion of students considered "outsiders." Again, this is not to suggest that some teachers do not intervene to protect students who are vilified as "bombers" or "fundamentalists," but that the lack of a safe climate within schools functions to create uncomfortable and hostile spaces for students who negotiate South Asian, Arab, Muslim, and Sikh identities. The lack of response and the silence around racial violence sanction the production of a citizenship discourse that makes distinctions between "us" and "them."

VIOLATING COMMUNITY SPACES

Lipsitz (1999) maintains that whites are socialized into possessively investing in whiteness (as property) and consciously or unconsciously work against gains made by people of color. For example, when the U.S. faces economic competition from Asia (China, Japan, etc.), whites feel the loss of white entitlement and Asian Americans often become objects of white anger. In the post-9/11 context, numerous cultural and educational institutions negotiated by South Asians and Arab, Muslim, Sikh, and other ethnic Asian groups came under attack and were desecrated. These institutions were often perceived as being the embodiment of the gains made by Asian Americans or Arab Americans, and were seen as interfering with traditional ways of imagining the nation-state as white and Christian. It was also assumed that Muslim and Sikh educational institutions were promoting anti-U.S. policies or promoting terrorism.

As a way to reclaim whiteness as property or as a marker of authentic citizenship, property destruction has been a recurring symbol of racial violence against South Asian Americans. In the post-9/11 racial context, the religious and cultural sites negotiated by South Asian American youth have been defaced and vandalized. "Get out," "Not here," and "Go home" have been common forms of hate messages being written on properties. Indeed, as Maira (2010) argues, South Asian American youth have felt the psychological impact on how their families and the larger communities they associate with have been represented in such attacks and realize that the cultural institutions they negotiate have come under surveillance. Maira explores the dissenting forms of citizenship that South Asian American youth engaged in to counter the racism they faced in everyday contexts. Dissenting citizenship is an "engagement with the nation-state that is based on a critique of its power and rhetoric, and not automatically or always in compliance with state policies" (p. 35). For instance, Maira writes about youth intentionally writing pro-Muslim terms or words in their backpacks to critique the dominant racialization of Islam. Similarly, the study documents youth organizing events addressing violations of civil rights after anti-Muslim incidents in high schools. The study documents how youth became "spokespersons in the public sphere engaging with the discourse of 'rights' and with civil and immigrant rights debates in the local community" (p. 36).

The attack on homes or cultural/religious spaces signifies a direct threat to a community's belief system and serves to destroy or desecrate institutions that are deemed as a threat to mainstream society. As Puar (2008) argues, Sikh and Muslim communities have endured various forms of racial violence, including perpetrators urinating and defecating in temples, throwing gasoline bombs at homes and religious centers, and so on. Thus, the living facilities, educational centers, mosques, or temples have become objects of white resentment. Because of racist perception, Sikh temples or *gurdwaras*, Hindu temples, and Islamic mosques have historically been seen as deviant institutions and, through various zoning laws, have been barred from being constructed in areas that are considered white spaces.

It is worth noting that too often instances of racial violence, including attacks at home, are not investigated by local officials as hate crimes. Racism or the racialization of religion is often not taken seriously in U.S. society in relation to Asian Americans, and such events are often read as pranks or events with limited or no social meaning. For example, when a cross was burned in the home of an Indian American family in a Midwestern, suburban area, the media quickly labeled it as a prank. Such events are interpreted as events taking place in isolation or as not being connected to racism or white hatred.

The mainstream interpretation simply forecloses the need to interrogate such events as racial violence. We can read such violence as attempts to reclaim neighborhoods as white spaces. Unfortunately, such events are consistently written as being unfortunate and having limited consequences or impact in society, considering the economic and political changes taking place within the nation-state.

CONCLUSION

I know many Asian American educators who speak about the white resentment they have encountered in classrooms. A common trope of the resentment narrative seems to center around Asian American educators' view on racialization and white complicity in perpetuating racial violence. White students often seem to claim that Asian Americans are not suitable subjects to speak about such racial discourses. My own experience suggests that white students are often in denial about the impact of the War on Terror on racialization. It is because of the imperial policies of the U.S. nation-state that Asian American educators' views on empire and neo-colonialism are represented as being radical and as being against the U.S. nation-state. This debate frames Asian Americans as being the foreign Other(s) who desire the disuniting of the U.S. nation-state.

CRT is a critical space to examine how racialization functions in relation to Asian Americans and how various master narratives operate as disciplinary mechanisms to codify who Asian Americans are and what they should be. Questions of war cannot be situated outside of discussions on race, considering the War on Terror has unleashed new and old forms of racism. I have suggested that local as well as global events have influenced how South Asian Americans have been racialized. The implication of the current context has led students to mobilize themselves to resist dominant politics, however small the resistance might be. The burden has been placed on youth to resist and to claim their cultural citizenship in schools.

As CRT scholars have noted, concepts such as interest convergence and whiteness as property enable us to recognize the function of racialization in U.S. society. As I have argued, both categories are relevant in analyzing the experiences of South Asian Americans within and outside of schools. Whites may be (temporarily) willing to consider the nation-state as a diverse entity if it can reinforce the difference between "domestic" and "foreign" or if it can reinforce a white interpretation of diversity that subsumes the racialization of people of color. Similarly, the attempts to represent the nation-state and schools as white spaces produce South Asian American students and their communities as the anti-norm, foreign, and a threat to the nation-state.

The post-9/11 call for tolerance is a form of intolerance. It is through the rhetoric of multicultural democracy, cultural preservation, and freedom that racial violence is justified against South Asian Americans in school and in society. The trauma faced by the U.S. nation-state often becomes a platform to justify white anger. Such interpretation of violence frames the real victim as being whites and South Asian Americans (particularly Muslims and Sikhs, etc.) as victimizers. The thesis on white victimhood subsumes the rightful claims made by Asian Americans for racial justice. CRT can be a critical space of uncovering narratives that traces the relationship between the racialization of citizenship and the rhetoric of war that positions South Asian Americans as suspects, potential terrorists, and foreign subjects who are defiling white culture.

REFERENCES

Abu-Lughod, L. (2002). Do Muslim women really need saving? Anthropological reflections on cultural relativism and its others. *American Anthropologist, 104*(3), 783–790.

Ahmad, M. (2002). Homeland insecurities: Racial violence the day after September 11. *Social Text, 20*(3), 101–115.

Asher, N. (2003). At the intersections: A postcolonialist woman of color considers western feminism. *Social Education, 67*(1), 47–50.

Bell, D. (1980). Brown v. Board of Education and the interest-convergence dilemma. *Harvard Education Review, 93*(3), 518–533.

Brayboy, B.M.J. (2006). Toward a tribal critical race theory in education. *Urban Review, 37*(5), 425–446.

Chang, R.S. (1993). Toward an Asian American legal scholarship: Critical race theory, post-structuralism, and narrative space. *California Law Review, 18*, 1243–1323.

Coloma, R.S. (2006). Disorienting race and education: Changing paradigms on the schooling of Asian Americans and Pacific Islanders. *Race, Ethnicity and Education, 9*(1), 1–15.

Dixson, A., & Rousseau, C. (2005). And we are still not saved: Critical race theory in education ten years later. *Race, Ethnicity and Education, 8*(1), 7–27.

Eisenstein, Z. (2008). Resexing militarism for the globe. In R.L. Riley, C.P. Mohanty, & M.B. Pratt (Eds.), *Feminism and war: Confronting US imperialism* (pp. 27–46). London: Zed Books.

Giroux, H.A. (2002). Democracy, freedom, and justice after September 11th: Rethinking the role of educators and the politics of schooling. *Teachers College Record, 104*(6), 1138–1162.

Hardt, M., & Negri, A. (2000). *Empire.* Cambridge, MA: Harvard Education Press.

Hashad, D. (2004). Stolen freedoms: Arabs, Muslims, and South Asians in the wake of post 9/11 backlash. *Denver University Law Review, 81*(4), 735–747.

Joshi, K.Y. (2006). *New roots in America's sacred ground: Religion, race, and ethnicity in Indian America.* New Brunswick, NJ: Rutgers University Press.

Ladson-Billings, G., & Tate, W.F. (1995). Toward a critical race theory of education. *Teachers College Record, 97*(1), 47–68.

Lee, S.J. (2005). *Up against whiteness: Race, youth and immigrant youth.* New York: Teachers College Press.

Leonardo, Z. (2002). The souls of white folk: Critical pedagogy, whiteness studies, and globalization discourse. *Race, Ethnicity and Education, 5*(1), 29–50.

Lewis, A.E. (2001). There is no "race" in the schoolyard: Color-blind ideology in an (almost) all-white school. *American Educational Research Journal, 38*(4), 781–811.

Lipsitz, G. (1999). *The possessive investment in whiteness.* Philadelphia, PA: Temple University Press.

Lowe, L. (1996). *Immigrant acts: On Asian American cultural politics.* Durham, NC: Duke University Press.

Lynn, M., & Jennings, M.E. (2009). Power, politics, and critical race pedagogy: A critical race analysis of black male teachers' pedagogy. *Race, Ethnicity and Education, 12*(2), 173–196.

Maira, S.M. (2010). Citizenship and dissent: South Asian Muslim youth in the US after 9/11. *South Asian Popular Culture, 8*(1), 31–45.

Mamdani, M. (2004), *Good Muslim, bad Muslim: America, the Cold War, and the roots of terror.* New York: Pantheon.

Mohanty, C.P. (2003). *Feminism without borders.* Durham, NC: Duke University Press.

Nair, M. (2003). *11'09"01: September 11.* Empire Pictures.

Ng, J.C., Lee, S.S., & Pak, Y.K. (2007). Contesting the model minority and perpetual foreigner stereotypes: A critical review of literature of Asian Americans in education. *Review of Research in Education, 31*, 95–130.

Okihiro, G. (1994). *Margins and mainstream: Asians in American history and culture.* Seattle: University of Washington Press.

Omi, M., & Winant. H. (1994). *Racial formations in the United States.* London: Routledge.

Osajima, K. 1988. Asian Americans as the model minority: An analysis of the popular press image in the 1960s and 1980s. In G. Okihiro, S. Hune, A. Hansen, & J. Liu (Eds.), *Reflections on shattered windows: Promises and prospects for Asian American studies* (pp. 165–174). Pullman: Washington State University Press.

Palumbo-Liu, D. (1999). *Asian/American: Historical crossings of a racial frontier.* Stanford, CA: Stanford University Press.

Pang, V.O., Han, P.P., & Pang, J.M. (2011). Asian American and Pacific Islander students: Equity and the achievement gap. *Educational Researcher, 40*(8), 378–389.

Prashad, V. (2007). Teaching by candlelight. *Social Text, 25*(1), 105–115.

Puar, J.K. (2008). "The turban is not a hat": Queer diaspora and practices of profiling. *Sikh Formations, 4*(1), 47–91.

Puar, J.K., & Rai, A.S. (2002). Monster, terrorist, fag: The war on terrorism and the production of docile patriots. *Social Text, 20*(3), 117–148.

Rhee, J. (2006). Re/membering (to) shifting alignments: Korean women's transnational narratives in US higher education. *International Journal of Qualitative Studies in Education, 19*(5), 596–615.

Rizvi, F. (2005). Representation of Islam and education for justice. In C. McCarthy, W. Crichlow, G. Dimitriadis, & N. Dolby (Eds.), *Race, identity and representation in education* (pp. 167–178). New York: Routledge.

Said, E. (1979). *Orientalism*. New York: Vintage Books.

Scheurich, J., & Young, M. (1997). Coloring epistemologies: Are our research epistemologies racially biased? *Educational Researcher, 26*(4), 4–16.

Solórzano, D., & Yosso, T. (2002a). A critical race counterstory of race, racism and affirmative action. *Equity and Excellence in Education, 35*(2), 155–168.

Solórzano, D.G., & Yosso, T.J. (2002b). Critical race methodology: Counter-storytelling as an analytical framework for education research. *Qualitative Inquiry, 8*(1), 23–44.

Spivak, G.C. (1988). Can the subaltern speak? In C. Nelson & L. Grossberg (Eds.), *Marxism and the interpretation of culture* (pp. 271–313). Urbana: University of Illinois Press.

Subedi, B. (2008). Contesting racialization: Asian immigrant teachers' critiques and claims of teacher authenticity. *Race, Ethnicity and Education, 1*(11), 57–70.

Tate, W.F. (1997). Critical race theory and education: History, theory, and implications. In M.W. Apple (Ed.), *Review of Research in Education* (pp. 195–247). Washington, DC: American Educational Research Association.

Teranishi, R.T., Behringer, L.B., Grey, E.A., & Parker, T.L. (2009). Critical race theory and research on Asian Americans and Pacific Islanders in higher education. *New Directions for Institutional Research, 142*, Summer, 57–68.

Tuan, M. (1998). *Forever foreigners or honorary whites? The Asian ethnic experience today*. New Brunswick, NJ: Rutgers University Press.

Verma, R. (2011). Unlearning the silence in the curriculum: Sikh histories and post-9/11 experiences. In B. Subedi (Ed.), *Critical global perspectives: Rethinking knowledge about global societies* (pp. 181–197). Charlotte, NC: Information Age Press.

Yoshino, K. (2006). *Covering: The hidden assault on our civil rights*. New York: Random House.

Yosso, T.J. (2005). Whose culture has capital? A critical race theory discussion of community cultural wealth. *Race, Ethnicity and Education, 8*(1), 69–91.

Zia, H. (2001). Oh, say, can you see? Post September 11. *Amerasia Journal, 27*(3), 2–12.

13

BLURRING THE BOUNDARIES
The Mechanics of Creating Composite Characters
Daniella Ann Cook

As Pharaoh drew near, the sons of Israel looked, and behold, the Egyptians were marching after them, and they became very frightened; so the sons of Israel cried out to the Lord. Then they said to Moses, "Is it because there were no graves in Egypt that you have taken us away to die in the wilderness? Why have you dealt with us in this way, bringing us out of Egypt? Is this not the word that we spoke to you in Egypt, saying, "Leave us alone that we may serve the Egyptians"? For it would have been better for us to serve the Egyptians than to die in the wilderness.

(Exodus, 14:11–12)

We are voices in the wilderness, trying to talk to the powers that be ... that some of the issues that you must take care of, we need to have some input into.

(Sarah Steve,[1] veteran African American educator)

The words spoken by Sarah Steve, regarding school reforms in post-Katrina New Orleans, call into memory the images of the Jewish people wandering in the wilderness after 400 years of slavery in Egypt. In the Biblical passage from Exodus, the newly freed Israelites are venting their anger and fear about being led into the wilderness by Moses. In many ways, this captures the plight of black educators in New Orleans after Katrina. As with the Israelites being led to the Promised Land, the wilderness experience tested their faith and belief. The wilderness in Biblical texts represents a place of remoteness and isolation. From one perspective, the wilderness is a place to be avoided or a sign of being out of favor with the powers that be. Yet the wilderness was also a place of miracles. In the Biblical account, over 40 miracles happened during the wilderness journey. In this sense, the wilderness is a place where miracles can happen, where a people can be restored.

Black educators in New Orleans after Katrina are voices crying out in the wilderness of school reform. In the wilderness of school reform in New Orleans, listening to black educators can lead toward a vision of public schooling that restores rather than just reforms public education. The stories and experiences of African American[2] educators are an important starting point for seeing and understanding the complexities and nuances of schooling in New Orleans after Katrina. With Hurricane Katrina and the subsequent school reforms capturing and sustaining national attention there is an urgent need for the counterstory of black educators to be told in a compelling and accessible manner.

This chapter expands on an earlier article I co-authored with Adrienne Dixson (Cook & Dixson, 2012), which employed composite counterstories to recount the experiences of black educators in post-Katrina New Orleans. Research methods are always a methodological preoccupation for those seeking to do rigorous and meaningful race research. A significant nuance of critical race theory (CRT) lies in its blurring the boundary between theory and method as an essential challenge to dominant methodological and epistemological canons in education research. In this chapter, I delve more deeply into the mechanics of constructing composite counterstory characters. Specifically, I want to expand this dialogue by detailing how to develop composite characters from data in composite counterstories and how this development is distinct from traditional narrative renderings of research participants.

Two assumptions undergird this chapter. First, meeting rigorous methodological standards matters even more for those doing critical work. Second, meaningful race research and high quality, rigorous research methods are not mutually exclusive. CRT scholars in education must continually develop the capacity not only to meet those rigorous research standards but also to expand beyond them in meaningful, precise ways. In the forthcoming discussion of composite counterstorytelling as a method and my goal is to continue to build upon the important dialogue with others seeking to do rigorous, high quality research that draws upon CRT as both a theory and a method.

Composite counterstorytelling as a critical race methodological tool exposes the ways in which race and racism affect the lives of racial minorities in education. According to Cook and Dixson (2012), composite counterstorytelling as a unique innovation of CRT methodology adds to critical race qualitative research in three ways. First, composite counterstories provide empirical space for researchers to recount the stories and experiences of people in political vulnerable positions. Second, composite counterstories as a vehicle to present counterstories necessarily require descriptions of rich, robust contexts in which to understand those stories and lived experiences while maintaining the complexity of meaning. The use of composite characters turns the focus from individual participants to the larger issues faced by groups (in this case African American educators in New Orleans post-Katrina) and deepens our analysis of how race and racism affect the lived experiences of people of color as a group in schools. Finally, an important contribution of composite counterstorytelling is the appeal of making research accessible beyond academic audiences.

After a brief discussion of critical race theory in education, I will discuss the use of composite counterstories within critical race methodology within the context of contemporary work on researching race, which is instructive for how the use of composite character counterstorytelling in CRT addresses some of the dilemmas of researching race. I present an excerpt of the composite counterstory "Something Sweet," followed by a discussion of lessons from the counterstory for deepening the dialogue about innovation in critical race theory methodology.

CENTERING RACE AND RACISM IN EDUCATION RESEARCH

CRT emanated from a need for "an adequate critical vocabulary for articulating … an alternative account of racial power" (Crenshaw et al., 1995, p. xxi). Informed by critical legal studies' insufficient accounting for race, critical race theorists maintained that the permanence of race, and racism, must be central to any serious critique and understanding of the American legal system, thus placing the realities of the oppressed at the center of analysis (Cook, 1995; Crenshaw et al., 1995; Matsuda, 1995). Thus, a key aspect of CRT is to articulate how race, particularly white supremacy, operates within structures and institutions (Crenshaw et al., 1995).

Beginning with the germinal work by Ladson-Billings and Tate (1995), CRT in education argues that race remains under-theorized in education (Ladson-Billings & Tate, 1995; Tate, 1997). In this sense, educational inequity and inequality could only be explained with a more robust racial analysis. Using CRT as a lens, scholars in education have engaged race more substantively in an interdisciplinary, multi-epistemological project focused on the complex and multiple ways in which race is connected to create predictable outcomes in the education of students of color in the United States (Chapman, 2007; DeCuir & Dixson, 2004; Ladson-Billings & Tate, 1995; Lynn & Parker, 2006; Solórzano & Yosso, 2001; Tate, 1997). Dixson and Rousseau (2006) in their review of CRT research in education found direct links to the legal CRT literature specifically in regard to attention to voice, challenging notions of colorblindness in education and exploring how restrictive and expansive views of equality are constructed in schools. Not only has CRT informed the analysis of the intersection of multiple oppressions in education (Buras et al., 2010; Cook, 2008; Dixson, 2011; Donnor, 2006; Duncan, 2002; Yosso, 2005), but it has informed and pushed our understanding of research methodology.

COMPOSITE COUNTERSTORYTELLING AS CRITICAL RACE METHODOLOGY

CRT intentionally blurs the boundary between theory and method. As a theoretical frame, CRT centers race and racism as essential to understanding how systems of inequality, disparity, and inequity continue to function. Maintaining the centrality of race elucidates the fluid, shifting, yet consistent message of white supremacy and how it operates in the policies, practices, and everyday schooling experiences of students, teachers, and the larger community. As a methodological frame, it embodies an epistemology for how and why particular methods are chosen, with particular attention to centering the stories and lived experiences of people of color. Solórzano and Yosso (2002) understand that methodology "is the nexus of theory and method in the way praxis is to theory and practice" (p. 143). There are at least five components to CRT methodology: (1) recognizing the intersectionality of race and racism with other forms of oppression (Crenshaw, 1991; Parker & Lynn, 2002; Solórzano and Yosso, 2002); (2) confronting dominant ideology, thus intentionally deconstructing the notions of objectivity and neutrality in research (D. Bell, 1987; Crenshaw et al., 1995; Ladson-Billings, 2000); (3) acknowledging the various ways that oppression is resisted (Delgado, 1989, 1993); (4) exposing deficit-based research by centering the lived, everyday experiences of people of color (Delgado, 1989; Delgado and Stefancic, 2001); and (5) drawing from multiple disciplines to analyze race and racism within particular historical and contemporary contexts (Pillow, 2003; Solórzano, 1997; Solórzano and Yosso, 2000, 2001; Tate, 1994). As a methodological frame, critical race methodology "generates knowledge by looking to those who have been epistemologically marginalized, silenced, and disempowered" (Solórzano & Yosso, 2002, pg. 142). Thus, CRT methodology in education advocates choosing methods (e.g. specific research practices and procedures) that intentionally push against further marginalizing those often rendered silent or invisible as subjects of the research.

As CRT scholars in education seek models and frames for their work, it is important to provide methodological frameworks for a method of CRT without being prescriptive. This is one of the crucial questions for CRT methodology. Those who say they do CRT, more often than not, are referring to their theoretical frames, although the actual practices and procedures of their research speak to the contrary. If a significant nuance of CRT lies in its blurring boundaries between theory and method as an essential strategy for challenging the dominant canon, then doing CRT research requires an understanding of how critical race theory in education functions as both a theory and a method. This necessitates turning to how researching race and race research have been taken up by other critical scholars.

Representation, Race, and Research

Woven throughout both recent and early work on race is the notion of representation. Zuberi and Bonilla-Silva (2008b) in their edited volume are concerned with:

> how White racial logic influences the life chances of all "racial subjects" and the sociological imagination. Thus, we regard this as our first collaborative effort to attack White supremacy in contemporary research on race as well as in the methods most sociologists employ to examine, according to the logic that parades as "objectivity," the so-called race effect.
>
> (p. 4)

Unapologetically drawing on their personal journeys as researchers, the authors proceed to critically examine how white logic and methods function to suppress, including the erroneous treatment of race as fixed, while simultaneously ignoring race and racism. Drawing on an African proverb, Zuberi and Bonilla-Silva (2008a) conclude:

> sociological hunters still parade the game they collect (data and arguments about people of color) with their objective rifles (White methods) and it is very likely they will continue doing so in the near future. However, in this volume the prey had a chance to tell the tale of the hunt. And the "prey" ("prey" from the perspective of the hunters) showed the weakness of the hunters as well as the many calibration problems of their rifle.
>
> (p. 329)

In essence, the collective response in this volume draws attention to how purportedly objective methods and methodology misrepresent matters of race, and racism, in research.

Representation is concerned with not only how questions of race are articulated but by whom and for whom. In their edited volume, *Racing Research Researching Race* (2000), Twine and Warren's exploration of "race as a concept … as having [a] special synergistic feature in getting at a collective version of reality" (p. xiv) is particularly useful in thinking about race and representation. Twine (2000) notes: "another aspect of conducting research in racialized terrains involves the issues of representations, or writing culture" (p. 22). In this sense, within the realm of race research in education, CRT methodology, particularly the focus on narrative and counterstory, addresses these issues, providing race researchers an avenue to represent people of color, and ourselves, in our full complexity as human.

Role of Narrative in Critical Race Methodology

The possibility and necessity of translating analyses into active resistance against oppressive and racist structures must be foundational for CRT research and scholarship. Matsuda (1995) calls for "grassroots philosophers who are uniquely able to relate theory to the concrete experience of oppression" (p. 63). In this sense, scholars are not passive producers of knowledge; they must become active in the struggle for social justice within education. CRT offers education researchers the opportunity to be intellectuals who not only are interested in "explicating an unjust social order" but will also be active participants "in reconstructing a just community" (Cook, 1995, p. 85). Fundamentally, CRT insists on both the necessity of theorizing race and researchers being *active* participants in the struggle for justice and equity.

This active struggle begins with the acknowledgement that all social science research tells a story. CRT not only acknowledges and actively pushes back against the dominant story told about those marginalized in education but is committed to doing so in accessible ways. Pillow (2003) aptly captures this commitment, noting that "a case for understanding and utilizing race-based methodologies [must be understood] as not simply new methods, but work that raises consciousness of, and asks critical questions about, our most fundamental epistemological practices" (p. 195). So the use of narrative is an essential tool utilized by CRT to dismantle hegemonic knowledge and discourse (D. Bell, 1987; Crenshaw et al., 1995; Ladson-Billings, 2000).

CRT scholars' use of narrative originates with Derrick Bell's (1987) assertion that narrative corresponds more closely to how the human mind makes sense of experience. A particular set of narratives, emerging from the experience of dominant groups, informs institutions charged with the creation, maintenance, and exchange of knowledge. The creation and exchange of stories about individual situations not only collectively creates social reality (Delgado, 1989) but also informs our understanding of that reality. The stories, or narratives, of the dominant group justify its power and privilege by the creation of "a form of shared reality in which its own superior position is seen as natural" (Delgado, 1989, p. 2412). If "stories create their own bonds, represent cohesion, shared understandings, and meanings" (Delgado, 1989, p. 2412), it is necessary to create stories to counter the dominant narratives.

In the tradition of CRT, stories are important in challenging traditional explanations of power relationships vis-à-vis an emphasis on the role of context in meaning-making (Guinier and Torres, 2002). Context is informed by the position, and thus perspective, of the teller. In this sense, narrative can provide the perspective of those at the bottom, and thus potentially challenge normative assumptions about power relationships (Matsuda, 1995). Narratives that "look to the bottom" acknowledge that "those who lack material wealth or political power still have access to thought and language, and their development of those tools ... differs from that of the most privileged" (Matsuda, 1995, p. 65). This way of storytelling is grounded in the experiences of those with the least advantage and privilege.

Accordingly, counterstorytelling uses the grounded everyday experiences of marginalized people coupled with actual data in contextualized social situations as a way to generate knowledge by looking to the bottom, thus epistemologically centering those most often rendered invisible and silent in research. Noblit et al. (2004) state it this way: "Methods are ideas and theories in themselves. They have histories, are best understood as tentative, and are not separate from the theories they are used to test or explore. Method and theory are linked by people in concrete historical and ideational contexts" (p. 3). In this sense, using counterstories or counter-narratives links theory to methods of CRT in one important aspect: the stories of the marginalized are foundational to both its method and its theory.

Solórzano & Yosso (2002) discuss three types of counterstories: personal narratives, other people's narratives, and composite narratives that (a) build community between those at the bottom and on the margins of society; (b) challenge the taken-for-granted understanding of those at the center; and (c) are pedagogical teaching and learning tools that use story to expand our understanding of reality and possibility. Those choosing to represent oppressed people must be wary of creating a homogenized version of the marginalized that does not take account of the diversity and complexity of those "at the bottom" (Matsuda, 1995, p. 65) with the least privilege and advantage. In this sense, counterstories, and the use of composite characters, centers the humanity of those at the margins of society.

An essential component of white supremacy in the United States has been affirming democratic principles while simultaneously denying the humanity of people of color. Within race research, countering this pervasive sentiment must be done through not only our methods and methodologies but also our writing. Although racism is permanent and ubiquitous, so is the possibility and potential for challenging racist practices and structures. From a CRT perspective, one powerful way is through counterstorytelling. The use of counterstorytelling and development of composite characters is one way to address our anxiety as race researchers committed to challenging racist structures and practices in research. What follows is an excerpt from "Something Sweet," the first story in a trilogy, and then a discussion of how the composite characters were created from the data in the stories, drawing on the excerpt as an example.

COMPOSITE CHARACTER COUNTERSTORYTELLING: AN EXCERPT FROM "SOMETHING SWEET"

"Something Sweet" is the first story in a series of three composite character counterstories based on my yearlong ethnography of black educator experiences with school reform in New Orleans post-Katrina. The setting of the counterstory trilogy is Community Coffeehouse (CC's) on Esplanade Avenue in the Mid-City area of New Orleans. A locally owned, family coffeehouse chain, CC's also packages and sells its own roasted coffee, specializing in the New Orleans favorite, chicory coffee. To ground the excerpt, I will provide a brief context of New Orleans and the contours of the public schools before and after Katrina.

Public education in New Orleans has been shaped by the racial, cultural, and economic complexity of the community. According to the 2000 Census, the population of New Orleans was 66.6 percent black and 26.6 percent white. Coincidently, the state of Louisiana's racial composition is the direct opposite, with 62.6 percent being white and

32.3 percent black. Although understanding the historical context of the city is necessary for understanding New Orleans post-Katrina, it is beyond the scope of this chapter to delve deeply into this history.[3] However, it is vital to bear in mind two aspects of post-Katrina school reforms in New Orleans.

First, the single largest displacement of black educators since desegregation was an unintended and historically significant consequence of Hurricane Katrina (Cook, 2010; Cook & Dixson, 2012). With the mass dismissal of educators, during the 2006–07 school year, the first full school year after Katrina, the black teaching force alone was cut in half, shrinking from 2,759 teachers in the 2004–05 school year to 801 in the 2006–07 school year (Cook, 2010). Research has documented how the desegregation process systematically disregarded conceptions of school quality valued by the African American community (Noblit & Dempsey, 1996; St. John & Cadray, 2004), so it comes as no surprise that the voices, knowledge, and experiences of black teachers are not explicitly included in urban school reform practice and research. Second, rather than a single, centralized governance system, a decentralized-system approach was adopted to govern public schools in Orleans Parish. Of the 53 schools open during the 2006–07 school year, the first full school year after Hurricane Katrina, 21 different entities (each charter school functions autonomously) operated schools, with ten using selective admission policies (Dingerson, 2006).

What follows is the opening of "Something Sweet," a dialogue between two veteran African American educators, Sarah Steve and Lewis Snyder. It is my hope that, in reading this composite story, we might become more conscious of the current reality of African American educators in New Orleans after Katrina from their perspective.

Something Sweet[4]

"I have so much work to finish. This new electronic grading and attendance system is really getting on my last nerve. And who has time?" thought Sarah as she got out of her car. She noticed the trees swinging lightly in the breeze and said out loud to no one in particular *"Dang, this is November 7th and who could ask for anything better than what the day looked and felt like? I mean, nowhere in the world other than Florida and Jamaica will you feel this type of breeze. How could anyone give this up? I love this city."*

As she opened the door to CC's Coffeehouse on Esplanade Avenue, a woman was walking out at the same time. They greeted each other warmly with a chorus of "How ya doin'? Fine an' you?" *Katrina may have flooded the city wreaking untold damage but it didn't take her soul or the heart and passions of her people. How could you not get stuck in the gumbo that is New Orleans?*

Reaching the counter, Sarah ordered her cup of coffee. *She decided to get a quick cup while waiting for the professional development workshop to begin. She was actually looking forward to this one. She had heard so much about the Bread Loaf/Students at the Center[5] training from one of her colleagues at another school.*

"Afternoon," she said to the tall skinny young man at the counter. "Umm … Can I have a tall house blend with room for cream?" *Maybe she should think of the sweeping changes happening in the school as the folks in charge ordering coffee. One tall charter with laptops or one venti open admissions house blend. She chuckled to herself. Like ordering a coffee, these schools are different sizes and names but in reality versions of the same coffee with room for cream.*

"Here is your coffee. That will be $2.60." As she took the steaming cup from the young man at the counter she said "Thank you, baby" with the baby sounding more like bey-bay to those ears not native to the Crescent City. She dropped the change into the jar with "TIPS" handwritten in large red letters. *She had tips for those people running the schools. "How about thanking the teachers who came back after the storm? How about showing some appreciation for the work we had been doing before the storm without all these resources? The only thanks we got was being told over the Internet that we were going to be terminated. In other parishes, teachers got paid throughout the storm, and they were just as impacted as we were. Jefferson Parish people never missed a check, but we had to go to a Western Union or Moneygram to get a check that wasn't even cor-rect. And that was one check.*

Lost in her thoughts, Sarah had not noticed the person who had walked up to the table where she was sitting near the glass window that extended the length of the wall giving patrons a view of Esplanade. "Good afternoon, Mrs. Steve," a voice called out. Sarah looked up from her musings to Mr. Snyder with his characteristic smile that was known to light up any room.

"Hey Mr. Snyder. How you doing?"

"Fine, I suppose. Or as fine as I could be given the circumstances."

(Cook & Dixson, 2012, pp. 19–20)

CREATING COMPOSITE CHARACTERS

In coding the interviews, field notes, and documents, I paid attention to not only the counterstories and dominant stories but also the specific ways in which black educators articulated their agency and resistance. After receiving the transcriptions, I coded the interviews regarding participants' pre-, post- and both pre- and post-Katrina school-ing experiences. Following this initial coding of the data, I mined the data for how the research question "What stories do these educators tell about schooling in pre- and post-Katrina New Orleans?" was addressed. After identifying three major themes in the data—loss and anger, isolation, and the importance of education—I went back and overlaid these three themes over historical/temporal codes (pre-Katrina, post-Katrina, both pre- and post-Katrina) to develop a thematic story. These thematic stories would provide the foundation for the composite counterstories. These emerging themes were then analyzed for whether and how they corresponded with the tenets of CRT, specifi-cally counterstorytelling and the permanence of racism.

The challenge with this etic approach was the possibility of privileging my interpreta-tion and understanding. This was countered by staying close to the interview data. In addition to coding the data for themes, I also wrote the narrative of each participant, mirroring traditional narrative writing. This was an important step in creating the com-posite characters. These individual narratives focused on creating a three-dimensional image of the participants that not only captured their words and sentiments but also would give insight into the personalities and histories. Given that story is understood and constructed out of exchanges, experiences, and observations (Emerson et al., 1995; Goodall, 2000), it was critical to capture the essence of each individual before construct-ing composite characters.

The process of composing the individual narratives before creating the three com-posite characters also yielded a crucial insight—the importance of New Orleans as a crucial character to the story. Incorporating how the city was and is talked about in the majoritarian and counterstories provided readers a visceral sense of the context of New Orleans. The relationship that participants had with the city needed to be fully present within the text of the counterstory, demonstrating another aspect of composite character building—the role of context.

Creating composite characters was an important aspect to shaping counterstories, with the goal of creating what LaPlante (2007) calls modular stories. Quoting M. Bell (1997), LaPlante (2007) defines modular stories as "stories ... composed as a mosaic, a design made up of component parts: What modular design can do is liberate the writer from linear logic, those chains of cause and effect, strings of dominoes always falling forward" (p. 158). In short, employing composite characters to move away from a *telling* to a *showing* in counterstories required coupling my training as an ethnographer and qualitative researcher with engaging the creative writing literature. In an effort to weave a coherent narrative, I created a storyline of the composite counterstory that would embed themes gleaned from the transcripts, field notes, and other data. Blending aspects of various participants into composite characters included taking aspects of body language, phrasing, and personal backgrounds. Each composite character simultaneously represented and introduced one of the three themes (anger and loss: "Something Sweet"; isolation: "Blocked"; and the importance of education: "Technical Difficulties"), with their internal thoughts giving insight into how people understood their relationship to the context of New Orleans and the people of New Orleans (see Figure 13.1). Drawing on Faulkner's (1929/1994) use of stream of consciousness in *The Sound and the Fury*, the internal thoughts of the characters, indicated by italics within the stories, became a crucial avenue for including relevant background data.

For consistency of representation throughout, I read each counterstory, individually and as a whole, for consistency of character, depth of character, and how well specific aspects from each theme were shown rather than told. Each composite character had

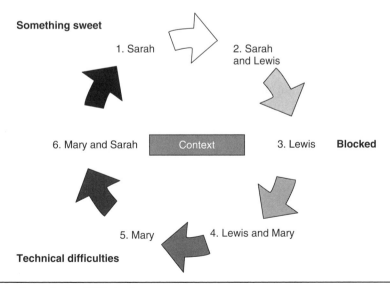

Figure 13.1 Composite counterstory (CCS) storyline

distinct gestures, speech patterns, and personality quirks based on my blending of participants in the study. An important component of revising the composite characters and their interactions in the context in which they were embedded was voice. A key question guiding this process was whether each character had a well-developed, distinct voice that was multidimensional and therefore captured the most complete representation of the data.

Within this frame, the voice of the researcher is acknowledged, problematized, and fully present,[6] acknowledged in the sense that researchers are not immune to the distress, heartache, joys, and pain of the people who share their stories and experiences. Self-reflexivity allows us as race researchers and researchers of race to trouble our individual stances, ideas, and assumptions to move beyond positivistic bounds of objectivity and subjectivity. This troubling opens the door to be fully present, and represent the findings from our analysis. To be fully human is the privilege of having faults and favorable attributes without your humanity being stripped as a consequence of the former. Composite character counterstorytelling methodologically provides a mechanism for honoring the humanity of participants, who are often marginalized into how we understand and, more importantly, write our research findings.

Using composite characters in counterstories focuses on central ideas in CRT and answers the call by Ladson-Billings (2005) to provide "richer, more detailed stories that place our stories in more robust and powerful contexts" (p. 117). Intentionally three-dimensional in their rendering, composite counterstories are not simply fictionalized narratives drawn from interview transcripts, field notes, memos, and other research data. As Solórzano and Yosso (2002) note, "we are not developing imaginary characters that engage in fictional scenarios. Instead, the 'composite' characters we develop are grounded in real-life experiences and actual empirical data and are contextualized in social situations that are also grounded in real life, not fiction" (p. 36). Given that within CRT experiential knowledge is an asset, composite character counterstories remind us of the importance of gaining a thorough understanding of how people understand their current reality before attempting any meaningful analysis about the meaning of their stories.

IMPLICATIONS FOR CRITICAL RACE METHODOLOGY

Three-dimensional portrayals of people and their stories and experiences embrace the contradictions and complications of their humanity. Although rich in detail, traditional ethnographies may inadequately embody the complexity of the people whose stories we share. In politically precarious contexts, it is even more important to center the humanity of participants in our research. Although the use of composite characters creates space to explore the agency and resistance of participants, another key aspect is the creation of a safe, yet uncomfortable space to examine the problematic places without falling into the familiar trope of blaming the victim (Ryan, 1976). Twine (2000) observes that, "In addition to the question of authority, the issue of representation seems to be a particularly agonizing and complicated one for those researching communities vulnerable due to racial and ethnic inequalities. A dilemma that often emerges is, how does one 'realistically' represent racially subordinate communities without conforming to idealized tropes" (p. 23). Composite characters representing several participants rather than a single participant that captures collective history and experience with racist structures and practice (Cook & Dixson, 2012) is one way to do this. This collective portrayal can more fully speak to the cumulative impact of race and racism, drawing attention to how individual experiences are representative of collective experiences with racial structures.

LaPlante (2007) notes that, "by being both surprising and convincing, and by choosing to render things that resist easy summary, we may, if we're lucky, avoid those twin hobgoblins of creative writers: sentimentality and melodrama" (p. 31). Although she was referring to creative writing, the same can be said for narrative writers, especially those who seek to write narratives that counter dominant stories and expose the daily injustices experienced by those marginalized by society. LaPlante's (2007) point is not to remove emotion and experience from the writing process but rather to focus on "creating an exact and believable context for that response within the world of the story" (pp. 31–32). This focus relies on the writer embracing the complexity of the characters within the story: their contradictions, tensions, hopes, fears, and ultimately humanity.

On the one hand, critical race researchers have a deep commitment to telling the stories of the oppressed and marginalized, exposing the mechanisms of racial dominance while not minimizing how people resist in their everyday lives. On the other, as researchers, we glean the themes from our data, deciding what is of interest, import, and significance, usually grounded in how the story confirms, informs, or deepens existing literature on a particular subject. The stories we choose to tell may not necessarily be the ones most important to the community from which the stories emanate (Twine, 2000). The use of composite character counterstorytelling balances the need for both complexity and simplicity in interpretation and presentation of research findings. In their simple complexity, composite characters are a valuable mechanism for sharing knowledge.

Referring to indigenous methodologies, Smith (1999) notes:

> Sharing knowledge is also a long-term commitment. I use the term "sharing knowledge" deliberately, rather that the term "sharing information" because to me the responsibility of researchers and academics is not simply to share surface information (pamphlet knowledge) but to share the theories and analyses which inform the way knowledge and information are constructed and represented.
>
> (pp. 15–16)

To be clear, the use of composite characters within counterstories is not *the* answer but rather an approach to the many, multi-faceted dilemmas of researching race. Composite counterstories, do, however, address several aspects, particularly for those interested in representation, voice, and sharing academic knowledge with a broader audience.

Finally, good academic writing does not necessarily translate into good creative writing, a necessity for this type of composite character counterstorytelling I've described. For critical race scholars, reading a broad range of literature will enhance the craft of our writing. Octavia Butler, the most prolific African American science fiction writer, explored the intersections of race, class, gender, and sexuality. It is no coincidence that I was reading her oeuvre while writing the counterstories. Her rich characters were my inspiration for how to tell compelling stories with characters full of depth and contradictions. From Butler, I learned that compelling storytelling is not about denying that we are telling and crafting the story. Powerful stories result from our acknowledging that we are a part of every story we tell. In short, good writers read well.

CONCLUSION

I've been particularly troubled about genre and style in academic writing, because the conventional modes of writing and reporting I was taught as a beginning scholar just don't have the elasticity for that kind of [authentic] audience contact. In fact, academic writing worldwide is becoming increasingly exclusive and atomistic, researchers reporting on more and more narrowly defined matters to an ever shrinking audience of readers, readers who become limited in their numbers because they need a specialized vocabulary and exotic base of shared knowledge.

(Banks & Banks, 1998, p. 12)

The composite counterstory speaks to the parallels between preoccupation with methodology for those doing race research and the difficulties experienced by black educators in New Orleans post-Katrina. In the realms of both school reform and race research, we often do not have clear, accessible avenues for transferring knowledge. Our collective technical difficulties, especially for those espousing similar beliefs in justice and equity, are often buttressed by our inattentiveness to explicitly sharing how we do what we do. Those of us preoccupied with race research methodology must have accessible space to question, probe, and dialogue about our collective ways of knowing and writing. Although this space must move beyond detailing a particular method, it is clear that not explicitly sharing our methods makes it more difficult for current and future researchers to innovate and expand them.

There is utility in distinguishing the methodological versus theoretical use of critical race theory (e.g. using numbers in and of itself does not make research quantitative, or using open-ended questions on a survey does not make research qualitative). Thus, using CRT as a theoretical lens does not necessarily mean that one's methods use CRT methodology. Not all race research is critical. Likewise, not all race research in education effectively or systematically employs a critical race theory approach.

Future generations of critical race theorists in education, and arguably current ones, need tools and guidance on how critical race theory functions as both theory and method if we are truly vested in producing powerful, impactful, and critical race research. By writing in more accessible ways without compromising methodological rigor, we will continue to transform academic writing as well as research through innovations in critical race theory methodology. Given that the broader public regularly reads about education, it is crucial that empirical work is shared in ways that resonate with a broader audience, especially marginalized communities. By developing our capacity to tell compelling stories with and from data, we as critical race scholars will greatly enhance the likelihood that research findings will permeate beyond the walls of the academy.

NOTES

1 Pseudonyms are used in this chapter to represent participants in the study.
2 In this chapter, I use black and African American interchangeably.
3 For a full discussion of the background of New Orleans and the history of its public schools, see Cook (2010) and DeVore and Logsdon (1991).
4 The full version of "Something Sweet" was published in the *International Journal of Qualitative Studies in Education* (Cook & Dixson, 2012).
5 Students at the Center (SAC) is an independent writing-based program directly serving high schools and middle schools that works within the Orleans Parish public school system.

6 As an African American female researcher from a working class background, I often felt that traditional methodologies required me to downplay and mediate the intensity of emotions (both my own and participants') present in the course of collecting data. The notion of being fully present recognizes the shared humanity and collective experience shared between race researchers and participants. So, in the writing of research, researchers must recognize, rather than distance themselves from, the emotive aspect of the stories on the hearers of participants' experiences (including the researcher).

REFERENCES

Banks, A., & Banks, S.P. (1998). *Fiction and social research: By ice or fire* (vol. 4). Lanham, MD: AltaMira Press.

Bell, D. (1987). *And we are not saved: The elusive quest for racial justice.* New York: Basic Books.

Bell, M.S. (1997). *Narrative design: A writer's guide to structure.* New York: W.W. Norton.

Buras, K., Randels, J., and Salaam, K. (Eds.). (2010). *Pedagogy, policy, and the privatized city: Stories of dispossession and defiance from New Orleans.* New York: Teachers College Press.

Chapman, T.K. (2007). Interrogating classroom relationships and events: Using portraiture and critical race theory in education research. *Educational Researcher, 36*(3), 156–162.

Cook, A.E. (1995). Beyond critical legal studies: The reconstructive theology of Dr. Martin Luther King, Jr. In K. Crenshaw, N. Gotanda, G. Peller, & K. Thomas (Eds.), *Critical race theory: The key writings that formed the movement* (pp. 85–102). New York: New Press.

Cook, D.A. (2008). Voices crying out from the wilderness: The stories of black educators on school reform in post Katrina New Orleans. Unpublished doctoral dissertation, University of North Carolina at Chapel Hill.

Cook, D.A. (2010). Disrupted but not destroyed: Fictive kinship networks among black educators in post Katrina New Orleans. *Southern Anthropologist, 35*(2), 1–25.

Cook, D.A., & Dixson, A.D. (2012). Writing critical race theory and method: A composite counterstory on the experiences of black teachers in New Orleans post-Katrina. *International Journal of Qualitative Studies in Education,* iFirst article, 1–21 (DOI:10.1080/09518398.2012.731531).

Crenshaw, K. (1991). Mapping the margins: Intersectionality, identity politics, and violence against women of color. *Stanford Law Review, 43*(6), 1241–1299.

Crenshaw, K., Gotanda, N., Peller, G., & Thomas, K. (Eds.). (1995). *Critical race theory: The key writings that formed the movement.* New York: New Press.

DeCuir, J.T., & Dixson, A.D. (2004). "So when it comes out, they aren't that surprised that it is there": Using critical race theory as a tool of analysis of race and racism in education. *Educational Researcher, 33*(5), 26–31.

Delgado, R. (1989). Storytelling for oppositionists and others: A plea for narrative. *Michigan Law Review, 87*, 2411–2441.

Delgado, R. (1993). On telling stories in school: A reply to Farber and Sherry. *Vanderbilt Law Review, 46*, 665–676.

Delgado, R., & Stefancic, J. (2001). *Critical race theory: An introduction.* New York: New York University Press.

DeVore, D.E., & Logsdon, J. (1991). *Crescent City schools: Public education in New Orleans, 1841–1991.* Lafayette: University of Southwestern Louisiana.

Dingerson, L. (2006). *Dismantling a community.* Washington, DC: Center for Community Change.

Dixson, A.D. (2011). Whose choice: A critical race perspective on charter schools. In Cedric Johnson (Ed.), *The Neoliberal Deluge: Hurricane Katrina, Late Capitalism, and the Remaking of New Orleans.* Minneapolis: University of Minnesota Press.

Dixson, A.D., & Rousseau, C.K. (2006). *Critical race theory in education: All God's children got a song.* New York: Routledge.

Donnor, J.K. (2006). Parent(s): The biggest influence in the education of African American football student-athletes. In A. Dixson & C. Rousseau (Eds.), *Critical race theory in education: All God's children got a song* (pp. 153–166). New York: Routledge.

Duncan, G.A. (2002). Critical race theory and method: Rendering race in urban ethnographic research. *Qualitative Inquiry, 8*(1), 85–104.

Emerson, R.M., Fretz, R.I., & Shaw, L.L. (1995). *Writing ethnographic fieldnotes.* Chicago: University of Chicago Press.

Faulkner, W. (1929/1994). *The sound and the fury* (David Minter, Ed.). A Norton Critical Edition. New York: W.W. Norton.

Goodall, H.L., Jr. (2000). *Writing the new ethnography.* Lanham, MD: AltaMira Press/Rowman & Littlefield.

Guinier, L., & Torres, G. (2002). *The miner's canary: Enlisting race, resisting power, transforming democracy.* Cambridge, MA: Harvard University Press.

Ladson-Billings, G. (2000). Racialized discourses and ethnic epistemologies. In N.K. Denzin & Y.S. Lincoln (Eds.), *Handbook of qualitative research* (2nd ed., pp. 257–277). Thousand Oaks, CA: Sage.

Ladson-Billings, G. (2005). The evolving role of critical race theory in educational scholarship. *Race, Ethnicity and Education, 8*(1), 115–119.

Ladson-Billings, G., & Tate, W.F., IV. (1995). Toward a critical race theory of education. *Teachers College Record, 97*(1), 47.

LaPlante, A. (2007). *The making of a story*. New York: W.W. Norton.

Lynn, M., & Parker, L. (2006). Critical race studies in education: Examining a decade of research on U.S. schools. *Urban Review, 38*(4), 257.

Matsuda, M. (1995). Looking to the bottom: Critical legal studies and reparations. In K. Crenshaw, N. Gotanda, G. Peller, & K. Thomas (Eds.), *Critical race theory: The key writings that formed the movement* (pp. 63–79). New York: New Press.

Noblit, G.W., & Dempsey, V.O. (1996). *The social construction of virtue: The moral life of schools*. New York: SUNY Press.

Noblit, G.W., Flores, S.Y., & Murillo, E.G. (2004). *Postcritical ethnography: Reinscribing critique*. Cresskill, NJ: Hampton Press.

Parker, L., & Lynn, M. (2002). What's race got to do with it? Critical race theory's conflicts with and connections to qualitative research methodology and epistemology. *Qualitative Inquiry, 8*(1), 7–22.

Pillow, W. (2003). Race-based methodologies: Multicultural methods or epistemological shifts? In G.R. López & L. Parker (Eds.), *Interrogating racism in qualitative research methodology* (pp. 181–202). New York: Peter Lang.

Ryan, W. (1976). *Blaming the victim*. New York: Vintage.

Smith, L.T. (1999). *Decolonizing methodologies: Research and indigenous peoples*. London: Zed Books.

Solórzano, D.G. (1997). Images and words that wound: Critical race theory, racial stereotyping, and teacher education. *Teacher Education Quarterly, 24*, 5–19.

Solórzano, D., & Yosso, T. (2000). Toward a critical race theory of Chicana and Chicano education. In C. Tejada, C. Martinez, & Z. Leonardo (Eds.), *Charting new terrains: Chicana(o)/Latina(o) education* (pp. 35–65). Cresskill, NJ: Hampton Press.

Solórzano, D.G., & Yosso, T.J. (2001). Critical race and LatCrit theory and method: Counter-storytelling. *International Journal of Qualitative Studies in Education* (*QSE*), *14*(4), 471–495.

Solórzano, D.G., & Yosso, T.J. (2002). Critical race methodology: Counter-storytelling as an analytical framework for education research. *Qualitative Inquiry, 8*(1), 23–44.

St. John, E.P., & Cadray, J.P. (2004). Justice and care in postdesegregation urban schools: Rethinking the role of teacher education programs. In V.S. Walker and J.R. Snarey (Eds.), *Race-ing Moral Formation: African American Perspectives on Care and Justice*. New York: Teachers College Press.

Tate, W.F. (1994). From inner city to ivory tower: Does my voice matter in the academy? *Urban Education, 29*(3), 245–269.

Tate, W.F. (1997). Critical race theory and education: History, theory, and implications. *Review of Research in Education, 22*, 195–247.

Twine, F.R. (2000). Racial ideologies and racial methodologies. In F.R. Twine & J.W. Warren (Eds.), *Racing research researching race* (pp. 1–34). New York: New York University Press.

Twine, F.R., & Warren, J.W. (2000). *Racing research researching race*. New York: New York University Press.

Yosso, T.J. (2005). Whose culture has capital? A critical race theory discussion of community cultural wealth. *Race, Ethnicity and Education, 8*(1), 69–91.

Zuberi, T., & Bonilla-Silva, E. (2008a). Telling the real tale of the hunt: Toward a race conscious sociology of racial stratification. In T. Zuberi & E. Bonilla-Silva (Eds.), *White logic, white methods: Racism and methodology* (pp. 329–342). Lanham, MD: Rowman & Littlefield.

Zuberi, T., & Bonilla-Silva, E. (2008b). *White logic, white methods: Racism and methodology*. Lanham, MD: Rowman & Littlefield.

14

EDUCATION AS THE PROPERTY OF WHITES
African Americans' Continued Quest for Good Schools
Jamel K. Donnor

INTRODUCTION

Historically, White people, and by default whiteness (i.e., White racial hegemony/White supremacy), have played a central role in determining Black people's[1] access to education in the United States (Anderson, 1988; Du Bois, 1973/2001; Woodson, 1933/1993). Beginning with the country's founding, with the outlawing of teaching slaves how to read and write to the imposition of the Hampton model of industrial education, which emphasized "an ideology [that was] inherently opposed to the political and economic advancement of [B]lack southerners" (Anderson, 1988, p. 53), to state-authorized and enforced public school racial segregation (i.e., Jim Crow), White people have shaped the educational fortunes of their Black counterparts. Despite African Americans being the first racial group in the US to advocate for universal public schooling, Whites have traditionally sought to maintain an inherently separate and unequal public schooling system (Anderson, 1988).

In more contemporary times, using rhetorical devices and discursive narratives such as metaphors, analogies, and euphemisms, Whites continue to adversely shape Black people's collective access to quality learning environments (Donnor, 2011). Significantly less hostile in veracity than Jim Crow but no less impactful, the aforementioned methods of racial exclusion frame policies and institutionalized practices meant to foster racial equality in education as inherently discriminatory toward White people (Donnor, 2011). According to this racially conservative line of reasoning, educational policies, such as public school integration and affirmative action, which consider race among a multitude of factors (i.e., plus-one) in pupil placement assignments or college admissions, are considered a "special consideration above and beyond a perceived baseline of equal treatment" (Bracey, 2006, p. 1272). In other words, policies and practices intended to formally expand people of color's access to quality educational environments are deemed unfair because they run counter to the American ideal of individualism and the capitalistic principle of choice (Brown et al., 2003; Flagg, 1998; Winant, 1997a, 1997b).

196 • Jamel K. Donnor

The assertion that policies in education that use race as a plus-one factor are antithetical to the country's founding tenets of individualism and choice is specious when one considers how the foregoing policy constructs have been utilized to secure and advance the privileges and self-interests of Whites over the needs of African Americans. For example, rather than comply with federal court desegregation orders, Whites in the South engaged in massive resistance, through policies such as freedom-of-choice plans. In theory, freedom-of-choice plans were intended to provide Black and White parents interested in racial integration an equal opportunity to send their children to the school of their choice (Crespino, 2006; Ogletree, 2004). In practice, however, freedom-of-choice plans shifted the responsibility of school desegregation onto Black families, because Black families had to formally apply for admission into White schools. Moreover, White parents "almost never" chose to enroll their children at schools with Black students (Kotlowski, 2005, p. 175). As a result, the pace of school desegregation in the South was not just slow; for nearly a decade after the *Brown v. Board of Education* decision of 1954 and 1955, "not a single [B]lack child attended an integrated public school in South Carolina, Alabama, or Mississippi" (Klarman, 1994, p. 84).

In addition to serving as political and racial code words, individualism and choice advance a restricted conception of equal opportunity that obfuscates entrenched ideological practices, ontological meanings, and structural arrangements that advance the self-interests and racial privileges of Whites over the educational needs of non-Whites, especially African Americans. Along with ignoring history and complexity, individualism and choice function as discursive policy instruments that evoke a set of mythic beliefs and behavioral assumptions on the part of White people that allow them: (1) to oppose large-scale efforts that attempt to equitably expand social opportunity; and (2) to justify an inequitable educational status quo.[2] Consequently, the target populations for policies meant to foster racial equity in public education, such as integration, are framed as undeserving. In a cruel irony, proponents of choice and individualism argue that the aforementioned policy constructs are best equipped to allocate social resources and opportunities more evenly, because they are neutral regarding race or blind to color (i.e., colorblind). Stated differently, by requiring people to act as if race does *not* exist, colorblind policies are considered as the "fairest way to mediate certain widely shared public values that clash sharply when victims of racial subordination seek legal preferences in redress for America's undeniable history of racial and ethnic injustice" (Boger, 2000, p. 1722).

A publicly stated objective of the Civil Rights movement of the 1950s and 1960s, colorblindness as a method for distributing resources and opportunities through choice and individualism does appear to be fair. However, a more critical examination of colorblindness, choice, and individualism reveals that the foregoing policy constructs are rife with inconsistencies, paradoxes, and contradictions, most notably the ability to reify the educational racial status quo, which for the purposes of this chapter includes the capacity to exaggerate the supposed harm of education policies, such as integration, incurred by Whites. Hence, the purpose of this chapter is to discuss how choice, individualism, and colorblindness, when used by Whites, foreclose access to quality learning opportunities for people of color. Moreover, the foregoing policy constructs ensure that access to quality educational environments remains the property right of people of European descent in the United States. To support this assertion, I examine the US Supreme Court's 2007 decision in *Parents Involved in Community Schools (PICS) v. Seattle School District No. 1,* using Cheryl Harris's whiteness as property construct. An anti-public school integration case, the Supreme Court's majority in *PICS v. Seattle School District No. 1* declared that the Seattle school district's voluntary efforts to diversify the region's best and most sought-after high schools were unconstitutional. According to the high court, the plaintiff, a group of mostly White families, had an interest in "not being forced to compete for seats at certain high schools in a system that uses race as a deciding factor in many of its admissions decisions" (PICS v. Seattle School District No. 1, 2007, Section II, p. 10, para. 2). The author contends that not only does the Supreme Court's position secure the historical advantages accorded to Whites over people of color, but by using the whiteness as property construct one is better able to see how people who are phenotypically White are surreptitiously redefined as a social group needing special protection.

ORGANIZATION OF THE CHAPTER

What follows in this chapter is organized into four sections. The first presents an overview of the Supreme Court's decision in *PICS v. Seattle School District No. 1*. The second discusses Cheryl Harris's whiteness as property construct in order to set the stage for how choice, individualism, and colorblindness are linked to a "set of expectations, assumptions, privileges, and benefits associated the with social status of being White" (Harris, 1995, p. 277). The third examines the high court's decision in *PICS v. Seattle School District No. 1* through the whiteness as property construct. My goal here is to articulate how access to quality public institutions of learning is the property of White people. The fourth section discusses the sociopolitical implications of the maintenance of quality public schools as the property of White people.

Parents Involved in Community Schools v. Seattle School District No. 1

Decided by a five to four margin in 2007, the US Supreme Court in *PICS v. Seattle School District No. 1* declared that voluntary public school integration programs are unconstitutional (PICS v. Seattle School District No.1, 2007). Specifically, citing the prospective harm to students and injury their families might incur from the denial of admission to the public school of their choice, the Supreme Court ruled that the Seattle school district's use of race as a categorical variable in assigning students to oversubscribed or over-selected schools in the region was "fatally flawed" (PICS v. Seattle School District No. 1, 2007, Section II, p. 15, para. 3). According to the Court's majority, the Seattle school district's Open Choice Plan, which consists of a series of tiebreakers, including an integration tiebreaker, to assign students to oversubscribed schools, "works backwards" toward achieving student racial diversity, rather than "working forward from some demonstration" that diversity provides an educational benefit to all students (PICS v. Seattle School District No. 1, 2007, Section II, p. 15, para. 4). In the Court's view, very little evidence exists supporting the policy assumption that a racially diverse classroom has an educative value for all students. The following is a synopsis of the Seattle school district's Open Choice Plan.

Open School Choice in Seattle

The Seattle school district's Open Choice Plan was established as an effort: (a) to systematically racially integrate its public schools; (b) to stem White flight from the city's public schools and assuage feelings of being forced to integrate; and (c) to allay Black Seattlites' concerns that they would be paying the bulk of the human and institutional costs of busing (Donnor, 2011; PICS v. Seattle School District No. 1, 2006). Under the Open

Choice Plan, area students ranked their attendance preferences for the district's ten public high schools. When too many students selected a particular high school, the district utilized a series of tiebreakers to assign students. The first tiebreaker was the sibling priority (PICS v. Seattle School District No. 1, 2006). In this particular instance, a student with a sibling in a chosen high school was given priority, because the district believed that students who attended school with their sibling were more likely to encourage parental engagement (PICS v. Seattle School District No. 1, 2006). The second tiebreaker implemented was geographic proximity. Here, the district granted admission priority to students who lived close to their preferred schools. As with the sibling tiebreaker, the district postulated that parents with children attending schools close to home are more likely to develop long-term partnerships with teachers. The third tiebreaker of the Open Choice Plan applied to pupil placement assignments was an "integration tiebreaker" (PICS v. Seattle School District No. 1, 2006). According to school district officials, when an oversubscribed or over-selected school's student enrollment deviated by "15 percentage points," plus or minus, from the district's overall student demographic composition, a student's race was considered in determining pupil placements (PICS v. Seattle School District No. 1, 2006). In fact, the Seattle school district used the integration tiebreaker *only* when the particular high school became racially homogeneous (PICS v. Seattle School District No. 1, 2006; Seattle Public Schools, 2007).

THE SUPREME COURT'S DECISION

For the affirming justices, the Seattle school district's integration tiebreaker "offer[ed] no evidence that the level of racial diversity necessary to achieve the asserted educational benefits happen to coincide with the racial demographics of the respective school districts—or rather the white/nonwhite or black/'other' balance of the districts, since that is the only diversity addressed by the plans" (PICS v. Seattle School District No. 1, 2007, Section II, p. 15, para. 4). For the Court's majority, if the racial composition of the Seattle metropolitan area were to shift, the school district would be compelled to continue considering race in assigning students to the city's most sought-after public high schools, meaning that the Seattle school district's policy on integration did not have a "logical stopping point" (PICS v. Seattle School District No. 1, 2007, Section II, p. 15, para. 4). Stated differently, allowing the school district to use race as a categorical variable in pupil assignments would "effectively assure that race will always be relevant in American life" (PICS v. Seattle School District No. 1, 2007, Section II, p. 16, para. 1).

In a separate concurring opinion, Justice Clarence Thomas, the lone African American on the Supreme Court, contended that the Seattle School Board did not "have [an] interest in remedying past segregation" (PICS v. Seattle School District No. 1, 2007, Section II, p. 25, para. 1). According to Justice Thomas, because the Seattle school district has never operated a *de jure* segregated school system or been subjected to federal court orders to integrate area schools, the school district could not proactively ameliorate the disparate impact of *de facto* racial inequality regarding pupil assignment. For Justice Thomas (and the Court's majority), racial segregation in education is the product of explicit governmental policies or identifiable actors who purposely intend to separate students "solely on the basis of race" (PICS v. Seattle School District No. 1, 2007, Section II, p. 25, para. 1). For the Court's majority, upholding the Seattle school district's integration tiebreaker as constitutional would "give school boards a free hand to make decisions on the basis of race—an approach reminiscent of that advocated by the seg-regationist in *Brown v. Board of Education*, 1954" (PICS v. Seattle School District No. 1, 2007, Section II, p. 25, para. 1).

In a consideration of the Supreme Court's decision in *PICS v. Seattle School District No. 1* within the nexus of race, education, opportunity, and exclusion, a more critical analytical approach is necessary in order to articulate how racial inequity is not only the byproduct of individual actors or specific institutionalized practices, but also a dynamic phenomenon and complex process involving "seemingly objective conditions [and the] [un]consciousness associated with those conditions" (Freeman, 1978, p. 1053), such as the cumulative effect of race (Katz et al., 2005; Katznelson, 2006; Walters, 2001). This is where Cheryl Harris's construct of whiteness as property is particularly useful.

WHITENESS AS PROPERTY

An analytical construct of critical race theory (CRT), whiteness as property posits that ensconced within people of Western European ancestry in the United States (and glo-bally) are a distinct set of ideological assumptions and dispositions, privileges, and expectations inextricably linked to their phenotypical appearance and sociopolitical sta-tus (Harris, 1995). White people over time and by virtue of their existence have come to expect and rely upon a unique and exclusive set of benefits, predispositions, and socioe-conomic privileges associated with their whiteness, which have been established through a legacy of conquest and domination of people of color globally (Harris, 1995; Lopez, 1996; Mills, 1997; Winant, 2001). Stated more pointedly, through force, coercion, con-sent, custom, and jurisprudential edifice, white skin and whiteness have become exclu-sive forms of private property (Harris, 1995; Lopez, 1996; Mills, 1997). According to Harris (1995), "whiteness—the right to white identity … is property if by 'property' one means all of a person's legal rights" (p. 279). In other words, whiteness is more than a set of specific physical traits and ancestry, although important. Rather, whiteness is a racial-ized system of meaning and domination composed of ideological adherents and material components (Lopez, 1996).

As a racialized system of meaning and domination, whiteness must be constantly "affirmed, legitimated, and protected" (Harris, 1995, p. 277). Indeed, one of the primary ways in which the aforementioned is accomplished is by ensuring White people's absolute right to exclude non-Whites from social resources and meaningful life opportunities or chances (Harris, 1995). For example, during the colonial era "only white [people's] pos-session and occupation of land was validated" (Harris, 1995, p. 278) by the federal gov-ernment. In addition to conflating the interrelationship between race and property, the federal government's recognition of White people as the sole bearers of property served as the genesis for an unjust and exploitative society designed to maintain and advance White supremacy (Harris, 1995; Mills, 1997). According to Harris (1995), property as

> conceived in the founding era included not only external objects and people's rela-tionship to them, but also all of those human rights, liberties, powers, and immunities that are important for human well-being, including freedom of expression, freedom of conscience, freedom from bodily harm, and free and equal opportunities to use personal faculties.
>
> (p. 280)

Indeed, "part of the point of bringing society into existence, with its laws and enforcers of the law, is to protect what you have accumulated" (Mills, 1997, p. 32). For example, the ideas of the "freeborn Englishman" and liberty not only served as the foundational pillars for Anglo-American culture and nationhood in Britain, but, once both constructs were conjoined, also "helped to legitimize the colonization of North America" (Foner, 1998, p. 5).

In summary, whiteness, like conventional material property, derives its value primarily from exclusivity, because the boundaries it creates "enforce or reorder existing regimes of power" (Harris, 1995, p. 280). As a consequence, the racial disparities and inequalities created, reproduced, and reified by whiteness, like property, not only establish a unique set of explicit and tacit rules, expectations, and practices regarding access and deployment, but governing institutions, such as the judicial and educational systems, are also instrumental in assigning their societal value. To put it bluntly, whiteness is characterized more by who *is* White than who is not (Harris, 1995). Furthermore, because whiteness is continuously fortified through social institutions and structural interactions, the political, economic, and educational status of superiority that has been historically assigned to Whites by White people naturalizes the existing state of affairs, which absolves them of responsibility for creating and maintaining an unjust society. Thus, for all intents and purposes, whiteness and White people are not just the societal norm. In addition, both social constructs require constant protection (Harris, 1995). With this understanding of whiteness as property, the following section will discuss how the high court's ruling preserves access to quality public schools as the property of people of European descent.

PARENTS INVOLVED IN COMMUNITY SCHOOLS V. SEATTLE SCHOOL DISTRICT NO. 1 AS SEEN THROUGH THE EYES OF WHITENESS AS PROPERTY

Upon first glance, the Supreme Court's decision to abolish race as a relevant aspect of public education and American life appears well intentioned. For sure, not only is the very notion that race be consciously employed in governmental administrative decisions and policy-making (i.e., pupil placement assignments) presumptively demeaning, because it is the "abrogation of individuality, through stereotyping and prejudice" (Carlon, 2007, p. 1173), but the conscious use of race in public policy decision-making processes can reintroduce formal racial caste systems of subordination, such as Jim Crow (Alexander, 2010; Carlon, 2007). Thus, the Supreme Court's anti-classificationist approach toward race (i.e., the removal of explicit racial designations) is an attempt to transform society into an idyllic place where extant racial disparities and disadvantages are redefined as the byproduct of individual dysfunctional behavior, rather than the manifestation of historical inequities or structural discontinuities.

Regrettably, the Supreme Court's application of a colorblind paradigm in *PICS v. Seattle School District No. 1* does nothing more than provide a protective veneer over White people, their self-interests, and their possessive investment in whiteness (Lipsitz, 1988). While more benign in appearance and more subtle in tone when compared to Jim Crow, the high court's "racial coding" (Wilson & Nielsen, 2011, p. 176) of integration, a policy intended to foster racial equality, as a barrier to the educational opportunities of White students and their families reinforces the American racial hierarchy, because the "values, perspectives, and practices traditionally associated with White institutions" (Crenshaw, 1997, p. 106) are affirmed. Furthermore, conscious policy efforts to disrupt or ameliorate the legacy of structural racism irrespective of its impact on White people collectively are interpreted as a violation of the American ideal (Mills, 1997). Indeed, the end-game on the part of the parent organization and the Supreme Court is maintaining White supremacy. Consider the schizophrenic rationale advanced by the Court.

Despite acknowledging that it is "factually possible that the plaintiff's children will not be denied admission to a school based on their race" (PICS v. Seattle School District No. 1, 2007, Section II, p. 10, para. 2), the Court's majority validated PICS's injury claim as previously mentioned. Not only does this validation frame individual Whites' cognitive and dispositional expectation of uninhibited access to quality learning environments as morally equivalent to Black people's mistreatment and marginalization, historically and contemporaneously, but the Supreme Court's affirmation of the mostly White organization's claim of harm fortifies entrenched racial advantages and existing structural patterns of racial inequality. For instance, in the only year that the integration tiebreaker was used (2000–01), "80.3%" of the total number of ninth graders were assigned their first choice of school compared to "80.4%" when the tiebreaker was not utilized (PICS v. Seattle School District No. 1, 2006, p. 9). Also, when one considers that "more than 75% of the District's non-white students live in the southern half of the city, while 67% of the white students live in the northern half" (PICS v. Seattle School District No. 1, 2006, p. 2), and the racial composition of Seattle public schools mirrors the city's residential patterns, the Supreme Court's decision to endorse PICS's claim that the integration tiebreaker intrudes on a student's individual right to select the high school of his or her choice is grossly overstated, and essentially inscribes racial segregation as a matter of law.

CONCLUSION: SEEING THROUGH WHITENESS

The Supreme Court's decision to depart from its *Brown v. Board of Education* precedent of 1954 in *PICS v. Seattle School District No. 1* teaches policy-makers, scholars, and activists concerned with the educational fortunes of African American students a lesson that is neither new nor unique (Bell, 2004; Donnor, 2011). When viewed from a historical perspective, the high court was adhering to a higher jurisprudential edict. Unspoken and subconscious, the Supreme Court's ruling in *PICS v. Seattle School District No. 1* is the latest iteration of what constitutional scholar Derrick Bell (2004) termed a "racial-sacrifice covenant" (p. 29). The product of a "convergence of interests" (Bell, 1980, p. 522), the racial-sacrifice covenant is a compromise whereby the sociopolitical fortunes of African Americans are *only* validated when they "secure, advance, or at least [do] not [interfere with] societal interest" (Bell, 1980, p. 523) deemed important by society's ruling elite. According to Bell (1980), the overall unwillingness of Whites, irrespective of socioeconomic status and political affiliation, to recognize that "true equality for blacks will require the surrender of racism-granted privileges for [W]hites" (p. 523) means legal remedies for racism and policy efforts to foster racial equality are not intended to systematically combat the practices, policies, and structures that adversely affect the life chances and experiences of people of color in the United States. Equally important, educational policies heralded as promoting equal racial opportunity are designed to be temporary (Bell, 1980).

From a whiteness as property perspective, the Supreme Court's decision in *PICS v. Seattle School District No. 1* reflects society's governing institutions' ability to schematize how public policies intended to help non-Whites are an axiological encroachment on White people's proprietary right to exclude non-Whites from meaningful social opportunities and resources. As such, the violations must be rectified. Because the interrelationship between white skin, ideology, epistemology, and expectation creates a "phantom objectivity" (Harris, 1995, p. 281), which is rooted in pre-Enlightenment conceptions of race, the Supreme Court's decision to prioritize the personal choices of White families over the educational opportunities of African Americans is expected (Mills, 1997; Vander Zanden, 1959). In other words, the prioritizing of personal choice within the context of education over racial equity recapitulates the educational and concomitant political economic status quo, because "White people's private choices [always] outweigh concern for Black people's equal status" (Roberts, 1996, p. 367). Moreover, the form of non-competitive individualism put forth by the highest court in the land renders members of historically marginalized groups, such as African Americans, "unable to compete without compensatory support" (Bell, 1987, p. 236). Perhaps the greatest lesson the Supreme Court's decision in *PICS v. Seattle School District No. 1* teaches is that whiteness is enduring.

NOTES

1 Black and African American are used interchangeably.
2 By educational status quo, I am referring to the educational reality that African Americans (and Latino/as), particularly males, are less likely to graduate from high school than their White and Asian American counterparts and more likely to be incarcerated as a result of their educational shortcomings (Children's Defense Fund, 2007; Donnor & Shockley, 2010; Justice Policy Institute, 2007; Mauer & Scott King, 2004).

REFERENCES

Alexander, M. (2010). *The new Jim Crow: Mass incarceration in an age of colorblindness.* New York: New Press.
Anderson, J.D. (1988). *The education of Blacks in the South, 1860–1935.* Chapel Hill: University of North Carolina Press.
Bell, D. (1980). Brown v. Board of Education and the interest-convergence dilemma. *Harvard Law Review, 93,* 518–533.
Bell, D. (1987). Law, litigation, and the search for the promised land. *Georgetown Law Journal, 76*(1), 229–236.
Bell, D. (2004). *Silent covenants: Brown v. Board of Education and the unfulfilled hopes for racial reform.* New York: Oxford University Press.
Boger, J.C. (2000). Willful colorblindness: The new racial piety and the resegregation of public schools. *North Carolina Law Review, 78*(1), 1719–1796.
Bracey, C.A. (2006). Article: The cul de sac of race preference discourse. *University of Southern California Law Review, 79*(6), 1231–1325.
Brown, M.K., Carnoy, M., Currie, E., Duster, T., Oppenheimer, D.B., Shultz, M.M., & Wellman, D. (2003). *Whitewashing race: The myth of a color-blind society.* Berkeley: University of California Press.
Carlon, A. (2007). Racial adjudication. *Brigham Young University Law Review, 2007,* 1151–1202.
Children's Defense Fund. (2007). America's cradle to prison pipeline: Summary report (retrieved June 24, 2008 from http://www.childrensdefense.org).
Crenshaw, K.W. (1997). Color-blind dreams and racial nightmares: Reconfiguring racism in the post Civil Rights era. In T. Morrison & C.B. Lacour (Eds.), *Birth of a nation'hood: Gaze, script, and spectacle in the O.J. Simpson case* (pp. 97–168). New York: Pantheon.
Crespino, J. (2006). The best defense is a good offense: The Stennis Amendment and the fracturing of liberal school desegregation policy, 1964–1972. *Journal of Policy History, 18,* 304–325.
Donnor, J.K. (2011). Whose compelling interest? The ending of desegregation and the affirming of racial inequality in education. *Education and Urban Society, 20*(10), 1–18.
Donnor, J.K., & Shockley, K. (2010). Leaving us behind: A political economic interpretation of NCLB and the

miseducation of African American males. *Journal of Educational Foundations*, Summer–Fall, 43–54.

Du Bois, W.E.B. (1973/2001). *The education of Black people: Ten critiques, 1906–1960.* New York: Monthly Review Press.

Flagg, B.J. (1998). *Was blind, but now I see: White race consciousness and the law.* New York: New York University Press.

Foner, E. (1998). *The story of American freedom.* New York: W.W. Norton.

Freeman, A.D . (1978). Legitimizing racial discrimination through antidiscrimination law: A critical review of Supreme Court doctrine. *Minnesota Law Review, 62,* 1049–1119.

Harris, C.I. (1995). Whiteness as property. In K.W. Crenshaw, N. Gotanda, G. Peller, & K. Thomas (Eds.), *Critical race theory: The key writings that formed the movement* (pp. 276–291). New York: New Press.

Justice Policy Institute. (2007). Education and public safety (retrieved June 24, 2008 from http://www.justicepolicy.org).

Katz, M.B., Stern, M.J., & Fader, J.J. (2005). The new African American inequality. *Journal of American History, 92,* 76–108.

Katznelson, I. (2006). When is affirmative action fair? On grievous harms and public remedies. *Social Research, 73*(2), 541–568.

Klarman, M.J. (1994). How Brown changed race relations: The backlash thesis. *Journal of American History, 81,* 81–118.

Kotlowski, D. (2005). With all deliberate delay: Kennedy, Johnson, and school desegregation. *Journal of Policy History, 17,* 155–192.

Lipsitz, G. (1998). *The possessive investment in whiteness: How White people profit from identity politics.* Philadelphia, PA: Temple University Press.

Lopez, I.F. (1996). *White by law: The legal construction of race.* New York: New York University Press.

Mauer, M., & Scott King, R. (2004). Schools and prisons: Fifty years after Brown v. Board of Education. The Sentencing Project (retrieved June 24, 2008 from http://www. sentencingproject.org).

Mills, C.W. (1997). *The racial contract.* Ithaca, NY: Cornell University Press.

Ogletree, C.J. (2004). *All deliberate speed: Reflections on the first half century of Brown v. Board of Education.* New York: W.W. Norton.

Parents Involved in Community Schools v. Seattle School District No. 1 (2006) (Brief for Respondents, No. 05-908).

Parents Involved in Community Schools v. Seattle School District No. 1 (2007), 127 S. Ct. 2738.

Roberts, D.E. (1996). The priority paradigm: Private choices and the limits of equality. *University of Pittsburgh Law Review, 57*(2), 363–404.

Seattle Public Schools. (2007). Student demographics (retrieved January 6, 2007 from http://reportcard.ospi.k12. wa.us/?schoolId=100&reportLevel=District&orgLinkId=100&yrs).

Vander Zanden, J.W. (1959). The ideology of White supremacy. *Journal of the History of Ideas, 20*(3), 385–402.

Walters, P.B. (2001). Educational access and the state: Historical continuities and discontinuities in racial inequality in American education. *Sociology of Education* (Extra Issue), 35–49.

Wilson, G., & Nielsen, A.L. (2011). "Color coding" and support for social policy spending: Assessing the parameters among Whites. *Annals of the American Academy of Political and Social Science, 634,* 174–189.

Winant, H. (1997a). Behind blue eyes: Whiteness and contemporary U.S. racial politics. *New Left Review, 225,* 73–88.

Winant, H. (1997b). Racial dualism at century's end. In W. Lubiano (Ed.), *The house that race built: Black Americans, U.S. terrain* (pp. 87–115). New York: Pantheon Books.

Winant, H. (2001). *The world is a ghetto: Race and democracy since World War II.* New York: Basic Books.

Woodson, C.G. (1933/1993). *The miseducation of the negro.* Trenton, NJ: Africa World Press.

15

THE INCLUSION AND REPRESENTATION OF ASIAN AMERICANS AND PACIFIC ISLANDERS IN AMERICA'S EQUITY AGENDA IN HIGHER EDUCATION

Robert T. Teranishi and Loni Bordoloi Pazich

Utilizing critical race theory (CRT), this chapter examines the ways in which Asian Americans and Pacific Islanders (AAPIs) are positioned in mainstream discourse on access and equity in American higher education. More specifically, this chapter demonstrates how existing tenets of CRT (e.g., interest convergence, intersectionality, and social justice) play a role in understanding the positionality of the AAPI population relative to key debates about race and the stratification of college opportunities. This chapter demonstrates that the study of AAPIs—particularly through the lens of CRT—is relevant to understanding the changing contours of race, ethnicity, and immigration in the twenty-first century.

Amidst racially charged debates about selective college admissions and affirmative action, trends in educational attainment and college enrollment among AAPIs have become the contemporary foundation for a perception of an "Asian Invasion" in U.S. higher education (Teranishi, 2010). This perception is driven in part by the presence of AAPI undergraduates in some of America's most elite and selective universities. Consider that, in 2005, while AAPIs made up 14.1 percent of California's high school graduating class, they constituted 41.8 percent of the freshman class at University of California (UC) campuses; at seven of the nine UC undergraduate campuses AAPIs were the single largest racial group.

In the high-stakes world of selective college admissions, AAPI enrollment trends have been coupled with a perception that AAPIs are succeeding to such an extent that it is occurring at the expense of other minorities. Conversely, there is a growing sentiment that, if affirmative action were to be overturned, it would have its greatest impact on the opportunities for AAPIs, because their access is being most suppressed (e.g., they are viewed as being held to a higher standard compared to other applicants). This idea has become the focus of two recent inquiries regarding the admissions practices at Princeton and Harvard by the U.S. Department of Education, Office of Civil Rights (Slotnik, 2012). This was also an assertion made by the petitioners in the ongoing U.S. Supreme Court case *Fisher v. University of Texas*, which is under the court's consideration at the time of writing.

The ongoing tension around the role of race in college admissions, coupled with the significant demographic changes in the nation, where AAPIs are the fastest growing racial group (Hoeffel et al., 2012), demonstrates a need for a deeper understanding of how and why AAPIs are a factor in legal and societal discourse on race and the stratification of college opportunities. Utilizing CRT, this chapter examines the ways in which AAPIs are positioned in mainstream discourse on national concerns related to access and equity in American higher education. This chapter advances an understanding of the ways in which existing tenets of CRT are important to the study of AAPIs relative to access, equity, and diversity issues in higher education. More importantly, the chapter offers a perspective on how CRT is a conceptual tool for understanding how issues of race impact the educational experiences, opportunities, and outcomes of AAPI students. Ultimately, this chapter demonstrates that the study of AAPIs—particularly through the lens of CRT—is relevant to understanding the changing contours of race, ethnicity, and immigration in the twenty-first century.

This chapter begins with a discussion about key tenets of CRT in education relevant to understanding AAPIs in higher education. Utilizing these tenets, we then discuss how AAPIs are positioned in broader concerns about America's commitment to equity in higher education. We conclude with a discussion about how this analysis demonstrates the relevance of AAPIs in a broader understanding of how race operates in U.S. society.

AAPIS AND CRITICAL RACE THEORY

As discussed in the Introduction of this handbook, CRT views racism as a "means by which society allocates privilege and status" (Delgado & Stefancic, 2012, p. 17). CRT in education examines how "educational theory, policy, and practice are used to subordinate certain racial and ethnic groups" (Solorzano, 1998, p. 122) and serves a "powerful explanatory tool for the sustained inequity that people of color experience" (Ladson-Billings, 1998, p. 18).

A CRT lens uncovers the ways in which structural racism operates, not only through exclusionary policies and practices, but also through the normative construction of racial inequality that sustains superiority for dominant groups. While CRT initially emerged as a means to consider Black–White power relations, it has increasingly been used to consider the experiences and outcomes of other minority groups, including AAPIs (e.g., R. Chang, 1999; Chew, 1994; Ng et al., 2007). While all racial minority groups have faced a history of challenges associated with race and racism, each individual group has dealt with unique experiences, challenges, and histories. From a historical perspective, AAPIs have endured racism that ranges across the exclusionary laws against Chinese immigrants in the 1880s, the internment of Japanese Americans during World War II, and acts of violence against Sikhs following 9/11. While these are just a few examples of racism against AAPIs, they demonstrate that forms of racial intolerance and stereotyping have evolved over time as political conditions have changed (R. Chang, 1999; Lowe, 1996).

AAPIs have experienced nativist racism through exclusion acts and internment camps, as well as "racist love" through stereotyping as a model minority (Chin & Chan, 1972). The model minority myth positions AAPIs as successful and high achieving, despite their marginalized status as a racial minority group. The focus on AAPI enrollment in higher education, particularly in the most selective universities in American higher education, is a key mechanism for touting AAPIs as a successful minority. Again, the positioning of AAPIs as a model minority is emblematic of different forms of racism over time and in different political and social contexts.

Below are some key CRT tenets we use in this chapter to reflect on the positioning of AAPIs in affirmative action discourse, and the racialization inherent in that positioning. The three tenets briefly described below and later elaborated upon in the sections that follow are by no means an exhaustive list of how CRT is applicable to AAPIs; rather, these tenets represent some key analytical tools for understanding AAPIs relative to their position in broader discourse on race, equity, and the stratification of college opportunities.

- *Interest convergence.* Introduced by Derrick Bell (1980), interest convergence suggests that the interests of racial minorities are accommodated only when they "converge" with the interests of Whites. In his analysis of *Brown v. Board of Education*, Bell (1980) asserts that the end of state-sponsored desegregation was achieved at least in part because it offered benefits to the White majority by furthering the South's transition from an agrarian to an industrialized economy and improving America's social justice credentials in the midst of the Cold War. Put another way, interest convergence implies that "the majority group tolerates advances for racial justice only when it suits their interest to do so" (Delgado & Stefancic, 2012, p. 165).
- *Intersectionality.* Intersectionality draws attention to how factors other than race can be separately disadvantaging factors, in addition to their impact, in combination with race, to disenfranchise individuals (Delgado & Stefancic, 2012). In other words, various aspects of identity do not necessarily act independently of one another, and forms of oppression related to race, class, gender, and sexual orientation, among other aspects of identity, can collectively exert a more powerful form of oppression greater than the subordination associated with the sum of individual forms of oppression (e.g., racism, sexism, etc.) (Crenshaw, 1989, 1991). While intersectionality has mainly been applied to Black women in the context of feminist thought, it is also a useful analytical tool for critically examining the relevance of social categories, and the boundaries between them, to understand how various forms of oppression impact the lives of other minority groups (Nash, 2008), including AAPIs (Teranishi, 2002). This is particularly important given the forces of oppression related to ethnicity, immigration status, and the unique racialization of AAPIs that is unique to their community.
- *Social justice.* Critical race theorists make their own ideological stance explicit by embracing a commitment to social justice. In the context of education CRT seeks to explicate and overcome racial subordination and other forms of discrimination (Matsuda, 1987; Solorzano, 1997). This is an important and necessary tenet for exposing and understanding the powerful forces of interest convergence that subjugate the voice and agency of the AAPI community in issues of race, inequality, and higher education policy (Teranishi, 2010).

The following sections of the chapter examine the role of interest convergence, the importance of intersectionality, and the embrace of ideologically oriented inquiry to achieve social justice in understanding AAPIs within the context of contemporary discourse on equity in education generally, and affirmative action more specifically.

Interest Convergence

The unique and relative position of AAPIs along the color line and within the equity agenda is predicated upon the confluence of key conceptual problems. At the most basic level, normative framing is often the basis for examining equity in America, invoked to identify populations that may warrant resources or services that can help close the gap identified in the research. Essentially, the goal of normative framing is to identify how different racial groups are unevenly distributed across particular outcomes (e.g., distribution of enrollment vs. graduation rates, etc.). Within this racially triangulated framing, the experiences, outcomes, and representation of AAPIs are examined vis-à-vis Blacks and Whites, which defines race in American society as a dichotomy, with Blacks at one end of the racial spectrum and Whites on the other (M. Chang et al., 1999).

Within the Black–White paradigm, AAPIs—along with Latinos and Native Americans—have problematic positions. In the years following the Civil War, for example, a small cadre of abolitionists and radical Republicans pushed for color-blind rights to be enshrined in American law, but the presence of Chinese immigrants complicated debates around citizenship and naturalization. The landmark legislation of the Reconstruction Congress, including the 1866 Civil Rights Act and 14th Amendment, has typically been read as a color-blind effort, but a historical analysis by Anderson (2007) suggests that this legislation in fact "gave race a place in the new constitutional order … and encoded race as a proxy without a name" (p. 251). In the congressional debates of that time, "Chinese were considered in congressional debates as a pagan race incapable of assimilating into American life" (Anderson, 2007, p. 253) who should therefore be denied access to the protections afforded by naturalization, unlike their African counterparts (predominantly newly freed slaves), who were eligible for naturalization. However, the population of native-born Chinese eligible for birthright citizenship was believed to be small enough to have an inconsequential impact on the national fabric, enabling a small cadre of abolitionists and radical Republicans to push for birthright citizenship to be extended to those of both Chinese and African descent.

The racial positioning of AAPIs within the Black–White paradigm shifted in the twentieth century. Consider that, in a 1927 Supreme Court ruling on how to position Asian Americans in racially segregated schools, the court ruled that Blacks and Asian Americans were "equivalent and interchangeable" (Wu, 2002, referring to Gong Lum v. Rice, 275 U.S. 78, 1927). This decision influenced the historical framing of educational access as a matter of Whites vs. non-Whites in which AAPIs are explicitly placed in the latter grouping. However, toward the end of the twentieth century, the treatment of AAPIs relative to Blacks and Whites shifted yet again, occupying a more liminal space as a "non-minority minority."

The racial construction of AAPIs as a "model minority" was coined in 1966 at the height of the civil rights movement (Zia, 2001). A representative example from the *U.S. News and World Report* from the time notes: "At a time when Americans are awash in worry over the plight of racial minorities, one such minority [AAPIs] is winning wealth and respect by dint of its own hard work—not from a welfare check" ("Success story of one minority group in the U.S.," 1966). Here, AAPIs were positioned against Blacks as a "deserving" minority, not to celebrate their accomplishments, but to reinforce negative stereotypes against Blacks. The struggles of the civil rights movement were accompanied or followed by a phenomenon in which AAPIs were "'racially triangulated' vis-à-vis Whites and Blacks through two interrelated processes of 'relative valorization' (Whites valorizing Asian Americans relative to Blacks) and ... 'civic ostracism' (Whites constructing Asian Americans as foreign and Other)" (Ng et al., 2007, p. 96).

We also find the placement of AAPIs on the "White" end of the Black–White spectrum. For example, according to sociologist Andrew Hacker's (2003) *Two Nations: Black and White, Separate, Hostile, Unequal,* AAPIs symbolically fall under the "White umbrella" in a racial paradigm that continues to be reduced to two groups, Whites and non-Whites. His claim is based on a belief that AAPIs do not fall within the "out-group," which he defines as those groups that face structural barriers. Similarly, in Bowen et al.'s (2005) book *Equity and Excellence in American Higher Education,* as in many other important scholarly debates about access and equity in higher education, the "non-minority" category groups Whites with AAPIs together, while the "minority" category continues to be occupied by Blacks and now also includes Latinos under its umbrella. Sociologist Douglas Massey has even suggested that "Whites and Asian Americans are jumbled together in a way that is making the distinctions between the groups less obvious" (Massey, 2008).

A deeper consideration of why AAPIs are cast as a model minority in contemporary discourse helps us understand why interest convergence is so persistent and damaging for the AAPI community. One such space where interest convergence has been particularly active is in recent debates about selective college admissions and affirmative action. AAPIs first came to the debate by way of inquiries into UC Berkeley's and other campuses' admission policies in the 1980s, became even more prominent with debates over Proposition 209 (also in California), and continued through the most recent Supreme Court cases on affirmative action. In these debates, we find AAPIs positioned as a group that is adversely affected by affirmative action, and that it is AAPIs, not Whites, who have the most to gain with ending affirmative action. Essentially, AAPIs are presented as the biggest "victims" of affirmative action.

Ward Connerly, the influential architect of the California Civil Rights Initiative, made this point in 2006 when reacting to the number of Black students admitted to UC Berkeley and UCLA, which appeared to be rebounding from the damage caused by Proposition 209. He claimed that the increase in Black enrollment at these campuses has meant "kicking out" Asian students (Connerly, 2006). This perspective was further popularized by a number of news stories about Jian Li, an applicant to Princeton University who filed a civil rights complaint with the Office for Civil Rights for not being admitted to the institution despite being in the top 1 percent of his high school class.[1]

In 2009 the University of California approved a new admission policy which intended to eliminate the requirement that applicants take two SAT subject tests and reduce the number of students guaranteed admission. Ling-Chi Wang called the change "affirmative action for Whites" (Chea, 2009, para. 5), because internal research by the UC system projected a 20 percent decrease for AAPIs, with most gains found among Whites. Ward Connerly, in the wake of a considerable outcry from AAPI advocacy organizations, reached out to the community through newspaper commentaries. In one such commentary, he wrote: "The proposed UC admissions policies are so egregious and so dramatically discriminatory against Asians ... There is one truth that is universally applicable in the era of 'diversity,' especially in American universities: an absolute unwillingness to accept the verdict of colorblind policies" (Connerly, 2009, paras. 10, 11).

Yet the assertions made by opponents to race-conscious admissions policies were not supported by survey and polling data on AAPIs relative to affirmative action. One source for gauging the level of support for or against affirmative action among AAPIs is a multicity, multiethnic, and multilingual survey of political attitudes and behavior administered by the Inter-university Consortium for Political and Social Research (Lien, 2004). The results show that 63.1 percent of Asian Americans indicated that affirmative action "is a good thing" as opposed to 5.7 percent who reported that it is a "bad thing" and 18.6 percent who reported that it "doesn't affect Asian Americans." These findings are consistent with a 2004 survey of 701 Asian American college students attending 169 colleges and universities. This study found that 62.6 percent of Asian American college students disagreed with the notion that affirmative action should be eliminated (Park, 2009a). Both of these survey results are consistent with exit polls during votes on state referendums to end affirmative action. In 1996, 61 percent of Asian American voters rejected Proposition 209 in California (*Los Angeles Times*, 1996) and, in 2006, 75 percent of Asian American voters rejected Proposal 2 in Michigan (*The Nation*, 2007).

The positioning of AAPIs within affirmative action debates has not only occurred in politics, the media, and the mainstream public, but also been the focus of a number of empirical studies. Daniel Golden (2006), author of *The Price of Admission*, asserts that AAPIs are deliberately held to a higher standard in selective college admissions to maintain an acceptable level of AAPI enrollment. Espenshade and Chung (2005) claim that, if Princeton University were to end affirmative action, AAPIs would be the "biggest winners," occupying four out of every five seats created by accepting fewer African American and Hispanic students. In these analyses, merit is narrowly conceived as involving only grades and test scores and gives no consideration to diversity of culture or experiences. Moreover, the decline of Black and Latino students throughout selective colleges that do not consider race for admissions decisions has resulted in AAPIs assuming the identity of conspicuous adversaries of diversity in higher education.

Again, while studies are quick to position AAPIs as "losers" in selective college admissions because of affirmative action, there is almost no acknowledgement to how AAPIs can benefit, and have benefited, from the basic goals of the policy, that is, to reap the educational benefits of a diverse campus setting, which includes exposure to divergent viewpoints and perspectives and preparing students to be leaders in a diverse democracy in an increasingly competitive and global society. Yet studies have found that exposure to diversity is linked to positive learning and civic outcomes (Gurin et al., 2002), improved intergroup attitudes (Bowman & Griffin, 2012), and higher levels of satisfaction with the racial diversity of the student body at more racially diverse institutions among AAPI undergraduate students (Park, 2009b).

Beyond the discourse of selective college admissions and affirmative action, we also see AAPIs selectively included in studies that have posited a cultural explanation for the racial achievement gap in America's schools. Anthropologist John Ogbu's theory of oppositional culture posits that Blacks experience "low-effort syndrome" as an oppositional response to subordination and oppression (e.g., Ogbu & Simons, 1998). The "oppositional culture" thesis is colloquially understood as a Black "attitude problem." A hypothesis about Black "attitude" being implicated in low achievement implies that a "good" (i.e., White) attitude is associated with high achievement.

The liminality of AAPIs positioning in the racial continuum can be seen in how AAPIs often straddle two "peg-holes" depending on the issue at hand. For example,

Coloma (2006) finds that when AAPIs perform well in school they are generally considered to be "acting White," yet when behavioral problems arise among AAPIs these individuals are seen to be "acting Black." How AAPIs are positioned in debates about racial stratification in U.S. society depends on how they can support or refute the position of the interests of others. Thus, AAPIs are examined within these paradigms not to explain AAPI achievement, but to provide an example of why these theoretical propositions hold true for others. In the context of Ogbu's theory of opposition, if it can be validated by the study of how culture operates among AAPIs then the theory has greater validity in, and is not an anomaly for, explaining the underachievement of Blacks (Lee, 1996; Lei, 2003).

The model minority myth not only is problematic for how it invidiously pits minority groups against each other, but blinds Americans to the ongoing discrimination experienced by AAPIs. Empirical evidence shows that "those in the general public who hold positive model minority stereotypes of Asian Americans ... tend to be complacent about any discrimination that Asian Americans face" (McGowan & Lindgren, 2006, p. 374). As a result, AAPIs are excluded from policy discussions about race and racism, and routinely omitted by scholars and policymakers in their pursuit of the equity agenda (Kiang, 2006). A prominent example of this pattern can be seen in the report *Changing America: Indicators of Social and Economic Well-Being by Race and Hispanic Origin*, produced by President Bill Clinton's Initiative on Race (Council of Economic Advisers for the President's Initiative on Race, 1998). Although the report's goals were purportedly in part "to educate Americans about the facts surrounding the issue of race in America" (p. 1), the AAPI population was almost completely excluded from the analysis, providing a perspective on race in America that was narrowly defined in a Black–White frame. These frames of race lose the complexity of race when it comes to AAPIs, which have a more complex racialization that is impacted by factors associated with their ethnic backgrounds, immigration histories, and language backgrounds, and other aspects of their identity that intersect with their experience with race.

Intersectionality

The concept of *intersectionality* captures CRT's sensitivity to the interplay and impact of various strands of identity relative to gauging opportunities and outcomes for AAPIs. Intersectionality as a frame through which to examine subordination and discrimination is important for AAPIs, because their representation is challenged by the limitations of more common frames for understanding race in America. For AAPIs, normative constructions of race lead to the prevailing idea that AAPIs are a monolithic and universally successful group relative to education, a perspective that overlooks the extent to which the population is very diverse, covering many cultures, histories, languages, and religions. Several AAPI sub-groups experience significant inequities that are masked when they are grouped with the larger population. For example, sub-groups such as Southeast Asians, Native Hawaiians, and Pacific Islanders, which have experienced refugeeism and colonization, face significant economic, political, cultural, and linguistic challenges that adversely impact their education and social mobility. Thus, in addition to negotiating forms of subordination enacted because of race, AAPIs in the United States are forced to straddle other intersecting identities: those of ethnicity and nationality, "foreign" status, being first-generation immigrants and children of immigrants, and their unique immigration histories that vary by sub-group.

Understanding the position of AAPIs within the racial frame of the United States begins with an understanding that defines race. Race is a concept that exists through, and only has meaning because of, differences between groups. Put another way, it is the gap between groups, when it comes to status attainment and other social indicators, which largely defines the social boundaries of race. It is these concerns among sociologists—the causes and consequences of racial stratification in our society and the conditions through which opportunities and mobility occur for different groups—that make comparative research essential to social science on racial inequality.

While there is certainly a place for the use of comparative race studies, it should not be the only basis for understanding racial groups in American society. Problems of comparisons between racial groups arise when researchers, policymakers, and practitioners attempt to find solutions for the racial gap by drawing inferences from the size and magnitude of the racial achievement gap. Higher education policy has been driven by conclusions about racial differences based solely on cross-sectional, normative framing. More specifically, results of cross-sectional research are commonly used to reach conclusions about the relative differences that exist between groups, and the between-group differences are often used to determine the treatment of a particular group by educators, practitioners, and policymakers (Teranishi, 2007).

In fact, historically, it is exactly an overreliance on comparative race research that has concerned scholars in the past, who have noted that this perspective can lead to a system of deficit thinking. Richard Valencia (1997) describes deficit thinking as a narrow set of assumptions about marginalized groups, which is "tantamount to 'blaming the victim' … [and is] founded on imputation, not documentation" (p. xi). As discussed earlier, Blacks and Latinos are viewed as a problem in comparative research, while Whites—and in some cases Asians—are viewed as a solution. While a gap in educational outcomes between groups is certainly an indicator that should be addressed, the gap does not necessarily tell us what is the problem, nor does it point to where solutions can be found.

The underlying assumption in these lines of inquiry is that studying the behaviors or experiences of White and AAPI students vis-à-vis those of Black and Latino students will not provide insights into how to better serve Black and Latino students and, just as importantly, does a disservice to struggling AAPI sub-groups whose experiences are camouflaged. For example, relative to higher education, Southeast Asians and Pacific Islanders consistently experience lower college matriculation and graduation outcomes compared to other AAPI sub-groups (Teranishi, 2010), and AAPI immigrants face challenges associated with language and immigration policies in schools and colleges (Teranishi et al., 2011).

Intersectionality moves traditional comparative approaches to acknowledge that racial categories as a whole are not consistently homogeneous across groups, and the actual educational experiences and processes of students can be concealed by looking solely at one aspect of their identity. This means that research on AAPIs needs to be approached with some caution, with attention to the fact that they are not equally comparable, given their unique composition, and the instruments used to measure differences across groups are universally applicable.

Social Justice for AAPIs

In keeping with the tradition of critical studies to which it belongs, CRT asserts that an ideologically neutral stance in any research endeavor is impossible. Critical race theorists make their own ideological stance explicit by embracing a commitment to social justice. The ultimate goal of research informed by CRT is the "abolition of … racial subordination [as] part of the broader goal of ending other forms of subordination such as gender, class, and sexual orientation" (Solorzano, 1997, p. 7). To reach that goal, CRT scholars are skeptical of claims of objectivity, meritocracy, and equal opportunity, and carefully consider how supposedly neutral practices and policies can enact discriminatory and inequitable outcomes. For example, contemporary jurisprudence regarding claims of discrimination rely on an apparently neutral standard of demonstrating intent to discriminate, a standard that is very difficult for victims to meet, because much of contemporary racism tends to be unconscious or to flow from larger structural forces that disadvantage people of color. By "looking to the bottom," or adopting the perspectives of those who have seen and felt discrimination, the AAPI community has a means of countering the hegemonic forces that shape claims of neutrality and color-blindness (Matsuda, 1987).

For AAPIs, a social justice perspective on their inclusion in affirmative action debates needs to be critical of the motivation and interests of parties involved in asserting claims about the population. As discussed earlier, interest groups who assert AAPIs have an anti-affirmative action claim are also trying to maintain access to higher education for dominant groups (e.g., Whites, legacy applicants, etc.). Social justice for AAPIs commands a deeper understanding of not only how they experience discrimination, but also how data is collected on the population and represented in studies. Researchers and policy analysts who study AAPIs often have to contend with inaccurate, incomplete, misleading, or unreliable information, which does not serve the population well relative to other groups. Many studies have been found to poorly accommodate distinctions within the AAPI population. More specifically, very few studies and policies acknowledge the ethnic, language, and other unique demographic distinctions within the population, and how these affect their comparability to other racial groups in the United States (Omi, 2000). In addition to being mischaracterized in comparative racial analysis or, worse, excluded from analysis, AAPIs are often also mixed with "other" or "international" categories (Teranishi, 2007).

The concept of "looking to the bottom" is an appropriate perspective on how the AAPI community is responding to how the population is treated in data. Most of the well-established community advocacy groups have worked diligently to demonstrate that current forms of population are not designed to critically examine, acknowledge, or appreciate the heterogeneity that exists among AAPIs. The data issues for AAPIs are particularly problematic in a data-driven culture that assumes a high degree of objectivity in numerical analysis to inform educational practice and policy. The data is simply misrepresenting and concealing the experiences and outcomes of the AAPI community.

A social justice approach to AAPIs also commands a closer examination of how the community is being represented by public policy and government programs. Just as troubling as the misrepresentation and exclusion of AAPIs in research are the ways in which the community is being overlooked, underserved, and misrepresented in broader concerns about the nation's education priorities. There is almost no recognition of AAPIs in the community college sector, for example, which is where AAPIs have their highest enrollment in U.S. higher education (National Commission on Asian American and Pacific Islander Research in Education, 2008). There is also slow progress in the inclusion and representation of Asian American Native American Pacific Islander Serving Institutions (AANAPISIs)—a federal program to support institutions serving low-income AAPI students—in efforts to invest in other minority-serving institutions (MSIs). Finally, AAPIs are seldom represented in important debates about immigration and language polices related to higher education (Teranishi et al., 2011). The blatant exclusion of AAPIs in some instances and the ambiguous positioning of the community in other instances demonstrate the powerful forces of racial triangulation and interest convergence, which was discussed earlier.

CONCLUSION

Positioning AAPIs within America's equity agenda requires transcending the intellectual boundaries that have severely limited—and even undermined—the knowledge about the intersection of race and educational opportunities and outcomes generally, and for the AAPI experience specifically. Existing research paradigms that are commonly applied to the study of racial inequality neither promote a better understanding about any individual racial population nor provide a perspective that allows us to constructively improve their educational experiences or outcomes. Particular tenets of CRT are particularly relevant to a better understanding of AAPIs relative to equity in higher education.

Interest convergence has been a powerful force in the origin and maintenance of the model minority myth. As a case in point for how interest convergence can be problematic for racial minorities, this "positive" stereotype has been damaging for the AAPI population. Quite simply, the model minority myth has resulted in the population being mischaracterized, overlooked, and underserved. The narrow and inaccurate characterization of AAPIs as a universally successful model minority has concealed the heterogeneity in the population and the ways in which unique aspects of the population—their diverse demography, wide range of immigration histories, and challenges associated with language, poverty, and discrimination—are a factor in the differences in access to and success in education, which vary tremendously within the population.

Intersectionality for AAPIs means acknowledging that normative constructions of race lead to the prevailing idea that AAPIs are a monolithic and universally successful group relative to education. This narrow approach to studying AAPIs conceals the extent to which the population is very diverse, covering many cultures, histories, languages, and religions. Perhaps most importantly, attention to intersectionality enables research to raise awareness for the most marginalized and vulnerable AAPI sub-groups. These are populations that experience significant inequities that are masked when they are grouped with the larger population.

Social justice for AAPIs needs to be derived from the unique needs and challenges of the population. For example, the AAPI population is in need of more and better research that utilizes data that can capture the distinct demographic features of the population. In conclusion, it is not a matter of simply improving their level of inclusion, but expanding the discourse about race in a way that accommodates the unique racialization of the AAPI community relative to other groups.

NOTE

1 The *Daily Princetonian* published an opinion column using the pseudonym "Lian Ji" that said, "I so good at math and science … Princeton the super dumb college, not accept me … I love Yale. Lots of bulldogs here for me to eat."

REFERENCES

Anderson, J.D. (2007). Race-conscious educational policies versus a "color-blind Constitution": A historical perspective. *Educational Researcher, 36*(5), 249–257 (doi:0.3102/0013189X07306534).

Bell, D. (1980). Brown v. Board of Education and the interest-convergence dilemma. *Harvard Law Review, 93*, 518–533.

Bowen, W.G., Kurzweil, M.A., & Tobin, E.M. (2005). *Equity and excellence in American higher education.* Richmond: University of Virginia Press.

Bowman, N.A., & Griffin, T.M. (2012). Secondary transfer effects of interracial contact: The moderating role of social status. *Cultural Diversity and Ethnic Minority Psychology, 18*, 35–44.

Chang, M., Witt-Sandia, D., Jones, J., & Hakuta, K. (Eds.). (1999). *The dynamics of race in higher education: An examination of the evidence.* Palo Alto, CA: Center for Comparative Studies on Race and Ethnicity, Stanford University.

Chang, R. (1999). *Disoriented: Asian Americans, law, and the nation-state.* New York: New York University Press.

Chea, T. (2009). University of Calif. admissions rule angers Asian-Americans. *USA Today*, April 24 (retrieved from http://www.usatoday.com/news/education/2009-04-24-university-california-asian_N.htm).

Chew, P.K. (1994). Asian Americans: The "reticent" minority and their paradoxes. *William and Mary Law Review, 36*(1), 1–94.

Chin, F., & Chan, J. (1972). Racist love. In R. Kostelanetz (Ed.), *Seeing through shuck.* New York: Ballantine Books.

Coloma, R.S. (2006). Disorienting race and education: Changing paradigms on the schooling of Asian Americans and Pacific Islanders. *Race, Ethnicity and Education, 9*(1), 1–15.

Connerly, W. (2006). Ward Connerly: We're saying race should not be used. *Oakland Tribune* (Oakland, CA), November 3.

Connerly, W. (2009). "Study, study, study"—A bad career move. *Minding the campus: Reforming our universities*, June 2 (retrieved August 10, 2012 from http://www.mindingthecampus.com/originals/2009/06/by_ward_connerly_about_five.html).

Council of Economic Advisers for the President's Initiative on Race. (1998). *Changing America: Indicators of social and economic well-being by race and Hispanic origin.* No. PR 42.8:C 36. Washington, DC (retrieved from http://www.gpo.gov/fdsys/pkg/GPO-EOP-CHANGINGAMERICA/pdf/GPO-EOP-CHANGINGAMER-ICA.pdf).

Crenshaw, K. (1989). Demarginalizing the intersection of race and sex: A Black feminist critique of antidiscrimination doctrine, feminist theory, and antiracist politics. Presented at the University of Chicago Legal Forum, Chicago.

Crenshaw, K. (1991). Mapping the margins: Intersectionality, identity politics, and violence against women of color. *Stanford Law Review, 43*(6), 1241–1299.

Delgado, R., & Stefancic, J. (2012). *Critical race theory: An introduction* (2nd ed.). New York: New York University Press.

Espenshade, T.J., & Chung, C.Y. (2005). The opportunity cost of admission preferences at elite universities. *Social Science Quarterly, 86*(2), 293–305 (doi:10.1111/j.0038-4941.2005.00303.x).

Golden, D. (2006). *The price of admission: How America's ruling class buys its way into elite colleges—And who gets left outside the gates.* New York: Crown (retrieved from http://www.amazon.com/The-Price-Admission-Americas-Colleges/dp/1400097967).

Gurin, P., Dey, E.L., Hurtado, S., & Gurin, G. (2002). Diversity and higher education: Theory and impact on educational outcomes. *Harvard Educational Review, 72*(3), 330–367.

Hacker, A. (2003). *Two nations: Black and White, separate, hostile, unequal.* New York: Scribner.

Hoeffel, E.M., Rastogi, S., Ouk Kim, M., & Shahid, H. (2012). *The Asian population: 2010.* 2010 Census Briefs No. C2010BR-11. Washington, DC: U.S. Census Bureau (retrieved from http://www.census.gov/prod/cen2010/briefs/c2010br-11.pdf).

Kiang, P.N.-C. (2006). Policy challenges for Asian Americans and Pacific Islanders in education. *Race, Ethnicity and Education, 9*(1), 103–115.

Ladson-Billings, G. (1998). Just what is critical race theory and what's it doing in a nice field like education? *Qualitative Studies in Education, 11*(1), 7–24.

Lee, S.J. (1996). *Unraveling the "model minority" stereotype: Listening to Asian American youth.* New York: Teachers College Press.

Lei, J.L. (2003). (Un)Necessary toughness? Those "loud Black girls" and those "quiet Asian boys." *Anthropology and Education Quarterly, 34*(2), 158–181.

Lien, P. (2004). *Pilot national Asian American political survey (PNAAPS), 2000–2001.* Ann Arbor, MI: Inter-university Consortium for Political and Social Research.

Los Angeles Times. (1996). Los Angeles Times poll study #389: Exit poll: The general election, November 5 (retrieved from http://www.latimes.com/media/acrobat/2008-10/43120439.pdf).

Lowe, L. (1996). *Immigrant acts: On Asian American cultural politics.* Durham, NC: Duke University Press.

Massey, D.S. (2008). *Categorically unequal: The American stratification system.* New York: Russell Sage Foundation.

Matsuda, M.J. (1987). Looking to the bottom: Critical legal studies and reparations. *Harvard Civil Rights–Civil Liberties Law Review, 22,* 323–399.

McGowan, M.O., & Lindgren, J. (2006). Testing the model minority myth. *Northwestern University School of Law, 100*(1), 331–377.

Nash, J.C. (2008). Re-thinking intersectionality. *Feminist Review, 89*(1), 1–15.

National Commission on Asian American and Pacific Islander Research in Education. (2008). *Asian Americans and Pacific Islanders: Facts, not fiction: Setting the record straight.* New York: National Commission on Asian American and Pacific Islander Research in Education (CARE) and the College Board (retrieved from http://www.nyu.edu/projects/care/rp.html).

Ng, J.C., Lee, S.S., & Pak, Y.K. (2007). Contesting the model minority and perpetual foreigner stereotypes: A critical review of literature on Asian Americans in education. *Review of Research in Higher Education, 31,* 95–130.

Ogbu, J.U., & Simons, H.D. (1998). Voluntary and involuntary minorities: A cultural-ecological theory of school performance with some implications for education. *Anthropology and Education Quarterly, 29*(2), 155–188 (doi:10.1525/aeq.1998.29.2.155).

Omi, M. (2000). Racial identity and the state: Contesting the federal standards for classification. In M. Adams, W. Blumenfeld, R. Castaneda, H. Hackman, M. Peters, & X. Zuniga (Eds.), *Readings for diversity and justice* (pp. 73–78). New York: Routledge.

Park, J.J. (2009a). Taking race into account: Charting student attitudes towards affirmative action. *Research in Higher Education, 50*(7), 670–690 (doi:10.1007/s11162-009-9138-7).

Park, J.J. (2009b). Are we satisfied? A look at student satisfaction with diversity at traditionally White institutions. *Review of Higher Education, 32*(3), 291–320.

Slotnik, D.E. (2012). Discrimination investigations end at Princeton and Harvard. *New York Times,* February 17 (retrieved from http://thechoice.blogs.nytimes.com/2012/02/17/discrimination-investigations-end-at-princeton-and-harvard/).

Solorzano, D.G. (1997). Images and words that wound: Critical race theory, racial stereotyping, and teacher education. *Teacher Education Quarterly, 24,* 5–19.

Solorzano, D.G. (1998). Critical race theory, race and gender microaggressions, and the experience of Chicana and Chicano scholars. *International Journal of Qualitative Studies in Education, 11*(1), 121–136 (doi:10.1080/095183998236926).

Teranishi, R.T. (2002). Myth of the super minority: Misconceptions about Asian Americans. *College Board Review, 195,* 16–21.

Teranishi, R.T. (2007). Race, ethnicity, and higher education policy: The use of critical quantitative research. In F.K. Stage (Ed.), *Using quantitative data to answer critical questions.* New Directions for Institutional Research. San Francisco: Jossey-Bass.

Teranishi, R.T. (2010). *Asians in the ivory tower: Dilemmas of racial inequality in American higher education.* New York: Teachers College Press.

Teranishi, R.T., Suárez-Orozco, C., & Suárez-Orozco, M. (2011). Immigrants in community colleges. *The Future of Children, 21*(1), 153–169.

The Nation. (2007). Asian Americans for affirmative action. January 8 (retrieved from http://www.thenation.com/blog/asian-americans-affirmative-action#).

Valencia, R.R. (Ed.). (1997). *The evolution of deficit thinking: Educational thought and practice.* Stanford Series on Education and Public Policy. Abingdon, Oxon, UK: Routledge (retrieved from http://www.amazon.com/The-Evolution-Deficit-Thinking-Educational/dp/0750706651).

Wu, F.H. (2002). *Yellow: Race in America beyond Black and White.* New York: Basic Books.

Zia, H. (2001). *Asian American dreams: The emergence of an American people.* New York: Farrar, Straus and Giroux.

16

LET'S BE FOR REAL
Critical Race Theory, Racial Realism, and Education Policy Analysis (Toward a New Paradigm)

Kristen L. Buras

At University Anywhere, the following exchange is unfolding between two education policy researchers—Polly C. Whitewash and B. F'Real:

Whitewash: That's the thing with charter schools. When research shows they are more efficient and effective than traditional public schools, state policymakers will lift caps that limit their formation. They'll flourish and so will students.

F'Real: Where's the evidence? As far as I know, many states are charter school-friendly, even though there's little evidence that they outperform regular public schools. It seems like policymakers have their own agenda.

Whitewash: I hear this often. But it really comes down to data—data-driven decision making. Besides, how can anyone defend the public schools?

F'Real: *The* public schools? For the most part, charter school operators target urban school districts. They're not setting up shop in the suburbs. I mean, it's mostly poor black kids who attend …

Whitewash: I don't think race has anything to do with it. It just so happens that city schools are the ones in need of reform. If suburban schools were troubled, we'd see the expansion of charter options for those children, too.

F'Real: I think that history is important here. On the face of it, *Brown v. Board of Education* was supposed to improve education for black students. Then there was foot dragging and white flight—white parents didn't want their children in desegregated schools. It seems like the new racial remedy is charter schools, but who is running them? Many white entrepreneurs say they're out to "help" poor kids of color, but it seems like they're lining their own pockets while …

Whitewash: Again, what matters is performance data. I'm sorry to interrupt, but I have an editorial meeting for the School Reform Journal. I need to decide which manuscripts will be published in a special issue on charter schools. Then

I've got a conference call with the Thomas B. Fordham Institute. I'll see you later ... [voice trails off].

F'Real: Why wasn't I invited to contribute an article? The students and parents I know say that school choice isn't working out the way that policymakers claim. Wait a minute! Did she say Fordham? Fordham spends most of its resources pushing charter schools.

This conversation between Polly C. Whitewash and B. F'Real exemplifies some of the tensions that characterize education policy research. As a traditional policy analyst, Whitewash embraces a "rational" paradigm for understanding education reform— one that presumes policy formation is based on the neutral and systematic collection of evidence to develop and refine interventions that promote the widest possible good. Whitewash is challenged by B. F'Real, a critical race theorist who underscores the racial dynamics of urban school reform and recognizes the constitutive elements of a race-conscious approach to policy analysis, including: (1) situating policy within a history of white supremacy, (2) mapping the racial-legal infrastructure that presently shapes education policy, (3) using and developing critical race constructs to analyze policy formation and implementation, (4) centering the counterstories of the racially oppressed in assessing policy effects, and (5) acting in alliance with communities affected by racially destructive policies in order to challenge those policies. Taken together, these elements constitute a new paradigm based on the philosophy of *racial realism* or the tenet that racism is endemic and infects all aspects of social life (Bell, 2005).

In this chapter, I explore each of these elements and offer concrete illustrations of what it means to "do" education policy analysis in the critical race tradition (and what doesn't constitute such work). More specifically, I provide a critical race response to a policy report (Smith, 2012) issued by the conservative Thomas B. Fordham Institute on educational reform in New Orleans. Through comparison of competing paradigms—rational versus racial realist—I reveal the shortcomings of the dominant model of policy analysis, which valorizes the color-blind, seemingly disengaged analyst who gathers data and writes policy reports without acknowledging the "for real" racial dynamics that shape school reform. The chapter concludes with a call for racial realism in education policy analysis and underscores the contributions of the still newly developing field of critical race education policy studies in advancing a new paradigm.

EDUCATION POLICYMAKING AND RESEARCH—NICE AND NEUTRAL?

Education policymaking is frequently understood as a rational process: decisions are shaped by evidence and ongoing assessment of which intervention promotes the widest possible good. Mary Lee Smith (Smith et al., 2004) explains that most textbooks provide the following description of the policy process:

Rational and democratic politics yield policies that respond to real social and educational needs and problems. Policy makers consider a range of solutions to these problems and select the best alternatives that can bring about the best outcomes. They conduct an adequate analysis of the outcomes of policies so they can make refinements and reports to the public (through media without vested interests) so that citizens can subsequently act in the political process in more informed ways.

Not without significance, Smith asks, "Outside of textbooks in the policy sciences, it this the way things really work?" (p. 3).

The rational understanding of policy formation and implementation does not account for dynamics of unequal power or the ways in which relations of supremacy and subordination influence education reform. Politics cannot be separated from policy—education policy is the product of disparate and competing interests between differently and often unequally situated groups. It is a site of struggle generating intended as well as unintended consequences and contradictions. Race and racial power are part and parcel of the policymaking process.

Recognition of these dynamics first inspired the development of critical race theory in the field of law. In the early 1980s, Kimberlé Crenshaw and other students of color (Crenshaw et al., 1995) noted the limitations of mainstream race analysis at Harvard's Law School where Derrick Bell, a critical race scholar who linked legal argumentation with the Black Power movement, had resigned over the absence of female faculty of color. Harvard's administration denied the need for replacing Bell with another black scholar, prompting law students to reflect: "We knew that we lacked an adequate critical vocabulary for articulating exactly what we found wrong with their arguments. It was out of this intellectual void that the impetus for a new conceptual approach to race and law was based" (p. xxi). In much the same way, scholars of color in the field of education grew frustrated with the lack of race-conscious analysis. Gloria Ladson-Billings (2009a) recollects her collaboration with William Tate in the early 1990s as they explored critical race theory in the field of law and its relevance to education. She reports: "Outside the supportive confines of our own institution, we were met with not only the expected intellectual challenges, but also outright hostility. Why were we focusing on race? What about gender? Why not class? Are you abandoning multicultural perspectives?" (p. 17).

Ladson-Billings doubts whether or not the vast majority of educational researchers will assume a subaltern position, especially "because of its dangers, its discomforts, and because we insist on thinking of ourselves as permanent residents in a *nice* field like education" (p. 34).

The exchange that opened this chapter represents one such challenge. Critical race policy analysis centers race and racial power in the examination of education reform. In doing so, however, this approach confronts researchers, such as Polly C. Whitewash, who not only value their position in a *nice* field like education, but conceive the process of policy formation to be *neutral* as well. That is to say, policymaking and policy research are viewed as nice, race-neutral processes where rational thought shapes argumentation and action.

Derrick Bell (2005) points out that, in the field of law, legal formalists have reasoned abstractly about law and analyzed juridical decision making as an objective process guided by precedent and the "rule of law." By comparison, legal realists "were a group of scholars in the early part of the twentieth century who challenged the classical structure of law as a formal group of rules that, if properly applied to any given situation, lead to a right—and therefore just—result." More to the point, "Realists accept a critical and empirical attitude towards the law, in contrast to the formalists who insist that law is logically self-evident, objective, a priori valid, and internally consistent" (p. 73). In the end, Bell concludes, "Racism provides a basis for a judge to select one available premise rather than another when incompatible claims arise" (p. 74). Thus he calls for racial realism or an orientation that recognizes racism as an indisputable force in policymaking.

In this chapter, I call for racial realism in education policy analysis. As critical race scholars in the fields of law and education have emphasized, we are too often left asking, "What about race?" It remains the absent presence in a seemingly neutral examination of policy, rendered subaltern even when school reform is unintelligible without its consideration.

LET'S BE RATIONAL? TRADITIONAL EDUCATION POLICY ANALYSIS AND ITS PROBLEMS

Before the elements of a race-conscious approach to education policy analysis are introduced, it is important to more thoroughly describe the "rational" approach that has traditionally characterized examinations of policymaking and research. Although I can only offer a few illustrations here, they do represent many of the overarching assumptions and tendencies that inform the rational and purportedly apolitical tradition.

In an edited book entitled *Charter School Outcomes*, Berends et al. (2008) join contributors in assessing the effects of charter schools on student achievement, among other things, and the relevance of such research to education policymakers. Notably the book is the first in a series on Research on School Choice sponsored by Vanderbilt University's National Center on School Choice—a center supported by the U.S. Department of Education's Institute of Education Sciences. The reference to *education sciences* is an important one to understand, as only particular approaches to policy analysis are viewed as credible by those working in the rational tradition.

Walberg (in Berends et al., 2008) explains that *Charter School Outcomes* is meant to "help set the stage for scientifically based charter school policy and practice." What precisely does this mean? On one hand, he underscores that "philosophy and theology—ancestors of the social sciences—were concerned with the moral value of ends and the ethical justification of means." On the other hand, he emphasizes, "The equally difficult issue is causality: Do the means indeed causally affect the ends?" (p. 1). The "objective" assessment of cause and effect is Walberg's foremost concern. In fact, he laments that the social sciences are "a half-century behind" the applied natural sciences in "drawing causal inferences necessary to base policy and practice decisions on scientific conclusions" (p. 2). Ultimately Walberg asserts that the "gold standard" of research is the "random assignment of units" to experimental and control groups. Moral and political questions—such as those pertaining to the historical role of racial power in shaping education policy and practice—are outside the immediate purview of legitimate education research. The fact that racially oppressed communities may have stories of their own to tell about what causes them to fare in school as they do is not relevant. In this research tradition, race is simply another variable to be controlled for purposes of statistical precision rather than a pervasive set of power dynamics that require contextualization and critical action to challenge inequities.

Along these same lines, Hoxby and Murarka (2008), who partly inspired Walberg's commentary, explore methods for assessing the achievement of students in charter schools. In painstaking detail, they discuss the primary forms of analysis used for evaluation, including "comparison with controls based on observable variables" (pp. 14–18). Reading and math scores on standardized tests are used to compare performance between traditional and charter schools; they are presumed to be a race-neutral means for gauging student achievement. Other ways of understanding school culture, knowledge, and achievement are never seriously considered, and the force of white supremacy in shaping what counts as knowledge at the outset is ignored. Perhaps most significant are the assumptions that Hoxby and Murarka (2008) make about the "rational" process of education policymaking. They proclaim the following without hesitation:

> Policymakers wish to have evidence on the effects of charter schools on their students' achievement. Such evidence has [several] potential uses. First, a policymaker who is considering expanding or contracting the availability of charter schools in his state may wish to know whether parents' desire to send their children to charter schools is based on their observations of achievement or based on other criteria.
>
> (p. 7)

In this case, objective metrics are assumed to guide charter school policy. That is to say, researchers gather, analyze, and report data in a seemingly disinterested fashion, and policymakers, without any specific set of interests, racial or otherwise, use this evidence to formulate and revise policy with the goal of advancing student achievement. But is this the way things *really* work?

The racial history that has shaped and continues to shape educational policy and law—a reality that critical race policy analysts emphasize—is an absent presence in the rational model. Why the achievement gap exists and how it has been shaped by racial formations and policies are not the kind of issues addressed by comparison-with-controls methods, even as these issues pertain to cause, effect, and state policy formation. Truth be told, the assumption that policymakers use student achievement data when making decisions about whether or not to support charter schools is highly questionable; the increasing power of wealthy white philanthropists and entrepreneurs in advocating laws that support private management of public schools in urban areas has been documented (Buras, 2011b; Scott, 2009, 2011). The failure to close low-performing charter schools has been documented as well and suggests that other interests may be operating (Lubienski & Weitzel, 2010). In *Charter School Outcomes*, Hill and Lake (2008) evaluate the research literature on charter school governance. They underscore that policymakers have not adequately funded charter school authorizers, which are the entities responsible for issuing charters and monitoring performance. "Charter school governance," they conclude, "has not been thought through thoroughly" (p. 117). Hill and Lake do not entertain the possibility that ensuring the achievement of students of color is not policymakers' greatest concern. Outside of providing data, researchers in the rational tradition purposefully distance themselves from anything that may be construed as race-conscious analysis of existing policies; this would, after all, compromise the metrics that policymakers presumably need to act upon when making rational decisions.

For critical race policy analysts, it turns out that the "gold standard" isn't so golden. Not only does it threaten to produce a truncated understanding of complex issues because of reductive formulae, but it also fails to address the fact that policymakers don't act neutrally in a world where color and cash matter. These matters cannot be addressed (and traditionalists do not desire to address them) through "rational" analyses of education policy.

What is needed is a new paradigm or racial realist approach, which I turn to now.

TOWARD A RACIAL REALIST APPROACH IN EDUCATION POLICY ANALYSIS

In light of competing paradigms, it is necessary to be explicit about what constitutes critical race policy analysis and what doesn't. In what follows, I delineate key aspects of critical race policy analysis by responding to a report by the Thomas B. Fordham Institute on school reform in New Orleans (see also Buras, 2012b).

The Fordham Institute is a generously endowed think tank and policy shop that sponsors "a growing portfolio of charter schools in Ohio" (Thomas B. Fordham Institute, 2012a). It claims to offer "independent, thoughtful criticism" of policies, but also says it remains "willing to change our minds when presented with new evidence." Its policy priorities include advancing choice, stretching the school dollar, and rethinking governance (Thomas B. Fordham Institute, 2012b).

Authored for Fordham by Nelson Smith (2012), founding president and former CEO of the National Alliance for Public Charter Schools, the aforementioned report examines the "lessons" that Ohio policymakers can learn from the Louisiana Recovery School District (RSD).

In the case of New Orleans, the vacuum created by Hurricane Katrina in 2005 provided policymakers with an unprecedented chance to address dismal student performance and the $30 million deficit of the city's public schools through mass restructuring (see Buras, 2005, 2011b). New Orleans is on track to become the nation's first all-charter school district. Prior to August 2005, the locally elected Orleans Parish School Board (OPSB) controlled 128 public schools in New Orleans. After August 2005, the state-run RSD assumed control of 107 of the city's public schools and chartered the majority of them, while only a handful remained under local governance through OPSB. Thus, by 2009–10, the majority of schools were charters (51 of 88 schools, enrolling 61 percent of students), with more than 30 different providers in two different school districts—the RSD in New Orleans governed by the state's Board of Elementary and Secondary Education (BESE) and New Orleans Public Schools governed by OPSB (Cowen Institute, 2010). While a small number of traditional, state-run schools remained in each district, the operation of charter schools by education entrepreneurs took precedence (New Schools for New Orleans, 2010). A comprehensive program of alternative teacher recruitment was also undertaken (United Teachers of New Orleans et al., 2007).

The report's foreword explains that historically public schools were overseen by "an elected group of civic-minded leaders ... with the help of expert professionals" (Ryan & Partin, 2012, p. 2). Regarding this arrangement, it warns:

> This system of local control may have worked well in a lot of communities around the U.S. and across the Buckeye State during much of the 20th century, but in recent decades some major urban school districts have fallen into fiscal and academic disaster with elected school boards in charge ...
>
> It is hard to revitalize gravely ill schools, however, without tackling the governance arrangements that led them—or at least enabled them—to fail in the first place.
>
> (p. 2)

From the outset, the report suggests that failed systems of management and governance—locally elected school boards and teacher unions—are responsible for many of the problems that plague urban school districts.

The report's foreword hails Louisiana's RSD as a bold alternative that has accomplished "significant gains in student achievement and consequential impacts on district-level standards and governance" (Ryan & Partin, 2012, p. 3). Ultimately, the report concludes that Ohio's policymakers have a great deal to learn from the RSD in New Orleans, where the vast majority of schools are privately managed charter schools staffed by newly recruited teachers and school leaders.

Situating Policy within a History of White Supremacy

In thinking about the Fordham report and its account of why urban school districts are faltering, it may help to recall the exchange that opens this chapter. B. F'Real challenges Polly C. Whitewash to consider the weight of history when she claims, "It just so happens that city schools are the ones in need of reform." F'Real responds by reflecting on *Brown v. Board of Education*, which he says led only to foot dragging and white flight. Such a move signals his recognition that present-day racial inequities and policies cannot be understood apart from the history of white supremacy. The conditions that plague urban schools today were produced in part by state abandonment of schools attended by blacks and the simultaneous flight of whites to newly built suburbs beginning in the 1950s.

In policy circles nowadays, however, history is a thing of the past. The Fordham report (Smith, 2012) provides one clear example. It opens with a section entitled "Essential Background: Why Was the RSD Created?" and emphasizes that the "story begins well before the floods of 2005" (p. 4). Yet the history of financial and academic distress in New Orleans public schools is only charted from 1998 onward. Based on a truncated account of "dysfunction" and "corruption," the report presumes the charter school-driven RSD is an appropriate solution; it defines centralized management of public schools as the problem and advocates privately managed charter schools as a more accountable alternative.

In contrast, a more extensive history of the city's public schools would be the starting point for a critical race analysis and would illuminate other possible explanations for the district's problems. For most of their history, public schools in New Orleans were not intended to support children of color or their black teachers but were instead considered the property of southern whites. The history of slavery, legalized segregation, ongoing racism, and white flight from the city has translated into strategic state neglect and disinvestment in African American education (DeVore & Logsdon, 1991; see also Buras, 2007).

Until 1917, the state did not provide a publicly funded high school education, not even an unequally funded one, for black students in New Orleans. In the late 1930s, a white teacher with ten years of experience and a B.A. degree received a yearly salary of $2,200; a black teacher with the same training and experience only earned $1,440. In addition, black teachers often had student loads 50 percent higher than their white counterparts (DeVore & Logsdon, 1991). In 1954, *Brown* led to mass white flight from the city's public schools. In 1960–61, there were approximately 53,000 black students and 38,000 white students in New Orleans public schools; by 1980–81, there were 72,000 and 13,000, respectively (Baker, 1996). Despite shifting racial demographics, the district did not have its first black superintendent until 1985 (DeVore & Logsdon, 1991).

Throughout the 1990s the district suffered ongoing financial crises, and by 2005 had a $30 million deficit. Why? Failing to consider the role that historical and racially targeted neglect has played in producing these conditions and relying on narratives of mismanagement and corruption, especially when such narratives focus only on local black governance of New Orleans public schools in recent years, seem purposefully partial. Fordham's account is far from neutral, as it avoids discussion of the legacy of racism in generating current problems.

This kind of dehistoricized appraisal of the urban education crisis is what prompted Ladson-Billings (2006) to argue that a focus on the achievement gap, which reflects only year-to-year test score disparities among racial groups, is unwise. Instead she called for analyzing the "education debt" or the "foregone schooling resources that we could have (should have) been investing in (primarily) low income kids" since the nation's founding.

Without an understanding of the education debt, we are vulnerable to any number of policy interventions based on incomplete knowledge of what caused existing racial inequities and what is required to resolve them.

Mapping the Racial-Legal Infrastructure that Presently Shapes Education Policy

In the opening exchange, Whitewash asserts, "When research shows [charter schools] are more efficient and effective than traditional public schools, state policymakers will lift caps that limit their formation." F'Real points out that most states have passed legislation supportive of charter schools, even in the absence of positive performance data. Importantly, he suggests there may be other agendas at play. F'Real thus recognizes that advancing white racial interests requires a legal infrastructure that accommodates those interests.

In the Fordham report, the RSD is lauded for "very positive" evidence of success (Smith, 2012, p. 4). Interestingly, the report relies on the School Performance Score (SPS) to measure the impact of reforms on student achievement; SPS is a creation of the state legislature in Louisiana and is largely based on standardized test scores from the Louisiana Educational Assessment Program (LEAP). A critical race analysis would show that using these scores to measure school performance is problematic on several fronts.

The first version of the LEAP program was implemented in 1986. In the late 1990s, LEAP was redesigned under Louisiana Governor Mike Foster, with the new version called LEAP 21 (or Leap for the twenty-first century). LEAP 21 introduced test scores as a factor in student promotion and graduation. What the report neglects to mention is that Foster, the son of a wealthy sugar planter, was endorsed by Ku Klux Klan member David Duke in 1995, and pled guilty to paying $150,000 to Duke for a mailing list of Duke's supporters. When the newly revised LEAP tests were administered in 1999, an insider in the Foster administration reported that the new LEAP eighth grade tests were more difficult than the existing high school exit exam (DeCuir, 2012).

A New Orleans-based group named Parents for Educational Justice formed in response to LEAP testing in 2000. Its legal representative sent letters to the state education superintendent under public records law for information on test development, old and new copies of LEAP tests, and names of the contractors responsible for developing the test. In turn, the House Education Committee introduced legislation protecting LEAP from the public records law, and a resolution was passed exempting LEAP from inspection in 2000. While education officials and lawmakers claimed the LEAP would most benefit black students, members of the African American community had grave doubts. "The secrecy … and [graduation] penalties associated with the LEAP," writes education historian Erica DeCuir (2012), "fueled Blacks' skepticism of high stakes testing as a school excellence reform model."

Most recently LEAP tests have been used to establish the "success" of the RSD. It may be more accurate to say that such "success" has been legislatively contrived, as the RSD has capriciously shifted its definition of academic "success" and "failure" since assuming control of public schools in Orleans Parish in 2005. The report ignores this fundamental point in its discussion of the "legal framework" associated with the RSD (Smith, 2012, pp. 5–6).

In November 2005, Act 35 redefined what counted as a failing school in Louisiana, raising the bar from an SPS cut-off of 60 to just below the state average of 87.4. This enabled 107 of 128 public schools in New Orleans to be folded into the RSD, whereas only 13 schools could have been assumed before the legislation was passed (United Teachers of New Orleans et al., 2006). Under these terms, most of the public schools in New Orleans were designated as failing, taken over by the RSD, and ultimately chartered.

In 2009 the standard shifted downward to SPS 75. In 2010—the year that conditions for transferring RSD schools back to the locally elected Orleans Parish School Board were to be set by the state board of education—a failing school was defined as having an SPS below 60; this enabled the RSD to establish its "success" and thereby justify ongoing experimentation with charter schools, which might lose their "autonomy" under local governance (Pastorek & Vallas, 2010). In 2011 the bar was set to SPS 65 and in 2012 was raised to SPS 75 (Louisiana Legislative Auditor, 2011). Under these terms, a greater number of RSD schools would still be defined by a "successful" trajectory upward when compared to Act 35 standards.

Notably by Act 35 standards (SPS 87.4), which were used to take over "failing" schools in New Orleans, all but a handful of schools *continue to fail*; this includes state-run schools as well as charter schools in the RSD (see attachment A in Pastorek & Vallas, 2010). In fact, school performance data in a state audit of the RSD, which is selectively discussed in the Fordham report, shows that all but ten schools in the RSD in New Orleans—whether state-run or charter—have an SPS below 75; SPS 75 means that roughly 54 percent of students are still below grade level (see appendix E in Louisiana Legislative Auditor, 2011). Thus more than half of the students in nearly all of the RSD schools in New Orleans *remain* below grade level despite the implemented reforms. Despite this, the RSD and private charter management organizations maintain control of these schools.

Critical race policy analysis seeks to unearth the indeterminate nature of the law and the racial interests undergirding its manipulation. In this paradigm, test scores are not regarded as a neutral means for measuring school performance, but are instead a legislative instrument for justifying the takeover and charterization of New Orleans public schools and the ongoing dispossession of black working-class communities who have little say in their governance.

Using and Developing Critical Race Constructs to Analyze Policy Formation and Implementation

When F'Real suggests that policymakers have an alternative agenda in advocating charter schools and that the white entrepreneurs running them care less about black students' well-being and more about lining their own pockets through control of public schools, he indirectly alludes to Cheryl Harris's (1995) theory of whiteness as property. For Harris, white identity has historically enabled its possessors to use and enjoy a host of benefits and assets and to exclude communities of color from such entitlements. Of course, Whitewash claims that the decision to establish charter schools is data-driven.

Using theoretical constructs such as whiteness as property, however, enables critical race education policy analysis to delve below taken-for-granted understandings and provide a reading of the policy formation and implementation process that accounts for the very real power that whites exercise to their own benefit.

Consider once more the Fordham report. It praises the RSD's "human capital strategy," which enables a non-governmental approach to recruiting and hiring personnel, particularly teachers. The emergent "blend" of new and veteran teachers is presented as an ideal mix for academic success in the RSD (Smith, 2012, pp. 12–13). While a critical race analysis acknowledges that the proportion of new and veteran teachers has important implications for student achievement, such considerations are absent from the report.

The Southern Education Foundation (2009) indicates:

> In Recovery School District schools … 47 percent of all teachers were entering the classroom for the first time in 2007 … Experience does not assure excellence in teaching, but it is well-established that students are often ill-served when most teachers in a school have little or no teaching experience.

While black veteran teachers were fired *en masse* in 2006 and the union's collective bargaining was no longer recognized, the city simultaneously became the site of one of the most comprehensive alternative teacher recruitment initiatives in the nation. Teach-NOLA, a teacher recruitment project organized by the RSD and New Schools for New Orleans, assumed a "no experience necessary" posture for hiring (Goodman, 2006; Robelen, 2007; United Teachers of New Orleans, 2007). Before 2005 only 10 percent of the city's teachers were in their first or second year of teaching; in 2008, 33 percent met that description (United Teacher of New Orleans, 2010). More specifically, in 2007–08, 60 percent of teachers in state-run RSD schools had 0–1 years of experience (only 1 percent had 25 or more years); by contrast, 4 percent of teachers in state-run schools under Orleans Parish School Board had 0–1 years (an entire 48 percent had 25 years or more). RSD charters also had a higher percentage of inexperienced teachers than charters under Orleans Parish School Board (41 percent had 0–3 years' experience versus 29 percent, respectively) (Cowen Institute, 2009). Many of the new and inexperienced teachers were white (Nelson, 2010) and assumed positions once held by the city's black veteran teachers—a testament to how whiteness functions as a form of property.

While hailed as progressive in the report, the RSD's human capital strategy presents some serious concerns. The National Academy of Education (2008) issued an education policy white paper on "Teacher Quality" and reported that the empirical evidence on the knowledge and performance of teachers recruited through alternative certification programs is mixed at best. Additionally, a number of these programs have substantially higher attrition rates, meaning that those recruited do not remain in the teaching profession (National Academy, 2008). In the case of Teach for America, students are grossly underprepared (Veltri, 2010). Perhaps most importantly, white teachers often have little appreciation for community cultural wealth (Yosso, 2006), whereas veteran educators from the community generally possess the heritage knowledge necessary to teach in historically rooted and culturally relevant ways (King, 2005; Ladson-Billings, 2009b). Regarding policies that affect teachers and teaching, and students of color in particular, a critical race analysis is most apt to question "Who benefits?"

While RSD superintendent, Paul Vallas touted charter schools without unionized teachers, announcing: "I don't want the majority of my teaching staff to work for more than 10 years. The cost of sustaining those individuals [with healthcare and retirement] becomes so enormous" (Conway, 2010). Such statements shed light on the "real" determinants of education policy and reveal that the human capital strategy endorsed in the report may have more to do with the dispossession of black veteran teachers and cost savings than innovations to raise student achievement.

In their groundbreaking book on critical race theory in education, Dixson and Rousseau (2006) assert that "examining the material effects of whiteness and the manner in which it is deployed and maintained materially ... has yet to be fully pursued by CRT scholars in education" (p. 50). Consideration of whiteness as property and other constructs developed in the critical race legal tradition have much to offer a racial realist paradigm in education policy analysis and should inform such work.

Centering the Counterstories of the Racially Oppressed in Assessing Policy Effects

When Whitewash says she is editing a special issue on charter schools for the School Reform Journal, F'Real questions why he wasn't invited to contribute. After all, he emphasizes, he has worked closely with students and parents whose experiential knowledge of school choice greatly differs from the accounts offered by policymakers. More to the point, critical race policy analysis requires that the testimony of the racially oppressed be part of what legal scholar Charles Lawrence (1995) calls the *evidentiary record*. Through counterstories (Delgado, 2000; Solórzano & Yosso, 2002), majoritarian policy narratives are challenged and their presumptions and limitations are rendered more transparent.

According to the Fordham report, the RSD has enjoyed "sustained support" in New Orleans because of "its success in creating new opportunities for students, schools, and communities" (Smith, 2012, p. 14). The report, which one would assume is based on a balanced analysis of data, relies on limited sources, including interviews with elite white stakeholders who installed the current policies.

A critical race policy analysis would consider the substantial criticism that charter schools have provoked in New Orleans, where not all students have been provided with the "new opportunities" alluded to in the report.

In a book that I coauthored with veteran teachers and students in New Orleans, firsthand accounts document discontent with charter schools, alternative teacher recruitment, and recovery-style reform in many parts of the African American community (Buras et al., 2010; see also Buras, 2011a, forthcoming). One student shares her concerns about the selective practices of charter schools and RSD endorsement of such reform:

> Now, with all schools being charters, no one will have the choice of a truly public, neighborhood-based education ...
>
> I've lost my home, my friends, my school. I'm always on the verge of tears. But the worst part of it all is that the public officials—both elected and hired—who are supposed to be looking out for my education have failed me even worse than the ones who abandoned me in the Superdome [during Katrina].
>
> (Hernandez, 2010, p. 86)

A veteran educator reflects on the troubling dynamics that have shaped the human capital strategy of the RSD, writing:

Many highly qualified educators are not working in the new charter schools and the Recovery School District because these are using unfair tactics to undermine the professionalism and the respect of veteran teachers … I worry these new schools only want to hire teachers who have never taught before. They want to hire inexperienced teachers so that they can pay them little or no money.

(Jackson-Ndang, 2010, p. 88)

The book from which these testimonies are drawn was written in order to circulate a fuller account of the concerns and criticisms that community members, who are the targets of these reforms, have articulated.

The tensions surrounding RSD takeover of most of New Orleans' public schools were evident during a public hearing before the state board of education in late 2010 regarding the possible transfer of schools from the RSD back to the locally elected Orleans Parish School Board (Buras, 2012a). It is beyond the scope of this chapter to enumerate the range of grievances expressed by large segments of the black community before the mostly white officials of the state board and the RSD. One representative statement will have to suffice. It comes from a longstanding community member, who charged:

What we're talking about here tonight is a simple question of democracy. We want in Orleans Parish what every other parish has in this state and that's the right to control our own schools. High crimes and misdemeanors have been carried out against the people of New Orleans … by the RSD and the people who run these charter operations. We don't believe that these schools have served the best interests of the majority of our African American students.

(In Buras, 2012a, p. 171)

There is a palpable sense that education entrepreneurs in New Orleans, assisted by white lawmakers in Baton Rouge, have been the real beneficiaries of reform.

Perhaps more than any other aspect of the Fordham report, its near complete silence regarding the viewpoints and experiences of community members who are "living through" these reforms reveals the deeper interests shaping this "independent" policy report. It is difficult not to ask what else may be missing from the report, which portrays contested reforms as having widespread support. This is where critical race policy analysis intervenes.

Acting in Alliance with Communities Affected by Racially Destructive Policies

As Whitewash discloses, she has built a relationship with the Fordham Institute, which supports and funds the charter school movement and other market-based solutions to problems in urban schools. In contrast, F'Real works with students and parents on the ground, exemplifying what may be called *critical race praxis*. Critical race praxis refers to the dialectical relationship between theory and practice or the commitment not only to analyze racial dynamics but to challenge inequities by acting in alliance with racially oppressed groups. Indeed, one of the things that animated critical race theorists in the field of law was a shared commitment to a political program. Dalton (1995) explains: "No matter how smart or bookish we were, we could not retreat from the sights, sounds, and smells of the communities from which we came … We learned from the start to harness our brains to the problems of the day" (pp. 80–81). Similarly, Dixson and Rousseau

(2006) stress: "In addition to uncovering the myriad ways that racism continues to marginalize and oppress people of color, identifying strategies to combat these oppressive forces and acting upon those strategies is an important next step within CRT" (p. 50).

In the context of New Orleans, veteran teachers, students, parents, and community organizers, cultural and educational organizations, and critical researchers established the Urban South Grassroots Research Collective for Public Education (2010). The collective develops and investigates questions focused on equity and accountability in public education. Countering the educational vision advocated by elite policy actors, the collective's research highlights the voices, experiences, and concerns of racially and economically dispossessed communities. The focus of this work is threefold: (1) government transparency, policy, and public education; (2) democratic curriculum, pedagogy, and assessment; and (3) grassroots school improvement and community engagement. By the provision of an alternative vision through locally and nationally disseminated research, combined with grassroots actions and initiatives, it may be possible to influence the direction of education policymaking and unearth the racially disparate effects of public school privatization in urban districts.

Critical race policy research and ongoing activism in multiple spaces are crucial. According to Stovall (2006), this is "where the rubber hits the road." In his own work in Chicago, Stovall has theorized the racial politics of school reform and built close relationships with community-based organizations focused on social justice issues. It is time for critical race policy scholars to nurture such alliances.

LET'S BE FOR REAL: THE PROMISE OF A RACIAL REALIST PARADIGM

It is time to "get real" about the racial politics of education policy. Those operating within a formal or rational paradigm overlook the actually existing role of racism and racial power in shaping the policymaking process. On one hand, the Fordham report could be read as a neutral and objective analysis of data on the RSD, which suggest that policymakers in Ohio and elsewhere should embrace charter schools and alternative teacher recruitment as remedies for the problems in urban school districts. On the other hand, a racial realist paradigm places the report in context and finds the following to be relevant:

- For more than a decade, the Fordham Institute has attacked multicultural education. One book (Leming et al., 2003) is entitled *Where Did Social Studies Go Wrong?* Its cover includes a young white boy surrounded by Abraham Lincoln and other white male leaders from U.S. history lamenting the damage wrought by multiculturalism. Contributors criticize multicultural theorists who "constantly focus upon the racism of the dominant (white) majority" (Ellington & Eaton, 2003, p. 72). It is regrettable, they point out, that such theorists "advocate using the public school classroom as a forum to promote the notion that there must be redress *now* for injustices that whites perpetrated, in some cases, centuries ago against people of color" (p. 75).
- For more than a decade, the Fordham Institute has advocated charter schools in urban districts. In a book entitled *Sweating the Small Stuff: Inner-City Schools and the New Paternalism* (Whitman, 2008), charter schools are praised for their "custodial culture." For example, the book's foreword, which is coauthored by

Fordham's president Chester Finn, explains that schools and teachers "are supposed to civilize … children," and those "serving inner-city kids may need to do more of that and do it more intensively" (Finn & Kanstoroom, 2008, p. xii). Alluding to associated policy priorities, Finn writes, "It is hard … to recreate these conditions in a traditional district school that is subject to central-office rules and collective bargaining agreements, which is why most efforts to create paternalistic schools are taking place under the banner of charter schooling" (pp. xiv–xv).

- For more than a decade, the Fordham Institute has advocated alternative teacher recruitment despite the lack of empirical evidence to support this policy. In 1999, for example, a "Manifesto" entitled "The Teachers We Need and How to Get More of Them" was issued (Thomas B. Fordham Foundation, 1999). Programs such as Teach for America and Troops to Teachers were praised.

In light of these facts, it is difficult to read the Fordham report as a rational and color-blind examination of school reform based on data alone. The desire to discipline communities of color through a market-based policy regime controlled by white entrepreneurs is more than apparent.

In her research on venture philanthropy in charter school policy and advocacy, Scott (2009) reminds us that "there is a long history of wealthy, mostly White philanthropists funding and shaping the education of African Americans and other communities of color in the United States" (p. 111). That's for real. And so is the fact that the Fordham Institute is part of a much wider policy network that includes charter schools, management organizations, advocacy groups, alternative leadership and teaching development programs, and research units—all advocating decentralized education reforms (Scott, 2009). As part of a critical research agenda, Scott calls for investigations to "determine the systematic effects of philanthropies on educational policies in particular urban 'markets'" (p. 131). Critical race policy analysis has much to offer here. A racial realist paradigm holds great promise for unveiling the ways that racism shapes education policy. As critical race theory comes into its own, the so-called rational paradigm will be exposed as a farce. Make no mistake about it: the money men are teleconferencing with Polly C. Whitewash at this very moment.

REFERENCES

Baker, L. (1996). *The second battle of New Orleans.* New York: HarperCollins.

Bell, D. (2005). Racial realism. In R. Delgado & J. Stefancic (Eds.), *The Derrick Bell reader* (pp. 73–77). New York: New York University Press.

Berends, M., Springer, M.G., & Walberg, H.J. (Eds.). (2008). *Charter school outcomes.* New York: Lawrence Erlbaum.

Buras, K.L. (2005). Katrina's early landfall: Exclusionary politics behind the restoration of New Orleans. *Z Magazine, 18*(12), 26–31.

Buras, K.L. (2007). Benign neglect? Drowning yellow buses, racism, and disinvestment in the city that Bush forgot. In K. Saltman (Ed.), *Schooling and the politics of disaster* (pp. 103–122). New York: Routledge.

Buras, K.L. (2011a). Challenging the master's plan for the Lower Ninth Ward of New Orleans. *Z Magazine, 24*(5), 19–22.

Buras, K.L. (2011b). Race, charter schools, and conscious capitalism: On the spatial politics of whiteness as property (and the unconscionable assault on black New Orleans). *Harvard Educational Review, 81*(2), 296–330.

Buras, K.L. (2012a). "It's all about the dollars": Charter schools, educational policy, and the racial market in New Orleans. In W. Watkins (Ed.), *The assault on public education* (pp. 160–188). New York: Teachers College Press.

Buras, K.L. (2012b). *Review of "The Louisiana Recovery School District: Lessons for the Buckeye State."* Boulder, CO: National Education Policy Center (retrieved March 20, 2012 from http://nepc.colorado.edu/thinktank/review-louisiana-recovery-buckeye).

Buras, K.L. (forthcoming). *Charter schools, race, and urban space: Where the market meets grassroots resistance.*

Buras, K.L., Randels, J., Salaam, K.Y., & Students at the Center. (2010). *Pedagogy, policy, and the privatized city: Stories of dispossession and defiance from New Orleans.* New York: Teachers College Press.

Conway, Z. (2010). Education "revolution" in New Orleans. *BBC News,* April 8 (retrieved from http://news.bbc.co.uk/go/pr/fr/-/2/hi/americas/8608960.stm).

Cowen Institute. (2009). Is education reform in New Orleans working? A few facts swimming in a sea of unknowns [PowerPoint], October. New Orleans, LA: Cowen Institute.

Cowen Institute. (2010). *The state of public education in New Orleans.* New Orleans, LA: Cowen Institute.

Crenshaw, K., Gotanda, N., Peller, G., & Thomas, K. (Eds.). (1995). *Critical race theory: The key writings that formed the movement.* New York: New Press.

Dalton, H.L. (1995). The clouded prism: Minority critique of the critical legal studies movement. In K. Crenshaw, N. Gotanda, G. Peller, & K. Thomas (Eds.), *Critical race theory: The key writings that formed the movement* (pp. 80–84). New York: New Press.

DeCuir, E.L. (2012). The Louisiana Educational Assessment Program (LEAP): A historical analysis of Louisiana's high stakes testing policy. Unpublished doctoral dissertation, Georgia State University.

Delgado, R. (2000). Storytelling for oppositionalists and others: A plea for narrative. In R. Delgado & J. Stefancic (Eds.), *Critical race theory: The cutting edge* (pp. 60–70). Philadelphia, PA: Temple University Press.

DeVore, D.E., & Logsdon, J. (1991). *Crescent City schools: Public education in New Orleans, 1841–1991.* Lafayette: Center for Louisiana Studies, University of Southwestern Louisiana.

Dixson, A.D., & Rousseau, C.K. (Eds.). (2006). *Critical race theory in education: All God's children got a song.* New York: Routledge.

Ellington, L., & Eaton, J.S. (2003). Multiculturalism and social studies. In J. Leming, L. Ellington, & K. Porter (Eds.), *Where did social studies go wrong?* (pp. 70–93). Washington, DC: Thomas B. Fordham Foundation.

Finn, C.E., & Kanstoroom, M. (2008). Foreword. In D. Whitman, *Sweating the small stuff: Inner-city schools and the new paternalism* (pp. ix–xvii). Washington, DC: Thomas B. Fordham Institute.

Goodman, A. (2006). All New Orleans public schools teachers fired, millions in federal aid channeled to private charter schools. *Democracy Now,* June 20 (retrieved from www.democracynow.org).

Harris, C.I. (1995). Whiteness as property. In K. Crenshaw, N. Gotanda, G. Peller, & K. Thomas (Eds.), *Critical race theory: The key writings that formed the movement* (pp. 276–291). New York: New Press.

Hernandez, M. (2010). Worse than those six days. In K.L. Buras, J. Randels, K.Y. Salaam, & Students at the Center, *Pedagogy, policy, and the privatized city: Stories of dispossession and defiance from New Orleans* (pp. 85–86). New York: Routledge.

Hill, P.T., & Lake, R.J. (2008). Charter school governance. In M. Berends, M.G. Springer, & H.J. Walberg (Eds.), *Charter school outcomes* (pp. 113–129). New York: Lawrence Erlbaum.

Hoxby, C., & Murarka, S. (2008). Methods of assessing achievement of students in charter schools. In M. Berends, M.G. Springer, & H.J. Walberg (Eds.), *Charter school outcomes* (pp. 7–37). New York: Lawrence Erlbaum.

Jackson-Ndang, K. (2010). Does anybody know? In K.L. Buras, J. Randels, K.Y. Salaam, & Students at the Center, *Pedagogy, policy, and the privatized city: Stories of dispossession and defiance from New Orleans* (pp. 87–88). New York: Routledge.

King, J.E. (Ed.). (2005). *Black education: A transformative research and action agenda for the new century.* New York: Routledge.

Ladson-Billings, G. (2006). From the achievement gap to the education debt: Understanding achievement in U.S. schools. *Educational Researcher, 35*(7), 3–12.

Ladson-Billings, G. (2009a). Just what is critical race theory and what's it doing in a *nice* field like education? In E. Taylor, D. Gillborn, & G. Ladson-Billings (Eds.), *Foundations of critical race theory in education* (pp. 17–36). New York: Routledge.

Ladson-Billings, G. (2009b). *The dreamkeepers: Successful teachers of African American students* (2nd ed.). San Francisco, CA: Jossey-Bass.

Lawrence, C. (1995). The word and the river: Pedagogy as scholarship as struggle. In K. Crenshaw, N. Gotanda, G. Peller, & K. Thomas (Eds.), *Critical race theory: The key writings that formed the movement* (pp. 336–351). New York: New Press.

Leming, J., Ellington, L., & Porter, K. (Eds.). (2003). *Where did social studies go wrong?* Washington, DC: Thomas B. Fordham Foundation.

Louisiana Legislative Auditor. (2011). *Louisiana Department of Education Recovery School District: Performance audit,* September 14. Baton Rouge, LA: Louisiana Legislative Auditor.

Lubienski, C.A., & Weitzel, P.C. (Eds.). (2010). *The charter school experiment: Expectations, evidence, and implications.* Cambridge, MA: Harvard Education Press.

National Academy of Education. (2008). *Teacher quality* [education policy white paper]. Washington, DC: National Academy of Education.

Nelson, F.H. (2010). *Teacher quality and distribution in post-Katrina New Orleans*, September. Washington, DC: American Federation of Teachers.

New Schools for New Orleans. (2010). *Our impact.* New Orleans, LA: New Schools for New Orleans (retrieved April 22, 2010 from http://newschoolsforneworleans.org/).

Pastorek, P.G., & Vallas, P. (2010). *Conditioning for success: A process to transfer schools placed in the Recovery School District*, September 14. Baton Rouge, LA: Louisiana Department of Education.

Robelen, E.W. (2007). New teachers are New Orleans norm. *Education Week*, November 12 (retrieved from www.edweek.org).

Ryan, T., & Partin, E. (2012). Foreword. In N. Smith, *The Louisiana Recovery School District: Lessons for the Buckeye State* (pp. 2–3). Washington, DC: Thomas B. Fordham Institute.

Scott, J. (2009). The politics of venture philanthropy in charter school policy and advocacy. *Educational Policy, 23*(1), 106–136.

Scott, J.T. (2011). Market-driven education reform and the racial politics of advocacy. *Peabody Journal of Education, 86*(5), 580–599.

Smith, M.L., Miller-Kahn, L., Heinecke, W., & Jarvis, P.F. (2004). *Political spectacle and the fate of American schools.* New York: Routledge Falmer.

Smith, N. (2012). *The Louisiana Recovery School District: Lessons for the Buckeye State*, January. Washington, DC: Thomas B. Fordham Institute.

Solórzano, D., & Yosso, T.J. (2002). Critical race methodology: Counter-storytelling as an analytical framework for education research. *Qualitative Inquiry, 8*(1), 23–44.

Southern Education Foundation. (2009). *New Orleans schools four years after Katrina: A lingering federal responsibility*, November. Atlanta, GA: Southern Education Foundation.

Stovall, D. (2006). Where the rubber hits the road: CRT goes to high school. In A.D. Dixson & C.K. Rousseau (Eds.), *Critical race theory in education: All God's children got a song* (pp. 231–240). New York: Routledge.

Thomas B. Fordham Foundation. (1999). *The teachers we need and how to get more of them: A manifesto.* Washington, DC: Thomas B. Fordham Foundation.

Thomas B. Fordham Institute. (2012a). About us (retrieved from www.edexcellence.net/about-us/).

Thomas B. Fordham Institute. (2012b). Policy priorities (retrieved from www.edexcellence.net/policy-priorities/).

United Teachers of New Orleans. (2010). *The New Orleans model: Shortchanging poor and minority students by over-relying on new teachers* [issue brief], March. New Orleans, LA: United Teachers of New Orleans.

United Teachers of New Orleans, Louisiana Federation of Teachers, & American Federation of Teachers. (2006). *"National model" or flawed approach? The post-Katrina New Orleans Public Schools*, November. New Orleans, LA: United Teachers of New Orleans, Louisiana Federation of Teachers, and American Federation of Teachers.

United Teachers of New Orleans, Louisiana Federation of Teachers, & American Federation of Teachers. (2007). *No experience necessary: How the New Orleans school takeover experiment devalues experienced teachers*, June. New Orleans, LA: United Teachers of New Orleans, Louisiana Federation of Teachers, and American Federation of Teachers.

Urban South Grassroots Research Collective for Public Education. (2010). *Overview.* New Orleans, LA: Urban South Grassroots Research Collective for Public Education.

Veltri, B.T. (2010). *Learning on other people's children: Becoming a Teach for America teacher.* Charlotte, NC: Information Age Publishing.

Whitman, D. (2008). *Sweating the small stuff: Inner-city schools and the new paternalism.* Washington, DC: Thomas B. Fordham Institute.

Yosso, T.J. (2006). Whose culture has capital? A critical race theory discussion of community cultural wealth. In A.D. Dixson & C.K. Rousseau (Eds.), *Critical race theory in education: All God's children got a song* (pp. 167–189). New York: Routledge.

17

EXAMINING BLACK MALE IDENTITY THROUGH A RACED, CLASSED, AND GENDERED LENS

Critical Race Theory and the Intersectionality of the
Black Male Experience

Tyrone C. Howard and Rema Reynolds

It has been well established in the professional literature that Black[1] males face myriad challenges in the nation's schools and society writ large (Anderson, 2008). The academic achievement and social outcomes of Black males in PreK-12 and postsecondary schools have been the subject of a number of scholarly works over the past three decades (Duncan, 2002; Harper & Harris, 2010; Howard, 2008, 2010; Jackson, 2007; Mincy, 2006; Noguera, 2008; Polite & Davis, 1999). A look at outcome data reveals how schools have fallen terribly short in engaging Black males academically, and providing the appropriate structures to foster their maximum performance. A cursory summary of these data would reveal that less than half of Black males graduate within four years from U.S. high schools, compared to 78 percent for White males (Schott Foundation for Public Education, 2010). Reading and math scores of Black males at the elementary and middle school levels have increased over the past decade; however, they still significantly trail their White, Latino, and Asian male counterparts in disturbing ways (U.S. Department of Education, 2009a, 2009b).

At the high school level, Black males are among the subgroups least likely to take and pass Advanced Placement (AP) courses and exams (College Board, 2012). Over the past three decades, the ACT and SAT scores of Black males have been notably lower than for their White, Latino, and Asian counterparts (U.S. Department of Education, 2009a, 2009b), Black males are the subgroup of students most likely to be retained during their K-8 education (Aud et al., 2010), and they are three times more likely than Latino and Asian males to be suspended from elementary and secondary schools (Aud et al., 2010; Gregory et al., 2010). Furthermore, data reveals that, even for Black males who do make a successful transition to postsecondary education, their completion rates and overall experiences are not on a par with those of their counterparts from other racial groups (Harper & Harris, 2010).

A number of explanations have been offered to shed light on the many challenges that Black males face in schools. Some of the more notable research in the 1960s on Black males focused on their families and communities and was centered on cultural deficits (Moynihan, 1965; Reynolds, 2010). Subsequent works in the 1980s and 1990s made the call for more of a cultural analysis of how Black students were not adequately being educated in schools (Gay, 1991, 1992; Irvine, 1990). Many of these arguments centered on cultural mismatch theory and led some researchers to make the call for more culturally responsive learning environments to improve the schooling outcomes of Black students (Irvine, 1990; Ladson-Billings, 1994). E. Gordon et al. (1994) called for scholars to move away from genetic and cultural explanations of Black male underachievement, and to examine structural causes. Using the lens of institutional racism and discrimination they suggested that drugs, crime, violence, inferior schooling, and economic instability provided more reliable insights into why Black males struggle to adapt in schools. Noguera (2001) contends that there are both structural *and* cultural factors that play out in detrimental ways for Black males that must be further analyzed and addressed if we are to disrupt patterns of school underperformance Black males experience. He suggested a further investigation of how identity is shaped within school contexts for Black males which takes into consideration race, gender, class, and place as essential for educational researchers and practitioners to understand if they are to effectively engage them in the learning process.

The focus of this work is not to debate the merits of previously proposed explanations for Black male underperformance. One of the problems in examining Black male performance is the consistent pursuit to find the single explanation for the current state of affairs. The depths and breadth of the challenges faced currently and historically defy the single explanation approach, and require a more thoughtful, nuanced, and complex set of explanations which rest on a wide range of variables. Moreover, a limitation with the work on Black males has been a failure to unpack what it means to be *Black* and *male*. Much of the literature has operated as though Black males are a monolithic group and assumes that there is a common or universal set of encounters that all Black males experience. Much of the previous work on Black males has fallen short in producing new knowledge because it has failed to problematize the diversity of social factors Black males face, which are often mitigated by socioeconomic conditions and normative gendered sociocultural expectations (Swanson et al., 2003) that can shape their experiences in and out of school. These works have frequently ignored or overlooked the multiple layers of Black male identity.

The scope of this work examines the plight of Black males through a critical race theory (CRT) lens, and more specifically through an intersectionality framework, to explore how research on Black males can help to inform the knowledge base by taking a more comprehensive and complexified account of Black males. CRT is used within this field to examine issues of racism and educational inequity. However, it also calls for an analysis of racism and its intersection with other forms of oppression such as sexism, classism, homophobia, and nativism (Delgado & Stefancic, 2001). CRT scholars have developed the following five tenets to guide research and inquiry on educational equity and racial justice:

1 *Centrality of race and racism.* All CRT research within education must centralize race and racism, including intersections with other forms of subordination such as gender, class, and citizenship.

2 *Challenging the dominant perspective.* CRT research works to challenge dominant narratives and re-center marginalized perspectives.

3 *Commitment to social justice.* CRT research must always be motivated by a social justice agenda.

4 *Valuing experiential knowledge.* CRT builds on the oral traditions of many indigenous communities of color around the world. CRT research centers the narratives of people of color when attempting to understand social inequality.

5 *Being interdisciplinary.* CRT scholars believe that the world is multidimensional, and similarly research about the world should reflect multiple perspectives.

(Solórzano and Delgado Bernal, 2001)

Using these tenets as guideposts, accompanied with the utility of intersectionality, this chapter offers a critical, holistic discussion of Black males' varied experiences.

CRT AND BLACK MALE INTERSECTIONALITY

In 1989 Professor Kimberlé Crenshaw introduced the concept of intersectionality in her work "Demarginalizing the Intersection of Race and Sex: A Black Feminist Critique of Antidiscrimination Doctrine, Feminist Theory, and Antiracist Politics." In this work, she describes the multidimensionality of Black women's experiences as being complicated, based on their gender (in a patriarchal society), race (in a predominately White society), and poverty (in a capitalistic society). Crenshaw's works spurred a plethora of works from dominated groups who argued that traditional approaches to examining equity and discrimination did not effectively capture the full spectrum of their experiences. Intersectionality is a way to conceptualize how oppressions are socially constructed and affect individuals differentially across multiple group categories. Crenshaw's explanation of intersectionality is central to understanding the complex and marginalized aspects of identity of which women in communities organizing for social change have long been aware.

Intersectionality—the interaction of multiple identities and varied experiences of exclusion and subordination (K. Davis, 2008)—provides a suitable framework to examine the experiences of Black males, because it not only centers race at the core of its analysis, but also recognizes and examines other forms of oppression and identity markers, namely class and gender, which have important implications for Black males as well (Patterson, 1995). The concept of intersectionality is based on the idea that the typical conceptualizations of discrimination and oppression within society, such as racism, sexism, homophobia, and class-based discrimination, do not act independently of one another; instead, these forms of oppression interrelate, creating a system of oppression that reflects the "intersection" of multiple forms of exclusion, prejudice, and discrimination (McCall, 2005). The intersections of race, class, and gender have manifested themselves in a multitude of complex and harmful ways within the U.S. that have profoundly influenced the manner in which Black males experience schools and society (Polite & Davis, 1999). This intersectionality is rarely examined and, as a result, opportunities to authentically capture the breadth and depth of Black males are missed, and efforts to capture their stories and reform schools are misinformed and misguided.

Identity politics, discussed in Crenshaw's work (2009), often characterizes the collective identity for people of color and recognizes as social and systemic what was formerly perceived as isolated and individual. Crenshaw contends that "the problem with identity politics is not that it fails to transcend difference, as some critics charge, but rather the opposite—that it frequently conflates or ignores intragroup differences" (p. 213). Hence, one of the goals of this work is to shed light on the dynamic intragroup differences that exist among Black males and their respective identities.

Interlocking oppressions (McCall, 2005) expands the idea of intersectionality, names the mechanisms of social construction more concretely, and explicitly allows for a deeper examination of intragroup differences among identities. Interlocking oppressions considers how interactions between individuals and social factors shape their subjectivities. Specifically, interlocking oppressions names how one person's sources of privilege or subordination can construct another's marginalized identity. In this way, the concept of interlocking oppressions explains how the oppressions associated with different socio-economic locations are socially constructed, and calls on individuals to take responsibility for their roles in the oppression of others as well. Examining the interlocking oppressions Black males may be subject to and explicating their experiences within those socially constructed locations of marginalizing subjugation could prove fruitful in widening the discourse around Black male identity. Heterosexual Black men, for example, though oppressed in many forms for varied reasons, possess the privilege that heteronormativity (Yep, 2003) brings. This privilege, accounting for interlocking oppressions, can serve to marginalize homosexual Black men in unintended and largely unexamined ways (Brown, 2005; Hill Collins, 2004; Hutchinson, 1999). Again, this intricate level of examination and discourse is necessary in order to better understand the complexity within the experiences of Black males.

CRT speaks to this intersectionality, providing a focused lens on the intersection or connectedness between race and other mitigating factors that influence Black males. The emergence of CRT as a theoretical, methodological, and analytical framework has provided a much needed and long overdue tool for researchers and practitioners alike to examine racial inequity in the United States (Bell, 1992, 1995; Delgado, 1995, 1999). Despite the progress that has been made in race relations and in the social and economic position of people of color over the last half-century, the remnants of racism remain strong in everyday life for millions of people of color (McLaren et al., 2010). CRT offers a probing theoretical construct to problematize race and racism. However, one of the challenges of the progressive agenda that analyzes race is the failure to critically examine the other identity markers that come with it, namely gender and class. Needless to say, the essentialization of any group presents a host of challenges. However, the failure to peel back the thick layers of oppression that afflict various groups ignores the complexity of identity in the twenty-first century. In many ways, the adoption of monolithic categorizations of racialized groups can further marginalize vicitimized groups (McCready, 2004). Further, the failure to unpack the multiple layers of identity markers inadvertently leads researchers to narrow and often misguided understandings of the lived experiences of certain groups—particularly those on the margins, in this case Black males. As a result, inquiry, interventions, or means to disrupt their realities fall short because of the failure to see, describe, examine, and understand the rich differences that exist within groups.

Exploring the intersectionality of race, gender, and class in a more nuanced fashion than much of the previous work has attempted is a necessary endeavor for this population. In his book *Thirteen Ways of Looking at a Black Man*, Gates (1997) unpacks the diversity and complexity of what it means to be Black and male in the United States. Gates's work is important, because he attempts to capture through a narrative account the myriad variables that define the lives of Black men in the U.S. He states: "We agree that the notion of a unitary black man is as imaginary (and as real) as Wallace Stevens' blackbirds are; and yet to be a black man in the twentieth century is to be heir to a set of anxieties: beginning with what it means to be a black man" (p. xvii). Gates speaks to the complexity of Black male identity, which is both located in a collective identity, yet influenced by individual experiences. The collective identity can produce a conundrum for researchers who seek to understand this group, Black males, as a whole. The diversity of experiences that influence the *individual* identity Black males develop in the U.S. would find that, while obvious social identities such as race and gender are prominent as provided in Gates's accounts, equally as captivating are the ways that religion, sexual orientation, political persuasion, ethnic origins, age, and geographical location also paint an intricate picture of how all Black males define themselves and ultimately live their lives. Ferguson's (2003) account of public schools and the making of Black masculinity is an example of work tied to the importance of intersectionality and identity, as it delineates the many ways Black males struggle to construct their own identity within a cultural framework that views the nexus of Black and male as being criminal, deviant, and problematic. She contends that for Black males:

> Identification is a process of marking off symbolic boundaries through embodied performances of self that call up and draw on idealized figures and cultural representations as a reference to one's rightful membership and authenticity. Identification in this sense is a series of public acts of commitment to a subject position.
>
> (p. 211)

Black males find themselves in perpetual negotiation as they seek to reconcile their own individual lived experiences with prescribed societal expectations and limitations. This negotiation can prove fatiguing and taxing mentally, physically, and emotionally for Black males (Smith, 2010; Smith et al., 2007) and may influence their social and academic outcomes in schools.

One of the challenges in examining the lived experiences and academic outcomes of Black males has been the narrow and often static manner in which they are viewed, and how their identities have been constructed (Flennaugh, 2011). Future research on Black males should explore what it is like to exist within these symbolic boundaries, and engage in inquiry that encourages Black males to step outside of these restrictive constructions and instead create narratives, from their standpoints, which can serve to disrupt the traditional narrative (Allen, 1996). Researchers need to consider that efforts to disrupt Black male underperformance have fallen short in producing new knowledge and unique insights, because the approaches taken historically have fallen short in incorporating, addressing, and examining the full scope of Black male identity (Howard & Flennaugh, 2011). If this is the case, if researchers have indeed been shortsighted in their examinations of Black males, then a plausible explanation as to why only minimal progress, if any, can be evidenced despite an increasing number of summits, special sessions of Congress, various calls to action, special issues in academic journals, and a host of other forums dedicated to the study of Black males may be found in the limited frames prior research has used. Therefore, this work attempts to move the conversation and to make a call for a more multi-faceted approach by looking at Black males through a race, class, *and* gendered lens. CRT has applicability in this discussion, because it draws upon paradigms of intersectionality. Delgado and Stefancic (2001) state that:

> Perspectivalism, the insistence of examining how things look from the perspective of individual actors, helps us understand the predicament of intersectional individuals. It can enable us to frame agendas and strategies that will do justice to a broader range of people and avoid oversimplifying human experience. Another critical tool that has proven useful in this respect is the notion of multiple consciousness.
>
> (p. 55)

Recognizing that race and racism work with and through gender, ethnicity, class, sexuality, and nation as systems of power, contemporary critical race theory often relies upon investigations of these intersections (Hill Collins, 1986; Solórzano, 1998). Furthermore, the utility of CRT is appropriate in this discussion, because one requisite tenet calls for the examination of racism alongside forms of subordination that have a profound influence on people's realities (Solórzano & Delgado Bernal, 2001).

Research on the educational experiences of Black males has to recognize the complexity that is Black male identity within the context of learning institutions and social spaces (Nasir, 2012). The intersectionality of race, class, and gender and other identity markers are fundamentally critical in research concerned with young Black males, as they are in the case of any subgroup. Each marker in its own way profoundly influences identity construction, self-concept, interactions with the world, and meaning making. Again, Black males possess multiple identities that are profoundly shaped by race, socio-economic status, and gender in all of their complex manifestations. Among the questions that need to be posed are: How do diverse notions of Black maleness play out in schools? What are the advantages and disadvantages of diverse masculinities in schools? Do school structures, policies, and practices suppress complex or strong racial identities? Patricia Hill Collins (2004) refers to the intersectional paradigm as an analytical framework that explains the interrelationships of political and social systems of race, class, gender, and other social divisions that may capture the complex realities of multiple forms of oppression, exclusion, and marginalization for non-dominant groups. The fields of education and psychology have struggled for well over a century to adequately address the significant challenges Black males face in constructing identities that function in institutions of education (Kumashiro, 2001; Reeser, 2010).

DOUBLE CONSCIOUSNESS AND INTERSECTIONALITY

Du Bois (1903) paid particular attention to the internal conflict that Black people faced in the United States at the turn of the twentieth century. His notion of double consciousness recognized the psychological and sociohistorical realities of American oppression and sought to shed light on the complex ways Black people develop notions of self in a social, economic, and racial milieu that is hierarchical and exclusionary. Although Du Bois did not problematize gender in his analysis of double consciousness, his ability to raise the importance of multiple identities is important in this context. More contemporary work on Black males has encouraged educational researchers and identity theorists to acknowledge the often complex ways masculinity, for example, plays out among

Black males in today's schools (Harper & Nichols, 2008). Harper and Harris (2010) have suggested "moving beyond singular notions of gender" (p. 5) and state that this static understanding of what it means to be Black and male excludes a large number of Black males who do not locate their identities in such narrow characterizations. These works are important, because they operate from a framework that Black males are not monolithic. Nasir et al. (2009) call for "the need for a nuanced conception of African American racial identity that considers both the strength of the identity and the local meaning of the identity" (p. 107). The local meaning of identity therefore should consider space, place, age, race, ways of being, and ways of knowing among other factors. In their sociocultural and ecological theory analysis of achievement, identity, and race for Black students, they discovered that African American students endorsed a range of identity meanings, and that these meanings varied according to the context in which they were shaped.

The exploration of intersectionality for Black males is complicated on several levels. As they are racialized beings in a predominately White supremacist society, issues tied to race and racism work to their detriment and bring a multitude of challenges with them. It is notable to identify the different ways that people of color experience life in the U.S. In many cases, Black people are more likely to be victimized targets of racism, discrimination, and exclusion from mainstream opportunities. However, as gendered beings, many Black males benefit from the privileges of living in a patriarchal society. Yet, as they are a racial minority, their male privileges are not at parity with those of their White male peers socially, politically, and economically (Anderson, 2008; Wilson, 2008). One of the challenges of these complex intersections, in thinking of interlocking oppressions, is that Black male privileges often lead to distorted notions of masculinity and can lead some to overlook the manner in which sexism harms the life experiences of Black men and women (hooks, 2000).

In their work *Cool Pose: The Dilemmas of Black Manhood in America*, Majors and Billson (1992) provide an intricate look at why and how Black men develop coping mechanisms to maintain a sense of pride and identity in the face of the onslaughts of discrimination in employment, housing, and skyrocketing rates of incarceration. This work was pivotal in unpacking the social, cultural, and historical factors which contribute to the development of Black male identity, and how it is divergent from mainstream accounts in some ways, familiar in others, yet interrogating while expanding the scope of the meanings of masculinity, maleness, and manhood for Black men.

Black male identity to a large extent stems from a distorted notion of masculinity within the traditional context of many Black communities and has been treated largely as one-dimensional and universal, meaning men play the role of being primary provider and disciplinarian, and possess a dearth of emotion and affective filters. Much of this construction is perpetuated within Black culture and life, and is a by-product of Eurocentric patriarchy that has defined maleness in distinct and confining ways (hooks, 2000). Harper and Harris (2010) argue that definitions of masculinity contribute to the exclusion of Black males who do not fit the hyper-masculine construct.

McCready (2004) suggests that Black males experience troubling social conflicts that may affect their academic outcomes. He contends that researchers need to take into account multiple categories of difference and oppression to understand and suggest interventions for gay and gender-nonconforming Black male students in urban schools. Therefore, a more complete analysis of how Black males experience schools needs to engage a discourse about how masculinity is often narrowly defined within Black cultural contexts, thus making it difficult for many Black males to display alternate forms of masculinity. Furthermore, McCready accesses Black feminist epistemology to apply intersectionality for documenting the experiences of Black males while acknowledging the limitation in using a feminist framework to unpack the experiences of men:

> The problem here is divorcing intersectionality from a distinctly feminist agenda and treating it instead as a normative enterprise. The persistence of uncritical, patriarchal, "additive," theoretical frameworks in urban education compel us to experiment and see what intersectionality, as a feminist framework, can bring in terms of developing a more socially just praxis for all stakeholders in urban schools.
>
> (pp. 14–15)

We employ intersectionality despite its limitations to further understand hyper-masculine and heteronormative ideologies and practices that are pervasive in many Black communities and the larger society. These ideologies characterize what it means to be male and Black in disturbing ways that are inconsistent with the manners in which countless numbers of Black males display their own identities (J. Davis & Jordan, 1995).

Hill (2005) used an intersectionality approach to examine how social class positionalities affect race and gender beliefs of Black parents and their children's reading practices and discovered that, while parents had notions of racial and gender equality, social class was also an important consideration in terms of breadth and depth of support for gender equality. The survey findings revealed that the more Blacks moved up the social class ladder, the greater their beliefs and convictions were toward gender equality, and conversely more limited beliefs in the idea of gender equality existed for lower-income Blacks. Further, Hill also maintained that, for low-income Black males, notions of masculinity are more narrowly defined, because many Black men have the traditional avenues used to construct masculinity (e.g. job and career, fiscal independence, provider); therefore they rely on stereotypical ideas tied to physical prowess such as size, athletic ability, and physical strength to operationalize their understanding of masculinity.

Watts and Everelles (2004) suggest that schools use the oppressive ideologies associated with race, class, gender, and disability to justify the social construction of certain students as deviant or rule-breaking, thereby making it an individual rather than a social or systemic problem. Using an intersectionality analysis, Watts and Everelles (2004) contend that material school conditions exist which compel students, especially African American and Hispanic students from low-income backgrounds, to feel vulnerable, angry, and viewed as resistant to normative expectations. Also incorporating aspects of critical race theory, Watts and Everelles (2004) further asserted that, in U.S. public schools, Whiteness continues to be constructed in such a way that material conditions produce and perpetuate difference to such a marked degree that both African American and Hispanic students experience segregation and discrimination through schools' sorting practices and discipline, especially for Black and Latino males. Moreover, their research highlights the complex nature upon which multiple identity markers become conflated and do not bode well for Black and Latino males, and disability labels become the norm.

Lacy (2008) argues that the intersectionality paradigm in most social science and legal research is limited, because, while it examines dual identities of subordinated groups (e.g. poor Black women), Black males are excluded from the paradigm despite the fact that they suffer the effects of racial and gender politics in a unique way. He contends that scholars have failed to take up the case of Black males in the intersectionality paradigm, and he offers an "exponential framework" in response to this void. He contends that, while Black men should enjoy the privileges that come with being male in a patriarchal society, the coupling of male with Blackness creates a burden, and undermines the so-called male privileges afforded in the U.S. to White men. He documents the disproportionality in educational outcomes, unemployment, crime, and incarceration rates as indicators that suggest that, even although Black males are members of a dominant group (men), the intersectionality paradigm has utility in examining the experiences of this population. Thus he argues for an exponential framework, because he contends that, as maleness and Blackness converge, evidence of prejudice and discrimination increases exponentially for this particular group in ways that it does not for others.

Purdie-Vaughns and Eibach (2008) contend that androcentric, ethnocentric, and heterocentric ideologies frequently cause people who have multiple subordinate group identities to be defined as non-prototypical members of their respective identity groups. Their contention is that the debate about who suffers more, individuals from one subordinate group (e.g. Black males) or persons from multiple subordinate groups (e.g. Black women), is counterproductive, and because of these multiple, subordinate, and frequently complex identities people can suffer from intersectional invisibility. They contend that there is a tendency to define the standard person as male (ethnocentric), there is the tendency to define a person as a member of the dominant ethnic group (White), and there is the tendency to define the person as hetereosexual (heterocentric). These prevalent ideologies will cause people who have multiple subordinate group identities to be defined as non-prototypical members of their respective identity groups. The aim, then, is to conduct "research on intersectionality that attempts to move beyond the question of 'whose group is worse off' to specify the distinctive forms of oppression experienced by those with intersecting subordinate identities" (p. 4). They contend that individuals who possess intersecting subordinate-group identities oftentimes are defined, described, and perceived as non-prototypical members of their constituent identity groups, thus rendering them invisible.

King (1988) postulates in her work in Black feminism that intersectionality is indeed critical in examining the "multiple jeopardies" people of color face when interfacing with a society that most often fails to individualize the multiple forms of oppression and subjugation with which they must contend, much like the double consciousness Du Bois describes. Similar to Purdie-Vaughns and Eibach (2008), King suggests that concepts of intersectionality have been overly simplistic in assuming that the relationships among various discriminations are merely additive—a mathematical equation of sorts; "racism plus sexism plus classism equals triple jeopardy" (p. 47). This simple incremental process does not represent the nature of Black women's oppression but, rather, I would contend, leads to nonproductive assertions that one factor can and should supplant the other. For example, class oppression is the largest component of Black women's subordinate status; therefore the exclusive focus should be on economics. Such assertions ignore the fact that racism, sexism, and classism constitute three, interdependent control systems. King, instead of dismissing the use of intersectionality as a tool for understanding Black women's identities, promulgates the use of the term *multiple*:

The modifier "multiple" refers not only to several, simultaneous oppressions but to the multiplicative relationships among them as well. In other words, the equivalent formulation is racism *multiplied* by sexism *multiplied* by classism. To reduce this complex of negotiations to an addition problem (racism + sexism = Black women's experience) is to define the issues, and indeed Black womanhood itself, within the structural terms developed by Europeans and especially white males to privilege their race and their sex unilaterally. Sojourner's declaration, "ain't I a woman?" directly refutes this sort of conceptualization of womanhood as one dimensional rather than dialectical.

(pp. 47–50)

Black males faced with compounding and sometimes confounding factors require research that can account for and sift through the complexity of both their collective and their individual identities through a dialectical process engaging intersectionality.

STRUCTURAL INTERSECTIONALITY

While competing forms of oppression can manifest themselves in problematic ways, another layer of Black male identity is socioeconomic status. In a society where capital is germane to one's life opportunities and overall life quality, Black males find themselves at or near the bottom of most social and economic indices (Anderson, 2008). A thorough analysis of Black males' experiences in the United States needs to recognize interlocking forms of oppression that have had a profound influence on the ability of this population to become self-actualized, and perhaps no other system of oppression has had a more adverse impact on Black males than capitalism and perhaps its most adverse manifestation—poverty. Different structures, systems, laws, and policies have combined to have a nefarious effect on how individuals participate in the nation-state (Massey & Denton, 1993). In a society that stresses the value of meritocracy, fairness, and egalitarian efforts, needless to say Black men have been members of one of the subgroups consistently on the outside looking into the structures that contribute to economic and social mobility.

Structural intersectionality refers to the creation, operation, maintenance, and synthesis of various systems and structures in society that maintain privilege for some groups or individuals while restricting or denying the rights and privileges of others (Swanson et al., 2003). Structural intersectionality also encompasses the political, economic, representational, and institutional forms of discrimination, oppression, exploitation, and domination, highlights the connectedness of systems and structures in society, and helps us understand how each system affects or impacts others (Wilson, 2008). To contextualize how structural intersectionality affects Black males in a capitalistic society, one need not look further than today's burgeoning prison industrial complex. Alexander (2010) unpacks how mass incarceration over the last three decades has disproportionately affected Black males more than any other group. Alexander also uncovers the varied obstacles that most Black males face as they attempt to re-enter society post-incarceration. The prolonged stigma that comes with incarceration has a direct effect on the ability to access public housing, public assistance, political participation, and most importantly the securing of employment. Each of these systems has a devastating effect on Black men and their families and communities that results in them frequently being denied options and opportunities for participation in mainstream society. Upon encountering repeated obstacles, many Black males in a quest for survival return to the behavior that led to their incarceration, thus explaining the 80 percent recidivism rate among Black men in the United States.

The interconnectedness of different structures has an impact on poor Black men that is more real and lasting than for any other segment of society. Any particular disadvantage or disability is sometimes compounded by another disadvantage, reflecting the dynamics of a separate system or structure of subordination. Thus, the analysis of Black males must problematize what it means to be Black in a White supremacist society and to be located as a subordinate, yet also what it means to be male in a patriarchal society, where there are clear advantages of being male, yet not on the same level as other males. Furthermore, complexifying this arrangement can also entail looking at citizenship status outside the U.S.

Historically, being Black and male has raised serious challenges in terms of recognition as a full citizen, and the ability to participate as an equal in a racist, capitalistic society. From the inception of chattel slavery in the United States to the exploitation of Black male labor through sharecropping and the subsequent Jim Crow laws that proclaimed separate but equal conditions were the law of the land, it is apparent that, from the initial encounter with North America, Black men were structurally locked out of pathways of participation; thus oppression and disenfranchisement have contributed to the historical and current social conditions researchers seek to explain. "Because Black men did hard manual labor, justifying the harsh conditions forced upon them required objectifying their bodies as big, strong and stupid" (Hill Collins, 2004, p. 56).

An additional reason to examine Black males within a more intersected context centers on the fact that much of the work on Black males has classified them as poor and residing in inner cities (Anderson, 2008). Unquestionably, a large number of Black males are growing up in the midst of economic challenges that are part of urban and rural America. Absent from this discourse are explanations of upward mobility and how it has shaped the manner in which Black males experience schools and society. B. Gordon (2012) raises important questions that seek to understand the experiences of middle- and upper-class Black students in general, and Black males in particular, that have facilitated conditions under which they are woefully overlooked, ignored, and under-studied in educational research. Her research reveals that approximately one-third of African American families live in suburban communities, and send their children to middle-class schools, where they still underperform compared to their White peers. Thus, even the promises of social and economic mobility do not seem to thwart the presence of race and racism when it comes to the schooling experiences. Therefore, understanding the challenges of race, gender, and social class for Black males is crucial to any thorough examination of their schooling experiences. Gordon (2012) documents that, "By living, growing up in, and attending schools in suburban communities, these students cannot help but absorb the culture of the schools and society of which they are a part, yet in which they remain the 'other'" (p. 10). Her analysis calls for additional investigation into the challenges Black males encounter in predominately White suburban schools. What is unique about these experiences is the need for Black males to negotiate the majority and minority cultures. Not only is the challenge for researchers then to examine the lived experiences and school outcomes in overcrowded, low-performing schools, but it is also paramount to document how Black males in high-performing schools, from middle-class to affluent neighborhoods, make meaning of these experiences.

Reynolds's (2010) work, for example, looks at the challenges that middle-class Black parents encountered when they sought to advocate on behalf of their children and discovered that the most notable obstacle was the issues that their sons faced from peers, teachers, and administrators. Parents in her study consistently noted the low expectations educators held for their Black sons. These parents distinguished between the treatment their Black daughters received juxtaposed with the experiences both they and their sons had in schools working with educators who were primarily from the dominant group. In this study, class proved to be less of a mediating factor in the disparate treatment Black boys received in predominantly White middle-class schools. In this case, race and gender seemed to overshadow capital as an explanative factor in understanding the discrimination Black males face.

The intersection of race along with other identity markers raises important insights into how our questions, analysis, and understanding of Black males shift when social class shifts. Moreover, this analysis of class and race brings important considerations to bear, as research consistently reveals that Black and Brown students in middle-class and affluent schools find themselves at a distinct disadvantage compared to their White and Asian counterparts (Howard, 2010). Thus inherent in the analysis is that, while the dominant community has its fears and concerns with poor Black males, there is a degree of comfort in seeing them as restricted within a poverty context. However, when Black males are not located exclusively within a poverty context, the response to race and class can have deleterious effects for Black males. Thus, we find that complexifying race and class in educational theory and practice contributes a richer, more comprehensive examination of the challenges Black males encounter in schools. This is imperative if we wish to engage in the authentic democratic tradition that the educational system was founded upon initially.

MOVING FORWARD: NEXT STEPS

As researchers continue to examine the lived realities of Black males in all of their complexity, we call for more extensive and comprehensive examinations of their experiences and identities. McCall (2005) offers a framework that encompasses three useful approaches that can help researchers in this pursuit of intersectionality complexity: 1) anticategorical complexity, 2) intercategorical complexity, and 3) intracategorical complexity. Each of these approaches serves to represent a broader spectrum of current methodologies that are used to better understand and apply the intersectionality theory. McCall (2005) outlines these approaches methodologically and conceptually in more detail:

- *Anticategorical complexity:* The anticategorical approach is based on the deconstruction of categorical divisions. It argues that social categories make up an arbitrary construction of history and language and that they contribute little to understanding the ways in which people experience society. Furthermore the anticategorical approach states that "inequalities are rooted in relationships that are defined by race, class, sexuality, and gender" (p. 1774); therefore the only way to eliminate oppression in society is to eliminate the categories used to section people into groups. This analysis claims that society is too complex to be reduced to finite categories and instead recognizes the need for a holistic approach in understanding intersectionality. Within this framework, one might find Black males who do not believe that their racial or gender identities are salient, would dismiss any notions of being viewed in racial terms, and would view themselves in a more human-istic approach devoid of the social and political factors associated with race and gender.

- *Intercategorical (aka categorical) complexity:* The intercategorical approach to inter-sectionality begins by addressing the fact that inequality exists within society, and then uses this as the base of its discussion of intersectionality. According to inter-categorical complexity, "the concern is with the nature of the relationships among social groups and, importantly, how they are changing" (p. 1777). Proponents of this methodology use existing categorical distinctions to document inequality across multiple dimensions and measure its change over time. Black males within this paradigm are located within their racial, ethnic, gendered, and class locations, and the intersections of these realities are unpacked to understand the manifesta-tion of oppression.
- *Intracategorical complexity:* The intracategorical approach can best be explained as the midpoint between the anticategorical and intercategorical approaches. It recognizes the apparent shortcomings of existing social categories and it questions the way in which they draw boundaries of distinction. Yet this approach does not completely reject the importance of categories like the anticategorical approach; rather the intracategorical approach recognizes the relevance of social categories to the understanding of the modern social experience. Moreover it attempts to reconcile these contrasting views by focusing on people who cross the boundaries of constructed categories, in an effort to understand the ways in which the com-plexity and intersectionality of the human experience unfold. Here, Black males are seen within their complex categorical locations, but individuals who have chal-lenged these spaces (e.g. homosexual or transgendered Black males, bi-racial Black males, or academically high-performing Black males) are also examined.

It is our hope that this framework and chapter make a thought-provoking and com-pelling, call to rethink the manner in which we study Black males. What is abundantly clear from data is that our knowledge base, theory, practice, policy, and research con-tinue to fall woefully short in informing educators about how to best address the needs of Black males. It is not our intention to claim that an intersectionality framework on its own will undo the years of oppression, exclusion, and emasculation that countless numbers of Black males have experienced and continue to experience in U.S. schools and society. It has been our goal to push for a more probing level of analysis which would enable us to have Black males define, describe, and analyze their realities on their terms, without being placed in restrictive categories informed by narrow constructions of race, class, and gender. Most importantly, it is vital for educational researchers and practition-ers to allow for multiple manifestations and iterations of those experiences and identities to be an integral part of the discourse on Black males.

NOTE

1 The terms *Black* and *African American* are used interchangeably throughout this text.

REFERENCES

Alexander, M. (2010). *The new Jim Crow: Mass incarceration in the age of colorblindness*. New York: New Press.

Allen, B.J. (1996). Feminist standpoint theory: A Black woman's review of organizational socialization. *Communication Studies*, *47*(4): 257–271.

Anderson, E. (2008). *Against the wall: Poor, young, Black and male*. Philadelphia, PA: University of Pennsylvania Press.

Aud, S., Fox, M., and KewalRamani, A. (2010). *Status and trends in the education of racial and ethnic groups*. NCES 2010-015. U.S. Department of Education, National Center for Education Statistics. Washington, DC: U.S. Government Printing Office.

Bell, D.A. (1992). *Faces at the bottom of the well*. New York: Basic Books.

Bell, D.A. (1995). Racial realism: After we're gone: Prudent speculations on America in a post racial epoch. In R. Delgado (Ed.), *Critical race theory: The cutting edge* (pp. 2–8). Philadelphia, PA: Temple University Press.

Brown, E. (2005). We wear the mask: African American contemporary gay male identities. *Journal of African American Studies*, *9*(2), 29–38.

College Board (2012). 8th annual AP report to the nation (retrieved from http://media.collegeboard.com/digital-Services/public/pdf/ap/rtn/AP-Report-to-the-Nation.pdf).

Crenshaw, K. (1989). Demarginalizing the intersection of race and sex: A Black feminist critique of antidiscrimination doctrine, feminist theory, and antiracist politics. *University of Chicago Legal Forum*, *1989*, 139–168.

Crenshaw, K. (2009). Mapping the margins: Intersectionality, identity politics, and violence against women of color. In E. Taylor, D. Gillborn, & G. Ladson-Billings (Eds.), *Foundations of critical race theory in education* (pp. 213–258). New York: Routledge.

Davis, J.E., & Jordan, W.J. (1995). The effects of school context, structure, and experiences on African American males in middle and high school. *Journal of Negro Education*, *63*, 570–587.

Davis, K. (2008). Intersectionality as buzzword: A sociology of science perspective on what makes a feminist theory successful. *Feminist Theory*, *9*(1), 67–85.

Delgado, R. (Ed.). (1995). *Critical race theory: The cutting edge*. Philadelphia, PA: Temple University Press.

Delgado, R. (1999). *When equality ends: Stories about race and resistance*. Boulder, CO: Westview.

Delgado, R., & Stefancic, J. (2001). *Critical race theory: An introduction*. New York: New York University Press.

Du Bois, W.E.B. (1903). *The souls of black folk*. Chicago: A.C. McClurg.

Duncan, G.A. (2002). Beyond love: A critical race ethnography of the schooling of adolescent Black males. *Equity and Excellence in Education*, *35*(2), 131–143.

Ferguson, A.A. (2003). *Bad boys: Public schools in the making of Black masculinity*. Ann Arbor: University of Michigan Press.

Flennaugh, T.K. (2011). Mapping me: A mixed-method approach to understanding academic self-concept among Black males in today's urban schools. Unpublished dissertation, University of California, Los Angeles.

Gates, H.L. (1997). *Thirteen ways of looking at a Black man*. New York: Random House.

Gay, G. (1991). Culturally diverse students and social studies. In J.P. Shaver (Ed.), *Handbook of research on social studies teaching and learning* (pp. 144–156). New York: Macmillan.

Gay, G. (1992). The state of multicultural education in the United States. In K.A. Moodley (Ed.), *Beyond multicultural education: International perspectives* (pp. 41–65). Calgary, Alberta: Detseting Enterprises.

Gordon, B.M. (2012). "Give a brotha a break!" The experiences and dilemmas of middle-class African American male students in White suburban schools. *Teachers College Record*, *114*(5) (retrieved on July 6, 2011 from http://www.tcrecord.org, ID no. 16416).

Gordon, E.T., Gordon, E.W., & Gordon-Nembhard, J.G. (1994). Social science literature concerning African American men. *Journal of Negro Education*, *63*(4), 508–531.

Gregory, A., Skiba, R.J., & Noguera, P.A. (2010). The achievement gap and the discipline gap: Two sides of the same coin? *Educational Researcher*, *39*, 59–68.

Harper, S.R., & Harris, F. (2010). *College men and masculinities: Theory, research and implications for practice*. San Francisco, CA: Jossey-Bass.

Harper, S.R., & Nichols, A.H. (2008). Are they not all the same? Racial heterogeneity among Black male undergraduates. *Journal of College Student Development*, *49*(3), 199–214.

Hill, S.A. (2005). *Black intimacies: A gender perspective in families and relationships*. Lanham, MD: Rowman & Littlefield.

Hill Collins, P. (1986). Learning from the outsider within: The sociological significance of Black feminist thought. *Social Problems*, *33*, S14–S32.

Hill Collins, P. (2004). *Black sexual politics: African Americans, gender, and the new racism*. New York: Routledge.

hooks, b. (2000). *All about love: New visions*. New York: Perennial.

Howard, T.C. (2008). "Who really cares?" The disenfranchisement of African American males in PreK-12 schools: A critical race theory perspective. *Teachers College Record, 110*(5), 954–985.

Howard, T.C. (2010). *Why race and culture matter.* New York: Teachers College Press.

Howard, T.C., & Flennaugh, T. (2011). Research concerns, cautions and considerations on Black males in a "post racial society." *Race, Ethnicity, and Education, 14*(1), 105–120.

Hutchinson, E.O. (1999). My gay problem, your Black problem. In D. Constantine-Simms & H.L. Gates (Eds.), *The greatest taboo: Homosexuality in Black communities* (pp. 2–6). Los Angeles, CA: Alyson Publications.

Irvine, J. (1990). *Black students and school failure.* Westport, CT: Greenwood.

Jackson, J.F.L. (2007). Introduction: A systematic analysis of the African American educational pipeline to inform research, policy, and practice. In J.F.L. Jackson (Ed.), *Strengthening the African American educational pipeline: Informing research, policy, and practice* (pp. 1–14). Albany: State University of New York Press.

Kumashiro, K.K. (2001). Queer students of color and antiracist, antiheterosexist education: Paradoxes of identity and activism. In K.K. Kumashiro (Ed.), *Troubling intersections of race and sexuality: Queer students of color and anti-oppressive education* (pp. 1–25). Lanham, MD: Rowman & Littlefield.

King, D.K. (1988). Multiple jeopardy, multiple consciousness: The context of a Black feminist ideology. *Signs, 14*(1), Autumn, 42–72.

Lacy, D. (2008). The most endangered Title VII plaintiff: Exponential discrimination against African American males. *Nebraska Law Review, 86*(3), 552–594.

Ladson-Billings, G. (1994). *The dreamkeepers: Successful teachers for African-American children.* San Francisco, CA: Jossey-Bass.

Majors, R., & Billson, J. (1992). *Cool pose: The dilemmas of Black manhood in America.* New York: Touchstone.

Massey, D., & Denton, N. (1993). *American apartheid.* Cambridge, MA: Harvard University Press.

McCall, L. (2005). The complexity of intersectionality. *Journal of Women in Culture and Society, 30*(3), Spring, 1771–1800.

McCready, L. (2004). Understanding the marginalization of gay and gender non-conforming Black male students. *Theory into Practice, 43*(2), Spring, 136–143.

McLaren, P., Macrine, S., & Hill, D. (Eds.). (2010). *Revolutionizing pedagogy: Educating for social justice within and beyond global neo-liberalism.* London: Palgrave Macmillan.

Mincy, R.B. (Ed.). (2006). *Black males left behind.* Washington, DC: Urban Institute Press.

Moynihan, D.P. (1965). *Negro family: The case for national action.* Washington, DC: Office of Policy Planning and Research, U.S. Department of Labor.

Nasir, N.S. (2012). *Racialized identities: Race and achievement among African American youth.* Stanford, CA: Stanford University Press.

Nasir, N., McLaughlin, M., & Jones, A. (2009). What does it mean to be African American? Constructions of race and academic identity in an urban public high school. *American Educational Research Journal, 46*(1), 73–114.

Noguera, P. (2001). The role and influence of environmental and cultural factors on the academic performance of African American males. *Motion Magazine*, February 11.

Noguera, P. (2008). *The trouble with Black boys … And other reflections on race, equity, and the future of public education.* San Francisco, CA: Jossey-Bass.

Patterson, O. (1995). The crisis of gender relations among African-Americans. In A. Hill & E.C. Coleman (Eds.), *Race, gender, and power in America: The legacy of the Hill-Thomas hearings* (pp. 56–104). New York: Oxford University Press.

Polite, V.C., & Davis, J.E. (Eds.). (1999). *African American males in school and society: Practices and policies for effective education.* New York: Teachers College Press.

Purdie-Vaughns, V., & Eibach, R.P. (2008). Intersectional invisibility: The distinctive advantages and disadvantages of multiple subordinate-group identities. *Sex Roles, 59*(5–6), 377–391 (doi 10.1007/s11199-008-9424-4).

Reeser, T.W. (2010). *Masculinities in theory: An introduction.* Malden, MA: Wiley-Blackwell.

Reynolds, R. (2010). "They think you're lazy," and other messages Black parents send their Black sons: An exploration of critical race theory in the examination of educational outcomes for Black males. *Journal of African American Males in Education, 1*(2), 144–163 (retrieved from http://journalofafricanamericanmales.com).

Schott Foundation for Public Education. (2010). *Yes we can: The Schott 50 state report on public education and Black males.* Cambridge, MA: Schott Foundation for Public Education.

Smith, W.A. (2010). Toward an understanding of Black misandric microaggressions and racial battle fatigue in historically White institutions. In V.C. Polite (Ed.), *The state of the African American male in Michigan: A courageous conversation* (pp. 265–277). East Lansing: Michigan State University Press.

Smith, W.A., Allen, W.R., & Danley, L.L. (2007). "Assume the position … You fit the description": Psychosocial experiences and racial battle fatigue among African American male college students. *American Behavioral Scientist, 51*, 551–578.

Solórzano, D. (1998). Critical race theory, racial and gender microaggressions, and the experiences of Chicana and Chicano scholars. *International Journal of Qualitative Studies in Education, 11*, 121–136.

Solórzano, D., & Delgado Bernal, D. (2001). Examining transfomational resistance through a critical race and LatCrit framework: Chicana and Chicano students in an urban context. *Urban Education, 36*(3), 308–342.

Swanson, D.P., Cunningham, M., & Spencer, M.B. (2003). Black males' structural conditions, achievement patterns, normative needs, and "opportunities." *Urban Education, 38*(5), 608–633.

U.S. Department of Education, Institute of Education Science, National Center for Education Statistics, National Assessment of Educational Progress (NAEP). (2009a). *Mathematics.* Washington, DC: U.S. Department of Education.

U.S. Department of Education, Institute of Education Science, National Center for Education Statistics, National Assessment of Educational Progress (NAEP). (2009b). *Reading.* Washington, DC: U.S. Department of Education.

Watts, I.E., & Everelles, N. (2004). These deadly times: Reconceptualizing school violence by using critical race theory and disability studies. *American Educational Research Journal, 41*, 271–299.

Wilson, W.J. (2008). The economic plight of Black males. In E. Anderson (Ed.), *Against the wall: Poor, young, Black and male* (pp. 55–70). Philadelphia: University of Pennsylvania Press.

Yep, G.A. (2003). The violence of heteronormativity in communication studies: Notes on injury, healing, and queer world-making. *Queer Theory and Communication, 45*(2/3/4), 11.

18

EXPANDING THE COUNTERSTORY

The Potential for Critical Race Mixed Methods Studies
in Education

Jessica T. DeCuir-Gunby and Dina C. Walker-DeVose

Critical race theory (CRT) allows for the challenging of systematic manifestations of White privilege that subordinate people of color (Bell, 1992). Specifically, CRT places race at the center of analysis and explores the transformations of the relationships among race, racism, and power in various social, economic, political, and educational contexts (Crenshaw et al., 1995). A strength of CRT is that it allows for the capturing of counterstories or the narratives of marginalized groups that counter the perspectives of the majoritarian (Delgado, 1989). Because of CRT's focus on the in-depth understanding of stories, studies using a CRT lens often utilize qualitative methods (Parker, 1998; Parker & Lynn, 2002). However, in recent years, scholars have begun to contemplate whether or not CRT and quantitative methods are compatible. One perspective is that the positivistic/post-positivistic approach that is associated with quantitative methods is incompatible with the critical approach of race-based theories such as CRT; in addition, it does not allow for the telling of individual and multiple stories (Zuberi, 2003). The alternative perspective feels that critical quantitative approaches allow for the telling of "group" or "composite" counterstories, although through the use of numbers, and are therefore compatible with CRT (Carter & Hurtado, 2007).

Thus, the purpose of this chapter is to elaborate on this debate by exploring the feasibility of combining CRT and quantitative methods. We begin the chapter by examining how researchers have combined CRT and quantitative methods in the education literature. Next we explore the compatibility of quantitative methods and CRT through the discussion of the philosophical underpinnings of quantitative methods (positivism/post-positivism) and qualitative methods (critical paradigm). Then we explain the role of counterstorytelling in CRT research from both quantitative and qualitative perspectives. Next we explicate how mixed methods research can be used as a viable alternative to traditional quantitative methods. We end by providing implications for the conducting of critical race mixed methods studies in education.

CRT AND QUANTITATIVE METHODS

There is a growing interest among CRT researchers in exploring the use of alternative methodologies, such as quantitative methods, in conducting critical race studies. Despite the increased interest in combining CRT and quantitative methods, there is still limited published research that combines the approaches. In fact, in a literature search, we found a paucity of published research articles that combine CRT and quantitative methods. The research we did find largely came from the research fields of educational leadership/policy (e.g. Aleman, 2007), ethnic studies (e.g. Covarrubias, 2011), and higher education (e.g. Brady et al., 2000; Jayakumar et al., 2009; Teranishi, 2007; Villalpando & Delgado Bernal, 2002). In the various arenas, the researchers used critical quantitative analyses in a variety of ways in order to help create composite stories.

One of the most common approaches of combining CRT and quantitative methods is to use the tenets of CRT to explore descriptive quantitative data. Researchers using this approach often examine and critique descriptive data such as financial figures, racial demographics, or test scores using the major tenets of CRT. For example, Aleman (2007) used such an approach in his study on Texas school finance policy. Specifically, he used critical race policy analysis to describe discrepancies in school funding in Texas based upon race and SES. He combined CRT and Latina/o critical (LatCrit) theoretical frameworks to conduct both a historical analysis regarding school finance equity and an analysis of the effects of the school finance system on communities of color. In doing so, he presented the financial and demographic data and then critiqued the findings using principles of CRT and LatCrit.

Another way of combining CRT and quantitative methods is to use tenets of CRT to examine and critique findings from descriptive statistics. For example, using U.S. census data, Covarrubias (2011) examined the educational attainment of people of Mexican descent using CRT's tenet of intersectionality. He disaggregated the data according to multiple factors including class, gender, and citizenship and examined their intersectional effects. Doing so allowed him to examine the multiple factors individually as well as their intersections. Covarrubias (2011) was able to demonstrate that, in order to understand the educational attainment of people of Mexican descent, it is necessary to examine the intersectionality of various variables.

In addition to the use of descriptive statistics, CRT and quantitative methods can be combined in more complex ways. For example, in a study examining racial climate, job satisfaction, and retention among faculty of color, Jayakumar et al. (2009) combined CRT and various univariate statistical procedures including cross-tabulation and hierarchical blocked regression analyses. Several tenets of CRT, particularly the pervasiveness of White privilege and racism, were used to interpret the research findings as well as provide general conclusions regarding the study.

Although researchers have combined CRT and quantitative methods in a variety of ways, there is still some debate regarding the compatibility of CRT and quantitative methods. The central argument is that CRT is better aligned with qualitative methods because of the focus on individual narratives, a core component of CRT. Quantitative methods generally focus on groups rather than individuals. Thus, in order to better understand this argument, it is necessary to examine the philosophical underpinnings of both quantitative methods and critical qualitative approaches.

UNDERSTANDING THE PHILOSOPHICAL FOUNDATIONS

Positivism/post-positivism and critical paradigms are rooted in distinct philosophical traditions. In order to examine the philosophical foundations of both paradigms, it is necessary to discuss the ontological and epistemological beliefs of each paradigm as well as common methodological strategies used in each. Ontology speaks to the form and nature of truth or reality and to what extent it can be known; epistemology speaks to the relationship between the knower (e.g. the researcher, the teacher, the clinician) and knowledge itself; and methodology refers to the process the knower uses to discover whatever is to be known (Guba & Lincoln, 1994). While positivism and post-positivism are discussed together, distinctions between the two are made as necessary.

Positivism/Post-Positivism

Ontology

Positivists and post-positivists believe that there is a universal truth or reality that exists within the world. Both paradigms are thought to be deterministic in that they hold the belief that there is a *cause* that determines an *effect*, as well as reductionistic in that the goal is to reduce a thought or an idea to a discrete set of variables that can be empirically tested in order to obtain truth. Although both paradigms suggest that there is an absolute truth, the two paradigms differ in their beliefs in the accessibility and understandability of that truth. While positivists believe that truth is understandable, identifiable, and measurable (Ponterotto, 2005), post-positivists believe that the truth of human experiences can only be apprehended imperfectly and "must be subjected to the widest possible critical examination to facilitate apprehending reality as closely as possible" (Guba & Lincoln, 1994, p. 110).

Epistemology

Positivists and post-positivists view the relationship between the researcher and research subjects as distant and impartial. The notions of dualism and objectivism guide the positivist perspective. In this paradigm, the researcher and the researched are independent of each other. The researcher sees him/herself as completely objective and without bias. To a positivist, replicated findings are believed to be true. Post-positivists do not adhere to the notion of dualism and embrace objectivity as a "regulatory ideal." Under this paradigm, researchers acknowledge that there may exist some influence between the researcher and the researched, but that objectivity remains an important guideline in the research process. On the other hand, to a post-positivist, replications of findings are probably true, but are always subject to falsification (Guba & Lincoln, 1994).

Methodology

The knowledge that is gained from a positivist/post-positivist lens is based on careful observation and measurement of the reality that exists in the world (Creswell, 2009). The methods used to obtain this knowledge are largely experimental and manipulative, and the "researcher's own emotional or expectant stance on the problem under study is irrelevant" (Ponterotto, 2005, p. 132). Positivists and post-positivists use quantitative methods, relying largely on true experimental methods and, when not possible, quasi-experimental methods. They often use a variety of self-report questionnaires, behavioral observations, and tests (e.g. standardized tests). However, it must be added that some post-positivists do use qualitative methods, oftentimes as a means to supplement quantitative findings (Johnson & Turner, 2003) or as part of the scale creation process (Benson & Clark, 1982). In such cases, emphasis is placed on the quantitative portions of the research. In addition, there are qualitative researchers that embrace post-positivism, using qualitative research to extend or complement quantitative research (Maxwell, 2010; Prasad, 2005). From this perspective, emphasis is placed on the qualitative portions of the research. While both paradigms value the scientific method of deduction and theory verification, post-positivists embrace the collection of more situational information to determine the meanings and purposes that people ascribe to their actions (Guba & Lincoln, 1994).

Critical Theory

The critical paradigm is quite distinct from the positivist/post-positivist paradigm. Critical theory grew out of the need to reconceptualize assumptions that democratic societies were free and unproblematic (Kincheloe & McLaren, 2005). Separating it from positivist and post-positivist assumptions that did not fit the marginalized individuals in society, these researchers began to advocate for a more active and participatory agenda. Basic assumptions of critical theory include the following beliefs: that all thought is mediated by power relations that are situated both socially and historically; that certain groups in society have privilege over other groups and that privilege is reproduced when subordinates accept their position as a natural state; that oppression is seen in many forms and those forms are interrelated; and that mainstream research practices help to reproduce systems of class, race, and gender oppression (Kincheloe & Steinberg, 1997). The aim of inquiry in critical research is to both critique and transform the "social, political, cultural, economic, ethnic, and gender structures that constrain and exploit humankind" (Guba & Lincoln, 1994). This focus on critiquing power structures is at the core of CRT.

Ontology

In critical theory, reality is thought to be historically based, with a sense of historical realism. That is, reality is shaped by a convergence of social, political, cultural, economic, ethnic, and gender factors that are refined into a set of "truths" that are viewed as real (Guba & Lincoln, 1994). This multi-layered reality changes over time, and these changes are often rooted in the tensions, conflicts, and contradictions of social relations and institutions. Although portions of these aforementioned aspects can be observed, structures of power are deeply rooted and are thereby unobservable (Neuman, 1997).

Epistemology

In stark contrast to the positivist and post-positivist paradigms, critical theory asserts that the researcher and the researched are impossible to separate. Ponterotto (2005) describes the researcher's values as central to the task, purpose, and methods of the research itself, and the relationship between the researcher and the research participant is transactional, subjective, and dialectic in nature. Since the connection between the researcher and the researched is so entangled, critical researchers enter into the research relationship with their assumptions known (Kincheloe & McLaren, 2005). The knowledge that comes from such research is thought to be value mediated (Guba & Lincoln, 1994).

Methodology

Given the nature of the inquiry and the role of the researcher, criticalists value more natu-ralistic methods of data collection. Researchers engaged in critical research are immersed in the participant's world over longer periods of time and often engage in qualitative research methods. Because the aim of critical research is one of transformation, the inter-actions between the researcher and the participant must be dialectical in nature in order to facilitate the transformation from the current set of socially constructed and power-laden "truths" and misapprehensions into a more informed consciousness (Guba & Lin-coln, 1994). Qualitative methods used in critical research include individual interviews, focus group interviews, and participant observation (Ponterotto, 2005). It is important to add, however, that, although critical researchers most often use qualitative methods, not all qualitative research is rooted in a critical framework (Koro-Ljungberg et al., 2009).

THE MULTIPLE ROLES OF COUNTERSTORIES

In order to combine CRT and quantitative methods, there is a need to reconcile the dif-ferent research traditions. The manner in which this can most easily be done is through the examination of methodology and the specific research methods used. Both posi-tivist/post-positivist and critical approaches attempt to tell some type of "story" from their analyses. The differences largely exist in the way the stories are captured and told. Positivists/post-positivists tell group stories that are captured and told in the form of numbers, while critical theorists capture oral stories and focus on discussing individual perspectives. Thus the combining of CRT and quantitative methods requires focusing on what constitutes a story or counterstory.

Counterstorytelling

Traditionally, CRT studies employ qualitative methods, focusing on the use of counter-stories. Counterstories are the "stories of those individuals and groups whose knowl-edges and histories have been marginalized, excluded, subjugated or forgotten in the telling of official narratives" (Peters & Lankshear, 1996, p. 2). Counterstorytelling pulls from the rich storytelling tradition in African-American, Chicano, and Native American communities and is a tool used in qualitative research to expose, analyze, and challenge the "majoritarian stories of racial privilege" (Solórzano & Yosso, 2002, p. 32). In coun-terstorytelling, the narratives of personal accounts, stories of other people, and compos-ite stories are developed into a narrative that is grounded in real-life experiences and empirical data and contextualized within a specific social setting. The use of countersto-ries allows for the telling of untold stories. In doing so, the utilization of counterstories "can open new windows into reality, showing us that there are possibilities for life other than the ones we live" (Delgado, 1989, p. 2414). Counterstories also play theoretical, methodological, and pedagogical roles in the research process. According to Solórzano and Yosso (2001), counterstorytelling enables the building of community among mar-ginalized groups, allows for challenging the views of the majoritarian by providing alter-nate realities, provides comfort to marginalized groups by showing that they are not alone and that they can learn from the experiences of others, and demonstrates that the stories of marginalized groups can be used to help create change.

Critical race theorists often present counterstories in three different ways: personal stories or narratives, other people's stories or narratives, and composite stories or narratives (Solórzano & Yosso, 2002). In personal stories or narratives, a personal story is told regarding an individual's experience with racism. These stories are often autobiographical and provide social-political critiques based upon the experiences described in the stories. Many of the works by critical race theorists take this approach, such as Lani Guinier's *Lift Every Voice: Turning a Civil Rights Setback into a New Vision of Social Justice* (1998). The second type of counterstory is other people's stories or narratives. This type of counterstorytelling allows for the telling of another person's experiences with racism. Such stories are biographical and situated within the sociohistorical context. The majority of CRT studies in education use this approach (for examples see Dixson & Rousseau, 2006). The last type of counterstory is composite stories or narratives. With this type of storytelling, a variety of sources of data are used in order to create a group story regarding experiences with racism. This group story is situated within historical, social, and political context and can draw from autobiographical and biographical events. Derrick Bell's *Faces at the Bottom of the Well: The Permanence of Racism* (1992) is a good illustration of this type of counterstory. Although composite stories draw from a variety of qualitative data, it can be argued that composite stories can even be created from quantitative data. Composite stories can be created and/or told in the form of numbers. It is from this perspective that some CRT researchers support the combining of CRT and quantitative methods (Carter & Hurtado, 2007).

Composite Stories and Quantitative Methods

As described earlier in this chapter, a growing number of CRT researchers are utilizing or contemplating the use of quantitative methods. Such researchers acknowledge some of the differences in the theoretical foundations of qualitative and quantitative methods; however, they contend that the quantitative methods themselves are useful in examining race-based problems if critical approaches are taken. Such researchers focus on CRT to help shape the types of research questions posed, interpretations of the analyses, and implications for the research, including any policy decisions. In the process, the numbers (quantitative results) are used to tell composite stories of marginalized groups and are interpreted by means of a CRT lens.

Although there is growing support for the use of CRT and quantitative methods, many researchers continue to question the compatibility of the approaches. Specifically, there are researchers who are not in support of combining CRT and quantitative methods because of its racist history. Modern statistical methods are rooted in the eugenics movement, which attempted to establish White racial superiority based upon supposed genetic differences (Zuberi, 2003; Zuberi & Bonilla-Silva, 2008). Because of this, the very use of quantitative methods to examine race-based constructs is viewed as problematic. Quantitative methods use majoritarian assumptions that allow for the hiding, manipulation, and exploitation of data (e.g. control away differences), which in turn helps to de-racialize the experiences of people of color (Gillborn, 2010). Specifically, many researchers have issues with quantitative methods because of the assumptions of objectivity and generalizability. Quantitative methods are assumed to be objective, although the researcher is in control of the research process and makes subjective decisions, including the choice of instruments, the sample composition, the statistical procedures utilized, and the conclusions that are drawn. Quantitative methods are also assumed to be generalizable. This assumption is questionable, because statistical methods rely on the quality of the instruments used, and many instruments have not been properly normed using people of color, yet these instruments are often used to make decisions regarding people of color (Bonilla-Silva & Baiocchi, 2001). In addition to race-based problems, there exists a sexist bias in quantitative research in that most statistical methods and approaches were created by men (Eichler, 1991).

Although using quantitative methods allows for the telling of composite stories, such an approach does not enable the examination of individual experiences. A major strength of CRT research is that readers can hear specific stories of marginalized groups. Storytelling is most powerful when individuals are able to voice their own experiences. Thus mixed methods research is a viable alternative to both quantitative methods and qualitative methods in that it combines both approaches and allows for the exploration of both composite and individual stories.

MIXED METHODS AS AN ALTERNATIVE METHODOLOGY

Mixed methods research is rooted in Campbell and Fiske's (1959) multitrait–multi-method approach, which suggests that, in order to understand a "trait" or phenomenon, researchers need to view it from various perspectives. Although Campbell and Fiske's discussion centered on quantitative methods, methodologists have expanded their perspective to include the use of multiple qualitative methods, as well as the combining of qualitative and quantitative methods or mixed methods research. Thus, mixed methods research can be defined as "research in which the investigator collects and analyzes data, integrates the findings, and draws inferences using both qualitative and quantitative approaches or methods in a single study or program of inquiry" (Tashakkori and Creswell, 2007, p. 4). Mixed methods studies can be either quantitative- or qualitative-dominant, with the mixing of data occurring at any point throughout the research process (Rocco et al., 2003), as well as within a single study, sequentially within a program of research, or in an area of research (Schutz et al., 2003). However, it must be stated that most mixed methods research is conducted from a quantitative-dominant perspective (Giddings, 2006).

Combining multiple and different types of data sources allows for a more nuanced view and interpretation of the research findings. Specifically, using a mixed methods approach to a research study allows for three general types of data analysis and interpretation: corroboration, elaboration, and initiation (Rossman and Wilson, 1985, 1994). Corroboration allows for the convergence of the quantitative and qualitative research findings. One type of data is used to support or triangulate the findings of another data source (Jick, 1979; Mathison, 1988). Similarly, elaboration enables one type of data to expand upon or complement the other. With this approach, one type of data helps to better explain the other type of data. The last approach is initiation, where the findings are contradictory or paradoxical. Because there are contradictions to the findings, no conclusive interpretations can be made. Instead, new research questions must be posed and possibly new research methods should be employed.

In order to best combine methods, it is necessary to follow the fundamental principle of mixed methods research which states that data collection methods should be combined in a manner to balance the strengths and weaknesses of qualitative and quantitative methods (Johnson & Turner, 2003, p. 299). The strengths of qualitative methods include the reflection of participants' understanding and in-depth explorations, among others, while the strengths of quantitative research include generalizability and breadth of explorations, among others. The weaknesses of qualitative research include the lack of generalizability and the intensiveness of data analysis, while quantitative research has questions concerning the researcher's conceptualizations of participants' understanding or experience of the constructs being examined. Mixed methods involve the aforementioned strengths as well as the ability to generate and test theory, the capability to answer complex research questions, and the possibility of corroborating findings. However, there are several weaknesses to mixed methods research, including the need for knowledge of multiple methods and the requirement for extensive amounts of time (Johnson & Onwuegbuzie, 2004). Despite the many weaknesses, mixed methods research is a useful approach to help expand CRT research in education (McKinney & Plano Clark, forthcoming).

Combining CRT and Mixed Methods

Mixed methods research is often characterized as methods-centric, focusing on the specific role of the methods in the data collection and analysis processes and paying little attention to theoretical perspectives (Hesse-Biber, 2010a). In essence, theoretical perspectives are often isolated from the research design. This is to be expected, since the majority of mixed methods research is quantitative-dominant and influenced by positivism/post-positivism, which does not require the examination of theoretical perspectives (Giddings, 2006). However, there is a growing movement in the mixed methods research arena to place more emphasis on theoretical perspectives and their impact on the specific research methods used in a study. Specifically, the push is to focus on how theoretical perspectives shape all areas of the research process, including the examination of the research literature, the creation of research questions, the implementation of research methods, the strategies used to analyze data, the manner in which data is interpreted, and the conclusions that are drawn from the data, including implications and possible policy decisions.

In addition to advocating for the stronger role of theoretical perspectives in mixed methods research, there is a movement to focus more on social inquiry issues related to sociopolitical awareness and commitment (Greene, 2006) as well as issues of power and social justice (Mertens, 2007). This movement calls for the shift from emphasizing singular voices to the focusing on the multiplicity of experiences, particularly of marginalized groups. Also, this requires being receptive to using a variety of research methods and theoretical perspectives. In order to focus on sociopolitical issues as well as issues of power, Mertens (2009) suggests using a transformative-emancipatory mixed methods focus. Such an approach consists of using mixed methods that are guided by an emancipatory framework, which is a framework that is designed to challenge power structures and to create change. Using a transformative-emancipatory framework requires situating research around a social problem that attempts to address issues of power as well as involves active community participation. It is from the perspective of the transformative-emancipatory framework that we see the potential alignment between CRT and mixed methods. This is because CRT is in itself a transformative theory that is designed to provide critiques regarding social inequities and to help create systemic change. In addition, a common goal of critical race studies is to involve community engagement through counterstorytelling. Thus, in order to best align CRT and mixed methods, it is necessary to use an approach that emphasizes counterstorytelling. One way to do so is to use qualitative-dominant mixed methods research designs (McKinney & Plano Clark, forthcoming).

Qualitative-Focused Mixed Methodology Designs: Emphasizing the Counterstory

Although the majority of mixed methods research is quantitative-dominant, there are numerous researchers who engage in qualitative-dominant designs. A qualitative-dominant mixed methods design is defined as the following: "the type of mixed research in which one relies on a qualitative, constructivist-poststructuralist-critical view of the research process, while concurrently recognizing that the addition of quantitative data and approaches are likely to benefit most research projects" (Johnson et al., 2007, p. 124). This type of research design places the emphasis on the qualitative methodology and incorporates the researcher's assumptions regarding the nature of knowledge into all stages of the research design, implementation, and analysis (Hesse-Biber, 2010b). Qualitative-dominant mixed methods designs emphasize the qualitative component regardless of the order in which the data is collected. There are three common mixed methods research designs that can be utilized from a qualitative-dominant perspective with a CRT lens: exploratory, explanatory, and multiphase.

The first design that readily adheres to a qualitative-dominant approach with a CRT lens is an exploratory mixed methods design (QUAL → quant).[1] In the exploratory mixed methods design, the qualitative data is collected first and is followed by quantitative data. In such a design, the qualitative data dictates how the quantitative data is to be collected (Creswell & Plano Clark, 2011). Although both qualitative and quantitative data is being collected, in a qualitative-dominant design, the qualitative data is emphasized while the quantitative data serves as support. This design is useful for CRT researchers in education. For example, many teacher educators are interested in pre-service teachers' perspectives on race. Using this design, researchers could conduct a study in which interviews are conducted with pre-service teachers regarding their views on the influence of race in the classroom. The interviews would then be analyzed using a CRT lens. The findings from the qualitative analyses can then be employed to identify appropriate quantitative measures to more broadly examine the themes that emerged from the interviews using a larger sample. The quantitative research findings can be utilized as a means of addressing the validity and trustworthiness of the qualitative data (Hesse-Biber, 2010b).

The second mixed methods design that is conducive to qualitative methodology with a CRT lens is an explanatory mixed methods design (quant → QUAL). In an explanatory design, quantitative data is collected first and is followed by qualitative data. The goal is for the qualitative data to explain the results of the quantitative data (Creswell & Plano Clark, 2011). In this design, the quantitative data provides trends that are to be more deeply explored by the qualitative data. For example, many researchers are interested in high school students' experiences with racism in schools. In order to study this phenomenon, researchers could first use Likert surveys to assess a sample of students' experiences with racism. The researcher could then use the results of the surveys to follow up with interviews. This would enable the researcher to capture additional information by allowing students to share their personal stories regarding their experiences with racism in schools. This design is particularly useful in addressing paradoxes found in the quantitative data (Hesse-Biber, 2010b).

The last design that can be used from a qualitative-dominant perspective is a multiphase mixed methods design. In this design, both quantitative and qualitative data is collected in multiple phases, with each phase informing the next phase (Creswell & Plano Clark, 2011). The type of data collected as well as the order in which it is collected will vary dependent upon the research goals. This type of design is most appropriate for more long-term projects such as program design/evaluation studies. For example, in education, many researchers are interested in developing, implementing, and evaluating culturally relevant curricula. In order to engage in such a study, a researcher can begin with the analysis of current curricula from a CRT perspective (QUAL). This analysis will lead to the second phase in which the researchers interview experts in the field regarding their thoughts on what is needed in a culturally relevant curriculum (QUAL). Based upon the analyses, the researcher will then create the new curriculum (QUAL). After the curriculum has been created, it will be implemented using a sample of students. Once the new curriculum has been implemented, the researcher can collect focus group interviews (QUAL) with the students to capture their perspectives on the new curriculum as well as gather achievement data such as test scores (quant). As demonstrated, this type of design is complex and time-consuming (QUAL → QUAL → QUAL → QUAL + quant). However, its intricate design most allows for the triangulation of data (Hesse-Biber, 2010b).

CONCLUSION

In this chapter, we discussed the compatibility of CRT and quantitative methods. Specifically, we suggested that critical race mixed methods are a plausible alternative to combining CRT and quantitative methods. As CRT continues to flourish within the discipline of education, we suggest the need to expand the traditional counterstory to include a variety of methodological approaches, including critical quantitative methods, particularly through the use of mixed methodology. The use of qualitative-dominant mixed methods designs (exploratory, explanatory, and multiphase) will enable the combination of critical quantitative methodological approaches while focusing on narratives, a central part of CRT. We are aware that in many circles the very discussion of combining CRT and quantitative methods in any form is seen as controversial. It is our belief that such a conversation is necessary to help to continue to move the field methodologically.

NOTE

1 This is the common nomenclature used in mixed methods research. The capitalization represents the place of emphasis. Also, the arrow signifies sequential data collection, while a plus sign suggests that the data is collected simultaneously or concurrently. See Morse (2003) for more details.

REFERENCES

Aleman, E. (2007). Situating Texas school finance policy in a CRT framework: How "substantially equal" yields racial inequality. *Educational Administration Quarterly, 43*(5), 525–558.

Bell, D.A. (1992). *Faces at the bottom of the well: The permanence of racism.* New York: Basic Books.

Benson, J., & Clark, F. (1982). A guide for instrument development and validation. *American Journal of Occupational Therapy, 36*(12), 789–800.

Bonilla-Silva, E., & Baiocchi, G. (2001). Anything but racism: How sociologists limit the significance of racism. *Race and Society, 4*(2), 117–131.

Brady, K., Eatman, T., & Parker, L. (2000). To have or not to have? A preliminary analysis of higher education funding disparities in the post-Ayers v. Fordice era: Evidence from critical race theory. *Journal of Education Finance, 25*(3), 297–322.

Campbell, D.T., & Fiske, D.W. (1959). Convergent and discriminant validation by the multitrait–multimethod matrix. *Psychological Bulletin, 56*(2), 81–105.

Carter, D.F., & Hurtado, S. (2007). Bridging key research dilemmas: Quantitative research using a critical eye. *New Directions for Institutional Research, 133*, 25–35.

Covarrubias, A. (2011). Quantitative intersectionality: A critical race analysis of the Chicana/o educational pipeline. *Journal of Latinos and Education, 10*(2), 86–105.

Crenshaw, K., Gotanda, N., Peller, G., & Thomas, K. (1995). *Critical race theory: The key writings that formed the movement* (pp. 85–102). New York: New Press.

Creswell, J.W. (2009). *Research design: Qualitative, quantitative, and mixed methods approaches* (3rd ed.). Thousand Oaks, CA: Sage.

Creswell, J.W., & Plano Clark, V. (2011). *Designing and conducting mixed methods research* (2nd ed.). Thousand Oaks, CA: Sage.

Delgado, R. (1989). Storytelling for oppositionists and others: A plea for narrative. *Michigan Law Review, 87*(8), 2411–2441.

Dixson, A.D., & Rousseau, C.K. (2006). *Critical race theory in education: All God's children got a song.* New York: Routledge.

Eichler, M. (1991). *Nonsexist research methods: A practical guide.* New York: Routledge.

Giddings, L.S. (2006). Mixed-methods research: Positivism dressed in drag? *Journal of Research in Nursing, 11*(3), 195–203.

Gillborn, D. (2010). The colour of numbers: Surveys, statistics and deficit-thinking about race and class. *Journal of Educational Policy, 25*(2), 253–276.

Greene, J. (2006). Towards a methodology of mixed methods social inquiry. *Research in the Schools, 13*(1), 93–98.

Guba, E.G., & Lincoln, Y.S. (1994). Competing paradigms in qualitative research. In N.K. Denzin & Y.S. Lincoln (Eds.), *Handbook of qualitative research* (pp. 105–117). London: Sage.

Guinier, L. (1998). *Lift every voice: Turning a civil rights setback into a new vision of social justice.* New York: Simon & Schuster.

Hesse-Biber, S. (2010a). *Mixed methods research: Merging theory with practice.* New York: Guilford Press.

Hesse-Biber, S. (2010b). Qualitative approaches to mixed methods practice. *Qualitative Inquiry, 16*(6), 455–468.

Jayakumar, U.M., Howard, T.C., Allen, W.R., & Han, J.C. (2009). Racial privilege in the professoriate: An exploration of campus climate, retention, and satisfaction. *Journal of Higher Education, 80*(5), 538–563.

Jick, T.D. (1979). Mixing qualitative and quantitative methods: Triangulation in action. *Administrative Science Quarterly, 24*(4), 602–611.

Johnson, R.B., & Onwuegbuzie, A.J. (2004). Mixed methods research: A research paradigm whose time has come. *Educational Researcher, 33*(7), 14–26.

Johnson, R.B., & Turner, L.A. (2003). Data collection strategies in mixed methods research. In A. Tashakkori and C. Teddlie (Eds.), *Handbook of mixed methods in social and behavioral research* (pp. 297–320). Thousand Oaks, CA: Sage.

Johnson, R.B., Onwuegbuzie, A.J., & Turner, L.A. (2007). Toward a definition of mixed methods research. *Journal of Mixed Methods Research, 1*(2), 112–133.

Kincheloe, J.L., & McLaren, P. (2005). Rethinking critical theory and qualitative research. In N.K. Denzin & Y.S. Lincoln (Eds.), *Handbook of qualitative research* (pp. 303–342). Thousand Oaks, CA: Sage.

Kincheloe, J.L., & Steinberg, S.R. (1997). *Changing multiculturalism: New times, new curriculum.* London: Open University Press.

Koro-Ljungberg, M., Yendol-Hoppey, D., Smith, J.J., & Hayes, S.B. (2009). (E)pistemological awareness, instantiation of methods, and uniformed methodological ambiguity in qualitative research projects. *Educational Researcher, 38*(9), 687–699.

Mathison, S. (1988). "Why triangulate?" *Educational Researcher, 17*(2), 13–17.

Maxwell, J.A. (2010). Using numbers in qualitative research. *Qualitative Inquiry, 16*(6), 475–482.

McKinney, T.R.F., & Plano Clark, V.L. (forthcoming). Use of mixed methods and critical race theory in educational research: A methodological review. Manuscript submitted for publication.

Mertens, D.M. (2007). Transformative paradigm: Mixed methods and social justice. *Journal of Mixed Methods Research, 1*(3), 212–225.

Mertens, D.M. (2009). *Transformative research and evaluation.* New York: Guilford Press.

Morse, J. (2003). Principles of mixed methods and multimethod research design. In A. Tashakkori and C. Teddlie (Eds.), *Handbook of mixed methods in social and behavioral research* (pp. 189–208). Thousand Oaks, CA: Sage.

Neuman, W.L. (1997). *Social research methods: Qualitative and quantitative approaches* (3rd ed.). Needham Heights, MA: Allyn & Bacon.

Parker, L. (1998). "Race is … Race ain't": An exploration of the utility of critical race theory in qualitative research in education. *Qualitative Studies in Education, 11*(1), 45–55.

Parker, L., & Lynn, M. (2002). What's race got to do with it? Critical race theory's conflicts with and connections to qualitative research methodology and epistemology. *Qualitative Inquiry, 8*(1), 7–22.

Peters, M., & Lankshear, C. (1996). Postmodern counternarratives. In H. Giroux, C. Lankshear, P. McLaren, & M. Peters (Eds.), *Counternarratives: Cultural studies and critical pedagogies in postmodern spaces* (pp. 1–39). New York: Routledge.

Ponterotto, J.G. (2005). Qualitative research in counseling psychology: A primer on research paradigms and philosophy of science. *Journal of Counseling Psychology, 52*(2), 126–136.

Prasad, P. (2005). *Crafting qualitative research: Working in the post-positivist traditions.* New York: M.E. Sharpe.

Rocco, T.S., Bliss, L.A., Gallagher, S., & Perez-Prado, A. (2003). Taking the next step: Mixed methods research in organizational systems. *Information Technology, Learning and Performance Journal, 21*(1), 19–29.

Rossman, G.B., & Wilson, B.L. (1985). Numbers and words: Combining quantitative and qualitative methods in a single large-scale evaluation study. *Evaluation Review, 9*(5), 627–643.

Rossman, G.B., & Wilson, B.L. (1994). Numbers and words revisited: Being shamelessly eclectic. *Quality and Quantity, 28*(3), 315–327.

Schutz, P.A., Chambless, C.B., & DeCuir, J.T. (2003). Multimethods research. In K.B. deMarrais and S.D. Lapan (Eds.), *Foundations for research: Methods of inquiry in education and the social sciences* (pp. 267–282). Hillsdale, NJ: Lawrence Erlbaum.

Solórzano, D.G., & Yosso, T.J. (2001). Critical race and LatCrit theory and method: Counter-storytelling. *Qualitative Studies in Education, 14*(4), 471–495.

Solórzano, D.G., & Yosso, T.J. (2002). Critical race methodology: Counter-storytelling as an analytical framework for education research. *Qualitative Inquiry, 8*(1), 23–44.

Tashakkori, A., & Creswell, J.W. (2007). The new era of mixed methods. *Journal of Mixed Methods Research, 1,* 3–7.

Teranishi, R.T. (2007). Race, ethnicity, and higher education policy: The use of critical quantitative research. *New Directions for Institutional Research, 133,* 37–49.

Villalpando, O., & Delgado Bernal, D. (2002). A critical race theory analysis of barriers that impede the success of faculty of color. In W.A. Smith, P.G. Altbach, & K. Lomotey (Eds.), *The racial crisis in American higher education: Continuing challenges for the twenty-first century* (pp. 243–269). New York: State University of New York Press.

Zuberi, T. (2003). *Thicker than blood: How racial statistics lie.* Minneapolis: University of Minnesota Press.

Zuberi, T., & Bonilla-Silva, E. (2008). Toward a definition of White logic and White methods. In T. Zuberi & E. Bonilla-Silva (Eds.), *White logic, White method: Racism and methodology* (pp. 3–27). Lanham, MD: Rowman & Littlefield.

19

A CRITICAL RACE POLICY ANALYSIS OF THE SCHOOL-TO-PRISON PIPELINE FOR CHICANOS

Brenda Guadalupe Valles and Octavio Villalpando

> Regrettably, students of color are receiving different and harsher disciplinary punishments than whites for the same or similar infractions, and they are disproportionately impacted by zero-tolerance policies—a fact that only serves to exacerbate already deeply entrenched disparities in many communities.
>
> (Thomas E. Perez, Assistant Attorney General for Civil Rights,
> U.S. Department of Justice, September 27, 2010)

School discipline policies such as zero tolerance have not proven to be an effective way to keep schools safe (NCES, 2009). In a more recent report on school crime and safety, the National Center for Education Statistics (NCES, 2011) found that, even while discipline policies are becoming broader and more punitive, they have not resulted in decreased crime or increased school safety. For instance, even while stricter school discipline policies have been enacted in our Mountain West[1] state, there has been an increase of 4 percent in injuries or threats with weapons while at school (p. 89). The increase in crime has been attributed primarily to African American and Chicano students, resulting in high suspension and expulsion rates for these two male groups, creating a pattern of exclusion (Reyes, 2006). Patterns of exclusion are drawn from on- and off-campus suspensions and expulsions that lead to the removal of students from instructional settings (Morrison & D'Incau, 1997) and increased school push-out (Skiba et al., 2002), which frequently lead to increased criminalization (Casella, 2003; Reyes, 2006).

Speaking on behalf of President Obama, Assistant Attorney General Thomas E. Perez outlines how school discipline policies such as zero tolerance are creating damaging trends for many "already deeply entrenched disparities" in communities. We read this to refer to the ways in which school disciplinary policies and practices are impacting communities of color. Perez (2010) described brief statistics and pointed to a school-to-prison pipeline that must be derailed; however, in this chapter, we seek to go a step further from Perez's critique and center our analysis on Chicanos.

In Mountain West, the overall academic performance of Chicana/o students is well below that of their White counterparts. In 2002, 3.2 percent of Chicano male students (including pan-Latino, male students) graduated high school, while 6.7 percent of their White male counterparts graduated high school (OCR, 2006). It is estimated that the overall Chicana/o population in Mountain West is currently at 13 percent (Pew Hispanic Center, 2010), while school-aged Chicana/o youth make up 17 percent of the Mountain West population.

Chicana/o youth are the fastest growing population nationally, and also within the prison system. Thus it is imperative that we center Chicanos in the conversation of school discipline policies and their effects, particularly because of the drastic impact that policies like zero tolerance are having on Chicanos. Furthermore, it is important to dissect how we got here, that is to say, we need to understand the history of the policy within a state context. To inform our understanding of discipline policy history and context, we follow it from a proposed bill to legislation (or law) to implementation. We believe that, by closely analyzing school discipline policies in an isolated environment such as one state, Mountain West, we are able to transparently present the process by which policies become racialized and thus racially/ethnically disproportionate in their distribution.

Historically, the educational experience for Chicana/o students has been one of marginalization and racially fueled policies and practices that have paved the way for the current educational status of Chicana/o students. Racially based policies such as school segregation (Donato et al., 1991), school tracking into vocational or remedial education programs (Oakes, 1985), lack of access to advanced placement courses (Solórzano & Ornelas, 2002), and poorly funded schools and resources have contributed to the significantly high rates of school failure that Chicana/o students experience today (Kozol, 1992).

School discipline policies have undergone extreme shifts over the last two decades. The purpose and outcome goals for school discipline policies have changed so dramatically that it is difficult to unfold the original intent of such policies. Additionally, as the policies have changed so have the boundaries of implementation and key stakeholders in school discipline policies. As such, school discipline policies and practices are complex, contradictory, and multidimensional. Using a race-conscious theoretical framework to analyze these policies is important in that this study centers Chicano students (Delgado Bernal, 2002).

While much research has been conducted on the topic of school discipline, oftentimes research focuses on African American males, given the alarming rates at which they are suspended and expelled from school as a result of zero tolerance policies (Raffaele Mendez, 2003; Skiba et al., 2002; Townsend, 2000). Furthermore, research seldom examines the long-term academic implications of zero tolerance policies (Casella, 2003). Further, while we support the continued empirical investigation of the way school discipline policies affect African American male students, we also seek to join other scholars who are examining the impact of school discipline policies on Chicano males (Covarrubias, 2011; Malagon, 2010; Solórzano et al., 2005; Villalpando, 2005, 2010).

DISCIPLINE POLICIES: A CONTEXT AND HISTORY

Discipline policy research indicates key findings that are unpacked further in this study. The first finding is that students targeted the most by zero tolerance policies are youth of color (Noguera, 2003; Reyes, 2006; Skiba et al., 2004). Researchers (Reyes, 2006; Skiba et al., 2002; Verdugo, 2002) suggest there is evidence of disproportionate implementation of discipline policies such as zero tolerance and out of school suspensions directed at male students of color, specifically African American males (Children's Defense Fund, 1975; Raffaele Mendez, 2003; Skiba et al., 2002). Second, these afore-mentioned studies have found that, by experiencing discipline policies at a disproportionate rate, students suffer lower academic achievement, less college readiness, increased likelihood of becoming a push-out, and racial disparities which impede students from participating in the college pipeline (Reyes, 2006). The disproportionate implementation of discipline policies fuels the school-to-prison pipeline (Casella, 2003; Osher et al., 2003).

METHODOLOGY: CRITICAL RACE POLICY ANALYSIS

We utilize LatCrit as a methodological framework to capture the nuanced experiences of Chicano students. LatCrit lends itself to a more in-depth analysis and for the centering of Chicano students by accounting for issues of language, and the intersection of Latinidad and gender, phenotype, and so on (Hernandez-Truyol, 1997). According to researchers who have advocated for a CRT policy analysis (Lopez, 2003; Parker & Villalpando, 2007) and those who have carried out this new methodological analysis (Alemán, 2006; Parker, 2003), a critical race theory policy analysis is helpful in centering race and racism, and thereby unmasking the process and ways in which policies marginalize and oppress communities of color.

Color-Blindness

It is important to understand the ways in which color-blindness plays a significant role in school discipline policies and implications. Gotanda (1991) outlines the way that color-blindness as a function in society is not just a "positive racial social vision" but rather a form of "racial privileging" (p. 1139). He goes on to point out: "Colorblindness is often described as a race-neutral process. However, 'racial nonrecognition,' the technique as the heart of our understanding of colorblindness, is by its nature not a 'neutral' process, since certain characteristics were recognized, calculated, and then discounted" (p. 1135). In other words, through a critical race policy analysis, the guise of color-blindness, fairness, and equality of discipline policies and practices is lifted to reveal the biased material nature of the policy which privileges White students over all other students of color, specifically in this case Chicano students. Lynn and Parker (2006) support this point when they suggest that "color-blind interpretations of the law or meritocracy are 'unmasked' by critical race theorists to be precursors for White, European American hegemonic control of the social and structural arrangements in U.S. society" (p. 9).

Race and Racism Intersecting

When the context and history of zero tolerance discipline policies are coupled with trends and current rates of racial/ethnic discipline distribution, a pattern of racial/ethnic disproportionality emerges that negatively impacts Chicanos in Mountain West (MWSOE, 2006; OCR, 2006) and questions the alleged fairness and color-blindness of these policies. More concerning still, the very policies and practices that prohibit Chicana/o students from an unobstructed educational pathway are protected under a veil of color-blindness and meritocracy (DeCuir & Dixson, 2004; Solórzano & Ornelas, 2002; Villalpando, 2010), allowing oppressive discipline policies to continue (Valencia, 1997).

While working to conduct a critical race policy analysis, we also incorporate LatCrit into our analysis. We feel the need to do so given that LatCrit works explicitly to center the Latina/o experiences (Valdes, 2002). LatCrit is inclusive of the diversity among and within Latinos' pan-ethnic (Valdes, 1997) and poly-ethnic (Hernandez-Truyol, 1997; Iglesias & Valdes, 1998) make-up. Secondly, LatCrit embraces the complexity of identity through recognizing multidimensional aspects and intersectionality of identity across race/ethnicity (Valdes, 1997), immigration (Johnson, 1995), sexuality and gender (Hernandez-Truyol, 1997), phenotype (Valdes, 1997), religion (Iglesias & Valdes, 1998), language (Johnson & Martinez, 2000), global equity (Hernandez-Truyol, 1997; Iglesias, 1997), and others. In this study, LatCrit speaks to the larger educational policy questions CRT has explored (Parker, 2003) and to the sensitivity to intersectionality between gender, race/ethnicity, and phenotype of Chicanos of LatCrit.

Research Design

As a critical race policy analysis, this study includes a thorough examination of discipline policies holistically, that is to say, we looked at discipline policies historically, and contextually (Parker & Lynn, 2002). This primary step to our critical race policy analysis included researching how discipline policies came about nationally and in our state and to include the process used to approve these policies. Second, it is imperative to learn who the key stakeholders to discipline policies are and have been, and what their motives and rationale are for supporting it or not supporting it. Third, we applied a discourse analysis using CRT and LatCrit to guide the analysis used to unpack drafted legislation and policies. Whenever we analyzed text, we applied this CRT informed discourse analysis. Last, we analyzed the impact to the implementation of the policy. In our case, this called for collecting and analyzing district disciplinary data and talking with legislators about these impacts.

This approach includes descriptive data and interview data. The qualitative component includes student narratives and interviews with a juvenile judge and state legislator. The narratives in this research work to create a counterstory in this study to re-tell or counter-tell the existing stock stories about Chicano experiences with discipline in schools. In this study, CRT and LatCrit counterstorytelling allows us to understand how participants of this study responded to disciplinary policies and practices through their own narratives (Fernandez, 2002). This part of the study seeks to inform the statistical data with the experiential knowledge students bring. In addition the juvenile judge and state legislator provide insight into the policy making and implementation process for discipline policies.

CRITICAL RACE POLICY ANALYSIS

According to researchers who have advocated for a CRT policy analysis (Lopez, 2003; Parker & Villalpando, 2007) and those who have carried out this new methodological analysis (Alemán, 2006; Parker, 2003), a critical race theory policy analysis is helpful in centering race and thereby unmasking the process and ways in which policies marginalize and oppress communities of color.

In this study, by centering race within a school discipline critical race theory policy analysis, the following examination can be conducted on school discipline policies:

1 A context is provided, which includes tracing the policy and policy relationships and those historical legacies. The development of discipline policies under zero tolerance was intended to protect students from firearms and drugs; however, the policy as it is implemented now is laden with racial bias and the personal interpretation of school officials (Reyes, 2006; Skiba et al., 2002). Locally, the development of discipline policies within zero tolerance, when analyzed through a critical race theory lens, took a clear target in legislative hearings and outlined specific groups that would use this policy. Knowing the history and context of the local policy development provides a better understanding of how the practice and implementation of such policies are not free of bias or prejudices.

2 The guise of color-blindness, fairness, and equality is lifted to reveal the biased material nature of the policy (Gotanda, 1991). When the context and history of zero tolerance discipline policies are coupled with trends and current rates of racial/ethnic discipline distribution, a pattern of racial/ethnic disproportionality emerges that negatively impacts Chicanos (OCR, 2006; MWSOE, 2006) and questions the alleged fairness and color-blindness of these policies.

3 Voices that are traditionally marginalized in the policy making process are incorporated into the analysis in an effort to disrupt traditional policy-actor narratives through the use of counterstorytelling. This critical policy analysis will incorporate the voices of a policy maker, a Chicano legislator, and a street-level bureaucrat, a Chicano juvenile judge. These voices are traditionally marginalized in the larger education policy discourse (Alemán, 2006) and research. In this way, critical policy analysis serves to incorporate the traditionally underrepresented voices into the policy discourse on Chicanos.

Through CRT guideposts, this study offers an alternative lens that centers marginalized experiences within a historical context and current race-conscious landscape.

Similarly, the role of LatCrit is as important to a critical race policy analysis. Given that this study centers Chicano students, LatCrit serves to bring forth a deeper focus on intersectionalities of experiences and identities within and across Latinidades. LatCrit contains the CRT tenets as part of the theoretical make-up, and brings forth additional and more complex analysis on Latinas/os that serves to illuminate the multiple dimensions of Chicano students as they navigate discipline policies as both male and brown.

DISCIPLINE POLICY DEVELOPMENT

In our Mountain West state, discipline policies have continued to develop through legislative amendments. While most states have a statewide discipline policy, including Mountain West, in 2007 the Mountain West discipline policy was connected with juvenile courts. This policy amendment now creates a policy bond between schools and juvenile courts which are directly linked to juvenile detention centers, thus institutionalizing the schools-to-prison pipeline. Furthermore, the policy also now includes juvenile judges among discipline policy actors.

Discourse Analysis

In 2007, when State Representative White took office, his agenda included an effort to indicate to his conservative counterparts that he was committed in the tradition of conservative politics and to education. Through this, he took the experiences of his wife as a teacher in a highly racially/ethnically diverse school in her husband's district, and drafted and proposed legislation that would connect school districts directly to juvenile justice courts. His idea was to make schools safer and spaces that were conducive to learning. When Representative White's bill was on the house floor for a hearing, he vividly described the rationale for his proposed legislation and began by describing current discipline policy implementation and practices:

> It was explained to me that there is what I call "no man's land."
>
> You have students that the district can go to a certain point and school can go to a certain point and they will respond very well to all sorts of interventions that the schools can do and the courts can come down to a certain point. And then there is a "no man's land" in between—a little collection of kids that know exactly where those borderlands are. They know that as long as they don't cross the line the district really can't do anything and the courts are not going to touch them.
>
> And so, my intent with this legislation is just to close that gap and let our kids know—we care an awful lot about kids showing up to school, we have laws based on truancy making sure kids get to school so that they can get educated.
>
> My concern is very simple, what about that punk kid that just loves coming to school? He doesn't want to come to school to get educated, he just wants to hang out with his yo-yo homies and he doesn't want to be there to get educated, he's just there because that's his stage and he's there to perform.
>
> (Utah State Legislative Hearing of House Bill 286, 2/7/2007)

This amendment in Mountain West is analyzed through a CRT lens by taking sections from the legislative hearing presentation by the Representative. The legislator authoring this proposed bill was in his freshman term when this bill was drafted. Within the bill, his language to describe the need for this legislation is blatantly discriminatory and explicitly targeted at Chicano students. With phrases like "no man's land," "borderlands," and "yo-yo homies," Representative White makes it clear who his target population is with this proposed bill. Through a critical race theory policy analysis, it is clear how this policy was racially biased in its inception. The way the bill is described and written, it explicitly targets a specific demographic of students; in this way there is a high likelihood that it will yield higher infractions for the population it seeks to target, that is, the population of color. This bill institutionalizes that "a school-age minor who receives a habitual disruptive behavior citation is subject to the jurisdiction of the juvenile court" (p. 1, lines 24, 25).

Stakeholder Interviews

The idea that policies are never fair and objective is a critique that other legislators observe; for instance, Representative Arias describes the legislature as one operating through a color-blind framework, making his efforts of advocacy for underrepresented students more challenging in a predominantly republican, White, and male legislature:

> A lot of the legislators who sit on the education committee don't believe it should be relevant whether or not somebody is a Chicano or African American, or Native American. They think it's just "about the children." But we know through history and

through having grown up in this community that it does matter and it's important to make sure that we know the statistics because they generally have a negative effect on our populations or they seem to be compounded.

Similarly, Judge Rodriguez describes the prevalence of color-blindness by also acknowledging his own investment in color-blindness:

I always, I have always kind of resisted that it is all based on race but you know, race comes to play. We can't be race-blind, I mean, or racism-blind. We want to be race-blind and say we are making a decision just based on the facts and the conduct ... but there is; we can't be racism-blind. There is a level of profiling.

Both participants here describe the policy climate that promotes a color-blind positionality, and yet performs in a contradictory fashion that includes centering the dominant population of the state as well as profiling students of color.

The Impact: Student Discipline Patterns

Chicano students make up about a third of the population in the sample for district 2, yet they represent nearly double of the zero tolerance violations, which include expulsions or long term suspensions or other violations when contrasted with their White peers. (See Table 19.1.)

Preliminary analysis of student data found dramatic patterns of disproportionality among discipline infractions for Chicano and White students. For instance, Table 19.2 indicates that Chicano students represent 34 percent of the sample for district 1 and made up 69 percent of discipline infractions. The rate for Chicano discipline is quite significant when contrasted with that of White students, who make up 66 percent of the sample representation but 36 percent of discipline infractions. Chicano students made up half of what Whites did in the sample representation, however double of the zero

Table 19.1 District percentages of all discipline infractions: distribution by race/ethnicity, 2007 and 2008

	Sample representation %	Infraction 2007 %	Infraction 2008 %
Chicano	27	13	17
White	73	5	6
Total	100	18	23

Table 19.2 Type of disciplinary infraction by race/ethnicity and violation type, 2007–08

	Sample representation %	Zero tolerance violation %	Other violation %
Chicano	34	15	54
White	66	6	30
Total	100	21	84

tolerance infractions and nearly double of all other infractions. Table 19.1 illustrates similar patterns of disproportionality to the data from district 1. In this table Chicanos make up slightly over a quarter of the sample and nearly three times the disciplinary infractions that their White counterparts make. Thus the first significant finding is that, in Mountain West, two large school districts indicate an overrepresentation of Chicano students receiving disciplinary infractions. Furthermore, the disproportionality is evident across severe zero tolerance citations and more general disciplinary infractions.

These tables describe the racial/ethnic breakdown of the two participating school districts and the disciplinary infractions by type and across two years. These brief snapshots present the imbalance in discipline patterns between Chicanos and their White peers. Although there is disproportionate presence between male students of color and their White peers, by centering Chicano students in this study we find the overrepresentation in discipline by Chicano students. The tables suggest differential application rates of disciplinary policy.

THE STORY DATA PAINTS OF DISCIPLINE AND CHICANOS

Consistent with the CRT and LatCrit lenses that inform this study, there were various steps taken to center Chicano students through this statistical analysis. Findings from this analysis are triangulated with qualitative data to provide a richer set of findings with the dimension of experience. This data is presented in a series of student narratives describing each of the participants. Following is an analysis with themes and key concepts. Within the research reviewed (Casella, 2003; Reyes, 2006; Skiba et al., 2002), there are apparent links between the increases in juvenile incarceration of students of color and the decrease in persistence within educational institutions. Casella (2003) found that many adults he interviewed who were incarcerated were also illiterate and had begun getting into formal "trouble" when they were in middle school. Through a CRT lens, we can identify parallels between Chicano student experiences with education discipline practices and practices in juvenile detention centers and jails (see Kim et al., 2010).

CONCLUSION

This critical race theory policy analysis seeks to look at discipline policies as they occur in Mountain West through a race-conscious framework. This is an important way to look at policy for the format that CRT provides, that is, a context and history, the interruption of dominant ideologies in policy formation and implementation, and unique, traditionally marginalized voices in the forefront.

The development of discipline policies under zero tolerance was intended to protect students from firearms and drugs; however, the policy as it is implemented now is laden with racial bias and personal interpretation of school officials (Reyes, 2006; Skiba et al., 2002). A critical race theory policy analysis exposes and turns the guise of color-blindness, fairness, and equality on its head, thereby revealing the biased nature of the policy. When the context and history of zero tolerance discipline policies are transparent, and presented with trends and current rates of racial/ethnic discipline distribution, a pattern of racial/ethnic disproportionality emerges that negatively impacts Chicanos and questions the alleged fairness and color-blindness of these policies, in the process exposing the racist nature of disciplinary policies and practices.

This study has significant implications for policy. By providing an analysis of discipline policy this study explores the ways in which policies can inherently be designed in a racist manner and target a specific group of people. This study also analyzes discipline policies and makes them transparent for the ways in which they are racially biased, subjective, unequally distributed, and unfair.

The policy implications of this study call for a re-consideration of the utility and benefits of zero tolerance and other discipline policies. It has been proven in this study and in national research that zero tolerance does not make schools safer, and it results in an increase in juvenile justice detention, further resulting in an increase in incarcerated adults in jails and prisons, rather than making schools non-violent spaces.

NOTE

1 To protect the anonymity of participants in our study, we refer to our state with the fictional pseudonym of "Mountain West."

REFERENCES

Alemán, E. (2006). Is Robin Hood the "prince of thieves" or a pathway to equity? Applying a critical race theory to school finance political discourse. *Educational Policy, 20*, 113–142.

Casella, R. (2003). Zero-tolerance policy in schools: Rationale, consequences, and alternatives. *Teachers College Record, 105*(5), 872–892.

Children's Defense Fund. (1975). *School suspensions: Are they helping children?* Washington, DC: Children's Defense Fund.

Covarrubias, A. (2011). Quantitative intersectionality: A critical race analysis of the Chicana/o educational pipeline. *Journal of Latinos and Education, 10*(2), 86–105.

DeCuir, J.T., & Dixson, A.D. (2004). "So when it comes out, they aren't that surprised that it is there": Using critical race theory as a tool of analysis of race and racism in education. *Educational Researcher, 33*(5), 26–31.

Delgado Bernal, D. (2002). Critical race theory, Latino critical theory, and critical raced-gendered epistemologies: Recognizing students of color as holders and creators of knowledge. *Qualitative Inquiry, 8*, 105–124.

Donato, R., Menchaca, M., & Valencia, R.R. (1991). Segregation, desegregation, and integration of Chicano students: Problem and prospects. In R. Valencia (Ed.), *Chicano school failure and success: Research and policy agendas for the 1990s* (pp. 27–63). New York: Falmer Press.

Fernandez, L. (2002). Telling stories about school: Using critical race and Latino critical theories to document Latina/Latino education and resistance. *Qualitative Inquiry, 8*(1), 45–65.

Gotanda, N. (1991). A critique of "Our constitution is color-blind." *Stanford Law Review, 44*, 1–68.

Hernandez-Truyol, B. (1997). Borders (en)gendered: Normativities, Latinas and a LatCrit paradigm. *New York University Law Review, 72*, 882–927.

Iglesias, E.M. (1997). International law, human rights, and LatCrit theory. *University of Miami Inter-American Law Review, 28*, 177–213.

Iglesias, E.M., & Valdes, F. (1998). Afterword: Religion, gender, sexuality, race and class in coalitional theory: A critical and self-critical analysis of LatCrit social justice agendas. *UCLA Chicano–Latino Law Review, 19*, 503–588.

Johnson, K.R. (1995). Celebrating LatCrit theory: What do we do when the music stops? *UC Davis Law Review, 33*, 753.

Johnson, K.R., & Martinez, G. (2000). Discrimination by proxy: The case of Proposition 227 and the ban on bilingual education. *UC Davis Law Review, 33*, 1227.

Kim, C., Losen, D., & Hewitt, D. (2010). *The school to prison pipeline: Structuring legal reform.* New York: NYU Press.

Kozol, J. (1992). *Savage inequalities: Children in America's schools.* New York: Harper Perennial.

Lopez, G. (2003). The (racially neutral) politics of education: A critical race theory perspective. *Educational Administration Quarterly, 39*(1), 69–94.

Lynn, M., & Parker, L. (2006). Critical race studies in education: Examining a decade of research on U.S. schools. *Urban Review, 38*(4), 257–290.

Malagon, M. (2010). Trenches under the pipeline: The educational trajectories of Chicano male continuation high school students. Thinking Gender Papers. UCLA Center for the Study of Women.

Morrison, G.M., & D'Incau, B. (1997). The web of zero-tolerance: Characteristics of students who are recommended for expulsion from school. *Education and the Treatment of Children, 20*, 316–335.

MWSOE (Mountain West State Office of Education). (2006). *Annual report.*

NCES (National Center for Educational Statistics). (2009). *Indicators of school crime and safety: 2009.* Washington, DC: U.S. Department of Education.

NCES (National Center for Educational Statistics). (2011). *Indicators of school crime and safety: 2011.* Washington, DC: U.S. Department of Education.

Noguera, P. (2003). Schools, prisons, and social implications of punishment: Rethinking disciplinary practices. *Theory into Practice, 42*(4), 341–350.

Oakes, J. (1985). *Keeping track: How schools structure inequality.* New Haven, CT: Yale University Press.

OCR (Office of Civil Rights). (2006). *State and national projects for enrollment and selected items by race/ethnicity and sex.* Washington, DC: U.S. Department of Education.

Osher, D.M., Quinn, M.M., Poirier, J.M., & Rutherford, R.B. (2003). Deconstructing the pipeline: Using efficacy and effectiveness data and cost–benefit analyses to reduce minority youth incarceration. In J. Wald & D.J. Losen (Eds.), *New direction for youth development: Deconstructing the school-to-prison pipeline* (pp. 91–120). San Francisco, CA: Jossey-Bass.

Parker, L. (2003). Critical race theory and its implications for methodology and policy analysis in higher education desegregation. In G.R. López & L. Parker (Eds.), *Interrogating racism in qualitative research methodology* (pp. 145–173). New York: Peter Lang.

Parker, L., & Lynn, M. (2002). What's race got to do with it? Critical race theory's conflicts with and connections to qualitative research methodology and epistemology. *Qualitative Inquiry, 8*(1), 7–22.

Parker, L., & Villalpando, O. (2007). A Race(cialized) perspective on educational leadership: Critical race theory in educational administration. *Educational Administration Quarterly, 43*(5), 519–524.

Perez, T. (2010). The civil rights and school discipline. Addressing Disparities to Ensure Equal Educational Opportunities Conference. Assistant Attorney General for Civil Rights, Washington, DC.

Pew Hispanic Center. (2010). *Population counts 2010, Census 2010.* Washington, DC: Pew Hispanic Center.

Raffaele Mendez, L.M. (2003). Predictors of suspension and negative outcomes: A longitudinal investigation. *New Directions for Youth Development, 99*, 17–33.

Reyes, A. (2006). *Discipline, achievement and race: Is zero tolerance the answer?* Lanham, MD: Rowman & Littlefield.

Skiba, R.J., Michael, R.S., Nardo, A.C., & Peterson, R. (2002). The color of discipline: Sources of racial and gender disproportionality in school punishment. *Urban Review, 34*, 317–342.

Skiba, R., Rausch, K., & Ritter, S. (2004). Children left behind: Series summary and recommendations. *Education Policy Briefs from Indiana Youth Services, 2*(4).

Solórzano, D.G., & Ornelas, A. (2002). A critical race analysis of advanced placement classes: A case of educational inequalities. *Journal of Latinos and Education, 1*(4), 215–229.

Solórzano, D., Villalpando, O., & Oseguera, L. (2005). Educational inequities and Latina/o undergraduate students in the United States: A critical race analysis of their educational progress. *Journal of Hispanic Higher Education, 4*(30), 272–294.

Townsend, B.L. (2000). The disproportionate discipline of African American learners: Reducing school suspensions and expulsions. *Exceptional Children, 66*(3), 382–384.

Valdes, F. (1997). LatCrit theory: Naming and launching a new direction of critical legal scholarship. *Harvard Latino Law Review, 2*, 1–501.

Valdes, F. (2002). Under construction: LatCrit consciousness, community, and theory. *La Raza Law Journal, 10*, 3–56.

Valencia, R. (1997). Conceptualizing the notion of deficit thinking. In R.R. Valencia (Ed.), *The evolution of deficit thinking: Educational thought and practice.* London: Falmer Press.

Verdugo, R.R. (2002). Race-ethnicity, social class, and zero-tolerance policies: The cultural and structural wars. *Education and Urban Society, 35*(1), 50–71.

Villalpando, O. (2005). Conditions that affect the participation and success of Latino males in college. Policy study commissioned by the Joint Center for Political and Economic Studies and the Kellogg Foundation, for the Dellums Commission, Washington, DC.

Villalpando, O. (2010). Latinos/as in higher education: Eligibility, enrollment, and educational attainment. *Handbook of Latinos and education.* New York: Routledge Press.

20

CRITICAL RACE QUANTITATIVE INTERSECTIONALITY

An Anti-Racist Research Paradigm that Refuses to "Let the Numbers Speak for Themselves"

Alejandro Covarrubias and Verónica Vélez

"Show me the data!" "The numbers" are omnipotent and often the only valid sources of data for many academicians, policymakers, and those most influential in the field of education (Kamil, 2004). Both private and public funding sources demand that the "hard facts" of outcomes are provided through quantitative data (Simonson, 2005). Politely, struggling non-profit agencies and public institutions comply. We give this data so much power, celebrating its purported objectivity and neutrality, that oftentimes we forget data—any data—is shaped by the sociopolitical context within which it arose, by the scientists who "discovered" it (Gould, 1996; Said, 1978; Zuberi, 2001). The over-reliance in mainstream policy and research arenas on quantitative data leads many to proclaim, "Let the numbers speak for themselves." Our training as critical race scholars has taught us that the numbers never "speak for themselves" and that, in fact, the numbers are given voice largely by the theoretical underpinnings upon which they rest. Bonilla-Silva and Zuberi (2008), for example, argue that claims of impartiality regarding statistical research fail to recognize its historical roots in white supremacy and the eugenics movement. They contend that "statistical analysis was developed alongside a logic of racial reasoning. That the founder of statistical analysis also developed a theory of [w]hite supremacy is not an accident" (Bonilla-Silva & Zuberi, 2008, p. 5). Consequently, a white logic has formed in quantitative methods, blinding social scientists in their contemporary research regarding race, especially its causal findings and its applications (Bonilla-Silva & Zuberi, 2008). The result? Rather than challenge racial stratification, social science becomes the justification for it. Framed as "objective" and "neutral," this misguided research has gone on to shape educational policy, allocate resources, and guide programming and practices that impact the education of low-income communities of color. We assert that a critical race quantitative intersectionality (CRQI) in the field of education challenges the lasting legacy of an erroneous, and arguably racist, application of statistical methods in the social sciences and expands the utility and transformative potential of critical race theory (CRT).

Over the last two decades of CRT's emergence and maturation in education, powerful work has surfaced that informs the field about the experiences of students of color in primary and secondary education, undergraduate studies, and graduate programs across the country. We have learned about the multifaceted forms of microaggressions and their influence on: students' experiences (Solorzano, 1998; Solorzano et al., 2000; Yosso et al., 2009); racial battle fatigue, or the cumulative impact of racial assaults (Smith et al., 2006); the unequal distribution of advanced placement courses, which often gives white students unfair GPA advantages and a head start in college (Solorzano & Ornelas, 2002, 2004); the range and depth of cultural wealth within communities of color (Yosso, 2005, 2006); and the intersection of nativism and racism and its impact on Latina/o immigrant communities, particularly the undocumented[1] (Perez Huber et al., 2008). While far from exhaustive, these examples of educational research provide a glimpse of the breadth of work that has advanced how we use CRT to explore the educational experiences of students of color at all levels of the educational pipeline. Still, our work is not complete.

Our efforts to challenge deficit portrayals and highlight the experiences of those most neglected in academic discourses have led to most of the aforementioned studies' reliance on qualitative research methods, from person centered and critical ethnographies, to case studies and portraitures, and from *testimonios* to autoethnographies, to name a few. This collection of work has disrupted the more traditionally self-ascribed objectivity in most educational literature and created spaces of creativity and resistance both within and outside academic settings. CRT has begun to receive well-deserved acknowledgement as the literature expands. Yet the lessons from this work have not translated well to widespread improved policy to enhance educational conditions. Perhaps misinformed policymakers and practitioners challenge the qualitative findings' generalizability or the rigor of the research. Simonson (2005) claims, "some assert that the vast quantity of research studies published, especially doctoral dissertations, have had little if any impact on the practice of education," and that the U.S. Department of Education's new "stress on the importance of quantitative research designs, especially randomized trials, is a victory of sorts for educational traditionalists and, for many, is long overdue (Simonson, 2005, p. ix). These same critics' limited interpretation of the value of qualitative work is what restricts its ability to have a wider impact. Regardless of why, much of the lessons arising from qualitative CRT research have, unfortunately, gone without a major policy impact.

This chapter makes the argument that critical race quantitative intersectionality has the potential to provide a greater impact in the areas of research, policy, and practice, as it transforms the manner in which "the numbers" are derived and framed while, at the same time, aligning with the type of methodological expectations of research that policymakers are looking for. As a framework rooted in CRT, CRQI guides our questions, our sources of data, our analysis, and ultimately how we disseminate our work and put it to use. The examples of work highlighted here illustrate the possibility of a CRT approach for quantitative research, and were, thus, instrumental in the development of CRQI. We explore each of these examples as we define several guiding principles that we argue should direct the practice of CRQI. First, though, we contemplate the value of quantitative research as a first step in theorizing a working definition of CRQI.

CRITICAL RACE QUANTITATIVE RESEARCH—CAVEATS TO CONSIDER

There exists a false dichotomy between quantitative and qualitative research that often positions researchers to choose. Much of the research conducted from a critical race perspective has utilized qualitative research, as highlighted above, positioning quantitative work in the minority of studies published from a CRT perspective, particularly in education. While the importance of critical race qualitative work goes without question, the value of quantitative work is equally important. Kamil (2004) asserts that "progress in research is made by asking different questions (and thus using different methods) at different stages of knowledge about particular research areas" (p. 101). We assert that it is time for CRT to develop a framework to guide quantitative research that, we argue, adds value to the overall impact CRT has in the field of education. Doing this, though, requires several considerations.

First, it is imperative to avoid misusing race as a variable that reifies the logic of a biologically based construction of race (James, 2008). Zuberi (2001) traces how the white supremacist, Eugenicist movement in the U.S. after emancipation, led to the development of the modern fields of statistics, genetics, demography and psychology, in order to affirm and rank racial categories. The data, its analysis, methods, and dissemination were flawed and biased from the beginning. According to Zuberi (2001), "the act of enumeration was an act of defining the colony for the civilized European world. The premodern censuses were a key element in the colonial process of transforming the identity of the African [American Indian, Asian, and Latina/o] subject" (p. 118). He goes on to warn well-intentioned anti-racists about inadvertently solidifying the notion of biological race (as opposed to the social construction of race) when they apply race as a predicting variable. Instead, he calls for a "causal theory of manipulative causation," through which race should be considered an attribute of individuals in a population, but not a causal variable that can be manipulated (Zuberi, 2001, pp. 126–134). Still, this does not suggest that those interested in an anti-racist agenda should not engage racial statistics, but that we should be aware of their uses and limitations. Zuberi (2001) insists that "we place our statistical analysis of race within a historical context" and use it to come up with important associations that can form the "basis for support of a causal theory" (p. 133), and that, "[b]efore the data can be deracialized, we must deracialize the social circumstances that have created racial stratification" (p. 102). Thus, in our view, CRT must consider the possibility of using statistical methods as "scientific tools [of the master] and [recast] them for different purposes [that] can benefit both science and subordinate groups" (Hill Collins, 1998, p. 123).

Second, we must remember that statistics, as a form of applied mathematics, relies on a system of estimation that is inherently based on a statistician's understanding of the world and tells us more about statistical modeling than the "real" world itself (Zuberi, 2001). Thus, we cannot separate analysis from analyst (Bonilla-Silva & Zuberi, 2008). According to Bonilla-Silva and Zuberi (2008), "accepted practices of statistical analysis unfortunately are not the result of the logic of the methods, but a result of the consensus-making process within the discipline" (p. 8). Consequently, "numbers" not only fail to speak for themselves, but speak about the underlying views and biases of those who generated them. Based on this argument, is it possible, then, to conduct critically minded quantitative research if everyone, arguably, holds particular beliefs and understandings of society? We believe that the potential of this work rests not in its ability to be "objective" and "un-biased" but in how we foreground our positionality in connection to the research and contextualize our findings and analysis in relationship to our causal theories of how the world operates. Masking our intentions any other way gives undue power to statistical methods, when, in actuality, power rests in the theories used to interpret social data, whether implicitly or explicitly.

Last, and building from the first two, is recognizing that the disciplinary context in which we operate, as critical race quantitative researchers, remains primarily defined and led by white scholars (Bonilla-Silva & Zuberi, 2008). Although CRT work in the field of education has greatly benefited from critical white allies (Wise, 2010, 2012), the legacy of white supremacy in the social sciences remains alive and well (Bonilla-Silva & Zuberi, 2008). Should it surprise us when statistical methods continued to be (mis)used and racial categories rigidly defined to perpetuate an understanding of the world that further solidifies racial hierarchies? Conversely, though, scholars of color employing quantitative methods aren't necessarily immune to reproducing the same problematic ends as their white counterparts. While a challenge to the dominant practice of quantitative work on race is sorely needed, we must first question the normative training we have received from the very institutions and individuals that fail to engage the legacy of racism in quantitative work, and continue to unproblematically apply what they believe to be "objective" science to the study of race. Looking to scholars who have provided alternative models is a start (Hill Collins, 1998; Smith, 1999; Zuberi, 2001), but a constant vigilance on our part is critical, as researchers who have been trained by and are simultaneously working to challenge our institutions, which still operate under a white logic (Bonilla-Silva & Zuberi, 2008) (Bonilla-Silva & Zuberi, 2008) to methodologically prepare young scholars, even if they refuse to recognize it as such.

LAYING THE GROUNDWORK FOR CRQI: EXAMPLES AND LIMITATIONS

One example that points to the possibility and necessity of a critically informed model of quantitative research in education is the work of Petruccelli, who explores race relations and racial categorization in Brazil. Petruccelli (2007) finds that, in Brazil, the *Pardo* (brown) designation, while granting those who use it the ability to self-identify, hinders an accurate analysis of the racialization of people of African descent, which makes addressing racial injustice difficult. Specifically, he highlights how Brazilians of African ancestry use hundreds of different terms to identify themselves, making it difficult to implement recent affirmative action policies aimed at addressing racial injustice. By suggesting a social analysis that combines the *Pardo* (brown) and *Preto* (black) categories, Petruccelli (2007) argues that Brazil is better positioned to capture the experiences of individuals with similar contemporary experiences related to racism and discrimination. This alternative approach of enumerating historically marginalized populations unmasks the elusive racial categories that have been hidden by dominant assertions of race neutrality and ambiguity in Brazil (Pagano, 2006), and provides some interesting considerations for addressing racial injustice in the U.S. This work also avoids the unintended trap that Zuberi (2001) warns of, by not casting racial data as a variable that can lead to causal effect findings, but providing racial statistics that can lead to a more equitable approach to addressing past injustices.

Focused on a context outside of the U.S., Petruccelli did not explicitly use CRT as a guiding frame, but his work is arguably an example of critical race work that challenges us to find creative ways of reassessing data. Similarly, in education, critical race work on the educational pipeline has offered us a useful, parsimonious framework to examine the educational trajectories of students of color in the U.S., using census data. Not only does it provide a snapshot of educational attainment for various racialized communities, but it also offers us a framework for contextualizing other educational research, as it provides national or statewide data that highlight the "leakage points" where students exit from the educational system. Over time, the pipeline has been used to summarize the trends in educational outcomes and help us predict potential areas where we might focus our energies and resources to seal the "leakage points"; it has also pointed to new "entry points" to create greater access and opportunity for historically underrepresented communities. Many use it as a descriptive model that provides solely context and trending information, which is a useful approach that is the most used in social sciences (Zuberi, 2001). However, its functionality is much more than this. We argue that CRQI can lead us to glean greater transformational utility from this and other quantitative models, but first we must explore the type of data we use and how it has been defined.

National datasets, like the census, help us understand changing demographics across time and space for the U.S., but are not without shortcomings. When viewed from a critical stance, these types of data are limited because of how racial/ethnic communities have been historically categorized and analyzed. This is particularly true when it comes to Latina/o ethnic groups, such as those of Mexican origin. From a U.S. census or mainstream demographic standpoint, individuals of Mexican origin are discussed as an ethnic or national group, but not viewed as a historically racialized group who constitute the numeric majority in many large cities throughout the American Southwest and a growing proportion in cities throughout the country. The U.S. census has not provided a racial category "box" for the Mexican population, or any other Latina/o ethnic group for that matter, with the exception of the 1930 decennial census.[2] This has resulted in many categorizing themselves as either "white" or "other," which, we argue, has operated to misrepresent the realities of ethnic groups *within* the Latina/o diasporas (Pew Hispanic Center, 2008). Since many Latinas/os identify themselves as white, owing to the narrow categories provided, and many Mexican origin populations are collapsed within a broader Latina/o category, we find it difficult to address issues of injustice for this group over time and/or within geographic boundaries. Furthermore, when you add the issue of how to account for those considered undocumented among those of Mexican origin, things become even more complicated and obscure. The ambiguity that exists about the undocumented U.S. population makes it difficult to fully capture the extent of injustice they face, because the count of undocumented individuals within the U.S. is a rough estimate at best. The census falls short in its predictive ability to help us understand their educational attainment rates among other social indicators. Hence, we are challenged to apply race centered analyses or policy recommendations for particular populations using census data. Furthermore, we must be clear that race and ethnicity data non-critically collected by the census is essentializing and has had a history of homogenizing heterogeneous groups (Zuberi, 2001). This should be taken into account when collecting and analyzing data.

Despite the aforementioned challenges, our search for a critically informed quantitative methodology has allowed us to capture what we feel is the most reliable intersectional analysis of the influence of race, class, gender, and citizenship for the undocumented Mexican origin population in the U.S. (Covarrubias & Lara, forthcoming). While others have provided important data about this population (Abrego & Gonzales, 2010; Perez, 2010; Pew Hispanic Center, 2008), the intersectional nuances of educational attainment have been missed by research not guided by critical theoretical frameworks. Teranishi's (2007) work begins to fill this gap, providing an important analysis in building a case for the value of quantitative work within CRT. He argues that a critical race centered quantitative approach can elucidate the hidden diversity that exists within the Asian American population, and other racialized populations. Often made "invisible" for their high visibility within institutions of higher education, Asian Americans are often ignored when policies are adopted to address educational injustice. Assumed as collectively having "made it," the Asian American population is often not disaggregated to reveal the high rates of poverty, low educational attainment, and general lack of resources that some Asian subgroups experience (Covarrubias & Liou, forthcoming; Lui et al., 2006). Thus, the model minority myth that pervades mainstream discussions about super-achieving Asians limits our ability to make sound policy recommendations that address the low educational outcomes of low-income Southeast Asian subgroups (Teranishi, 2007; Thrupkaew, 2002). These and other limitations of work that homogenizes historically diverse populations with unique histories and particular educational experiences demand that we call for a quantitative research methodology that is both critical and intersectional. Critical race quantitative intersectionality is about finding ways to address this concern by offering creative solutions to more accurately account for communities of color and intersectionally disaggregate populations. CRQI, delineated in the next section, aims to disentangle data that often camouflages the interests of the dominant group.

TOWARD CRITICAL RACE QUANTITATIVE INTERSECTIONALITY: A WORKING FRAMEWORK FOR QUANTITATIVE RESEARCH

CRQI is a framework to guide our quantitative research and one that challenges us to explore the material impact of intersectionality.[3] It is a working framework, far from definitive and complete, yet an important step in re-imagining quantitative work for social justice ends. We offer it as a starting point for advancing quantitative research in education that is guided by CRT. With its origins in CRT, the guiding principles of CRQI are intentionally framed in such a way as to parallel CRT's guiding tenets and thus add to the critical body of research already being produced by CRT scholars in education.

It is important to first underscore the relationship between CRQI and CRT. As a theory, CRT is grounded in a set of principles based on facts, observations, and/or experiences that help us understand, explain, and predict phenomena centered on race and its intersection with other social categories and guide anti-racist and anti-oppressive scholarship. In addition, in challenging the traditionally proclaimed neutrality of research, critical race scholars assert that theory can also aim to transform, which makes our theory praxis. CRQI, on the other hand, is not a theory, but rather a framework guided by CRT. As a framework, CRQI offers a set of principles grounded in CRT that provide the basis for incorporating quantitative research in our work, and it is intended to be developed further, along with the methods that it utilizes. It is a framework that has developed from our desire to expand CRT and the impact of our research in transforming educational policy and practice. Given our objectives, we first provide the following working definition of CRQI to aid us in defining its guiding principles in the next section:

> Critical race quantitative intersectionality is an explanatory framework and methodological approach that utilizes quantitative methods to account for the material impact of race and racism at its intersection with other forms of subordination and works toward identifying and challenging oppression at this intersection in hopes of achieving social justice for students of color, their families, and their communities.

Through our efforts to define CRQI we hope to extend a theoretical examination of racism and intersectionality by focusing on its material impact. We look to CRQI to help us explore the material conditions created at the intersection, not only the discursive impact of intersectionality. It is about shedding light on how social constructions shape the lived experiences of people of color. For example, how does education impact earning power for different racial groups of different citizenship statuses (Covarrubias & Liou, forthcoming)? These and other similar, materially grounded questions can and should be addressed by CRQI.

CRQI exposes the "racial compensation" that over time has led to disparate racial surpluses and racial deficits accumulated by a racial tax imposed on people of color and the racial shelters provided whites (Carbado, 2011, pp. 1608–1609). The accumulated racial compensation transferred over generations helps define the economy of the racial hierarchy that has resulted in the typical white family having 20 times the net worth of African American and 18 times the net worth of Latina/o families (Wise, 2012). Still, this homogenizing narrative of communities of color hides the lower average income and education levels of different sex Latina/o couples in California when compared with same sex Latina/o couples in the state (Konnoth, 2011), the types of "opportunities" available to citizens compared to undocumented students (Abrego & Gonzales, 2010), the advantages continuing-generation students have compared to first-generation college students in institutions of higher education (Stephens et al., 2012), and the disparate compensation afforded Asian American men and women with similar educational attainment to white men and women (Covarrubias & Liou, forthcoming). In the end, non-intersectional analyses conceal the intra-group differences and elide the fact that "different status identity holders within any given social group are differently situated with respect to how much, and the form of, discrimination they are likely to face" (Carbado & Gulati, 2001, p. 702).

Critical race scholarship produced over the last two decades re-evaluates race and racism in education. We have not only witnessed greater attention granted to the impact of racism, but we have also seen evidence of new conceptualizations about the concept. Scholars have not only illuminated the intersectional nature of race, but paid closer attention to the growing significance of race at all levels of the educational pipeline. It is within this context that we offer the following guiding principles of CRQI, which are inspired by the guiding tenets of CRT in education (Delgado Bernal, 2002; Ladson-Billings, 1998; Ladson-Billings & Tate, 1995; Solorzano, 1998; Yosso, 2006). For each of the principles we delineate below, we offer examples of current work employing CRQI in an effort to better illuminate how CRQI builds from and extends CRT work in education and provides scholars additional tools for conducting anti-racist research.

I Quantifying the Material Impact of Racism at Its Intersections: Intersectional Data Mining

Since quantitative research is ultimately about searching for answers by collecting, computing, analyzing, and synthesizing data, CRQI focuses on the critical manipulation and contextualizing of data that can be measured or expressed in numerical terms. We start from the belief that no data, including numerical data, can in and of itself explain anything—in other words, the numbers cannot "speak for themselves." Even the analytical strategies and tools used to manipulate and analyze quantitative data are inventions created within a specific context, and one that was openly white supremacist (Bonilla-Silva & Zuberi, 2008; Gould, 1996; Zuberi, 2001). Furthermore, just as the earlier quantification of the biological sciences was fraught with errors in measurement (Kuhn, 1961), a modern version of these errors is found in today's social sciences, in the form of errors of causality with weak causal theories (Zuberi, 2001). This context shapes the meaning of these numbers and the strategies and tools used for analyses. Thus we argue that the theoretical assumptions of any quantitative research should be made explicit and guide the collection, computation, analyses, and reporting of data.

Our first assumption is that the "intersection" is not only an ideological and discursive idea, but also a real space that is shaped by and shapes the material conditions for those who exist within it, be it temporarily or permanently (Covarrubias, 2005). This intersection is created by the interconnected social constructions[4] that have been used to categorize and define those within it. These social constructions are both flexible enough to quickly transform in the interest of the dominant group, and permanent enough so that they create longstanding hierarchies that benefit those with power and privilege. Social constructions are typically set up in binaries or rigid, essentializing categories, but are probably best explored with a critical eyeing of their existence as continuums. These social constructions are mechanisms by which society and its institutions disseminate resources, status, and power, often privileging one group over all others, but arranging all in existing interlocking hierarchies.

With these social constructions as the basis, we often create ideologies that can create and sustain inequality. For example, gender is a social construction that has been shaped over time to privilege men above women, or the masculine over the feminine (Lorber, 1995). We also know that these constructions are homogenizing, because they mask the diversity that exists within them, and these omissions often serve to prioritize the interest of the most dominant within the category. For example, women of color have long critiqued the early feminist movement as rigidly focused on the interest of white, middle-class, straight women, concealing the interests and experiences of diverse women of color. CRQI calls for a multidimensional analysis of power-based relationships. This methodology challenges the use of singular analytical lenses that reduce people to essentialized and homogenizing units of larger ambiguous, political, social, and often legal categories used to distribute power. Instead we see people as being multidimensional and having various power-based relationships with other individuals, groups, and institutions (Covarrubias, 2011a).

Thus, when we are presented with crudely homogenizing data, we heed the call of Mari Matsuda, to "ask the other question" (Matsuda, 1991, 1996). Although Chicanas/os collectively have the lowest educational attainment rates compared to other racial and ethnic groups, we challenge ourselves to search for within-group differences. For example, in previous work on the educational pipeline, Covarrubias and Lara (forthcoming) have been able to isolate groups by citizenship status (i.e. U.S. born and foreign born naturalized citizens compared to those considered undocumented non-citizens), gender, and class. By asking the other question, our intersectional analysis of the Chicana/o educational pipeline reveals that citizenship status has a unique influence on educational attainment that helps account for the low outcomes at all levels of the pipeline for undocumented students of Mexican origin. Without this intersectional analysis, we confound many of the constructions that result in unique, within-group differences. This analysis also demonstrates the significant advantages that Chicanas/os of middle- to upper-class status have over their working-class counterparts, a revelation often lost in general reporting on the aggregated Chicana/o population.

II Challenging the Neutrality of Quantitative Data: Numbers Do Not "Speak for Themselves"

When measurement departs from theory, it is likely to yield mere numbers, and their very neutrality makes them particularly sterile as a source of remedial suggestions. But numbers register the departure from theory with an authority and finesse that no qualitative technique can duplicate, and that departure is often enough to start a search.

(Kuhn, 1961, p. 180)

The epigraph above demonstrates both the over-reliance on "numbers" and the fact that the numbers mean little without their framing narrative. Often, numbers are framed by people who use them in such a way as to protect those in power, or the constructions that maintain their privilege, like whiteness, masculinity, and loyalty and submission to the nation-state. CRQI argues that quantitative analyses must be contextualized by a critical theoretical framework that is able to deconstruct their traditional use and claims of neutrality and objectivity.

For example, the model minority myth that has been used to explain the high level of Asian American educational attainment exemplifies how numbers are often utilized to protect overarching ideologies that maintain inequality. The myth holds that, despite their "foreignness" and presumed language and cultural barriers, Asians have been able to overcome prejudice. Furthermore, their success suggests that prejudice may no longer be a formidable barrier in America if this ethnic minority group is able to overcome it (Thrupkaew, 2002). In contrast, the academic "failure" of African Americans and Latinas/os often signals to mainstream observers their lack of effort, their cultural deficiency, or the non-existent assets of their community. Of course, this is a non-critical and non-intersectional analysis. Covarrubias and Liou's (forthcoming) intersectional disaggregation of the Asian American educational pipeline uncovers wide within-group differences within this population that are shaped by gender, citizenship, and class. Teranishi (2007) found that recent Southeast Asian immigrants have low educational outcomes that are restricted by poverty rates that exceed those of Latinas/os and African Americans, limited economic opportunities, high unemployment rates, little English-speaking ability, and neglect by policymakers.

III Originating from the Experiential and Material Experiences of People of Color

Our ongoing quantitative research is grounded in experiential knowledge. Covarrubias's work organizing high school push-outs in East and South Los Angeles (Covarrubias,

2011b), for example, has guided his research on this population, as have the experiences of many members of his family and friends with failing schools. Similarly, Vélez's work organizing with migrant parents in northern and southern California guides her critical race spatial analyses of the hostile social, political conditions these communities encounter. We draw from what Delgado Bernal (1998) describes as cultural intuition, the theoretical sensitivity developed through personal experience (including community memory and collective experience), literature review, professional experience, and the analytical research process which Chicana/o scholars utilize to gain a deeper insight of their research site and their informants. As Chicana/o scholars who have worked several years as organizers and allies within communities, we employ our intuition to understand the experiences of low-income, migrant communities of color as they are impacted by the "intersection" in a historically contextualized manner.

While this principle closely mirrors the tenet of CRT qualitative research that insists on drawing from experiential knowledge in both research and the classroom, we offer additional considerations when conducting quantitative research. Similarly to other standpoint analyses (Delgado Bernal, 1998; Harding 1990, 1992, 1994; Hartsock, 1987; Hill Collins, 1986, 1991; Smith, 1987), critical race scholars argue that starting from the lived experience of communities of color, or those at the bottom of the well (Bell, 1992), is not only valid and relevant for understanding inequality in American education, but necessary (Pizarro, 1998; Solorzano, 1998; Yosso, 2006). Along these lines, we argue that the "bottom" is a mobile and relative position, as it is shaped by both time and space. Thus we seek an intersectional analysis rather than one that is solely guided by a race-based, or gender-based, investigation (Covarrubias, 2011a), and we are not limited by dichotomous conceptualizations of social constructions, like the black–white paradigm of race, which is often presented as a limiting framework for understanding race and racism in America, but is also mainly constructed by those in power who authored it with an interest in protecting whiteness (Carbado, 2011).

For example, Covarrubias and Liou's (forthcoming) investigations of the Asian American educational pipeline's impact on earning power reject the idea that racism only happens to the most vulnerable. Often, some Asian American subgroups' experiences with racism are diminished because of their relative educational and occupational success when compared to other communities of color (Sethi, 1994). We have found that, relative to their white counterparts, educationally successful Asian Americans' earning power is depressed, even when the educational attainment is controlled (Covarrubias & Liou, forthcoming), demonstrating the mobility of the "bottom."

In other work, our cultural intuition has led us to investigate the impact of space on Chicana/o educational attainment. Using a developing CRQI methodology within CRT known as critical race spatial analysis (Pacheco & Velez, 2009), our findings demonstrate that there is a correlation between a state's percentage of Chicanas/os and the rate of Chicana/o high school push-outs, such that there is a higher rate of push-outs in states where there is a larger concentration of people of Mexican origin (Covarrubias & Velez, 2011). This data calls into question the educational policy, structure, and practices that shape educational conditions where Mexican origin individuals are largely concentrated. Lastly, in a study of over 400 Los Angeles high school push-outs, Covarrubias (2011b) found that Chicanos were significantly much more likely to have internalized deficit-based frameworks to explain their premature school exit compared to Chicanas, helping shed light on differential outcomes based on the intersection between race and gender.

Not only were all these studies quantitative, but they were all originally conceived from our lived experiences as English-language-learning children of immigrants and first-generation college graduates and our working-class experiences as students of color. Additionally, the guiding questions for all these projects were developed together with those on whom our research was based, demonstrating our commitment to transforming the research process by collaborating with agents outside of academic institutions. Our research questions, our data analysis, and the transformative intent of our scholarship are rooted in our personal and professional experiences.

IV Being Intentionally Committed to Addressing Injustice and Seeking Transformation

CRQI is guided by a commitment to social justice that aims to transform educational policy and practice. Our work has never been only about understanding, explaining, and predicting educational inequities. It is primarily driven by the goals of educational and social transformation. Through our work, we look to shape funding and other resources that will move us towards educational and broader social equity. We understand that typically quantitative data is privileged in terms of justifying broad policy change because of its assumed value for scaling up educational interventions. Although we have unpacked and critiqued these assumptions above, we believe in its utility for educational reform if employed through a critical lens. CRQI aims to do just that.

By grounding quantitative analyses through a CRT lens, we argue CRQI offers a more appropriate and more authentic portrayal of the material intersections affecting students of color. By challenging the homogenizing tendencies of traditional quantitative research, CRQI allows us to better understand the conditions affecting those whose interests are lost within data that relies on singular dimensions of reality. Thus, when data analyzed through CRQI is shared in the form of research articles, reports, and/or presentations, its impact on policy will yield greater returns for better understanding and addressing the educational issues facing these diverse communities.

But our work is not only intended for academic publication. We also strive to work with and collaborate with community members whose voices are often unheard in academic discourse, to participate in the creation, implementation, analyses, and dissemination of research. While methodological approaches like community-based action research are uncommon in quantitative work, within a CRQI frame they are not only important to consider, but encouraged. In our recent work using critical race spatial analysis (CRSA), we employed action research and collaborated with Latina/o immigrant families in the production and dissemination of maps that quantitatively captured the historical legacy of racism in their school district. These families not only identified unrecognized, but critical, data sources to construct a powerful counter-cartographic narrative of racism and resistance in their community, but their involvement in each step of the research process ensured that the final product had value for their efforts in schools as much as it had value for challenging deficit portrayals of Latina/o families in educational research. They went on to use these maps in a community forum they organized to shed light on oppressive practices in their local district *and* presented at a national educational conference about their efforts to disrupt the majoritarian narrative of Latina/o immigrant families in public schools (Asociación de Padres de Pasadena Luchando por la Educación, 2011).

Highlighted by the previous example, we argue that CRQI actively pursues unexplored questions from the standpoint of those who have been marginalized and encourages engaged models of research in creating products that can be useful on the ground. Our grassroots work attests to the importance we both feel in making sure our work is accountable to the students and parents we serve. Thus, in considering possible readership and audiences for our work, CRQI calls on scholars to develop strategies from the start to ensure that students, parents, and communities will not only have access to, but will be able to make use of, their research. This includes identifying vehicles for publication that speak to a broader public and will, thus, have greater reach for using data in ways that bring about reform.

V Taking a Transdisciplinary Perspective and Methods for Revealing Elusive and Hidden Patterns

As social scientists, we have learned from our training and professional experiences that our work must draw from and contribute to multiple disciplinary traditions in order to be most effective in its transformative intent and in its ability to provide a more complete account of our social world. CRQI engages the theoretical and methodological traditions of ethnic studies, women's studies, queer studies, geography, sociology, psychology, and other fields both inside and outside education. Our transdisciplinary stance has led us to utilize effective tools for considering new problematics in education.

As briefly highlighted above, critical race spatial analysis, a research approach that informs and is informed by CRQI, draws heavily from the fields of geography, urban planning, and visual sociology, in addition to critical race scholarship in education. By bringing together critical work on space from different disciplines, CRSA illuminates how specific spatial features or markers, like a street or freeway, can become inscribed with important racial meaning that has particular consequences for the schools that co-exist near these spatial features or are affected by how these features are used. It builds from the recent work of other education scholars who are exploring the relationship between spatial arrangements and opportunity structures through the use of geographic information systems (GIS) technologies (Hogrebe & Tate, 2012; Tate & Hogrebe, 2011), but extends this work using CRT explicitly in order to craft a spatial, counter-cartographic narrative about the central role of race and racism in mediating this relationship.

CRSA affords critical race scholars in education an opportunity to explore space and the socio-spatial dimensions of race and racism in innovative and creative ways. The benefit of CRSA's capacity to explore spatial patterns related to critical race inquiry rest, in large part, on its ability to draw from these multiple disciplines and extend its analytical power to include fields not commonly used in critical race research. For example, our current work looks to employ CRSA to conduct a community-based action research project on the spatial identities and experiences of undocumented students on college campuses and in their communities. Using GIS technologies, a group of undocumented college students will use mobile GIS devices to identify which spaces, both in and outside of school, are particularly critical to their survival and successful navigation in higher education. They will also identify those spaces, on the flipside, that have been especially hostile toward the same ends. Yet, because of the tracking and analytical capacities of GIS, the project also intends to monitor the physiological responses of these students as they enter and leave certain spaces, drawing from recent work in social psychology (Blascovich et al., 2001; Purdie-Vaughns et al., 2008; Steele, 1997, 2010; Steele & Aronson, 1995; Tomaka et al., 1993). Using heart rate monitoring devices along with GIS tools, the goal is to determine whether these students experience a physiological change as they engage with particular spaces. Combined with recorded narrative that simultaneously captures their experiences as they move in and through spaces, the physiological and spatial data gathered from this project will contribute powerfully to recent critical race scholarship on racial battle fatigue (Smith et al., 2006). We highlight this current study not only to demonstrate the transformative potential of this work but to underscore its transdisciplinary nature, which extends into the field of medicine and psychology in addition to the several fields from which CRSA already draws.

CONCLUSION

When we set out to employ quantitative approaches in our work, we do so not in place of qualitative inquiry, but rather along with it. CRQI seeks to provide a guide to expand the functionality of CRT in understanding the material impact of intersectionality, but it also seeks to grant us greater opportunities to effect change at the policy level. Both quantitative and qualitative methods are essential for capturing the specific nuances of educational trends—the lives behind the numbers. These numbers mean little unless we delve into the processes and stories about those living "at the bottom of the well" and their relationship to institutions and society. CRQI-framed research must start and end from the stories of people's lives; they are not mutually exclusive. Indeed, we are calling for more quantitative work in critical race scholarship that adds to and complements the extensive body of qualitative work that currently exists. But it is important that we understand CRQI work as not independent of qualitative work, but necessarily informed by it. As we have attempted to articulate above, we see ourselves at the intersection of quantitative work and qualitative work. By grounding ourselves at this intersection, we argue that CRQI extends our critical race research toolbox and helps us develop the necessary skills that satisfy the tenets of critical race scholarship, both quantitatively and qualitatively, and supports our efforts to transform the lives of the communities we serve through our work, in large part, because of its ability to impact policy.

Not only is CRQI about how we capture, analyze, report, and disseminate data, but it is also about how we ask questions and what methods we use to pursue those queries. This work seeks to de-homogenize diverse communities of color and find creative ways to "mine" the data. Through it, we seek to better understand and transform how power divides communities and how these demarcations shape the material experiences and opportunities at the intersection. A power-blind approach to understanding our divisions leads many to blindly accept the deep fissures that are created to sustain the current power relationships between groups and with institutions. Only by engaging in a more complete and authentic understanding of power and how it shapes our realities along intersecting dimensions can we truly begin to work toward a more comprehensive commitment to loosening the vice grip of that power.

NOTES

1 In this chapter, *undocumented* is used to refer to immigrants who come to the U.S. without "proper" documentation that would otherwise permit them legal authority to reside within the borders of the U.S. It is important to note that this label is highly contested. We use this term cautiously, recognizing its problematic nature in defining or framing U.S. immigrants from a nation-state position without adequately recognizing global conditions that have led many individuals to risk their lives to cross the border without this documentation. We have chosen to use this term in lieu of other terms in public discourse, such as *illegal* or *alien*, because the latter

serve to inhumanely criminalize and demonize the immigrant population, particularly Latina/o immigrants in contemporary U.S. society.

2 This historic moment was marked by large numbers of unemployed Americans as a result of the Great Depression, which offered racist policymakers the excuse for blaming Mexicans for the worst economic conditions in American history. Presumably, this initiated two decades of repatriation efforts that resulted in over one million Mexican origin Americans being deported to Mexico, many of whom were U.S. born citizens who had never set foot in Mexico (Balderama & Rodríguez, 1995).

3 Intersectionality refers to the simultaneous impact of systems of power that result in privilege and marginalization, neglect, or omission for distinctly constructed groups. Intersectionality lies at the points of overlap between racism, sexism, classism, nativism, and other interconnected systems. Although the theorizing around intersectionality has been thorough, it is still incomplete, and the field is largely debating its utility, application, and definition (Bowleg, 2008; Carbado, 2011; Carbado & Gulati, 2001; Crenshaw, 1989, 1991).

4 Social constructions are the context-specific, hierarchically arranged categories that we have used to define and assign value to difference. Rothenberg describes social constructions as "culturally constructed differences that maintain the prevailing distribution of power and privilege in society, and they change in relation to changes in social, political, and economic life" (Rothenberg, 2010, p. 8).

BIBLIOGRAPHY

Abrego, L.J., & Gonzales, R.G. (2010). Blocked paths, uncertain futures: The postsecondary education and labor market prospects of undocumented Latino youth. *Journal of Education for Students Placed at Risk, 14,* 144–157.

Asociación de Padres de Pasadena Luchando por la Educación. (2011). Analyzing Paulo Freire's problem-posing methodology in a Latina/o immigrant parents' organization. American Educational Research Assocation Conference, New Orleans, LA.

Balderama, F., & Rodríguez, R. (1995). *Decade of betrayal: Mexican repatriation in the 1930s.* Albuquerque: University of New Mexico Press.

Bell, D. (1992). *Faces at the bottom of the well: The permanence of racism.* New York: Basic Books.

Blascovich, J., Spencer, S.J., Quinn, D., & Steele, C.M. (2001). African Americans and high blood pressure. *Psychological Science, 13*(3), 225–229.

Bonilla-Silva, E., & Zuberi, T. (2008). Toward a definition of white logic and white methods. In T. Zuberi & E. Bonilla-Silva (Eds.), *White logic, white methods: Racism and methodology* (pp. 3–27). Lanham, MD: Rowman & Littlefield.

Bowleg, L. (2008). When black + lesbian + woman ≠ black lesbian woman: The methodological challenges of qualitative and quantitative intersectionality research. *Sex Roles, 59,* 312–325.

Carbado, D.W. (2011). Afterword: Critical what what? *Connecticut Law Review, 43*(5), 1593–1643.

Carbado, D.W., & Gulati, M. (2001). The fifth black woman. *Journal of Contemporary Legal Issues, 11,* 701–729.

Covarrubias, A. (2005). Agencies of transformational resistance: Transforming the intersection of race, class, gender, and sexuality oppression through Latino critical race theory (LatCrit) and praxis. Unpublished doctoral dissertation, University of California, Los Angeles.

Covarrubias, A. (2011a). Quantitative intersectionality: A critical race analysis of the Chicana/o educational pipeline. *Journal of Latinos and Education, 10*(2), 86–105.

Covarrubias, A. (2011b). The busted educational pipeline: Examining the leakage points in our educational pipeline. (Covarrubias, Alejandro, Performer.) California State University, University Student Union, Los Angeles Room, Los Angeles, CA.

Covarrubias, A., & Lara, A. (forthcoming). The undocumented (im)migrant educational pipeline: The influence of citizenship on educational attainment for people of Mexican origin. *Urban Education.*

Covarrubias, A., & Liou, D. (forthcoming). Asian American educational and income attainment in the era of post racial America.

Covarrubias, A., & Velez, V. (2011). The Chicana/o educational pipeline "in space": Using GIS to explore the socio-spatial dimensions of Chicana/o educational attainment. Unpublished paper presented at Annual Conference of the American Educational Research Association, April, New Orleans, LA.

Crenshaw, K. (1989). Demarginalizing the intersection of race and sex: A black feminist critique of antidiscrimination doctrine, feminist theory and antiracist politics. *University of Chicago Legal Forum, 1989,* 139–166.

Crenshaw, K. (1991). Mapping the margins: Intersectionality, identity politics, and violence against women of color. *Stanford Law Review, 43,* 1241–1252.

Delgado Bernal, D. (1998). Using a Chicana feminist epistemology in educational research. *Harvard Educational Review, 68*(4), 555–582.

Delgado Bernal, D. (2002). Critical race theory, Latino critical theory, and critical race-gendered epistemologies: Recognizing students of color as holders and creators of knowledge. *Qualitative Inquiry, 8*(1), 105–126.

Gould, S.J. (1996). *The mismeasure of man.* New York: W.W. Norton.

Harding, S. (1990). Feminism and theories of scientific knowledge. *Women, 1*(1), 87–89.

Harding, S. (1992). After the neutrality ideal: Science, politics, and "strong objectivity." *Social Research, 59*(3), 567–587.

Harding, S. (1994). Is science multicultural? Challenges, resources, opportunities, uncertainties. In D.T. Goldberg (Ed.), *Multiculturalism: A reader.* Oxford: Blackwell.

Hartsock, N. (1987). The feminist standpoint: Developing the ground for a specifically feminist historical materialism. In S. Harding (Ed.), *Feminism and methodology* (pp. 157–180). Bloomington: Indiana University Press.

Hill Collins, P.H. (1986). Learning from the outsider-within: The sociological significance of black feminist thought. In M.M. Fonow & J. Cook (Eds.), *Beyond methodology: Feminist scholarship as lived research.* Bloomington: Indiana University Press.

Hill Collins, P.H. (1991). *Black feminist thought: Knowledge, consciousness, and the politics of empowerment.* New York: Routledge.

Hill Collins, P. (1998). *Fighting words: Black women and the search for justice.* Minneapolis: University of Minnesota Press.

Hogrebe, M., & Tate, W.F. (2012). Geospatial perspective: Toward a visual political literacy project in education, health, and human services. *Review of Research in Education, 36*, 67–94.

James, A. (2008). Making sense of race and racial classification. In T. Zuberi & E. Bonilla-Silva (Eds.), *White logic, white methods: Racism and methodology* (pp. 3–27). Lanham, MD: Rowman & Littlefield.

Kamil, M.L. (2004). The current state of quantitative research. *Reading Research Quarterly, 39*(1), 100–107.

Konnoth, C.J. (2011). *Testimony on the demographic characteristics of gay, lesbian and bisexual Latinos and Latinos in same-sex couples.* UCLA, UCLA School of Law. Los Angeles: Williams Institute.

Kuhn, T.S. (1961). The function of measurement in modern physical science. *Isis, 52*(2), 161–193.

Ladson-Billings, G. (1998). Just what is critical race theory and what is it doing in a nice field like education? *Qualitative Studies in Education, 11*(1), 7–24.

Ladson-Billings, G., & Tate, W.F. (1995). Toward a critical race theory of education. *Teachers College Record, 97*(1), 47–68.

Lorber, J. (1995). "Night to his day": The social construction of gender. In *Paradoxes of gender* (pp. 13–35). New Haven, CT: Yale University Press.

Lui, M., Robles, B., Leondar-Wright, B., Brewer, R., & Adamson, R. (2006). The perils of being yellow: Asian Americans as perpetual foreigners. In *The color of wealth: The story behind the US racial wealth divide* (pp. 177–224). New York: New Press.

Matsuda, M. (1991). Beside my sister, facing the enemy: Legal theory out of coalition. *Stanford Law Review, 43*, 1183–1189.

Matsuda, M. (1996). *Where is your body? And other essays on race, gender and the law.* Boston, MA: Beacon Press.

Pacheco, D., & Velez, V.N. (2009). Maps, mapmaking, and critical pedagogy: Exploring GIS and maps as a teaching tool for social change. *Seattle Journal for Social Justice, 8*(1), 273–302.

Pagano, A. (2006). The "Americanization" of racial identity in Brazil: Recent experiments with affirmative action in a "racial democracy." *Journal of International Policy Solutions, 5*, 9–25.

Perez, W. (2010). Higher education access for undocumented students: Recommendations for counseling professionals. *Journal of College Admission, 206*, 32–35.

Perez Huber, L., Benavidez Lopes, C., Malagon, M., Velez, V., & Solórzano, D. (2008). Getting beyond the "symptom," acknowledging the "disease": theorizing racist nativism. *Contemporary Justice Review, 11*(1), 39–51.

Petruccelli, J.L. (2007). Brazilian ethnoracial classification and affirmative action policies: Where are we and where do we go? *International conference on social statistics and ethnic diversity: Should we count, how should we count, and why?* Québec, Montréal: Interuniversitaire Québécois de Statistiques Sociales, Université du Québec, Montréal.

Pew Hispanic Center. (2008). *Pew Hispanic Center tabulations of 2008 American Community Survey (1% IPUMS).* Washington, DC: Pew Hispanic Center.

Pizarro, M. (1998). Chicana and Chicano power! *Qualitative Studies in Education, 11*(1), 43–55.

Purdie-Vaughns, V., Steele, C.M., Davies, P.G., Ditlmann, R., & Randall Crosby, J. (2008). Social identity contingencies: How diversity cues signal threat or safety for African Americans in mainstream institutions. *Journal of Personality and Social Psychology, 94*(4), 615–630.

Rothenberg, P.S. (2010). *Race, class and gender in the United States: An integrated study* (8th ed.). New York: Worth Publishers.

Said, E. (1978). *Orientalism.* New York: Vintage Books.

Sethi, R.C. (1994). Smells like racism: A plan for mobilizing against anti-Asian bias. In K. Aguilar-San Juan (Ed.), *The state of Asian America: Activism and resistance in the 1990s* (pp. 235–249). Boston, MA: South End Press.

Simonson, M. (2005). Quantitative research returns: Why did it leave? *Quarterly Review of Distance Education*, *6*(3), ix–x.

Smith, D. (1987). Women's perspective as a radical critique of sociology. In S. Harding (Ed.), *Feminism and methodology* (pp. 84–96). Bloomington: Indiana University Press.

Smith, L.T. (1999). *Decolonizing methodologies: Research and indigenous peoples*. New York: Zed Books.

Smith, W., Yosso, T., & Solorzano, D. (2006). Challenging racial battle fatigue on historically white campuses: A critical race examination of race-related stress. In C.A. Stanley (Ed.), *Faculty of color: Teaching in predominantly white colleges and universities* (pp. 299–327). Bolton, MA: Anker Publishing.

Solorzano, D. (1998). Critical race theory, race and gender microaggressions, and the experience of Chicana and Chicano scholars. *Qualitative Studies in Education*, *11*(1), 121–136.

Solorzano, D., & Ornelas, A. (2002). A critical race analysis of advanced placement classes: A case of educational inequality. *Journal of Latinos in Education*, *1*, 215–229.

Solorzano, D., & Ornelas, A. (2004). A critical race analysis of Latina/o and African American advanced placement enrollment in public schools. *High School Journal*, *87*(3), 15–26.

Solorzano, D., Ceja, M., & Yosso, T. (2000). Critical race theory, racial microaggressions, and campus racial climate: The experiences of African American college students. *Journal of Negro Education*, *69*(1/2), 60–73.

Steele, C.M. (1997). A threat in the air: How stereotypes shape intellectual identity and performance. *American Psychologist*, *52*(6), 613–629.

Steele, C.M. (2010). *Whistling Vivaldi: And other clues to how stereotypes affect us*. New York: W.W. Norton.

Steele, C.M., & Aronson, J. (1995). Stereotype threat and the intellectual test performance of African Americans. *Journal of Personality and Social Psychology*, *69*(5), 797–811.

Stephens, N.M., Fryberg, S.A., Markus, H.R., Johnson, C.S., & Covarrubias, R. (2012). Unseen disadvantage: How American universities' focus on independence undermines the academic performance of first-generation college students. *Journal of Personality and Social Psychology*, *102*(6), 1178–1197.

Tate, W.F., & Hogrebe, M. (2011). From visuals to vision: Using GIS to inform civic dialogue about African American males. *Race, Ethnicity and Education*, *14*(1), 51–71.

Teranishi, R.T. (2007). Race, ethnicity, and higher education policy: The use of critical quantitative research. *New Directions for Insititutional Research*, *133*, 37–49.

Thrupkaew, N. (2002). The myth of the model minority. *American Prospect*, *13*(7), 38–41.

Tomaka, J., Blascovich, J., Kelsey, R.M., & Leitten, C.L. (1993). Subjective, physiological, and behavioral effects of threat and challenge appraisal. *Journal of Personality and Social Psychology*, *65*(2), 248–260.

U.S. Census Bureau. (2010). *Current population survey (CPS)* (retrieved August 4, 2010 from http://www.census.gov/cps/).

U.S. Census Bureau. (2010). *Census.gov* (retrieved October 12, 2011 from http://factfinder.census.gov/home/saff/aff_transition.html).

Wise, T. (2010). *Colorblind: The rise of post-racial politics and the retreat from racial equity*. San Francisco, CA: City Lights Books.

Wise, T. (2012). *Dear White America: Letter to a minority*. San Francisco, CA: City Lights Books.

Yosso, T. (2005). Whose culture has capital? A critical race theory discussion of community cultural wealth. *Race, Ethnicity and Education*, *8*(1), 69–91.

Yosso, T. (2006). *Critical race counterstories along the Chicana/o educational pipeline*. New York: Routledge.

Yosso, T., Ceja, M., Smith, W., & Solorzano, D. (2009). Critical race theory, racial microaggressions, and campus racial climate for Latina/o undergraduates. *Harvard Educational Review*, *79*, 659–690.

Zuberi, T. (2001). *Thicker than blood: How racial statistics lie*. Minneapolis: University of Minnesota Press.

Part III

Critical Race Praxis in Communities, Schools, and the University

21

"FIGHTIN' THE DEVIL 24/7"

Context, Community, and Critical Race Praxis in Education

David O. Stovall

About a year ago, I was invited by a friend who is deeply involved in education organizing to talk to a community group about a speak-out that was to take place at a local community center. Chicago Public Schools was in full-blown attrition mode, closing schools and replacing them with charters or some other educational management organization contract situation. The weather was bad that day, damp and dreary. In Chicago it's the type of weather that can delay people from getting to meetings on time. Since my office was up the street, I walked over figuring that I would probably get there before everyone else. When I arrived at the building where the meeting was scheduled to take place, I walked to the office of the community organization that was sponsoring the event. The executive director opened the door for me and let me know that she needed to take care of a couple of things before she could come to the meeting. She pointed to where the meeting would be held and told me that people should be filing in shortly. While sitting by myself in the conference room, I began to wonder about the times I have been in meetings of two or three people when 30 or 40 were expected. I didn't know how many folks were expected, but I constantly have to remind myself of a key component of community organizing: mass movements often start extremely small.

Following my short reflection, I noticed that people began to file in the room. I was the unfamiliar face, but everyone smiled at me, while a few asked me who I was. One gentleman in particular asked me how things were going. I replied with my usual "All good—just tryin' to make it work." When I asked him how he was doing, he replied "Aw, you know, still fightin' the devil 24/7." Instantly I thought, "You couldn't have said it any better." Sometimes in our lives those brief/clear statements are all we need to remind us of the necessity of the simple realities that influence our work. His inference made perfect sense: in the world of big-city education, organizing for educational justice can sometimes make you feel like you're up against evil incarnate—the devil.

In light of the aforementioned narrative, the following chapter takes from a popular euphemism used in many African-American communities to remind people of the intensity of the day-to-day work in the fight for quality public education. Instead of accusatory language negatively identifying a particular person or group of people, "the devil" speaks to the forces at play that work to prevent historically underrepresented, under-resourced, and disinvested groups or communities from attaining equitable, quality education. Using the colloquial statement to provide context, I seek to revisit a challenge presented by Eric Yamamoto in the mid-1990s with regard to critical race theory (CRT) and what he coined critical race praxis (CRP). As he challenges legal scholars concerned with justice for historically underserved communities to do "less abstract theorizing" and more work with communities that are experiencing injustice, I am suggesting a return to Yamamoto's assessment in education. Where we have Freire's notion of praxis in education as "action and reflection in the world in order to change it," Yamamoto's assertion should be considered on the same continuum (Freire, 1973).

By framing the discussion in CRP, the chapter has three sections. Section one provides a framework for the challenge to CRT in the form of critical race praxis. By way of merging a constellation of theoretical constructs from educational, sociological, anthropological, legal, and public health scholarship, I will posit a framework for critical race praxis in education. Section two returns to Yamamoto's tenets, suggesting a shift in the thoughts and actions of education scholars regarding our participation in educational justice work. These challenges allow us to suspend our "expertise" and substitute it with the process of listening to members of communities with whom we work with the specific intent to address the identified issues. It provides examples of current critical race praxis work happening in the United States, ending with an example of counternarrative that engages the contradictions and tragic mistakes often made in educational justice work by those who work in the academy in solidarity with communities. Section three offers a meditation on the messiness of CRP in community spaces, coupled with the willingness to engage in such work.

In Opposition to Traditional Scholarship: Process and Context in the Current Moment

This type of thinking stands in opposition to how we are traditionally trained in the academy. When Crenshaw et al. declared CRT "insurgent scholarship" the term resonated with me in that it was intentionally resisting the status quo while posing an alternative to "business-as-usual" mainstream approaches to scholarship (Crenshaw et al., 1995). For the purposes of this account, I am suggesting a return to the Crenshaw et al. use of the concept, understanding that established national governments have not been collectively responsive to needs of disenfranchised, under-resourced, and disinvested communities of color. Individual triumphs assumed as qualifiers for the advancement of racial justice (e.g. the election of Barack Obama as the 44th President of the United States or the rise in the number of African-American billionaires, etc.) are not reflective of the local realities of low-income communities of color in urban areas. If scholars are going to stand in solidarity with such communities, it is imperative that they take an "insurgent" stance to traditional scholarly approaches. This is required to re-direct the efforts of our work.

CRT and CRP scholars do not claim to be purveyors of the holy grail to the investigation of race and racism in education. Nevertheless, the current wave of "post-racial" rhetoric flies in the race of the material realities experienced by communities of color in the U.S. and across the planet. Coupled with classism, ageism, homophobia, and patriarchy, racism remains salient and relevant. "Post-racial" is utilized to obfuscate the concrete understandings of disproportionate sentencing, the school-to-prison pipeline, and the prison industrial complex (Alexander, 2010). Until these issues are addressed substantively and formatively, we remain far from post-racial.

Identified in the work of Lipman (2011), Saltman (2010), and Buras et al. (2010), the trend to convert the work of educational scholars or justice workers to market economies should be considered part of the larger neoliberal project in education. On a broader scale, the neoliberal trend in education has called for the marketization of goods and services once located in the public sector (i.e. education, city services, state-sponsored health care provision, etc.) as products to be privatized and sold to students and families as consumers (Lipman, 2011; Pedroni, 2007; Saltman, 2000). Public private partnerships are fashioned as "necessary engagements" to support states in financial peril. Educational management organizations (EMOs), testing companies, and textbook publishers have capitalized on a broad and deep market to wrestle states to engage in practices that are more in compliance with the federal government than in the best interests of students and families (e.g. the U.S. Department of Education's "Race to the Top" initiative). "Value added" and "results driven" rhetoric drives the conversation surrounding student achievement, placing teachers, administrators, and families in high-pressure situations that could result in school closure if compliance with local, state, or federal entities is deemed inadequate.

The purpose of this chapter is to recruit and retain community-minded scholars to join the struggle to responsibly engage communities with the goal of educational justice. However, to do so requires engaging methods that are not always sanguine to the annals of traditional educational research. Because this reality is intimate to our day-to-day functions in the world, CRP stands as a challenge for us to engage in ways focused on developing tangible solutions connected to the material realities of the communities we work with. The ability for low-income, working-class communities of color to access quality public education is in the balance. This being the case, the quest is not for universal objectivity. Instead, the following account is an attempt to provide insights, however limited, on the possibility of CRP as a weapon in the struggle for educational justice.

SECTION ONE: A HUMBLE ATTEMPT TO ENGAGE AUTHENTICALLY

From the basic tenets of challenging dominant ideology while maintaining a commitment to social justice and valuing experiential knowledge, I was drawn to the commitment of CRT scholars in educational research (Parker & Lynn, 2002; Skrla & Scheurich, 2004; Solórzano & Villalpando, 2005; Yosso, 2005; etc.). Critical to my engagement with the construct were the seminal writings of Ladson-Billings and Tate (1995), Solórzano and Yosso (2000), and Harris (1993). Each of these writings challenged my insights on how to critically engage and join the struggle against systemic oppression.

Returning to the legal construct, I agree with Yamamoto's assertion that justice, as an "experienced" phenomenon, involves grappling with the often "messy and conflictual racial realities" often absent in theoretical analysis (Yamamoto, 1997, p. 875). Yamamoto's critical race praxis was the bridge by which to take the construct and apply it to real-life issues facing communities that have been historically disenfranchised and under-resourced. It requires the marriage of theoretical and practical components, in the attempt to "heal disabling intergroup wounds and forge intergroup alliances" (Yamamoto, 1999, 139). At the same time, the process is often messy: mistake-laden, fraught with contradictions, tempered and curtailed by life-events. I agree with Sudbury and Okazawa-Rey's work on activist scholarship suggesting that critical engagements with "emancipatory intentions are inevitably troubled by unequal power relationships" (Sudbury & Okazawa-Rey, 2009, p. 3). In light of these realities, I argue that an authentically grounded critical race praxis in education moves toward the contradictory spaces with the intent of naming the risks and rewards of developing a form of engaged scholarship that is both activist and insurgent.

Towards Intersectionality: Pairing Theoretical Constructs to Propose CRP in Educational Research

Yamamoto suggests that critical race praxis should "signal the continual rebuilding of theory in light of the practical experiences of racial groups engaged in particular antiracist struggles, the recasting of the conceptual, performative, and material aspects of (critical) race praxis" (Yamamoto, 1999, p. 132). To this day, where many education scholars have identified the reality that social justice should be an operative tenet of the construct, few have specifically mentioned critical race praxis regarding education. The influential work of Ladson-Billings (2003), Lynn (1999), and Jennings and Lynn (2005) speaks to the necessity of developing critical race pedagogy through praxis, but a void continues to exist when explicitly naming CRP in education. To date, there is only one collected journal volume dedicated to the investigation of CRP in education (Stovall et al., 2009). Included in this journal issue are the attempts of scholar-activists to put theory into practice in school and community settings. Considered by some to be a grounded approach to theorizing our experiences as activist scholars, it also allows for researchers to engage communities from a level that acknowledges a commitment to community spaces and K-20 institutions. Instead of relying on assumptions, CRP in education positions the researcher to continually question her/his practice with community stakeholders.

For these reasons, it is important to engage in research with students and families in school and community spaces from the perspective of co-constructor or co-collaborator. Doing so requires us to work at the intersection of multiple theoretical and methodological approaches that coalesce in our work on the ground and with/in communities (Cammarota & Fine, 2008; Ibanez-Carrasco & Meiners, 2004; Jennings & Lynn, 2005; Parker & Lynn, 2002). By interrupting the traditional research paradigm suggesting "objectivity" and "validity," CRP, like grounded theory, engaged scholarship, youth participatory action research (YPAR), critical ethnography, and community-based participatory research before it, encourages scholars to get "close" to our work. This will sometimes require making tough, uncomfortable decisions that often have the potential to isolate scholars from the groups they work with (Tuhiwai Smith, 1999). As Yamamoto has offered a working definition of CRP in legal scholarship, I am posing a combination of existing tenets of CRT in education and CRP from legal studies to propose working tenets for critical race praxis in education. I am noting the term "working," because I do not contend that my definition provides the comprehensive explanation of the concept. Instead, my offering of a working definition invites malleability as needed to address conditions in the spaces we have chosen to actively engage such communities.

From critical race praxis in legal studies I incorporate the tenets of Yamamoto's working definition of race praxis from *Interracial Justice* (1999):

- *Conceptual:* Examining the racialization of a controversy and the interconnecting influences of heterosexism, patriarchy, and class while locating that examination in a critique of the political economy (p. 130).
- *Performative:* Answering the question as to what practical steps are responsive to the specific claim and who should act on that claim (p. 131).
- *Material:* Inquiring into changes, both socio-structural and concerning the remaking of the democratic structure of public institutions, in the material conditions of racial oppression. Examples would include access to fair housing, health care, quality education, employment, etc. (p. 132).
- *Reflexive:* Commitment to the continual rebuilding of theory in light of the practical experiences of racial groups engaged in particular antiracist struggles (p. 132).

From CRT in education, I utilize the tenets suggested by Yosso and Solórzano (2005) to create a framework for a critical race theory of sociology. All incorporate an intimate understanding of race and racism from micro- and macro-levels. Similar to the tenets of Yamamoto, Solórzano and Yosso speak to the current concerns of scholars in the field. The italicized portion is directly from the Yosso and Solórzano text. I offer my interpretations of the tenets following the italicized print:

- *Intercentricity of race and racism with other forms of subordination:* Racism, in its systemic and individual iterations, is intimately connected with other forms of oppression (e.g. classism, sexism, adultism, ableism, heterosexism, etc.) and should be named when it converges with the aforementioned concepts. It is wrong to assume that one group is more oppressed than another. Instead, our responsibility is to identify how such oppressions converge and diverge depending on the context.
- *Challenge to dominant ideology:* CRT challenges dominant ideology surrounding the ability of students of color to excel inside and outside of K-20 spaces. This problematizes over-reliance on standardized test performance and normalizing views associated with White, western-European Christian male standpoints as the standards for culture and academic achievement.
- *Commitment to social justice:* Social Justice broadly defined should include a dedication to the physical/material, social, and intellectual support of the efforts of historically marginalized groups to self-determine. This includes destinies of their schools and communities on their own terms, as opposed to conscripted solutions offered by those outside of said contexts.
- *Centrality of experiential knowledge:* Similar to how lawyers view the rules of evidence, the experiential knowledge of historically marginalized groups is given little credence both individually and collectively. Taking this into account, one of the responsibilities of the CRT scholar in education is to de-center the common White, western-European Christian male perspective and re-center the stories of students and families of color in working towards tangible ways to address the issues facing the aforementioned groups.
- *Utilization of interdisciplinary approaches:* CRT in education incorporates the use of numerous theoretical approaches (ethnic studies, humanities, social sciences,

gender and women's studies, public health, medicine, urban planning, etc.) to name and work with others in solidarity against racist, oppressive structures in education.

(Yosso and Solórzano, 2005, pp. 122–123)

In the attempt to coalesce the Yosso and Solórzano with the Yamamoto tenets, I offer the following to be considered in developing CRP in education:

• *Commitment to on-the-ground work:* Our theorizing should deal less with abstract concepts and should be rooted in a tangible commitment to the physical/material, social, and intellectual support of communities that are experiencing educational injustice. An explicit understanding of the political economy of the moment is critical to perform such tasks, while working with communities to unpack how the realities of the current political economy are relevant to the situation at hand.
• *Social justice as an experienced phenomenon:* Social justice requires a material commitment by scholars to work with communities in reaching tangible goals, while understanding that the spaces in which we work are "grounded in concrete and often messy and conflictual racial realities" (Yamamoto, 1999, p. 129).
• *Utilization of interdisciplinary approaches:* A commitment to continue to utilize theoretical and methodological approaches (e.g. ethnic studies, humanities, social sciences, gender and women's studies, public health, medicine, urban planning, etc.) to specifically address the racial, social, political, and economic concerns of the communities with whom we work.
• *Training others to move beyond the intellectual exercise of challenging dominant ideologies:* Continuing the work of CRT scholars like Solórzano and Ladson-Billings, CRP requires a commitment to develop the capacity of up-and-coming CRT scholars (e.g. graduate students, new faculty, etc.) to engage communities and groups working for educational justice.
• *Commitment to self-care:* In order to engage the larger project of justice in education, it is imperative to commit ourselves to physical, mental, and spiritual well-being. Because justice work in education can be extremely taxing to our minds and bodies, we must engage in individual and collective efforts aimed at taking care of ourselves (Rager, 2005).

Where the first four tenets operate as a revisionist interpretation of the Yamamoto and Yosso and Solórzano tenets, critical to the discussion of CRP in education is the necessity of self-care. Rejecting the unspoken expectation of academics who are "serious" about their work, we need not compromise our physical, mental, and social well-being. Noted by Rager in her seminal account of research with breast cancer patients who engaged in self-directed learning, the work we are concerned with can be taxing as a result of its intense nature. In Rager's situation, the participants in her study are living in the throes of a potentially deadly disease (Rager, 2005, p. 26). During her process she notes how critical it was to understand how her work slowly became an act of solidarity instead of a distanced ethnographic account of their struggles.

In the case of educational justice in low-income, working-class communities of color, our work rests in the realities of communities losing their neighborhood schools or being wrongfully displaced through gentrification, eminent domain, or other state-sanctioned policies with long-term negative effects on these communities. Owing to the intensity of the situation, taking care of oneself can be a daunting task. For these reasons, late nights, early mornings, travel schedules, faculty responsibilities (i.e. teaching load, committee work, student support, support of new faculty, research/writing, promotion, and tenure), community meetings, and time to attend to family concerns should not be considered outside of the realm of justice work in education. Paying attention to our physical, mental, and spiritual selves is critical if we are to remain fully present in our participation with communities.

SECTION TWO: CRITICAL RACE PRAXIS ON THE GROUND— COUNTERSTORY AND THE LAYERS OF COMMUNITY ENGAGEMENT

In the aforementioned special edition on CRP in education (Stovall et al., 2009), the contributing authors dedicated their accounts to articulate the ways in which their work incorporates theoretical understandings into their praxis. Of particular importance to this chapter and the 2009 edited volume is the work of Augustine Romero, Sean Arce, and Julio Cammarota in Tucson, Arizona. Currently they are experiencing an onslaught of negative media and problematic policy implementation resulting in the elimination of the Social Justice Education Project and Raza Studies Program in the Tucson Unified School District (TUSD). Engrained in the efforts of local and state officials, instruction in the Social Justice Education Project and Raza Studies Program is wrongly assumed to teach students to "resent or hate other races or classes of people" (www.saveethnicstudies.org). Every aspect of the program has been demonized, despite an independent audit refuting the district's notion that content and instruction in the program are threatening to non-Latino/a students or staff in TUSD (ibid.). A series of books including *Critical Race Theory: An Introduction* by Richard Delgado and Jean Stefancic, *A People's History of the United States* by Howard Zinn, *Occupied America* by Rudolfo Acuna, and *The Tempest* by William Shakespeare have been banned from the district. Nevertheless, members of the Social Justice Education Project and Raza Studies Program continue to engage in efforts to humanize students through a critical examination of the experiences of Latino/as in the Southwestern U.S. We believe in the power and necessity of counterstory as a tool to analyze and understand the reality of students in a state that is deeply hostile to the development of their intellectual, social, and physical capacities (Romero et al., 2009, pp. 218–219).

Their focus on students as creators of knowledge and belief in their capacity to "change the racial and social order inherent within the US educational system" are practices I have tried to emulate in my practice as a critically conscious, justice-minded scholar/educator (Romero et al., 2009, p. 220). My work over the last nine years at Social Justice High School in Chicago, which has attempted to develop curricular units with the Social Studies faculty centered in critical consciousness and praxis, serves as my attempt to develop CRP with community and students. The following counterstory, in its success and failure, is an attempt to stand in solidarity with my Tucson comrades.

Success and Failure in Community Critical Race Praxis

Over the past nine years I have been involved in a community-based effort to solidify quality education for African-American and Latino/a residents in Chicago. Culminating in the development of a high school with a social justice focus (SOJO hereafter), students, faculty members, and families have worked tirelessly to ensure that the spirit of the 19-day hunger strike initiated to create the school are maintained in its curriculum and implementation. Enveloped in the political economy of a city that utilizes mayoral control of public schools, Chicago has been flooded with a series of policies (e.g. Renaissance 2010) and EMOs (KIPP, Academy for Urban School Leadership, United Neighborhood Organization, etc.) that attempt to flood the district with charter and contract schools (Lipman, 2004, 2011).

The current situation is particularly difficult for neighborhood schools, as public dollars are siphoned away from their budgets to fund the new bevy of charter and contract schools. Because SOJO is a neighborhood public school that serves fewer than 400 students, the city has used its current $700 million budget shortfall to deem the school "too expensive" to operate. Because it shares building space with three other schools, its existence is perpetually contested owing to a "failure" to meet Chicago Public Schools (CPS) requirements for annual progress. Primarily centered in high-stakes test performance, this gatekeeping strategy has created another set of pressures on families and students. If a school has a history of declining test scores, it is placed on probation. If a school is on probation for more than three years, the Board of Education (under the guise of CPS's CEO, with final approval from the Mayor's office) could choose to close the school or subject it to "turnaround," where all the staff is fired and invited to re-apply.

Noting the various layers of the political economy of public schools in Chicago at the district and local levels, I work with SOJO on a few different levels. In addition to the aforementioned curriculum development with faculty and students, I serve as a member of the Advisory Local School Council (ALSC). Serving as a derivative of the Local School Councils developed as part of the 1988 school reforms in Chicago, the ALSC only serves in an advisory capacity in terms of approving the school budget and principal hiring. The following offering is an account of a recent ALSC experience regarding the hiring of SOJO's new principal. In it lie the messy and conflicting realities of race and class in K-12 settings.

October 21, 2011, Minneapolis, Minnesota: While having dinner the night before a workshop presentation for Minneapolis public school teachers, I noticed a text on my phone from a trusted friend who is also on staff at SOJO. It read, "the principal came in and announced his resignation today." My first response was to curse and yell out loud, but I looked across the table to my partner and told her the news. As her eyes widened with shock, I excused myself to call my friend. During our conversation he explained to me that the principal called an emergency faculty meeting and explained to everyone that he had had enough of his position as principal and was calling it quits. Granted, I knew that there had been tensions amongst the staff regarding our new attention to test scores and college readiness standards, and that the principal was not pleased with his relationship with the staff, many of whom he became close with before his transition to principal (he had moved up the ranks at SOJO from teacher to assistant principal to principal).

This put the school in a serious predicament; not only were we on academic probation, but we would have to engage in a principal search in the first quarter of the school year. It is especially difficult to do this with the fact that the most viable candidates traditionally make themselves eligible for hiring in the summer. Complicating this fact is the reality of the new CPS Office of Principal Professional Development (OPPD), which has a new battery of qualifications for principal candidates. If you don't pass this set of requirements (which includes a series of observations and tests), you cannot become "principal eligible." For the ALSC, this became a problem because we could only choose people to interview who were currently on the principal eligibility list. Coupled with the idea that we were already "too expensive" by CPS standards we entertained a worst-case scenario. Our inability to find a viable principal could put us in a series of interim administrators who would not understand the mission and vision of the school, which could deeply affect teacher and student efficacy and could make the environment hostile and toxic. Closure became an immediate reality. CPS schools placed on probation are perpetually fearful of closure. Over the last eight years, over 70 schools have been closed or declared "turnaround," where the entire faculty is removed in favor of a new supply of teachers. Ironically, this development has not resulted in any sort of improvement in school achievement (Lipman, 2011).

Upon returning to Chicago, we met as the ALSC, understanding the particular restraints placed on us by the new CPS policies. As the ALSC we dedicated ourselves to learning as much as we could about the principal hiring process while following leads with people we knew across the city who might consider taking the position. Simultaneously, the outgoing principal created a timeline with a turnaround date that was untenable. Once we got the timeline pushed back, we were able to maneuver to buy ourselves more time. We were offered a stop-gap solution in the interim, where the school would have what CPS refers to as an "administrator-in-charge" (AIC), who is essentially a retired school principal who has enough work days left to keep the school running while a new principal is hired. As a blessing in disguise, the administrator-in-charge was an extremely competent and transparent person. Students and staff were impressed with her ability to address school issues in a fair but critical manner. Demonstrative of her commitment was her promise to assist the new principal in becoming acclimated to the school.

As the AIC came closer to making her transition, the search process did not yield the type of results we had hoped for. The applications submitted for the position were moderate at best. However, members of the community used their resources and found a potential candidate for the position. Remaining responsible to the efforts of the hunger strike, four of the 14 hunger strikers are members of the ALSC. Because of their deep ties to the community they were able to use their networks to locate a potential candidate. Members of the ALSC met with her informally, to get an idea of what she brought to the table. She was Latina, from the neighborhood where SOJO resides, bilingual, and had some success in math and science education at the K-8 level. One of the ALSC members went to high school with her and had good things to say about her. Our concern was that she didn't seem well versed on what social justice/liberatory education meant to her. This was significant given that our school was on probation—potentially facing closure. Nevertheless, we encouraged her to apply for the position.

As more applications came in, we noticed another person who sparked our interest. She had high school experience as a principal and was known for her ability to challenge central office. Her situation was one where her school was closed without warning. Owing to this experience, she led a collective of parents, teachers, students, and administrators to the state capital to change legislation on school closings. Because of her efforts with others, CPS schools cannot be closed without proper warning. This resonated with the ALSC because it appeared as if she had a sense of justice in her understanding of schools. I promised the ALSC that I would try to find out as much as I could about her, but my efforts were unsuccessful.

Both candidates were called in for interviews. The first candidate (Ms. Valentino—not her actual name) was the Latina with whom members of the ALSC met informally. Ms. Jackson (also a pseudonym) was the candidate whose application resonated with the ALSC. She was African-American, with a 30-year history in CPS. As the ALSC, we knew we needed someone with experience who was willing to stand up to CPS while able to execute a strategy to get us off of probation.

While we agreed on these points, there was division on the ALSC as to who could best fulfill these needs. The SOJO student body is close to 85 percent Latino/a and 15 percent African-American. Of the ten members of the ALSC, seven are Latino/a, one is mixed-race, and two are African-American. Where there haven't been any racial divisions on the ALSC, the school struggles to attract and retain African-American students, owing to the explosion of charter schools in their community. At the same time, Latino/a members of the ALSC hold steadfast to the fact that the school is for all students, no matter the race or neighborhood of origin.

All of the aforementioned ideals were understood as foundational to our function as the ALSC. Nevertheless, divisions in the group were realized in terms of what members thought was best for students. Many of the LSC members (including three of the hunger strikers) were concerned about the school's current probation status. Where they liked the outgoing principal as a person, they expressed their disdain for probation. Because the community has witnessed a legacy of under-resourced, disinvested schools, SOJO is viewed as a space that should provide the opportunity to reverse the trend. Complicating matters was the fact that this would be the third principal in three years. Despite promises made by the outgoing principal to remain at the school, many members of the faculty and the ALSC felt burned by his sudden departure. Ms. Valentino, as someone from the neighborhood who knew the struggles of the community intimately, presented an opportunity to return to keeping the issues and concerns of the community at the center.

In our discussions as the ALSC, I agreed with a number of members that an experienced person who had a plan to get us off probation would be critical in keeping the school open. Owing to the rash of current closings in Chicago, we knew that many educational management organizations would be salivating at the opportunity to be in the building and benefit directly from SOJO's closing. Where some seemed to agree, they also wanted a person who had community concerns at the center of their analysis. Because both sides were correct, we decided to see how the candidates would fare during the interview process.

After our rounds of interviews, the two finalists, Ms. Valentino and Ms. Jackson, were brought in for full-day interviews and a community forum. During this process each candidate met with students, faculty, community members, and community partners. The community forum at the end of the day was particularly for parents who would not be able to attend the meetings. After fielding feedback via survey and various one-on-one interactions, everyone seemed to be lukewarm to both candidates. At the same time, we were alerted that there were major problems at Ms. Valentino's current school with faculty and community members. She didn't have a grasp on social justice. She also lacked a concrete plan on how to recruit and retain African-American students (a lingering problem) and she was not clear about how to address the academic probation situation. This drew a red flag from some of the ALSC members, students, faculty, and community partners.

The concerns with Ms. Jackson were rooted in her expressed belief that one of the pathways to justice included contact with local and state legislators. Coupled with the fact that she was monolingual and had a nominal view of what justice meant in education, she displayed a number of strengths. One was her well-articulated plan on recruiting African-American students and concrete short-term and longitudinal strategies on how to address probation. Members of the ALSC felt this was important as we moved forward in finding a long-term principal.

All of these concerns clashed in our ALSC meetings. Because we had the responsibility of submitting a single candidate to CPS, there was a struggle as to whose name would be the final submission. To Ms. Valentino's supporters, I noted that she didn't have a concrete plan. Where Ms. Jackson was not the ideal candidate for some, her strengths were evident in her plan. Many returned to the fact that it would be difficult for her to understand the concerns of Spanish-speaking parents as a monolingual English speaker. This was a central community concern, as schools that serve Latino/a students with Spanish-speaking parents have experienced rampant paternalistic leadership that has not addressed their concerns of transparency with school policy. To Ms. Jackson's credit, she was the principal of a school that was 50 percent Latino/a and 50 percent African-American. During her tenure she kept a robust student population, while the three other schools in the building had dwindling student bodies. One of her letters of recommendation was from a Latino/a parent who expressed his satisfaction with her ability to address the concerns of the community despite her inability to speak Spanish.

The final development in the principal hiring culminated in an open meeting with a closed session vote by the ALSC. In attendance were members of community partner organizations, parents, and a central office representative, specifically from the office that supervised LSCs and ALSCs. He informed us that all we needed was a simple majority vote. Because the student ALSC member cannot vote, there were nine eligible voters. As the community representatives expressed their concerns and their support for both candidates, the meeting was closed for the vote. Each member voted by a show of hands. With nine members present, the vote was 5–4 for Ms. Jackson. To the credit of everyone on the ALSC, there was no dispute of the vote. However, the lines were drawn in the sand; the person felt by some to have the community's concerns at heart was not selected.

This left a rift in the ALSC. Some felt that some of us had illegally conspired outside of ALSC meetings to strategize on how to get Ms. Jackson elected. Those who voted for Ms. Jackson were also accused of making Ms. Valentino's supporters the enemy by bringing in reinforcements by way of community partners and central office staff. Where this was furthest from the truth, the perception became the reality in terms of ALSC relations. This was expressed to the new principal in her second ALSC meeting. Where Ms. Jackson respectfully replied that she didn't need to know all of the particulars, Ms. Valentino's supporters expressed that there were no personal feelings of ill will towards her. They believed in her ability to do her job as SOJO principal, but they would not apply for membership to the ALSC in the next year.

All of this left a bitter taste in the mouths of all who participated in the principal election. Our decisions, where not solely guided by race and ethnicity, were heavily seasoned by them in the end. At the same time, the schools doors are open, but we don't know for how long. Our fight is still there, but we have potentially lost community input that was so instrumental to the process of creating the school.

SECTION THREE: NOTE OF CAUTION—REAL WORK, REAL CONSEQUENCES

The above account is reflective of the realities when the messiness of human interactions, tethered by the political economy of race and class, is in play. At the same time, it should not discourage us from engaging work in a way that remains responsible to community concerns. In the field of battle, allies are sometimes lost, but several are gained if we continue to remain responsible. For my particular situation, I cannot make the claim that what we did was right. Instead, I must be responsible for the mistakes made in the process that could potentially place the school in jeopardy of closing. Unfortunately we might know this sooner rather than later.

At the same time I remain confident in the community members and teachers who remain on the ALSC. There will definitely be a fight ahead, but I am trustful that they will not surrender. In our praxis we must remain responsible to our victories and mistakes while embracing a commitment to make them nonetheless. Because this work is intimately tied to the life and death of community-centered public education as we know it, I remain willing to work in solidarity with those concerned with creating quality, viable schools for young people and their families. It is a struggle that I am honored to take part in. With that blessing I must know that the results are not even or sometimes fair. If I have contributed in any way to those injustices, the mistakes are mine.

BIBLIOGRAPHY

Alexander, M. (2010). *The new Jim Crow: Mass incarceration in the age of colorblindness.* New York: New Press.

Buras, K.L., Randels, J., & Salaam, K.Y. (Eds.). (2010). *Pedagogy, policy and the privatized city: Stories of dispossession and defiance from New Orleans.* New York: Teachers College Press.

Cammarota, J., & Fine, M. (Eds.). (2008). *Revolutionizing education: Youth participatory action research in motion.* New York: Routledge.

Crenshaw, K., Gotanda, N., Peller, G., & Thomas, K. (Eds.). (1995). *Critical race theory: Key writings that defined the movement.* New York: New Press.

Fabricant, M. (2010). *Organizing for educational justice: The campaign for public school reform in the South Bronx.* St. Paul: University of Minnesota Press.

Fabricant, M., & Fine, M. (2012). *Charter schools and the corporate makeover of public education: What's at stake?* New York: Teachers College Press.

Freire, P. (1973). *Pedagogy of the oppressed.* New York: Continuum.

Gillborn, D. (2008). *Racism and education: Coincidence or conspiracy?* New York: Routledge.

Hale, C. (Ed.). (2008). *Engaging contradictions: Theory, politics and methods of activist scholarship.* Los Angeles: University of California Press.

Harris, C. (1993). Whiteness as property. *Harvard Law Review, 106*(3), 1710–1793.

Ibanez-Carrasco, F., & Meiners, E. (Eds.). (2004). *Public acts: Disruptive readings on making curriculum public.* New York: Routledge.

Jennings, M., & Lynn, M. (2005). The house that race built: Critical pedagogy, African-American education and the reconceptualization of a critical race pedagogy. *Educational Foundations, 19*(3), 13–45.

Ladson-Billings, G. (Ed.). (2003). *Critical race perspectives on the social studies: The profession, politics and curriculum.* Charlotte, NC: Information Age Press.

Ladson-Billings, G., & Tate, W. (1995). Towards a critical race theory of education. *Teachers College Record, 97*(1), 47–68.

Lipman, P. (2004). *High stakes education: Inequality, globalization and urban school reform.* New York: Routledge.

Lipman, P. (2011). *The new political economy of urban education: Neoliberalism, race and the right to the city.* New York: Routledge.

Lynn, M. (1999). Toward a critical race pedagogy: A research note. *Urban Education, 33*(5), 606–626.

Parker, L., & Lynn, M. (2002). What's race got to do with it? Critical race theory's conflicts with and connections to qualitative research methodology and epistemology. *Qualitative Inquiry, 8*(1), 7–22.

Pedroni, T. (2007). *Market movements: African American involvement in school voucher reform.* New York: Routledge.

Rager, K.B. (2005). Self-care and the qualitative researcher: When collecting data can break your heart. *Educational Researcher, 34*(4), 23–27.

Romero, A., Arce, S., & Cammarota, J. (2009). A barrio pedagogy: Identity, intellectualism, activism and academic achievement through the evolution of critically conscious intellectualism. *Race, Ethnicity and Education, 12*(2), 217–234.

Saltman, K. (2000). *Collateral damage: Corporatizing public schools—A threat to democracy.* Lanham, MD: Roman & Littlefield.

Saltman, K. (2010). *The gift of education: Public education and venture philanthropy.* New York: Palgrave Macmillan.

Skrla, L., & Scheurich, J. (2004). *Educational equity and accountability: Paradigms, policies, and politics.* New York: Routledge.

Solórzano, D., & Villalpando, O. (2005). Educational inequalities and Latina/o undergraduate students in the United States: A critical race analysis of their educational progress. *Journal of Hispanic Higher Education, 4*(3), 272–294.

Solórzano, D., & Yosso, T. (2000). Critical race methodology: Counter-storytelling as an analytical framework for educational research. *Qualitative Inquiry, 8*(1), 23–44.

Soyini Madison, D. (2005). *Critical ethnography: Method, ethics, and performance.* Thousand Oaks, CA: Sage.

Stovall, D., Lynn, M., Danley, L., & Martin, D. (Eds.). (2009). Special issue: Critical race praxis. *Race, Ethnicity and Education, 12*(2), 131–266.

Sudbury, J., & Okazawa-Rey, M. (Eds.). (2009). *Activist scholarship: Antiracism, feminism and social change.* Boulder, CO: Paradigm.

Tuhiwai Smith, L. (1999). *Decolonizing methodologies: Research and indigenous peoples.* New York: Zed Books.

Valdes, F., McCristal Culp, J., & Harris, A.P. (Eds.). (2002). *Crossroads, directions and a new critical race theory.* Philadelphia, PA: Temple University Press.

Vaught, S.E. (2011). *Racism, public schooling, and the entrenchment of White supremacy: A critical race ethnography.* Albany, NY: SUNY Press.

Yamamoto, E.K. (1995). Rethinking alliances: Agency, responsibility and interracial justice. *UCLA Asian Pacific American Law Journal, 3*(33), 1–65.

Yamamoto, E.K. (1997). Critical race praxis: Race theory and political lawyering practice in post civil-rights America. *Michigan Law Review, 95*(7), 821–900.

Yamamoto, E.K. (1999). *Interracial justice: Conflict and reconciliation in post-civil rights America.* New York: NYU Press.

Yosso, T. (2005). Whose culture has capital? A critical race theory discussion of community cultural wealth. *Race, Ethnicity and Education, 8*(1), 69–91.

Yosso, T.J., & Solórzano, D.G. (2005). Conceptualizing a critical race theory in sociology. In M. Romero & E. Margolis (Eds.), *The Blackwell companion to social inequalities* (pp. 117–146). Malden, MA: Blackwell.

22

ARIZONA ON THE DOORSTEP OF APARTHEID[1]
The Purging of the Tri-Dimensionalization of Reality
Augustine F. Romero

INTRODUCTION

The Tucson Unified School District's (TUSD) Raza Studies[2] Department (Hispanic Studies at the time of its establishment) was created in July of 1998 as a result of a grassroots movement that advocated for greater levels of academic achievements for the Latina/o children in the district. In 2002, on the heels of No Child Left Behind (NCLB), I was charged with the task of creating a program that would alleviate the achievement gap for Latina/o students in TUSD. As a result, I implemented the critically compassionate intellectualism model[3] (CCI) as the theoretical model for the Raza Studies program. CCI became the framework for the Social Justice Education Project,[4] the Raza Studies classes at all levels, the redemptive remembering team,[5] and the Institute for Transformative Education.[6] I did this as a means of ensuring an equitable and excellent educational experience for our Latina/o students and for that matter any and all students who took part in our program. I, like the community elders and the youth who struggled for the creation of this program, was able to envision the creation of this program because of our capacity to tri-dimensionalize our realities. In this reconstructed reality we have recognized the hegemonic group's perpetuation of racial realism (Bell, 1993) and of its understanding of common sense (Haney Lopez, 2003), all of which have contributed to the intentional placement of the majority of American people of color at the bottom of society's well (Bell, 1992).

One of the key pedagogical methodologies used in the CCI classroom is Freire's idea of the tri-dimensionalization of reality. Freire (1994) states that, "Through their continuing praxis, men and women simultaneously create history and become historical-social beings. Because—in contrast to animals—people can tri-dimensionalize time into the past, the present, and the future, their history, in function of their own creations, develops as a constant process of transformation" (p. 82). Through the tri-dimensionalization of reality we are able to help our students to a newfound state of organic intellectualism, a state of tri-dimensionalized intellectualism. The tri-dimensionalization of reality is grounded in the process of challenging the epistemological and ontological understandings of the student's social condition with the intent of transforming them as a means of transforming not their social condition and future but that of their community. In this ongoing exercise we, as a means of challenging the hegemonic order, ask our students unapologetically to insert issues of race and racism into their critiques and their analysis. This re-contextualized analysis has helped our students develop stronger critiques of the racial and cultural deficits discourse responses that have been constructed by the hegemonic group to explain away the racial social structures that perpetuate the oppressor group's historical privilege and social advantages, while simultaneously constructing people of color as unfit, undeserving, and/or less than human.

These deficit models have prejudicially and historically plagued and mislabeled communities of color as places of inherent inanity and futility. I firmly believe that communities of color are places of "blossoming intellectualism" (Romero, 2008), and places that are inherently perseverant, imaginative, and highly intellectualized. The tri-dimensionalization of reality helps students nurture this understanding of our present-day capacities, our past realities, and our future potential.

Recent events in Arizona have disrupted the work that I began over a decade ago. The permanence and the depth of racism have heaved themselves in Tucson's educational and political reality. In this historical moment both so-called (fair-weather) liberals and racist conservatives at the state and local level are attempting to purge the teaching of historical truths from public schools and for all intents and purposes the teaching of culture from a counter-hegemonic and anti-racist perspective. These racists and their oppressive legacy will not stop our movement forward. We are not fooled by the rhetoric and we fully recognize their hypocrisy. Moreover, we realize that, although we were born as members of the human race, it does not mean that these racists recognize, much less acknowledge, our humanity. Despite the dismay resulting from this understanding, we as true progressives shall continue to confront, struggle against, and find ways to overcome the evils of these oppressors. It is our responsibility to ensure that we continue our struggle towards the materialization of the dream[7] and its manifestation in a new world.

Many of those who helped establish the TUSD Mexican American/Raza Studies Department (Raza Studies) and the academic program and theoretical framework I created for the Department and the children we serve share the beliefs offered above. These are the same beliefs that led to the establishment of the Department and these are some of the beliefs that drive the struggle for its prolongation.

CCI: AN ELUCIDATION

CCI is grounded not just in Freirean theory (Freire, 1994) but also in critical race theory (Bell, 1992; Delgado, 1999; Ladson-Billings & Tate, 1995), authentic caring (Valenzuela, 1999), and funds of knowledge (Moll et al., 1992). It also uses youth participatory action research as one of the mechanisms by which it engages and encourages its students (Cammarota & Romero, 2006) to begin the process of problem-posing (Cammarota & Romero, 2008), and sets the stage for the tri-dimensionalization of reality.

CCI converges these theoretical understandings into three student-centered areas: curriculum, pedagogy, and student–teacher–parent interactions. The curriculum is socially, culturally, and historically relevant while being aligned to state standards (state honor standards when applicable). The pedagogy is heavily framed in the Freirean

notion of critical literacy wherein students are recognized and engaged as equal partners in the construction of knowledge, identification of problems of social injustice,
and implementation of solutions to these problems. Equally important to the nurturing and implementation of pedagogy is the understanding that students possess knowledge and have created knowledge in their own personal, cultural, and organic spaces
(Delgado Bernal, 2002). Also within this frame is a pursuit of social justice. In this pursuit
of social justice the voice of the student in the naming of the social toxin(s) is important.
Equally important is the student voice in deciding how to challenge the oppressive social
toxin(s) (Cammarota & Romero, 2006). Student–teacher–parent interactions are based
upon Valenzuela's (1999) notion of authentic caring. Authentic caring requires educators to interact with students on a genuine emotional level and nurture a strong sense of
empathy for their deepest concerns and feelings about the students' lived realities.

CCI does not focus on grades, test scores, or other arbitrary socially constructed measures. This model uses the above triad as a method by which students develop a strong
sense of identity, purpose, and hope (Romero, 2008). It is through this evolutionary
state that students challenge their ontological and epistemological understandings. It
is in the transformed and tri-dimensionalized state that students name and challenge
their social condition with a critical praxis that is transformative (Solórzano & Delgado
Bernal, 2001) and redemptive (Romero, 2008) in nature.

CCI is unapologetically critical and progressive. As a result, its success is based upon
our ability as educators to maintain a strong focus on the equitable needs and interests
of the students, families, and communities we serve. This understanding supports John
Dewey's belief that education should center on "student interest, student activity, group
work, and cooperation" (Spring, 2008, p. 282). Another prominent Deweyan perspective that intersects with CCI is the construction and relevance of the "social imagination." According to Spring (2008), "Social imagination is the ability to relate isolated
ideas to the actual conditions that have given them their original meaning" (p. 282). CCI
advocates for students to be critical of their reality, and in their pursuit of understanding
they must search for root causes of social toxins rather than simply addressing symptoms
of those toxins.

CCI AND RAZA STUDIES DATA

From the academic year 2005 to the academic year 2010, CCI students outperformed all
other students at the four sites where it was being implemented on Arizona's high stakes
graduation exam. Over the same time frame CCI students graduated from high school
at a higher rate than their peers at these four sites, and CCI students have matriculated
to college at a rate that is 179 percent greater than the national average for Chicana/o
students.

Over these six academic years something unique happened. CCI students did not
close the achievement gap; in many ways they inverted the gap. CCI students were three
times more likely to pass the Reading section, four times more likely to pass the Writing
section, and two and a half times more likely to pass the Math section of the high school
graduation exam than their peers not in our program (Romero, 2011).

At these same four sites over the same time frame, we graduated 93 percent of our
students. During that same time and at the same sites, the graduation rate for non-CCI
students was 82.5 percent. In addition, slightly more than 67 percent of our students

were enrolled in post-secondary education after they graduated high school. This is 179 percent greater than the national average of 24 percent for Chicano/Mexican American students (Romero, 2011).

While CCI was being implemented, more than 1,900 CCI students completed pre- and post-course surveys that I mandated as a means of better understanding how CCI students felt about the CCI experience. Some of the highlights revealed by these surveys are: 1) 96 percent of the students agreed or strongly agreed that they talk to their parents and/or other adults about "what I've learned on this project or in this class"; 2) 95 percent of the students agreed or strongly agreed that they were willing to do homework "in order to keep the project moving along on time or to ensure participation in the class"; 3) 97 percent of the students agreed or strongly agreed that the project or the class "has better prepared me for college"; and 4) 98 percent of the students agreed or strongly agreed that "working on this project or taking this class" had helped them believe that they have something worthwhile to contribute to society (Romero, 2008, 2011).

TRI-DIMENSIONALIZATION OF REALITY: ON THE GROUND

As mentioned previously, CCI does not focus on test scores, grade point averages, classroom management, objectives on the board, and so on. The principal objective of CCI and the tri-dimensionalization of reality is to instill a strong sense of identity, purpose, and hope in students (Romero, 2008). I believe that, if we can accomplish this objective and fulfill these human capacities, then the academic capacities of our students will simultaneously establish a different trajectory towards an end that only the students can define (Romero, 2008).

To achieve the above objective, I engaged in the process of helping the students gain the ability to tri-dimensionalize their realities. In essence the tri-dimensionalization of reality is the nexus between the students' social context, the students' historical understandings, and the students' vision of the future.

The primary methods by which CCI students tri-dimensionalize their realities is through the exercise of generative words and generative themes and the intellectual exercise of critical racial praxis. In these intellectual exercises students are encouraged to intellectually engage the realities of their social condition, and they are required not only to identify the social issues that impact their lives but to research and analyze these issues. Upon completing their research, students are required to create a plan of action to address a problem, identify key potential allies who could help implement their plans, educate and recruit those key allies, and implement the plan of action. Finally, students engage in analyzing and evaluating their action. Originally Julio Cammarota and I took these understandings from Freire (1970), Smith-Maddox and Solórzano (2002), Yosso (2006), and Duncan-Andrade and Morrell (2008). During our reflections after each exercise, we adapted our own understandings based upon the voices and input from CCI students.

It is only appropriate that the tri-dimensionalization of reality be constructed in a third space. This third space (Bhabha, 1994; Moje et al., 2004) is created in the CCI classroom via the convergence of the barrio and the institution. The CCI third space challenges the inequities and their inherent injustices that exist within the American educational institution. This is a newly created tri-dimensionalized space that is driven by the need to challenge the epistemological and ontological understandings of our students and in many cases their parents. Furthermore, the ideological framework and our critical praxis are grounded in the understanding that race and racism are dominant variables within the tri-dimensionalized reality of our students, their parents, and our communities, and even within us as emancipatory educators (Romero, 2008).

By no stretch of the imagination is this process easy. Connecting a student's social condition to the historical reality of the student's ancestors, and then connecting the nexus of these two spaces to the student's vision of the future is not easy; however, it is critical to the development of his or her critical consciousness and ability to transform his or her epistemological and ontological perspectives. At times it is a true struggle, but the day when you see that look in students' eyes or that confident nod, both saying "I get this," is the moment that you know they have moved to a space wherein they are able to transcend their state of uni-dimensionalism. I found that, as students gained a deeper epistemological and ontological contextualization of their realities and their histories, the CCI students were able to construct visions of a future wherein they are better able to challenge and negotiate the constructions of Delgado's theory of surplus equality.[8] They are also better able to challenge the constructions of racial realism and Haney Lopez's (2003) notion of common sense.

As CCI moves deeper into the construction and representation of students' true words and the tri-dimensionalization of their realities, students often enter into a state that Solórzano and Delgado-Bernal (2001) refer to as transformational resistance. In this state, the students' praxis articulates a strong critique of oppression and they demonstrate a profound desire for social justice.

As I reflect upon the voices of CCI students, it is clear that their critical praxis influenced their ability to find their true words, and through their true words they are able to tri-dimensionalize their realities. I have interpreted true words to mean the actions that are informed by a high level of reflection and transformational actions that take place through a lens of respect and love in the pursuit of a stronger sense of identity, purpose, and hope within the CCI student (Romero, 2008).

> You all helped us understand how our history, the history of our gente was important to understand what is going on now. After me and the other students realized this, it all got more interesting. It got to be more real, it wasn't just something that happened in the past. It meant something now. We could do things now that could change our future. Our education was never about that kinda shit.
>
> (Tito)

Tito articulates upon his experience in the CCI classroom. In this articulation he explains how the courses helped him recognize the intersectionality of his history, his social condition, and potential actions that could change his future.

> I have this precious knowledge. I have this consciousness. Now I have to make it worth me having all of this. I am sure that all the people who struggled before me would want me to do something with it. I know our crew wants me to do something with it. I am sure that my teachers, and you need us to do something, and I want to make sure that the little ones after me get this education so that they can have a better life, more knowledge, and deeper consciousness than we do. This is not a choice. It's a commitment.
>
> (Jakob)

Jakob articulates about the value of his tri-dimensionalized reality and his consciousness, and the importance of taking actions that will ensure a better life for him and also for those who come after him.

> This helps you understand, if something is wrong right now, what in the past were the building blocks that led to this wrong. We understand that we need to research the past to understand this moment. Then when we have a better understanding, then we must take the actions that will make things better in the future.
>
> (Lelani)

Lelani offers a great explanation of the tri-dimensionalization of reality. She touched upon the importance of understanding how the ills of the past were constructed, and how understanding these constructs helps students better understand their social condition. Equally importantly, she connects these dimensions to actions that must be taken to build a better future.

The tri-dimensionalization of reality reveals for the CCI student the political and anti-humanistic battles that have been and are being waged in the name of patriotism (covert racism), (im)morality, and values (of hypocrisy). Moreover, the tri-dimensionalization exercise helps the CCI student develop a counternarrative to the anti-humanistic and pro-racist notions of the right and fair-weather liberals. In addition, it illuminates the social and cultural transformations that are taking place in the lives of the CCI students.

COMMON SENSE AND RACIAL REALISM

It is with a tri-dimensionalized awareness that CCI classes focus on and question what Haney Lopez (2003) refers to as a commonsense understanding of each of the three dimensions: the historical dimension, the social dimension, and the futuristic dimension. Haney Lopez (2003) defines common sense as "a complex set of background ideas that people draw upon, but rarely question in their daily affairs" (p. 6). The background ideas are the references we depend upon as we make our daily decisions and as we seek to understand and engage our world. This process is historical and, as such, it has created a societal process of oppression and racism. This is a process that is neither sightless nor unconscious, despite the notion that the masses who subscribe to this process may be unconscious and/or without critical sight; this process has created a structure, a process, and a belief (in many cases unconscious or dysconscious) for the perpetuation of oppression and subordination that the masses of American society pursue without question. According to Haney Lopez (2003), common sense is an ideology and practical process that is consumed with racism that leads many to engage in racist practices that ensure the maintenance of the racial hierarchy of White oppression.

Ironically the racist right and even some dysconscious racists on the left have labeled me as racist because I advocate for an education that challenges and exposes commonsense racism. It is this everyday kind of racism that is most prevalent and insidious; it is the racism of the status quo, it is the racism of disregard, and it is the racism of privilege that force the halting of racial progress or awareness because of the discomfort it causes the privileged group (who are in many cases members and beneficiaries of the oppressor group). In fact, in the State of Arizona's case against TUSD's Mexican American Studies program lawyers for the state cited my 2010 *Hamline Law Review* article wherein I articulate upon my decision to deliberately insert race into the CCI students' problem-posing process. It is my belief that it is only the naïve, the dysconscious, or the oppressor group who would denounce the reality that the examination of racism is fundamental to developing a deep understanding of the United States' political, social, economic, and educational reality.

Therefore, within the intellectual exercises of problem-posing and the tri-dimensionalization of reality, as an authentic carer and as a barriorganic (barrio and organic) intellectual how could I offer truth to these intellectual exercises if I did not help CCI students develop a race-critical consciousness? How could I advocate for a tri-dimensional understanding if I failed to recognize the historical and present-day realities and manifestations of racism, and how it influences the construction of tomorrow's structure of the United States?

As I reflected upon these understandings and their implication within the intellectual exercise fostered by CCI along with Haney Lopez's common sense, Derrick Bell's racial realism weighed heavy on my thoughts. Bell's (1993) notion of racial realism significantly influences my praxis as a *critical* race educator.[9] If the *critical* race educator understands racial realism, we understand that, despite the rhetoric of both the fair-weather left and nearly every element of the right, racism in American society has not diminished; rather today it is more sophisticated, equally damaging, and perilous. Moreover, as *critical* race educators we must recognize issues of race and racism, and we must understand how they impact how we teach, what we teach, and in many ways how we interact with our students, our parents, and the community (Romero, 2008). In essence, for *critical* race educators, racial realism impacts all aspects of our praxis.

As CCI students come to understand Haney Lopez's common sense and Derrick Bell's racial realism and how these understandings are intersected in the intellectual execution of problem-posing and tri-dimensionalizing, the students transform the way in which they see and engage the world. The transformational understanding of the world is something that is expected within the CCI experience rather than the passivity and false promise of the traditional American educational system where most students wait for the oppressor group's transformation to be imposed upon them. This shift of epistemology and ontology has created a new reality for the overwhelming majority of our students, and it has led to the ethnic studies movement in Arizona.

EXAMINATION OF THE INTERSECTIONALITY OF RACISM, EDUCATION, AND LAW: ARIZONA REVISED STATUTE §15–112: THE CURRENT REALITY

Despite its compliance with NCLB, the inversion of the achievement gap for CCI students, and its exceptional college matriculation record, Mexican American Studies (MAS), with the CCI model and the tri-dimensionalization of reality, has fallen victim to the racist and fascist agenda of the state's attorney general, the state's Republican superintendent of public instruction, the Republican-led state legislature, the Republican governor, and the majority of the TUSD governing board. (It must be noted that governing board member Adelita Grijalva has been and continues to be an ardent supporter of CCI and the MAS program. Adelita Grijalva and the late Judy Burns are among the true champions of CCI and the MAS program.) On May 12, 2010 House Bill (HB) 2281 (the anti-ethnic studies bill) was signed into law, and on January 3, 2011 it became Arizona Revised Statute §15–112.

The intent of HB 2281 is the purging of the MAS program and any other similar program that utilizes methodologies such as tri-dimensionalization of reality. The guardians of the status quo and even those who seek to move full circle back into a state of overt and de jure oppression consciously act with the intent of denying our children the cognitive tools that can be used to liberate their souls, minds, and bodies from the oppression of American education and the American system of social, economic, political, and medical oppression (Agency for Healthcare Research and Quality, 2005, 2010; Smedley, 2012).

For those seeking a critical and a real understanding of the construction of America, it should be understood that, regardless of the rhetoric of "opportunity" and "equality," America was founded and constructed on an ideology of racism (Bell, 1999). As a method of its perpetuation, the reproduction of the racial oppression within America's social, political, economic, and educational structures is most often and most effectively conducted through state policy or activity (Omi & Winant, 1994; Spring, 2008). Historically and presently, racism in America has led to egregious levels of unjust treatment of those who do not belong to the privileged group or oppressor group. Most often those that bear the greatest burden of the privileged and oppressor groups' atrocities have been people of color. These atrocities lie in the fact that "race continues to signify difference and structure inequality" (Omi & Winant, 1994, p. 57). From its inception, America and Americans have operated on the belief that Whites were superior to all other races, especially those of the tawny persuasion (Takaki, 1994).

Omi and Winant (1994) state, "The hallmark of this [American] history has been racism … The U.S. has confronted each racially defined minority with a unique form of despotism and degradation" (p. 1). The American reality (versus the American Dream) for people of color has been one of inequality, injustice, and exclusion. These experiences run from expulsion, to slavery, to invasion, to occupation, to colonization, to deculturalization, to genocide. Therefore, despite its rhetoric of morality and social mobility (Spring, 2008), American schools for children of color (primarily those of Indigenous, Latino, or African American descent) have been a space of exclusion (Roithmayr, 1999), repudiation (Roithmayr, 1999), dishonesty (Villenas et al., 1999) and false generosity (Freire, 1994). Moreover, the American education system, through the use of each of these characteristics, has been used as a vehicle for the reproduction of oppression and subordination.

The ideology of racism fosters and perpetuates a discourse that maintains and justifies the continual production of injustice, inequality, and oppression. These products lead to the creation of a system of ignorance wherein historical and present-day people of color are exploited and oppressed (Delgado, 1995; Solórzano & Yosso, 2000). Racism is the sum of programs, practices, institutions, and structures that are deeply rooted within America's fabric. These programs, practices, institutions, and structures maintain America's social and racial order wherein White oppression is perpetuated and intensified (Delgado & Stefancic, 2001; Ladson-Billings & Tate, 1995; Pine & Hilliard, 1990). Racism is reflected in entrenched policies and practices, a biased curriculum, and standardized testing. Traditionally the aforementioned methods concomitantly and deliberately benefit the White students and victimize students of color (Haymes, 2003; Pine & Hilliard, 1990; Yosso, 2002).

These methods presently and historically have been used to ensure that students of color remain in position as an underclass that is ripe for economic exploitation (Delgado, 1995;

Spring, 2008). Moreover, the methods of the oppressor group are a method of decultur-alization that intends to strip people of their history, culture, and language, with the intent of preparing them for acceptance by the oppressor group. According to Spring (2008), "It combines education for democracy and political equality with cultural genocide—the attempt to destroy cultures" (p. 190). This fascist and racist method of homogenization has been and currently is an attempt to render people of color voiceless in their struggles, thereby making them easy prey for the cultural predators (McLaren & Gutierrez, 1995). This form of racist discourse intentionally excludes the voices, the thoughts, and the values of the non-White, and those of non-Western European descent (Said, 1979). This deliber-ate exclusion enunciates racist ideals, and it makes claims of White superiority (Baez, 2000; Garcia, 2001; Rodriguez, 2001; Said, 1979). This discourse of racism often becomes the discourse of the institutions (political, educational, economical, and social). These institu-tions foster the structures that perpetuate the racial order: the racial order that historically and presently places people of color at the bottom of society (Bell, 1992). Moreover, the racist discourse of these institutions often takes on the belief (within themselves or those they oppress) that this relegation of people of color to the bottom rung of society is not oppressive, but rather a form of liberation (Said, 1979). This is what is supposed to happen to students, even those who are academically successful. This historically has been one of the primary functions of American education (Spring, 2008).

However, when education is being used not only to intellectualize students (not that traditional American education truly does this for students of color), but to expose the inequities, inequalities, and injustices within the lived conditions of students who have been historically labeled for exploitation and oppression, it is then that education, regard-less of how successful it is, becomes a problem for the oppressor group and its conscious, dysconscious, and unconscious supporters within the privileged group. Those students who have been marked for subordination are not supposed to become aware of this real-ity and most importantly they should not be taught that they can resist and transform this preordained social and racial order.

It is in this intellectualized moment of tri-dimensionalization, resistance, and transfor-mation that the problem of the oppressor group is created. In the mind of the oppressor group, students who have been labeled for exploitation, oppression, and subordination or those who have been labeled as less than human are not supposed to graduate at higher rates than the children of the oppressor or the privileged, they are not supposed to do bet-ter on the oppressor's test than the children of the oppressor or the privileged, and they are not supposed to matriculate to college at a higher rate than the children of the oppressor or the privileged. Most importantly, not only are the CCI students experiencing newly found academic successes, but they are also equipped with a stronger state of identity, purpose, and hope, which has been fostered through the CCI model, CCI teachers, and intellectual exercises such as the tri-dimensionalization of reality. They have now developed a coun-ter-hegemonic lens, and are ready and willing to act upon their new understandings of inequity, inequality, and injustice. This is where the racist and fascist see the problem.

NOTES

1 I need to thank Cathy Amanti for her intellectual support during the dark times in which this chapter was written.
2 One the first things I did upon taking over the Hispanic Studies Department in 2002 was to change the name of the Department to Mexican American/Raza Studies. This was done in collaboration with Lorraine Lee, Gustavo Chavez, and Albert Soto, members of the Mexican American/Raza Studies Community Advisory Board.

3 The critically compassionate intellectualism model is a model that I created in response to the voices and the needs of the students in our Social Justice Education Project.

4 The Social Justice Education Project was a creation of Lorenzo Lopez, Jr., Julio Cammarota, our students, and myself. In its origin it was designed as an 11th and 12th grade experience.

5 Redemptive rememberings were transformative teacher learning communions that I created as a method of educating, mentoring, and recruiting teachers. The focuses of the redemptive rememberings were critical pedagogy, critical race theory, and authentic caring. The redemptive rememberings existed from 2002 to 2009, and during that same time period all but one of the Raza Studies staff members were redemptive remembering participants. Also, when we expanded into the elementary and middle school levels I tapped redemptive remembering members for these opportunities.

6 I created the Institute for Transformative Education as a means of constructing a four-day learning community that offered its participants the latest and most relevant educational theory and educational research. This four-day institute also gave participants the opportunity to intimately dialogue with the leading scholars in the areas of urban education, critical multicultural education, critical pedagogy, cultural studies, cultural responsive pedagogy, participatory action research, ethnic studies, urban youth engagement, equity pedagogy, and critical race theory in education.

7 Dr. Martin Luther King's dream of a time when people will not be judged by the color of their skin but by the content of their character.

8 Through the theory of surplus equality Delgado (1999) argues that more equality exists in our national principles than can be accommodated at any time. Therefore, not all Americans will experience equality. Given this reality and the reality of historical and present-day oppression in the United States, Native Americans, Blacks, and Latinos have been and are constructed as unequal through the hegemony of White oppression.

9 I have italicized the word "critical" to emphasize how I have fused the essential theoretical frames of both critical race theory and critical pedagogy. Both frameworks have heavily influenced my understanding of equity and excellence in education. It was through this understanding that I constructed the foundational elements of the critically compassionate intellectualism model of transformative education, and subsequently the theoretical framework of Tucson Unified School District's Mexican American Studies Department.

REFERENCES

Agency for Healthcare Research and Quality. (2005). *National healthcare disparities report* (retrieved from http://www.ahrq.gov/qual/nhdr05/fullreport/Index.htm).

Agency for Healthcare Research and Quality. (2010). *National healthcare disparities report* (retrieved from http://www.ahrq.gov/qual/nhdr10/nhdr10.pdf).

Baez, B. (2000). Agency, structure, and power: An inquiry into racism and resistance for education. *Studies in Philosophy and Education, 19*(1), 329–348.

Bell, D. (1992). *Face at the bottom of the well: The permanence of racism.* New York: Basic Books.

Bell, D. (1993). Racial realism. *Connecticut Law Review, 24,* 363–379.

Bell, D. (1999). Property rights in whiteness: Their legal legacy, their economic costs. In R. Delgado & J. Stefancic (Eds.), *Critical race theory: The cutting edge* (pp. 71–79). Philadelphia, PA: Temple University Press.

Bhabha, H. (1994). *The location of culture.* London: Routledge.

Cammarota, J., & Romero, A. (2006). A critically compassionate intellectualism for Latina/o students: Raising voices above the silencing in our schools. *Multicultural Education, 14*(2), 16–23.

Cammarota, J., & Romero, A. (2008). The social justice project: A critically compassionate intellectualism for Chicana/o students. In W. Ayers, T. Quinn, & D. Stovall (Eds.), *Handbook of social justice in education* (pp. 465–476). New York: Routledge.

Delgado, R. (1995). *The Rodrigo chronicles: Conversations about America and race.* New York: New York University Press.

Delgado, R. (1999). *When equality ends.* Boulder, CO: Westview.

Delgado, R., & Stefancic, J. (2001). *Critical race theory: An introduction.* New York: New York University Press.

Delgado Bernal, D. (2002). Critical race theory, Latino critical theory, and critical raced-gendered epistemologies: Recognizing student of color as holders and creators of knowledge. *Qualitative Inquiry, 8*(1), 105–126.

Duncan-Andrade, J., & Morrell, E. (2008). *The art of critical pedagogy: Possibilities for moving from theory to practice in urban schools.* New York: Peter Lang.

Freire, P. (1970). *Pedagogy of the oppressed.* New York: Continuum.

Freire, P. (1994). *Pedagogy of the oppressed.* New York: Continuum.

Garcia, J. (2001). Racism and racial discourse. *Philosophical Forum, 32*(2), 125–145.

Haney Lopez, I. (2003). *Racism on trial: The Chicano fight for justice.* Cambridge, MA: Belknap Press of Harvard University Press.

Haymes, S. (2003). Toward a pedagogy of place for Black urban struggle. In S. May (Ed.), *Critical multiculturalism: Rethinking multicultural and antiracist education* (pp. 42–76). Philadelphia, PA: Falmer Press.

Ladson-Billings, G., & Tate, W., IV. (1995). Toward a critical race theory of education. *Teachers College Record, 97*(1), 47–63.

McLaren, P., & Gutierrez, K. (1995). Pedagogies of dissent and transformation: A dialogue with Kris Gutierrez. In P. McLaren (Ed.), *Critical pedagogy and predatory culture: Oppositional politics in a postmodern era* (pp. 145–176). New York: Routledge.

Moje, E.B., McIntosh Ciechanowski, K., Kramer, K., Ellis, L., Carrillo, R., & Collazo, T. (2004). Working toward third space in content area literacy: An examination of everyday funds of knowledge and discourse. *Reading Research Quarterly, 39*(1), 38–70.

Moll, L., Amanti, C., Neff, D., & González, N. (1992). Funds of knowledge for teaching: Using a qualitative approach to connect homes and classrooms. *Theory into Practice, 31*, 132–141.

Omi, M., & Winant, H. (1994). *Racial formation in the United States: From the 1960s to the 1990s.* New York: Routledge.

Pine, G., & Hilliard, A. (1990). Rx for racism: Imperative for America's schools. *Phi Delta Kappan, 71*(8), 593–600.

Rodriguez, I. (2001). Reading subaltern across texts, discipline, and theories: From representation to recognition. In I. Rodriguez (Ed.), *The Latin American subaltern studies reader.* Durham, NC: Duke University Press.

Roithmayr, D. (1999). Introduction to critical race theory in educational research and praxis. In L. Parker, D. Deyhle, and S. Villenas (Eds.), *Race is … Race isn't: Critical race theory and qualitative studies in education.* Boulder, CO: Westview.

Romero, A. (2008). Towards a critically compassionate intellectualism model of transformative education: Love, hope, identity, and organic intellectualism through the convergence of critical race theory, critical pedagogy, and authentic caring. Unpublished doctoral dissertation, University of Arizona.

Romero, A. (2011). At war with the state in order to save the lives of our children: The battle to save ethnic studies in Arizona. *Black Scholar Journal, 40*(4), 7–15.

Said, E. (1979). *Orientalism.* New York: Vintage Books.

Smedley, B. (2012). The lived experience of race and its health consequences. *American Journal of Public Health, 102*(5), 933–935.

Smith-Maddox, R., & Solórzano, D. (2002). Using critical race theory, Paulo Freire's problem-posing method, and case study research to confront race and racism in education. *Qualitative Inquiry, 8*, 66.

Solórzano, D., & Delgado-Bernal, D. (2001). Examining transformational resistance through a critical race theory and LatCrit theory framework: Chicana and Chicano students in an urban context. *Urban Education, 36*(3), 308–342.

Solórzano, D., & Yosso, T. (2000). Toward a critical race theory of Chicana and Chicano education. In C. Tejada, C. Martinez, & Z. Leonardo (Eds.), *Charting new terrains: Chicana(o)/Latina(o) education* (pp. 35–65). Cresskill, NJ: Hampton Press.

Spring, J. (2008). *The American school: From the Puritans to No Child Left Behind.* New York: McGraw-Hill Higher Education.

Takaki, R. (1994). Reflection of racial patterns in America. In R. Takaki (Ed.), *From different shores: Perspectives on race and ethnicity in America.* Oxford: Oxford University Press.

Valenzuela, A. (1999). *Subtractive schooling: U.S.-Mexican youth and the politics of caring.* Albany: State University of New York Press.

Villenas, S., Deyhle, D., & Parker, L. (1999). Critical race theory and praxis: Chicano(a)/Latino(a) and Navajo struggles for dignity, educational equity and social justice. In L. Parker, D. Deyhle, & S. Villenas (Eds.), *Race is … Race isn't: Critical race theory and qualitative studies in education* (pp. 31–52). Boulder, CO: Westview.

Yosso, T. (2002). Toward a critical race curriculum. *Equity and Excellence in Education, 35*(2), 93–107.

Yosso, T. (2006). *Critical race counterstories along the Chicana/Chicano educational pipeline.* New York: Routledge.

23

OTHER KIDS' TEACHERS

What Children of Color Learn from White Women and What This Says about Race, Whiteness, and Gender

Zeus Leonardo and Erica Boas

In recent research on schooling, much attention has been paid to the growing demographic divide between the teaching and student population. According to a 2011 report by the National Center for Education Information, as the number of students of color in public schools rises, the teaching profession develops in the opposite direction as it becomes more White (Feistritzer, 2011). There is a reasonable concern that the gulf between them will grow, spelling greater difficulties for struggling minority students whose culture and experience already mismatch their teachers' milieu and upbringing, captured by Lisa Delpit's (1995/2006) symptomatic book title, *Other People's Children*. By 2050, it is widely predicted that public schools will boast a majority of students of color in trend-setting states like California and Texas (Banks, 2004). Because they are two of the largest states, their development often represents projected patterns for the future of education. The growing racial divide between White teachers and students of color is worrisome for critical race theorists because it means the implementation of culturally relevant pedagogy (Gay, 2000; T. Howard, 2010; Ladson-Billings, 1995) faces serious challenges.

However, an important detail rarely makes it into the prognosis. Teachers are not only predominantly White; they are overwhelmingly *White women*. The National Center for Education Information released a 2011 report stating that over 80 percent of the teaching force in the United States was White and female. Up from 69 percent in 1986, the numbers seem to keep growing. A 2007 National Center for Education Statistics report states, "In 2004, minorities made up 42 percent of public prekindergarten through secondary school enrollment" (KewalRamani et al., 2007, p. iv). With each of these groups reportedly growing, the interface between White female schoolteachers and students of color has a significant bearing on education policies, outcomes, and teaching practices. Therefore, a specificity to the situation needs to be highlighted and interrogated. White women's particular role in the racial formation (Omi and Winant, 1994) becomes an important node of analysis, because it forms a basic architecture for the unique interaction between White women teachers and students of color of any gender. This chapter explores this particular tendency in the field of education. The specific relationship between White women teachers and their students of color is under-theorized. Yet this relationship is structural and has strong historical roots that affect the future of education. To create a basis for understanding these roots and the subsequent structures they take on, this chapter draws from historical texts, statistics, literary analysis, film, and social theories pertaining to education. In the spirit of critical race theory, the chapter narrates from these different perspectives to tell a "story" of the White woman teacher's significant social position and impact.

The majority of teachers in U.S. public schools are White, most of whom are women. This necessitates that critical race education entails a thoughtful analysis of both the White and the woman-dominant teaching force. This means that the interaction between White women and children of color needs to be understood in order to explain the concrete and historical dynamics between these groups. For example, what is the historical relationship between White women and women of color? What is the relationship between White women and men of color? Undoubtedly, in this analysis we discuss children of color and adult White women, but it remains significant that children of color are linked to adults of color and become implicated in the histories with White women. This suggests that an ungendered analysis of whiteness and a White-absent, let alone colorblind, analysis of gender during the educational interaction will be limited in their scope and ability to shed light on the development of both children of color and White women teachers. This is an endorsement for an intersectional analysis in general, but an interrogation of a specific relationship between subgroups within the matrix of race and gender. Not only will race and whiteness become central themes for the analysis, but also the historical development of femininities and masculinities. Together race, whiteness, and gender create a complex relationship with multiple contradictions that benefit from critical analysis. First, this chapter presents several key publications concerning the whiteness of the teaching population. In addition, key research in Whiteness Studies will be highlighted. Second, the chapter imagines how the arguments put forth in these works become complicated when the specific role of White women is accounted for. Third, informed by a woman of color feminist perspective, we provide a short history of White women in the making of race, their investments in racialization, and their contradictions. Last, the chapter concludes with some thoughts on how an articulated uptake of the racialized/gendered dimensions of teaching helps educators understand and explain, if not change, schooling's current and future institutional appearance.

If it is consistent with CRT to argue that the current racial formation is dominated by whiteness and its structures, then it requires a nuanced understanding of the many dimensions of whiteness. This means that, even if whiteness is, as Ellsworth (1997) notes, many things at once and never the same thing twice, we may go a long way with Ian Haney Lopez (2006), who argues that the differences within whiteness do not prevent it from converging in order to produce one overarching condition: White domination. In our estimation, Lopez comes closest to providing the theoretical understanding that synthesizes the apparently irreconcilable differences between scholars who argue for whiteness's multiplicity (Dyer, 1997; Giroux, 1997; G. Howard, 1999; Kincheloe and Steinberg, 1998; McIntyre, 1997; McLaren and Torres, 1999; Twine and Gallagher, 2008) and those who argue for whiteness's singularity (Ignatiev and Garvey, 1996; Leonardo,

2009; Roediger, 1994). On one side, Giroux and others argue that whiteness cannot be reduced to the main trope of social domination based on the evidence that whiteness has been performed in multiple ways by different Whites across the political spectrum. Therefore, if Whites historically have deployed whiteness with multiple and divergent consequences, it does not hold up conceptually to characterize it in an essentialist manner.

On the other side, Roediger and others define whiteness as an ideology based on the evidence that it functions for the purposes of White domination as well as obfuscating the real mechanisms responsible for the lot of otherwise oppressed Whites, such as the working class or, for our specific argument, White women. This does not suggest that White workers or women suffer from the classical Marxist affliction of "false consciousness" because they are not merely duped into whiteness but actively endorse it. Lopez provides a third option, which recognizes whiteness in the multitude while staking a claim that these variegations lead to the essence of whiteness, which is the ability to determine the configurations of race power. These machinations of whiteness take shape in historically specific ways with the contradictions that are different for White men, women, and other identities under the aegis of whiteness.

THE WHITE RACIAL ARMY AND WHITE WOMEN'S PLACE IN IT

Just as every army is composed of different tactical positions in order to secure or conquer a territory, so does whiteness consist of its own foot soldiers, officers, and generals who perform different functions but whose allegiance to whiteness is not the question. With respect to White women, although they may not call the shots, they often pull the trigger (Leonardo, forthcoming). Understanding their role in the upkeep of whiteness is critical if educators wish to explain the specific battleground called schooling. Often, White women are drafted to carry out the reproductive work of whiteness as education becomes a para-caring profession, not unlike nursing. For centuries, as the "caring gender," White women have occupied a space different from White men within the enactment of racism. From enslavement to colonialism, White women have done the work of White supremacy specific to their own place in the hierarchy, producing their own contradictions in the process. As part of an oppressed gender, White women have been relegated to reproductive roles—social and biological—in society (Arnot, 2002; Lamphere, 1987; MacKinnon, 1989; Milkman, 1987). Despite the fact that the history of teaching did not always follow this script and men were once dominant in the teaching profession (Apple, 1986), and the fact that Black teachers of Black and other children of color exercise their own influence on education (e.g., see Foster, 1998; Lynn & Jennings, 2009), the current dynamic makes White women ideal subjects for maintaining race relations within the field of education today. Their specific history with men and women of color interpellates their involvement with boys and girls of color in schools. Several key works have highlighted the dominant role of whiteness in society and schools. We present a few influential exemplars here, whose research participants have been White women, some of whom are located in the field of education.

In 1988, Peggy McIntosh wrote a "little" working paper for Wellesley College (see McIntosh, 1992). Now popularly known as the "White knapsack" argument, McIntosh's essay is acknowledged by Rothenberg (2002), whose dedication page credits McIntosh for having "led the way" to interrogate White privilege. In it, McIntosh speaks in compelling terms about the obliviousness of most Whites toward their mundane racial privileges and institutional normativity. Producing an original list of 46 White privileges (it appears elsewhere in shorter versions), McIntosh (1992) intended the essay to provide a correspondence theory between White *and* male privilege. She writes:

> I think whites are carefully taught not to recognize white privilege, as males are taught not to recognize male privilege . . . I have come to see white privilege as an invisible package of unearned assets that I can count on cashing in each day, but about which I was "meant" to remain oblivious.
>
> (p. 71)

Although there may be problems with McIntosh's overuse of the passive tone to describe her own, and other Whites', oblivion to race privilege, rather than focusing on their active investment in it (Leonardo, 2004), McIntosh captures powerfully the dynamics of such privileges.

In the intellectual and activist scene, McIntosh's original points about male privilege have all but dropped off the interpretive radar, and the essay has produced an industry focusing solely on her indictment of whiteness. This is unfortunate if a gender–race correspondence regarding privilege is helpful in illuminating both social forces. However, in using the correspondence, because McIntosh's main thrust is to compare men's experience with White privilege, her target of analysis becomes Whites in general, on one hand, and men in general, on the other. Although her list includes taken-for-granted privileges unearned by White women, such as finding store-bought stockings in their skin color, the specific role that White women play in promoting White domination is not one of her deep concerns. Since McIntosh bases her racial explications on her own daily experiences, some of the examples are conveniently specific to White women, while others arguably include White men and children, such as expecting that store managers are usually White and school curricula attest to their social contributions. In all, despite basing the list on her personal confessions, the different role that White women play in the transaction of an otherwise universal White privilege, or withholding resources from people of color, does not enter the framework on other than a superficial level. McIntosh's knapsack argument fails to interrogate White women's specific role in the upkeep of White supremacy, or its feminized form (see Leonardo, 2005).

Only several years later, Ruth Frankenberg (1993) produced another classic text in the uptake of whiteness. Her research participants are exclusively White women, also signaled in the book's title, *White Women, Race Matters*. Like McIntosh, this time based on interviews with research subjects, Frankenberg unveils the inner workings of White perspectives on race and racism. Extending some of McIntosh's initial thoughts, Frankenberg produces discursive repertoires deployed by White women in her study, ranging from essentialist racism, to color- or power-evasiveness, to race-cognizance. In the first, Frankenberg discovers White women's interpellation into traditional or classical racism, participating in a more or less biological understanding of how "*race was made into a difference*" (p. 139, italics in original). In the second, she traces the more dominant mode of race discourse of color of power-evasion, more popularly known as colorblindness (Bonilla-Silva, 2003), where Whites feign indifference (Chesler et al., 2003; Dixson, 2008; Leonardo, 2007) to racial difference. What perhaps distinguishes Frankenberg's findings from McIntosh's initial argument is the inclusion of a third moment, a more hopeful one, wherein White women express the ability to speak directly to race power and recognition of racist relations. In her writing as a color-conscious feminist, Frankenberg's relational analysis, inclusion of the women's family narratives, and emotional investments in their racial perspectives retain some of the central themes of a gender-sensitive research program. However, as with McIntosh, these themes are rarely turned inward toward White women's specific contributions to racism, since Jim Crow racism, colorblindness, and race awareness are repertoires also deployed by White men. As a result, an undifferentiated picture or racism ironically comes forth. The significance of the interview data is that Frankenberg discovers White discursive moves and use of language to apprehend race. The fact that her participants happen to be women does not change fundamentally the analysis. It is their whiteness that matters in the end, not their White womanness.

In a set of essays on White teachers, one of the leaders in anti-racist education, Christine Sleeter (1993, 1995; Landsman, 2009), comes closest to touching this chapter's central concern. Early in the turn to whiteness, Sleeter takes up White women teachers' understanding of race as one filled with tensions and ambivalence. One of her women teacher-participants indicates, "So I feel the first main objective to help make a change for the young African American male is to work with the white female teacher and work to change their perceptions about the African American male" (in Sleeter, 1995, p. 421; see also Ferguson, 2001). In a more recent essay, Sleeter (2011) traces her personal history to her great-great-grandmother's immigration to the U.S. in the mid-1800s. Aligning herself with the Confederacy, Sleeter's ancestor, whom she calls C.B.C., like many women before her, becomes the keeper of home culture, where she maintains Swiss-French as the family's primary language. This retelling of one's family history with a woman as the main protagonist emphasizes White women's specific role in the reproduction of whiteness, particularly in the domestic sphere. Fighting against the tide of sexism that targets her gender on one front, C.B.C. clutches onto the oar of whiteness in order to make headway in the antebellum South. As Sleeter poignantly ponders:

> One might wonder whether a white woman who fought to protect girls would include non-white girls, or would identify with non-white women. These possibilities did not happen. It appears that because of the strength of the racial classification system and laws based on that system, a newly learned identity as white trumped identifying with anyone not classified as white, including other immigrants and other women.
>
> (2011, p. 430)

Sleeter's accounting for White women's role in the racial army provides a necessary history of the specificities and contradictions of an under-studied relationship in U.S. education, that between White women teachers and students of color. Sleeter expands McIntosh and Frankenberg's earlier insights on White privilege by shining a light on the dark moments in White women's investment in race making. In particular, she extends the invitation to teachers and other educators to excavate similar family histories. We want to take up this challenge and enter a general historical accounting for White women within the racial formation and the educative lessons therein.

"TRUE WOMAN" AND THE WHITE MOTHER–TEACHER: FROM DOMESTIC TO EDUCATOR

Soon, in all parts of our country, in each neglected village, or new settlement, the Christian female teacher will quietly take her station, collecting the ignorant children around her, teaching them habits of neatness, order and thrift; opening the book of knowledge, inspiring the principles of morality, and awakening the hope of immortality.

(Catharine E. Beecher [1800–1878], U.S. educator and author)

American educator and harbinger of women in the teaching profession Catharine E. Beecher made this declaration in 1846, at a time when the role for most White women was as caretakers and nurturers of children and husbands within the home. The "cult of true womanhood," or the "cult of domesticity" as it has been termed by Barbara Welter in her 1966 article "The Cult of True Womanhood: 1820–1860," was a social standard maintained by the White, Protestant majority. It maintained that "proper" women possessed four virtues: piety, purity, obedience to men, and domesticity (Welter, 1966). As Anne McClintock (1995) more recently points out, "Until 1964, the verb to domesticate also carried as one of its meanings the action 'to civilize'" (p. 35). Women were necessary in the home, it was argued, because through these four "cardinal" virtues they would serve as a civilizing force. Married women would bring home the word of God, teach their own children to be virtuous and good, and keep their husbands content in the home. Men, in turn, would provide financial and physical protection for their wives, who were understood to be both physically and intellectually weaker than their male counterparts. This belief was bolstered by scientific studies of the time, found in phrenology, anatomy, and psychology. The trade-off was this: men would protect women from harm by others, and women would save men from themselves (Welter, 1966, p. 156).

Beecher's support for women to enter the realm of teaching did not so much challenge the ideal of domesticity as it extended the ideal into schools, where the nurturing mother figure could reach into a rapidly expanding school system in industrializing America (Preston, 1993). Domesticating remained the project of women. The vocation of the White female schoolteacher in America, according to Beecher, would be to bestow gracefully the "ignorant children" with a new knowledge system based on principles of Christianity. That is, this new teacher figure would, in effect, benevolently save her children.

A century and a half later, this White female schoolteacher remains a familiar figure, this time embodied in a pair of dynamic teachers, Erin Gruwell and LouAnne Johnson. The former is a college graduate who enters Teach for America. She is the high school student who writes in her statement of purpose to her college of choice that she "always wanted to be a teacher to help those less advantaged." Full of good intentions, she is needed in a system that fails repeatedly in retaining good teachers. Her positionality has a history—a gendered and racialized one—complicated by the fact that she is frequently the teacher of students of color. Unlike the teaching figure of the late nineteenth century, more often than not in states like California, today's White, female teacher instructs what Delpit (1995/2006) refers to as "other people's children." Her objective remains the same, but, instead of White children of farmers, this time it is to save children of color through education. She is part of a larger social structure steeped in co-forming systems of race and gender that play out in significant ways within the institution of public schooling.

The traces of the White female schoolteacher in the U.S. since the Victorian era are represented in modern women such as Gruwell and Johnson. These women hold all the promise of education that Beecher sought in her day. While today's White women may not exude the fragile femininity of years past, their maternal love comes through their tenacity, a steadfast belief that they have important roles in educating their black, yellow, red, and brown students. They are embodiments of what Fiol-Matta (2002) has named the "mother–teacher" (p. 44), writing that the mother–teacher is not only the literal maternal figure to her students, but also served in the "absence of the 'national' man" (p. 38). That is, the mother–teacher held the positions of the father and the male teacher, as she raised children in both the public and the private realm. She is therefore removed from the perceived femininity of the non-working mother, inhabiting a more masculinized position. In this role, however, she is always incomplete, because she takes the place of someone else, a man who would likely do better in her position if he were there. Men's lives would be better spent in professions of higher rank, politics, finance, or business, perhaps. But because the schoolteacher is seen as a profession of middling social status, it is an inferior position. Women are good enough for teaching. The White and female teacher is afforded the privilege of inhabiting this "honorable" role, but she will never wholly succeed in it. She is told that she is fit for teaching, and she takes up the post righteously, but the system is bound to fail, especially when she teaches students of color.

In the 2007 film *Freedom Writers*, based on the book with the same title, there is a frequently quoted dialogue. One male student, Marcus, says to Ms. Gruwell, "No, that don't fly, Ma." Gruwell responds, "First of all, I'm not anybody's mother." Here Gruwell rejects the label "mother," demonstrating her thin understanding of the students' vernacular and directing a defensive speech act toward her students and the ostensive audience. Her purpose seems to be to distance herself relationally from her students in a tactical move to reassert herself professionally as a teacher. Conscious of her gender, and regardless of any misunderstanding she might have about the term "Ma," she is quick to reject the position of mother, first and foremost, as she tells her students. Having vocalized this desire, she is able to inhabit the figure of the "national man," positioning herself away from the maternal schoolteacher while remaining female and White bodied, and therefore continuing to benefit from the privileges of feminized whiteness. In verbally rejecting a maternal role, she can claim for herself the position of a tough, respectable, and serious disseminator of education. As her gender is called into focus, she subverts the historical perspective of woman as mother, naturally maternal. Instead, her femininity is based on her ability to "reach" her students, making them believe in themselves and the goodness of school. By distancing herself from them, she can uphold her position as interlocutor between her students and the state, which is further explained in the following section.

VENTRILOQUIST ACTS

LouAnne Johnson: You asked me once how I was gonna save your life. This is it. This moment.

(From the film *Dangerous Minds*, 1995)

If the U.S. education system, in fact, manufactures failure at greater rates than it does success (Varenne and McDermott, 1999), and if the U.S. education system is also an institution that supports whiteness (Leonardo, 2009), then students of color will be, by design, the failing demographic of the system. And relatively speaking, they are (Ferguson, 2001; Noguera, 2009; Valenzuela, 1999). The White, female teacher is thus charged with a population that is set up to fail within a greater system that relies on the systematic failure of the majority to reproduce an expendable labor pool and a capitalist class that benefits from it. However, the fact that the majority of the teaching force is White is significant—her whiteness represents benevolence, signifying her value and a natural proclivity for the job. In this way, she is also in a prime position to defend whiteness as good and well intentioned. So, in spite of any teaching failures, she is best suited for a job that requires the show of goodness and virtue. Through her whiteness, then, and also through the continued, routine failure of the education system, the White female schoolteacher defends patriarchy, which is co-implicated with racism, even if she does not benefit from it. As Audre Lorde (1984) wrote, "In a patriarchal power system where whiteskin privilege is a major prop, the entrapments used to neutralize Black women and white women are not the same . . . white women face the pitfall of being seduced into joining the oppressor under the pretense of sharing power" (p. 118). The White female teacher benevolently serves the nation through her good intentions of saving children of color. Her feminized whiteness is a kinder, gentler whiteness, an "imperial feminism" of sorts (Coloma, 2011), which allows her to reproduce the White, patriarchal nation, or what Audre Lorde (1984) has named a "mythical norm." She writes:

> Somewhere, on the edge of consciousness, there is what I call a *mythical norm*, which each one of us within our hearts knows "that is not me." In america [*sic*], this norm is usually defined as white, thin, male, young, heterosexual, Christian, and financially secure. It is with this mythical norm that the trappings of power reside within society.
>
> (p. 116)

In her unique position, the White female schoolteacher is able to serve as a representative of the state and of the racialized other. In effect, she performs ventriloquist acts for both. Her perceived benevolence and privilege in a system of whiteness afford her the power to speak to, and more significantly on behalf of, "the other." With well-intentioned White women being in the privileged position of representing the needs and desires of others through charity, politics, and schooling, they have also been granted the power to speak for their students. Gruwell and Johnson both wrote books that document their experiences teaching low-income students of color. In some circles, these youth would be called "at-risk." Gruwell's (1999) book tells the story of changing students' lives through writing as her students produced works under her heartfelt guidance. (Her second book is aptly titled *Teach with Your Heart* [2008].) While these students were the representative beneficiaries of her efforts, ultimately she reaps the major recognition and rewards. To her credit, many of her 150 students went on to college, and some actively participate in the Freedom Writers Foundation Gruwell founded in 1997. However, it is Gruwell who remains the heroine and spokesperson for her students and a method of teaching that can "tap the untapped potential of our future: our students!" (see www.freedomwritersfoundation.org).

The White and female teacher speaks to the world for her students, and she speaks to the students for the racialized nation state. Determined to "make a difference," she toils endlessly to effect change in her band of students. Her position as schoolteacher automatically implicates her within the institution of schooling, which maintains a core objective of producing proper citizens for the nation. Like all public schoolteachers, she must represent the state's interests, and if she does not the stakes are high. That the teaching majority is made up of White women demonstrates their "fitness" for the occupation, where she continues to instill virtue through feminized whiteness, creating conditions for a feminized White supremacy. Her whiteness is a currency of power that is aligned with White, patriarchal state power. Yet, as a woman, she is marginalized from the absolute power of the masculine state, positioning her well for ventriloquist acts for the state to her students of color and, likewise, for her students of color to the state.

Certainly not a novel observation, third world feminists and U.S. feminists of color have long taken seriously this aspect of White women's privilege. The preface to the second part of *This Bridge Called My Back: Writings by Radical Women of Color* (Moraga & Anzaldúa, 1983), contains the following lines:

We are the colored in a white feminist movement
We are the feminists among the people of our culture.
We are often then lesbians among the straight.
We do this bridging by naming our selves and by telling our stories in our own words.

(p. 23)

"In our own words" bears significance historically and today. The third world feminist movement rejected the entitlement of White/Western feminists to speak on their behalf. Instead, in the words of Mohanty (Mohanty & Russo, 1991), they called for the dismantling of "the production of the 'third world woman' as a singular monolithic subject" and for the construction of "autonomous, geographically, historically, and culturally grounded feminist concerns and strategies" (p. 51). The feminist project, put simply, is a struggle against patriarchy, yet, with power gained through their whiteness, White/Western women have greater access to power in the race/gender system. This is not true only within feminism. The historical legacy of White women benevolently speaking on behalf of others, such as students of color, endures. White women's positions of power persist in the racial order, and they continue to produce and support a discourse of rescue for those they aim to save.

THE ENDURING SIGNIFICANCE OF THE WHITE FEMALE SCHOOLTEACHER

To understand the import of the relationship between White women teachers and their charges today and into the future, it makes sense to trace what Ann Stoler (2006) has called "tense and tender ties." The White, female teacher inherits and inhabits a social position that originates, as they all do, in the past. She embodies the ideal of the "true woman," benevolent protector of a moral state with a will and a duty to domesticate children. As an extension of the mother for the nation, she falls short of achieving the state's desires. She is stuck in a structural quandary as she educates children who, by design, are bound to fail. She is a female figure emptied of the national man. Yet she perseveres, ever vigilant, caring for her students and rallying on their behalf. She becomes a heroine, in some cases through the figure of the White, female schoolteacher. In the film *Dangerous Minds*, Callie tells Ms. Johnson as she tries to convince her not to quit her teaching post: "See, 'cause we see you as being our light."

We began with the premise that White women teachers' role as benevolent saviors of children in need is one deeply embedded in history. White women have been teachers in an ever developing education system that is, at base, a civilizing institution that has roots in a colonial past and a continuing coloniality of power (Quijano, 2000). The growing numbers of students of color taught by White women reflect a relationship structured by ideologies of racial superiority. White women teachers and children of color constitute a historical relationship that continues and deepens today as the number of students of color and White female teachers increases at both ends. As history has been made, children in schools have learned how to participate in the current social configurations. These teachings happen inside and outside of schools as networks of social institutions intertwine and interact, instructing future adults on race and gender relations.

It is also important for all to remember that the educational project is, as Omi and Winant (1994) imply, at the same time a racial project. The statistics offered above regarding the overrepresentation of White women in the teaching force and the representations of White women teachers in popular culture presented in this chapter confirm Omi and Winant's claim that the racial formation is constituted through both material, institutional arrangements and cultural politics. Furthermore, the racial project is not by accident but by design. Ladson-Billings and Tate (1995), defining the significance of critical race theory for education, wrote that it is "a radical critique of both the status quo and the purported reforms" (p. 62). That is, critical race theory offers a method to contextualize current manifestations of inequalities for knowledge production on education. It helps those concerned with education understand the historical roots of differentiated racial outcomes, and it can make more clear the causes of the effects. CRT is therefore a way to see that the suggested reforms are extensions of patterns of racial hegemony and "an important intellectual and social tool for deconstruction, reconstruction, and construction" (Ladson-Billings, 1998, p. 9). Reforms for education are hastily enacted with uncritical regard for race as a historical and ongoing structuring force. Instead, it is understood as an outcome of problems with the education system or, worse, a variable in research rather than a central principle. Thus, to accept the special position of White women teachers as having a unique impact on the education system and its outcomes may lead to a better understanding of educational problems.

With the knowledge that teaching must be an application of principles, values, and integrity, we conclude with critical race suggestions for all teacher candidates:

- Critically reflect on racialized and gendered histories and how you are implicated in them.
- Make race and race history part of the curriculum, and fight for its maintenance within the curriculum.
- Teach race as a structural and systemic construct with material, differential outcomes that are institutionally embedded not reducible to identities.
- Work to understand and teach race not as a personal crusade but as a socio-historical construct through which we are all (unequally) produced.

All Whites play a part in the reproduction of racism. If it were only a problem of White elites, racism would be more transparent and perhaps easier to explain. But it requires recruiting Whites from all walks of life, from divergent statuses with their own cleavages of power. The process of racial hegemony creates alliances among different White interest groups wherein they surrender certain ideal goals, such as gender or class equality, in exchange for White racial domination. In education, the specificities of the racialized state apparatus (Leonardo, 2009; cf. Althusser, 1971) require a particular analysis. It is not the case that the profession is plainly dominated by White teachers, but more specifically by White women teaching in a school system with a steady rise in minority students. Therefore we suggest that critical race theory would need to pay attention to the role that White women have played in enabling racism, even as oppressed members of a gender group. This chapter represents that attempt.

REFERENCES

Althusser, L. (1971). *Lenin and philosophy* (B. Brewster, Trans.). New York: Monthly Review Press.

Apple, M. (1986). *Teachers and texts*. New York: Routledge & Kegan Paul.

Arnot, M. (2002). *Reproducing gender: Selected critical essays on educational theory and feminist politics*. New York: Psychology Press.

Banks, J. (2004). Teaching for social justice, diversity, and citizenship in a global world. *Educational Forum, 68,* 289–298.

Beecher, C.E. (1846). *The evils suffered by American women and American children: The causes and the remedy: Presented in an address by Miss C.E. Beecher, to meetings of ladies in Cincinnati, Washington, Baltimore, Philadelphia, New York & other cities*. New York: Harper & Brothers.

Bonilla-Silva, E. (2003). *Racism without racists: Color-blind racism and the persistence of racial inequality in the United States*. Lanham, MD: Rowman & Littlefield.

Chesler, M., Peet, M., & Sevig, T. (2003). Blinded by whiteness: The development of White college students' racial awareness. In A. Doane and E. Bonilla-Silva (Eds.), *White out* (pp. 215–230). New York: Routledge.

Coloma, R. (2011). White gazes, brown breasts: Imperial feminism and disciplining desires and bodies in colonial encounters. *Paedagogica Historica* (DOI: 10.1080/00309230.2010.547511).

Delpit, L. (1995/2006). *Other people's children*. New York: New Press.

Dixson, A. (2008). "Taming the beast": Race, discourse, and identity in a middle school classroom. In S. Greene (Ed.), *Literacy as a civil right* (pp. 125–150). New York: Peter Lang.

Dyer, R. (1997). *White*. London: Routledge.

Ellsworth, E. (1997). Double binds of whiteness. In M. Fine, L. Weis, L. Powell, & L. Wong (Eds.), *Off white* (pp. 259–269). New York: Routledge.

Feistritzer, C.E. (2011). *Profile of teachers in the U.S. 2011*. Washington, DC: National Center for Education Information.

Ferguson, A. (2001). *Bad boys*. Ann Arbor: University of Michigan Press.

Fiol-Matta, L. (2002). *Queer mother for the nation: The state and Gabriela Mistral* (1st ed.). Minneapolis: University of Minnesota Press.

Foster, M. (1998). *Black teachers on teaching*. New York: New Press.

Frankenberg, R. (1993). *White women, race matters: The social construction of whiteness*. Minneapolis: University of Minnesota Press.

Gay, G. (2000). *Culturally responsive teaching: Theory, research, and practice*. New York: Teachers College Press.

Giroux, H. (1997). Rewriting the discourse of racial identity: Towards a pedagogy and politics of whiteness. *Harvard Educational Review, 67*(2), 285–320.

Gruwell, E. (1999). *The Freedom Writers diary*. New York: Broadway.

Gruwell, E. (2008). *Teach with your heart: Lessons I learned from the Freedom Writers*. New York: Broadway.

Howard, G. (1999). *We can't teach what we don't know*. New York: Teachers College Press.

Howard, T. (2010). *Why race and culture matter in schools*. New York: Teachers College Press.

Ignatiev, N., & Garvey, J. (1996). Abolish the White race: By any means necessary. In N. Ignatiev and J. Garvey (Eds.), *Race traitor* (pp. 9–14). New York: Routledge.

KewalRamani, A., Gilbertson, L., Fox, M., & Provasnik, S. (2007). *Status and trends in the education of racial and ethnic minorities*. NCES 2007–039. Washington, DC: National Center for Education Statistics, Institute of Education Sciences, U.S. Department of Education.

Kincheloe, J., & Steinberg, S. (1998). Addressing the crisis of whiteness: Reconfiguring White identity in a pedagogy of whiteness. In J. Kincheloe, S. Steinberg, N. Rodriguez, & R. Chennault (Eds.), *White reign* (pp. 3–29). New York: St. Martin's Griffin.

Ladson-Billings, G. (1995). Toward a theory of culturally relevant pedagogy. *American Educational Research Journal, 32*(3), 465–491.

Ladson-Billings, G. (1998). Just what is critical race theory and what is it doing in a "nice" field like education? *Qualitative Studies in Education, 11*(1), 7–24.

Ladson-Billings, G., & Tate, W.F., IV. (1995). Toward a critical race theory of education. *Teachers College Record, 97*(1), 47–68.

Lamphere, L. (1987). *From working daughters to working mothers: Immigrant women in a New England industrial community.* Ithaca, NY: Cornell University Press.

Landsman, J. (2009). *A White teacher talks about race.* Lanham, MD: Rowman & Littlefield.

Leonardo, Z. (2004). The color of supremacy: Anti-racist education and White domination. *Educational Philosophy and Theory, 36*(2), 137–152.

Leonardo, Z. (2005). Through the multicultural glass: Althusser, ideology, and race relations in post-Civil Rights America. *Policy Futures in Education, 3*(4), 400–412.

Leonardo, Z. (2007). The war on schools: NCLB, nation creation, and the educational construction of whiteness. *Race, Ethnicity and Education, 10*(3), 261–278.

Leonardo, Z. (2009). *Race, whiteness, and education.* New York: Routledge.

Leonardo, Z. (forthcoming). *Critical frameworks on race: Toward a multidimensional theory of racism and education.* New York: Teachers College Press.

Lopez, I.H. (2006). *White by law.* New York: New York University Press.

Lorde, G.A. (1984). *Sister outsider.* Freedom, CA: Crossing Press.

Lynn, M., & Jennings, M. (2009). Power, politics, and critical race pedagogy: A critical race analysis of Black male teachers' pedagogy. *Race, Ethnicity & Education, 12*(2), 173–196.

MacKinnon, C.A. (1989). *Toward a feminist theory of the state.* Cambridge, MA: Harvard University Press.

McClintock, A. (1995). *Imperial leather: Race, gender, and sexuality in the colonial contest* (1st ed.). New York: Routledge.

McIntosh, P. (1992). White privilege and male privilege: A personal account of coming to see correspondences through work in women's studies. In M. Andersen & P.H. Collins (Eds.), *Race, class, and gender: An anthology* (pp. 70–81). Belmont, CA: Wadsworth Publishing.

McIntyre, A. (1997). *Making meaning of whiteness.* Albany: State University of New York Press.

McLaren, P., & Torres, R. (1999). Racism and multicultural education: Rethinking "race" and "whiteness" in late capitalism. In S. May (Ed.), *Critical multiculturalism: Rethinking multicultural and antiracist education* (pp. 42–76). Philadelphia, PA: Falmer Press.

Milkman, R. (1987). *Gender at work: The dynamics of job segregation by sex during World War II.* Champaign: University of Illinois Press.

Mohanty, C.T., & Russo, A. (1991). *Under Western eyes.* Bloomington: Indiana University Press.

Moraga, C., & Anzaldúa, G. (1983). *This bridge called my back: Writings by radical women of color.* New York: Kitchen Table/Women of Color Press.

Noguera, P.A. (2009). *The trouble with Black boys.* San Francisco, CA: Jossey-Bass.

Omi, M., & Winant, H. (1994). *Racial formation in the United States: From the 1960s to the 1990s* (2nd ed.). New York: Routledge.

Preston, J.A. (1993). Domestic ideology, school reformers, and female teachers: Schoolteaching becomes women's work in nineteenth-century New England. *New England Quarterly, 66*(4), 531–551 (DOI: 10.2307/366032).

Quijano, A. (2000). Coloniality of power, Eurocentrism, and Latin America. *Nepantla, 1*(3), 533–580.

Roediger, D. (1994). *Toward the abolition of whiteness.* New York: Verso.

Rothenberg, P. (Ed.). (2002). *White privilege: Essential readings on the other side of racism.* New York: Worth Publishers.

Sleeter, C. (1993). How White teachers construct race. In C. McCarthy and W. Crichlow (Eds.), *Race, identity, and representation in education* (pp. 157–171). New York: Routledge.

Sleeter, C. (1995). Reflections on my use of multicultural and critical pedagogy when students are White. In C. Sleeter and P. McLaren (Eds.), *Multicultural education, critical pedagogy, and the politics of difference* (pp. 415–437). Albany, NY: SUNY Press.

Sleeter, C. (2011). Becoming White: reinterpreting a family story by putting race back into the picture. *Race, Ethnicity and Education, 14*(4), 421–433.

Stoler, A.L. (2006). *Haunted by empire.* Durham, NC: Duke University Press.

Twine, F.W., & Gallagher, C. (2008). The future of whiteness: A map of the "third wave." *Ethnic and Racial Studies, 31*(1), 4–24.

Valenzuela, A. (1999). *Subtractive schooling.* Albany: State University of New York Press.

Varenne, H., & McDermott, R. (1999). *Successful failure.* Boulder, CO: Westview.

Welter, B. (1966). The cult of true womanhood: 1820–1860. *American Quarterly, 18*(2), 151–174 (DOI: 10.2307/27111790).

24

CRITICAL RACE METHODOLOGICAL TENSIONS
Nepantla in Our Community-Based Praxis
Enrique Alemán, Jr., Dolores Delgado Bernal, and Sylvia Mendoza

And I now call it *Nepantla*, which is a Nahuatl word for the space between two bodies of water, the space between two worlds. It is a limited space, a space where you are not this or that but where you are changing … It is very awkward, uncomfortable and frustrating to be in that *Nepantla* because you are in the midst of transformation.

(Anzaldúa, 1987, p. 237)

Emphasizing the moral and ethical responsibilities of critical race scholarship, Ladson-Billings and Donnor (2005) bridge methodology and praxis by effectively arguing that committed intellectuals must move outside of academic walls to engage in critical race practice. They state that "We must learn to be 'at home' on the street corners and in the barrios, churches, mosques, kitchens, porches, and stoops of people and communities, so that our work more accurately reflects their concerns and interests" (p. 298). We, like many CRT scholars, take their point to heart and are literally, not just figuratively, "at home" in the barrios and community spaces they name. For example, seven years ago we formed a partnership with Jackson Elementary and introduced ourselves to students, parents, and school community members. Spurred by our desire to apply our scholarly expertise, tap into our professional networks, and exhibit "parental involvement" in our children's school,[1] we initiated a partnership between the University of Utah and Jackson Elementary when a call for proposals was released encouraging partnerships on the Westside of Salt Lake City, an area that has been historically underserved (Buendia & Ares, 2006; A. Solórzano, 2005).[2]

However, even as we find comfort and a sense of belonging in the community in which we continue to work and live, we often experience the type of methodological discomfort, awkwardness, and frustration that Anzaldúa describes in the introductory quote. These tensions are not the result of the many beneficial and rewarding relationships we've forged with parents, students, educators, and community members. Rather, they result from being in spaces where theory and practice often clash and from wrestling with ethical responsibilities as members of this community and as scholar-activists striving to develop trusting and reciprocal relationships.

Given our seven years of partnership development and community-engaged research, our goal is to contribute to this volume by offering a methodological discussion of some of the challenges we confront while *doing* critical race praxis. While CRT has always informed and shaped our program development, we continue to struggle with the methodological messiness of our research. Understanding the way schools work—or don't work—for students of color, CRT has been especially useful in providing the tools and language to critique and push back against racist structures, policies, and discourses. However, we have also found that CRT's tenets and its well-cited constructs do not always provide us with all the methodological tools to make sense of the tensions we experience in our praxis.

Indeed, our praxis is wrought with methodological tensions that result from the material realities of the parents and students with whom we partner, our limited capacity to reform educational systems and practices that continue to privilege and reify Whiteness, and the concerted state efforts to institute policies that increase surveillance and dehumanize immigrants. Although we are constantly negotiating the methodological uneasiness that results from these dilemmas, it is in illuminating our methodological frictions and contradictions and by expanding our use of other critical conceptual tools that, we argue, our experience in community-engaged research may continue to push the boundaries of CRT, and critical race praxis scholarship in particular. Therefore, it is in our drawing upon Chicana feminist thought that we introduce the indigenous concept of *nepantla*—a space of tension and a space of possible transformation—as one way of articulating and theorizing the awkward, uncomfortable, and frustrating methodological tensions that are inevitable in critical race praxis.

In the remaining sections of this chapter, we will first contextualize our critical race praxis by introducing *Adelante*, our university–school–community partnership, and the background and context of the community in which it is situated. Next, we discuss how CRT is foundational to and grounds all of our partnership development. By introducing how *nepantla* as a conceptual tool informs our methodology simultaneously, we seek to theorize the "messiness" of critical race praxis. We then present an abbreviated counterstory that illustrates some of the tensions and ethical dilemmas we confront while living and working in this school community. Finally, we discuss the complications that arise with our insider–outsider positionalities when working to enhance *confianza*, or trust building, and the power dynamics that ensue. We seek to describe how our work with *Adelante* not only necessitates focusing on the messiness of engaging communities, families, and schools as critical race praxis, but also requires that we embrace the *nepantla* of our methodology as we continue to struggle for more just schools, policies, and practice.

ADELANTE AND JACKSON: SETTING THE CONTEXT

I like everything about *Adelante*! The immersion in college awareness as well as in the (Spanish and English) languages is the best thing that could happen at Jackson. I like that from such a young age we prepare and teach about college.

(Clara, *Adelante* parent)

In Fall 2005, we formed a partnership with Jackson Elementary, one of only two English–Spanish dual immersion programs in the Salt Lake City School District at that time. "*Adelante*:[3] A College Awareness and Preparatory Partnership" seeks to raise awareness of higher education opportunities and to increase the expectation of university attendance and success among students, families, and teachers at Jackson Elementary. It was formed as a counter-space, to directly confront the racist and historically oppressive role that schools play in the lives of students and families of color (Anderson, 2007; San Miguel & Valencia, 1998). The partnership's main goals are: 1) to prepare students and their families for college by integrating higher education into their school experience; and 2) to help establish a college-going culture within the school. We attempt to meet these goals in our development and implementation of five interconnected components: university visits and science camps; academic and cultural enrichment; university service learning and mentoring; parental and community engagement; and research informing practice (see Figure 24.1).

Our work with *Adelante* is set in a context where growing state diversity continues to be thwarted by an overwhelmingly White legislative and educational policymaking apparatus. As in other states that have failed to provide equal educational access and opportunities to Latina/o and Chicana/o students (Alemán & Rorrer, 2006), Utah has been contending with a shift in demographics and increases in student enrollment over the last decade (Perlich, 2008).[4] In the Salt Lake City School District, where Jackson is located, 40 percent of the total student enrollment is Latina/o and, despite the fact that they are the numerical majority, the district classifies 53 percent of the student population as "ethnic minorities." Jackson's current enrollment includes approximately 550 students, 68 percent of whom are Latina/o and 81 percent of whom are students of color. Fifty-six percent of its students are classified as English language learners (ELLs), and 86 percent qualify for free or reduced lunch. Although the students at Jackson are predominantly Latina/o, all students participate in the *Adelante* Partnership.

Figure 24.1 *Adelante* goals and programmatic components

CRITICAL RACE EPISTEMOLOGIES AND *NEPANTLA*

Even though racial fatalism continues to be an important part of Critical Race Studies—mainly because it "keeps things real"—Critical Race Studies, nonetheless, embraces key liberal traditions. Predictably this creates tension, but it is this uneasy coexistence between critical fatalism and liberal optimism that distinguishes Critical Race Studies from countervailing postmodernist movements that drift toward a nihilistic bent.

(Lazos Vargas, 2003, p. 4)

As stated previously, critical race theory undergirds our methodological perspective and provides a framework from which to understand *Adelante*'s initial development and subsequent evolution. Engaging with critical race literature, we first and foremost adhere to the notion that racism is historical and embedded structurally into society's institutions, systems, and policies, such as in health care, housing, criminal justice, and education (Bell, 1992; Crenshaw et al., 1995). For schools in particular, macro-level, institutionalized racism and the inequity that it creates not only manifest themselves as systemic "gaps" in educational achievement, cyclical poverty, and dropout rates, but also result in micro-level, individual "gaps" in the K-16 educational pipeline that are part of the Black and Brown educational experience (Alemán, 2009a; Ladson-Billings, 1998; D. Solórzano, 1998). Derrick Bell contends that racial fatalism or racial realism is the notion that racism is a permanent aspect of our society, embedded in the everyday lives of all persons in the U.S., and corrosive to all of society's institutions and structures (Bell, 1995). Thus we use the idea of racial realism to aid in our confrontation of these realities and the formulation of strategies that push back against the educational, economic, and sociopolitical conditions that marginalize families and students in our school community.

Although our work is informed by a racial realist view of the way schools work for our community, we are simultaneously guided by Bell's (1995) words that the "fight itself has meaning and should give us hope for the future" (p. 308). It is in this continued struggle and hope—a critical hope that West (2005) distinguishes from "cheap optimism" or what Duncan-Andrade (2009) calls "hokey hope"—that unexpected benefits and gains in the face of permanent indestructible racism justify and sustain our endeavors. Hokey hope "ignores the laundry list of inequities that impact the lives of urban youth" (Duncan-Andrade, 2009, p. 182). It is based on a false narrative of meritocracy that suggests if young students of color just work hard and pay attention in school then they will make it to college. While *Adelante* encourages young people to work hard to make it to college, it is not based on a hokey hope that ignores the very real material conditions of students at Jackson. Rather, *Adelante* is guided by racial realism *and* a critical hope that allows us collectively to move towards action without assurance that educational structures will indeed change.

To help us explore the methodological tensions and the contradictions of our critical race praxis that is grounded in both racial realism and critical hope we introduce the idea of *nepantla*, a Nahuatl word meaning the space between two worlds or the land in the middle. It is a "place where different perspectives come into conflict" (Anzaldúa, 2002, p. 548). Our methodological perspective understands *nepantla* as the rupture between elements of critical race theory and conceptions of critical hope or the uneasy coexistence of critical fatalism and liberal optimism. It is that space where practice and theory meet and often grate against each other, requiring a researcher's tolerance for ambiguity.

Burciaga's (2007, 2010) exploration of graduate school as *nepantla* positions Chicana graduate students as *nepantleras*—women who negotiate a transitional in-between space and understand their role as individuals in the collective search for social transformation. "As such *nepantla* is also a bridge to possibility, a bridge to aspirations; a bridge one crosses voluntarily and involuntarily to draw from the rivers of lived and learned experiences" (2007, p. 147). Similarly, Elenes (2011) says *nepantleras* are constantly shifting, "from single goal reasoning to divergent thinking. This shift is characterized by a movement away from set patterns and goals and toward a holistic perspective ... This is a central aspect of 'spiritual activism' which connects the mind, body, soul, and spirit" (pp. 51–52).

In many ways, the scholar-activists involved with *Adelante* are *nepantleras/os* who constantly negotiate and shift between the overarching goals of the educational partnership and the everyday realities of parents, students, and institutional constraints. Indeed, our methodology allows us to weave together our intellectual, political, and spiritual work into a kind of spiritual activism (Delgado Bernal, 2008). We have reflected on our own educational experiences as multiple generation Chicanas and Chicanos, and each of us has personal and familial knowledge of inequity in public schools and has witnessed firsthand the damaging and "subtractive" (Valenzuela, 1999) nature of schooling for Chicanas/os or Latinas/os. Therefore, our methodology is rooted in our previous experiences of "being child translators, of experiencing racist nativism and racial name-calling, and struggles with normative gender roles in our families" (Prieto & Villenas, 2012). It is a methodology born from our own ways of knowing, learning, and teaching. It is a methodological approach of *nepantla* that includes a space of discomfort, dissonance, and possibilities.

ALVARO: THE COST OF CENTERING EXPERIENTIAL KNOWLEDGE

Adelante's cultural enrichment component was conceptualized with the understanding that the cultural knowledge, pedagogies of the home, and family histories of students and families of color are often negated, silenced, and ignored in traditional school settings. The *Adelante* Oral History Project (AOHP) is one part of the cultural enrichment component and operates from the belief that Jackson students and families embody wisdom, knowledge, and traditions that can contribute to the core curriculum as well as enhance students' education. Jackson students, teachers, and families collaborate to co-produce migration stories and community histories, and to re-tell the stories of their elders as part of the core curriculum. Students also share their work back with the school's families via blogs, videos, or after-school presentations, and as a result students are able to learn from one another and teachers become acquainted with students and their families in new ways (Flores Carmona & Delgado Bernal, 2012). The methodological reflection below was primarily written by co-author Sylvia Mendoza and is not a composite story. Rather, it is a counterstory of the actual interactions she has had with Alvaro, a third grader who participates in the AOHP. We share it as a way of illuminating the *nepantla* of our critical race praxis.

As a co-coordinator for AOHP my research interests have been informed by our work with the students at Jackson Elementary and I have come to view the AOHP as a decolonizing pedagogy. The students' final presentations of their projects have always impacted me profoundly and overwhelmed me emotionally. Watching the students share their research of self and present the narrative of their family members, cultures, and histories is validating not only because of the hours of collaborative work shared between students, teachers, and families to complete the projects, but also because, for me, the presentations represent a disruption—if only for a moment—of the colonial legacy of schooling that has intentionally omitted the life experiences of students of color (Calderón, 2010). At these final presentations, students are literally and meta-phorically at the center of the curriculum and school. As their parents or other family members acknowledge and validate their stories, the students' voices fill the room, talking back (hooks, 1999) to a history of schooling that has aimed to silence them, to drown out their experiences with a dominant narrative which does not represent their everyday lives.

However, despite our best intentions to provide a space that centers the voices and experiences of the students with whom we work, I was quickly reminded of the realities and limitations of the AOHP and of critical race praxis when recently facilitating a presentation for our third grade group. While most Jackson students and their families were in attendance, one student was noticeably absent. Alvaro, a student from Gua-temala, was resistant from the start of the project. Even though he was in a bilingual dual immersion program, he had consistently expressed insecurities with his English abilities and struggled with his writing. Appearing to have internalized deficit notions of himself as a student, he would berate himself, commenting that his project would be the shortest and the worst. Rather than focus on the assignment, Alvaro would leave his desk, walking around the classroom, talking to other students, and avoiding his opportunity to write his oral history. When he did sit down to write, he would ask us to sit right next to him to help him write.

During one of these sessions when Alvaro asked for individual attention, he began to share his concerns with the project, school, and the challenges he faced in his daily life. For this particular project, students were asked to bring a photo from home or to draw a picture of a memory they had, and to then write a story about that particular image. Alvaro shared that he was unable to bring in any photos. "Can you draw a pic-ture for me, then? Maybe a drawing of you with your family?" I asked. Alvaro decided that he would draw a picture of his brother and his brother's girlfriend. As he took out a blank sheet of paper to begin drawing, he quickly changed his mind. "I can't. My brother will get mad at me." Alvaro was reluctant to share private information about his brother with strangers. When it seemed as though he did not fit into the purpose and goals of the assignment, Alvaro's frustration mounted.

Sensing this, I asked Alvaro to draw a picture of anything he was interested in, and to write a story about it. He continued to be frustrated with the instructions and had a difficult time deciding on a topic. In the midst of this frustration, he shared: "I hate school. School is boring. And I hate living here." Alvaro expressed that he missed home, where most of his family continued to live, and lamented on how things were much better in Guatemala. When I asked him to elaborate, he said, "At least in Gua-temala we can walk outside in the streets." In the U.S., and Utah in particular, Alvaro said he feared his family could at any moment be deported. Unsure of how to console or validate his experience and feelings in such a vulnerable moment where he had enough trust to open up to an adult, I tried to continue the conversation. "What are some things you do like about school and living in the U.S.?" I asked. Thinking for a moment, he quickly shared that his favorite thing about the U.S. was Halloween—a holiday that allowed him not only to walk freely in the streets with his friends and family members but also to receive candy from friends and neighbors. At the end of our time together, Alvaro had drawn a picture (see Figure 24.2) and written a story:

> I was born in Guatemala, I came when I was 6 years old. Then I came to Jackson Elementary. I was in 1st grade now I'm in 3rd grade, now it's boring here and now I want to go to Guatemala because all my family is there. I do like the snow and Halloween. What I like about the USA is that you get to trick or treat at people's houses.

For me as a doctoral student and an emerging critical race and community-engaged scholar, coordinating the AOHP and working with students like Alvaro exemplify the moments of methodological tension inherent in our critical race praxis. While the projects provide a space for students to research and share their experiences and histories, they also provide opportunities to develop meaningful relationships with students. Yet we are limited in how much we can do, what we can really change, and how, in the end, society's institutions and their policies continue to destabilize and foster hostility in the lives of our students and their families. While I felt touched that

Figure 24.2 Alvaro's picture story

Alvaro was comfortable enough to share such intimate and personal details about his emotions and his life, I also felt conflicted that through this project I was asking him to open up and reveal inner feelings and confidential information about himself and his family. When he shared his real life experiences, I was not in a position to assist or help directly with his situation. Further, while focusing on Alvaro's life experience as a disruption within a colonial schooling project, it did little in the way of reforming immigration policy or of personally putting him at ease from his fears of deportation. It did not remove the fear that Alvaro feels daily when experiencing the mundane or, as he put it, just trying to "walk outside in the streets." While I am exploring the possibilities of critical race praxis in education in my privileged position as a U.S. citizen and graduate student, Alvaro and his family confront real issues of citizenship, safety, and fear on a daily basis.

ETHICS AND RESPONSIBILITY: UTILIZING *NEPANTLA* AND CRITICAL RACE THEORY

Unlike some academic disciplines, critical race theory contains an activist dimension. It not only tries to understand our social situation, but to change it; it sets out not only to ascertain how society organizes itself along racial lines and hierarchies, but to transform it for the better.

(Delgado & Stefancic, 2001, p. 3)

Alvaro and his family are representative of the students and families with whom we interact. As for so many others, their lives have been impacted by an unforgiving economy, a harrowing migration experience, and an unequal and disadvantaging public schooling system. This methodological reflection provides a glimpse into the *nepantla* of our critical race praxis. For us, the story of Alvaro epitomizes the layered and messy nature of our methodology, and the interactions between Alvaro and Sylvia reflect a number of complex interactions that occur while trying to sustain and build our partnership. While we experience many spaces of *nepantla*, in this section we highlight just two sites of dissonance we experience in doing critical race praxis. That is, our purpose here is to utilize the story of Alvaro to illustrate sites of tension between critical race theory and critical race praxis.

Centering Experiential (and Dangerous) Knowledge

Utilizing arguments for providing spaces and valuing the knowledges of marginalized people to challenge deficit notions and promote social transformation (D. Solórzano & Yosso, 2001), we often ask students and their parents to share their experiences as part of AOHP. Understanding students, parents, and communities of color as holders and creators of knowledge (Delgado Bernal, 2002), we allow our praxis to be shaped by community needs and aspirations. Our goal is to provide a counter to the manner by which marginalized communities, parents, and students are treated in the schooling process—a process that often fails to recognize and utilize the positive attributes and skills, as well as the rich and valuable histories, traditions, cultures, and languages, that are brought with them into the educational setting (Garcia & Guerra, 2004). However, while we listen and attempt to institutionalize the home and cultural knowledges brought to school by these students, the implementation of this goal is ripe with contradictions and limitations.

In asking students to reflect about and document their story as a culturally relevant exercise, we are simultaneously asking some of them to share student or parent realities that could jeopardize their very security or freedom. Although we attempt to mitigate this danger or fear by helping the school improve its relationships with undocumented parents and families, we are still left with contradictory understandings of our role(s) as scholar-activists: How should we as the researchers confront our emotions or feelings of powerlessness when we are unable to respond in meaningful ways with strategies that might actually alter the oppressive conditions that parents and students encounter?

Lest we be unclear, there has been much success in listening to and incorporating familial and communal knowledge into the school curriculum via the AOHP. Family history has been shared in public spaces. Students have bilingually honored their home knowledge and traditions. Teachers have had university students aiding with literacy and writing in their classrooms. The Brown bodies of undergraduate and graduate students have benefited from connections to this community and influenced the culture of the school. However, Alvaro (and possibly other students) has also experienced discomfort in sharing his experiential knowledge. While Sylvia listened and worked with him by modifying the assignment, there was a clear sense that focusing on his life and revealing personal family information were not empowering for him. In fact, sharing his experiential knowledge that was shaped by acts of racism, colonialism, and anti-immigrant sentiments was painful. For those who are the most susceptible, there is an added fear of being exposed and experiencing retaliation (Latina Feminist Group, 2001). Whether it be a kindergartner who shares how he and his mother were apprehended by immigration agents (Delgado Bernal et al., 2008) or a parent who feels a teacher behaves in a racist manner or feels that the school is not a welcoming space (Alemán, 2009b), there is often a personal sense of vulnerability and possible exposure when these experiences are centered. So, while AOHP attempts to institute a value of experiential knowledge throughout the partnership and within the classroom space, Alvaro highlights the threats that he and others face on a daily basis. His example challenges us to complicate and problematize our development of CRT praxis in schools. And, although it also requires us to acknowledge the methodological tensions and embrace the *nepantla* that we as researchers are thrust into, his example does not absolve us from the ethical and moral responsibility of ensuring his anonymity and the protection of his rights and the rights of those who are most vulnerable to society's racist policies and practices.

The work of all of those involved with *Adelante*, and critical race praxis more generally, must seek to cultivate meaningful, caring, and ethical relationships with the students and their parents or family members. However, cultivating these relationships requires being aware of the local context and the realities of our partners. At times, our students' projects must be modified if there is a sense that their safety may be compromised because of the assignment. Many times additional and one-on-one communication is needed to better explain the purpose of the projects and to ensure that student and family situations will not be overtly shared. To practice reciprocity and develop *confianza*, the oral history project staff also share intimate details of their own histories and experiences, regularly creating templates based on their own lives to share with the students before asking the students to share their personal histories. These examples contribute to the development of *confianza* between *Adelante* and the Jackson community and contribute to the creation of a space where students and family members feel they can share personal details about their selves and their lives.

While these are small ways that we attempt to mediate contradictions that emerge, Sylvia's reflection demonstrates a larger point—listening and truly hearing marginalized experiences does not necessarily mean one can do something to alter those experiences. Sylvia felt real frustration in knowing that the overall structure and colonial legacy of schooling, combined with the very real socioeconomic factors affecting the community, severely limited her capacity to significantly and substantially alter Alvaro's life situation. As she pointed out, listening and focusing on his life experiences "did little in the way of reforming immigration policy or of personally putting him at ease from his fears of deportation." The geopolitical effects of migration, immigration, and a global economic crisis have impacted Alvaro's family as they have so many other Latino families in the United States. The families have to contend with a surveillance that limits their freedom of movement, participation, and engagement with societal institutions such as schools (López & López, 2010). Moreover, the families sometimes view the *Adelante* team as having more power to limit this surveillance and address or improve school concerns than we actually have. So, while our research and the partnership attempt to impact school culture, the curriculum, and the awareness of higher education with a backdrop of racial realism and a colonial legacy, we are reminded daily of how little institutional and systemic impact we can have on the material realities of many of the families with whom we work. Sylvia's reflection demonstrates our *nepantla*—that space where practice and theory scrape up against one another and where we wrestle with our understandings of the research and practice that we seek to conduct. As a result of this uncertainty, we are forced to be *nepantleras/os* who constantly negotiate and shift between the overarching goals of our educational partnership and the everyday realities of parents, students, and institutional constraints.

Striving for Reciprocity and Confianza *while Acknowledging Insider–Outsider Privileges*

We have taken special care to not replicate the manner by which universities and educational researchers have conducted their research historically—exploiting marginalized communities as research sites and students and people of color as research "subjects," taking from them without giving anything back (Denzin & Lincoln, 2003). As scholars of color, we are well aware of this colonial history and struggle with the ways that we may be complicit and fail to "give back" in meaningful ways. We approach our research "in solidarity with urban communities" and an understanding that "their pain is our pain" (Duncan-Andrade, 2009, p. 190), but we are also keenly aware that, as university professors and graduate students, we enter our community with power and privilege. Although we are insiders who live in this neighborhood and have children who attend this school, we are also positioned as outsiders with privileges afforded by location of birth and socioeconomic status denied to many in the community we are a part of. We hold contradictory identities as the colonizer and colonized and embody what Villenas (1996) describes as "hav[ing] a foot in both worlds; in the dominant privileged institutions and in the marginalized communities" (p. 231). Many scholars of color have noted the methodological tensions that can emerge when doing research in our "own" communities (Baca Zinn, 1979; Russel y Rodriguez, 1998; Téllez, 2005). Power and the dynamics of its use are inescapable and central to the transformative work being conducted in schools. So while we as critical race scholars wrestle with the unequal distribution of privileges—of which we are holders—we also attempt to build trusting, reciprocal, and non-hierarchal relationships with our partners. This methodological process does not subdue the tensions we feel as scholar-activists. Rather it places special emphasis on our development of trust and our ethical responsibility in supporting parents to negotiate their harsh realities.

Alvaro's story points to the very real tensions we experience when trying to build trusting and reciprocal relationships. Sylvia speaks to her discomfort with the idea that her academic endeavors are sometimes at odds with what is most relevant to the students and families. For example, the *confianza* Sylvia developed with Alvaro allowed her to travel to his world, if even momentarily (Lugones, 1987). Their relationship of *confianza* developed over time and was based on reciprocity in that both Sylvia and Alvaro contributed to it and benefited from it. Sylvia was attaining teaching and research expertise in a community that she was invested in and one that she wanted to give back to. At the same time, Alvaro received mentoring and support with his writing skills and was nurtured with individual, culturally competent instruction. However, this relationship of *confianza* also contributed to Sylvia's discomfort as a CRT scholar-activist. Not able to alter the structural barriers that he was up against, she felt inadequate and unable to reciprocate in a meaningful way precisely because she had developed trust with Alvaro and occupied a more privileged status or position than he.

So, although fostering *confianza* and reciprocity is foundational to *Adelante*'s work in that partnership activities strive to benefit all partners, structural and geopolitical barriers often do not allow us to overcome the contradictions that are present when there is no symmetry in the reciprocity. In other words, reciprocity is often conceived as being 50–50 or looking the same for all partners. However, in our experience, reciprocity cannot be symmetrical given the nature of our privilege and the state of racism in a racial realist view of society. Oftentimes, "doing" critical race praxis benefits the activist-scholar in qualitatively and quantitatively different ways than it benefits the student or community of color. One can argue that the outcome is hardly fair or equitable. In fact, the community outcome of partnership work or community-engaged scholarship is but a brief disruption, a moment in a legacy of oppressive structures imbedded in school and society. In the case of Alvaro, immigration reform was not achieved via the oral history project or other aspects of the partnership. Alvaro and his family continue to live in fear of deportation. For Alvaro, Utah and the larger U.S. sociopolitical context continue to represent an unsafe and unwelcoming place to live. While the *Adelante* Partnership aims to develop ethical, caring, and reciprocal relationships, we continue to be confronted with methodological tensions created by our privileged positions as faculty and graduate students. We see ourselves advance in the academy without knowing the final outcomes of the students and families with whom we work. This methodological tension we will continue to wrestle with, and the questions that arise will prompt us to further develop strategies for reciprocity in our research.

CONCLUSION

During nepantla, individual and collective self-conceptions and worldviews are shattered. Apparently fixed [methodological] categories ... begin eroding. Boundaries become more permeable, and begin to break down. This loosening of previously restrictive labels and beliefs, while intensely painful, can create shifts in consciousness and opportunities for change.

(Keating, 2005, p. 9)

Committed to social change, community engagement, and activism, we are situated in complex, nuanced dilemmas in heeding Ladson-Billings and Donnor's (2005) call for a moral and ethical responsibility of conducting critical race scholarship "at home on the street corners and in the barrios" (p. 298). Even as we feel "at home" with our communities, engaged with parents and students, applying the skills and privileges garnered in our time in the academy, we often experience methodological discomfort in our critical race praxis. As stated earlier, it is not a discomfort or unease we have with the community members or the community spaces in which we live and work. Rather, our discomfort emerges from the *nepantla* we find ourselves in—the methodological space where theory and practice clash, requiring us to embrace ambiguity, compromise, and discomfort all at the same time. *Nepantla* is, in part, that uneasy feeling of being involved in transformational work.

While space (and the story of Alvaro) did not allow us to engage all of the many methodological tensions we have encountered in our critical race praxis, we want to argue that CRT and *nepantla* work in tandem to help us make sense of these tensions and the compromise that is always present in this type of praxis. For example, as CRT scholars, we know that an understanding of racial realism and the inequities it creates influences all aspects of how we negotiate critical race praxis within or alongside educational institutions. Our challenge is naming and pointing to racist practices and policies that are present in a university or school setting, while also attempting to build a sustainable partnership with individuals who work in these institutions. In other words, in order to continue our work from *within* these institutions we often find ourselves having to diplomatically negotiate the ways in which we call out racism. Different than the discomfort we explained in regard to Alvaro and the many students and families like him, we have also found uneasiness and dissonance in that space between calling out racial realism and maintaining critical hope. However, we remain optimistic in our implementation of the *Adelante* Partnership, and part of being "realistic" is the idea that activism comes in very different forms and transformation happens at many different levels.

Attempting to critically reflect on our roles as members of a community of color seeking to maintain our positions as academic researchers in a predominantly White research-intensive institution, we utilize *nepantla* as a space for emancipation and empowerment, rather than oppression or schizophrenia. In wrestling with the complexities of embodying Brownness and privilege, and struggling with the normalcy of frustration and tension that pervades in the "in-betweenness" that Anzaldúa alludes to, we draw upon our understanding of *nepantla* as a supplementary construct with the potential to complement a critical race methodology. With this, we challenge the false binaries (good/bad or activist/sellout) that we too fall victim to and attempt to place our praxis in the in-between spaces that constantly test and challenge us and provide moments of frustration along with success. By embracing these points of rupture and discomfort, we see the real potential of using critical race praxis in tandem with *nepantla*.

NOTES

1 Both Alemán and Delgado Bernal and their partners reside in the local community and have children who attend Jackson Elementary.
2 University Neighborhood Partners (UNP) (http://www.partners.utah.edu/), the University of Utah's unit responsible for promoting and facilitating community-engaged research and partnerships, sponsored the call

for proposals and provided $5,000 start-up funds for two years. Since this initial grant, UNP has served as integral partner and provided numerous opportunities for us to continue our work.

3 We use the Spanish word *Adelante*, which translates to "forward," "forward moving," or "looking forward," as a reinforcement of the goals and purpose of the partnership.

4 Utah and western U.S. states in general have been undergoing a significant shift in demographics over the last several years. According to the U.S. Census Bureau, the western region of the U.S. is made up of 13 states, of which Utah is one. See http://2010.census.gov/news/pdf/apport2010_map3.pdf for a visual representation of the percentage increase in population for each state. Utah's population has increased by 23.8 percent since 2010. The Census Bureau also projects that 90 percent of all population growth will occur in the south and west regions of the U.S.

REFERENCES

Alemán, E., Jr. (2009a). LatCrit educational leadership and advocacy: Struggling over Whiteness as property in Texas school finance. *Equity and Excellence in Education, 42*(2), 183–201.

Alemán, E., Jr. (2009b). Leveraging conflict for social justice: How "leadable" moments can transform school culture. *Journal of Cases in Educational Leadership, 12*(4), 1–16.

Alemán, E., Jr., & Rorrer, A.K. (2006). *Closing educational achievement gaps for Latino students in Utah: Initiating a policy discourse and framework.* Salt Lake City: Utah Education Policy Center.

Anderson, J.D. (2007). Race-conscious educational policies versus a "color-blind constitution": A historical perspective. *Educational Researcher, 36*(5), 249–257.

Anzaldúa, G. (1987). *Borderlands/La frontera: The new mestiza.* San Francisco, CA: Aunt Lute Books.

Baca Zinn, M. (1979). Field research in minority communities: Ethical, methodological and political observations by an insider. *Social Problems, 27*(2), 209–219.

Bell, D.A. (1992). Racial realism. *Connecticut Law Review, 24*(2), 363–379.

Bell, D.A. (1995). Racial realism. In K. Crenshaw, N. Gotanda, G. Peller, & K. Thomas (Eds.), *Critical race theory: The key writings that formed the movement* (pp. 302–312). New York: New Press.

Buendia, E., & Ares, N. (2006). *Geographies of difference: The social production of the east side, west city, and central city school.* New York: Peter Lang.

Burciaga, R. (2007). Chicana Ph.D. students living nepantla: Educación and aspirations beyond the doctorate. Doctoral dissertation (retrieved from Proquest, AAT 3280937).

Burciaga, R. (2010). Aspiring to profess: Chicana Ph.D. students' aspirations of tenure-track careers. Paper presented at the annual meeting of the American Educational Research Association, May, Denver, CO.

Calderón, D. (2010). Making explicit the jurisprudential foundations of multiculturalism: The continuing challenges of colonial education in US schooling for indigenous education. In A. Kempf (Ed.), *Breaching the colonial contract: Anti-colonialism in the US and Canada* (pp. 53–78). New York: Springer.

Crenshaw, K.W., Gotanda, N., Peller, G., & Thomas, K. (Eds.). (1995). *Critical race theory: The key writings that formed the movement.* New York: New Press.

Delgado, R., & Stefancic, J. (2001). *Critical race theory: An introduction.* New York: New York University Press.

Delgado Bernal, D. (2002). Critical race theory, Latino critical theory, and critical raced-gendered epistemologies: Recognizing students of color as holders and creators of knowledge. *Qualitative Inquiry, 8*(1), 105–126.

Delgado Bernal, D. (2008). La trenza de las identidades: Weaving together our personal, professional, and communal identities. In K. Gonzalez & R. Padilla (Eds.), *Doing the public good: Latina/o scholars engage civic participation* (pp. 135–148). Sterling, VA: Stylus.

Delgado Bernal, D., Alemán, E., Jr., & Flores, J. (2008). Transgenerational and transnational Latina/o cultural citizenship among kindergarteners, their parents, and university students in Utah. *Social Justice, 34*(2), 28–49.

Denzin, N.K., & Lincoln, Y.S. (Eds.). (2003). *The landscape of qualitative research: Theories and issues* (2nd ed.). Thousand Oaks, CA: Sage.

Duncan-Andrade, J.M.R. (2009). Note to educators: Hope required when growing roses in concrete. *Harvard Educational Review, 79*(2), 181–194.

Elenes, A.C. (2011). *Transforming borders: Chicana/o popular culture and pedagogy.* Lanham, MD: Lexington Books.

Flores Carmona, J., & Delgado Bernal, D. (2012). Oral histories in the classroom: The Latina/o home as a pedagogical site. In C.E. Sleeter & E. Soriano Ayala (Eds.), *Building solidarity between schools and marginalized communities: International perspectives.* New York: Teachers College Press.

Garcia, S., & Guerra, P. (2004). Deconstructing deficit thinking: Working with educators to create more equitable learning environments. *Education and Urban Society, 36*(2), 150–168.

hooks, b. (1999). Talking back: Thinking feminist, thinking Black. Cambridge, MA: South End Press.

Keating, A. (Ed.). (2005). *Entre mundos/Among worlds: New perspectives on Gloria E. Anzaldúa*. New York: Palgrave Macmillan.

Ladson-Billings, G. (1998). Just what is critical race theory and what's it doing in a *nice* field like education? *Qualitative Studies in Education, 11*(1), 7–24.

Ladson-Billings, G., & Donnor, J. (2005). The moral activist role of critical race theory scholarship. In N.K. Denzin & Y.S. Lincoln (Eds.), *Sage handbook on qualitative research* (3rd ed., pp. 279–301). Thousand Oaks, CA: Sage.

Latina Feminist Group. (2001). *Telling to live: Latina feminist testimonios*. Durham, NC: Duke University Press.

Lazos Vargas, S.R. (2003). Introduction: Critical race theory in education: Theory, practice and recommendations. In G.R. López and L. Parker (Eds.), *Interrogating racism in qualitative research methodology* (pp. 1–18). New York: Peter Lang.

López, M.P., & López, G.R. (2010). *Persistent inequality: Contemporary realities in the education of undocumented Latina/o students*. New York: Routledge.

Lugones, M. (1987). Playfulness, "world"-traveling and loving perception. *Hypatia, 2*(2), 3–19.

Perlich, P.S. (2008). Utah's demographic transformation: A view into the future. *Utah Economic and Business Review, 68*(3), 1–11.

Prieto, L., & Villenas, S. (2012). Pedagogies from nepantla: Testimonio, Chicana/Latina feminisms and teacher education classrooms. *Equity and Excellence in Education, 45*(3), 411–429.

Russel y Rodriguez, M. (1998). Confronting the silencing praxis in anthropology: Speaking of/from a Chicana consciousness. *Qualitative Inquiry, 4*(1), 15–40.

San Miguel, G., & Valencia, R.R. (1998). From the Treaty of Guadalupe Hidalgo to *Hopwood*: The educational plight and struggle of Mexican Americans in the Southwest. *Harvard Educational Review, 68*(3), 353–412.

Solórzano, A. (2005). At the gates of the kingdom: Latino immigrants in Utah, 1900 to 2003. In E.M. Gozdziak & S.F. Martin (Eds.), *Beyond the gateway: Immigrants in a changing America* (pp. 177–212). Lanham, MD: Lexington Books.

Solórzano, D.G. (1998). Critical race theory, racial and gender microaggressions, and the experiences of Chicana and Chicano scholars. *International Journal of Qualitative Studies in Education, 11*, 121–136.

Solórzano, D.G., & Yosso, T.J. (2001). From racial stereotyping and deficit discourse: Toward a critical race theory in teacher education. *Multicultural Education, 9*(1), 2–8.

Téllez, M. (2005). Doing research at the borderlands: Notes from a Chicana feminist ethnographer. *Chicana/Latina Studies, 4*(2), 46–70.

Valenzuela, A. (1999). *Subtractive schooling: U.S.-Mexican youth and the politics of caring*. Albany: State University of New York Press.

Villenas, S. (1996). The colonizer/colonized Chicana ethnographer: Identity, marginalization, and co-optation in the field. *Harvard Educational Review, 66*(4), 711–731.

West, C. (2005). *Democracy matters: Winning the fight against imperialism*. New York: Penguin.

25

CRITICAL RACE THEORY, INTEREST CONVERGENCE, AND TEACHER EDUCATION

H. Richard Milner IV, F. Alvin Pearman III, and Ebony O. McGee

In this chapter, we discuss Bell's (1980) interest convergence, a key concept in critical race theory,[1] as a useful analytic and strategic tool to analyze, critique, make sense of, and reform sites in teacher education that we argue should be studied and interrogated to improve policies and practices in the field. The tenet "interest convergence" originated with the work of Derrick Bell (1980), who argued that the *Brown v. Board of Education* (1954) decision, in which the Supreme Court outlawed *de jure* segregation of public schools, was not the result of a moral breakthrough of the high court but rather a decision that was necessary: (1) to advance American Cold War objectives in which the United States was competing with the Soviet Union for loyalties in the third world; (2) to quell the threat of domestic disruption that was a legitimate concern with Black veterans, who now saw continued discrimination as a direct affront to their service during WWII; and (3) to facilitate desegregation in the South, which was now viewed as a barrier to the economic development of the region. In other words, the interests of Black civil rights coincided for a brief time with the interests of White elites, thus enabling a decision that benefited the interests of Black people. In Bell's (1980) words, "the interests of Blacks in achieving racial equality will be accommodated only when it converges with the interests of Whites" (p. 523).

In 1995, Ladson-Billings and Tate argued that race was under-theorized in education. We argue that race is grossly under-theorized in teacher education. Racial apathy and color blindness permeate as leading orientations to race within mainstream teacher education research, policy, and practice. Therefore thinking seriously about how interest convergence can be used as a tool to explain the intersections of race and teacher education has potential implications for how we construct and deconstruct knowledge in the field. Although race has been investigated and theorized about in teacher education for several decades (Dixson, 2006; Ladson-Billings, 1999; Sleeter, 2008; Tatum, 2001), we stress that the field has yet to develop a research agenda with consistent language and problem spaces to build a more robust conceptual and empirical literature base about race. It is important for those of us in teacher education to name the multiple realities regarding race that exist in the field, and the conceptual tools and the categorical language and concepts that can be used to study, analyze, discuss, explain, and ultimately name the realities that may contribute to the raced policy, research, and theory that govern teacher education policies and practices.

In *The Report of the AERA Panel on Research and Teacher Education*, Cochran-Smith and Zeichner (2005) emphasized that researchers in the field of teacher education need to situate their research and conceptual discussions more solidly in theory. They wrote, "without locating empirical studies in relation to appropriate theoretical frameworks regarding teacher learning, teacher effectiveness, and pupil learning, it will be difficult to explain findings about the effects of particular teacher education practices" (p. 32) and policies. Similarly, Johnston-Parsons (2007) wrote, "Accounts of teacher education programs and research are often light on theoretical explanations" (p. 1).

Thus, how we theorize about race, what we focus on regarding it, and what we believe counts as useful knowledge about race, as well as who constructs and deconstructs knowledge in teacher education regarding race, have the potential to profoundly influence the field and move it forward (Chapman, 2007; Howard, 2008; Ladson-Billings, 1999; Lynn & Parker, 2006; Milner, 2007; Ryan & Dixson, 2006; Tillman, 2002). We argue that using interest convergence as an analytic tool in teacher education can help us address and potentially disrupt structural inequity, racist policies and practices, and hegemonic forces that perpetuate and maintain the status quo in the field and beyond. In this chapter, we focus on four sites that we argue need additional exploration in the field: (1) curriculum and instructional practices; (2) racial demography of teacher educators; (3) routes into teaching; and (4) school–university partnership incentives. We suggest that policies, reform movements, and practices related to these sites have meaningful implications for the field of teacher education. In short, because issues of race and racism are deeply rooted in U.S. society (Bobo & Kluegel, 1993), they are also ingrained and deeply imbedded in the policies, practices, procedures, and institutionalized systems and practices of teacher education.[2]

We begin the chapter by providing a brief summary of the literature base. We then define and discuss what we mean by interest convergence. Next, we conceptualize and expound upon four analytic sites in teacher education, applying the interest convergence tenet. With each site we provide examples and strategies of how interest convergence can serve as a timely mechanism for understanding and challenging current teacher education policies and practices that mirror those found in the larger society. Interest convergence suggests that educational policy makers, curriculum developers, and practitioners can no longer deny the role of race and assists in providing evidence that meritocratic ideals and political conservatism fueling persistent inequities are not in the best interest of teacher education. We further argue that the interest convergence concept establishes the means of investigating and generating alternative lenses and approaches on behalf of all teachers. In the final section of the chapter, we provide a brief summary and final thoughts about interest convergence as an analytic tool and strategic tool moving forward.

SUMMARY OF ARTICLES AVAILABLE IN THE LITERATURE

While there have been a growing number of researchers who have employed critical race theory as an analytic tool in teacher education in general, our search of the databases revealed a paucity of research concerning the precise intersection of interest convergence and teacher education. For example, a search with the keywords "critical race theory" and "teacher education" revealed over 200 results in ERIC. Yet, when we limited these searches to articles that included "interest convergence" *anywhere in the article*, this robust list of 200 was reduced to just seven articles. Thus, even with the increase of research in teacher education employing a critical race theory lens, the research base has largely ignored the value of interest convergence as an analytic and strategic tool within teacher education. Because this chapter is about interest convergence and teacher education, we focus our attention on literature in this area.[3]

Using the keywords "interest convergence and teacher education" as well as "interest convergence and education," we conducted a search in several educational, psychological, social science, and legal databases (i.e., ERIC, PsycINFO, Sociological Abstracts, and Lexis-Nexis). The search with the descriptors "interest convergence and teacher education" *anywhere in the article* revealed three publications in ERIC, 28 publications in PsycINFO, six publications in Sociological Abstracts, and eight publications in Lexis-Nexis. The search with the descriptors "interest convergence and education" *anywhere in the article* revealed 23 publications in ERIC, 92 publications in PsycINFO, 40 publications in Sociological Abstracts, and 845 in Lexis-Nexis.

The search with descriptors "interest convergence and teacher education" *in the title of the article* revealed one publication in ERIC, no publications in PsycINFO, no publications in Sociological Abstracts, and no publications in Lexis-Nexis. The search with the descriptors "interest convergence and education" *in the title of the article* revealed five publications in ERIC, one publication in PsycINFO, two publications in Sociological Abstracts, and one in Lexis-Nexis.

Owing to sufficient and manageable results from our first search ("interest convergence and teacher education" *anywhere in the article*), we identified a total of 19 articles that gave what we perceived as sufficient treatment of interest convergence within the field of education. For a collective body of research primarily concerned with educational policies, the authors of these 19 articles, mostly found in legal studies, argued that accounts of educational reforms in the U.S. have been, and will always be, contingent upon the interests of White people in power. We attempt to summarize our review in Tables 25.1 and 25.2.

Table 25.1 Summary of keyword search: "anywhere"

Keywords anywhere in article	ERIC	PsycINFO	Sociological Abstracts	Lexis-Nexis
interest convergence and teacher education	3	28	6	8
interest convergence and education	23	92	40	845

Table 25.2 Summary of keyword search: "title"

Keywords in title of article	ERIC	PsycINFO	Sociological Abstracts	Lexis-Nexis
interest convergence and teacher education	1	0	0	0
interest convergence and education	5	1	2	1

INTEREST CONVERGENCE

The interest convergence principle stresses that racial equality and equity for people of color[4] will be pursued and advanced when they converge with the interests, needs, expectations, benefits, and ideologies of White people. By way of an interest convergence example, Ladson-Billings (1998) wrote:

> Originally, the state of Arizona insisted that the King Holiday was too costly and therefore failed to recognize it for state workers and agencies. Subsequently, a variety of African American groups and their supporters began to boycott business, professional and social functions in the state of Arizona. When the members of the National Basketball Association and the National Football League suggested that neither the NBA All-Star Game nor the Super Bowl would be held in Arizona because of its failure to recognize the King Holiday, the decision was reversed.
>
> (p. 12)

Ladson-Billings's (1998) analysis of the state's reversed decision exemplifies the concept of interest convergence. The state of Arizona did not want to lose revenue; it wanted in fact to increase revenue and was willing to compromise and negotiate to satisfy its financial interests. In this sense, the interests of Black people (and others) who supported and advocated for the Martin Luther King holiday converged with the interests of the state that supported and advocated increased revenue.

From a policy perspective, difficult race-central decisions can be linked to revenue. In their analyses of university mascot policies, Castagno and Lee (2007) declared that:

> the potential losses to the university are significantly increased if the policy … *prohibited* the use of mascots and the sale of athletic wear with Native logos and refused to schedule any games with teams with Native mascots, they would most likely also experience a loss of revenue from missed games, alumni discontent, and disapproval from other conference schools.
>
> (p. 7, emphasis in original)

However, the sacrifice that is necessary for real social change to occur is often painful; taking serious strides toward racial, social, and economic justice is often too difficult for White people in power in the U.S. because it means that they may have to give up something of interest to them: their systems of White privilege (Bell, 1980; Ladson-Billings, 2000) that they may or may not admit that they benefit from. The problem is that many worry about how change and social justice can threaten their position, status, benefits, and lifestyles, and the interests that their children, grandchildren, and future generations should (in their worldview) reap currently and in the future. As B. Gordon (1990) maintained, it is difficult for a group of people to critique and work to change and transform the world when the world works for that group of people. Thus, as Bell (1980) rationalized, changes in policy that benefit people of color in systems of oppression occur when they converge with and benefit White people.

Aleman and Aleman (2010) conceptualized two main ways interest convergence is constructed in the literature: "scholarship that uses interest convergence as a conceptual tool and scholarship that encourages tactical application of theory" (p. 5). Some authors use interest convergence as an explicatory tool to make sense of specific educational policies (Bell, 2003; Brady et al., 2000; Castagno & Lee, 2007; Lee, 2007; Leigh, 2003; Morris, 2001; Muhammad, 2009; Taylor, 2000). For example, Bell (2003) argued that the 2003 *Grutter* decision,[5] in which the Supreme Court upheld the affirmative action admission policy of the University of Michigan Law School, is an example of interest convergence in that employers now have a vested interest in having their White employees better prepared to work in "an increasingly diverse workforce and society" (Grutter v. Bollinger, 2003). Additionally, Muhammad (2009) analyzed the allocation of higher education funding in Mississippi and contended that, while policies are promoted ostensibly to rectify historical discrimination, the asymmetrical desegregation funding primarily benefits White students and "the playing field will remain unleveled" (p. 333).

Other researchers attempted to utilize interest convergence to provide specific educational reforms and to shed light on the experiences of people of color in relation to policy realities on various levels of education (Adamson, 2006; Beratan, 2008; Milner, 2008; Schmidt & Block, 2010; Singleton, 2007; Skrla et al., 2001; Su, 2007). For instance, describing the potential interest convergence between advocates for social justice and proponents of accountability standards, Skrla and colleagues (2001) discussed the pervasiveness of systemic racism and its negative effects on students of color, while advocating the use of state accountability systems to achieve educational equity for children of color and low-income students. And, despite the ubiquity of unsuccessful attempts in practice, the remainder of the articles we reviewed advocated for broad "coalition building" (Murray, 1997, pp. 207–208) between and among communities of color and those of Whites (Araujo, 1996; Cashin, 2005; Murray, 1997; Smith, 2008; Weinstein, 2006).

While several authors explored interest convergence in higher education (Brady et al., 2000; Castagno and Lee, 2007; Donnor, 2005; Milner 2008; Muhammad, 2009), we found that only Milner (2008) addressed the influence of interest convergence specifically in teacher education programs. Overall, while this body of research revealed the usefulness of interest convergence as an analytic and strategic tool within education *in general*, and while critical race theory has made significant inroads in theorizing about teacher education more broadly, we argue that there is a near absence of literature concerning the intersection of interest convergence and teacher education.

It is our belief that, while the use of alternative tenets of CRT highlights the importance of considering the role of race and racism in teacher education policies and practices, and advocates for the importance of voices of color to be included in authoritative conversations regarding teacher education programs, interest convergence, as an analytic tool and also as a site for critical reflection in teacher education practices, is pivotal in underscoring the past and present inequities in education and the larger maintenance of privilege led by a concentrated few that impacts the vast majority of Americans, including middle-class White Americans. The interest convergence thesis recognizes that educational advancements will occur for marginalized students in conjunction with the interests of Whites, realizing that Whites do not necessarily have a vested interest in full educational, social, and economic equality of these marginalized students of color. The interest convergence concept can serve as a catalyst toward understanding that the educational experiences of White students and teachers have been co-opted to appear to be a venue for intellectual challenge, curiosity, and social justice reform, while in reality they perpetuate forms of dominant cultural reproduction that undermine independent thought and go against the best interests of critical teacher education (Milner, 2010; Sleeter, 2001). Thus, while critiquing aspects of teacher education that may be overlooked by other tenets of CRT, the interest convergence concept provides an expedient and pragmatic approach to uncovering and reforming racist policies and practices in teacher education.

We next discuss two interrelated themes that emerged from our review and conceptualization of interest convergence in the literature. In conceptualizing the literature, we refer to and discuss what we call *self and systemic interests* and a *loss/gain binary*. Leigh (2003) explained that, when the interests of Black people are in opposition to or at "odds with those in power" (p. 277), namely White people, it becomes increasingly difficult to expose racism and to pursue racial equality. Further, inherent in the interest convergence principle are matters of loss and gain; typically, someone or some group, often the dominant group, has to negotiate and give up something and simultaneously see the benefits to him, her, or it in order for interests to converge or align (Bell, 1980). Self and systemic interests and the loss/gain binary are intensified by a permeating pace imperative, which means that convergence and change are often at the moderately slow pace of those in power, namely White people. For example, Lopez (2003) wrote that "racism always remains firmly in place but that social progress advances at the pace that White people determine is reasonable and judicious" (p. 84). Change is often *purposefully, skillfully,* or even *subconsciously* slow and at the will and design of White people, those who make up the rules historically and change them as they find necessary, depending on what is necessary for them to maintain their power, their perceived dominance, and the status quo.

Self and Systemic Imperative

Individuals change systems and, according to Bell (1980), Whites may support social justice and equity-oriented policies and practices yet still believe that injustice can be "remedied effectively without altering the status of whites" (p. 522). In this way, in rhetoric, theory, or philosophy, White people may reject racism, injustice, or inequity but refuse to recognize how their own privileges and benefits are individually, collectively, structurally, and systemically shaped to propel them, even at the expense of non-White people. Castagno and Lee (2007) explained that those in the majority will advance social justice agendas "when such advances suit" (p. 4) their own self-interests. The point is that people in power are sometimes, in theory, supportive of policies and practices that do not oppress and discriminate against others as long as they—those in power—do not have to alter their own ways, systems, statuses, and privileges of experiencing life. Lopez (2003) explained that interest convergence centralizes "the belief that Whites will tolerate and advance the interests of people of color only when they *promote the self-interests of Whites*" (p. 84, emphasis added).

In short, the problem of convergence of interests is that many worry about how change can threaten their position, status, property, and economic resources (Bell, 1980). Castagno and Lee (2007) wrote that interest convergence "exposes the selfishness behind many policies and practices that may advance greater equity" (p. 10). In her historical analyses of segregation and desegregation of two Midwestern districts in Cincinnati, Leigh (2003) concluded:

> Social justice, in this case access to equal educational opportunities, was afforded the Black children of the Lincoln Heights community only when doing so benefited the neighboring White communities and districts. Avoiding the threat of legal suit and

the accompanying negative publicity was a compelling benefit that was a significant factor in causing the interests of Whites to converge with the interests of Blacks.

(p. 294)

The idea here is that it is difficult for systems to change because individuals (the self) can interpret what people know to be just; however, they struggle with losing, sharing, or negotiating the advantages, privileges, and benefits they have enjoyed that might transform the system.

A Loss/Gain Binary

A critical race theory perspective would suggest that the ability, will, and fortitude of White people to negotiate and make difficult decisions in providing more equitable policies and practices might mean that they lose something of great importance to them, including their propensity to control others, and their ability to reproduce and maintain their self-interests—which can be viewed as the status quo. Such loss would be deeply troubling, because their property of Whiteness (Harris, 1993; Ladson-Billings & Tate, 1995) may depreciate and be compromised at best. A decrease in this type of currency could mean they lose material possessions that many White people believe they have legitimately earned; they buy into a meritocratic way of seeing the world.

There is a tension in the idea that institutions and "schools, through their organization, structure, and curriculum (both formal and hidden), aid in the maintenance of hegemony by acculturating students to the interest of the dominant group and the students are encouraged and instructed, both explicitly and implicitly, to make those interests their own" (Jay, 2003, p. 7).[6] This idea relates to Ladson-Billings and Tate's (1995) point that "curriculum represents a form of 'intellectual property …'" and that 'intellectual property' must be undergirded by 'real' property" (p. 54) such as curriculum materials, school zoning, funding, property taxes, and instructional tools and resources in schools. Lynch (2006) explained that the intellectual property argument suggests that "those with 'better' property are entitled to [and experience] 'better' schools" (p. 56). Thus, some in the U.S. have adopted and nurtured a competitive, binary milieu wherein a caste system is set up such that only some students will have the property they will need to develop, acquire, inherit, and earn more elaborate forms of property, and consequently transcend poverty and racial oppression, for instance. In this sense, racial inequity in schools can be seen as intentionally designed—not accidental or happenstance.

With an explanation of interest convergence complete, in the next section of this chapter we outline several analytic sites, both micro and macro, that we believe it is essential to consider in studying, analyzing, and theorizing about teacher education. We offer these sites as analytic spaces for further development and consideration as the field deepens its knowledge base and understandings about the complex intersections of interest convergence, teacher education, and policy.

ANALYTIC SITE NO. 1: CURRICULUM AND INSTRUCTIONAL PRACTICES

Policy decisions around the curriculum[7] and instruction in teacher education can have the interests of White students and faculty at the core. In Agee's (2004) study, she explained that "the teacher education texts used in the course made recommendations for using diverse texts or teaching diverse students based on the assumption that preservice teachers are White" (p. 749). Dixson (2006) declared that the curriculum of teacher education mirrors, in many ways, the P-12 curriculum in that it is Eurocentric and White dominated, to the exclusion or marginalization of people of color. This reality can alienate teachers of color, because they may feel that their worldview is marginalized, not central to what matters in the classroom. Policy makers—that is, teacher educators who have the power to make policy decisions in the classroom (and also through programmatic policy decisions)—can focus their attention on the needs and interests of White students in their courses but also through the fabric of an entire teacher education program. What about the curricular and instructional needs of Black or Brown teachers, for instance?

From a broader curricular and instructional perspective, research suggests that it is not enough to have one standalone course on race, urban education, or equity in a teacher education program (Ladson-Billings, 1999; Milner 2010). Goals of understanding *all* P-12 students and their experiences, and developing racialized knowledge, as well as understanding trends and issues where race and racism are concerned without reinforcing stereotypes, should be at the very core of the teacher education programs themselves. Thus, while increasing the number of race-based courses and experiences may be needed and could be advantageous, such an increase in the number of courses is not enough.[8] Later in this chapter we will discuss another analytic site, *routes into teaching*, that can be interrogated to increase the number of teachers of color with the dispositions and capabilities to adequately teach these courses.

Curricular and instructional experiences in teacher education throughout the program as well as the structure of teacher education programs, we argue, need to change. In her review, Ladson-Billings (1999) found that "most [teacher education] programs were satisfied with adding 'multicultural content' rather than changing the philosophy and structure of the teacher education programs" (p. 221). The core of teacher education programs, the nature and focus of the programs, and the interests and emphases on certain issues over others are policy matters that White faculty and administrators often control.

ANALYTIC SITE NO. 2: RACIAL BACKGROUND OF TEACHER EDUCATORS

An excellent example of how the educational system aids in the maintenance of inequalities in this country is the privilege and access associated with being and becoming a White female teacher. Teacher educators are overwhelmingly White and female. Similarly to what happens in P-12 educational institutions, this fact can negatively impact what gets addressed, fought against, and advocated for in policy discourses, decision making, and consequently practices. Bales (2006) astutely proclaimed that teacher educators need to become more centrally involved in policy discussions that are increasingly being shifted from teacher education programs and state levels to national platforms. Moreover, Bales (2007) and Zeichner (2005) reminded us that policy matters are deeply ideological, political, and worldview-centered. In Bales's (2007) words, "reform effort can originate from a range of self-interests" (p. 1). These self-interests, we argue, are shaped in part by the interests that people have that are racially centered and constructed. Thus, increasing participation of teacher educators in broader policy conversations is an important endeavor for the field; however, if the voices participating in these policy conversations are all or mostly White, with colonized epistemologies, ideologies, and ideas, this participation could actually harm populations or students of color rather than help.

Thus policies embedded within and beyond teacher education programs to recruit more teacher educators of color are essential. Our point here is not that all teacher educators of color are exactly the same. We recognize the variation of teacher educators of color in terms of their thinking, beliefs, worldviews, and practices. Using interest convergence, White teacher educators could benefit from having teacher educators of color in their cohort, to better understand how race influences the day-to-day experiences of teachers of color and to provide more substance for unpacking the experiences of students of color. For example, White teacher educators can learn from teacher educators of color to understand and co-opt the ways teacher educators of color may draw on their culture as a basis for fostering the academic achievement of students of color (Lynn, 2006). White and Black teachers, for example, will be able to share their narratives and both groups could confront and deconstruct stereotypes, biases, and other assumptions that impede overall learning and achievement of their students and themselves. Analytically, researchers can examine these forms of interplay to help make sense of and illuminate discourse patterns and practices in teacher education.

Additionally, the probability of a teacher educator of color speaking on behalf of other people of color is more likely, especially because teacher educators of color have an interest in their own families and ancestry, and also because they are likely to have experienced some forms of oppression, racism, and/or discrimination in their own life experiences, personally and professionally (Milner, 2010). Their voices at the very least will add to the diversity of the teacher education paradigm and provide a catalyst to possibly create or support teaching methods that discourage marginalized students of color from conforming to an inherently White curriculum and promote educators to consider conforming to the unique cultural and racial identities of the students.

Consider the racial demography of teacher educators identified in Figures 25.1 and 25.2. The racial demographic information in the figures is representative of both full-

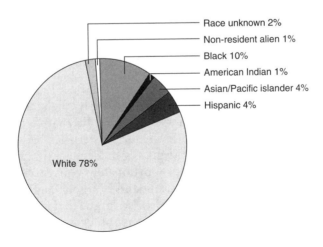

Figure 25.1 An emerging picture of the teacher preparation pipeline: race and ethnicity of full-time faculty in professional education programs, Fall 2007

Source: Adapted from Ludwig et al. (2010)

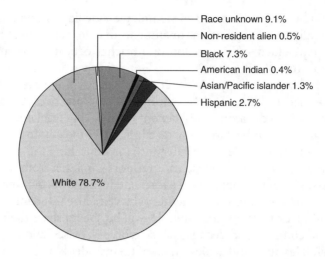

Race unknown 9.1%
Non-resident alien 0.5%
Black 7.3%
American Indian 0.4%
Asian/Pacific islander 1.3%
Hispanic 2.7%
White 78.7%

Figure 25.2 An emerging picture of the teacher preparation pipeline: race and ethnicity of adjunct faculty in professional education programs, Fall 2007

Source: Adapted from Ludwig et al. (2010)

time and adjunct faculty in teacher education programs. We have included racial demographic data of adjunct faculty in addition to full-time faculty, considering the fact that a representative number of teacher education programs across the U.S. rely on adjunct instructors to teach in teacher education and they in fact should have some voice and perspective in policy matters. These demographic data suggest that we should be concerned about increasing the numbers of teachers of color not only in P-12 social contexts but in teacher education as well.

ANALYTIC SITE NO. 3: ROUTES INTO TEACHING

A third site for analysis in teacher education concerns the various preparation routes into teaching. Beginning in the late 1980s, alternative teacher "education" programs, such as Teach for America, New York Teaching Fellows, Teach NOLA, and Teach Tennessee, intensified their visibility and, concurrently, their relevance in U.S society. Debates that focus on whether there should be alternative teacher certification programs are somewhat obsolete. However, recent statistics hailing from Teach for America have raised issues related to the grossly inadequate training of teachers who teach in environments which are disproportionately concentrated in schools and classrooms serving low-income students, students of color, English language learners, and students with disabilities (Labaree, 2010). We argue that an analytic site for additional exploration will reveal how these various routes into teaching are developed, what they focus on in these programs, and where the graduates of these programs are placed. In what ways do various teacher education programs prepare teachers to meet the complex needs of all students, especially students of color? What policies are in place to ensure that routes into teaching serve the interests and needs of the students they serve? How diverse are the participant pools from which these programs recruit and what factors contribute to the matriculation of students into particular teacher education programs?

The interest convergence thesis would shed light on the nature and extent of these programs and how they are or are not serving their White teacher candidates or the teacher candidates of color by preparing teachers who are unqualified, inexperienced, or teaching out of field in schools and classrooms serving students from low SES and students of color. We argue these programs weaken the standards of what all students, particularly students from already distressed communities, deserve: a highly qualified and highly capable teacher who recognizes the culture and identities of her or his students. We also argue and embrace the interest convergence thesis to demonstrate that these programs are not only doing a disservice to students but also not providing their mostly White teacher trainees the proper resources to become fully prepared effective teachers in any classroom. Using interest convergence we further suggest that it would be in the best interest and benefit of both parties involved (teacher educators and the students they serve) to be in programs that provide adequate settings for teacher development and culturally sensible training. Through interest convergence, White teachers in these programs can stand up with teachers of color and demand proper preparation and training, to become teachers who would aid in advancing the nation's teaching quality. Since teachers of color are in too short supply, the cultural diversity of many teacher education programs limited their ability to be attentive to issues of cultural responsiveness in teaching. Further, coalitions could fight to improve working conditions, to improve and equalize salaries, and to provide supports for talented and culturally sound teacher education programs for students residing in marginalized communities as well as those from the middle and upper class.

ANALYTIC SITE NO. 4: SCHOOL–UNIVERSITY PARTNERSHIP INCENTIVES

A fourth site for analysis is the nexus between and among teacher education, interest convergence, and policy in school–university partnership incentives. Teacher education programs sometimes establish partnerships with local school districts to provide tuition free or tuition assistance for teachers at either the undergraduate or the graduate level. For the tuition incentive, teachers are required to spend a specified number of years teaching in "resource-deprived schools," usually urban schools serving high numbers of students of color. The idea is that students benefit, as they are afforded the opportunity to earn educational credentials without incurring the monetary costs; districts benefit by having an assured influx of teachers in their most needy schools. While providing a promising policy alternative for increasing the number of teachers in particular schools, the recruitment in such programs is often limited by narrow information channels and rigid qualifications (such as the GRE) that delimit the number of people of color in such programs, which perpetuates an already appreciable imbalance of White teachers in schools. Interest convergence would propose that universities start early in preparing potential teachers to teach at urban schools, possibly by identifying teacher candidates who may have been former students of those urban schools or teachers who hail from similar school environments. Considering the particularly low attrition rates for teachers of color (Achinstein et al., 2010; Villegas & Irvine, 2010), school–university partners could serve as exemplars in developing successful retention strategies, to reconstruct a vision of teacher success that really does include the voice and experiences of teachers serving the unique needs of urban schools. School–university partnerships, through the framework of interest convergence, can redefine what it means to create supportive and successful learning environments for K-12 students and those who serve them, by offering inclusive education theories and practices that address issues of race, class, culture, language, and ability, as well as the intersection of these identity markers. CRT's interest convergence thesis is capable of critically exploring and scrutinizing the following questions: Whose interests are being served and met in these incentive programs? Proportionately, how do these programs serve populations of color? Whose voices are heard and engaged in partnerships that target populations of color?

CONCLUSION

In this chapter we have discussed the underutilization of interest convergence in extant teacher education research and its potential usefulness as a problematizing and reformatory tool. Crenshaw et al. (1995) described one of the common themes that cut across critical race scholarship as the "desire not to merely understand the vexed bond between law [in our particular analysis, policy and practice] and racial power but to *change* it" (p. xiii, emphasis in original). Thus, we have suggested that those of us in teacher education need to become more serious about interrogating, exposing, and challenging racist policies and practices in teacher education. We provide four analytic sites that we believe need additional attention in order not only to expose how race works within them, but also to change areas that undermine the success of people of color. Indeed, we argue that it is critical that we continue to understand interests and the convergence of interests in order to improve teacher education and, as Cochran-Smith (1995) wrote, "open up this discourse among teacher-education faculty and staff and examine our own efforts to teach those who are like and not like us." Interest convergence can serve as a valuable analytic tool to study policy and practice in teacher education and to fill the void of the under-theorization of race in the field. Interest convergence is grounded in perspectives that conceptualize teacher education as prearranged by the relations of race that exist in the larger culture. Such a perspective draws attention to the fact that all teachers— not just those identified as marginalized—could benefit from a critical understanding of race and its adverse conditions, under which some teachers are frequently forced to teach and students are often forced to learn. Our ability to gauge the interests of teachers and teacher educators is important because, until interests converge, it will be difficult to have policies and practices that place race, racism, and equity on the agenda. In short and in essence, we believe that we need to be more focused on building theory in teacher education about race. Indeed, as Bell (1992) declared, "we are attempting to sing a new scholarly song [in teacher education]—even if to some listeners our style is strange, our lyrics unseemly … we do not expect praise for our scholarship that departs from the traditional. We simply seek understanding" (pp. 144, 146). Finally, as Ladson-Billings (1998) explained, "we will have to take bold and sometimes unpopular positions" (p. 22) in order to bring the still sensitive topic of race and racism to the fore of our thinking, and to consider how we might address the convergence and divergence of interests in policy and practice.

NOTES

1   In order to understand how interest convergence is situated within the framework of critical race theory (CRT), it is helpful to review CRT's historical origins and emergence from critical legal studies (CLS). CLS developed in the 1970s as a small group of scholars decided to reevaluate the tenets of a realist tradition in legal discourse (Tate, 2005). According to Livingston (1982), legal realists synthesized principles of pragmatism, instrumentalism, and progressivism to establish a model of legal scholarship centered around a rational, scientific method in order to implement pragmatic policy reform. Consequently, CLS evolved out of this movement in an attempt to reveal inconsistencies in social and political theory; moreover, their efforts were linked to a radical political agenda (Livingston, 1982). The CLS movement aimed to expose and challenge "the ways American law served to legitimize an oppressive social order" (Crenshaw et al., 1995, p. xvii). CLS attacked American social and legal institutions, legal reasoning, human rights, doctrine, hierarchy, meritocracy, and conventional views of the free market (Brosnan, 1986; Delgado, 1987; R. Gordon, 1984; Hutchinson & Monahan, 1984; Stick, 1986). However, CLS's handling of human rights issues became problematic for people of color within the movement. First was CLS's emphasis on class and economic structure and its "failure to come to terms with the particularity of race" (Crenshaw et al., 1995, p. xxvi). Delgado (1987) offered three other components of CLS that were a challenge for people of color in the movement: first was the emphasis on incremental rather than sweeping reform; second, CLS seemed to be more ideological than practical; third, CLS endorsed the concept of "false consciousness" which suggests that people of color support the systems that oppress them. These factors precipitated the outgrowth of CRT. At its foundation, CRT was to be an intersection of "racial theory" and activism against racism (Cole, 2009). CRT begins with the assertion that racism is "normal, not aberrant in American society" (Delgado, 1995, p. xvi). Second, CRT emphasizes personal narratives to "analyze the myths, presuppositions, and received wisdoms that make up the common culture about race and that invariably render blacks and other minorities one-down" (Delgado, 1995, p. xvii). The "voice of the other" is valuable in legal discourse for several reasons: social reality is constructed by the exchange of stories; stories provide members of marginalized groups a means for psychic self-preservation; the telling of stories can help overcome ethnocentrism and the unconscious need to view the world in one particular way (Delgado, 1989). Third, CRT critiques the protracted nature of liberalism in effecting social change. CRT argues that racism requires sweeping, not deliberate, social change (Ladson-Billings, 1999). Fourth, CRT is a problem-centered approach and thus an interdisciplinary approach (Matsuda et al., 1993). And fifth, CRT argues that, since Whites have surreptitiously been the chief beneficiaries of movements enacted to benefit minorities, the correct approach to lasting social change is to find places where the interests of people of color and Whites intersect, a concept called "interest convergence" (Bell, 1980).

2   It may seem a bit inconceivable, irrelevant, and unimportant to some that the field of teacher education likely suffers from deep-seated racism, because the field is often perceived as a "nice" field (Ladson-Billings, 1998) and a field that often suffers as "low-status" (Ladson-Billings, 1999). However, matters of race and racism are tainted in policies and practices in teacher education to such an extent that they often are normalized and quite frankly hidden from those in the field. The different and difference in teacher education are often viewed as abnormal, insufficient, substandard, and deficient. Just because racism may not be visible (explicit) to some, usually those in power (Delpit, 1995), it does not mean that it does not exist. Scheurich and Young (1997) maintained that racism exists on various levels explicitly and covertly.

3   For two good, broader reviews of teacher education and critical race theory, read Chapman (2011) and Vavrus (2002).

4   Throughout this chapter, we use "people of color" to refer to those individuals who are not White. We realize that this use is problematic, because there is variance between and among individuals of color. However, the use of "people of color" seems to be the most appropriate language at this time, as "minority" is also an inappropriate word choice.

5   In 2003 Barbara Grutter, a White Michigan resident, sued the University of Michigan Law School alleging that the school's use of race as a predominant factor in the application process discriminated against her based on her race in violation of the Equal Protection Clause of the 14th Amendment, Title VI of the Civil Rights Act of 1964, and 42 USC §1981. In a 5–4 decision, the Supreme Court upheld the use of race as one of many factors for admission decisions of public institutions of higher learning and ruled that the U.S. Constitution "does not prohibit the law schools' narrowly tailored use of race … to further a compelling interest in obtaining the educational benefits that flow from a diverse student body" (Grutter v. Bollinger, 2003, p. 343). In Fisher v. University of Texas (2012), a subsequent case which has yet to be ruled, two White females sued the University of Texas regarding similar admission policies. The Supreme Court's ruling on this case will determine the constitutionality of the Grutter decision, and perhaps affirmative action as we know it.

6   Students typically meet the expectations established by educators through curriculum and instructional practices (Milner, 2010). However, schools can structurally produce and reproduce inequity, poverty, and injustice for students (Anyon, 1980; Bowles & Gintis, 1976; Kozol, 2005).

7 The curriculum can be defined as what students have the opportunity to learn.
8 It is important to note there is no guarantee that teacher educators themselves actually have the knowledge and skill to teach the content, even if more courses are offered.

REFERENCES

Achinstein, B., Freitas, C., Ogawa, T., & Sexton, D. (2010). Retaining teachers of color: A pressing problem and a potential strategy for "hard-to-staff" schools. *Review of Educational Research, 80*(1), 71–107.

Adamson, B.L. (2006). The h'aint in the (school) house: The interest convergence paradigm in state legislatures and school finance reform. *California Western Law Review, 43*(1), 173–202.

Agee, J. (2004). Negotiating a teaching identity: An African American teacher's struggle to teach in test-driven contexts. *Teachers College Record, 106*(4), 747–774.

Aleman, E., & Aleman, S.M. (2010). "Do Latina interests always have to 'converge' with White interests?" (Re)claiming racial realism and interest-convergence in critical race theory praxis. *Race, Ethnicity and Education, 13*(1), 1–21.

Anyon, J. (1980). Social class and the hidden curriculum of work. *Journal of Education, 162*(1), 366–391.

Araujo, R.J. (1996). Critical race theory: Contributions to and problems for race relations. *Gonzaga Law Review, 32*, 537–575.

Bales, B.L. (2006). Teacher education policies in the United States: The accountability shift since 1980. *Teaching and Teacher Education, 22*, 395–407.

Bales, B.L. (2007). Teacher education reform in the United States and the theoretical constructs of stakeholder mediation. *International Journal of Education Policy and Leadership, 2*(6), 1–13.

Bell, D. (1980). Brown v. Board of Education and the interest-convergence dilemma. *Harvard Law Review, 93*(3), 518–533.

Bell, D. (1992). *Faces at the bottom of the well: The permanence of racism.* New York: Basic Books.

Bell, D.A. (2003). Diversity's distraction. *Columbia Law Review, 103*, 1622–1633.

Beratan, G.D. (2008). The song remains the same: Transposition and the disproportionate representation of minority students in special education. *Race, Ethnicity and Education, 11*(4), 337–354.

Bobo, L., & Kluegel, J.R. (1993). Opposition to race-targeting: Self-interest, stratification ideology, or racial attitudes? *American Sociological Review, 58*(4), 443–464.

Bowles, S., & Gintis, H. (1976). *Schooling in capitalist America: Education reform and the contradictions of economic life.* New York: Basic Books.

Brady, K., Eatman, T., & Parker, L. (2000). To have or not to have? A preliminary analysis of higher education funding disparities in the post-Ayers v. Fordice era: Evidence from critical race theory. *Journal of Education Finance, 24*, 297–322.

Brosnan, D.F. (1986). Serious but not critical. *Southern California Law Review, 60*, 259–296.

Cashin, S.D. (2005). Shall we overcome? Transcending race, class, and ideology through interest convergence. *St. John's Law Review, 79*(2), 253–291.

Castagno, A.E., & Lee, S.J. (2007). Native mascots and ethnic fraud in higher education: Using tribal critical race theory and the interest convergence principle as an analytic tool. *Equity and Excellence in Education, 40*(1), 3–13.

Chapman, T.K. (2007). Interrogating classroom relationships and events: Using portraiture and critical race theory in educational research. *Educational Researcher, 36*(3), 156–162.

Chapman, T.K. (2011). A critical race theory analysis of past and present institutional processes and policies in teacher education. In A.F. Ball & C.A. Tyson (Eds.), *Studying diversity in teacher education.* New York: Rowman & Littlefield.

Cochran-Smith, M. (1995). Color blindness and basket making are not the answers: Confronting the dilemmas of race, culture, and language diversity in teacher education. *American Educational Research Journal, 32*(3), 493–522.

Cochran-Smith, M., & Zeichner, K.M. (2005). Executive summary. In M. Cochran-Smith & K.M. Zeichner (Eds.), *Studying teacher education: The report of the AERA Panel on Research and Teacher Education* (pp. 1–36). Mahwah, NJ: Lawrence Erlbaum.

Cole, M. (2009). *Critical race theory and education: A Marxist response.* New York: Palgrave Macmillan.

Crenshaw, K., Gotando, N., Peller, G., & Thomas, K. (Eds.). (1995). *Critical race theory: The key writings that formed the movement.* New York: New Press.

Delgado, R. (1987). The ethereal scholar: Does critical legal studies have what minorities want? *Harvard Civil Rights–Civil Liberties Law Review, 22*, 301–322.

Delgado, R. (1989). Symposium: Legal storytelling. *Michigan Law Review, 87*(2073).

Delgado, R. (1995). *Critical race theory: The cutting edge.* Philadelphia, PA: Temple University Press.

Delpit, L. (1995). *Other people's children: Cultural conflict in the classroom.* New York: New Press.

Dixson, A.D. (2006). What's race got to do with it? Race, racial identity development, and teacher preparation (pp. 19–36). In H.R. Milner & E.W. Ross (Eds.), *Race, ethnicity, and education: The influences of racial and ethnic identity in education.* Westport, CT: Greenwood/Praeger.

Donnor, J. (2005). Towards an interest-convergence on the education of African-American football student athletes in major college sports. *Race, Ethnicity and Education, 8*(1), 45–67.

Gordon, B.M. (1990). The necessity of African-American epistemology for educational theory and practice. *Journal of Education, 172*(3), 88–106.

Gordon, R.W. (1984). Critical legal histories. *Stanford Law Review, 36,* 57–125.

Grutter v. Bollinger, 539 U.S. 330 (2003).

Harris, C.I. (1993). Whiteness as property. *Harvard Law Review, 106*(8), 1707–1791.

Howard, T. (2008). Who really cares? The disenfranchisement of African American males in preK-12 schools: A critical race theory perspective. *Teachers College Record, 110*(5), 954–985.

Hutchinson, A., & Monahan, P. (1984). The "rights" stuff: Roberto Unger and beyond. *Texas Law Review, 62,* 377–393.

Jay, M. (2003). Critical race theory, multicultural education, and the hidden curriculum of hegemony. *Multicultural Perspectives, 5*(4), 3–9.

Kozol, J. (2005). *The shame of a nation: The return of apartheid schooling in America.* New York: Crown Publishing.

Labaree, D. (2010). Teach for America and teacher ed: Heads they win, tails we lose. *Journal of Teacher Education, 61*(1–2), 48–55.

Ladson-Billings, G. (1998). Just what is critical race theory and what's it doing in a nice field like education? *Qualitative Studies in Education, 11*(1), 7–24.

Ladson-Billings, G. (1999). Preparing teachers for diverse student populations: A critical race theory perspective. *Review of Research in Education, 24,* 211–247.

Ladson-Billings, G. (2000). Fighting for our lives: Preparing teachers to teach African American students. *Journal of Teacher Education, 51*(3), 206–214.

Ladson-Billings, G., & Tate, B. (1995). Toward a critical race theory of education. *Teachers College Record, 97*(1), 47–67.

Lee, C. (2007). Cultural convergence: Interest convergence theory meets the cultural defense. *Arizona Law Review, 49,* 911–950.

Leigh, P.R. (2003). Interest convergence and desegregation in the Ohio Valley. *Journal of Negro Education, 72*(3), 269–296.

Livingston, D. (1982). 'Round and 'round the bramble bush: From legal realism to critical legal scholarship. *Harvard Law Review, 95,* 1669–1690.

Lopez, G.R. (2003). The (racially neutral) politics of education: A critical race theory perspective. *Educational Administration Quarterly, 39*(1), 68–94.

Ludwig, M., Kirshstein, R., Sidana, A., Ardila-Rey, A., & Bae, Y. (2010). *An emerging picture of the teacher preparation pipeline: A report by the American Association of Colleges for Teacher Education and the American Institutes for Research for release at the briefing: Teacher preparation: Who needs it? What the numbers say.* Washington, DC: American Association of Colleges for Teacher Education and American Institutes for Research.

Lynch, R.V. (2006). Critical-race educational foundations: Toward democratic practices in teaching "other people's children" and teacher education. *Action in Teacher Education, 28*(2), 53–65.

Lynn, M. (2006). Education for the community: Exploring the culturally relevant practices of Black male teachers. *Teachers College Record, 108*(12), 2497–2522.

Lynn, M., & Parker, L. (2006). Critical race studies in education: Examining a decade of research on US schools. *Urban Review, 38*(4), 257–290.

Matsuda, M., Lawrence, C., & Delgado, R. (Eds.). (1993). *Words that wound: Critical race theory, assaultive speech and the first amendment.* Boulder, CO: Westview.

Milner, H.R. (2007). Race, culture, and researcher positionality: Working through dangers seen, unseen, and unforeseen. *Educational Researcher, 36*(7), 388–400.

Milner, H.R. (2008). Critical race theory and interest convergence as analytic tools in teacher education policies and practices. *Journal of Teacher Education, 59,* 332–346.

Milner, H.R. (2010). *Start where you are, but don't stay there.* Cambridge, MA: Harvard Education Press.

Morris, J.E. (2001). Forgotten voices of Black educators: Critical race perspectives on the implementation of a desegregation plan. *Educational Policy, 15*(4), 575–600.

Muhammad, C.G. (2009). Mississippi higher education desegregation and the interest convergence principle: A CRT analysis of the "Ayers settlement." *Race, Ethnicity and Education, 12*(3), 319–336.

Murray, Y.M. (1997). Towards interest convergence: Coalition building requires connection within as well as without. *California Western Law Review, 33*, 205–208.

Johnston-Parsons, M. (2007). Where's the theory in teacher education? Researchers gazing from multiple theoretical perspectives. Paper presented at the Annual Meeting of the American Educational Research Association, Chicago, IL.

Ryan, C.L. & Dixson, A.D. (2006). Rethinking pedagogy to re-center race: Some reflections. *Language Arts, 84*(2), 175–183.

Scheurich, J.J., & Young, M.D. (1997). Coloring epistemologies: Are our research epistemologies racially biased? *Educational Researcher, 26*(4), 4–16.

Schmidt, C., & Block, L.A. (2010). Without and within: The implication of employment and ethnocultural equity policies for internationally educated teachers. *Canadian Journal of Educational Administration and Policy, 100*, 1–23.

Singleton, D.A. (2007). Interest convergence and the education of African-American boys in Cincinnati: Motivating suburban Whites to embrace interdistrict education reform. *Northern Kentucky Law Review, 34*, 663–677.

Skrla, L., Scheurich, J.J., Johnson, J.F., & Koschoreck, J.W. (2001). Accountability for equity: Can state policy leverage social justice? *International Journal of Leadership in Education, 4*, 1077–1093.

Sleeter, C.E. (2001). Preparing teachers for culturally diverse schools: Research and the overwhelming presence of Whiteness. *Journal of Teacher Education, 52*(2), 94–106.

Sleeter, C.E. (2008). Preparing White teachers for diverse students. In M. Cochran-Smith, S. Feiman-Nemser, & J. McIntyre (Eds.), *Handbook of research in teacher education: Enduring issues in changing contexts* (3rd ed., pp. 559–582). New York: Routledge.

Smith, C. (2008). Unconscious bias and "outsider" interest convergence. *Connecticut Law Review, 40*(4), 1077–1093.

Stick, J. (1986). Can nihilism be pragmatic? *Harvard Law Review, 100*, 332–401.

Su, C. (2007). Cracking silent codes: Critical race theory and education organizing. *Discourse: Studies in the Cultural Politics of Education, 22*, 195–247.

Tate, W.F. (2005). Access and opportunity to learn are not accidental: Engineering a mathematical revolution in your school. Monograph commissioned by the Southeastern Regional Vision for Education (SERVE), United States Department of Education.

Tatum, B.D. (2001). Professional development: An important partner in antiracist teacher education. In S.H. King & L.A. Castenell (Eds.), *Racism and racial inequality: Implications for teacher education* (pp. 51–58). Washington, DC: AACTE Publications.

Taylor, E. (2000). Critical race theory and interest convergence in the backlash against affirmative action: Washington state and Initiative 200. *Teachers College Record, 8*(3), 539–560.

Tillman, L.C. (2002). Culturally sensitive research approaches: An African American perspective. *Educational Researcher, 31*(9), 3–12.

Vavrus, M. (2002). *Transforming the multicultural education of teachers: Theory, research and practice.* New York: Teachers College Press.

Villegas, A., & Irvine, J. (2010). Diversifying the teaching force: An examination of major arguments. *Urban Review, 42*, 175–192.

Weinstein, S.M. (2006). A need for image makeover: Interest convergence and the United States' war on terror. *Roger Williams University Law Review, 11*, 403–430.

Zeichner, K.M. (2005). A research agenda for teacher education. In M. Cochran-Smith & K.M. Zeichner (Eds.), *Studying teacher education: The report of the AERA Panel on Research and Teacher Education.* Mahwah, NJ: Lawrence Erlbaum.

26

CRT'S CHALLENGE TO EDUCATORS' ARTICULATION OF ABSTRACT LIBERAL PERSPECTIVES OF PURPOSE

Kenneth Fasching-Varner and Roland Mitchell

When speaking of the "achievement gap" it is understood by virtually everyone that this does not refer to a gap between Africans and Asians or a gap between Africans and Latinos or a gap between Africans and anyone else other than Europeans. Therefore, right away, it seems something more than education is being discussed when the gap language is used.

(Hilliard, 2003, p. 137)

The above statement was taken from Hilliard's (2003) chapter "No Mystery: Closing the Achievement Gap" in *Young, Gifted and Black*. We open with this quote because Hilliard's problematizing the societal narrative concerning the "achievement gap" between blacks and whites draws attention to the way that racism functions in a conspicuous manner by, on the one hand, differentiating between whites' and non-whites' cognitive ability through a supposed objective measure (achievement/IQ test) (Arbuthnot, 2011; Gould, 1996; Steele & Aronson, 1995), while, on the other hand, simultaneously forwarding what we will refer to as a "seemingly expansive but inherently restrictive" discourse about racial hierarchies and relations. This discourse conflates the root cause of the dismal educational outcomes of African American children in U.S. schools with numerous issues, from biological considerations of intelligence (Herrnstein & Murray, 1994) to discussions of the inherent dysfunctionality of black families, communications styles, or communal beliefs about education (Asante, 2009; Delpit, 2008). Dominant narratives about the educational outcomes of African American students all but ignore the historical fact that our current educational system (established only decades after slavery and still 50 years removed from *Brown*) was designed in an era when the educability and actual humanity of African Americans was at issue (Watkins, 2001). This discourse also ignores the social, political, and moral debts levied against underrepresented students (Ladson-Billings, 2006). Our assertion is that this phenomenon is exacerbated by the fact that typically educators are socialized in a manner that hinders their ability to conceptualize their own racialized identities; we see understanding racial identity as an indispensable skill for building pedagogical relationships steeped in cultural knowledge and understanding about African American learners amongst and across racial barriers (Lewis et al., 2008).

The seemingly expansive rhetoric about race and the "achievement gap" has prompted numerous educational researchers, politicians, and consultants to announce that our twenty-first-century educational system is in crisis and failing children of color (Landsman & Lewis, 2006; Lewis & Moore, 2004; Moore, 2003; Obiakor & Beachum, 2006). Building on the work of social structural inequality scholars and critical educators informed by critical race theory (CRT), we assert that there is no crisis at all—that is to say, schools and children are not really failing, but the system is performing exactly as it was designed to function: creating gaps between racial groups as well as disparate opportunities in education and employment (Berliner & Biddle, 1996; Kozol, 1991, 2005; Ladson-Billings, 2006). Berliner and Biddle (1996) appropriately describe this manufactured crisis as "appearing within a specific historical context led by identifiable critics whose political goals could be furthered by scapegoating teachers" (p. 3). Therefore, Hilliard's "something more than education that is being discussed when the gap language is used" is actually a restrictive discourse concerning educational opportunities for students of color that represents the ongoing vestiges of white supremacy profoundly shaping the current and foreseeable educational outcomes for students of color (Ladson-Billings, 2006).

According to educational historian Anderson (1988) the Patrician class primarily responsible for establishing the U.S. public school system never intended the children of ex-slaves to receive the same quality of education or access to wealth as their former owners. Despite pervasive meritocratic notions of education as the key to affording impoverished communities access to the American Dream, the current neo-liberal incarnation of education was intended to produce an economic underclass of semi-skilled laborers to support the expanding base of industrial capitalism at the turn of the twentieth century. Keeping people of color subjugated through education, therefore, was intentional and protected white interests. As a result, post-*Brown*, white interests have maintained their place at the center of twenty-first-century desegregation efforts (Frankenberg, 2005; Orfield & Lee, 2004, 2006; Siddle-Walker, 2001; Watkins, 2001).

The proceeding paragraphs provide a drastically different and, might we add, damning critique of our educational system. Consequently, our inquiry into the seemingly expansive rhetoric concerning the manufactured educational crisis and resulting restrictive outcomes for students of color prompts us to ask: Are educators complicit with limiting opportunities for students of color? The short answer to this question is yes. We recognize, however, that it would be easy (and in some circles even fashionable) to pin the failings of public school systems on the individual motivations/actions of teachers. We believe there are much more complex social, political, and most importantly market-driven causes for this dilemma. As Lewis et al. (2008) noted, the education system is functioning in harmony with all other systems and institutions (i.e., economic, legal, family, religious, media, and government) in American society, benefiting students who are members of privileged social groups at the expense of less privileged students. Lacking critical knowledge of the fore-mentioned legacy of U.S. schooling and a well-informed purpose for entering the labor field of education, novice teachers cannot help but fall in line with hegemonic professional norms. Further, if the crisis is manufactured and ultimately a subterfuge to advance race- and class-driven hierarchies, answers fueled by for-profit learning management companies (KIPPS, TFA, etc.), currently championed as the best type of education for free-market enterprise, efficiently and effectively continue our legacy of being unresponsive to the needs of marginalized populations.

This chapter explores the experiences and preparation of pre-service teachers, who in most cases unknowingly occupy the precarious position of existing in the badlands of this manufactured crisis. We will draw on tenets of CRT to support our analysis of the ways in which pre-service teachers operate in crisis badlands. Our aim is to draw upon the tenets of CRT to propose why the vision, actions, and rhetoric of teacher preparation and teacher candidates serve to support manufactured crisis and its resulting neo-liberal answers.

CRITICAL RACE THEORY TENETS

CRT and CRT analyses are premised on a number of interrelated tenets. Many of the tenets of CRT are appropriate as mechanisms for analysis in our work, and have been taken up by the chapter authors in this volume. We are limiting our discussion to the two particular CRT elements that appear to be most fruitful in our analysis. In this chapter we draw from 1) whiteness as property and 2) expansive versus restrictive orientations. We explore each tenet briefly below.

Whiteness (and Blackness) as Property

Critical race theorist Harris (1993, 1995) articulates conditions by which we might understand whiteness as property. The first condition is that whiteness has a particular inalienability, precluding it from transfer to racial others. This exclusivity represents whiteness's absolute value. Inalienability often precludes property from having value, as value is believed to be garnered from one's ability to sell, trade, or otherwise negotiate the transfer of the property. Whiteness, however, has been given full regard as property given that white people have vested interests in protecting whiteness and keeping the benefits of whiteness from others while simultaneously experiencing a high sense of value for their own whiteness. Paradoxically, according to Harris (1993, 1995), whiteness is infinitely absolute, so that one drop of white blood never makes one white, yet one drop of black blood precludes someone from possessing whiteness, decreasing the overall property value of the person's identity. While Harris situates her discussion within the field of law, the application of whiteness as property has been taken up in a number of academic fields, including business (Beeman et al., 2010), political science (Tillery, 2009), history (Jay, 2012; Lentz-Smith, 2011; Roediger, 1999), philosophy (Mills, 1997; Owen, 2007), and art (Osucha, 2009), and for the purposes of this chapter has had a significant impact on the various fields of education (Alemán, 2009; Dixson & Dingus, 2007; Dixson & Rousseau, 2006; Fasching-Varner, 2009; Ladson-Billings & Tate, 1995; Vaught & Castagno, 2008).

Consequently the possession of whiteness, often falsely understood at the level of phenotype (Winant, 2000), is an absolute that garners a higher value as property than other races. As Lopez (1996) and Ignatiev (1995) highlight, the legalistic construction of whiteness has seen many groups petitioning courts and other authorities in a struggle to be identified as white in an attempt to access the fullness of the property value attributed to whiteness. Harris (1993, 1995) cites that white people capitalize on their whiteness for purposes of enjoyment, and place high value on the reputation of whiteness. Stating that a white person acts or is black, for example, causes harm to his/her reputation, devaluing his/her property value of whiteness. Contrastingly, saying that a black person acts or is white causes no harm given the "absolute and inherent goodness" of being white. In the landscape of the United States the court system has protected and maintained the sense of whiteness (DeCuir & Dixson, 2004). Finally, whiteness excludes, in that white peoples never have to define whiteness itself, but rather define what it is not. In defining what whiteness is not, white peoples continually exclude all whom they deem to not possess whiteness; all of these elements, in unison, help whiteness serve a property function for whites (Harris, 1993, 1995; Morrison, 1992).

Expansive and Restrictive Views of Anti-Discrimination

CRT scholars examine the distinctions between an expansive and a restrictive view of anti-discrimination and anti-discrimination law (Crenshaw, 1995; Dixson & Rousseau, 2006; Fasching-Varner, 2009; Tate & Rousseau, 2002). Crenshaw (1995) suggests that expansive views of the law locate their emphasis on equality as a result, and thus those with an expansive view of anti-discrimination look to stop the conditions and circumstances by which the subordination of people of color exists, working with courts and governmental agencies "to further the national goal of eradicating the effects of racial oppression" (p. 105). In the expansive view there is a full recognition that racism, discrimination, and subjugation work in concert such that discriminatory acts and practices are targeted to groups of people across difference representing systemic epidemics, not individualized instantiations of discrimination against individual people.

Restrictive legal views on anti-discrimination are oriented and focused on the process at hand, not the outcomes of the process (Crenshaw, 1995; Dixson & Rousseau, 2006; Tate & Rousseau, 2002). This view values a look toward the future, toward what anti-discrimination does in potential cases and circumstances, but makes no effort to "redress present manifestations of past injustice" (Crenshaw, 1995, p. 105). Restrictionists take the positions that discriminatory acts take place in isolation, targeted to individuals, and are not representative of "a social policy against an entire group" (Crenshaw, 1995, p. 105). This view protects restrictionists from dealing with race outside of very narrowly constructed and localized experiences (Crenshaw, 1995, p. 105).

The restrictionist position is parallel to Bell's notion (1995) of interest convergence insofar as whites' interests in redressing discrimination are always set against the "competing interests of white workers, even when those interests were actually created by the subordination of blacks" (Crenshaw, 1995, p. 105). Bell (1995) states that "the interest of blacks in achieving racial equality will be accommodated only when it converges with the interests of whites," supporting that white people engage in restrictive notions of anti-discrimination and value orientations that support restrictive stances. To engage with expansionist views oriented beyond process, to actual outcomes, comes into conflict with white interests.

THE PROBLEM OF PURPOSE AND CRT

The gaps between white and non-white students can be understood as being exacerbated by any number of factors associated with the educational debt that Ladson-Billings (2006) has pointed out. The combination of this gap and the resulting debt establish the groundwork for the "manufactured" crisis to have "material" effects on the lives of students of color. A significant problem exists, however, because we are searching for answers that cannot help but be faulty given that they are intended to address fictitious and at best ancillary problems. The challenges of U.S. schooling are not limited to the act of teaching or the most efficient approach for delivering instruction, as our current fixation on "standards," "accountability," and market-driven educational testing and assessment organizations would lead us to believe (Taubman, 2009). Instead these problems are actually microcosms of the larger gap in wealth, material worth, and employment opportunities between whites and non-whites throughout the nation and the world (Marable, 1983; Mitchell & Mitchell, 2007). The school then can be understood as a site where the gaps that persist into adulthood are formed.

Evidence of the strain associated with the influence of racism, classism, and neo-liberalism on schooling is not exclusively relegated to students of color. It can also be found in the experiences, high attrition rates, and overall level of dissatisfaction among teachers. For example, it is increasingly difficult to retain teachers in working-class communities (McLeod & Tanner, 2007). And, when considering the phenomenon of white flight (Hancock, 2006), or new white teachers rapidly leaving the profession, the interlocking maladies associated with race and class surface. The role of the teacher in remedying this systemic problem cannot be limited to stereotypic constructions of what a teacher is, if the challenge of paying off the debt is to be addressed. Ignoring the influence of institutional racism continues the debt by sending a majority white, female, and middle-class teacher population to work in public schools that are increasingly racially, culturally, and economically diverse (Hancock, 2006). The divergence in identity between students and teachers is not inherently a problem. In the hands of a skilled pedagogue this difference can serve as a powerful tool for innovative teaching and learning. The problem exists because there are few if any pedagogic spaces in which pre-service teachers are explicitly challenged or educated about their "implicatedness" in the continuance of the educational disenfranchisement of students of color.

Against this backdrop, educators across levels and particularly K-12 teachers struggle to articulate developed rationales for why they enter the profession. In our professional work in higher education and teacher education we engage significant numbers of pre-service educators and notice disturbing patterns of vagueness about why they want to enter this profession. In exchanges we often hear candidates struggle to articulate something substantive about why they chose to do this work. Their responses can be categorized into fairly consistent narratives concerning them viewing their calling to be "teachers as helpers," who found their ways into the profession through a convergence of personal interests and choice of content. To illustrate this point, we share data from qualitative research conducted with pre-service teachers that was aimed at understanding these educators' narratives (teacher as helper, interests–content convergence, and the overlap between the two) as they relate to teaching.

Teacher Helpers

The first and most pervasive narrative that we hear concerning why our participants chose to become teachers consists of fairly common clichés that frame teachers as helpers. One participant, Brian, commented that early on he knew he wanted to be a teacher but gave no specific rationale about why, stating "When I was in ninth grade I knew I wanted to be a teacher and I don't know why." Brian went on to say that he had a teacher he thought was "the coolest guy." Brian's remarks reflect that he had been interested in teaching for several years (since ninth grade); however, from that point to the present one would expect a more developed rationale other than his admiration of a former teacher ("the coolest guy") as a means to further develop his interests.

Another participant, Barbara, as opposed to discussing her perception of a former teacher, focused on what she could offer future students and subsequently qualities that she felt made her fit to teach. She said, "I want to help and being a teacher is a good way to do that. I want to be that positive role model because I never got in trouble and I'm not the bad kid." Barbara articulates the cliché of educator as helper, and then redirects the conversation away from the act of teaching and back toward herself and her own experience of never getting in trouble or being the "bad kid." Barbara's responses (like Brian's before) appear to indicate that she has not thought through the more serious implications of the profession, nor has she developed a discourse to articulate her true understandings of the profession.

Similarly to Brian and Barbara, other participants in the study, and other candidates we work with, struggle to provide a rationale for teaching beyond surface clichés that dominate the wider parlance about teachers and education. Additional examples of lacking a clearly articulated purpose for entering the profession included comments like "I want to be a teacher so I can make a difference in kids' lives; I loved the idea of guiding kids; choosing to become a teacher is me taking an oath to do my best to help them; I like to help people, like teaching … it makes me happy."

While clearly these remarks are far from malevolent, given the complexity of teaching in the twenty-first century more is needed. To help—or be a teacher helper—one must first be knowledgeable about, and in dialogic relation to, the students' communities. Next, teachers are challenged to have a sense of clarity about the systemic nature of the racist/classist challenges that their students from historically marginalized communities are facing. In not knowing why they enter their profession, pre-service educators have narratives that conveniently nestle into seemingly liberal and expansive views of education. Who after all wants to have a teacher who would say "I don't want to help kids; I don't like kids; I never thought this would be something I should do"? CRT ideas about expansive and restrictive approaches, however, suggest that merely articulating an expansive sounding narrative does not directly work against a restrictive approach. In the age of the marketization of education through Teach for America and KIPP (among other ideological approaches to education) the abstract liberal idea of "helping kids" is often articulated against a restrictive view of who students are, what communities look like, and other judgments of families and communities that seemingly serve to block educators from authentic engagement with the very students and families they are serving. If educators fundamentally do not understand the strength of the cultural capital students and families possess, and they have no substantive reason for doing the work, what they are left with is a seemingly expansive narrative clouded in the restrictionist approach of ignoring the effects of racism on the educational landscape.

It is our belief that, by informing the curriculums of teacher education programs with CRT, pre-service teachers will be provided opportunities to understand the hegemonic nature of U.S. schooling. In the process, vague conceptualizations of expansivity are replaced with authentic notions aligned with the expansive approach to understanding race. With a more profound and authentic base to understanding race and racial inequity, teachers with substantive purposes for their work are best positioned to challenge how restrictive approaches further exacerbate the perceived crisis. Subsequently teachers are able to develop a much more profound purpose for becoming teachers and responsibility in their practice as teachers.

Personal Interests and Subject Matter Convergence

Another theme that consistently turns up in our discussions is that, when pressed for a more clearly developed rationale for becoming teachers, participants and candidates in our programs provide responses that have little if any relation to the actual work of teachers. We are afforded what we describe as a convergence of personal and content or subject matter interests as a rationale for becoming teachers. As one example, Bob, comments, "I know that I want to do sports and I have always been good at sports. I just love it. It's relaxing to me and at the same time math came easy." Bob went on to share that he looked to either "be a physical education or math teacher, and that being a physical education teacher is just the easiest job ever, just play sports all day." Contrastingly, it is our belief that loving sports, being interested in math, and considering teaching an opportunity for extended leisure are a far cry from the ways that well-informed teachers describe schools. It appears that Bob lacks understanding of what happens in schools as well as the work of teachers. And in the end we do not see how his narrative would help educators understand the experiences of students from historically marginalized communities.

Cathy, on the other hand, commented: "I have always loved history and knew I wanted to do something with history; my dad and uncle were history majors; it runs in our family. Also, I have always taught at sports camps." Having family members in education, Cathy has the potential to make deeper connections to the profession, and even possibly have a language to explain why teaching makes sense. Like other participants, though, Cathy also framed teachers as helpers, and displayed a convergence between her personal interests and choice of content. Cathy stated, "I am very serious about the fact that I really do love history." The over-focus on content, particularly her personal affection for the content, coupled with a lack of discussion about the students in meaningful ways, limits her ability to connect with students. Being drawn to history does not automatically prepare one for the difficult work of building pedagogical relationships across racial, ethnic, and class divisions that is at the heart of addressing the debt.

Similar remarks about the convergence of personal and subject matter interests on the decision to teach by participants include: "I love social studies, politics, and history … I could talk about them until I'm blue in the face, so I think I should teach; there were engaging teachers and coaches and I was just like—I think I can do that." Therefore family relations and love of sports, politics, or content areas significantly influence our candidates' choices to become teachers, as well as their conceptions of exactly what teachers do.

We would like to point out, however, that when we were interviewing candidates none of our participants substantively discussed building relationships with their students. At best we were provided insight into what they hoped to provide, or how they hoped to serve students, but even in these limited instances student-to-teacher interactions were addressed in abstraction or through their own past experiences of schooling. We consider these disconnects as commonplace within the pre-service teacher population. The danger in this naiveté is that, lacking grounding in what happens in schools, purpose for entering the profession, or the ability to understand the experiences of students, educators often take the proverbial path of least resistance. As mentioned earlier they are susceptible to furthering the articulation of ideas that sound expansive, but work restrictively, on purpose. The system is designed to praise, encourage, and facilitate the lack of development in the narratives of educators so as to maintain a restrictive stronghold on marginalizing particular types of students to maintain the order of a free-market economy.

Because the United States is dependent on a free-market system, some segment of the population intentionally has to be withheld from advancing educationally so that they will work for low wages in the service industry so as to meet the needs of the chosen, overrepresented, dominant factions of the population. In the case of our current educational system this status quo path means becoming a cog in the system that, according to critical educational scholars, has disenfranchised working-class students of color for over 122 years (Watkins, 2001). To that extent the property value of whiteness operates through expansive articulations with restrictive actions to select out those who will have access and those who will not. Sending novice teachers to urban areas without proper supports, without developed rationales for being there, and without an understanding of the restrictive mechanisms to race that fuel free-market orientations intentionally maintains the marginalization of students from historically underrepresented groups.

More Complex Callings

Despite the fact that the bulk of the candidates we work with provide fairly surface rationales for becoming teachers, there are a few exceptions worth noting. These exceptions were not necessarily all positive, but they did provide instances of deeper reflection. For example, Angela discussed numerous reasons for becoming a teacher that coalesced into what she described as wanting to "make them care." Angela is not specific about what making students care means, or how as a teacher her role would allow her to develop an ethos of care among her potential future students. Angela elaborated: "I really try to make myself one of the teachers that I feel is there because they want to be there." While this sentiment is positive in nature it is still unclear why she wants to teach or the conditions that would demonstrate she has met the goal of wanting to be there. However, we found Angela's remarks intriguing because they hint at the sensibilities that we believe are essential for becoming a competent teacher.

It is our belief that these sensibilities evolve from Angela's aim to solicit what she describes as care or an excitement about the content from her students in combination with her espoused desire to be in the school with her students and colleagues. Both of these aims are in line with the mantra that before you can expect students to show you what they know you have to show them that you care (Delpit, 2008). Consequently, caring means that you must be informed about the ways that the students that you are teaching have experienced schooling. And, as we have previously stated, CRT provides a drastically different perspective about the racialized/classist nature of schooling. We consider the CRT vantage on schooling to be instrumental for understanding the current educational system. If teachers truly hope to be present and ultimately care, they cannot ignore the hegemonic functioning of white supremacy within our educational system, which becomes the next step for candidates like Angela.

Another participant, Todd, commented that he sees the role of teaching as being unique, asserting that, "from a legal standpoint my job is to teach them that curriculum, but more than that my job is to connect with them." Todd uses a reductionist approach, as he describes a main "legal" purpose of his work as content delivery. Content delivery is but one aspect of teaching and, ultimately, if the prospective teacher sees content delivery as the major purpose of his/her job, the conceptualization of teacher is reduced only to that of information specialist. However, we found in Todd's remarks, as in Angela's, attention, albeit limited, to his actual relationship with students. Todd's reference that more than content delivery his job is to connect with students suggests that he understands the significance of the need to build relationships, but he has not acquired the language to speak in concrete ways about exactly how these relationships will take place. We believe that the process of developing this language amounts to the deeper sense of purpose that we consider to be sorely lacking that might challenge the nature of whiteness as property that has undergirded most of his life experiences, while giving him a window into breaking apart restrictionist views.

Steven, like Todd, appealed to a reductionist notion of teaching, with a focus on educating students for the test. Specifically, Steven sees his role as helping to "educate them on information that they are gonna need to know for the test." The concept of teacher as test preparer becomes, in a way, a reification of an autocratic teacher as technician who must focus on test results as a measure of teacher efficacy. In essence Steven as test preparer espouses a self-regulated view of teaching that aligns with the lay discourse on what teachers' roles are, yet falls short of being a clear vision of what teacher education hopes to prepare teachers to be. This reductionist view of education illustrates Steven's ability to align his thinking about teaching with the dominant discourse that we consider has historically been to the detriment of marginalized communities.

Cathy was our only participant who spoke directly to the racial/cultural dimension of teaching. However, we found her remarks proof of a total ignorance on the part of our candidates, when considering the influence of race and racism on schooling. Cathy commented that her desire to become a teacher comes from having good model teachers. It is her explanation of what her models are, however, that gives one pause. Cathy said that teachers:

> influenced me especially the diverse teachers that I had, how I could have one history teacher that was an ex-Marine but he taught just as well as any teachers maybe of a different race. I thought it was cool that so many races and religions could still be good teachers and it didn't matter. [Pause] It doesn't matter?

Cathy asserted that race does not matter, then paused for a long second, and turned her statement into a question, as though seeking approval to ensure her that race did not, in fact, matter. It is interesting that, in her conceptualization of teacher, Cathy placed emphasis on aspects such as military service, and was surprised that either service or race could create a situation for the teacher to also be good. Cathy's position that this was the model that motivated her to pursue teaching is confusing analytically, as she did not really provide what it is about those teachers who served as models for her, beyond hypothetical and undefined race and military service.

Of all the participants, Pat shared what appeared to be the most in-depth and substantive ideas of why she wants to be a teacher. Pat cited that being a social studies teacher is important in order to help students "become better citizens." The response shows some thinking that matches the aims of promoting social studies and the goal of a free public education to promote democratic ideals of citizenship consistent with the National

Council for the Social Studies' standards. Pat was ultimately unable to describe how her role as a teacher would serve in pursuit of the development of the citizenry and future electorate, and consequently her articulation, while positive, matching the bulk of the responses, remains surface.

It is not our point to be overly critical of our participants, because we believe in many regards their desire to do good by students is admirable. Further we do not find their remarks to be remarkable or decidedly unique; and perhaps the problem lies with the fact that these narratives are common stock narratives articulated throughout the country by nearly all pre-service educators. Our contention, instead, is that, given the anesthetized state of the nation at large and education in particular, their surface level thought about why they want to be teachers and ultimately lack of purpose are typical of most entering the profession. Our current insistence on turning a blind eye to the ways that white supremacy undergirds this manufactured crisis promotes the property value of whiteness's narratives that inform these teachers, and that further embed the restrictionist approach while encouraging surface and vague articulations that appear to afford something more expansive. Teacher education programs can only do so much in terms of preparing teachers for their roles. Educators must be both informed and purposeful. Lacking critical sensibilities about the hegemonic functioning of our educational system, coupled with a lack of clarity about why they aspire to become educators, teacher candidates, and even many teacher educators, our data suggests, reduce instructional opportunities to issues of methods and approaches to delivering instruction, leaving the question and discussion of their identity, and particularly racial identity, unspoken. Left unspoken, the narratives further our society's engagement with restrictionist approaches cloaked in the sheep's clothing of expansive narratives.

In an approach with either too much focus on methods, to the exclusion of a broader perspective, or too much focus on sweepingly broad claims about the aims of education, without meaningful mechanisms for reaching these goals, a crucial aspect of race is left unsaid, and remains colorblind (Bonilla-Silva, 2006). When the racial identity of the teacher is left unexamined, and the teacher is unable to see her/his work as a teacher being that of a political agent of change with a developed and substantive rationale, the ability for the teacher to situate the work within a culturally relevant approach is lost. Our observation of the resulting conundrum has led us to believe that this loss amounts to falling in line with the taken-for-granted or status quo approach to teaching.

CONCLUDING THOUGHTS

Instead of thinking about how we need to fix students (which CRT would suggest is a restrictive approach to "dealing" with the "problems"), teacher educators and educational scholars need to help teachers develop their own sense of identity and purpose for teaching (which CRT might suggest is a more expansive approach to being real "agents of change"). We suggest that teachers in touch with their identity and purposes for teaching have a clearer sense of how they are like their students despite surface level differences between a predominately monocultural white teaching force and a predominantly multicultural and multiracial student body. We conclude then that the CRT critique of the "liberal" perspectives (perspectives that create actual distance between teachers and students) is addressed through an engagement with expansive orientations.

The gambit of educational policies spawned by but not limited to A Nation at Risk, No Child Left Behind, or the Spellings Commission provides illustrations of the base narrative that has been created in the U.S. educational landscape. The lack of purpose exhibited in teachers' narratives ultimately does nothing except to help to support them being a tool in the neo-liberal machine. We argue that alternative certification programs such as TFA and charter school approaches manipulated in urban contexts to support the corporatization of education really de-contextualize the realities of urban education while intentionally drawing in folks who have nothing but the "I want to help those people" mentality. All teacher preparation programs and certification paths have to demand that, before being certified or licensed, candidates have developed both sufficient pedagogical approaches and sufficient purpose for doing the work.

Because teacher preparation programs and corporatized approaches do not demand an authentic engagement with purpose, but rather encourage teachers to only articulate surface sounding expansive narratives while fitting into the restrictive approaches, in the twenty-first century the problem will continue to be a manufactured 147-years-in-the-making educational crisis, which articulates false expansive discourses of "helping" and wanting to "change to educate all" and "leave no child behind," all the while masking what is essentially a restrictive approach to education.

REFERENCES

Alemán, E. (2009). LatCrit educational leadership and advocacy: Struggling over whiteness as property in Texas school finance. *Equity and Excellence in Education, 42*(2), 183–201.

Anderson, J. (1988). *The education of blacks in the South 1860–1935.* Chapel Hill: University of North Carolina Press.

Arbuthnot, K. (2011). *Filling in the blanks: Standardized testing and the black–white achievement gap.* Charlotte, NC: Information Age.

Asante, M. (2009). *Speaking my mother's tongue: Introduction to African American language.* Fort Worth, TX: Temba House.

Beeman, A., Glasberg, D.S., & Casey, C. (2010). Whiteness as property: Predatory lending and the reproduction of racialized inequality. *Critical Sociology, 37*(1), 27–45.

Bell, D. (1995). Racial realism. In K. Crenshaw, N. Gotanda, G. Peller, & K. Thomas (Eds.), *Critical race theory: The key writings that formed the movement* (pp. 302–314). New York: New Press.

Berliner, D., & Biddle, B. (1996). *The manufactured crisis: Myths, fraud, and the attack on America's public schools.* New York: Perseus.

Bonilla-Silva, E. (2006). *Racism without racists: Color-blind racism and the persistence of racial inequality in the United States* (2nd ed.). Lanham, MD: Rowman & Littlefield.

Crenshaw, K.W. (1995). Race, reform, and retrenchment: Transformation and legitimating in anti-discrimination law. In K. Crenshaw, N. Gotanda, G. Peller, & K. Thomas (Eds.), *Critical race theory: The key writings that formed the movement* (pp. 103–126). New York: New Press.

DeCuir, J.T., & Dixson, A.D. (2004). "So when it comes out, they aren't surprised it is there": Using critical race theory as a tool of analysis of race and racism in education. *Educational Researcher, 33*(5), 26–31.

Delpit, L. (2008). *The skin that we speak: Thoughts on language and culture in the classroom.* New York: New Press.

Dixson, A.D., & Dingus, J.E. (2007). Tyranny of the majority: Re-enfranchisement of African-American teacher educators teaching for democracy. *International Journal of Qualitative Studies in Education, 20*(6), 639–654.

Dixson, A.D., & Rousseau, C.K. (2006). And we are still not saved: Critical race theory in education ten years later. *Race, Ethnicity, and Education, 8*(1), 7–27.

Fasching-Varner, K.J. (2009). No! The team ain't alright: The individual and institutional problematics of race. *Social Identities, 15*(6), 811–829.

Frankenberg, E. (2005). The impact of school segregation on residential housing patterns: Mobile, AL and Charlotte, NC. In John Boger & Gary Orfield (Eds.), *School resegregation: Must the South turn back?* Chapel Hill: University of North Carolina Press.

Gould, S. (1996). *The mismeasure of man* (2nd ed.). New York: W.W. Norton.

Hancock, S. (2006). White women's work: On the front lines of urban education. In J. Landsman & C. Lewis (Eds.), *White teachers/diverse classrooms: A guide for building inclusive schools, promoting high expectations and eliminating racism* (pp. 93–109). Sterling, VA: Stylus.

Harris, C. (1993). Whiteness as property. *Harvard Law Review, 106*(8), 1707–1792.

Harris, C. (1995). Whiteness as property. In K. Crenshaw, N. Gotanda, G. Peller, & K. Thomas (Eds.), *Critical race theory: The key writings that formed the movement* (pp. 276–291). New York: New Press.

Herrnstein, R., & Murray, C. (1994). *The bell curve: The reshaping of American life by difference in intelligence.* New York: Free Press.

Hilliard, A., III. (2003). No mystery: Closing the achievement gap between Africans and excellence. In T. Perry, C. Steele, & A. Hillard III (Eds.), *Young, gifted and black: Promoting high achievement among African-American students* (pp. 131–143). Boston, MA: Beacon Press.

Ignatiev, N. (1995). *How the Irish became white.* New York: Routledge.

Jay, G. (2012). Property rites: The Rhinelander trial, passing, and the protection of whiteness. *Journal of American Ethnic History, 31*(3), 109–110.

Kozol, J. (1991). *Savage inequalities.* New York: Crown.

Kozol, J. (2005). *The shame of the nation: The restoration of apartheid schooling in America.* New York: Three Rivers Press.

Ladson-Billings, G.J. (2006). From achievement gap to education debt. Presidential keynote address, American Educational Research Association, San Francisco, CA.

Ladson-Billings, G.J., & Tate, W.F., IV. (1995). Toward a critical race theory of education. *Teachers College Record, 97*(1), 47–68.

Landsman, J., & Lewis, C.W. (2006). *White teachers, diverse classrooms: A guide to building inclusive schools, promoting high expectations, and eliminating racism.* Sterling, VA: Stylus Publishing.

Lentz-Smith, A. (2011). Property rites: The Rhinelander trial, passing, and the protection of whiteness (review). *Journal of Interdisciplinary History, 41*(3), 478–480.

Lewis, C., & Moore, J.L., III. (2004). African American students in kindergarten through twelfth grade (K-12) urban settings: Implications for teachers, counselors, social workers, psychologists and administrators. *E-Journal of Teaching and Learning in Diverse Settings, 2*, 1–8 (retrieved from http://www.subr.edu/coeducation/ejournal/v2i1.htm).

Lewis, C., Hancock, S., James, M., & Larke, P. (2008). African American students and No Child Left Behind legislation: Progression or digression in educational attainment. *Multicultural Learning and Teaching, 3*(2), 9–29.

Lopez, I.H. (1996). *White by law: The legal construction of race.* New York: New York University Press.

Marable, M. (1983). *How capitalism underdeveloped black America.* Boston, MA: South End Press.

McLeod, K., & Tanner, T. (2007). Transitioning diverse classrooms toward education equality: A new model of teacher dependence and independence. *National Journal of Urban Education and Practice, 1*, 99–110.

Mills, C.W. (1997). *The racial contract.* Ithaca, NY: Cornell University Press.

Mitchell, R., & Mitchell, R.L. (2007). History and education mining the gap: Historically black colleges as centers of excellence for engaging disparities in race and wealth. In Beverly Moran (Ed.), *Race and wealth disparities* (pp. 82–109). New York: University Press of America.

Moore, J.L., III. (2003). Guest editorial. *Journal of Men's Studies, 12*, 1–2.

Morrison, T. (1992). *Playing in the dark: Whiteness and the literary imagination.* New York: Vintage Books.

Obiakor, F., & Beachum, F. (2006). *Urban education for the 21st century: Research, issues and perspectives.* Springfield, IL: Charles C. Thomas.

Orfield, G., & Lee, C. (2004). *Brown at 50: King's dream or Plessy's nightmare?* Cambridge, MA: Civil Rights Project at Harvard University.

Orfield, G., & Lee, C. (2006). *Racial transformation and the changing nature of segregation.* Cambridge, MA: Civil Rights Project at Harvard University.

Osucha, E. (2009). The whiteness of privacy: Race, media, law. *Camera Obscura, 24*(70), 66–107.

Owen, D.S. (2007). Towards a critical theory of whiteness. *Philosophy and Social Criticism, 33*(2), 203–222.

Roediger, D.R. (1999). The pursuit of whiteness: Property, terror, and expansion, 1790–1860. *Journal of the Early Republic, 19*(4), 579–601.

Siddle-Walker, V. (2001). African-American teaching in the South: 1940–1960. *American Educational Research Journal, 38*, 751–779.

Steele, C.M., & Aronson, J. (1995). Stereotype threat and the intellectual test performance of African-Americans. *Journal of Personality and Social Psychology, 62*(1), 26–37.

Tate, W., & Rousseau, C. (2002). Access and opportunity: The political and social context of mathematics education. In L. English (Ed.), *Handbook of international research in mathematics education* (pp. 271–299). Mahwah, NJ: Lawrence Erlbaum.

Taubman, P.M. (2009). *Teaching by numbers: Deconstructing the discourse of standards and accountability in education.* New York: Routledge.

Tillery, A.B. (2009). Tocqueville as critical race theorist: Whiteness as property, interest convergence, and the limits of Jacksonian democracy. *Political Research Quarterly, 62*(4), 639–652.

Vaught, S.E., & Castagno, A.E. (2008). "I don't think I'm a racist": Critical race theory, teacher attitudes, and structural racism. *Race, Ethnicity, and Education, 11*(2), 95–113.

Watkins, W. (2001). *The white architects of black education: Ideology and power in America, 1865–1954.* New York: Teachers College Press.

Winant, H. (2000). Race and race theory. *Annual Review of Sociology, 26,* 169–185.

27

POST-RACIAL CRITICAL RACE PRAXIS

*Sabina Vaught and Gabrielle Hernandez, with Ikenna Acholonu,
Amber Frommherz, and Ben Phelps*

In this country, lesbianism is a poverty—as is being brown, as is being a woman, as is being just plain poor. The danger lies in ranking the oppressions. *The danger lies in failing to acknowledge the specificity of the oppression.*

(Moraga, 1981, p. 29)

… power is exercised rather than possessed; it is not the "privilege," acquired or preserved, of the dominant class, but the overall effect of its strategic positions … this power is not exercised simply as an obligation or a prohibition on those who "do not have it"; it invests them, is transmitted by them and through them; it exerts pressure upon them, just as they themselves, in their struggle against it, resist the grip it has on them … [In these relations] there is neither analogy nor homology, but a specificity of mechanism and modality.

(Foucault, 1995, p. 27)

INTRODUCTION: SPECIFICITY

In the fall of 2012, we (one professor, seven graduate students in an educational foundations program, and two undergraduate American Studies majors) piloted a new graduate seminar, "Pedagogies," in which we asked, "What are the features of a critical race praxis in a White supremacist context that is ideologically post-racial?" As we will illustrate in this chapter, we did not arrive at a particular answer, but rather began to formulate a set of principles that we hope will contribute to the larger conversation on critical race pedagogy (Lynn, 1999; Lynn & Jennings, 2009). The guiding principle that emerged for all other principles was specificity.

We understood the current White supremacist context of schooling to be an assault on the specificity of the relationships between power and race. While we in fact developed this understanding over time, it was through a particular in-class discussion of critical praxis that its salience came into stark relief. We began this discussion by considering the ways in which practitioners might disrupt post-racial teaching and learning contexts in which race is constructed and mobilized as a de-powered category. In particular, we understood many such contexts to be organized around discourses and practices that formulate race as a neutral aspect of identity, or one that is attached to culture but not institutional and systemic power structures. So, in fidelity to our concerns with institutional power, we explored the example of one graduate student, Ikenna,[1] who identifies as Nigerian American and Black, but whose public, institutional racialization is consistently Black American. He discussed a praxis situation in which he helped facilitate a frequently used activity—often referred to as "the privilege walk"—in which teenagers were asked to stand in a shoulder-to-shoulder line. Facilitators asked these teenagers, who were participants in a leadership training program, to take a step forward or a step backward depending on the prompt. The group included students of various race, class, gender, and sexual identities. This activity was intended to show differences in "privilege" vis-à-vis social location within the group membership. However, the activity upset and frustrated a number of the teens, most particularly the only two young Black men. These two young men found themselves at the end of the activity occupying the most privileged position in the room. Given the raced and gendered power structures in the United States, students in the Pedagogies seminar were surprised at Ikenna's description of this conclusion to the privilege walk.

So, in attempting to discern how an activity designed to reveal power[2] in fact masked and grossly misrepresented power through and on the bodies of youth, we examined some of the prompts. One of the prompts was: "Take a step backward if you have ancestry in American slavery." Our class realized through dialogue that, if Ikenna were to participate, he would not step backward. Yet his public racialization as an African American male means he is consistently assigned by White institutional representatives the supremacist-constructed features of African American masculinity—namely, criminality and aggressive heteronormative hypersexuality (Ferguson, 2000; Williams, 1995). Conversely, if Professor Vaught were to participate, she would step backward. Although she has Black ancestry in American slavery, she is institutionally White and so is protected and afforded power through that racial status and its attendant assumptions in relation to law enforcement, school, and so on. Therefore, the result of locating Ikenna and Professor Vaught as imaginary privilege walk participants illustrated the way in which an activity aimed at revealing power differentials could reify post-racial notions that race itself is no longer attached to power. In other words, this use of ancestry to locate contemporary racial experience and institutional power failed to create a context in which current racial power structures and individual location within them might be legitimately understood. The privilege walk served to *rank* decontextualized notions of oppression and power rather than identify the *specificity* of that oppression and power.

In this chapter, we explore just one modal facet of specificity—that one expressing the public, institutional mechanisms of race. So, while students in the Pedagogies course understood racial specificity as multifaceted—including personal identification, familial and cultural practice, legal and political standing, and even blood quantum—we take up as the purview of this chapter one aspect of that larger conceptualization of specificity. We are interested in the public modalities by which institutionally racialized identity is acted on and through, and how those modalities shape education, broadly conceived, in this contemporary moment. Ancestry in U.S. slavery, for example, is personally, culturally, and familially important, but does not necessarily recognize the specific functioning of White supremacy on variously racialized people and cannot, alone, specifically locate the dynamic of White supremacist, institutional educational practice.

In failing to identify the specificity of institutional racial power and instead identifying the specificity of individual ancestral identity, the privilege walk activity in fact entrenched reigning ideological definitions of race as decoupled from real material, political, and cultural power, thus creating a supremacist context in spite of its intention to do otherwise. The two young Black men were dually assaulted by the denial of their specific experiences with and within power structures, particularly in relation to other students in the room. While individual people may have cultural origins in familial contexts that include racial identities that go institutionally unrecognized, these aspects of identity do not necessarily match the public, institutional racial identities that function along axes of power that post-racialism works to elide. Moreover, Ikenna was problematically positioned—as a facilitator of the activity and teacher in the program—as potentially being made complicit in the post-racial power relations the activity produced. The question of disruption of power dynamics, then, lies in mapping the specificities that reified a contemporary mechanism of White supremacy. In other words, how Ikenna might navigate such an activity, through his institutional racial position, is informed in part by his assessment of the specificity of power dynamics.

So, while we understand CRT to draw on personal experience, we also understand it to do so in ways that illustrate the larger racialized power context, even if those are seemingly contradictory narratives. Therefore, in this chapter, we have selected counterstories (Ladson-Billings, 2000; Solórzano & Yosso, 2002) from student praxis experiences that emphasize the tension between specificities, but ultimately highlight the specificity of institutional racial dynamics that young educators encounter and navigate to challenge current supremacist practices.

THEORY, CONTEXT, AND METHODOLOGY

CRT scholar Cho (2009) defines post-racialism as:

> a twenty-first-century ideology that reflects a belief that due to the significant racial progress that has been made, the state need not engage in race-based decision-making or adopt race-based remedies, and that civil society should eschew race as a central organizing principle of social action. According to post-racial logic, the move is to effectuate a "retreat from race."
>
> (p. 1594)

This conceptual frame articulates the emerging social order in which the prevailing liberal narrative imagines a nation free of racial barriers to success. And this narrative is being mechanized through law, policy, and practice. Cho argues that post-racialism possesses four key features: an assumption of racial progress; a race-neutrality that decouples race from power; a moral uniformity that constructs all races as morally equitable and so suggests that those who call attention to racism are as suspect as those who practice racism; and an overt effort at distance from political correctness, civil rights, and critical race scholarship. These features operate in overlapping and coordinating ways to assemble an ideology with vast systemic traction.

The theoretical concept of post-racialism highlights the ways in which, through the signifier of the election of President Obama (and perhaps the existence of Obama himself), Whiteness is reconstituting itself as redeemed. In this state of redemption, it can celebrate the fictive equitable outcome of what it constructs as its noble sacrifices to civil rights and to African Americans in particular. In the post-racial era, Whiteness no longer need defer to African American critiques, requests, or demands, as the redemption narrative suggests that the racial playing field has been leveled through decades of noble White sacrifice. In constructing this fantasy of the level playing field, the White narrative firmly relegates racial oppression to history. Moreover, this supposed leveling of the playing field denotes a societal condition in which legal (and, by proxy, policy and practice) remedy for racial disparity is no longer relevant and racialist approaches to institutional organization and understanding, such as affirmative action and critical race theory, respectively, are not only rendered moot but also cast as racist. This ideological shift lays fresh groundwork for an unchecked and normalized White supremacy.

Students in the Pedagogies class established Cho's (2009) conceptualization of post-racialism and the larger theoretical tenets of CRT as the scholarly and political context within which all other discussions, readings, and praxis were engaged. Within this context, we examined various strands of critical pedagogy central to our discussion of racialist education in a post-racial context: critical pedagogy (Apple, 2009; Ayers, 1988; Freire, 2000; Giroux, 2009a; Greene, 2009; McLaren, 2009); Indigenous and Red pedagogies (Battiste, 2008; Brayboy & Maughan, 2009; Grande, 2007, 2009; Kaomea, 2005); culturally relevant pedagogies (Ladson-Billings, 1994); critical race pedagogies (Jennings & Lynn, 2005; Lynn, 1999; Lynn & Jennings, 2009); critical feminist pedagogies (Alarcón, 1981; Cho, 2003; Crenshaw, 1991; Fine, 2009; hooks, 1989; Jamarillo, 2006; Lorde, 1984; Luttrell, 2003; Moraga, 1981; Weiler, 1988, 2009); queer pedagogies (Britzman, 1995; Kumashiro, 2001; Loutzenheiser, 2001; Mayo, 2009; McCready, 2010; Mercer, 1991; Rofes, 2005; Sumara & Davis, 1999); and materialist critical pedagogies (De Lissovoy, 2007; hooks, 1994; Monahan, 2009). Additionally, we explored readings that took up the dilemmas of both in-service and pre-service teacher training (Bartolomé, 2007; Delpit, 1988; Dixson & Dingus, 2007; Ellsworth, 1989; Giroux, 2009b; King, 1991; Solórzano, 1997; Vaught & Castagno, 2008), as well as those that detailed various literacies and related praxes (Duncan-Andrade & Morrell, 2007; Fisher, 2007; Green, 2008; Hill, 2009; Moses & Cobb, 2001; Winn, 2011).

Students actively encountered these strands by observing, implementing, and reflecting on them in the contexts of their respective praxis sites. These sites were selected by each student, and shared the characteristics of being purposefully outside core content area pK-12 classrooms though within educational classrooms or programs. At these sites, students worked directly with youth for several hours weekly and paid particular attention to the function and expression of race, racialization, racism, and White supremacy as they intersect with gender, sexuality, and other categories of power and identity (Crenshaw, 1991). Additionally, they paid attention to their own positions, actions, and understandings. Students recorded this work in field site journals. These weekly journals became contributing data for weekly electronic dialogues students produced with partners they maintained throughout the semester. These dialogues, designed to facilitate the dialogic/dialectic process at the heart of critical pedagogy, explored the interrelation of praxis site experience, weekly readings, and class discussion.

Students practiced the core critical pedagogical exercise of dialogue in weekly exchanges as a methodology grounded in counterstorytelling (Ladson-Billings, 2000; Solórzano & Yosso, 2002), and collaboratively constructed interacting experiential narratives that were inherently theorized, both in that they produced and interacted with theory (Brayboy, 2005) and in that they drew overtly from theoretical frames (Duncan, 2005). Students engaged dialogic counterstorytelling on multiple levels. First, they narrated experiences distinct from the dominant, post-racial narrative of schooling. Second, they narrated experiences that challenged and complicated reductive binary categories of experience and praxis. And, finally, they narrated experiences that consistently disrupted their own narratives. In this way, they methodologically problematized praxis at every level, from the institution to the body. Moreover, students recognized institutional contexts as unfixed, in that our institutional identities sometimes changed (to varying degrees) over time in a particular location. The evident multiplicity and contextually shifting nature of our identities challenged students to identify specificity as linked to power rather than to fixed categories of identity. This meant that, if one student could be institutionally read as Latina, White, straight, and gay, over a brief period of time in just one post-racial educational context, as we will illustrate later, she had to establish the specificity of power through critical race pedagogical practices that were not singularly linked to categories but rather fastened to supremacist power dynamics and the construction of meaning.

SILENCES AND ASSERTIONS

Many of the students in the Pedagogies seminar began the semester by theoretically mapping the racial organization of their praxis sites. For example, they asked how, when, and where Whiteness was constructed and exerted as a property (Harris, 1993). Furthermore, students considered how the particular supremacist organization and institutional architecture of their praxis sites shaped their negotiation of a critical race pedagogy. This illustrated their initial foray into formulating specificity. Ben, a White, male graduate student wrote about the impact of post-racialism on developing specificity at his praxis:

> This new iteration of racial ideology presents considerable barriers for the work toward praxis. Freire (2000) believed in the dialectic nature of pedagogy, and thus in the inextricable link between "reflection and action, in such radical interaction that if one is sacrificed—even in part—the other immediately suffers" (p. 87). Put more simply, he argued that both theory and practice are necessary for true praxis. Yet, post-racialism works to separate the two, as I found in my own praxis site over the course of the semester.

Ben worked as a one-on-one math tutor for an 8th grade African American boy through an organization that serves students of Color in a local urban school district. In the course of the program's tutor training, Ben was told that the organization relied on the "Socratic method" and drew on what he perceived to be many aspects of a critical pedagogy. "The goal," wrote Ben,

> is to value the knowledge that the students bring with them to the tutoring sessions by having the tutors act as guides rather than all-knowing authorities. Furthermore, by

making it "all about asking questions," the process is predicated on what Freire (2000) calls "problem-posing education," which takes dialogue as a foundational component of pedagogy. The method ... made me hopeful for working toward true praxis.

However, the actual work of tutoring was measured through a "log detailing what the student and I worked on and whether or not he achieved 'mastery' of the material." Ben was required to determine and assign a level of mastery that would be recorded and follow the student as a record of sorts. Moreover, during the training, "there was little mention of race. In the binder of tutoring materials I received, there were printouts of PowerPoint slides that discussed the achievement gap, but there was no discussion of my role as a White tutor working with a student of Color." Therefore Ben understood that, in the program's arrangement of power relations, he was established as the authority over mastery, and one who would contribute to the establishment of an academic record for an African American student, yet the only institutional recognition of race was a set of handouts that detailed achievement statistics. Race was constructed as a fact, but not as a factor in the educational process at the organization (Ladson-Billings & Tate, 1995; O'Connor et al., 2007, 2009). It was detached from power and decoupled from "Socratic" pedagogical methods.

In citing scholars (Delpit, 1988, 2006; Ladson-Billings, 1994; Lynn, 1999), Ben argued that "teachers must not only be aware of power differentials across multiple lines, but also 'aggressively name and interrogate potentially harmful ideologies and practices in the schools and classrooms where they work'" (Bartolomé, 2007, p. 264). Yet the organization "took a post-racial stance ... and the message was that individual racial locations do not matter in the classroom, as long as everyone works hard." Yet, in this very observation, the student narrated the contradiction of post-racialism. Racially locating himself would not—in a legal, material, discursive national moment when Whiteness can charade as decoupled from power—have necessarily accomplished any more of the aggressive naming and interrogating of power he identifies as so central to pedagogy above. In a post-racial era, where Whiteness is slippery, vague, and elusive in its relation to racial power, in fact that proclamation of Whiteness contains very little specificity. Increasingly overt, hollow self-assertions of White identity buttress the post-racial presumption that Whites are redeemed and now morally, politically, and otherwise equal to people of Color. Racial location in the post-racial educational contexts encountered by students in the Pedagogies course had to do with specific descriptions of power that begged newly conceived and complex language.

Grappling with this challenge, Ben realized that the specificity of racialized power dynamics did not reside simply in his assertion of a racial identity, but in the appropriation of superficial tenets of critical pedagogy in the post-racial masquerade of White supremacy. Ben wrote: "I never openly discussed race during our tutoring sessions. I am not necessarily suggesting that I needed to affirm Mauro's voice and experience as a Black student by discussing with him my White privilege, but there is power involved in my ability to deny my body" (hooks, 1994). However, as the semester went on, his understanding of location in relation to specificity became more nuanced. After the semester, he reflected:

> Although I did not explicitly name my racial location, I worked from a position of understanding dominant pedagogical practice as an embodiment of Whiteness.

Specifically, I worked to give my student ownership and agency over his work, affirming his own processes. I operated from and in resistance to a location that was post-racially linked in the organization's functioning to "mastery." In other words, I was the post-racial master, and I had to locate and dislocate myself there, rather than in the simple naming of my race.

Initially unable to locate himself with any specificity, Ben was at a loss as to how to engage a critical race praxis and instead did not identify himself at all. This conscious paralysis resulted in part directly from Pedagogies class discussions in which we complicated and contextualized assertions of White identity. While in recent colorblind educational contexts the assertion of Whiteness may have invoked a range of meanings from a challenge to colorblindness to a declaration of racial and cultural superiority, in the post-racial context simple assertions of Whiteness are claims to racial moral equivalence and erasure of structural, material realities. To claim Whiteness is to be redeemed. Hollow proclamations of Whiteness can in fact attenuate efforts to challenge supremacy. So having questioned the tools he learned about White privilege (McIntosh, 1989) as an undergraduate—locating yourself racially is to say "I am White"—he was faced with the inertia of racial power specificity attached to post-racial Whiteness. This meant he had to identify specificity in the modalities and mechanisms of a masked Whiteness, here in the form of master and mastery.

Live with your head in the lion's mouth.

(Ellison, 1995, p. 16)

Another graduate student, Amber, a Diné Navajo woman, undertook her praxis at a private Christian day school where her daughter was an elementary student and where she conducted portions of the high school Yearbook class, composed exclusively of White students. The school was overwhelmingly White and both politically and religiously extremely conservative. In considering how to navigate power in such a context, Amber wrote, "I never talked about my racial location or race and they never did and I never used [the term] 'White' in class." For some time, Amber was confounded by what she perceived as her own inaction and by the seeming absence of opportunities to interrupt Whiteness in the Yearbook class. This produced in Amber significant self-doubt about herself as a public, institutional being:

I feel that being in a post-racial society and even being here in Massachusetts as a student at Tufts(!), married to a White man who I met in the Navy is the epitome of post-racialism. By introducing myself via my history (Native–Navy–White spouse–on the east coast–Christian) the assumption could be that I'm striving for an honorary whiteness status.

However, by complicating restrictive notions of context—i.e., the Yearbook classroom—to include multiple contexts defined by power dynamics, Amber developed contextual specificity unrestricted by space and time, and formulated as a nexus of interdynamic mechanisms. This meant casting the net wide to yield specificity—something that initially felt counterintuitive to Amber.

Contextualizing herself, Amber wrote:

> In a post-racial society, when I talk with White people, I can be Native (Diné) but only as a token living artifact that automatically produces a "sympathy" statement: "Oh, I just hate what we (White dominant society) DID to you ... your people." So, I think my very presence erases the "legitimacy" of my structural complaints. By my very presence in the conversation, genocide is erased. I am alive. Then, I confirm post-racial notions of Indian deficiency. In other words, the dominant response can be, "If you can be here as a Native woman, then what's wrong with all those other Natives you're trying to return home to?" It's the level playing field argument of post-racialism. Once when invited to my friend's house for dinner, her dad said the most outrageous racist, post-racial thing to me about Natives being the only "ones" not complaining about the past. It's crazy, this post-racial era, for Native people because we can be as a collective so "tragic," yet, at the same time if living a "dominant" lifestyle, we're "productive and successful." So, we are living evidence that the colonizing society is fair. But, if I do separate myself from the mainstream, then I'm the angry activist,[3] who doesn't even speak Navajo (but probably because of Pratt's Carlisle Indian School). I make a mockery of Indianness through my supposed lack of authenticity. Native groups are forced to stay frozen in time and so forced to be invisible.

Amber developed a sense of context cultivated through a specificity around silence. Precisely, she conceived of her silence around direct comments about race as a negotiation with the new supremacist ideology—a negotiation she was in the midst of initiating during the early phases of her praxis. She attended to the dynamic in relation to both historical and contemporary power contexts, arriving at an understanding that her identity linked historical and contemporary racisms in specific ways that might embolden both. So she had to embark on reimagining a disruption to supremacy. Ultimately, well into her second semester in the Yearbook class, she did openly discuss race, but she did not posit that this described the praxis of a post-racial critical race pedagogy.

Instead, she characterized her emerging critical race praxis as a contextual dialogic. Widening the circle of praxis became important for establishing the specificity of her localized challenges to supremacy. Consequently, in describing her praxis navigation of race, she explained that she had to understand her work in an all-White context as occurring in tandem with multiple other endeavors, chief among those to learn about Whiteness so she could "return home" (both literally, to the reservation, and figuratively, to all-Native contexts), to collaborate in the efforts to disrupt colonial Whiteness in institutional systems and internalized belief. Not insignificantly, she also understood herself as engaging a praxis directly linked to cultural survival, in that she could resist post-racial supremacy and colonization by equipping her daughter (who is read by school personnel as White) with sophisticated navigational capital (Yosso, 2005). Amber perceived the multi-context praxis of disrupting post-racial supremacy as requisite for the self-humanizing project of a woman of Color teaching White students. Her expansion of context in fact heightened the specificity of her experience for her and her classmates and allowed a more dynamic, complex conceptualization of the principle of specificity. But, to be certain, Amber believed her decision to participate in educational contexts away from the reservation made her authenticity questionable, and so her efforts to learn about and challenge Whiteness also compelled her to negotiate her own contested legitimacy. "Red Pedagogies," Amber wrote,

> changes my perspective, for sure (Grande, 2004). First, it reminded me of all the teachings that my dad engrained in me while growing up. He would say, "Diné are not about the self. We believe in Ke'." He would also highlight our (Diné) difference from the "white man's culture" which is linear, "anthropocentric" (Grande used this word and I like it). So I have to learn about both ways, and challenge Whiteness in both places. But it does mean I have to constantly figure out how to be legitimate in both places so I can truly teach. I think all my teaching has a ripple effect, outside the sphere of the classroom or family relationship.

This decision to step squarely into liminality in a search for specificity was not a comfortable decision. Nor was it a certain one. However, it was one she took head on. After a year of praxis work, she undertook a TA position for a sociological survey course for pre-service teachers. There she confronted Whiteness in myriad ways, both challenging supremacy and gathering detailed information about colonial White post-racial society.

> I have strange experiences here in Massachusetts with people directly talking about my Native background. At the eye clinic the eyeglass guy said, "Oh, you're so beautiful. I wish I brought my daughter here today to meet a real Indian, like Pocahontas." I am not sure how this fits into my praxis site. Yet, it is the "cultural baggage" I carry everywhere, huh?

REPRESENTATION, RESISTANCE, AND PERSISTENCE: NAVIGATING INTERSECTIONALITY

These encounters with specificity signaled the possibility to the class for framing more nuanced representation. In examining what she describes as "intersectional identities" (p. 1243), CRT scholar Crenshaw (1991) writes: "the social power in delineating difference need not be the power of domination; it can instead be the source of social empowerment and reconstruction" (p. 1242). Crenshaw posits that difference be delineated expressly through ascertaining the particular power locations of multiple identities at the site of their intersection. In this way she explains that gender and race, for example, are not two separate categories that one possesses, but shape one another through dimensions of social power, so that race is gendered and gender is raced in the political economy of identity. Intersectionality suggests that the whole of identity is greater than the sum of its parts and so cannot be understood through a separate investigation of each part. As Crenshaw point outs, this mobilization of intersectionality is not meant just to locate individuals in a power order, but rather to identify the mechanisms of power functioning on and through identity groups, thereby highlighting complex power problems.

Crenshaw (1991) explores three dimensions of intersectionality—structural, political, and representational. In this discussion, we take up the frame of representational intersectionality, focusing our attention on the contemporary cultural production of post-racial supremacist narratives that function to represent dominant constructions of racial identity and power. In her explication of representational intersectionality, Crenshaw argues that the sexual violence concerns and experiences of women of Color are eclipsed by competing race and gender agendas. "But when one discourse fails to acknowledge the significance of the other," she writes, "the power relations that each attempts to challenge are strengthened" (p. 1282). As will become evident below, students found that this failure of acknowledgement was exacerbated in them and in educational contexts by the neutralizing force of post-racialism.

This emphasis on representation complicated specificity as it functioned and was contested by students. Rather than produce a conclusive taxonomy of representation, students in the Pedagogies class wrestled with representation as a permanently unresolved dilemma and yet a mechanism central to the task of critical race pedagogical relationships. While we attended to shifting, complex identities across multiple contexts, we were particularly interested in how those shifting identities could be understood as specific in relation to power in post-racial contexts.

In relation to intersectionality, Ikenna detailed a pedagogical interaction in which he withheld specificity about his identity in what he initially understood as an effort to challenge White supremacist educational practices. At a site unrelated to the one at which he helped to facilitate the privilege walk, Ikenna was assisting in running a program aimed at training youth of Color from one neighborhood to be leaders of "positive change" in their community. The program curriculum focused on issues ranging from police brutality to youth violence occurring in one ten-block area. The program directors were two straight, White females and a straight Black man (who was the only of the three directors to be from the community). Ikenna was troubled by the positioning of these two White women as directors, as their knowledge of the community was limited both racially and because they were outsiders. Moreover, their roles within the program and the way in which they embraced those presented to Ikenna as affirmative assertions of the redemptive and neutral features of post-racialism, namely the newly sanctified White, female savior. This was a newly minted iteration of the longstanding supremacist figure of the "true woman" (Carby, 1987; Welter, 1966). Yet he was posed with the difficulty of ascertaining the intersectional nature of their power and his. "As a queer identified Black male," wrote the graduate student, "I became aware of the heteronormativity that existed within the organization, as discussions often came up about relationships that the youth and directors had with the 'opposite gender.'"

During one of his first days working at this organization, Ikenna had to contend with the collapsing of sexism, racism, and homophobia, and make a pedagogical decision:

> It was down time within the office … two of the directors, Kit and John, were sitting in a room with a student, Deshawn, when I walked in. Kit was drawing on a white board in the office while Deshawn and John were discussing music. When Kit finished writing on the board it said, "Deshawn is beautiful, Love, your boy Blaze (pseudonym for John)" in fancy, bubble letters. John was sitting at a computer and did not notice. Deshawn on the other hand saw it and in a laughing but aggressive manner said, "Naw, you trying to mess with my life" and erased the words "Love, your boy Blaze." Kit looked at the change and said, "Mine was positive. I don't know what that is."

In this interaction, Kit, a White, straight woman, had imitated the stylized writing of many middle school girls and depicted a love note from the Black, straight, male director to the Black, male student. Ikenna understood Kit to be asserting her White female authority to impose a construction of masculinity on both Deshawn and John, and in so doing to emasculate them through a complex legacy of racial dynamics in which White women orchestrate the raced and gendered construction of Black masculinity—particularly in educational contexts. Moreover, he understood homophobia to be a tool in this power move. To disrupt Kit's conduct, Ikenna had to understand the intersecting identities of the groups represented by the individuals in the room. He wrote:

> Deshawn had to engage in action that demonstrated his definition of Black masculinity as being in opposition to loving another man. His act was a resistance to an identity that was being imposed on him by a White female. Kit was policing, mediating her supremacy as a White woman, through her ability to determine what relationships Black men should have and deem "positive."

In spite of this initial analysis, Ikenna explained that the conundrum produced by this dynamic was stark. "My silence in the eyes of the others in the room communicated to them that I was not offended by the statement and implied that I was a complacent participant in the joke." In a decidedly divided moment, Ikenna found his own difficulty in ascertaining the specificity of intersectionality somewhat paralyzing. He understood his immediate bifurcated choices as either to act against White supremacy as a Black male, and so challenge the aggressive representational actions of the White woman, or to act against homophobia as a gay male, and so contest the implicit anti-gay discourse in the room. The pedagogical challenge for Ikenna was to understand an intersectional identity from which he could enact a specificity that occluded neither the sexual nor the racial concern, but instead contested the particular liminality of queer men of Color.

In discussing the role of humor, Crenshaw (1991) argues that claims to humor pivot on reductive assertions of categories of identity and power, categories that lack specificity. Expressly, the use of humor reduced the situation into a representational contest between fractured categories of race, gender, and sexuality. The challenge for Ikenna was not just to identify the complex intersectional dynamics so that he could disrupt the specific homophobia that is leveraged by supremacist White women toward Black men, but to understand how to identify them in this particular historical, socio-cultural moment. He had to understand homophobia, supremacy, and sexism, in other words, not as stand-alone societal mechanisms, but as shifting constellations of power specific to their intersectional context and post-racial production.

This investigation was in part an exercise in fidelity to specificity, in which Ikenna pushed himself toward intersectionality. He said:

> Hybridity produces anxiety. People want to know, if you are bisexual, what percent of you is straight and what percent is gay? If you are mixed race, they want to know what percent is what thing. They want to divide you into existing categories instead of recognizing you as a different category that is equally specific but challenges oppressive norms.

He said later, "So, I have to understand how to be hybrid pedagogically in order to challenge intersectional power." This particular experience suggested to Ikenna and his classmates that specificity is not comprehensive. Again, we considered specificity in this instance to be in the intersectional disruption of power rather than in the assertion of a list of identities or in the mistaken choice of a singular identity. We also understood intersectional specificity to be always partial, as representational intersectionality occurs across dimensions of complex power difference. Furthermore, the Pedagogies class concluded that, in post-racial power contexts, we reify power as we are disrupting it. In particular, the class suggested that any pretense to full disruption is false and perhaps even stalls the important endeavor of persistence. Disruption of power through a critical race praxis requires a specificity of attention and action that is always complicated by the teacher's simultaneous participation in the system.

Ikenna translated this new understanding into numerous disruptions of the program's supremacist dynamic over the course of his time there. In one case, the program organized an event entitled "Choices." The emphasis of this event was on "meritocracy, and the message was that if the students made the right choices in school and worked hard, they would be successful." Ikenna designed poetry workshops that incorporated intersectionality at their core, guiding students to challenge meritocracy through complex intersectional locations of self and power structures, including law enforcement, school, and health care. As Crenshaw (1991) writes, "intersectionality might be more broadly useful as a way of mediating the tension between assertions of multiple identity and the ongoing necessity of group politics" (p. 1296). It was precisely this function that Ikenna took up in guiding students from understandings of multiple identities to challenging multiplex power structures of post-racial White supremacy. He has cultivated that critical race skill set and applied it to his work assisting in the creation of a university bridge program, illustrating the ripple effect of pedagogical practice identified by Amber.

SPECIFICITY, INTERSECTIONALITY, AND VIOLENCE: LOCATIONS AND INTERPOLATIONS

While intersectional representation (Crenshaw, 1991) served as a compelling tool for students developing an emerging critical race pedagogy, there was a substantive tension between locating and representing one's self in the Pedagogies classroom and locating and representing one's self in an educational organization or institution. The contradictions and tensions between and among various contexts produced a challenge to aligning reflection and action. While many students felt that Freire (2000) suggested that alignment must occur and must be synchronous, students found their intersectional identities were reductively constructed in the public post-racial world and that alignment would in fact thwart their very efforts to challenge post-racial White supremacy. In other words, the specificity of their identities shifted between the Pedagogies classroom and their respective praxis sites, making dialogue, reflection, and action asynchronous and dissonant. It took some time for them to understand that specificity as a principle could be constant while the content of that specificity might shift. In other words, specificity as a verb, as a doing, might not match specificity as descriptors of identity.

One of the two undergraduate students in the class, Gabrielle, who identified as lesbian, female, and variously as Latina, Chicana, and bi-racial, began to theorize and enact intersectionality as a form of specificity not exclusively linked to categories but rather more overtly linked to the power dynamics produced by those intersections as they interacted with contexts. In contemplating this she wrote, "Fanon regards

'difference' as a marker of colonial violence, describing it as 'an index of absolute cleav-
age of the social, the axis of a historical and active brutalization'" (De Lissovoy, 2007, p.
360). She applied this conceptualization of difference to her praxis site, an afterschool
SAT and college preparatory program with which she had worked for three years at various locations. The administering program is a not-for-profit that trains college students
to be "coaches" who will guide "motivated, low-income high school students" through
a course consisting of both content-specific SAT instruction and college preparation,
including familiarization with the application process among others. The organization
understood itself to be driven by social justice. "That said," wrote Gabrielle, "post-racialism shaped pedagogical structures operating in the organization, operating mostly by
virtue of the distancing move and a race-neutral universalism." Because the organization was based on a social justice model in a post-racial context, the student argued, it
used "language and constructs that only discuss power ambiguously and imprecisely
while, as De Lissovoy (2007) critiques, 'reserving for itself a vagueness which often acts
to obfuscate the very social forces that support the injustices that social-justice efforts
presumably aim to eliminate'" (p. 364).

As an illustration of the post-racial ambiguity of the site practices, this student detailed
an incident: "My students, from a variety of racial backgrounds, often made racial jokes
at one another's expense that I felt I had to then ensure I addressed in class." In response,
the site directors and her peers told her simply to "encourage students to respect me and
one another."

> "Respect," in this instance, became a vague, racially-neutral stand-in for an actual
> discussion and naming of the specifically racial structures creating these "jokes."
> Furthermore, the distinction between "me" and "one another" strategically removes
> coaches from this problem, locating the racial structures that create these comments
> squarely within the students.

It was indeed the intentional withdrawal from specificity as a power context rather than
the engagement of the specificity of the students' comments that emerged as central in
the post-racial effort to neutralize racial power relations and to "undercut that conversation" about institutional racism. The violence produced by supremacist constructions
of difference was ameliorated by White institutional practices. Consequently, Gabrielle's
efforts at a critical race praxis had to draw on multiple specificities of power.

"Though I spent a lot of time writing field notes in which I critique the problematic
practices of the institutions operating in my praxis site," she wrote,

> it took me all year to realize something I theoretically knew all along—I am very
> much a part of that same system … in moving through my coursework and engag-
> ing dialogue with my class partner, I found myself assuming dual roles as both
> "oppressor and oppressed," as Cherríe Moraga might say (Moraga, 1981, p. 32) …
> In working to create praxis, I found that while I was working to push back against
> the institution's set up to maintain the system of racial domination of the students
> in the program, my interactions with students simultaneously contributed to many
> of those same oppressive structures I thought I was resisting.

This same conflict, highlighted above, became more nuanced when Gabrielle was sud-
denly, abruptly outed during one class. When she challenged homophobic language, one

of the students turned to her and asked if she was gay, and she said, "Yeah." As Gabrielle later said, "I was forced to either lie or say 'yes'. That is being outed, and the power locations were hard for me to determine in that moment."

Gabrielle detailed this pedagogical exchange:

> Last year, a similar conversation arose around the exact same slur. Similarly, I told the two kids having the conversation that it wasn't a word I thought they should be using. This year, Mike D-Tech, the only White male student, said back to me, "Yo, I didn't mean it like that, you know I love the homos. Wait, you're not gay?" I flinched at being addressed so directly, but reflecting on my last experience made me feel like I wanted to be able to have this conversation with students without the assumption that everyone in the room was straight, so I said "Yeah, I am," back to him in front of the group. It was a response I felt very uncertain about, but it raised a lot of questions from students, some that I felt were pedagogically meaningful, and some that I thought were kind of invasive, which got deflected and we moved on. As we were finishing up class and starting to pack up, Emma, one of the girls in class, asked again if I was gay, and mentioned that she had a bisexual-identified teacher for a different class who'd drawn up a spectrum line on the board about sexual orientation, so she drew that same scale up.

Two things occurred in this moment. Emma initiated an opportunity that Gabrielle seized to disrupt heteronormative understandings of sexuality. However, simultaneously, some of the male students responded by saying they were cool with her sexuality and asking her if she thought certain girls were "hot"—questions she did not challenge or avoid overtly. Notably, Gabrielle doubted the criticality of her response and was quite tough on herself as she retold the story. In fact, she thought that by not challenging the sexism inherent in conversations about "hot women" she was again reinforcing dominant power structures. She later wrote:

> There was something to be said about intersectionality (Crenshaw, 1991) in this moment too—through naming my queerness and placing it in a body I'd already established as Latina, I might have suggested that non-dominant identities could co-exist and produce one singular identity with its own implications. That said, I don't remember any explicit discussions about this at my praxis site, and as Rofes (2005) might suggest, my body doesn't inherently promote a deconstruction of these structures.

While we were quick to point out that she was explicit in myriad and disruptive ways, and that the comfort of the young men in engaging her in sexist conversations could be read in multiple and ongoing ways, she remained uneasy with her attempts at specificity. Gabrielle, in fact, consistently disrupted the intersectional exercises of dominance, challenging supremacy with notable critical acuity.

Gabrielle later theorized her dilemma, ultimately theorizing the heart of our principle of specificity:

> Needing to name the lens is not the same as needing to exactly locate yourself, which is not the same as "implicating yourself" in engagement … As Mercer (1991) might

suggest, while we can develop critical lenses, resist as we might we also view through the lens of oppressive structures … [As we realized in our critical dialogues] "implicating yourself" isn't accomplished simply by means of being forced to place yourself on a series of axes … the message that I didn't really understand until the very end of trying to make praxis was the idea that power isn't as streamlined as I'd thought. There is no simple divide between domination and resistance. Instead, actors are involved in both resisting and administering power, in mediating and recreating institutional oppression.

In the end, she was unresolved not because she failed to engage a critical race pedagogy in specific, complex, and nuanced ways, but because the process of doing so heightened her sense of the open-endedness and constant contradiction of critical race praxis. Resolution would have denoted a satisfaction or solution that the class ultimately found incompatible with critical race pedagogy in post-racial times. It is in fact action and resistance, not resolution, that are foundational to critical race praxis.

CONCLUSION: MEDIATING CONFLICTING SPECIFICITIES

In conclusion, one student wrote:

> There are institutional forces that mediate personal agency and there is personal agency that challenges institutional structures. There are privileges that everyone possesses that may be tools for silencing others; and, there are aspects of our identities that will also be silenced regardless of who we are.

On this dynamic of specificity and power, he elaborated by exploring conceptualizations of critical race pedagogy and praxis, challenging us to constantly re-ask the questions. "The question, I realized, is more important than finding an exact answer," remarked one student. And the original questions are not old or resolved, but always in need of restating. It is the restatement that supports resistance, disruption, and challenge. So, in the end, the class concluded that the process and act of engaging specificity around power and race and of privileging the ongoing disruption of White supremacy were a central principle of an effective critical race praxis.

NOTES

1 We understand the multiple implications of using our individual names in this chapter. We are concerned with the tension between hyperindividualization and an argument for collective, systemic experience. We, as students, are also cognizant of the potential vulnerability related to making our identities and experiences public. However, we respect the editors' position that anonymity may be counter to the CRT project.
2 We understand received convention and application of the concept of privilege to be quite distinct from our collective conceptualization of power. Specifically, in class we referenced Leonardo's (2004) assertion that "the theme of privilege obscures the subject of domination, or the agent of actions, because the situation is described as happening almost without the knowledge of whites. It conjures up images of domination happening behind the backs of whites, rather than on the backs of people of color. The study of white privilege begins to take on an image of domination without agents" (p. 138). However, we also understand that privilege and power are conflated in exercises such as the privilege walk and so we view such exercises as efforts to identify, reveal, and sometimes challenge aspects of power.
3 Although the White construction of "the angry person of Color" is not a phenomenon new to post-racialism, the particular terrain has shifted so that the maps one uses to navigate the landscape must be redrawn. See

Collins (2000), among others, for a more comprehensive discussion of White supremacist constructions of people of Color that function explicitly to police and invalidate non-dominant epistemology, ideology, culture, and resistance.

REFERENCES

Alarcón, N. (1981). Chicana feminist literature: A re-vision through Malintzin/or Malintzin: Putting flesh back on the object. In C. Moraga & G. Anzaldua (Eds.), *This bridge called my back: Writings by radical women of Color* (pp. 182–190). New York: Kitchen Table/Women of Color Press.

Apple, M. (2009). Patriotism, pedagogy, and freedom: On the educational meanings of September 11. In A. Darder, M. Baltodano, & R. Torres (Eds.), *The critical pedagogy reader* (2nd ed., pp. 491–500). New York: Routledge.

Ayers, W. (1988). Problems and possibilities of radical reform: A teacher educator reflects on making change. *Peabody Journal of Education, 65*(2), 35–50.

Bartolomé, L.I. (2007). Critical pedagogy and teacher education: Radicalizing prospective teachers. In P. McLaren & J.L. Kincheloe (Eds.), *Critical pedagogy: Where are we now?* (pp. 263–286). New York: Peter Lang.

Battiste, M. (2008). The struggle and renaissance of Indigenous knowledge in Eurocentric education. In M. Villegas, S.R. Neugebauer, & K.R. Venegas (Eds.), *Indigenous knowledge and education* (pp. 85–91). Cambridge, MA: Harvard Educational Review.

Brayboy, B.M.J. (2005). Toward a tribal critical race theory in education. *Urban Review, 37*(5), 425–446.

Brayboy, B.M.J., & Maughan, E. (2009). Indigenous knowledges and the story of the bean. *Harvard Educational Review, 79*(1), 1–21.

Britzman, D.P. (1995). Is there a queer pedagogy? Or, stop reading straight. *Educational Theory, 45*(2), 151–165.

Carby, H. (1987). *Reconstructing womanhood: The emergence of the African American woman novelist.* New York: Oxford University Press.

Cho, S. (2003). Converging stereotypes in racialized sexual harassment: Where the model minority meets Suzie Wong. In A.K. Wing (Ed.), *Critical race feminism: A reader* (2nd ed., pp. 349–366). New York: New York University Press.

Cho, S. (2009). Post-racialism. *Iowa Law Review, 94,* 1589–1649.

Collins, P.H. (2000). *Black feminist thought: Knowledge, consciousness, and the politics of empowerment.* New York: Routledge.

Crenshaw, K. (1991). Mapping the margins: Intersectionality, identity politics, and violence against women of Color. *Stanford Law Review, 43*(6), 1241–1299.

De Lissovoy, N. (2007). Frantz Fanon and the materialist critical pedagogy. In P. McLaren & J.L. Kincheloe (Eds.), *Critical pedagogy: Where are we now?* (pp. 355–370). New York: Peter Lang.

Delpit, L. (1988). The silenced dialogue: Power and pedagogy in educating other people's children. *Harvard Educational Review, 58*(3), 280–298.

Delpit, L. (2006). *Other people's children: Cultural conflict in the classroom.* New York: New Press.

Dixson, A.D., & Dingus, J.E. (2007). Tyranny of the majority: Re-enfranchisement of African American teacher educators teaching for democracy. *International Journal of Qualitative Studies in Education, 20*(6), 639–654.

Duncan, G. (2005). Critical race ethnography in education: Narrative, inequality and the problem of epistemology. *Race, Ethnicity and Education, 8*(1), 93–114.

Duncan-Andrade, J., & Morrell, E. (2007). Critical pedagogy and popular culture in an urban secondary English classroom. In P. McLaren & J.L. Kincheloe (Eds.), *Critical pedagogy: Where are we now?* (pp. 183–199). New York: Peter Lang.

Ellison, R. (1995). *Invisible man* (2nd Vintage International ed.). New York: Random House.

Ellsworth, E. (1989). Why doesn't this feel empowering? Working through the repressive myths of critical pedagogy. *Harvard Educational Review, 59*(3), 297–324.

Ferguson, A.A. (2000). *Bad boys: Public schools in the making of Black masculinity.* Ann Arbor: University of Michigan Press.

Fine, M. (2009). Sexuality, schooling, and adolescent females: The missing discourse of desire. In A. Darder, M. Baltodano, & R. Torres (Eds.), *The critical pedagogy reader* (2nd ed., pp. 240–261). New York: Routledge.

Fisher, M.T. (2007). *Writing in rhythm: Spoken word poetry in urban classrooms.* New York: Teachers College Press.

Foucault, M. (1995). *Discipline and punish: The birth of the prison.* New York: Vintage Books.

Freire, P. (2000). *Pedagogy of the oppressed.* New York: Continuum.

Giroux, H. (2009a). Critical theory and educational practice. In A. Darder, M. Baltodano, & R. Torres (Eds.), *The critical pedagogy reader* (2nd ed., pp. 27–51). New York: Routledge.

Giroux, H. (2009b). Teacher education and democratic schooling. In A. Darder, M. Baltodano, & R. Torres (Eds.), *The critical pedagogy reader* (2nd ed., pp. 438–459). New York: Routledge.

Grande, S. (2004). *Red pedagogy: Native American social and political thought.* Lanham, MD: Rowman & Littlefield.

Grande, S. (2007). Red Lake Woebegone: Pedagogy, decolonization, and the critical project. In P. McLaren & J.L. Kincheloe (Eds.), *Critical pedagogy: Where are we now?* (pp. 315–336). New York: Peter Lang.

Grande, S. (2009). American Indian geographies of identity and power: At a crossroads of indigena and mestizaje. In A. Darder, M. Baltodano, & R. Torres (Eds.), *The critical pedagogy reader* (2nd ed., pp. 183–208). New York: Routledge.

Green, S. (2008). *Literacy as a civil right: Reclaiming social justice in literacy teaching and learning.* New York: Peter Lang.

Greene, M. (2009). In search of a critical pedagogy. In A. Darder, M. Baltodano, & R. Torres (Eds.), *The critical pedagogy reader* (2nd ed., pp. 84–96). New York: Routledge.

Harris, C. (1993). Whiteness as property. *Harvard Law Review, 106*(8), 1709–1791.

Hill, M.L. (2009). *Beats rhymes + classroom life: Hip-hop pedagogy + the politics of identity.* New York: Teachers College Press.

hooks, b. (1989). *Talking back: Thinking feminist, thinking Black.* Boston, MA: South End Press.

hooks, b. (1994). *Teaching to transgress: Education as the practice of freedom.* New York: Routledge.

Jaramillo, N. (2006). Hooters pedagogy: Gender in late capitalism. In C.A. Rossatto, R.L. Allen, & M. Pruyn (Eds.), *Reinventing critical pedagogy: Widening the circle of anti-oppression education* (pp. 191–205). New York: Rowman & Littlefield.

Jennings, M.E., & Lynn, M. (2005). The house that race built: Critical pedagogy, African American education, and the re-conceptualization of a critical race pedagogy. *Educational Foundations,* Summer–Fall, 15–32.

Kaomea, J. (2005). Indigenous studies in the elementary curriculum: A cautionary Hawaiian example. *Anthropology and Education Quarterly, 36*(1), 24–42.

King, J. (1991). Dysconscious racism: Ideology, identity, and the miseducation of teachers. *Journal of Negro Education, 60*(2), 133–146.

Kumashiro, K. (2001). Queer students of Color and antiracist, antiheterosexist education: Paradoxes of identity and activism. In K. Kumashiro (Ed.), *Troubling intersections of race and sexuality: Queer students of Color and anti-oppressive education* (pp. 1–25). New York: Rowman & Littlefield.

Ladson-Billings, G. (1994). *The dreamkeepers: Successful teachers of African American children.* San Francisco, CA: Jossey-Bass.

Ladson-Billings, G. (2000). Racialized discourses and ethnic epistemologies. In N. Denzin and Y. Lincoln (Eds.), *Handbook of qualitative research.* Newbury Park, CA: Sage.

Ladson-Billings, G., & Tate, W. (1995). Toward a critical race theory of education. *Teachers College Record, 97*(1), 47–68.

Leonardo, Z. (2004). The color of supremacy: Beyond the discourse of "White privilege." *Educational Philosophy and Theory, 36*(2), 137–152.

Lorde, A. (1984). Use of the erotic: The erotic as power. *Sister outsider: Essays and speeches.* Freedom, CA: Crossing Press.

Loutzenheiser, L.W. (2001). "If I teach about these issues they will burn down my house": The possibilities and tensions of queered, antiracist pedagogy. In K. Kumashiro (Ed.), *Troubling intersections of race and sexuality: Queer students of Color and anti-oppressive education* (pp. 195–214). New York: Rowman & Littlefield.

Luttrell, W. (2003). *Pregnant bodies, fertile minds: Gender, race, and the schooling of pregnant teens.* New York: Routledge.

Lynn, M. (1999). Toward a critical race pedagogy: A research note. *Urban Education, 33*(5), 606–626.

Lynn, M., & Jennings, M.E. (2009). Power, politics, and critical race pedagogy: A critical race analysis of Black male teachers' pedagogy. *Race, Ethnicity and Education, 12*(2), 173–196.

Mayo, C. (2009). The tolerance that dare not speak its name. In A. Darder, M. Baltodano, & R. Torres (Eds.), *The critical pedagogy reader* (2nd ed., pp. 262–273). New York: Routledge.

McCready, L.T. (2010). Black queer bodies, Afrocentric reform, and masculine anxiety. *International Journal of Critical Pedagogy, 3*(1), 52–67.

McIntosh, P. (1989). White privilege: Unpacking the invisible knapsack. *Peace and Freedom,* July/August, 10–12.

McLaren, P. (2009). Critical pedagogy: A look at the major concepts. In A. Darder, M. Baltodano, & R. Torres (Eds.), *The critical pedagogy reader* (2nd ed., pp. 61–83). New York: Routledge.

Mercer, K. (1991). Review: Looking for trouble. *Transition, 15,*184–197.

Monahan, T. (2009). The surveillance curriculum: Risk management and social control in the neoliberal school. In A. Darder, M. Baltodano, & R. Torres (Eds.), *The critical pedagogy reader* (2nd ed., pp. 123–134). New York: Routledge.

Moraga, C. (1981). La güera. In C. Moraga & G. Anzaldua (Eds.), *This bridge called my back: Writings by radical women of Color* (pp. 27–34). New York: Kitchen Table/Women of Color Press.

Moses, R.P., & Cobb, C. E. (2001). *Radical equations: Math literacy and civil rights.* Boston, MA: Beacon Press.

O'Connor, C., Lewis, A., & Mueller, J. (2007). Researching "Black" educational experiences and outcomes: Theoretical and methodological considerations. *Educational Researcher, 36*(9), 541–552.

O'Connor, C., Hill, L., & Robinson, S. (2009). Who's at risk in school and what's race got to do with it? *Review of Research in Education, 33*(1), 1–34.

Rofes, E. (2005). *A radical rethinking of sexuality and schooling: Status quo or status queer.* New York: Rowman & Littlefield.

Solórzano, D. (1997). Images and words that wound: Critical race theory, racial stereotyping, and teacher education. *Teacher Education Quarterly, 24,* 5–19.

Solórzano, D., & Yosso, T. (2002). Critical race methodology: Counter-storytelling as an analytical framework for education research. *Qualitative Inquiry, 8*(1), 23–44.

Sumara, D., & Davis, B. (1999). Interrupting heteronormativity: Toward a queer curriculum theory. *Curriculum Theory, 29*(2), 191–208.

Vaught, S., & Castagno, A. (2008). "I don't think I'm a racist": Critical race theory, teacher attitudes, and structural racism. *Race, Ethnicity, and Education, 11*(2), 95–113.

Weiler, K. (1988). *Women teaching for change: Gender, class, and power.* Westport, CT: Bergin & Garvey.

Weiler, K. (2009). Feminist analysis of gender and schooling. In A. Darder, M. Baltodano, & R. Torres (Eds.), *The critical pedagogy reader* (2nd ed., pp. 217–239). New York: Routledge.

Welter, B. (1966). The cult of true womanhood: 1820–1860. *American Quarterly, 18*(2), part 1, 151–174.

Williams, P. (1995). Meditations on masculinity. In M. Berger, B. Wallis, & S. Watson (Eds.), *Constructing masculinity* (pp. 238–249). New York: Routledge.

Winn, M.T. (2011). *Girl time: Literacy, justice, and the school-to-prison pipeline.* New York: Teachers College Press.

Yosso, T. (2005). Whose culture has capital? A critical race theory discussion of community cultural wealth. *Race, Ethnicity and Education, 8*(1), 69–91.

28

WHAT IS "URBAN"?

A CRT Examination of the Preparation of K-12 Teachers for Urban Schools

Celia Rousseau Anderson and Beverly E. Cross

> He has told you, O man, what is good; and what does the LORD require of you but
> to do justice, and to love kindness, and to walk humbly with your God?
> (Micah 6:8, English Standard Version)

One of the characteristics of the scholarship of critical race theorist Derrick Bell was the use of both spiritual texts and songs as a means to "better understand the fundamental question undergirding the theoretical formulation of many race-based analyses of social relations" (Tate, 2003, p. 123). For example, Bell (1987) used Jeremiah 8:20 to frame his book *And We Are Not Saved: The Elusive Quest for Racial Justice.* He asserted that three decades after the historic Supreme Court decision of 1954 regarding school desegregation, we were still not saved. According to Bell, the achievement of *Brown v. Board of Education* had been "so eroded as to bring us once again into fateful and frightful coincidence with Jeremiah's lament" (p. 3).

As a means to situate our discussion in this chapter of the preparation of teachers for urban schools, we also turn to a scriptural text. Specifically, we use a verse from the Old Testament to suggest the need to consider both disposition and distribution. In the verse from the book of Micah, the Israelites are given the direction not only to love kindness, but also to *do* justice. According to Brueggemann et al. (1986), the meaning of justice in this context was directly tied to material factors—to the equitable distribution of resources. Thus, according to Brueggemann et al., the message of Micah offered not only spiritual guidance but also a call to earthly social change.

In this chapter, we build on this dual message to consider how two different perspectives on critical race theory (CRT) can be used to frame an examination of urban teacher education. In so doing, we seek to illustrate the power of a hybrid perspective that considers issues of both disposition and distribution, seeking not just to love kindness but also to do justice. Our goal in doing this analysis is not merely to engage in a rhetorical exercise but rather engagement in challenging what Weiner (2007, p. 58) calls "imaginative inertia": "A state of intellectual paralysis which, if not remedied, will be the beginning of the end of critical pedagogy's struggle to attract educators and students, thereby curtailing its influence in educational theory and practice." It is in this intellectual space and conversation that we undertake this analysis and seek to outline an approach that moves beyond surface analyses and the identification of quick solutions.

TWO WAYS TO THINK ABOUT CRITICAL RACE THEORY

Legal scholar Richard Delgado (2003) asserts that there are two distinct schools of thought within CRT scholarship (i.e., idealist and materialist) that ultimately answer the question, "Are race and racism, at bottom, real or are they socially constructed?" Delgado characterizes the divide between these two schools as "deep, but largely unrecognized." We acknowledge these schools of thought and the significance of this question and use them as the essence of what we are asking about approaches to urban teacher preparation.

Delgado and Stefancic (2001) offer the following hypothetical story in order to highlight the distinctions between the two perspectives:

> Suppose a magic pill were invented or perhaps an enterprising entrepreneur developed The Ultimate Diversity Seminar, one so effective that it would completely eliminate unkind thoughts, stereotypes, and misimpressions harbored by its participants toward persons of other races. The president's civil rights advisor prevails on all the nation's teachers to introduce it into every K-12 classroom, and on the major television networks and cable network news to show it on prime time. Would life improve very much for people of color?
>
> (Delgado & Stefancic, 2001, p. 16)

For the purpose of our discussion, we could alter the concluding question to read: "Would the educational experiences of students in urban schools and the preparation of teachers for those schools improve very much as a result of the end of stereotypes, misimpressions, and prejudice?"

Attention to Disposition: CRT Idealist School of Thought

The idealist school of thought holds that "race and discrimination are largely functions of attitude and social formation. For these thinkers, race is a social construction created out of words, symbols, stereotypes, and categories" (Delgado, 2003, p. 123). According to Delgado, this school of thought within CRT scholarship tends to focus on discourse analysis and the ways that race and racism are socially constructed. The focus of the idealists is on the psychological; thus it is possible to rid society of racism and discrimination by changing "the system of images, words, attitudes, unconscious feelings, scripts and social teachings" (Delgado & Stefancic, 2001, p. 17) that support the beliefs that some people are superior to others. Thus, an affirmative answer to the hypothetical scenario would reflect idealist thinking. To set it in the context of this chapter, the idealist would hold the belief that, in the absence of racial animus, the educational experiences of students in urban schools would improve.

Attention to Distribution: CRT Realist or Materialist School of Thought

According to Delgado (2001, 2003), the early writings of critical race scholars in legal studies were largely "materialist" or "realist" in nature. According to this view, racism is the "means by which society [systematically] allocates privilege, status, and wealth" (2001, p. 2283). From the perspective of the materialist/realists, this attention to material forces sheds more light on the cycle of racial progress than consideration of more psychological conditions, such as attitude or intent. Racial realists acknowledge that lack of conscious malice or intent does not mitigate the oppressive effects of institutional racism and the impact on the material conditions of persons of color (Delgado, 2001, 2003). The core of the racial realist perspective is acknowledgement that discriminatory beliefs, stereotypes, and attitudes towards persons of color could disappear overnight, but the lives of persons of color would change only minimally (Delgado & Stefancic, 2001). Materialists acknowledge that ideology and social structures work together and that the connection is complex so that changes in material conditions may need to precede changes in attitude, rather than the reverse (Delgado, 2003). In response to the hypothetical scenario outlined above, materialists would claim that neither the magic pill nor the seminar would change the actual oppressive and marginalizing realities of people of color. Nor would there be any substantive change in the experiences and outcomes of students in urban schools.

Disposition and Distribution: A Hybrid Perspective

According to Delgado and Stefancic (2001), the distinctions between the materialists and the idealists are significant insofar as they influence how scholars from the two strands of CRT approach issues of racism and inequity. Those in the idealist "camp" are likely "to examine the role of ideas, thoughts, and unconscious discrimination" (p. 120). The idealist would focus on issues such as racist speech, diversity training, and visual representation of persons of color in the media. In contrast, the materialist focuses on changing the material circumstances of the lives of persons of color. According to Delgado and Stefancic, scholars in this group tend to examine issues such as "globalization, human rights, race and poverty, immigration, and the criminal justice system" (p. 120).

Yet, Delgado and Stefancic (2001) argue that the lines between the two perspectives, while distinct, are not rigid. In fact, they suggest the possibility of a middle ground that "would see both forces, material and cultural, operating together and synergizing each other, so that race reformers working in either area contribute to a holistic project of racial redemption" (p. 21). Further, they note that, while many scholars write from one perspective or the other, some have sought to straddle the divide by simultaneously examining issues that are both idealist and materialist (e.g., considering both unconscious and overt discrimination). Moreover, Delgado (2003) argues that this dualistic approach is not just a possibility. Rather, it is a necessity in order to address certain race-related issues. Delgado asserts that, while some racial problems can be examined from either perspective, other problems "will require analysis in both idealist and material terms; either alone will be incomplete" (p. 136). The idea of a dualistic approach incorporating the two stances is intriguing and compels us to ask how such a hybrid perspective might be relevant for teacher education.

CRT AND TEACHER EDUCATION

Preparing the nation's teachers is a widespread endeavor with approximately 1,400 teacher education programs across the nation. These programs have over the years received various levels of critique and scrutiny, often followed by various levels of reform and change, with varying levels of meaningful success, particularly for children in urban schools. Several organizations have engaged in the process of scrutinizing teacher education, including the American Association of Colleges of Teacher Education, the National Council for Accreditation of Teacher Education, the Holmes Partnership, the Interstate Teacher Assessment and Support Consortium (INTASC), and recently the National Council on Teacher Quality (NCTQ). Too much of this work has centered on compliance, standards, and aligning simple measures rather than a move toward liberatory ideas or practices. Ladson-Billings (1999) argues that one of the strengths of a CRT perspective on teacher education is its "ability to move us out of a cycle of detailing and ranking research and [teacher education] programs without a systematic examination of their paradigmatic underpinnings and practical strengths" (p. 219). In this way, a CRT perspective on teacher education is akin to applying a new prism that may provide a different vision of our notions of teacher preparation in a socio-political and socio-cultural context in which schools systematically and repeatedly fail diverse students in urban contexts. Haberman (2007) describes this situation as "not a series of accidental, unfortunate, chance events" but rather "a predictable, explainable phenomenon ... where the larger society provides the institutional and cultural setting which protects, preserves and enhances failing urban school systems for the purpose of providing a broad spectrum of constituencies with a priceless set of unearned privileges." CRT offers a means to bring into focus some of the predictable phenomena of teacher education that operate to preserve failing urban schools as oppressive institutions.

In the following sections, we consider how the idealist and the materialist/realist approaches to CRT could be used to examine issues related to urban teacher education. We then consider what the middle ground approach might look like and how it could be employed to inform the preparation of teachers for urban schools.

The Idealist at Work in Urban Teacher Education

As noted above, the idealist school of thought within CRT focuses on the role of language, images, and attitudes in the perpetuation of racism and inequity. Within the field of teacher education, one issue to which this approach could be applied is the definition of the terms that we use surrounding urban teaching and teacher education. From the idealist perspective, it is important to understand the meanings of the terms, such as "diversity" and "urban," that we use frequently in teacher education. Teacher educators and their students can spend semester after semester wrestling with these terms. Both groups often claim success when the terms flow freely, without discomfort, when faculty and students can spend time in "urban" and/or diverse schools, and when the terms adumbrate demographic statistics about the school's population. Doing these things and using certain terms with ease equate to urban preparedness. However, what is often left unexamined is the meaning ascribed to these terms and the ways through which such terms can serve as code for difference and deficit.

For example, scholars such as Akintunde (1999), Carlson (1995), Nieto (1995), and Pardini (2000) have challenged the ways in which the term "diversity" is used in teacher education literature. Ladson-Billings (1999) notes that "teachers refer to teaching in a diverse or multicultural setting when, in truth, they are teaching in predominantly African American or Latino schools. Diversity … is that 'thing' that is other than White and middle class" (p. 219). Similarly, some have challenged how the use of "diversity" in teacher education has led to practices of celebrating the "other" through simplistic distortions that can easily reinscribe subordination and imperializing statuses.

Another example is evident in the teacher education standards movement, which has similarly inserted narrow definitions of diversity as something that future teachers believe they can check off as completed on a degree sheet rather than approaching diversity or urban education as teaching for equity. At our own university, for example, teacher candidates are admitted into the teacher education program if they evidence a "clear social justice orientation and commitment to diversity" during a 20-minute interview with faculty. To receive the highest score on the interview rubric, they simply need to "appear to value diversity." Neither the meaning that the candidates ascribe to diversity nor the implications for classroom practice are specifically interrogated as part of this process.

Additionally, the significance of language use with regard to teacher preparation can be found in the multitude of meanings ascribed to the term "urban." For example, in a study of pre-service and early-career teachers who had participated in an "urban" teacher education program, Watson (2011) found that these teachers had particular meanings for "urban" which were tied to the characteristics of students. Specifically, the teachers used "urban" as a code for racial difference and deficit. This meaning is significant, insofar as the teachers used "urban" and "suburban" as cultural constructs, as opposed to geographic references. "When teachers did not have students with the cultural or symbolic capital of suburban students, they often expressed a desire to teach different kids" (p. 28). They wished to teach students who were "urban, but not too urban." When asked directly what they meant by "urban," the teachers indicated that urban "meant of color and, to a lesser degree, poor."

However, it is not only teacher education students who engage in the use of such coded language. We have witnessed multiple examples of the use by faculty and administrators of "urban" or "like urban" to describe schools that are geographically suburban or even rural. In such cases, the underlying meaning of "urban" is poor and/or of color. Such definitions allow the ascription of "urbanness" to schools that are only peripherally connected to cities and permit the justification for diverting resources from city schools. While this concern over the meaning ascribed to terms reflects an idealist perspective, the potential effect of disadvantaging already resource-poor schools turns attention from idealist considerations to more materialist ones.

The Materialist at Work in Urban Teacher Education

As noted above, the focus of the materialist is less on psychological concerns and more on critical social structures and resource allocation. For example, one of the issues with regard to education that can clearly be understood in materialist terms is segregation (specifically the role of segregation in defining opportunities to learn and receive quality education). McLaren (1994, p. 9) describes educational inequality as a "social lottery" in which "schools constitute a loaded social lottery in which the dice fall in favor of those who already have power and money." A manifestation of this social lottery is student-level segregation and the differential access to resources that it supports (Anderson,

2011; Mickelson, 2005). The same can be said for teacher segregation. While certainly not limited to urban schools, teacher segregation is an issue that, we would argue, must be considered in urban teacher preparation.

The segregation of the nation's teachers occurs across several levels. For example, on the basis of a national survey of over 1,000 teachers, Frankenberg (2006) found that white teachers, on average, teach in schools where almost 90 percent of the faculty are white and over 70 percent of the students are white. Schools where less than 10 percent of the population are students of color typically have almost all-white faculties (96.3 percent of teachers are white, on average). In contrast, in schools where over 90 percent of students are black and/or Latino, only 40 percent of the faculty is white, on average. Similarly, whereas the typical black teacher teaches in a school where nearly 60 percent of the students are from low-income families, the average white teacher teaches only 35 percent of low-income students. According to Frankenberg, these results show that white and non-white teachers, on average, teach different populations of students.

Just as with student segregation, the racial isolation of teachers is not in and of itself a material consideration. The segregation of students becomes significant from a material perspective as a result of the differential resources and outcomes associated with this isolation. Similarly, the significance of teacher segregation from a materialist perspective comes through its relationship to issues such as teacher longevity. In Frankenberg's (2006) study, for example, almost two-thirds of teachers in schools with the lowest shares of black and Latino students reported that they are not at all likely to leave teaching in the next few years, while less than half (40 percent) of teachers in high minority schools expressed similar confidence that they will be teaching in three years. Similarly, in a study of Georgia public schools, Freeman et al. (2005) found that teacher turnover (specifically, white teacher turnover) was much greater in schools with higher percentages of black students. The material impact of this kind of turnover was demonstrated in Frankenberg's (2006) study through the relative experience levels of teachers in different schools. She found that teachers with less than three years of experience were more likely to teach in high minority schools, whereas veteran teachers (those with more than 20 years of experience) teach in schools that are over 70 percent white. Given the relationship between teacher experience and achievement (Fetler, 1999), the higher levels of teacher turnover and lower levels of teacher experience point to different (material) opportunities in segregated minority schools. According to Frankenberg (2006), "these findings suggest that black and Latino students in this sample are systematically disadvantaged by the overrepresentation of inexperienced teachers in their schools" (p. 38). For the materialist, such systematic disadvantaging of students of color through teacher and student segregation is a critical issue, and one that demands attention with regard to teacher preparation.

For the sake of clarity, we must note that the segregation of students and teachers is not strictly an "urban" education issue. Such racial and socioeconomic segregation can, and does, take place in various types of schools. However, insofar as urban schools often experience additional challenges with regard to opportunity to learn, any issue, such as teacher segregation, that might contribute to those challenges is of importance for urban teacher education. Such is the view through the materialist lens.

Teacher educators operating from a materialist school of thought work to illuminate how social practices such as segregation are created with societies and how they inform educational opportunities, social identities, and relationships across social groups. For the materialist, deep social analysis is imperative. Any phenomenon or structure that plays a role in maintaining and reproducing disparities must not remain unexamined.

The Implications of a Hybrid Perspective for Urban Teacher Education

One of the hallmarks of CRT scholarship in education has been the application of various constructs from the legal literature on CRT. Scholars in education have considered how various ideas outlined by legal scholars could be applied to the examination of education. These constructs have included *whiteness as property, interest convergence,* and *restrictive versus expansive views of equality* (DeCuir-Gunby, 2006; Donnor, 2006; Milner, 2008; Rousseau & Tate, 2003; Solorzano, 2001). While CRT offers several powerful analytical tools such as these that can be applied to the study of education (Dixson & Rousseau, 2006; Gillborn, 2008), arguably one the most useful with regard to examining teacher education is the concept of *structural determinism.*

According to Delgado and Stefancic (2001), structural determinism engages both the materialist and the idealist dimension of CRT thought. Delgado and Stefancic (2001) describe structural determinism as the "idea that our system, by reason of its structure and vocabulary, cannot redress certain types of wrong" (p. 26). The structure of the law or other societal institutions imposes a particular framework upon the thought processes of those who operate under those structures. That framework can prevent members of society from being able to envision and name a new or different concept that could lead to greater racial justice.

One form of structural determinism identified by Delgado and Stefancic (2001) is what they refer to as "the empathetic fallacy":

> The idea that one can use words to undo the meanings that others attach to these very same words is to commit the empathetic fallacy—the belief that one can change a narrative by merely offering another, better one—that the reader's or listener's empathy will quickly and reliably take over … The idea that a better, fairer script can readily substitute for the older, prejudiced one is attractive, but falsified by history.
>
> (p. 28)

With regard to urban teacher education, we argue that this points to the potential flaws with efforts on the part of teacher educators to operate using terms with meanings that have been "co-opted" for use as racial code words. Terms such as "diversity" or "urban" can mean very different things to different members of the teacher education community (whether students, faculty, or administrators). Teacher educators who are committed to social justice may be committing a form of the empathetic fallacy when we strive to change the narrative about "diverse" students and "urban" schools.

Moreover, while this empathetic fallacy is largely an idealist consideration, we must also consider the materialist implications of continuing to operate within this structure. It is possible that our continued efforts to use these co-opted terms does more than simply prevent all parties involved in urban teacher preparation from having a shared vocabulary and thereby prohibits the challenging of dominating ideas. Issues involving resource allocation (e.g., pre-service teacher placements, in-service teacher professional development, curricular decisions, faculty hiring, etc.) can be impacted by the lack of a shared understanding of what is "urban" and what "diversity" means. In this way, a hybrid approach that integrates idealist considerations (e.g., the meaning ascribed to the terms we use) with materialist implications (e.g., resource allocation) is necessary to fully understand how urban teacher education might perpetuate inequity as opposed to alleviate it. It also "raises the stakes" for considering how we might seek to address the structural determinism represented in our continued commitment to co-opted language.

In addition to structural determinism, another key idea from the legal literature on CRT is the critique of colorblindness. CRT scholars seek to problematize the liberal construction of colorblindness:

> CRT indicates how and why the contemporary "jurisprudence of colorblindness" is not only the expression of a particular color-consciousness, but the product of a deeply politicized choice ... The appeal to colorblindness can thus be said to serve as part of an ideological strategy by which the current Court obscures its active role in sustaining hierarchies of racial power.
>
> (Crenshaw, Gotanda, Peller, & Thomas, 1995)

In other words, CRT scholars view colorblindness not as part of the solution but as part of the problem in an effort to achieve racial justice. In fact, Crenshaw (2001) refers to colorblind discourse as "the virtual lunch counter, the rationalization for racial power in which few are served and many are denied" (p. 1371).

The problematic features of colorblindness can be seen in an examination of segregation, both of teachers and of students. As various authors have noted (Lawrence, 2005; Orfield & Lee, 2007), very little attention at a policy level is paid to student-level segregation. According to Lawrence (2005), "fifty years after *Brown* ... the word 'segregation' is rarely spoken in public policy discussions" (p. 1358). Similarly, Orfield and Lee (2007) note that the relationship between segregation and educational outcomes is rarely mentioned by policy makers. The same can be said about teacher-level segregation. White students in the U.S. are substantially more likely than students of color to be taught by a white teacher (Frankenberg, 2006). So why is there not more attention paid to ongoing segregation?

We would argue that one reason can be found in the phenomenon of colorblindness. As Watson (2011) noted in the teachers that she studied, teachers can "code" racial preferences in nonracial terms. Moreover, conditions that are ostensibly racially neutral (such as a school's annual yearly progress status as determined by No Child Left Behind) can also be cited as reasons for white teacher attrition from high minority schools. So long as clearly defined racial animus is not the cause for teacher segregation, the racial isolation of white teachers can be constructed as colorblind or race neutral. In fact, recent Supreme Court decisions have pointed to the existence of a "radical colorblindness" in which race-based remedies for conditions of student segregation are prohibited in the absence of clear evidence of intentional and contemporary discrimination (Anderson, 2011).

Yet CRT challenges this picture of colorblindness or neutrality. The CRT lens highlights the material consequences of teacher segregation while reducing the focus on issues of intent. This attention to segregation absent intent is crucial. With regard to student-level segregation, Lawrence (2005) asserts that the tendency to ignore this racial isolation, to look the other way, ensures that persons with no measure of ill intent are nevertheless responsible. We would assert that the same can be said of teacher-level segregation. It would be easy for teacher education programs in general, and urban teacher education programs in particular, to apply a colorblind lens to the issue of teacher segregation—to take an approach of "that's just the way things are." Yet, from a CRT perspective, the material consequences of teacher segregation for students of color demand that we look more closely at our role in perpetuating this segregation. A materialist perspective demands that we reject the colorblind lens and examine the results of our failure to adequately prepare teachers for cross-racial instructional settings. However, this is not strictly a materialist issue. It is at this juncture that an idealist perspective might also inform our direction by focusing attention on the stereotypes and attitudes that are also related to teacher segregation. In this way, we engage both the materialist and the idealist perspective to critically examine issues of teacher segregation.

CONCLUSION

Although we have raised questions about the meaning ascribed to terms such as "urban," we take seriously the importance of the task of preparing teachers for success in city schools. Further, our analysis has been based on the assumption that the context in which teachers work is of consequence. As Ladson-Billings (1999) notes:

> A CRT perspective rejects the idea that the conditions under which urban teachers and suburban teachers work can be compared in a way that is fair and equitable. The context of the urban setting creates a challenging environment—issues of limited school funding, more inexperienced and underqualified teachers, greater teacher turnover, and more students assigned to special classes and categorical programs are endemic in urban schools.
>
> (p. 233)

It is our assertion that CRT offers a way to examine the preparation of teachers for urban schools in a potentially transformative way. In addition, CRT offers a new vocabulary for analyzing teacher preparation. Specifically, we assert that the process of making distinctions between materialist and idealist considerations in the preparation of teachers is of importance, particularly in an urban context, because it requires that consideration be given both to attitudes and to conditions. One danger that we have encountered in urban teacher education is the allure of concentrating primarily on more idealist factors with regard to future teachers. Our programs seek to address teacher dispositions (perhaps because these are characteristics that we, as teacher educators, believe we can influence) while largely ignoring the structural or materialist conditions. The CRT vocabulary offers a means to name these conditions and examine the interplay between the idealist and materialist forces and raises questions regarding the design of more equitable programs. Although having the vocabulary to name materialist factors does nothing to change these inequities, we view it as a potentially important first step to transforming teacher preparation for urban schools.

We suggest further exploration of a hybrid approach to CRT that conjoins the idealist and materialist perspectives for at least two reasons. First, a hybrid approach seeks to expand our thinking beyond teacher attitudes and beliefs to consider the complex interplay between dispositions and distribution. Thus it can broaden our view of what it means to prepare effective teachers for urban schools. Rather than simply asking "What is the candidate's attitude toward diversity?," this approach shifts the frame to consider the teacher candidate's understanding of the material forces shaping educational opportunities as well as the candidate's role in either perpetuating or disrupting those structures. A relevant question in evaluating candidates would then become: "How likely is the candidate to do justice (and not simply love kindness)?"

A second reason for pursuing a hybrid approach (as opposed to focusing strictly on one perspective or the other) is that this dual focus should position teacher educators to avoid balkanization and binary approaches to the important work of preparing teachers for urban schools. Because the hybrid approach pays attention to the complex interaction of dispositions and material conditions, it provides a space for persons from different perspectives to engage in meaningful discourse around the preparation of teachers for urban schools. In fact, a hybrid approach honors the need for multiple, related voices to be heard in a dynamic environment such as urban teacher preparation.

A primary goal of this chapter has been to explore how critical race theory might be employed to analyze urban teacher education. Yet our larger purpose is not simply to engage in analysis. Crenshaw et al. (1995) describe one of the common interests that cut across critical race scholarship as the "desire to not merely understand the vexed bond between law and racial power but to *change* it" (p. xiii, emphasis in original). Similarly, the goal of considering both disposition and distribution in teacher education is to catalyze change.

REFERENCES

Akintunde, O. (1999). White racism, white supremacy, white privilege, and the social construction of race. *Multicultural Education, 7*, 2–8.

Anderson, C. (2011). What do you see? The Supreme Court decision in PICS and the resegregation of two Southern school districts. *Teachers College Record, 113*, 755–786.

Bell, D. (1987). *And we are not saved: The elusive quest for racial justice.* New York: Basic Books.

Brueggemann, W., Parks, S., & Groome, T. (1986). *To act justly, love tenderly, walk humbly: An agenda for ministers.* New York: Paulist Press.

Carlson, D. (1995). Constructing the margins of multicultural education and curriculum settlements. *Curriculum Inquiry, 25*, 407–431.

Crenshaw, K. (2001). The first decade: Critical reflections, or "a foot in the closing door." *UCLA Law Review, 49*, 1343–1372.

Crenshaw, K., Gotanda, N., Peller, G., & Thomas, K. (Eds.). (1995). *Critical race theory: The key writings that formed the movement.* New York: New Press.

DeCuir-Gunby, J. (2006). "Proving your skin is white, you can have everything": Race, racial identity, and property rights in whiteness in the Supreme Court case of Josephine DeCuir. In A. Dixson & C. Rousseau (Eds.), *Critical race theory in education: All God's children got a song* (pp. 89–112). New York: Routledge.

Delgado, R. (2001). Two ways to think about race: Reflections on the id, the ego, and other reformist theories of equal protection. *Georgetown Law Review, 89*, 2279, 2283–2285.

Delgado, R. (2003). Crossroads and blind alleys: A critical examination of recent writings about race. *Texas Law Review, 82*, 121–152.

Delgado, R., & Stefancic, J. (2001). *Critical race theory: An introduction.* New York: New York University Press.

Dixson, A., & Rousseau, C. (Eds.). (2006). *Critical race theory in education: All God's children got a song.* New York: Routledge.

Donnor, J. (2006). Parent(s): The biggest influence in the education of African American football student-athletes. In A. Dixson & C. Rousseau (Eds.), *Critical race theory in education: All God's children got a song* (pp. 153–166). New York: Routledge.

Fetler, M. (1999). High school staff characteristics and mathematics test results. *Education Policy Analysis Archives, 79*(9), 1–22.

Frankenberg, E. (2006). *The segregation of American teachers.* Cambridge, MA: Civil Rights Project at Harvard University.

Freeman, C., Scafidi, B., & Sjoquist, D. (2005). Racial segregation in Georgia public schools, 1994–2001: Trends, causes, and impact on teacher quality. In J. Boger & G. Orfield (Eds.), *School resegregation: Must the South turn back?* (pp. 143–163). Chapel Hill: University of North Carolina Press.

Gillborn, D. (2008). *Racism and education: Coincidence or conspiracy?* New York: Routledge.

Haberman, M. (2007). Who benefits from failing urban schools? *Theory into Practice, 46*(3), 179–186.

Ladson-Billings, G. (1999). Preparing teachers for diverse student populations: A critical race theory perspective. In A. Iran-Nejad & P. Pearson (Eds.), *Review of research in education* (vol. 24, pp. 221–247). Washington, DC: American Educational Research Association.

Lawrence, C. (2005). Forbidden conversations: On race, privacy, and community. *Yale Law Journal, 114,* 1353–1403.

McLaren, P. (1994). *Life in schools: An introduction to critical pedagogy in the foundations of education.* New York: Longman.

Mickelson, R. (2005). The incomplete desegregation of the Charlotte–Mecklenburg schools and its consequences, 1971–2004. In J. Boger & G. Orfield (Eds.), *School resegregation: Must the South turn back?* (pp. 87–110). Chapel Hill: University of North Carolina Press.

Milner, H.R. (2008). Critical race theory and interest convergence as analytic tools in teacher education policies and practices. *Journal of Teacher Education, 59*(4), 332–346.

Nieto, S. (1995). From brown heroes and holidays to assimilationist agendas: Reconsidering the critiques of multicultural education. In Christine Sleeter and Peter McLaren (Eds.), *Multicultural education, critical pedagogy and the politics of difference* (pp. 191–220). New York: State University of New York Press.

Orfield, G., & Lee, C. (2007). *Historic reversals, accelerating resegregation, and the need for new integration strategies.* Los Angeles, CA: Civil Rights Project.

Pardini, P. (2000). Down but not out. *Rethinking Schools, 15*(1), 4–7.

Rousseau, C., & Tate, W. (2003). No time like the present: Reflecting on equity in school mathematics. *Theory into Practice, 42,* 211–216.

Solorzano, D. (2001). Critical race theory, racial microaggressions, and campus racial climate: The experiences of African American college students. *Journal of Negro Education, 69,* 60–73.

Tate, W. (2003). The "race" to theorize education: Who is my neighbor? *Qualitative Studies in Education, 16,* 121–126.

Watson, D. (2011). "Urban, but not too urban": Unpacking teachers' desires to teach urban students. *Journal of Teacher Education, 62*(1), 23–34.

Weiner, E.J. (2007). Critical pedagogy and the crisis of imagination. In P. McLaren & J.L. Kincheloe (Eds.), *Critical pedagogy: Where are we now?* (pp. 57–77). New York: Peter Lang.

INDEX

9/11 167, 172–3, 176–7

AAPIs: *See* Asian Americans; Pacific Islanders
accountability 148–9
achievement levels 1; Black students 154, 158–62, 232–3;
    CCI model 302–5, 308, 310; charter schools 219–29;
    Chicanos 261, 304–5, 308; emphasis on 291;
    gaps 155–7, 302–5, 308, 328, 355–6; Latinos 302,
    308; measuring 224; *Nepantla* (Nahuatl) 293, 328;
    pan-Latinos 261; race recognition 372–3; Raza
    study data 304–5; teachers of color 347; *See also*
    performance testing
activism 109–10, 227, 336; OWS movement 113;
    praxis 110, 332; scholarship 292; social justice 101–2;
    spiritual 329
Adelante partnership: CRT tensions 335; goals and
    components 326–8; Oral History Project 329–30, 333;
    racial realism 328–9, 336
admission practices 11, 16, 198, 204–6
AERA panel 129, 340
African Americans: *See* Black Americans
Africans 41–3, 369–70, 377–9
Ahmad, M. 176
Alfred, Gerald Taiaiake 97
Alridge, Derrick 82–3
American culture 16, 309, 340
American ideals 107–8, 195–8
ancestry assumptions 369
Anderson, James 90
Anglo-American culture 200
anomaly thesis 37
anticategorical complexity 243–4
anti-discrimination 26, 358
anti-essentiaism 39–40
anti-immigration lobby 132
anti-Muslim racialization 167
antiracists 19–20
Anzaldúa, Gloria 105, 107, 321, 325–6

apartheid: anti apartheid movements 74; Arizona 301–
    11; epistemic 69, 72, 74; South Africa 42
appearance 38–41, 133
Arce, M.S. 131, 133
Arizona: apartheid 301, 305–10; fascism 308;
    Freirean pedagogy 302; interest convergence 38,
    342; intersectionality 308–10; racial realism 302;
    statutes 129–38, 148, 295, 301; United Nations 132
armed forces, African Americans 143
Asian Americans: achievement levels 232;
    citizenship 167–8; demographics 144; dominant
    narratives 168–9; interest convergence 207–9;
    intersectionality 209–10; social justice 171, 210–1; war
    involvement 168–9; white resentment 178

Bakke v. Regents of the Univ. of Calif. 11
Ball, Stephen 130–1
Banfield, Edward C. 116
Beecher, Catherine E. 318
Bell, Derrick A. 14, 17–8, 24, 38, 42–3, 49–61, 101, 104,
    106, 108–9, 134–5, 143, 201, 206, 218–9, 237, 339,
    342–4, 350, 386
Bell, M. 189
Berends, M. 219
Bilson, J. 238
biology, racial 69, 72, 272, 316, 355
bi-racial students 379–82
Black Americans: armed forces 143; Chicago 295–0;
    citizenship 242; critical pedagogy 75, 79–83;
    cultural history 75–6; demographics 13; Du Bois
    on 69–70; education 55, 75, 79; educators 181–2,
    186–7; intellectuals 69; interest convergence 14;
    internal conflicts 237–8; knowing roots 75; LEAP
    tests 223; linked fate 122; Nigerian 369–70, 377–9;
    as property 119; race and racism 113; scholars 107;
    school access 113, 195, 195–202, 349, 390–4;
    stereotypes 155, 369; wariness 113; White female
    teachers 317; *See also* Du Bois, W.E.B.

Black educational inferiority, myths 153–5
Black elites, roles 123
Black feminist writers 108, 206, 239–40
Black male students: counter-narratives 160;
   dress codes 40–1; gay 238, 377–8; institutional
   expectations 157–8; intersectionality 234–5;
   LEAP tests 223; racial identity 234–44;
   underachievement 154, 158–62, 232–3; White female
   teachers 317
Black parents 196, 239, 243
Black Power movement 218
Black professionals 105, 198
Black Reconstruction in America 70
Black schoolchildren, protecting the rights of 17
Black schools, segregation era 157
Black teachers 225, 346
Black veterans 339
Black women 39–40, 105, 206, 234, 240
Blackness as property 119, 357–8
Boger, J.C. 196
Bonilla-Silva, E. 184
books, banned 107, 131–2, 295
books and essays, Du Bois on 70–1
Boyles, D. 102
Brainwashed 153
Brown v. Board of Education: Bell on 386; effects of 27–8,
   35, 221–3; interest convergence 17, 25, 143, 206, 339;
   school integration 3, 21, 136, 155, 196; significance 11;
   Supreme Court 20, 201; US image 171; White
   elite 134–5; whiteness as property 119
Buras, K.L. 227
Burkhart, Brian Yazzie 96
Burrell, Tom 153, 161
Bush, George 13

Cabral, Amilcar 77
capitalism: CRT 122; fairness 195–6; globalization 40,
   77; and racism 77, 114, 118; social inequalities 115–6
Cartesian coordinate system 63–4
Cartesian principle 96
Castagno, A.E. 342, 344
caste systems 200
CCI model 302–5, 310
centering on race: *See* race, centering on
Chan, J. 205
Charter School Outcomes 219
charter schools 216, 219–29, 289
Chicago 289, 295–300
Chicana feminists 326
Chicano students 260–7, 304–5, 308, 329–30
children 17, 43, 137, 145, 266–7, 313
Chin, F. 205
Cho, S. 370
choice 195–8, 379
Christian values 89, 140, 144, 293, 318–9
'The Chronicle of the DeVine Gift' 42
chronicles 18–9, 42–3
citizenship 134, 167–8, 242, 363
City of Richmond v. Croson 13–4
Civil Rights Act (1964) 10, 12, 14–8, 26
Civil Rights movement 14, 123, 135, 196, 339
Civil Rights Office 204
class, social: appearance 40; Black Africans 232–6,

239–40; classism 359; CRT priorities 121–4;
   exploitation 115; as a focus 118–9, 218;
   intersectionality 104; middle class, main stream 55,
   135, 175, 243; vs. race 40, 114; studies in education 83;
   UK White working class 137
CLS (critical legal studies) 12–8, 351.1
Cochran-Smith, M. 340, 350
coercion, cultural 77, 89, 92–3
Coffey, Wallace 97
Cohen, Cathy 122
Cold War 134, 206, 339
Cole, Mike 115, 117
Coleman report 155
colonialism 137, 199, 329–32, 375, 376
colonization 92–3, 334
color-blindness 393–4; critical race analysis 264; Crow,
   Jim 195, 242, 317; Fordham Institute 228; Mountain
   West 265–6; politics 196; power-evasion 316;
   radical 393; school discipline policies 262;
   schools 175; teacher education 339; who is
   White? 200; *See also* race neutrality
colored people: *See* people of color
common sense, racial realism 302, 307–8
communities: critical race praxis 294–0; tri-
   dimensionalization 303; vandalism in 177–8; working
   with 325, 329–34; working-class 359
competition 195–6, 202
complexity analyses 243–4
composite characters 188–90, 190–1
composite counter-narratives 183–6
composite narratives 186, 252–3
conformist resistance 63 fig
Congress Acts 9–10
consciousness, false 315, 351.1
consciousness of race: *See* race consciousness
conservatism (racial) 195, 244–5
contradiction-closing cases 28, 129, 135–6
contradictions: critical race praxis 382; No Child Left
   Behind Act 149; post racialism 373; race scholar
   roles 332–3; views of Latino immigrants 140–1; White
   female teachers 314–5
Cool 238
corporate capitalism 77
counter-narratives 41–3, 160, 186, 248, 252–3; 9/
   11 172–3; Black students 160, 234; centrality 293;
   Chicago 295, 295–6; collective 120; community 295–
   0; composite 183–6; from data 186, 252; education
   reforms 43, 186; legal principles 42; Native
   Americans 88–9; New Orleans, post-Katrina 186–7;
   policy effects 226; post-racial 371–2; qualitative
   research 255–6; whiteness as property 18–9;
   Whitewash 'n F'real 216–7, 226–7
courses, race-based 346
Crenshaw, Kimberlé Williams 5, 19–20, 26, 104, 106–7,
   111, 206, 218, 234–5, 290, 350, 358, 376–9, 393, 395
critical legal studies (CLS) 12–8, 351.1
critical race methodology 4, 184–5; chronicles 18–9,
   42–3; composite characters 188–90, 190–1; composite
   counter-narratives 183–6; composite narratives 186,
   252–3; data collection 252; dominant ideologies
   293–4; expansive articulations 358, 362; interest
   divergence 136–8, 293, 350; limitations 121, 239–40,
   326, 330–3; mixed method studies 254–6, 256–7;

Nepantla 325–8, 329–30, 332–5; post-racialism 371–2; qualitative research 252, 255–6, 271; quantitative methods 248–57; role contradictions 332–3; tensions 292, 325–7, 329–30, 332–6, 382; theory and method 184; tri-dimensionalization 190, 302–3, 305–7; vocabulary 341, 394–5; *See also* counter-narratives; critical race policy analysis; interest convergence; intersectionality; narratives; quantitative methods; racial realism; whiteness as property

critical race pedagogy: African Americans 75, 79–83; course description 368; dialogic process 371–2; inertia 387; Pedagogies class 371; praxis 302; *See also* Freirean pedagogy

critical race policy analysis 263–4; Chicano students 260–7; consciousness of race 219–20; data in 263; expanding and updating 121; hybrid perspective 388; LatCrit 141, 262–4; Louisiana RSD 226–7; Marxian critiques 114–8, 124.1; neutrality 217–8; policy effects 226; power 218; racial realism 221–7, 228–9; school-to-prison pipeline 260–7; United Kingdom 118, 120; Whitewash 'n F'real 216–7, 226–7

critical race praxis (CRP) 290–1, 293, 372–3; activism 110; CRT impediments 120; enactments of 109–10; ethics and responsibility 332–5; framework for education 291–5; F'real 227; post-racial 368–82, 371–2; reciprocity 335; teacher education 364–5; vs. theory 105, 289–90; training in 294

critical race scholars: activism 109, 292; difficulties faced by 109, 294, 332–5; expansive and restrictive views 358; idealists and realists 387–8; legal 12, 111, 290; on Marxian critiques 114, 118–21; roles 107–9, 332–3; White 120, 372–3

critical race scholarship 102, 105, 107

Critical Race Theory 132

critical race theory (CRT): benefits 20–1, 49–50, 111; concepts 56–7, 134–7, 233–4, 326, 357–8; definitions 122, 251–2, 339; education 2–3, 51–2, 58, 64, 110–1, 392; emergence 12–4; ethnic studies 51–2; hybrid perspective 388; ideal and real 391–5; idealists 387–8; intellectual roots 48–64; literature review 341–2; materialists 387–8; pre-history 9–12; purpose of 106; realists 387–8; social class 121–4; sociology of race 293–4; structural determinism 392–3

critically compassionate intellectualism model (CCI) 302

Cross, B.E. 156

Crow, Jim 195, 242, 317

CRP: *See* critical race praxis

CRQI: *See* quantitative methods

culture 94–5, 389–90; coercion 77, 89, 92–3; competitive 195–6, 202; deculturalization 309; Du Bois on 74–9; Louisiana RSD 225; mismatches 233; novice teachers 363; popular 114; sovereignty 97; urban/suburban 390; White American 16, 293, 309, 340

curriculums 175, 341, 345–6

Dalton, Harlan 13, 227

Darder, Antonio 115, 116–7

data 186, 252, 263, 270–1, 277–8

Davis, Angela 105

Dawson, Michael 122

Declaration of Independence 107–8

decolonizing pedagogy 329–30, 333

DeCuir, Erica 223

deculturalization, culture 310

Delgado, Richard 121–2, 132, 135–6, 137, 185, 205, 206, 237, 332, 387

Delgado Bernal, Dolores 37, 39, 59–60, 63–4, 107, 108, 233–4

Deloria, Vine Jr 95, 97

Delpit, Lisa 313

democracy: homogenization 310; ideals 363–4; liberal 37; Louisiana RSD 227; politics 217–8; throttling of 78–9; US image 134, 171; War on Terror 170; White supremacy 186

demographics: Asian Americans 144; Black Americans 13, 298; Chicano students 265; Latinos 137, 144, 298, 327; Pacific Islanders 144; people of color 327; student ratios 265, 327; teacher educators 341, 347–8; teachers and students 313; undocumented people 140, 144; 'urban' 389; White students 265

Denver, Colorado, Brown v. Board of Education 27–8

desegregation 9–12, 196, 339, 386

Detroit, segregation in schools 10

Devil 289–90

dialogue, power locations 381–2

discipline policies, schools 260–2

discrimination, forms of 11–2, 19; *See also* oppression; race discrimination

diversity and tolerance 168, 197, 389–90, 392–3

Dixson, A.D. 120, 226, 227–8, 346

dominant narratives: Asian Americans 168–9; Black male students 234, 355; challenging 293–4, 392–3; educational institutions 373–4; interest convergence 343–4; Native Americans 375

Donnor, J. 325

DREAM Act 148–9

Du Bois, Cruse 108

Du Bois, W.E.B. 1; Africana critical pedagogy 79–83; books and essays 70–1; culture 77–9; education 69–76, 107–8; human reasoning 107; sociology of race 75–6

economic downturns 114

economic interests: Black women 240; desegregation 339; entrepreneurs 221–2, 224, 227, 291; exploitation 309; free-markets 196, 362; inequalities 113–5, 387–8; interest convergence 38, 344; intersectionality 116; loss of income 38, 344; neoliberal 225; whiteness 119

education: African Americans 79, 113–4; big city 289; cross-cutting issues 123; CRP framework 291–5; CRT genealogy 2–3, 51–2, 58, 64; Du Bois on 69–76, 107–8; European 76; multicultural 131–2; and politics 52–3; as property 195–202; restrictive actions 364

education entrepreneurs 221–2, 224, 227, 291

education policies: assimilation 95; beneficiaries 225; British Government 143; contradictions 140–50; counter-narratives 226; discipline 260–2; hiring principals 297; Indigenous peoples 95–6; interest convergence 38; nature of 130–1; neutrality 217–8; racism case 130–8; recommendations 148–9; temporary 201; White supremacy 129–38, 222–3, 369–70

education policy analysis: *See* critical race policy analysis
education policy formulation: discipline 244–7; philanthropies 228; politics 109, 144; racial specificity 372–3; racial-legal infrastructure 223–4; racism influence 123, 144–5; RCMPC model 148; teacher participation 346–7; traditional 219–20; Tucson, Arizona 133; Whitewash 'n F'real 216–7, 226–7
education policymakers 93–4, 216–7, 222, 226–7
education reforms: counter-narratives 43, 186, 226–7; CRQI 280–1; CRT importance 322; Fordham Institute 221–3, 227–8; hegemony 322, 341; New Orleans, post-Katrina 181–2, 186, 227; status quo, preserving 102; urban renewal 43; Whitewash 'n F'real 216–7
education system 319
Elementary and Secondary Education Act 10
Elenes, A.C. 329
Emancipation Proclamation 17
empowerment 18, 105–6, 369
enrollment: *See* admission practices
entrepreneurs, education 221–2, 224, 227, 291
Against Epistemic Apartheid 72
equal opportunity 38, 196, 201, 204–13, 309
Equal Protection Clause 11, 16
equality: *See* racial equality
equity 204–5, 207–9
essentialism 39–40, 40
ethics and responsibility 332–5
ethnicity 5, 51–2, 104, 141, 293, 347–8
eugenics movement 36, 154, 253, 270, 272
Eurocentricity 77, 79, 92–3, 346
Europe 17, 40, 74, 76, 133
European-Americans 93
exclusion acts, AAPIs 205
Executive Orders 38
exploitation 309

Faces at the Bottom of the Well 18
failing schools 224
fairness 103, 195–6, 223, 264
false consciousness 315, 351.1
fascism 17, 42, 308
Faulkner, W. 189
federal government interests 291
feminist writers 19–20, 105–8, 206, 239–40, 320–1, 326
Finn, Chester 228
Fiol-Matta, L. 319
Fisher v. University of Texas 205–6
Flynn, Paul 129
Fordham Institute 221–3, 227–8
Fourteenth Amendment 9, 12
Frankenberg, Ruth 316
freedoms 79, 103, 171, 196, 320
Freeman, Alan 14, 15–6
free-market system 362
Freirean pedagogy 52–9; influence on CRT 50–2; postmodern politics 80–1; praxis 302; racial awareness 62–3; tri-dimensionalization 302–3, 305–7; visual models 51, 60–1; *See also* critical race pedagogy

Gates, H.L. 235–6
gay people 238, 377–8, 379–82

gender: Black males 232–44; as a focus 118–9, 218; intersectionality 19–20, 72, 104–5, 378; Native Americans 97–8; sociology of 81; studies 83; TribalCrit 97–8; White women 377–8; *See also* sexuality
genetics 38–9, 233, 253
Gillborn, David 118, 119, 120, 124
Gillman, Susan 72
Giroux, Henry 59, 60, 64
globalization 40, 77
Gotanda, N. 393
governmental policies 95
grassroots leadership 58–9, 61, 67, 227, 302, 377
grassroots movements 131, 228, 302
Green v. New Kent County 10
Griggs v. Duke Power Co. 11
Gruwell, E. 320
Guatemala, Alvaro's story 330–2, 334–5
Guerrero, M.A.J. 98
Guinier, Lani 136–7

Haberman, M. 189
Hall, Stuart 122
Hamdani, Mohammad Salman 172–3
Hamline Law Review 307
Hansard 136
Harris, Angela 26
Harris, Cheryl 18–9, 119, 196, 199, 357–8
Harris, S 142–3
Harvard Civil Rights–Civil Liberties Law Review 13
Harvard Law Review 136
Harvard Law School 17, 24, 104, 218
Harvard University 96, 204
Haudenosaunee 96
hegemony: Arizona 302–3; discourses 185; education reforms 322, 341; education system 322–3, 360, 364; institutions 345; narratives 310; power 195, 340
high schools, Black male students 232
higher education 146–7, 204–13
Hill, Dave 115
Hilliard, A. 355–6
Hispanic students 130, 239, 295, 301–11
historical events 74–5, 222, 302–3
Hitler, Adolph 17, 42
Hochschild, I.J. 37
homogenization 310
Hooks, B. 373
Horne, Tom 131–3
Hull, G. 105
human nature 79–80, 107, 185, 293
humor 378, 380
hybridity, anxiety 378

idealists 387–8, 394
identity, racial: *See* racial identity
identity-based politics 234–5; intersectionality 116; limitations 19–20; Marxian view 120; White women 317; whiteness 132–3; *See also* whiteness
ideology of race 69
Iglesias, Elizabeth 123
immigrants: *See* undocumented students
immigration policies 132–3, 144, 146, 330–2, 334–5

imperialism 74, 78, 93, 170, 320
income 103
Indigenous peoples: *See* Native Americans
individualism, concepts of 195–6
industrial imperialism 78
inertia, critical race pedagogy 387
Inheriting Shame 154
institutions, desecrations 177
insurgent scholarship 292
integration 196–8
intercentricity, race and racism 293
interdisciplinary approaches 234, 280–2, 293–4
interest convergence 14, 17–8, 37–8, 206, 339,
     342–4; AAPIs 207–10; Arizona 38, 342; Asian
     Americans 207–9; candidate teachers 361–2;
     catalyst 342; dominant ideologies 343–4; education
     policy 129, 134–5; equity 207–9; importance of 213;
     Latinos 141; literature review 341–2; loss/gain
     binary 344–5; Pacific Islanders 207–10; *PICS v. Seattle
     School District No. 1* 201; racialization 178; restrictive
     views 358; school-university partnerships 349–50;
     self and systematic 343–4; theory and praxis 350;
     tolerance and war 171; War on Terror 168, 171–3;
     White privilege 342
interest divergence 136–8, 293, 350
Interracial justice 293
intersectional identities 376
intersectionality 26, 116, 206, 234, 292–5; AAPIs 210–1,
     213; African American/Latino 298–9; anti-
     essentialism 39–40; Arizona statutes 308–10; Asian
     Americans 209–10; Black males 232–44, 234–5, 369;
     categorical complexity 243–4; Chicano students 262–
     3; Delgado & Stefancic 37; difficulties 378; double
     consciousness 237; equal opportunity 212;
     limitations 121, 239–40; multiple identities 376;
     navigating 376–9; Nigerian Americans 369–70;
     origins 5; position of race 114; racialization 369;
     resistance 376–9; vs. single focus theories 20;
     sociology 81; sources of concepts 104; structural
     241–3; *See also* CRQI
intragroup differences 19–20
Iowa Review 121
Iroquois Confederacy 96
Islamaphobia 172–3

Jackson Elementary 326–7, 329–30, 333
Jefferson, Thomas 154–5
Johnson, Lyndon 38
Johnston-Parsons, M. 340
Julian, L. 131
justice 79, 104–7, 117, 161–3

K-12 education 145–50, 157, 296, 359, 386–7
K-20 spaces 292–3
Keating, A. 335
Kennedy, John F. 38
Keyes v. School District No. 1 10
knowledge 94–5, 190–1

Lacy, D. 239–40
Ladson-Billings, G. 20, 118–9, 190, 205, 218, 322, 325,
     339, 342, 345, 346, 350, 394

land, taking 93
land rights 93
language 196, 299, 310, 348, 389; CRT vocabulary 341,
     394–5; racial code words 196, 309, 389–10, 392–3;
     racializing agent 4–5
LatCrit 141, 262–4
Latinos 149.1, 295; achievement levels 232, 261;
     Adelante partnership 326–7; Chicago 295–12;
     Chicano students 260–7, 304–5, 308, 329–30;
     demographics 137, 144, 327; gay students 379–82;
     male students 239; No Child Left Behind Act 302;
     segregation 239; undocumented students 140–1,
     140–4; *See also* Arizona
Lawrence, Charles 14, 16, 109
Lee, S.J. 342, 344
legal infrastructure 12, 130–8, 223–4
legal principles: argumentation 218; counter-
     narratives 42; discourses 16–9; manipulation of 93;
     neutrality 16; pure procedural justice 103; reliance
     on 97; restrictive views 358; rule of law 218; rules of
     evidence 293
Leigh, P.R. 344–5, 345
Leming, J. 227
Leonardo, Z. 132
levels of consciousness, (Freire) 62–3
liberals 37, 364, 370
liminality 89–94, 98
Lincoln, Abraham 17
linked fate, (Dawson) 122
Lopez, Henry 307
Lorde, Audre 320
loss/gain binary 344–5
Louisiana: *See* New Orleans, post-Katrina
Lumbee people 90–1
Lynn, Marvin 50, 157–60, 165, 171, 262–3, 291–2

Majors, R. 238
male privilege 316
Manifest Destiny 93
market economies 114, 123, 143, 291, 362
Martinez, George 137–8
Marxism 70, 114–8, 124.1
masculinity 238–9
mastery 373–4
material conditions 103, 118, 239, 277–8, 359, 386
Matsuda, Mari 102
McCall, L. 243–4
McCready, L. 239
McIntosh, P. 316
McLaren, Peter 80
Meacham, Evan 38
meritocracy 379
Mexican Americans 130, 140, 144; *See also* Chicano
     students; Raza studies
middle class 122, 135, 175, 243
Milliken v. Bradley 10
Mills, C.W. 199–202
minority groups, lists of 348
misrepresentation 184–5
model minority 168, 205
Moraga, C. 321
'mother-teacher,' teachers 319

Mountain West 261–2, 264–7
multicultural education 131–2
multicultural society 218
multiple identities 234–8, 376, 379
multiple oppressions 240–1
Muslims 133, 167, 171
Myrdal, Gunnar 37
myths: *See* racial myths

Nair, Mira 172–3
narratives 185–6, 248; *Adelante* Oral History
    Project 329–30, 333; Alvaro's story 330–2,
    334–5; Amber 374–5; Black males 234, 236;
    centrality 293; Ikenna 377; Native Americans 88–9;
    novice teachers 362–3, 364; Old Testament 386;
    personal 186; post-racial 371–2; songs 88–9, 386;
    spirituality 97, 329, 386; Whitewash 'n F'real 216–7,
    226–7; *See also* counter-narratives; dominant narratives
Native Americans 55, 90; education 92–3; gender 97–8;
    political/legal standing 94; Specificity 374–5; tribal
    critical race theory 88–98; U.S. government 92–3
Negroes 76, 78, 107
neo-liberalism 123, 130–8, 143, 291, 359
neo-racism 141
Nepantla (Nahuatl) 325–6; Chicano students 329–30;
    critical race praxis 327; ethics and responsibility 332–5
networks of markets 123
neutrality: *See* color-blindness; race neutrality
New Orleans, post-Katrina: charter schools 221–2;
    composite characters 188–90; counter-narrative 186–
    7; educators 181–2; predictions 43; RSD 221–8
New York Times 17
Next to the Color-Line 72
Nigerian Americans, Ikenna 369–70, 377–9
Nixon, Richard 10
No Child Left Behind 142, 147–8, 302, 364, 393
Noblit, G.W. 186
Norman Yoke 93
Notes on the State of Virginia 154

Obama, Barak 148–9, 260, 290, 371
objectivity 184–5, 202
Open Choice Plan (Seattle) 197–8
opportunity 103, 117, 309
oppositional behavior, model of 60–1
oppression 221–8; common ground 40; counter-
    narratives 226; economics 113; forms of 5, 116,
    233–9, 291, 293; intersectionality 206; multiple 240–1;
    school ideologies 239; White women 315; *See also* race
    discrimination; racial subordination
oral traditions 41–3, 96
Other People's Children 313

P-12 education 348
Pacific Islanders 144, 207–11
painful experiences, storytelling 42
parables 18–9
paradigm shifts: color-blindness 200;
    intersectionality 239–40; nepantla 335–6;
    neutrality 224; policy analysis 216–29; racial
    realism 226, 227–8; research 213; test scores 224;
    Yamamoto 290

Parents for Educational Justice 223
Parker, Arthur C. 89–90
pedagogues, postmodern 80
Pedagogy of the Oppressed 52, 131–2
Peller, G. 393
people of color 351.4; demographics 327; Du Bois
    on 78; Executive Orders 38; feminists/feminism 314,
    321; Harvard Law School 218; hegemony 302; levels of
    unjust treatment 309; teachers 347; voting rights 10,
    134; women 19–20
performance testing: charter schools 219–24; LEAP
    tests 223–4; over-reliance 293; race recognition 372–
    3; Raza study data 304–5; test scores 156, 232, 296,
    304; Whitewash 'n F'real 216–7
The Philadelphia Negro 69, 70
philanthropies 228, 320
philosophy 70, 96, 107–8
PICS v. Seattle School District No. 1 196–202
Plessy v. Ferguson 9, 155
Plyer v. Doe 145
politics: anti-racism 70; color-blindness 196;
    communism 70; democratic 217–8; and
    education 52–3, 217–8, 227–8; intersectionality 116;
    Labour Party (UK) 129; Marxism 70, 114–8,
    124.1; policy formulation 144; postmodern 80;
    progressive 81; racial 114, 121, 227–8; radical 72, 74,
    79, 80, 110; rational 217–8, 227–8; social change 134;
    socialism 70; *See also* activism; identity-based politics
popular culture 114
positive discrimination 11–2
positive racial identity 162, 232
positivism 248, 250–1
post-modernists 80, 104
post-positivism 248, 250–1
post-racialism 371; level playing field 375;
    neutrality 377; praxis 368–82; society 290–1, 375;
    teaching 368–9; White supremacy 368
post-structuralism 104
poverty 108, 137, 234
Powell, justice 12
power: battles over 110; Black Power movement 218;
    categories of 371; concept of 94–5; CR policy
    analysis 218; empowerment 18, 105–6, 369;
    evasion 316; exclusivity 200; institutional 368–9;
    interest convergence 206, 340, 344; intersectional 378–
    9; locations In dialogue 400–401 379–82; Marxian
    scholars on 115; mastery 373–4; material
    conditions 115; narrative and counterstory 185–6;
    race 315, 368–9, 373; race neutrality 370;
    racialized 373; relationships 185; reordering
    regimes 200; revealing 369; of scholarship 105, 334;
    shifting 378, 395; US Senate 118; White female 378;
    White people 119; whiteness 373; *See also* economic
    interests; hegemony; politics; White supremacy
Prieto, L. 329
principals, recruiting 296–8
privilege: allocation of 19, 119, 205; Black males 238;
    differences exercise 369; heteronormativity 235;
    insider-outsider 334–5; male 316; and
    oppressors 307, 309; race 315–6; of scholarship 334;
    White women 173–5, 316, 321, 346; *See also* White
    privilege

property 93, 119, 173–5, 195–202, 345, 357–8; *See also* whiteness as property
public schools 216, 221–3
pure procedural justice 103

qualitative research 96–7, 252, 255–6, 271
quantitative methods: compatibility with CRT 248–57; composite stories 252–3; discipline policies 265; mixed method studies 254–5; objectivity 184–5, 202; RCMPC model 148; student ratios 265; variables 20; views on 96
quantitative methods, CRQI 270–1; caveats 271–2; data, perceptions of 270; data mining 277–8; data neutrality 278; experiential knowledge 278–80; framework 275–6; limitations 274–5; multidisciplinary 280–2; social justice 280–1
quantitative research, the analysts 272–3
quotas, teachers of color 349

race 5; Black male identity 232–44; centering on 233, 293, 329–33, 340, 346, 363; dynamics of 121; Executive Orders 38; genetic difference 38–9, 233, 253; as an important variable 200–1, 272; intersectionality 104; silence 375; as a social construction 38–9; studies 51–2, 83; understanding 111; untheorized 118; *See also* Du Bois, W.E.B.
Race, Racism and American Law 49, 58
race and class 117, 123–4, 359, 360
race and color 369–70
race and education 212–3, 308–10
race and gender 19–20, 72, 104–5, 378
race and language: *See* language
race and law 308–10
race and racism 262–4, 298–9; Black people 113; centrality 233, 340; intercentricity 293; intersecting 262–4, 298–9; Marxian scholars on 114–8; novice teachers 363; social/material 387; US culture 340
race and whiteness and gender 314
race consciousness: commonsense 302, 307–8; critical race policy analysis 219–20; double 237; Freirean stages 54–5, 62–3; Horsford steps 162–3; liminality 90; mythical norm 320; *Nepantla* 325, 335–6; of racialization 380; raising 185, 189; revealing power 369; shifts in 335–6; tri-dimensionalization 302–3
race discrimination: economics 113; revealing 18–9; Supreme Court definition 14; unconscious 16–7, 388; victims and perpetrator's 15
race navigation 375
race neutrality: challenging 14–8; CRQI data 278; educational policies 218; post racialism 377; power 370; racial identity 369; racial realism 18–9, 219–20, 223; respect 380; *See also* color-blindness
race policy analysis, traditional 219–20
race recognition, achievement statistics 373
race scholars: *See* critical race scholars
race-based courses 346
race-relations 117
racial biology 69, 72, 272, 316, 355
racial classifications 12, 148
racial code words 196, 309, 389–10, 392–3

racial demography: *See* demographics
racial equality: critical race analysis 264; inequality 213, 309; interest convergence 17, 339; and justice in schools 161–3; racial realism 18; United Kingdom 136
racial identity 236; Black males 234–8; CCI students 310; importance of 120, 355–6; institutionalized 369, 388; intersectional 376; liminality 89–94, 98; multiple 234–8, 240; neutral 369; silencing 382; teachers 364; and whiteness 374
racial literacy 136–7
racial location 374–5
racial myths: Black educational inferiority 153–5; model minority 169–70, 205; mythical norm 320; White supremacy 119; *See also* stereotypes
racial power, whiteness 373
racial profiling 171
racial realism: *Adelante* partnership 327, 336; Arizona 302; Bell, Derrick A. 14, 18, 218–9; common sense 307–8; critical race policy analysis 221–7, 228–9; paradigm shifts 227–8; reconciliation 161–2
racial segregation: *See* segregation
racial spaces 123
racial specificity 368–70, 372–5, 378–82
racial subordination 14, 200, 205–6, 233, 240–1, 293, 310
racialization
AAPIs 206
Black males 238
interest convergence 178
intersectionality 369
power 373
in schools 362; *See also* hegemony
South Asian Americans: *See* South Asian Americans
War on Terror impact 178
White female teachers 314, 319–21
whiteness as property 178
racial-legal infrastructure 223–4
Racing Research Researching Race 184
racism 14, 205, 307; American culture 16, 309; Asian Invasion 204; and capitalism 77, 114, 118; effect on schools 359; ethno-racism 141; example 130–8; Marxian scholars on 114–8; narratives 19; as normal 16, 21, 37–8; persistence in America 108–9; as policy 123, 133, 144–5; racial realism 219; rejected as a system 119; understanding 111; writing about 105
racist ideologies: *See* White supremacy
racist love 205
racist policies and practice, exposing 141, 343–4, 380
radical color-blindness 393
radical politics 72, 74, 79, 80, 110
Ranson, S 142–3
rational politics 217–8, 227–8
Rawls, John 102–3
Raza studies program 130, 295, 301–11
reactionary behavior 63 fig
Reagan, Ronald 13
reciprocity, critical race praxis 335
recruiting principals 296–8
recruiting teachers 221, 228, 341–2, 348–9
reforms, education: *See* education reforms
representation 184–5

re-segregation 20
resentment 130–8
reservations, Indian 96
respect, racially neutral 380
restrictive actions 362
Richmond, Virginia 13–4
Rodriguez, Judge 265–6
Romero, A. 131, 133, 303
Rousseau, C.K. 120, 226, 227–8
Russia 134

safety in schools 260, 265, 267
Salt Lake City 326–7, 329–30, 333
Sanders, M.G. 160–1
scholarship, traditional 290–1
school admissions, 'tie breakers' 198
schools: Black people 113–4; charter and public 221;
    charter schools 219–29; color-blindness 262; critical
    race analysis 263–4; curriculums 345–6; discipline
    policies 260–4; failing 224; Freirean pedagogy 52–5;
    hidden curriculum 175; Jackson Elementary 326–7,
    329–30, 333; oppressive ideologies 239; as
    property 173–5; racial equality 161–3; resources 113,
    195, 349, 390–4; social justice in 161–3; urban
    renewal 43; War on Terror 174; White people 113–4;
    See also segregation
school-to-prison pipeline 20, 260–7, 291
school-university partnerships 341, 349–50
scientific basis of race: See eugenics movement; racial
    biology; racial genetics
scientific racism 154–5
scientific research: See quantitative methods
Scott, J. 228
Seattle 196–202
segregation: African Americans 239; desegregation 9–10;
    Latinos 239; re-segregation 20; in schools 136, 143,
    391, 393; scientific racism 154–5; teachers 391, 394;
    See also Brown v. Board of Education
segregation era 157, 195, 242, 317
Selden, Steven 154
self and systematic interests 343–5
self-defeating resistance 63 fig
self-determination 16–7, 94, 97
self-respect 103
'separate but equal' 9, 155, 195, 242, 317
sexism, writing about 105
sexuality 5; Black males 40–1, 238; gay people 238,
    377–8, 379–82; heteronormativity 235; sexism 81;
    white female authority 377–8; women of color 19–20;
    See also gender
silencing, Black male 232–44
Silent Covenants, (2004) 49
Slaughterhouse Cases 9, 12
slavery: abolition of 17–8; assumed ancestry 369;
    distance from 355; importance of 75, 77, 106;
    reading and writing 195; scientific racism 154–5;
    Slaughterhouse Cases 9
Sleeter, Christine 317
Smedley, A. 39
Smith, Adam 93
Smith, B. 105
Smith, Janet 123–4

Smith, Mary Lee 217–8
social categories 243–4
social class: See class
social justice 101–4, 110, 206, 293–4, 386, 395; Asian
    Americans 210–3; Black male students 234; Crenshaw
    on 105–8; CRT role 210–3; as motivator 63–4; Pacific
    Islanders 210–3; praxis 109–10; in schools 161–3;
    social movements 72, 74; SOJO 295–12
Social Justice Education Project 302
Social Justice High School, Chicago 295–300
social sciences 293
social studies teachers 363–4
social values 103
socialism 70, 80
socioeconomic status, Black males 241–2
sociology of gender 81
sociology of race 69–79, 81, 293–4
SOJO 295–12
Solorzano, D.G. 205, 206, 212, 233–4, 293
The Souls of Black Folk 1, 70
The Sound and the Fury 189
South, transitions 206
South Africa, apartheid 42
South Asian Americans 167–78, 168, 174, 176
sovereignty 94, 97
Soviet Union 134, 339
speaking out, paying the price 109
specificity: See racial specificity
spirituality 97, 329, 386
Spring, J. 310
Stanford Law Review 19
statistical analyses: See quantitative research
statistics: See demographics; performance testing
status quo, preserving 102, 196, 290
Stefancic, Jean 37, 39, 107, 108, 132, 135–6, 205, 206,
    332, 387
stereotypes: AAPIs 213; Black men 239, 378;
    Black people 55, 155, 369; effects of 387; media
    'spin' 144; model minority 169–70, 205; model
    teachers 363; Native Americans 376; racist
    love 205; reinforcing 346; slave ancestry 369; White
    women 318–22; See also myths
storytelling: See narratives
Stovall, David 118–21, 123–4
structural determinism 392–3
structural intersectionality 241–3
Su, J.A. 110
subordination: See oppression; racial subordination
successful minorities, AAPIs 205–6, 213
Supreme Court: Black members 198; Brown v. Board
    of Education 9–10, 143; decisions 9–11, 13–4, 145,
    196–202, 205–6; first impression cases 15; legal
    neutrality 16; limitations 17; race discrimination 14;
    radical colorblindness 393; White privilege 358
Sweating the Small Stuff 227
symbiosis thesis 37

Tate, Greg 113, 114
Tate, William F. 20, 110, 118–9, 322, 339, 345
Teach with Your Heart 320
teacher education: Black & Brown teacher needs 346;
    color-blindness 339–40; CRT vocabulary 341, 394–5;

ideal and real 391–5; idealist/materialist 386, 389–94; importance of 294; interest convergence 339–51; literature review 341–2; policy participation 346–7; praxis 364–5; racial code words 196, 309, 389–10, 392–3; research 350; school-university partnerships 349–50; teacher curriculums 346, 360–1
teacher helpers 359–60
teachers: Black 225, 346; candidate 361–2; of color 347; CRT suggestions 322; experienced 225; general dissatisfaction 359; interest convergence 361–2; language 389; maths 372–3; 'mother-teacher' 319; motivations 360; novice 225, 362–3, 391; perceptions of students 158–9; pre-service 359; racial background 346–8; racial identity 357–8, 364; recruitment 221, 228, 296–8, 341–2, 347–8, 348–9; role of 228; segregation 391, 394; student relationships 361–2, 391; White men 315; White women 313–22; working-class communities 359
Teacher's Manual 49
teachers of color, quotas 349
The Tempest 132
terrorism, post 9/11 144, 170
test scores: *See* performance testing
Texas 122, 148
theory and praxis: *See* critical race praxis
third world scholars 108, 320–1
Thirteen Ways of Looking at a Black Man 235–6
This Bridge Called My Back 321
Thomas, Justice Clarence 198–9
Thomas, K. 393
tolerance 168, 171–3, 178, 197, 389–90, 392–3
Toll v. Moreno 145
Torres, Adolfo 115, 116–7
Transcending the Talented Tenth 81
transformations 59–64, 325, 335–6
tribal critical race theory (TribalCrit) 88–98; counter-narrative 88–9; early influences 89–91; gender 97–8; liminality 89–94, 98; qualitative research 96–7
tri-dimensionalization 190, 302–3, 305–7
'true womanhood' 318–9, 321, 377
Tsosie, Rebecca 97
Tucson, Arizona: *See* Arizona statutes
Twine, F.R 184

underachievement, Black students 154, 158–62, 232–3
undocumented students 140–1, 144–8, 330–5
United Kingdom 118, 120, 129, 133, 136–7, 200
United Nations, Arizona 132
United States, social justice 102
United Teachers of New Orleans report 221–2
universities: AAAPIs 204–13; admission practices 11, 16, 204–6; economic interests 344; hiring policies 110, 296–8; University Anywhere 216–7
University of Pennsylvania 96
Urban Education 64
urban schools 386; districts 227; novice teachers 362–3; racial code words 196, 389–10, 392–3; teaching in 389–90; unique needs of 349–50; urban renewal 43; Whitewash 'n F'real 216–7, 226–7
U.S. v. Carolene Products Co. 12

Valdes, J.M. 106

Village Voice 113
Villenas, S. 329
violence 136, 177–8
voice: *See* counter-narratives
voting rights 10, 134

Walberg, H.J. 219
War on Terror 168, 171–4, 177–8
Warren, J.W. 184
Washington v. Davies 11, 15
And We Are Not Saved 18, 386
Weinbaum, Alys Eve 72
Western colonialism, notions 89
Where Did Social Studies Go Wrong? 227
White, State Rep. 244–5
White anti-racist scholars 120, 372–3
White children, discipline patterns 266–7
White civilization 78, 89, 228
White elite 14, 17–8, 134–5, 322, 339
White female teachers 313–22; privilege 346; racialization 315–21, 377; as saviors 377; today 321–2
White law schools 12
White men 293, 315, 319, 372–3
White parents, choosing schools 196
White people: anger displacement 175; boys and youths 136–7; dissatisfactions 113–4; middle class, main stream 55, 135, 175, 390; seeking racial justice 38; socialists and communists 70; UK 119, 133, 137; vs. White elite 322
White privilege: allocation of 19, 119, 205; identifying with 374; interest convergence 342; maintaining 344–5; Supreme Court 358; surrendering 201
White schools 195–6
White supremacy 71, 195, 309–10; centering on 14, 114–7, 314; conspiracy 118; entrepreneurs, education 224; ignoring 364; interest divergence 136–7; Marxian scholars on 116–8; politics of race 120–3; post-racial 368; preserving 136–8; social sciences 273; *See also* eugenics movement; racial biology; racial genetics; racial myths; racial subordination
White women: benevolent saviors 320–1; gender 377–8; philanthropies 320; stereotypes 318–22, 377; 'true womanhood' 318–9, 321, 377; White supremacy 315–8
White Women, Race Matters 316
whiteness 358; enduring 202; honorary 374; Horne and Arizona 132–3; imperial feminism 320; post-racial 374; redeemed 371, 373–4; studies 314
whiteness as property 119, 195, 199–200, 357–8; challenged 103; interest convergence 345; model minority 169–70, 205; narratives 18–9; philanthropies 228; *PICS v. Seattle School District No. 1* 196–202; racial realism 226; racialization 178; vandalism 177–8; War on Terror 168, 177–8
Whitewashing 216–7, 226–7
Whitman, D 227
Wilkins, Roger 108
Williams, Robert A. 93, 109–10
Willis, Paul 59, 64
Wiredu, Kwasi 76, 78
Women, Culture and Politics 105

women of color: Black women 39–40, 105; Harvard
Law School 218; intersectionality 26; Muslim 133;
research gaps 59; sexuality 19–20; *See also* feminist
writers
women's studies, influence on CRT 51–2, 104
World War II 17, 339
writings, importance of 107, 320

Yamamoto, E.K. 110, 290, 291–2, 294
Yosso, T. 293–4
Young, Gifted and Black 355

Zeichner, K.M. 340
zero tolerance 260, 264–6, 268
Zuberi, T. 184

Taylor & Francis

eBooks

FOR LIBRARIES

ORDER YOUR FREE 30 DAY INSTITUTIONAL TRIAL TODAY!

Over 23,000 eBook titles in the Humanities, Social Sciences, STM and Law from some of the world's leading imprints.

Choose from a range of subject packages or create your own!

Benefits for you

- ▶ Free MARC records
- ▶ COUNTER-compliant usage statistics
- ▶ Flexible purchase and pricing options

Benefits for your user

- ▶ Off-site, anytime access via Athens or referring URL
- ▶ Print or copy pages or chapters
- ▶ Full content search
- ▶ Bookmark, highlight and annotate text
- ▶ Access to thousands of pages of quality research at the click of a button

For more information, pricing enquiries or to order a free trial, contact your local online sales team.

UK and Rest of World: **online.sales@tandf.co.uk**

US, Canada and Latin America:
e-reference@taylorandfrancis.com

www.ebooksubscriptions.com

ALPSP Award for BEST eBOOK PUBLISHER **2009 Finalist** sponsored by

Taylor & Francis eBooks
Taylor & Francis Group

A flexible and dynamic resource for teaching, learning and research.